D1456861

Prepared under the

editorial supervision of

FREDERICK ERNST

First-Year French

A CONVERSATIONAL GRAMMAR AND READER

Revised Edition

EDMOND A. MÉRAS
Phillips Exeter Academy

MARIO A. PEI
Columbia University

A HOLT-DRYDEN BOOK
HENRY HOLT AND COMPANY, INC. NEW YORK

Library of Congress Catalog Card Number: 57-5146

35670-0117

Manufactured in the U.S.A.

FOREWORD TO THE REVISED EDITION

WHILE PRESERVING its original character of a complete text to introduce the student to French pronunciation, grammar, reading, and conversation, this REVISED EDITION of *First-Year French* differs in several important respects from the original work.

First, the book as a whole has been shortened to make it more easily usable in the three-hour-a-week college course. The exercises in each lesson have been pruned so that they can be covered readily in one recitation. The lessons have been further shortened by removing the readings and substituting for them nine new *Lectures,* one following each review lesson. These *Lectures* are adaptations of well-known works of French literature, the longest being Anatole France's *La Comédie de celui qui épousa une femme muette*. They provide sufficient material to satisfy the reading requirements of the average three-hour course.

Second, the REVISED EDITION uses fewer words than did the original. If the end-vocabularies give the appearance of lengthiness, it is because they include many words that the student will not have occasion to use —words (required by readings which have now been replaced) whose removal proved typographically impracticable.

Another notable feature of the REVISED EDITION is a new section on pronunciation, prepared by a phonetics specialist, Professor Dora Bashour of Hunter College.* The international phonetic symbols have been used in this section as a means to an end, rather than with any expectation that the student will learn to write in phonetic script. The symbols do not appear in the text proper, but in the French-English Vocabulary each word is phonetically transcribed.

At the request of many teachers, the grammar sections in each lesson have been supplied with headings and subheadings, to give their logical grouping a helpful typographical emphasis.

F. E.

January 1957

* A phonograph record of this *Introduction to French Pronunciation* is obtainable from Funk and Wagnalls, 153 East 24th Street, New York City.

PREFACE TO THE FIRST EDITION

THIS GRAMMAR is intended for the first-year college course in French. It stresses a modern conversational approach and embodies three considerations which the authors believe to be fundamental in language learning: (1) frequency of occurrence, (2) memorization, and (3) realism in conversation.

(1) Frequency of occurrence. More than half of the terms used in ordinary spoken language are ready-made clichés, and a few hundred of these tend to recur most frequently. Once the student has learned these clichés by memorizing them, he will have a real degree of confidence in speaking and understanding the foreign language.

The principle of frequency of occurrence applies not only to words and expressions but to grammatical forms and constructions as well. Consider, for example, the demonstrative adjective and the demonstrative pronoun. From the point of view of abstract logic it may be desirable to assign the demonstrative pronoun immediately after the demonstrative adjective; but the relative frequency of occurrence of these two forms warrants their presentation at widely different points in the text. The learner can always say "ce livre et le livre de mon frère" instead of "ce livre et celui de mon frère" if the need for such a construction arises in everyday speech.

Relative frequency of occurrence in actual conversation has been a primary guiding principle throughout this grammar. Verbs—both regular and irregular—and tense forms are arranged in accordance with this principle. Thus, irregular verbs such as *être, aller, avoir, vouloir,* and *prendre* precede even the regularly conjugated verbs. Tenses such as the present, the past indefinite, and the periphrastic future formed with *aller* are studied much earlier than the tenses which are used less frequently. Forms such as *ce dont, je tinsse,* and *nous eûmes parlé*—dear to the hearts of reference grammarians and compilers of final examinations—receive less attention than forms which recur frequently in everyday language.

(2) Memorization. The authors believe that memory, more than any

other faculty, is the basis of language learning. To help the student retain an essential vocabulary, they have presented words and phrases in a practical context which lends itself to dramatization. If the learner repeats orally the *Conversations* often enough, bearing in mind their setting, he will acquire a working vocabulary which should lead to rapid progress in his use of the language.

(3) Realism in conversation. Realism in conversation has been the third guiding principle in the preparation of this text. The grammar is developed from lifelike *Conversations* based on lifelike situations. The authors have scrupulously sought to avoid artificiality.

Teachers examining this textbook may be interested in the method by which the various aspects of language learning have been integrated. Each *Conversation* illustrates the grammatical points discussed in the lesson. To explain these grammatical points, numerous examples are given, most of which repeat the vocabulary of the lesson. Moreover, some grammatical points are often presented briefly, and then discussed in more detail later in the book. This method may make a deeper impression on the student than a single but more complicated discussion. The *Exercices* drill the student on the *same* points and the *same* vocabulary. The *Questions* train him in the oral use of the vocabulary and of the constructions discussed. The *Lectures,* especially in the early lessons, repeat once again the vocabulary and grammatical constructions while introducing new words and phrases—which the student will retain because of the context in which they are found. The *Thèmes,* written in a practical, conversational form, require a review of the vocabulary and grammar of the lesson. Finally, the *Compositions* give the student an opportunity to test what he has learned by using it freely—either in oral or in written form. Thus, every portion of the lesson fits in with every other portion. This multiple yet integrated approach, with its variety of drill, should facilitate the learning process with all types of students.

The vocabulary of the reading material is eminently practical. Occasionally new words or difficult expressions have been translated in the expectation that some of them may be subconsciously retained. The *Lectures* also present inductively some points of grammar which are discussed in subsequent lessons. In this way the expression may enter the student's consciousness before actual study—as occurs in any natural language-learning process.

The reading and conversational material leads naturally to the reading of dramatic literature (such as Tristan Bernard's *Franches Lippées,* a short scene from daily life in which the vocabulary is that of everyday speech); it leads likewise to the understanding of ordinary fiction, especially prose with dialogue. After completing the study of this text, the student should be able to read without difficulty any simple play or short story of the late nineteenth-century type.

If the *Conversations* are used orally and repeated until they are memorized, pronunciation can be effectively taught and oral comprehension developed. If the *Exercices* are covered thoroughly and if the *Questions, Lectures, Thèmes,* and *Compositions* are used to test the student's mastery of each lesson, at the end of one year's study he should be able to speak, read, write, and understand the basic vocabulary, idioms, and constructions presented in this book.

The varied elements presented in each lesson offer the teacher a great flexibility of method. He may stress the conversation, the reading, or the writing. He may use the *Questions* immediately after the students have memorized the *Conversation,* or wait until they have studied the sections dealing with verbs and grammar. He may even prefer to use the *Questions* after all the *Exercices* have been covered.

According to the time he has at his disposal, the teacher may give more or less importance to the *Lecture* and *Composition,* at the end of each chapter. He may finally decide to eliminate part of the *Exercices* or cover some of them at sight in the classroom.

This book purposely offers more material than is strictly needed in most first-year courses. While the authors have included all that they consider essential, and have indicated the order of presentation which they personally prefer, each teacher will make his own emphases and will organize his teaching to meet the specific needs of his students.

E. A. M.
M. A. P.

January 1950

Table of Contents

APPENDIX

VOCABULARY

Introduction to French Pronunciation

PHONETIC SYMBOLS

In this text, pronunciation is indicated by the phonetic symbols used by the International Phonetic Association.

Each phonetic symbol represents only one sound.

A single letter of the alphabet may have several different pronunciations. For example, s in phrase is pronounced [z], whereas s in simple is pronounced [s].

Several letters of the alphabet combined frequently represent only one sound, but a single sound can never be represented by more than one symbol. For example, beau has four letters but only two sounds, and will therefore be represented by only two symbols: [bo].

Sometimes there are several ways of spelling the same sound, but this sound is always represented by the same symbol.

Thus in [bo], [o] is spelled eau: beau
in [poːz], [o] is spelled o: pose
in [fo], [o] is spelled au: faux

VOWELS

General Instructions

Pronounce the English word I very slowly. You will notice that you are really saying a series of vowel sounds, starting with a as in father, with the mouth wide open, and ending with i as in machine, with the mouth almost closed. This composite sound is called a diphthong. English vowels are very often pronounced as diphthongs. French vowels are never pronounced as diphthongs. In pronouncing the English word I the open mouth produced an a as in father, the closed mouth produced an i as in machine. Each position of the mouth produces a different sound. Therefore, in pronouncing French vowels, be sure to keep tongue, lips and jaw tense and firm in exactly the same position throughout the entire sound. Otherwise you will produce a diphthong.

All French sounds are produced with the tongue convex (), never concave (). The tip of the tongue must not be permitted to turn up and back.

Vowel Sounds

A. There are sixteen vowel sounds in French. Four of these are nasal vowels.

Symbol	Tongue
i	Very high in front of mouth, tip pressed firml against lower teeth
e	Still very high in front, but not quite so high a for [i]. Tip still firmly against lower teeth
ɛ	A little lower in front than for [e]. Tip still against lower teeth
a	Only slightly raised, with tip still against lower teeth
ɑ	Lowered, with tip still against lower teeth
ɔ	Slightly raised toward back of mouth. Tip no longer touches teeth
o	A little higher in back of mouth than for [ɔ]. Tip a little further from teeth
u	Very high and pulled well back in the mouth
y	As for [i]
ø	As for [e]
œ	As for [ɛ]
ə[1]	Between [ø] and [œ]

[1] This sound is not to be pronounced by itself. It is heard only when surrounded by consonants.

Lips	Jaw	Examples
orners drawn well back	Almost closed	i si vi zit si vil
orners drawn back a little less than for [i]	Slightly more open than for [i]	si te e te i de
orners drawn back a little less than for [e]	More open than for [e]	bɛl ɛl mɛːm[2] vi lɛːn
orners drawn back a little less than for [ɛ]	Moderately open	ma dam sa lad la bal
elaxed	Well open	a ʃɑ la bɑ nɛs pɑ
ounded and slightly protruding	A little less open than for [ɑ]	pɔm bɔ nɔm pɔ sibl
uite far forward and tightly pursed	Very much more closed than for [ɔ]	ɔ poːz ʃa po o si
s far forward as possible	Almost closed	bluːz ʒa lu gu te
s for [u]	As for [i]	mi nyt py ni my zik
s for [o]	As for [e]	i døːz e mø de ʒø ne
s for [ɔ]	As for [ɛ]	ɛl vœːl il pœːv i mœbl
etween [ø] and [œ]	Between [e] and [ɛ]	ʒən se pɑ kɛl kə za mi ta blə doːt

[2] Dots (ː) after a vowel sound indicate that it is prolonged.

B. Nasal vowels.

There are no nasal vowels in English.

Open your mouth wide before a mirror. In the back of the mouth you will notice a small tongue-like extension of the soft palate, pointing downward. This is the uvula. It can be raised or lowered easily.

To produce a nasal vowel, lower the uvula just enough to allow a large part of the air rising from the throat to be expelled through the nose. Be sure that the back of the tongue does not touch the roof of the mouth, for this will add to the nasal vowel an English consonant sound (ng).

Symbol	*Tongue, Lips*	*Jaw*	*To Nasalize*	*Examples*
ɑ̃	As for [ɑ]	A little more open than for [ɑ]	Lower the uvula and force the air through the nose	ma mɑ̃ ɑ̃ fɑ̃ i mɑ̃:s
ɔ̃	As for [ɔ]	A little more closed than for [ɔ]		bɔ̃ bɔ̃ dɑ̃ sɔ̃ a lɔ̃
ɛ̃	As for [ɛ]	A little more open than for [ɛ]		mɛt sɛ̃ ɑ̃ fɛ̃ la mɛ̃
œ̃	As for [œ]	A little more open than for [œ]		œ̃ bɛ̃ œ̃ sɛ̃ kɛl kœ̃

SEMI-VOWELS

When the sounds [u, i, y] are pronounced immediately before any vowel, a new sound is produced which is halfway between a consonant and a vowel. This is called a semi-vowel. The semi-vowel and the accompanying vowel are always in the same syllable.[3]

[3] A semi-vowel cannot be pronounced by itself. It must be accompanied by a vowel.

Symbol	*Derived from*	*Examples*	
w	u	ui *becomes* wi	lwi:z (*not* lu i:z)
		uɛ *becomes* wɛ	swɛ te (*not* su ɛ te)
j	i	ia *becomes* ja	pja no (*not* pi a no)
		iɔ̃ *becomes* jɔ̃	de fi ni sjɔ̃ (*not* de fi ni si ɔ̃)
ɥ[4]	y	yi *becomes* ɥi	kɥi zin (*not* ky i zi:n; *not* kwi zi:n)
			lɛ̃ gɥist (*not* lɛ̃ gy ist; *not* lɛ̃ gwist)
		ye *becomes* ɥe	si tɥe (*not* si ty e; *not* si twe)
			a bi tɥe (*not* a bi ty e; *not* a bi twe)

CONSONANTS

General Instructions

French consonants, like French vowels, are pronounced with the tongue convex, the tip pointed downward.[5]

Try to pronounce each consonant with the tongue in the same position as the accompanying vowel. Do not permit the consonant to spoil the purity of the vowel.

The final consonant sound of a group of syllables must be very clearly and neatly articulated.

A. Breath consonants: In pronouncing consonants like [p, t, k], use as little breath as possible, saying the consonant and the accompanying vowel almost simultaneously, without any breath between them.
Examples: pa pa, ta pe, pa kɛ.

B. Dental consonants: [l, n, t, d, s, z] are produced with the tongue firmly against the upper teeth, the tip of the tongue pointing down towards the lower teeth. In English the tongue is concave, with the tip touching the upper gums.[5]
Examples: mad mwa zɛl, vi lɛ:n.

[4] Do not confuse with [w]. Be sure the tip of the tongue is firmly against the lower teeth as for [y].

[5] See page **xvii**.

C. The Parisian [r]: This sound is pronounced by forcing the air between the back of the tongue and the back of the palate pressed firmly together.[6] This sound resembles gargling. Be sure to keep the tip of the tongue lightly touching the lower teeth. If it curls up, you will probably pronounce an English r.
Examples: pa ri, mar sɛːj, la frɑ̃ːs.

D. Special consonants: The phonetic symbol for most consonants is the same as the corresponding small printed letter. Three consonant sounds have special symbols.
   1. [ʃ] pronounced like sh in she.
      Examples: ʃɛːz, aʃ te.
   2. [ʒ] pronounced like s in pleasure.
      Examples: aːʒ, ʒa mɛ.
   3. [ɲ]. Place the tip of the tongue against the lower teeth, pronounce [n] with the tongue touching the palate[7] as for [j]. The nearest English sound is [nj] as in onion. The French sound is like [nj] pronounced so close together that they form one sound.
      Examples: si ɲe, kɔ̃ pa ɲi, mɔ̃ taɲ.

SYLLABIFICATION

In English, most written letters are pronounced. French, on the other hand, is characterized by the fact that written letters are often silent.[8] It is particularly important to learn how to separate the letters of a French word into syllables, because the position of some letters in a syllable determines whether or not they are pronounced.

A single vowel sound, with or without accompanying consonants or semi-vowels, forms a syllable. Thus, in English, I is a syllable, tie is a syllable, so is twin. In French, [ɛ] is a syllable, so is [sɛ], as is [swɛt].

Each of the following groups of letters in French, with or without accompanying consonants or semi-vowels, forms just one syllable.

[6] There are regions in France where r is like a lightly trilled Italian or Spanish r.

[7] Not the upper teeth.

[8] Silent letters are indicated in this introduction by a slanted line, as in est and comme.

Spelling	*Pronunciation*[9]
ai	ɛ
au	o
eau	o
ei	ɛ
eu	œ
œu	œ
oi	wa
ou	u

Rules of Syllabification[10]

A. Whenever possible, a syllable starts with a consonant.
divisibilité — di vi si bi li té
inutile — i nu ti le[11]

B. Two consonants are generally separated.
partir — par tir
intacte — in tac te

1. However, r and l are combined with a preceding consonant to start the new syllable.
secrétaire — se cré tai re
probablement — pro ba ble ment
Exceptions: r, l are separated from a preceding r, l, n or m.
parlé — par lé
intelligent — in tel li gent
Henri — Hen ri

2. nn, mm, mn generally start the new syllable together.
immense — i mmen se
personne — per so nne
automne — au to mne

3. ss preceded by the prefix re generally start the new syllable together.
ressource — re ssour ce
ressentiment — re ssen ti ment

[9] This is the most frequent pronunciation. There are naturally some variants. These are indicated in the Reference List of Spellings, page **xxvii.**

[10] We are referring here to letters of the alphabet, not to their pronunciation.

[11] The method of syllabification used here will sometimes not correspond to the hyphenating method based on etymology. We are concerned only with pronunciation, not with meaning: inutile, from the point of view of meaning ("not useful") would be hyphenated in-u-ti-le.

4. ch, gn, ph, th represent only one consonant sound, so they must not be separated.

   achat — a chat
   signature — si gna tu re

C. When there are more than two consonants, separate the first consonant from the rest.

   surprendre — sur pren dre
   semblant — sem blant
   instructif — in struc tif

D. The letters i, u, and ou are in the same syllable as a vowel which follows.

   nation — na tion
   cuisinière — cui si niè re
   avoué — a voué

Spelling, Syllabification, and Pronunciation

A. A consonant or a group of consonants at the end of a *word* are generally silent.

   résultat — ré sul ta~~t~~ — pronounced re zyl tɑ
   palais — pa lai~~s~~ — pronounced pa lɛ
   portant — por ta~~nt~~ — pronounced pɔr tɑ̃

   Exceptions: c, f, l, r at the end of a word are frequently pronounced as in lac, actif, bal, amer — pronounced lak, ak tif, bal, a mɛːr.

B. When the letter e (without any accent marks) is the last letter of a *syllable,* it is called a *mute e* and is generally silent.

   avenir — a v~~e~~ nir — pronounced av niːr
   faire — fai r~~e~~ — pronounced fɛːr

   Sometimes, however, there are so many consonants surrounding the mute e that it would be difficult to omit it altogether without omitting one of the consonants too. In that case, it is pronounced [ə].

   bretonne — br(e) to nn~~e~~ — pronounced brə tɔn
   je ne vois pas — j(e) n~~e~~ voi~~s~~ pa~~s~~ — pronounced ʒən vwɑ pɑ

C. In all other positions the letter e (without any accent marks) is pronounced [ɛ].

   respect — res pe~~ct~~ — pronounced rɛs pɛ

D. When n or m is the last letter of the *syllable,* it is silent.

   menton — me~~n~~ to~~n~~ — pronounced mɑ̃ tɔ̃
   importe — i~~m~~ por t~~e~~ — pronounced ɛ̃ pɔrt

E. Whenever n or m is silent, no matter what the reason, the preceding vowel is nasalized.

menton — me~~n~~ to~~n~~ — pronounced mɑ̃ tɔ̃

important — i~~m~~ por ta~~nt~~ — pronounced ɛ̃ pɔr tɑ̃

F. The letter h is silent.

Homme — ~~h~~o mm~~e~~ — pronounced ɔm

G. Double consonants are generally pronounced like a single consonant.

confesseur — co~~n~~ fes seur — pronounced kɔ̃ fɛ sœːr

immense — i mme~~n~~ s~~e~~ — pronounced i mɑ̃ːs

LA LIAISON

Just as in separating the letters of a word into syllables we start each syllable with a consonant *letter*, so in pronouncing a series of syllables we start each syllable with a consonant *sound*. This is so basic to the flow of the music of a French phrase, that when a word starts with a vowel sound, if a consonant sound is available at the end of the preceding word, it is borrowed for the beginning of the next one. Comm~~e~~ il e~~st~~ gra~~nd~~ is not pronounced kɔm il ɛ grɑ̃, but comm~~e~~ il e~~st~~ gra~~nd~~[12] — kɔm il ɛ grɑ̃ (really pronounced kɔ mi lɛ grɑ̃).

The need for starting syllables with a consonant sound is so marked that even a final consonant that is normally silent is very frequently pronounced at the beginning of the following word if it starts with a vowel.

Do not say Qua~~nd~~ il e~~st~~ arrivé, j'étai~~s~~ trè~~s~~ occupé.
Kɑ̃ il ɛ a ri ve, ʒe tɛ trɛ ɔ ky pe.

Say Qua~~n~~d il e~~s~~t arrivé, j'étai~~s~~ très occupé.
Kɑ̃ til ɛ ta ri ve, ʒe tɛ trɛ zɔ ky pe.

This pronunciation of a normally silent final consonant before the initial vowel of the next word is called la liaiso~~n~~ (la ljɛ zɔ̃).[13]

In liaison d is pronounced [t] — pre~~n~~d-il prɑ̃ til.
g is pronounced [k] — sa~~n~~g i~~m~~pur sɑ̃ kɛ̃ pyːr.
s is pronounced [z] — pas ici pɑ zi si.
x is pronounced [z] — deux a~~n~~s dø zɑ̃.

[12] In this chapter as elsewhere, the linking of the final consonant sound of a word to the initial vowel of the next word is indicated by ⌢.

[13] The liaison is indicated by ‿.

The liaison is permissible only when the two words to be linked are in the same thought group and are closely connected grammatically. However, some people make the liaison more often than others, and on the whole it is less frequent in familiar conversation than in formal speech. Listen carefully to Frenchmen speaking or to French records. You will get the "feel" of the liaison as your fluency increases.

CONNECTED SPEECH

A French thought group is pronounced as a single unit composed of a series of syllables, and not as a series of words.

The following sentence contains nine words, but only three thought groups.

Je voudrais partir | par le premier train | pour Paris.

ʒə vu drɛ par tiːr | par lə prə mje trɛ̃ | pur pa ri

(*not* ʒə vudrɛ partir par lə prəmje trɛ̃ pur pari).

In pronouncing a series of French syllables, whether they form one word or a group of words, it is important to articulate clearly and accurately, saying exactly the vowel that the spelling requires, and no other. This is sometimes difficult for the English-speaking student, for in English, an unstressed vowel frequently deteriorates and becomes a mute [ə]: The English word attention is pronounced [ə tɛn ʃən]. A Frenchman with a heavy accent would pronounce it [a tɛn ʃɔn]. Ambassador is pronounced [am ba sə dər]. The same Frenchman would pronounce it [am ba sa dɔr].

Pronounce la sall~~e~~ d'atte~~n~~t~~e~~ — la sal da tɑ̃ːt (*not* lə sal də tɑ̃ːt).

Pronounce divisibilité — di vi zi bi li te (*not* də viz ə bil ə te).

STRESS

In English, it is difficult for a foreigner to determine which syllables to stress. We say em'phatic,[14] but 'emphasis; re'fer, re'ferral, but 'reference. In French, all syllables are of equal importance and should be pronounced with equal intensity.

Pronounce without stress.

Que voule~~z~~-vou~~s~~ fair~~e~~? Kə vu le vu fɛːr?

Il e~~st~~ v~~e~~nu m~~e~~ voir. Il‿ɛ vnym vwaːr.

[14] In this chapter as elsewhere, ′ is used before the stressed syllable.

In emphatic speech, the last syllable of the last word of a thought group is stressed.

Mais pourquoi | ne voulez-vous pas | me le donner?
mɛ pur 'kwa | nə vu le vu 'pɑ | məl dɔ 'ne?
C'est parce que j'en ai besoin | moi-même.
sɛ par skə ʒɑ̃ ne bə 'zwɛ̃ | mwa 'mɛːm.

INTONATION

There is no resemblance between English and French intonation. A good French pronunciation can be badly marred by English intonations. Listen carefully to Frenchmen speaking or to French records. You will notice that French intonation is generally a rising intonation. The voice rises smoothly throughout each thought group and in ordinary speech usually falls at the end of a sentence. Naturally, the greater the emphasis or the emotion, the higher the pitch of the stressed syllable. At such times the sentence may end on a high note instead of falling in the usual manner.

When practicing pronunciation, try not only to enunciate individual syllables perfectly, but try also to express the melody and rhythm of each thought group considered as a unit, and finally, the music of the entire sentence.

REFERENCE LIST OF SPELLINGS, WITH THEIR REGULAR PRONUNCIATION[15]

Spelling	*Pronunciation*	*Examples*
a	a	place — pla ce — plas
a before a silent final consonant	ɑ	achat — a chat — a ʃɑ
à	a	là-bas — là bas — la bɑ
â	ɑ	âme — â me — ɑːm
ai last letters of a *word*	e	serai — se rai — sre
ai elsewhere	ɛ	grammaire — gra mmai re — gra mɛːr

15 Naturally there are irregularities that must be learned separately.

Spelling	*Pronunciation*	*Examples*
aim̸ ain̸ } in the same syllable	ɛ̃	saint — sain̸t̸ — sɛ̃
am̸ an̸ } in the same syllable	ɑ̃	grande — gran̸ de̸ — grɑ̃ːd
au	o	autre — au tre̸ — oːtr
b, bb	b	banane — ba na ne̸ — ba nan
b before s	p	absent — ab sen̸t̸ — ap sɑ̃
c, cc	k	fracas — fra cas̸ — fra kɑ
c before e	s	lance — lan̸ ce̸ — lɑ̃ːs
cc before e	ks	accepte — ac cep te̸ — ak sɛpt
c before i	s	civile — ci vi le̸ — si vil
cc before i	ks	accident — ac ci den̸t̸ — ak si dɑ̃
c before y	s	cynique — cy ni que̸ — si nik
ç	s	français — fran̸ çais̸ — frɑ̃ sɛ
ch	ʃ	achat — a chat̸ — a ʃɑ
d, dd	d	madame — ma da me̸ — ma dam
d in liaison	t	quand il parle — quan̸d‿il par le̸ — kɑ̃ til parl
e last letter of a *syllable*	silent, or ə	serai — se̸ rai — sre parlera — par le ra — par lə ra
e before mm	a	femme — fe mme̸ — fam
e before nn	ɛ	antenne — an̸ te nne̸ — ɑ̃ tɛn
e not last letter of a *syllable*	ɛ	secret — se̸ cret̸ — skrɛ
é	e	dansé — dan̸ sé — dɑ̃ se
è	ɛ	achète — a chè te̸ — a ʃɛːt
ê	ɛ	rêverie — rê ve̸ ri e̸ — rɛːvri
eau	o	beauté — beau té — bo te
ei	ɛ	veine — vei ne̸ — vɛːn
eim̸ ein̸ } in the same syllable	ɛ̃	déteint — dé tein̸t̸ — de tɛ̃
em̸ en̸ } in the same syllable	ɑ̃	entendre — en̸ ten̸ dre̸ — ɑ̃ tɑ̃ːdr
en̸ last letters of a *word*	ɛ̃	lycéen — ly cé en̸ — li se ɛ̃

Spelling	*Pronunciation*	*Examples*
~~ent~~ verb ending	silent	ils désirent — il~~s~~ dé si r~~ent~~ — il de ziːr
e~~r~~, last letters of a *word*	e	parler — par le~~r~~ — par le
er, last letters of a few words	ɛːr	cher — ʃɛːr hiver — ~~h~~i ver — i vɛːr
~~es~~, verb ending	silent	tu parles — tu par l~~es~~ — ty parl
~~es~~, plural ending of noun	silent	trois livres — troi~~s~~ livr~~es~~ — trwɑ liːvr
e~~s~~, in mono-syllables	e	me~~s~~ — me
eu, last sound of a *word*	ø	dangereux — da~~n~~ g~~e~~ reu~~x~~ — dɑ̃ʒ rø
eu, before s	ø	dangereuse — da~~n~~ g~~e~~ reu s~~e~~ — dɑ̃ʒ røːz
eu, before t	ø	feutre — feu tr~~e~~ — føːtr
eu, elsewhere	œ	empereur — e~~m~~ p~~e~~ reur — ɑ̃ prœːr
e~~z~~, last letters of a *word*	e	fermez — fer me~~z~~ — fɛr me
f, ff	f	affaire — af fai r~~e~~ — a fɛːr
f in neuf, when linked	v	neuf ans — neuf a~~ns~~ — nœ vɑ̃
g, gg	g	grandeur — gra~~n~~ deur — grɑ̃ dœːr
g before e	ʒ	agent — a ge~~nt~~ — a ʒɑ̃
gg before e	gʒ	suggéré — sug gé ré — syg ʒe re
g before i or y	ʒ	Égypte — é gyp t~~e~~ — e ʒipt
g in liaison	k	sang impur — sa~~ng~~ i~~m~~ pur — sɑ̃ kɛ̃ pyːr
gn	ɲ	signé — si gné — si ɲe
gu	g	guichet — gui che~~t~~ — gi ʃɛ
~~h~~	silent[16]	haricot — ~~h~~a ri co~~t~~ — a ri ko
i	i	chemine — ch~~e~~ mi n~~e~~ — ʃmiːn
î	i	épître — e pî tr~~e~~ — e piːtr

[16] h is always silent. An initial h therefore leaves a vowel sound at the beginning of the word and we generally make the liaison with the final consonant of the preceding word: en ~~h~~iver ɑ̃ ni vɛːr. Sometimes, however, an initial h, though silent, prevents the liaison. This h is called "aspirated". Dictionaries and vocabularies indicate this type of h by placing a mark such as † before the word. For example †honte. Je n'ai pas honte j~~e~~ n'ai pa~~s~~ ho~~n~~ t~~e~~ — ʒne pɑ ɔ̃ːt. (Do *not* say ʒne pɑ zɔ̃ːt.)

Spelling	*Pronunciation*	*Examples*
i before a vowel	j	violet — vio le~~t~~ — vjɔ lɛ
il at the end of a *word* after any vowel but o	j	travail — tra vail — tra vaːj
ill after a vowel	j	travaillait — tra va illai~~t~~ — tra va jɛ
ill after a consonant	ij	famille — fa mi ll~~e~~ — fa miːj
i~~m~~, i~~n~~ } in the same syllable	ɛ̃	infinitif — i~~n~~ fi ni tif — ɛ̃ fi ni tif
j	ʒ	jamais — ja mai~~s~~ — ʒa mɛ
k	k	képi — ké pi — ke pi
l, ll	l	embellir — e~~m~~ bel lir — ɑ̃ bɛ liːr
m, mm	m	comment — co mme~~nt~~ — kɔ mɑ̃
mn	n	automne — au to ~~m~~n~~e~~ — o tɔːn
n, nn	n	personne — per so nn~~e~~ — pɛr sɔːn
o, before a final silent consonant	o	haricot — ~~h~~a ri co~~t~~ — a ri ko
o, before one s	o	arroser — ar ro se~~r~~ — a ro ze
o, elsewhere	ɔ	forteresse — for te res s~~e~~ — fɔr tə rɛs
ô	o	hôte — ~~h~~ô t~~e~~ — oːt
œu, last sound of a *word*	ø	nœud — nœu~~d~~ — nø
œu, elsewhere	œ	œuvre — œu vr~~e~~ — œːvr
oi	wa	voilà — voi là — vwa la
oi~~n~~ in the same syllable	wɛ̃	besoin — be soi~~n~~ — bə zwɛ̃
o~~m~~, o~~n~~ } in the same syllable	ɔ̃	chanson — cha~~n~~ so~~n~~ — ʃɑ̃ sɔ̃
ou	u	route — rou t~~e~~ — rut
ou, before a vowel	w	avouer — a voue~~r~~ — a vwe
p, pp	p	apparent — ap pa re~~nt~~ — a pa rɑ̃
p, between two consonants	silent	compter — co~~m~~ ~~p~~ter — kɔ̃ te
ph	f	camphre — ca~~m~~ phr~~e~~ — kɑ̃ːfr
q	k	coq — kɔk
qu	k	question — ques tio~~n~~ — kɛs tjɔ̃

Spelling	*Pronunciation*	*Examples*
r, rr	r	guerre — guer re̸ — gɛːr
s, ss	s	sagesse — sa ges se̸ — sa ʒɛs
s, between two vowels	z	caserne — ca ser ne̸ — ka zɛːrn
s, in liaison	z	pas ici — pas‿ici — pɑ zi si
t, tt	t	toilette — toi let te̸ — twa lɛt
th	t	thèse — thè se̸ — tɛːz
t, before the *sound* j	s	initial — i ni tial — i ni sjal définition — dé fi ni tion̸ — de fi ni sjɔ̃
t, before the *sound* j but after s	t	digestion — di ges tion̸ — di ʒɛs tjɔ̃
u	y	punition — pu ni tion̸ — py ni sjɔ̃
u, before a vowel	ɥ	intuition — in̸ tui tion̸ — ɛ̃ tɥi sjɔ̃
v	v	arrivera — ar ri ve̸ ra — a ri vra
w	v	wagon — wa gon̸ — va gɔ̃
x	ks	expert — ex pert̸ — ɛk spɛːr
x, before ce	k	exception — ex cep tion̸ — ɛk sɛp sjɔ̃
x, before ci	k	exciter — ex ci ter̸ — ɛk si te
x, before a vowel	gz or ks	examen — e xa men̸ — ɛg za mɛ̃ fixer — fi xer̸ — fik se
x, in liaison	z	deux amis — deux‿a mis̸ — dø za mi
y	i	typique — ty pi que̸ — ti pik
y, before a vowel	j	yeux — yeux̸ — jø
y, after a vowel=ii		paysan — pai i san̸ — pɛ i zɑ̃
y, between two vowels=ii		envoyez — en̸ voi iez̸ — ɑ̃ vwa je
ym̸, yn̸ } in the same syllable	ɛ̃	sympathie — sym̸ pa thi e̸ — sɛ̃ pa ti
z	z	douzaine — dou zai ne̸ — du zɛːn

First-Year French

REVISED EDITION

Lesson 1

Present indicative of *être*

Negative and two interrogative forms of *être*

Gender of nouns

Definite and indefinite articles

Plural of nouns and adjectives by adding *s*

Plural of *un, une*

Formation of interrogative sentence with *est-ce que*

CONVERSATION

Dans la Rue

(Read this and all subsequent conversations aloud over and over with a fellow-student or alone until you feel that you can carry on a similar conversation yourself.)

LE MÉDECIN: Bonjour, Marie.
MARIE: Bonjour, M. le docteur.
LE MÉDECIN: Comment ça va, aujourd'hui?
MARIE: Très bien, merci, et vous?
LE MÉDECIN: Pas mal. Mais, où est Henri? Comment va-t-il?
MARIE: Il est à la maison. Il ne va pas très bien aujourd'hui.
LE MÉDECIN: Est-il souvent malade?
MARIE: Non, pas trop souvent. De temps en temps, seulement.
LE MÉDECIN: Est-ce que Georges est malade aussi?

MARIE: Oui, il ne va pas très bien.
LE MÉDECIN: Est-ce qu'il est à la maison?
MARIE: Oui, M. le docteur.
LE MÉDECIN: A tout à l'heure.
MARIE: Au revoir, M. le docteur.

VOCABULAIRE ET EXPRESSIONS

un docteur a doctor
un médecin a physician
un homme a man
une femme a woman
un or **une enfant** a child
un étudiant a student
une étudiante a girl student, co-ed
un livre a book

une maison a house
une rue a street
une minute a minute
une heure an hour
Marie Mary
Henri Henry
Georges George
malade (*pl.* **malades**) ill, sick

je (**j'** before vowels) I
tu you (familiar)
il he (used also for "it" in referring to a noun which is masculine in French)
elle she (used also for "it" in referring to a noun which is feminine in French)

nous we
vous you (polite, sing. and pl.)
ils they (used when referring to nouns which are masculine in French)
elles they (used when referring to nouns which are feminine in French)

il (elle) va he (she) goes, he (she) is (referring to health)

je vais I go, I am going, I am (referring to health)
être to be

où where
ou or
dans in, within, into
à to, at
non no

que . . . ? (**qu'** before a vowel) what?
mais but
oui yes
bien well

mal badly, poorly
trop too
qui . . . ? who? whom?
ne . . . pas (before vowels **n' . . . pas**) not (if the verb is not used, "not" is often translated by **pas: pas bien** not well; **pas seul** not alone)

très very
souvent often

de (**d'** before a vowel) of
vite quickly, fast

seulement only
aussi also

aujourd'hui today

monsieur (abbreviated to **M.** in writing) sir, Mr.

à tout à l'heure I'll see you presently
bonjour good day, good morning, good afternoon
comment ça va? how are you? how are things?
tout à l'heure just now
de temps en temps from time to time
à bientôt I'll see you later, so long

merci thanks, thank you
un peu a little
au revoir goodbye
eh bien! well!
est-ce que (introduces a question)
s'il vous plaît please, if you please
comment va-t-il? how is he?
il va très bien he is very well
à la maison at home

VERBES

Present Indicative of être (to be)

je suis malade I am ill
tu es malade you are ill
il est malade he is ill
elle est malade she is ill

nous sommes malades we are ill
vous êtes malade(s) you are ill
ils sont malades they are ill
elles sont malades they are ill

→ Use *tu* for "you" only when addressing a single intimate friend, relative, child or animal. Use *vous* for "you" when addressing a single person with whom you are not on very familiar terms or when addressing two or more people.

je ne suis pas malade I am not ill
tu n'es pas malade you are not ill
il n'est pas malade he is not ill
elle n'est pas malade she is not ill
nous ne sommes pas malades we are not ill
vous n'êtes pas malade(s) you are not ill
ils ne sont pas malades they are not ill
elles ne sont pas malades they are not ill

→For the negative, use *ne* between the subject and the verb, and *pas* after the verb. Note that *ne* becomes *n'* before vowels.

est-ce que je suis souvent malade? am I often ill?
est-ce que tu es souvent malade? are you often ill?
est-ce qu'il est souvent malade? is he often ill?
est-ce qu'elle est souvent malade? is she often ill?
est-ce que nous sommes souvent malades? are we often ill?
est-ce que vous êtes souvent malade(s)? are you often ill?
est-ce qu'ils sont souvent malades? are they often ill?
est-ce qu'elles sont souvent malades? are they often ill?

→For the interrogative, prefix *est-ce que* (is it that) to the statement. Note that *que* becomes *qu'* before vowels.

suis-je à la maison? am I at home?
es-tu à la maison? are you at home?
est-il à la maison? is he . . . ?
est-elle à la maison? is she . . . ?
sommes-nous à la maison? are we at home?
êtes-vous à la maison? are you at home?
sont-ils à la maison? are they . . . ?
sont-elles à la maison? are they . . . ?

→Another way of asking a question is to put the subject pronoun after the verb, with a hyphen between. For the first person singular of most verbs, however, the *est-ce que* form is preferable.

est-ce que Jean est malade? is John ill?
Jean est-il malade? is John ill?

→If the subject is a noun, use either *est-ce que* with affirmative word order, or the noun subject by itself, followed by the interrogative word order with the appropriate pronoun.

GRAMMAIRE

Gender of Nouns—Definite Articles

le docteur the doctor
le médecin the physician
l'homme (*masc.*) the man
la femme the woman
l'enfant (*masc.* or *fem.*) the child
l'étudiant (*masc.*) the student
l'étudiante (*fem.*) the girl student, the co-ed
le livre the book
la maison the house
la rue the street
l'heure (*fem.*) the hour

→ French has only two genders, masculine and feminine.

Nouns denoting males are normally masculine, those denoting females are feminine.

For nouns which in English are neuter, the definite article indicates the French gender.

The singular definite article is *le* for masculine nouns, *la* for feminine nouns; but both masculine and feminine nouns beginning with a vowel or h mute take *l'* as a definite article; for such nouns the indefinite article (see later) will indicate the gender.

Plural of Nouns

le docteur the doctor	**les docteurs** the doctors
le médecin the physician	**les médecins** the physicians
l'homme the man	**les hommes** the men
la femme the woman	**les femmes** the women
l'étudiant (*masc.*) the student	**les étudiants** the students
l'étudiante (*fem.*) the girl student	**les étudiantes** the girl students
le livre the book	**les livres** the books
la maison the house	**les maisons** the houses
la rue the street	**les rues** the streets
l'heure (*fem.*) the hour	**les heures** the hours

→ The plural of the definite article is *les* for all nouns.
→ Most French nouns form the plural by adding a written *-s* which is silent in pronunciation.

Indefinite Articles

le docteur	the doctor	**un docteur**	a doctor
le médecin	the physician	**un médecin**	a physician
l'homme	the man	**un homme**	a man
la femme	the woman	**une femme**	a woman
l'enfant	the child	**un enfant or une enfant**	a child
l'étudiant	the student	**un étudiant**	a student
l'étudiante	the girl student	**une étudiante**	a girl student
le livre	the book	**un livre**	a book
la maison	the house	**une maison**	a house
la rue	the street	**une rue**	a street
l'heure	the hour	**une heure**	an hour

→ The indefinite article is *un* for the masculine, *une* for the feminine nouns.

Plural of Adjectives

l'homme malade	the sick man	**l'étudiant est malade**	the student is ill
les hommes malades	the sick men	**les étudiantes sont malades**	the girl students are ill

→ Most French adjectives, like nouns, form the plural by adding a written *-s* which is silent in pronunciation.

→ If a noun is plural, any adjective that describes it must also be plural.

Plural of **un, une**

un homme malade	a sick man	**des hommes malades**	sick men or some sick men
une femme	a woman	**des femmes**	women or some women

→ *Des* may be regarded as the plural of *un, une*. It is translated by "some," which is often understood in English, but which always appears in French.

QUESTIONS

(Answer in full sentences.)

1. Où est le médecin? 2. Où est Marie? 3. Où est Henri? 4. Comment va Marie? 5. Comment va Henri? 6. Est-ce qu'Henri est souvent malade? 7. Est-ce que Georges est souvent malade? 8. Est-ce que Marie va très bien? 9. Est-ce que le médecin va bien? 10. Est-ce que Georges est malade de temps en temps?

EXERCICES

A. Make the following sentences negative and repeat them orally:

1. Il est malade aujourd'hui. 2. Nous sommes à la maison. 3. Je suis souvent malade. 4. Vous êtes malade. 5. Ils sont dans la rue.

B. Make the foregoing statements interrogative.

C. Place the correct definite article before each of the following:

maison, rue, livre, médecin, heure, étudiant, homme, étudiante, enfant, docteur, femme.

D. Give the plural of the foregoing with the correct definite article.

E. Reclassify the foregoing as masculines and feminines with the correct indefinite article. Give the plural of these.

F. Complete the following conjugations:

1. je suis trop malade; tu es . . . . 2. je ne suis pas très souvent malade; tu n'es . . . . 3. est-ce que je suis à la maison? est-ce que tu es . . . . etc.

THÈME

—Good morning, doctor. How are you?
—Very well, thank you. Where is Henry today?
—Henry is not very well today. He is at home.
—Is he often ill?
—No, only from time to time. Today he is not well.
—Well, goodbye.
—See you soon.

Lesson 2

Present indicative of *aller*

Negative and interrogative negative of *aller*

Insertion of *-t-* in *va-t-il, va-t-elle*

Use of *aller* with reference to health

Use of *il est, elle est, c'est*

Preposition *à*

Contraction of *à* with *le* and *les*

Feminine and plural of adjectives ending in e

Agreement of adjectives with nouns

Position of adjectives

CONVERSATION

Au Téléphone

HENRIETTE: Allô!
ALBERT: Allô. C'est vous, Henriette?
HENRIETTE: Mais oui! C'est Henriette.
ALBERT: Comment allez-vous?
HENRIETTE: Assez bien. Et vous, comment vous portez-vous?
ALBERT: Bien, merci. Dites-moi, Henriette, est-ce que vous êtes libre ce soir?

HENRIETTE: Pourquoi?

ALBERT: Parce que je voudrais aller au cinéma. Mais pas seul. Il y a un film épatant, avec Charles Boyer. C'est un film français.

HENRIETTE: Entendu! J'accepte avec plaisir. A quelle heure?

ALBERT: A huit heures. Ça va? Marie et Henri vont aussi au cinéma.

HENRIETTE: Est-ce qu'Henri n'est pas malade?

ALBERT: Non, il va bien aujourd'hui. Alors, à ce soir, Henriette.

HENRIETTE: C'est bien. A ce soir.

VOCABULAIRE ET EXPRESSIONS

une nation a nation
une ville a city
une université a college, a university
un cinéma a movie theater
un film a motion picture
un téléphone a telephone
une table a table
un soir an evening
un plaisir a pleasure
Henriette Henrietta
Albert Albert
Charles Charles

grand tall, great, large, big
petit small, little
jeune young
seul alone
intelligent smart, clever, bright, intelligent
libre free
épatant wonderful
français French

aller to go
aller voir to go and see
voir to see

huit eight
quand? when?
comment? how?
beaucoup much
mieux better (only when used as an adverb)
pourquoi? why?
alors then
tard late
parce que because
sur on, upon
avec with

pour to, in order to (followed by an infinitive)

mais but! why! (in exclamations)

et and

allô! hello! (only on telephone)

c'est it is; **est-ce?** is it?

à ce soir see you tonight

assez bien well enough, fairly well

comment allez-vous? comment vous portez-vous? how are you?

dites-moi tell me

entendu! agreed! O.K.

à huit heures at eight o'clock

ce soir this evening, tonight

il y a there is, there are

est-ce qu'il y a? y a-t-il? is there? are there?

je voudrais (plus infinitive) I'd like to . . . .

à quelle heure? at what time?

ça va? all right? O.K.?

c'est bien all right, O.K.

VERBES

Present Indicative of **aller** (to go)

je vais au cinéma I go, I am going to the movies

tu vas au cinéma you go, you are going to the movies

il va au cinéma he goes, he is going . . .

elle va au cinéma she goes, she is going . . .

nous allons au cinéma we go, we are going to the movies

vous allez au cinéma you go, you are going to the movies

ils vont au cinéma they go, they are going . . .

elles vont au cinéma they go, they are going . . .

→ The present tense of French verbs (*je vais*) conveys both the English present (*I go*) and the English present progressive (*I am going*).

je ne vais pas à l'université I don't go, I'm not going to the university

tu ne vas pas à l'université you don't go, you're not going . . .

il ne va pas à l'université he doesn't go, he's not going . . .

elle ne va pas à l'université she doesn't go, she's not going . . .

nous n'allons pas à l'université we don't go, we're not going . . .

vous n'allez pas à l'université you don't go, you're not going .
ils ne vont pas à l'université they don't go, they're not going . .
elles ne vont pas à l'université they don't go, they're not going .

→ The auxiliary "do" which appears in English in questions and negative statements (*does he go? they do not go*) is not used in French.

est-ce que je ne vais pas à la maison? don't I go, am I not going to the house?
est-ce que tu ne vas pas à la maison? don't you go, aren't you going to the house?
est-ce qu'il ne va pas à la maison? doesn't he go, isn't he going . . . ?
est-ce qu'elle ne va pas à la maison? doesn't she go, isn't she going . . . ?
est-ce que nous n'allons pas à la maison? don't we go, aren't we going . . . ?
est-ce que vous n'allez pas à la maison? don't you go, aren't you going . . . ?
est-ce qu'ils ne vont pas à la maison? don't they go, aren't they going . . . ?
est-ce qu'elles ne vont pas à la maison? don't they go, aren't they going . . . ?

or

ne vais-je pas à la maison? don't I go, am I not going to the house?
ne vas-tu pas à la maison?
ne va-t-il pas à la maison?
ne va-t-elle pas à la maison?
n'allons-nous pas à la maison? don't we go, aren't we going to the house?
n'allez-vous pas à la maison?
ne vont-ils pas à la maison?
ne vont-elles pas à la maison?

→ The negative interrogative form of the verb is formed by placing *ne* before and *pas* after the verb if the *est-ce que* device is used. If the verb and the subject pronoun are inverted, *ne* goes before the verb, *pas* after the pronoun.

→ Note the insertion of *-t-* in *va-t-il?* and *va-t-elle?* This "glide-*t*" is inserted in questions to ease the pronunciation when the verb-form ends in a vowel and the subject pronoun begins with another vowel.

Aller with Reference to Health

je vais beaucoup mieux   I am much better
elle va assez bien   she is fairly well
comment **allez-vous?**   how are you?

→ *Je vais* and other forms of the same verb (which in the infinitive has the form *aller*) are used to translate the English "to be," with reference to health.

GRAMMAIRE

Translation of **it is**

Où est le livre? Il est sur la table   Where is the book? It's on the table
Où est la table? Elle est dans la maison   Where is the table? It's in the house

→ The English "it is" is translated by *il est* when the "it" replaces a specific masculine noun; by *elle est* when it replaces a specific feminine noun.

c'est vous   it's you
c'est bien   it's well, it's all right, it's O.K.

→ In most other cases, "it is" is rendered by *c'est.*

il est huit heures   it's eight o'clock
il est tard   it is late

→ In expressions of time, however, *il est* is used.

Preposition **à**—Contraction

Marie   Mary
l'homme   the man
le cinéma   the movie theater
l'université   the university
la maison   the house

à Marie   to Mary
à l'homme   to the man
au cinéma   at or to the movies
à l'université   at or to the university
à la maison   at or to the house, at home

→ *à* is a preposition meaning "to" or "at."
→ *à* contracts with the masculine definite article *le* in the form ***au.***
→ It does not contract with the feminine article *la* or with *l'*.

les hommes	the men	**aux hommes**	to the men
les cinémas	the movie theaters	**aux cinémas**	to or at the movie theaters
les maisons	the houses	**aux maisons**	to or at the houses

→ *à* always contracts with the plural definite article *les* in the form *aux.*

Adjectives: Gender—Number—Position

le jeune étudiant	the young student	**les jeunes étudiants**	the young students
la jeune femme	the young woman	**les jeunes femmes**	the young women
l'homme libre	the free man	**les hommes libres**	the free men
la nation libre	the free nation	**les nations libres**	the free nations

→ Adjectives ending in *e* do not change their form in the feminine, but add *s* to form the plural.

le grand livre	the large book	**les grands livres**	the large books
la grande maison	the large house	**les grandes maisons**	the large houses
le petit livre	the small book	**les petits livres**	the small books
la petite maison	the small house	**les petites maisons**	the small houses

→ Adjectives that do not end in *e* usually add *e* to form the feminine singular, *s* to form the masculine plural, *es* to form the feminine plural.
→ If the final consonant of the masculine singular form is silent, it becomes pronounced when the feminine *e* is added.

l'étudiant est intelligent the student is intelligent
l'étudiante est intelligente the girl student is intelligent
les étudiants sont intelligents the students are intelligent
les étudiantes sont intelligentes the girl students are intelligent

→ The adjective must take the same gender and number as the noun it modifies, even if separated from it by a verb.

l'homme libre the free man	**le grand homme** the great man
l'homme intelligent the intelligent man	**le jeune homme** the young man
l'homme malade the sick man	**le petit homme** the small man

→ Most French adjectives follow the noun they modify; but several frequently used adjectives precede the noun. Learn the position of adjectives by observation.

QUESTIONS

(Answer in full sentences.)

1. Qui téléphone à Henriette? 2. Comment va Henriette? 3. Comment va Albert? 4. Est-ce qu'Henriette est libre? 5. Où Albert voudrait-il aller? 6. Pourquoi? 7. Est-ce qu'Henriette accepte avec plaisir? 8. A quelle heure est le film? 9. Est-ce qu'Henri va au cinéma? 10. Est-ce qu'Henri est malade?

EXERCICES

A. Make affirmative statements of the following questions:

1. Est-ce qu'il va voir un film? 2. Est-ce que tu vas à l'école (*school*)? 3. Est-ce que nous allons au cinéma? 4. Est-ce que je vais au téléphone? 5. Est-ce que vous allez à la maison?

B. Change the affirmative to the negative in the foregoing questions.

C. Write questions requiring the following answers:

1. C'est Albert. 2. Je vais bien, merci. 3. Elle va au cinéma à huit heures. 4. Les étudiantes sont intelligentes. 5. Marie est libre ce soir.

D. Replace the blanks by *au, aux, à la, à l'*, whichever is correct:

1. Ils vont ________ maison. 2. Il passe (*passes*) le livre ________ homme. 3. Elle passe le livre ________ étudiants. 4. Nous allons ________ cinéma.

THÈME

—Are you free tonight?
—Why, yes!
—I should like to go to the movies. There is a French film.
—The French film with Charles Boyer is at the (*au*) Paramount.
—Why aren't you going with Mary?
—Mary is not well. But how is Henriette?
—Oh! She is well. She is going to the movies with Henry this evening.
—Goodbye. I'll see you tonight.

Lesson 3

Present indicative of *avoir*

Negative and interrogative of *avoir*

Present indicative of *vouloir*

Negative and interrogative of *vouloir*

Interrogative sentence with noun subject

Ce, cet, cette, ces

Use of demonstrative adjective

Use of *-ci* and *-là*

Use and meaning of *combien, combien de, assez, assez de, trop, trop de, beaucoup, beaucoup de*

Expressions of time

CONVERSATION

Dans une Boutique

MARIE: Combien vaut ce crayon, s'il vous plaît, monsieur?
LE VENDEUR: Trente francs, mademoiselle.
MARIE: Et cette plume?
LE VENDEUR: Cent dix francs, mademoiselle.
MARIE: C'est trop.
LE VENDEUR: Voulez-vous plutôt un stylo? Voici un excellent stylo à sept cent cinquante francs.

MARIE: Non, merci. Je n'ai pas assez d'argent sur moi. Mais, dites-moi, Paul. Quelle heure est-il?

PAUL: Il est deux heures et demie.

MARIE: Oh! il est tard. Allons-nous-en. Je ne veux pas ce stylo. Merci bien, monsieur.

LE VENDEUR: Il n'y a pas de quoi, mademoiselle. Au revoir.

VOCABULAIRE ET EXPRESSIONS

un vendeur a salesman
une boutique a shop
un crayon a pencil
une plume a pen
un encrier an inkwell
un stylo a fountain pen
l'argent (*masc.*) the money
un franc a franc
un centime a 1/100th part of a franc
mademoiselle Miss
Paul Paul
midi twelve o'clock, noon
minuit twelve o'clock, midnight
excellent excellent

avoir to have
vouloir to want

demi half
un quart a quarter, a fourth
un, une one
deux two
trois three
quatre four
cinq five
six six
sept seven
huit eight
neuf nine
dix ten
onze eleven
vingt twenty
trente thirty
quarante forty
cinquante fifty
soixante sixty
cent one hundred, a hundred
ce, cet, cette this, that
ces these, those
combien (de) how much, how many
assez (de) enough
trop (de) too much, too many
beaucoup (de) much, many, a great deal (of)
moins less
sur on, upon, with (only in the sense of "to have something with one")

voici here is, here are
plutôt rather
de of, from
pour for

merci bien thank you very much
allons-nous-en let's go (away)
il n'y a pas de quoi don't mention it
voulez-vous? do you want? will you have?
combien vaut? how much is . . . worth?

VERBES

Present Indicative of **avoir** (to have)

j'ai un stylo I have, I've got a fountain pen
tu as un stylo you have, you've got a fountain pen
il a un stylo he has, he's got . . .
elle a un stylo she has, she's got . . .
nous avons un stylo we have, we've got . . .
vous avez un stylo you have, you've got . . .
ils ont un stylo they have, they've got . . .
elles ont un stylo they have, they've got . . .

→ *Avoir* translates the English "have"; it also translates the colloquial English "have got."

je n'ai pas assez d'argent I haven't, I don't have, I haven't got enough money
tu n'as pas assez d'argent you haven't, you don't have, you haven't got enough money
il n'a pas assez d'argent he hasn't, he doesn't have, he hasn't got . . .
elle n'a pas assez d'argent she hasn't, she doesn't have, she hasn't got . . .
nous n'avons pas assez d'argent we haven't, we don't have, we haven't got . . .
vous n'avez pas assez d'argent you haven't, you don't have, you haven't got . . .
ils n'ont pas assez d'argent they haven't, they don't have, they haven't got . . .
elles n'ont pas assez d'argent they haven't, they don't have, they haven't got . . .

est-ce que j'ai dix francs? have I, do I have, have I got ten francs?
est-ce que tu as dix francs? have you, do you have, have you got . . . ?
est-ce qu'il a dix francs? has he, does he have, has he got . . . ?
est-ce qu'elle a dix francs? has she, does she have, has she got . . . ?
est-ce que nous avons dix francs? have we, do we have, have we got . . . ?
est-ce que vous avez dix francs? have you, do you have, have you got . . . ?
est-ce qu'ils ont dix francs? have they, do they have, have they got . . . ?
est-ce qu'elles ont dix francs? have they, do they have, have they got . . . ?

or

ai-je dix francs? have I, do I have, have I got ten francs?
as-tu dix francs? have you, do you have, have you got . . . ?
a-t-il dix francs? has he, does he have, has he got . . . ?
a-t-elle dix francs? has she, does she have, has she got . . . ?
avons-nous dix francs? have we, do we have, have we got . . . ?
avez-vous dix francs? have you, do you have, have you got . . . ?
ont-ils dix francs? have they, do they have, have they got . . . ?
ont-elles dix francs? have they, do they have, have they got . . . ?

→ Note again the *-t-* which is used in questions between the verb-form and the subject pronoun when the former ends and the latter begins in a vowel.

→ The negative is formed by putting *ne* before the verb and *pas* after the verb (in simple tenses).

→ The interrogative is formed 1) by prefixing *est-ce que* to the statement; 2) by inverting the subject pronoun and verb and placing a hyphen between them, remembering to insert *-t-* if the verb ends and the pronoun begins with a vowel (*a-t-il dix francs?*); 3) by placing the subject noun at the beginning of the sentence and have it followed by the inverted question with a pronoun, such as: *Marie est-elle malade?* or *le livre est-il sur la table?*

Present Indicative of **vouloir** (to want)

je veux ce crayon I want this pencil
tu veux ce crayon you want this pencil
il veut ce crayon he wants this pencil
elle veut ce crayon she wants this pencil
nous voulons ce crayon we want this pencil
vous voulez ce crayon you want this pencil
ils veulent ce crayon they want this pencil
elles veulent ce crayon they want this pencil

GRAMMAIRE

Demonstrative Adjectives

voulez-vous **ce** livre? do you want this book? do you want that book?
voulez-vous **cet** encrier? do you want this inkwell? do you want that inkwell?
voulez-vous **cette** plume? do you want this pen? do you want that pen?

→ French ordinarily makes no distinction between "this" and "that." Translate "this" or "that" by *ce,* before masculine nouns beginning with a consonant.

Use *cet* before masculine nouns beginning with **vowels or** (usually) h.

Use *cette* before feminine nouns.

voulez-vous **ces** livres? do you want these books? do you want those books?
voulez-vous **ces** encriers? do you want these inkwells? do you want those inkwells?
voulez-vous **ces** plumes? do you want these pens? do you want those pens?

→ "These" and "those" are translated by *ces,* before all plural nouns.

voulez-vous ce livre-ci ou ce livre-là? do you want this book or that book?
voulez-vous ces plumes-ci ou ces plumes-là? do you want these pens or those pens?

→ If a distinction must be made between "these" and "those," "this" and "that," use *-ci* after the noun for "this," "these"; and *-là* after the noun for "that," "those."

Preposition **de**—Contraction

j'ai **le stylo de Marie** I have Mary's pen
je viens **de la maison** I come from the house

→ *De* is a preposition meaning "of" or "from."
→ *De* must be used whenever English uses the possessive 's or '. This means that "Mary's" must be changed to "of Mary," "the physicians' pens" to "the pens of the physicians," etc.

j'ai **le stylo du médecin** I have the doctor's pen
j'ai **le stylo de l'enfant** I have the child's pen
j'ai **le stylo de l'homme** I have the man's pen
j'ai **le stylo de la femme** I have the woman's pen

→ *De* contracts with the masculine singular definite article *le* into *du.*
→ *De la* and *de l'* do not contract.

j'ai **les stylos des médecins** I have the doctors' pens, I have the pens of the doctors
j'ai **les crayons des enfants** I have the children's pencils
j'ai **les plumes des femmes** I have the women's pens

→ *De* contracts with the plural definite article *les* into *des.*

Some Expressions of Quantity

combien de crayons voulez-vous? how many pencils do you want?
combien d'argent voulez-vous? how much money do you want?

→ *Combien* means "how much" or "how many."
If a noun follows, *de* must be used.

c'est assez it's enough, that's enough
avez-vous **assez de crayons?** have you enough pencils?
avez-vous **assez d'argent?** have you enough money?

→ *Assez* means "enough."
If a noun follows, *de* must be used.

c'est trop it's too much, that's too much
il a **trop d'enfants** he has too many children
il a **trop d'argent** he has too much money

→ *Trop* means "too much," "too many."
If a noun follows, *de* must be used.

c'est beaucoup it's much, it's many, it's a great deal, that's a great deal
il a **beaucoup d'enfants** he has many children
il a **beaucoup d'argent** he has a great deal of money

→ *Beaucoup* means "much," "many," "a great deal."
If a noun follows, *de* must be used.

Expressing Time

quelle heure est-il? what time is it?
il est deux heures it is two o'clock
il est deux heures et demie it is half past two
il est deux heures et quart it is quarter past two
il est deux heures moins le quart it is a quarter to two
il est deux heures dix it is ten minutes after two
il est deux heures moins dix it is ten minutes to two
il est midi it is twelve noon
il est minuit it is twelve midnight

QUESTIONS

1. Que dit (*says*) Marie? 2. Combien vaut le stylo? 3. Et la plume? 4. Est-ce que le stylo est bon? 5. Est-ce que Marie a assez d'argent? 6. Quelle heure est-il? 7. Est-ce qu'il est tard? 8. Est-ce que Marie veut le stylo? 9. Est-ce qu'elle dit merci au vendeur? 10. Que répond (*answers*) le vendeur? 11. Est-ce qu'il dit au revoir?

EXERCICES

A. I. Give the affirmative of the following:

1. il ne veut pas 2. nous ne voulons pas 3. il n'a pas 4. vous n'avez pas 5. je ne veux pas 6. ils ne veulent pas 7. ils n'ont pas 8. nous n'avons pas 9. vous ne voulez pas 10. tu ne veux pas 11. je n'ai pas 12. tu n'as pas 13. Marie n'est pas malade 14. Paul, ne veut-il pas beaucoup d'argent? 15. le livre n'est pas sur la table

II. Give the interrogative of the foregoing forms.

B. I. Use *ce, cet, cette* or *ces* with the following nouns:

1. franc 2. crayon 3. vendeur 4. stylo 5. plume 6. boutique 7. argent 8. heure 9. heures 10. crayons 11. plumes 12. homme 13. encrier 14. film 15. cinéma 16. étudiantes 17. étudiant

II. Use the foregoing nouns in their correct form after the following:

1. *assez* 2. *trop* 3. *beaucoup* 4. *combien*
(Change from the singular to the plural when necessary.)

III. Use *du, de l', de la* or *des* with each of the above nouns according to meaning and gender.

C. Substitute a suitable word for the blank in the following expressions of time:

1. ________ est deux heures. 2. Il ________ trois ________. 3. ________ heure est-il? 4. Il est trois heures ________ cinq. 5. Est-il deux heures ________? 6. Il est trois heures et ________. 7. Il est une heure ________ demie. 8. Il est deux heures ________ quart. 9. Il est cinq heures ________. 10. Est-il ________?

THÈME

—What time is it?
—It is half past two.
—Where are you going?
—I am going to a shop. I should like a fountain pen.
—How much money have you?
—I have six dollars but I haven't enough money.
—You have too much money. Do you want that pencil, too?
—No, I do not want that pencil. I have lots of pencils.
—It is late.
—To what shop are you going?
—To Henry Vollard's shop.

Lesson 4

Present indicative of *prendre*

Idiomatic use of *prendre*

Infinitive forms of regular verbs

Present indicative of *acheter*

Present indicative of *essayer*

Orthographic changes in verbs ending in *ayer, eyer, oyer,* and *uyer*

***Aller* and *vouloir* plus the infinitive**

Use of the article with names of languages

Partitive to translate "some" or "any"

Omission of partitive article after negative and when noun is preceded by adjective

Exceptions to foregoing

CONVERSATION

Dans un Magasin

LE VENDEUR: Mademoiselle désire?

JACQUES: Allons, Hélène. Parlez. Dites quelque chose. Que désirez-vous?

HÉLÈNE: Oh! non, Jacques. J'ai peur. Monsieur, parlez-vous anglais?

LE VENDEUR: Non, malheureusement, mademoiselle. J'en suis désolé.

HÉLÈNE: Eh bien! alors, parlez lentement, très lentement, s'il vous plaît.

LE VENDEUR: Oui, mademoiselle, avec plaisir.

HÉLÈNE: Je voudrais acheter un chapeau et des gants.

LE VENDEUR: Oui, mademoiselle. Malheureusement, nous n'avons pas de gants. Mais quant au chapeau, voici quelque chose de très chic.

JACQUES: Comprenez-vous, Hélène?

HÉLÈNE: Mon Dieu, non; je ne comprends pas.

LE VENDEUR: Voulez-vous essayer ce chapeau, mademoiselle?

JACQUES: Ce chapeau vous va à merveille, Hélène.

HÉLÈNE: Très bien. Je le prends. C'est combien, monsieur?

LE VENDEUR: Huit cent quatre-vingt-dix-huit francs. Mademoiselle ne veut rien d'autre?

HÉLÈNE: Merci, c'est tout.

LE VENDEUR: Au revoir, mademoiselle, et merci encore.

HÉLÈNE: Au revoir, monsieur.

VOCABULAIRE ET EXPRESSIONS

le pain the bread
le magasin the store
le chapeau the hat (*pl.* **les chapeaux**)
le gant the glove
le billet the ticket
l'eau (*fem.*) the water
la glace the ice cream
la peur the fear
la jeune fille the girl
les jeunes gens the young people
l'anglais English (language)
le français French
l'espagnol Spanish
l'allemand German
Hélène Helen
Jacques James

bon good, fine (the *fem.* is irregular, **bonne**; *masc. pl.* **bons**; *fem. pl.* **bonnes**)
chic elegant, stylish (this adjective is invariable; same form in the feminine and in the plural)

désirer to wish, to desire
accepter to accept
prendre to take
essayer to try, to try on **(j'essaie)**
parler to speak
acheter to buy **(j'achète)**
jeter to throw **(je jette)**
comprendre to understand

douze twelve
treize thirteen
quatorze fourteen
quinze fifteen
seize sixteen
dix-sept seventeen
dix-huit eighteen
dix-neuf nineteen
vingt et un twenty-one
vingt-deux twenty-two
vingt-trois twenty-three
soixante-dix seventy
soixante et onze seventy-one
soixante-douze seventy-two
quatre-vingts eighty
quatre-vingt-un eighty-one
quatre-vingt-dix ninety
quatre-vingt-onze ninety-one

encore still, yet, again
lentement slowly
malheureusement unfortunately
que? qu'est-ce que? what?
plus more

allons come, come now, come on
j'en suis désolé I'm very sorry
quelque chose (de) something
à merveille wonderfully
aller to fit, to suit, to be becoming
dites quelque chose say something
parlez lentement speak slowly
avoir peur to be afraid
mon Dieu! goodness! gracious!
c'est tout that's all
je le prends I'll take it
rien d'autre? anything else?
quant à as for

VERBES

Present Indicative of **prendre** (to take)

je prends le chapeau et les gants
I take, am taking the hat and the gloves
tu prends le chapeau et les gants
il prend le chapeau et les gants
elle prend le chapeau et les gants

nous prenons le chapeau et les gants
vous prenez le chapeau et les gants
ils prennent le chapeau et les gants
elles prennent le chapeau et les gants

Idiomatic Use

→ *Prendre* means "to take" but never in the sense of "to take a person or a thing somewhere."

It occasionally means "to buy" (*prendre un billet* means "to buy a ticket").

In shopping, *je le prends* is used idiomatically with the meaning "I'll take it."

Prendre has a large number of compounds, all conjugated in the same way. The most common of these are *comprendre* (to understand) and *apprendre* (to learn).

The Infinitive

être to be
avoir to have
aller to go, to be going to
vouloir to want
prendre to take
comprendre to understand

désirer to wish, to desire
parler to speak
accepter to accept
acheter to buy
essayer to try, to try on
finir to finish

→ The French infinitive corresponds to the English infinitive preceded by "to." The preposition "to" is usually not translated in French.

→ French has many irregular verbs. They occur frequently and must be learned separately; among these are *être, avoir, aller, vouloir, prendre.*

→ French also has regular verbs which fall into three classes, each marked by special endings: *-er, -ir, -re.*

Most French regular verbs have an infinitive ending in *-er.*

Present Indicative of a Regular Verb ending in **-er**: **parler** (to speak)

je parl-e français I speak, am speaking French
tu parl-es français you speak, are speaking, etc.
il (elle) parl-e français

nous parl-ons français
vous parl-ez français
ils (elles) parl-ent français

→ The present indicative endings of these verbs are:
Singular **-e, -es, -e** Plural **-ons, -ez, -ent**

Orthographic Changes in Verbs

Present Indicative of **acheter** (to buy)

j'achète un billet I buy a ticket
tu achètes un billet you buy, etc.
il achète un billet
elle achète un billet

nous achetons un billet
vous achetez un billet
ils achètent un billet
elles achètent un billet

→ Most verbs whose infinitive ending *-er* is preceded by a mute *e* plus a consonant (as in *lever, mener, acheter*) change this *e* mute of the stem to *è*. This occurs in the first, second, and third person singular and the third person plural of the present indicative. This is done to prevent the occurrence of two mute *e's* in two successive syllables in the same word, which would cause an unpleasant sound. Other similar verbs double the consonant before a mute *e* of the ending as in *jeter: je jette; appeler: j'appelle.*

Present Indicative of **essayer** (to try, to try on)

j'essaie un chapeau I try on a hat
tu essaies un chapeau
il essaie un chapeau
elle essaie un chapeau

nous essayons un chapeau
vous essayez un chapeau
ils essaient un chapeau
elles essaient un chapeau

→ Verbs ending in *-yer* generally change the *y* to *i* before a mute *e* in the ending. When this occurs, it naturally will affect the pronunciation. Verbs ending in *-ayer* and *-eyer* may retain the *y* throughout (*j'essaie* or *j'essaye*). Verbs ending in *-oyer* or *-uyer* must change *y* to *i* (*déployer,* to deploy: *je déploie; appuyer,* to support: *j'appuie*).

Aller + an Infinitive

je vais acheter un chapeau I am going to buy a hat

→ *Aller* with the infinitive has the same use as the English "to be going to."

GRAMMAIRE

Special Use of the Definite Article

je parle anglais I speak English
elles parlent français they speak French

→ Names of languages are not capitalized in French.

répondez en français, s'il vous plaît please answer in French
parlez-vous français? do you speak French?
il parle parfaitement le français he speaks French perfectly
je ne comprends pas le français I do not understand French

→ Except when the name of a language immediately follows *parler* (to speak) and after *en* (in), the masculine singular article is used with the names of languages.

Partitives

je désire du pain I want (some) bread
avez-vous du pain? have you (any) bread?
je veux de l'eau I want (some) water
avez-vous de l'eau? have you (any) water?
je voudrais de la glace I should like (some) ice cream
a-t-il de la glace? has he (any) ice cream?
je vais acheter des livres I am going to buy (some) books
ont-ils des livres? have they (any) books?

→ "Some" or "any," expressed or understood, is translated in French by the partitive article which consists of **de** *plus the definite article.* This partitive article must be used in French even where the "some" or "any" is only implied in English.

je ne désire pas de pain I want no bread, I don't want any bread
vous n'avez pas d'eau you don't have any water, you have no water
il n'achète pas de livres he doesn't buy any books, he buys no books

→ If the sentence is negative, *de* alone, without the definite article, is normally used for "some" or "any." The English "no" used before a noun with an affirmative verb (*he has no books*) is regularly translated into French by making the verb negative and using *de* before the noun (*il n'a pas de livres*).

il a d'excellents livres he has excellent books

→ If an adjective precedes a noun, in the plural especially, *de* alone without the article is used for "some" or "any," expressed or understood. This rule is seldom observed in the singular and one normally hears *il a du bon pain.*

Des jeunes gens (young people), *des jeunes filles* (girls), *des petits pois* (peas), *des petits pains* (rolls), and other expressions where the adjective does not have its customary value but forms a unit with the noun are exceptions to the rule.

QUESTIONS

1. Est-ce qu'Hélène parle français? 2. Est-ce qu'elle a peur? 3. Qui parle lentement? 4. Est-ce qu'Hélène veut acheter quelque chose? 5. Que veut-elle acheter? 6. Qu'est-ce qu'il y a dans le magasin? 7. Est-ce qu'Hélène comprend le vendeur? 8. Pourquoi Hélène achète-t-elle un chapeau? 9. Est-ce qu'Hélène veut autre chose? 10. Que dit-elle au vendeur? 11. Est-ce que vous parlez anglais? 12. Parlez-vous français?

EXERCICES

A. Fill in the blank using the correct form of *prendre*.

1. Il ______ le livre et je ______ le crayon. 2. Nous ______ ces gants. 3. Vous ______ trop de pain. 4. Ils ______ des billets. 5. Est-ce que tu ______ les chapeaux?

B. Write the present indicative of the following verbs: *parler, acheter, essayer.*

C. Write the negative of the foregoing verbs in the present indicative.

D. Fill in the blank with the correct partitive construction.

1. J'ai ______ pain mais je n'ai pas ______ eau. 2. Je veux ______ eau, mais je ne veux pas ______ pain. 3. Il va acheter ______ glace mais il ne va pas acheter ______ livres. 4. Il a ______ excellents livres. 5. Vous n'avez pas ______ eau, avez-vous ______ pain? 6. Nous n'avons pas ______ billets. 7. Il achète ______ gants et elle achète ______ chapeaux. 8. Nous n'avons pas ______ crayon.

E. Ask questions to which the following are the answers:

1. Non, malheureusement. 2. Non, j'en suis désolé. 3. C'est tout, merci. 4. Non, je veux quelque chose de très simple. 5. Oui, je le prends.

THÈME

—What do you wish, Miss?
—I should like some ice cream.
—I am very sorry, Miss, but we have no ice cream.
—Have you any bread?
—Yes, and we have sandwiches (*le sandwich*) and soup (*la soupe*).

Do you want some water, too?

—Yes, some water and some sandwiches. It is late.

—Yes, unfortunately. Will you have some soup, too?

—No, I want no soup now.

—And you, sir, what will you have (do you wish)?

—Some soup and sandwiches. Have you any peas?

—No, I am sorry.

—Tell me, Henry, do you speak French?

—No, I do not understand much and I speak slowly.

—But you speak Spanish and German.

—Yes. Mary is learning Spanish, too. Where is Mary?

—She is at the store. She is buying a hat. She has no hat now.

—That hat is very stylish.

—Yes, and she is stylish, too.

Review Lesson 1

A. Conjugate:

1. Je suis à l'école. 2. Je vais à la maison. 3. Je veux essayer ce chapeau. 4. Je jette mes gants. 5. J'appelle (*call*) Georges. 6. J'essaie (*ou* j'essaye) les gants. 7. J'achète un stylo. 8. J'ai un livre. 9. Je prends des billets.

B. Replace the blank by the correct partitive construction:

1. Il achète ________ glace. 2. Avez-vous ________ pain? 3. Voulez-vous ________ eau? 4. Ils ont ________ stylos. 5. Il n'y a pas ________ glace. 6. Je ne veux pas ________ pain. 7. Je ne prends pas ________ eau. 8. Nous n'avons pas ________ stylos. 9. Ils ont ________ excellents stylos. 10. Nous avons ________ gants.

C. Replace the blank by: *au, à l', à la, aux, du, de l', de la,* or *des.*

1. Voici le livre ________ vendeur. 2. Avez-vous le stylo ________ jeune fille? 3. Montrez-moi les crayons ________ étudiants. 4. Où sont les étudiants ________ école? 5. Nous allons souvent ________ école. 6. Il achète un livre ________ magasin. 7. Ils vendent les gants ________ jeunes filles. 8. Nous parlons français ________ vendeurs. 9. Nous allons ________ maison ________ vendeur. 10. Il jette le crayon ________ garçon.

D. Make the following sentences interrogative, then negative, and finally negative interrogative:

1. Vous êtes souvent malade. 2. Il comprend le français. 3. Nous parlons français. 4. Ils prennent des billets. 5. Nous voulons un bon stylo. 6. J'achète toujours de bons livres. 7. Il appelle Paul et Marie.

E. Translate the following words and then use the plural in a sentence:

1. fountain pen 2. store 3. glove 4. ticket 5. ice cream 6. house

7. city 8. table 9. evening 10. movie theater 11. telephone 12. film 13. book 14. man 15. student 16. pencil 17. street 18. hour 19. child 20. physician.

F. Study the spelling and meaning of the words of this and subsequent dictations before they are given in class.

G. *DICTÉE*

La France est une contrée riche et fertile. Il y a quatre grands fleuves en France: la Seine, la Loire, la Garonne et le Rhône. La Seine passe à Paris et à Rouen. La Loire passe à Orléans et à Nantes. La Garonne passe à Toulouse et à Bordeaux. Le Rhône passe à Lyon et à Avignon. Les montagnes qui séparent la France de l'Italie sont les Alpes. La France n'est pas si grande que le Texas mais l'Union française (la France et les colonies françaises) est plus grande que les États-Unis et ses possessions.

Lecture 1

RIVALITÉ

(D'après un conte de Max et Alex. Fischer)

A Beaulieu[1], dans la rue Lafayette, il y a[2] deux magasins de tissus (*dry goods, materials*). Le magasin de monsieur Petit est au numéro[3] six; le magasin de monsieur Legrand est au numéro onze. Dans les deux magasins il y a beaucoup de tissus de coton, de satin, de soie (*silk*). Naturellement (*naturally*), il y a une grande rivalité entre (*between*) les deux marchands.

Il est huit heures.[4] Monsieur Petit est dans son magasin avec Émile, son commis (*salesman, clerk*). Monsieur Legrand aussi a un commis: Eugène.

A huit heures et demie[5] Eugène entre dans[6] le magasin Petit.

—Bonjour monsieur Petit, dit-il (*says he*), je voudrais (*I would like*) un mètre[7] de ruban (*ribbon*) pour monsieur Legrand.

—Bonjour Eugène, dit monsieur Petit, vous désirez un mètre de ruban, mais de quelle couleur (*what color*)?

—La couleur n'a pas d'importance, monsieur Petit, dit Eugène.

—C'est bizarre, dit monsieur Petit. Mais il mesure (*measures*) un mètre de ruban rouge[8] et il donne (*gives*) le ruban à Eugène.

A midi,[9] madame Lenoir entre dans le magasin de monsieur Petit.

—Bonjour, monsieur Petit, dit-elle; comment allez-vous?

[1] A Beaulieu: *note that the preposition* à *is used with names of cities.*

[2] il y a: *this expression translates "there is" and "there are."*

[3] numéro *is used to number things in succession (for example, houses)*

[4] il est huit heures: *It's eight o'clock. Note that* il *is used in telling time.*

[5] demie: demie, *placed after a noun, agrees with it in gender; placed before it remains invariable:* une demi-heure.

[6] entre dans: entrer *is followed either by* dans *or* à *before a noun.*

[7] un mètre: *a meter (39.3 inches, a little more than a yard). Most European countries measure in meters, which have 100 parts, or centimeters.*

[8] ruban rouge: *note that adjectives of color follow the noun.*

[9] à midi, *at noon; similarly:* à minuit, *at midnight.*

—Je vais bien, merci, madame Lenoir. Que désirez-vous aujourd'hui?

—Je voudrais un mètre de soie orange; mais je suis pressée (*I am in a hurry*); envoyez (*send*) cette soie ce soir[10] à la maison, s'il vous plaît.

—Entendu (*agreed*), madame Lenoir, et merci bien!

Monsieur Petit cherche (*looks for*) la soie orange. Il y a sur sa (*his*) table des soies rouges, bleues,[11] blanches (*white*), noires (*black*), violettes, mais il n'y a pas de soie orange. Monsieur Petit est désolé. Que faire (*What is he to do*)? Madame Lenoir est une excellente cliente. C'est aussi[12] une cliente difficile (*hard to please*). Mais monsieur Petit a une idée, une excellente idée. Il va faire comme (*like*) son (*his*) rival monsieur Legrand, et acheter un mètre de soie orange. C'est la solution. Monsieur Petit dit donc (*therefore*) a son commis Émile:

—Tu vas aller au magasin Legrand acheter un mètre de soie orange à cent francs le mètre.[13]

Émile va donc au magasin Legrand. Il achète un mètre de soie orange; il donne cent francs à monsieur Legrand et il rapporte (*brings back*) la soie à monsieur Petit. Monsieur Petit est content, très content. Il a la soie orange pour madame Lenoir. Il va faire le paquet (*package*) et il va envoyer son commis avec le paquet chez (*to the house of*) madame Lenoir. Mais il a une idée bizarre. Il a l'idée de mesurer la soie. Il va chercher son mètre; il mesure le précieux morceau (*piece*) de soie orange et il trouve (*finds*) que ce morceau de soie ne mesure pas un mètre mais quatre-vingt-dix-sept centimètres. Il mesure une fois (*time*), deux fois, trois fois. C'est clair (*clear*) et c'est extraordinaire! Le morceau est trop court de (*by*) trois centimètres. Monsieur Petit est furieux, mais il est content aussi. Il est content parce qu'il a la preuve (*proof*) que son rival, monsieur Legrand, est un filou (*cheat, thief*).

10 ce soir, *this evening, tonight;* une soirée *means an evening's entertainment.*

11 bleues: *notice the feminine plural form for "blue." In French the* e *precedes the* u.

12 C'est aussi . . . , *She is also a customer who is hard to please. When a noun follows* c'est, c' *is translated by the pronoun representing the noun.*

13 le mètre: *the definite article is translated into English by* a *or* per.

A une heure, le professeur Dupont[14] passe devant le magasin Petit. Monsieur Petit est devant la porte de son magasin. Il arrête (*stops*) le professeur Dupont et dit:

—Comment vous portez-vous, monsieur le professeur? Avez-vous besoin de (*do you need*) quelque chose, aujourd'hui? Un beau tissu de coton, de satin, de soie?

—Non, merci, monsieur Petit, pas aujourd'hui.[15]

—Je regrette, monsieur le professeur; mais je voudrais vous donner un conseil (*piece of advice*). Quand vous avez besoin de tissus, n'allez pas (*don't go*) au magasin de monsieur Legrand. Je ne dis pas cela (*I don't say that*) parce que je suis un rival de monsieur Legrand. Je voudrais vous prouver (*prove*) que le conseil est bon. Voici cent francs. Vous allez entrer dans le magasin Legrand et acheter un mètre de soie bleue. Vous allez rapporter la soie et vous allez voir (*see*) une chose extraordinaire.

Le professeur Dupont est surpris, mais il accepte les cent francs et il va au magasin Legrand. Après cinq ou six minutes, il arrive au magasin Petit avec la soie. Monsieur Petit donne son mètre au professeur et dit:

—Vous avez un mètre de soie, n'est-ce pas? Un mètre, c'est cent centimètres, n'est-ce pas? Bon! Vous allez, s'il vous plaît, mesurer ce morceau de soie. (Le professeur mesure.)

Combien (*how much*) est-ce que ce morceau mesure? Quatre-vingt-dix-sept centimètres? C'est bizarre, n'est-ce pas? Oui, c'est extraordinaire.

A deux heures, le docteur Bonvent passe devant le magasin Petit. Monsieur Petit est devant la porte et il arrête le docteur.

—Bonjour Docteur, dit-il, comment allez-vous et comment va madame Bonvent? A-t-elle besoin de beaux[16] tissus de coton, de satin, de soie?

[14] le professeur Dupont: *speaking of a titled person in French, one says* le professeur Dupont, le général MacArthur; *but in direct address one says* monsieur le professeur, monsieur le président, *etc.*

[15] pas aujourd'hui: pas *is used without* ne *to express a negative with a noun not accompanied by a verb:* pas Henri, *not Henry;* pas ce livre, *not that book.*

[16] les beaux tissus: beau *is an irregular adjective; the feminine is* belle, *the masculine plural* beaux, *the feminine plural* belles.

—Non, merci, monsieur Petit, pas aujourd'hui.

—Je regrette, dit monsieur Petit. Mais, Docteur, je désire vous donner un bon conseil: n'allez jamais (*never*) acheter de tissus au magasin Legrand. Si je dis cela, ce n'est pas parce que monsieur Legrand est un rival. J'ai une bonne[17] raison. Voici cent francs. Pour me faire plaisir (*to do me a favor*), vous allez entrer dans le magasin de monsieur Legrand et acheter un mètre de soie noire; vous allez rapporter la soie ici et vous allez voir une chose extraordinaire.

Le docteur Bonvent est surpris, mais il est curieux. Il va donc chez Legrand[18] (*to Legrand's store*) et achète un mètre de soie noire. Il rapporte la soie chez Petit. Monsieur Petit va chercher son mètre. Il donne le mètre au docteur et dit:

—Docteur, vous avez bien (*really*) un mètre de soie, n'est-ce pas? Voici un mètre. Un mètre, c'est bien cent centimètres, n'est-ce pas? Mesurez!. (Le docteur mesure.) Combien est-ce que le morceau de soie mesure? Quatre-vingt-dix-sept centimètres? N'est-ce pas remarquable? N'est-ce pas extraordinaire? Voilà pourquoi, Docteur, il est préférable de ne pas acheter de tissus chez Legrand. Au revoir, Docteur, et merci!

Monsieur Petit est très content. Le capitaine Lemaître, le pharmacien Purgeon, le banquier Dorval passent devant son magasin. Monsieur Petit les arrête (*stops them*). A chacun (*to each*) il pose (*puts*) les mêmes questions. A chacun il donne cent francs pour (*in order to*) aller acheter un mètre de soie chez son rival, monsieur Legrand. Chacun rapporte le morceau de soie, chacun mesure et trouve (*finds out*) que le morceau ne mesure pas un mètre, mais quatre-vingt-dix-sept centimètres. Quel succès! Monsieur Petit est très content, parce que tout le monde dans la petite ville de Beaulieu va savoir (*know*) que monsieur Legrand

17 une bonne raison: *bon is an irregular adjective; masculine* bon, *feminine* bonne, *masculine plural* bons, *feminine plural* bonnes.

18 chez Legrand: chez *with a noun representing a proper name* (chez Marie, chez Paul) *or a title* (chez le professeur, chez le docteur) *is rendered in English by "at the store of," "at the office of," "at the house of," etc.*

est un filou. Le temps passe. Il est sept heures. Monsieur Petit va fermer (*close up*) son magasin. Il va aller prendre son apéritif (*have his before-dinner drink*) au Café du Commerce comme chaque soir (*each evening*). Il est très, très content. Au café il va trouver le professeur Dupont, le docteur Bonvent, le capitaine Lemaître, le pharmacien Purgeon, le banquier Dorval. Ils vont tous (*all of them*) le soir[19] au Café du Commerce prendre l'apéritif. Il va aussi trouver là monsieur Legrand. Monsieur Legrand aussi va chaque soir au Café du Commerce. C'est une situation parfaite pour monsieur Petit, car tous savent (*for all know*) que monsieur Legrand est un filou.

Monsieur Petit entre dans le café. A une table il voit (*sees*) le professeur Dupont, le docteur Bonvent, le capitaine Lemaître, le pharmacien Purgeon, le banquier Dorval. Ils jouent (*play*) aux cartes. Monsieur Petit va prendre un siège (*seat*) à la même table. Il est très content. Quelques minutes passent. Monsieur Legrand entre dans le café. C'est un moment très agréable pour monsieur Petit. Mais monsieur Legrand va prendre un siège à côté de (*next to*) monsieur Petit.

—Monsieur Petit, dit-il, je voudrais vous remercier (*thank you*).

—Vous désirez me remercier? Et pourquoi?

—Mais vous remercier du (*for the*) mètre de ruban de ce matin.

Et monsieur Legrand explique (*explains*):

—Ce matin, j'arrive à mon magasin à huit heures. J'ai besoin de mesurer des tissus et je cherche mon mètre. Pas de mètre! Alors (*then*) j'ai une idée. Je dis à mon commis: "Eugène, tu vas aller acheter un mètre de ruban chez monsieur Petit." Eh bien (*well*), depuis (*since*) huit heures du matin je mesure mes tissus avec le mètre de ruban de monsieur Petit.

[19] le soir: *expressions involving time, such as* le matin, l'après-midi, *and* le soir, *are translated as "in the morning," "in the afternoon," "in the evening," etc.*

Catastrophe! Monsieur Petit regarde (*looks at*) son apéritif. Les autres (*the others*) regardent monsieur Petit avec mépris (*contempt*) et monsieur Legrand avec sympathie. Et monsieur Legrand répète:

—Merci, monsieur Petit, encore une fois merci!

QUESTIONNAIRE

1. Quels sont les deux magasins de tissus qui sont dans la rue Lafayette à Beaulieu? 2. Qui sont Émile et Eugène? 3. Pourquoi Eugène entre-t-il dans le magasin de M. Petit? 4. Des soies de quelle couleur M. Petit a-t-il dans son magasin? 5. Pourquoi Émile va-t-il acheter un mètre de soie orange chez M. Legrand? 6. Quelle idée bizarre M. Petit a-t-il avant d'envoyer la soie à madame Lenoir? 7. Que trouve-t-il? 8. Pourquoi est-il content? 9. Pourquoi dit-il au professeur Dupont de ne pas acheter de tissus chez M. Legrand? 10. Pourquoi lui donne-t-il cent francs? 11. Quand le docteur Bonvent passe devant le magasin Petit, que lui dit M. Petit? 12. Qui sont les autres personnes qui passent devant le magasin Petit? 13. Quand ils vont tous prendre l'apéritif au Café du Commerce, quelle opinion ont-ils de M. Legrand? 14. Au café, quel siège M. Petit prend-il? 15. Quand M. Legrand entre dans le café, quel siège va-t-il prendre? 16. Que dit-il à M. Petit? 17. Qu'est-ce qu'il explique à tout le monde? 18. Que fait M. Petit et comment les autres le regardent-ils?

Lesson 5

Conjugation of -er verbs

Orthographic changes and conjugation of *appeler*

Reflexive pronouns

Position of reflexive pronouns in positive and negative statements and questions

Omission of article after *être* before nouns of profession, nationality, and religion

Possessive adjectives

CONVERSATION

L'Agent de Police et l'Étranger

L'AGENT: Un instant, Monsieur, s'il vous plaît.
L'ÉTRANGER: Qu'est-ce qu'il y a?
L'AGENT: Comment vous appelez-vous, Monsieur?
L'ÉTRANGER: Je m'appelle Victor Lambert.
L'AGENT: Vous êtes étranger?
L'ÉTRANGER: Oui, monsieur l'agent.
L'AGENT: Montrez-moi votre passeport, s'il vous plaît.
L'ÉTRANGER: Voici mon passeport.
L'AGENT: Quel âge avez-vous?
L'ÉTRANGER: J'ai trente et un ans.
L'AGENT: Depuis combien de temps êtes-vous ici?

L'ÉTRANGER: Dans cette ville?

L'AGENT: Non, Monsieur, en France.

L'ÉTRANGER: Depuis deux mois et une semaine.

L'AGENT: Êtes-vous Anglais?

L'ÉTRANGER: Non, je suis Américain.

L'AGENT: Et cette dame, c'est votre femme?

LA DAME: Oui, M. l'agent, je suis sa femme; Françoise Rosemarie Lambert.

L'AGENT: Je regrette, Monsieur, mais vos papiers ne sont pas en règle. Voulez-vous m'accompagner chez le commissaire de police?

L'ÉTRANGER: Allons donc! Vous plaisantez!

LA DAME: Pas possible!

L'AGENT: Pardon, Monsieur. Je ne plaisante pas. J'insiste. Accompagnez-moi.

VOCABULAIRE ET EXPRESSIONS

l'étranger (*fem.* **l'étrangère**) the foreigner
la femme the woman; the wife
la dame the lady
le passeport the passport
l'âge (*masc.*) the age
l'an (*masc.*) the year

le mois the month
la semaine the week
l'instant the instant
le temps the time
le papier the paper (but *not* newspaper)

l'agent, l'agent de police the policeman
le commissaire (de police) the chief of police
la police the police
l'amie the friend (*fem.*)
l'hospitalité (*fem.*) the hospitality
la France France
Anglais English, Englishman (capitalize if it refers to a person)
Américain American (capitalize if it refers to a person)

montrer to show
accompagner to accompany, to come with, to go with

s'appeler to call oneself, to be called, one's name to be
regretter to regret, to be sorry

plaisanter to joke
appeler to call **(j'appelle)**

insister to insist

mon, ma, mes my
ton, ta, tes your
son, sa, ses his, her

notre, nos our
votre, vos your
leur, leurs their

depuis since
chez to or at the home, office, place of business of
ici here

en in (*en* has particular uses, as with fem. sing, names of countries: *en France*)
dans in, within, into

un instant just a second
qu'est-ce qu'il y a? qu'y a-t-il? what's the matter?
quel âge avez-vous? how old are you?
j'ai trente ans I am thirty (years old)
comment vous appelez-vous? what is your name?
je m'appelle my name is
depuis combien de temps (or depuis quand) êtes-vous ici? how long have you been here?
je suis ici depuis— I have been here—

je suis Américain I am an American
montrez-moi show me, let me see
je regrette I'm sorry
en règle in order (especially in connection with documents)
voulez-vous? will you?
allons donc! come now! come, come!
pas possible! impossible! you don't say so!
pardon! pardon me!
accompagnez-moi come with me! come along!

VERBES

→ *Plaisanter* (to joke); *accompagner* (to accompany, come with, go with); *insister* (to insist); *montrer* (to show); *regretter* (to regret, to be sorry) are all regular verbs of the *-er* conjugation.

To conjugate them in the present indicative, drop the *-er* of the infinitive and add the endings *-e, -es, -e, -ons, -ez, -ent.* (See pp. 28, 29.)

Present Indicative of **appeler** (to call)

j'appelle I call
tu appelles you call
il appelle he calls
elle appelle she calls
nous appelons we call
vous appelez you call
ils appellent they call
elles appellent they call

→ Verbs ending in *-eler,* like *appeler,* generally double the l before a mute *-e* of the ending. This is done to prevent the sound of two mute *e's* in two successive syllables in the same word.

The Reflexive Verb

je m'appelle I call myself, I am called, my name is
tu t'appelles you call yourself, you are called, your name is
il s'appelle he calls himself, he is called, his name is
elle s'appelle she calls herself, she is called, her name is
nous nous appelons we call ourselves, we are called, our names are
vous vous appelez you call yourself or yourselves, you are called, your name is or your names are
ils (elles) s'appellent they call themselves, they are called, their names are

→ *S'appeler* is *appeler* used reflexively; that is, with the subject acting on himself or for himself or to himself. English uses many verbs reflexively (I hurt myself, I cut myself, etc.); and many verbs are reflexive in French which are not so in English, such as *je me lave,* I wash.

Reflexive Pronouns

me myself, to or for myself
te yourself, to or for yourself
se himself, herself, itself, themselves, to or for himself, herself, itself, themselves
nous ourselves, to or for ourselves
vous yourself, yourselves, to or for yourself, yourselves

→ Note the position of these pronouns. They normally precede the verb, coming between the subject pronoun and the verb-form.

Note that *me, te, se,* become *m', t', s'* if a vowel follows.

je ne m'appelle pas Jean I do not call myself, I am not called, my name is not John

→ In the negative, the reflexive pronoun follows *ne* and precedes the verb.

est-ce qu'il s'appelle Robert? s'appelle-t-il Robert?

→ In the interrogative, the reflexive pronoun comes immediately before the verb.

GRAMMAIRE

Omission of the Indefinite Article

je suis étranger I am a foreigner
il est Américain he is (an) American
ils sont médecins they are doctors
elle est protestante she is a Protestant

→ A predicate noun used after the verb "to be" and describing the subject's profession, nationality, religion, or class is generally used without the indefinite article or the partitive.

Possessive Adjectives

mon livre my book
mes livres my books
ma maison my house
mes maisons my houses

→ "My" is translated: 1. by *mon* before a masculine singular noun; 2. by *ma* before a feminine singular noun; 3. by *mes* before a plural noun.

ton livre your book
tes livres your books
ta maison your house
tes maisons your houses

→ "Your" (familiar singular) is translated: 1. by *ton* before a masculine singular noun; 2. by *ta* before a feminine singular noun; 3. by *tes* before a plural noun.

son livre his or her book
ses livres his or her books
sa maison his or her house
ses maisons his or her houses

→ "His" or "her" is translated: 1. by *son* before a masculine singular noun; 2. by *sa* before a feminine singular noun; 3. by *ses* before a plural noun. "Its" has the same translation.

notre livre our book
nos livres our books

notre maison our house
nos maisons our houses

→ "Our" is translated: 1. by *notre* before a singular noun; 2. by *nos* before a plural noun.

votre livre your book
vos livres your books

votre maison your house
vos maisons your houses

→ "Your" (singular or plural) is usually translated: 1. by *votre* before a singular noun; 2. by *vos* before a plural noun.

leur livre their book
leurs livres their books

leur maison their house
leurs maisons their houses

→ "Their" is translated by: 1. *leur* before a singular noun; 2. *leurs* before a plural noun.

mon amie, ton amie, son amie my friend (*fem.*), your friend, his or her friend
mon hospitalité, ton hospitalité, son hospitalité my hospitality, your hospitality, his or her hospitality

→ *Mon, ton, son* are used, however, instead of *ma, ta, sa,* before feminine singular nouns beginning with a vowel or (usually) h. This is done in order to avoid the break in the voice that would come if two vowels were to be pronounced successively.
→ Note that *mon, ton, son,* etc. are *adjectives* to be used only when a substantive follows.

QUESTIONS

1. Comment vous appelez-vous? 2. Êtes-vous Américain ou étranger? 3. Avez-vous un passeport? 4. Quel âge a Monsieur Lambert? 5. Quel âge avez-vous? 6. Depuis quand êtes-vous dans cette ville? 7. Êtes-vous Anglais? 8. Est-il Anglais? 9. Qui est la dame qui accom-

pagne M. Lambert? 10. Comment s'appelle-t-elle? 11. Est-ce que ses papiers sont en règle? 12. Où va-t-elle accompagner l'agent de police? 13. Que répond-elle à l'agent quand il lui dit (*tells her*) de l'accompagner? 14. Est-ce qu'il plaisante? 15. Est-ce qu'il y a un commissaire de police dans votre ville?

EXERCICES

A. Give the negative of the following forms:

1. il s'appelle Henri
2. vous vous appelez Marie
3. ils s'appellent Georges et Anna

B. Give the interrogative of:

1. il se montre aimable
2. nous nous montrons aimables
3. ils se montrent aimables

C. Use the correct pronoun in the following reflexive forms:

1. il __________ appelle
2. vous __________ appelez
3. ils __________ appellent
4. nous __________ appelons
5. elles __________ appellent
6. je __________ appelle
7. elle __________ appelle
8. tu __________ appelles

D. Conjugate the present indicative of *être* using each of the following as predicate nouns: a) étranger b) Américain c) Anglais d) Français e) médecin f) professeur g) catholique h) protestant

E. I. Use in turn *mon, ton, son, ma, ta, sa, mes, tes, ses*—whichever forms are correct, with the following nouns:

ami, livre, maison, médecin, âge, passeport, femme, amis, livres, papiers.

II. Use in turn *notre, votre, leur, nos, vos, leurs*—whichever forms are correct, with the following nouns:

commissaire, hospitalité, pain, gant, billet, chapeau, crayons, stylos, plumes, enfants, argent.

F. Find in the vocabulary the word best suited to fill in the blanks in the following sentences:

1. Victor Lambert est ________. 2. Quel ________ avez-vous? 3. J'ai trente ________. 4. Êtes-vous ________ de Monsieur Lambert? 5. Depuis combien de ________ êtes-vous dans cette ville? 6. Je suis ici depuis ________. 7. Voilà un ________ de police! 8. Je ________, je n'ai pas de passeport. 9. Comment ________ ce monsieur? 10. Mes papiers sont ________.

G. Ask questions to which the following are answers:

1. Je viens dans un instant. 2. J'ai vingt ans. 3. Je m'appelle Georges. 4. Il s'appelle Henri. 5. Nous nous appelons Smith. 6. Nous sommes ici depuis deux mois. 7. Ils sont à Paris depuis deux semaines. 8. Nous sommes Américains. 9. Je suis Anglais. 10. Ces documents sont en règle maintenant. 11. Il est malade et nous le regrettons. 12. Allons donc! pas possible!

THÈME

—Are you a foreigner?

—No, I am an American.

—Have you a passport?

—Yes, but I insist. I am not a foreigner.

—Show me your passport. Show me those papers, too. How long have you been in this city?

—I have been here twenty-five years.

—What is your name?

—Georges Lambert.

—Why, you're French.

—No, I am an American now and my wife is also an American.

—How old are you, sir?

—I am thirty-two years old.

—These papers are not in order. Accompany me to the chief of police.

—Why, you're fooling.

—No, I am not fooling. I insist.

Lesson 6

Present indicative of *pleuvoir, sortir,* and *faire*

Idiomatic uses of *faire*

Expressions of weather

Idiomatic uses of *avoir* to express physical sensations

Formation of the imperative

Interrogative pronouns translating "what"

Interrogative adjectives translating "what"

Agreement of interrogative adjectives

Qu'est-ce que c'est que cela?

CONVERSATION

Le Temps

MADELEINE: Quel temps fait-il dehors, René? Est-ce qu'il fait mauvais temps?

RENÉ: Il fait plutôt chaud dans la rue. Mais ici, dans la maison, il fait presque froid.

MADELEINE: Vraiment? Moi, j'ai très chaud.

RENÉ: Pourquoi ne sortons-nous pas? Il fait vraiment beau. Faisons une petite promenade.

MADELEINE: Avec plaisir. Attendez un instant. Je vais prendre mon chapeau et mon sac à main.

René: Prenez aussi votre manteau.

Madeleine: Mais vous dites qu'il fait chaud.

René: Oui, c'est vrai. Mais vous avez toujours froid quand vous sortez.

Madeleine: Eh bien, je suis prête. Sortons.

René: En route.

Madeleine: Ah, mon Dieu, mon chapeau! Il fait du vent aujourd'hui!

René: Oui, mais il fait aussi du soleil.

Madeleine: Et ces nuages là-bas?

René: Enfin, il ne pleut certainement pas encore.

Madeleine: Non, mais s'il pleut, qu'est-ce que je vais faire?

René: S'il fait mauvais temps, nous allons tout simplement rentrer. Mais il ne va pas pleuvoir. Il fait trop frais.

Madeleine: Je ne suis pas du tout de votre avis. Je suis en nage.

René: Écoutez, Madeleine; oublions un peu le temps. Mettons-nous d'accord. Autrement, nous allons rentrer trop tard pour le cinéma.

Madeleine: Bon! D'accord. Mettons-nous en route et oublions le temps. S'il fait chaud, il fait chaud. S'il fait froid, il fait froid. Voilà tout.

VOCABULAIRE ET EXPRESSIONS

le travail (*pl.* **travaux**) the work
le sommeil the sleep, the sleepiness
la soif the thirst
la faim the hunger
la promenade the walk
le voyage the trip
le lit the bed
le soleil the sun
le vent the wind
le nuage the cloud
le manteau the woman's coat
le sac the woman's bag
le sac à main the handbag
Madeleine Madeleine
René René (*masculine name*)
vrai true, real
froid cold

chaud warm, hot
frais (*fem.* **fraîche**) cool
prêt ready
mauvais bad

beau (change to **bel** before vowel or h; *fem. sing.* **belle;** *masc. pl.* **beaux;** *fem. pl.* **belles)** beautiful, handsome, fine

pleuvoir (il pleut) to rain
penser to think
oublier to forget
arriver to arrive, to happen

sortir to go out
rentrer to come back, to come home, go home
écouter to listen, to listen to

dehors out, outside
presque almost, nearly
là-bas over there, down there
vraiment really, truly
pas encore not yet
(ne . . . pas) du tout (not) at all
un peu a little, a while
que that (*conjunction*)
que? qu'est-ce que? qu'est-ce qui? quoi? what? (*pronouns*)

quel? quelle? quels? quelles? what? which? (*adjectives*)
toujours always, still
enfin after all, in short, finally, at last
si if (becomes **s'** before **il, ils**)
pas du tout not at all
autrement otherwise
certainement certainly, surely
bien very, quite

quel temps fait-il? what kind of weather is it? how is the weather?
il fait (très) chaud (froid, frais) it is (very) warm (cold, cool)
il fait du vent it is windy
il fait du soleil it's sunny
il fait (très) beau (temps) it is (very) fine weather, the weather is fine
il fait (très) mauvais (temps) it is (very) bad weather, the weather is bad
j'ai (très) chaud (froid, sommeil, faim, soif) I am (very) warm (cold, sleepy, hungry, thirsty)
tout simplement simply
d'accord agreed
voilà tout that's all
mettons-nous d'accord let's come to an understanding, let's get together
mettons-nous en route let's get started, let's get going

faire une promenade (un voyage) to take a walk (a trip)
attendez! wait!
en route let's go
être en nage to be dripping with perspiration
être de votre avis to be of your opinion, to agree with you

VERBES

Present Indicative of **pleuvoir** (to rain)

il pleut it rains, it is raining

→ *Pleuvoir* is an impersonal verb. Such verbs appear only in the third person singular.

Present Indicative of **sortir** (to go out)

je sors de la maison I go out, I am going out of the house
tu sors de la maison
il sort de la maison
elle sort de la maison

nous sortons de la maison we go out of the house, etc.
vous sortez de la maison
ils sortent de la maison
elles sortent de la maison

Present Indicative of **faire** (to do, to make)

je fais I do, I make, I am doing, I am making
tu fais
il fait
elle fait

nous faisons we do, we make, we are doing, we are making
vous faites
ils font
elles font

qu'est-ce que vous faites? que faites-vous? what are you doing?
il fait son lit he is making his bed

Idiomatic Uses of **faire**

il fait chaud it is warm
il fait mauvais (temps) it is bad weather, the weather is bad
je fais une promenade I am taking a walk

→ In addition to its basic meanings of "do" and "make," *faire* has a variety of idiomatic usages. One is to describe the state of the weather; another is to translate "to take," in such expressions as "to take a walk" (*faire une promenade*), "to take a trip" (*faire un voyage*), etc.

Idiomatic Uses of **avoir**

j'ai froid	I'm cold	**j'ai soif**	I'm thirsty
j'ai chaud	I'm warm	**j'ai sommeil**	I'm sleepy
j'ai faim	I'm hungry	**j'ai peur**	I'm afraid

→ *Avoir* is used to express a number of physical sensations.

Imperative

nous faisons	we do, we make	**faisons**	let us do, let us make
nous allons	we go, we are going	**allons**	let's go
nous sortons	we are going out	**sortons**	let's go out

→ For the English imperative "let us" followed by the infinitive French uses the same form as the first person plural of the present indicative, with the subject pronoun omitted.

vous faites	you are doing	**faites**	do
vous allez	you are going	**allez**	go
vous sortez	you are going out	**sortez**	go out

→ For the second person imperative, French uses the second person plural of the present indicative, with the subject pronoun omitted.

GRAMMAIRE

What? (Pronoun)

qu'est-ce qu'il y a dans le sac? what is (there) in the bag?
que désirez-vous? what do you wish?
qu'est-ce que vous voulez? what do you want?

→ "What?" when it does not immediately precede a noun but is the *object* of a verb is translated by *que* or *qu'est-ce que*.

Que requires inversion of verb and subject pronoun.

Qu'est-ce que requires normal declarative order.

qu'est-ce qui va arriver? what is going to happen?
qu'est-ce qui est sur la table? what is on the table?

→ "What" when it does not immediately precede a noun and is the *subject* of a verb is translated by *qu'est-ce qui.*

quoi? what? what did you say?
quoi? vous avez peur? what? you are afraid?
avec quoi faites-vous votre travail? with what do you do your work?

→ "What" standing by itself or used as the object of a preposition is *quoi.*

quel temps fait-il? what (sort of) weather is it?
quelle heure est-il? what time is it?
quels livres voulez-vous? what (*or* which) books do you want?
quelles maisons allez-vous voir? what (*or* which) houses are you going to see?
montrez-moi quels livres vous désirez show me what (*or* which) books you wish
quels sont les livres que vous allez lire? what are the books you are going to read?
quels beaux livres! what fine books!

→ "What," used interrogatively or not, when it is an adjective modifying a noun is *quel, quelle, quels, quelles,* agreeing with the noun it modifies. This is true even when the adjective "what?" is separated from the noun it modifies by the verb "to be."

In this use, "what" is often the equivalent of "which."

Qu'est-ce que c'est que cela? means "what is that?"

QUESTIONS

1. Quel temps fait-il dans la rue? 2. Fait-il chaud dans la maison? 3. Pourquoi René veut-il sortir? 4. Que veut-il faire dehors? 5. Pourquoi Madeleine prend-elle un manteau? 6. Pourquoi dit-elle "Sortons"? 7. Pourquoi pensent-ils qu'il va pleuvoir? 8. S'il pleut, que vont-ils faire? 9. Pourquoi Madeleine et René ne sont-ils pas d'accord sur le

temps? 10. Pourquoi ne veulent-ils pas rentrer trop tard? 11. Est-ce qu'il fait du soleil aujourd'hui? 12. Est-ce qu'il va pleuvoir? 13. Aimez-vous sortir quand il fait du vent? 14. Est-ce qu'il fait toujours frais quand il fait du vent?

EXERCICES

A. Conjugate:

1. je sors quand il fait beau
2. je fais mon lit tous les jours
3. je ne fais pas de promenade quand il pleut

B. Translate:

1. Henry is thirsty. 2. Mary is sleepy. 3. We are hungry. 4. Are you cold? 5. They are very warm. 6. It is sunny. 7. The weather is bad. 8. What kind of weather is it? 9. The weather is very fine. 10. The weather is warm. 11. It is windy. 12. Is it cool? 13. It is very cold. 14. Let's take a walk! 15. Let's make the beds! 16. Let's go out! 17. Go out! 18. It is not very warm. 19. I am not very thirsty.

C. Use the correct form of *que, qu'est-ce que, qu'est-ce qui, quoi,* in the following:

1. ________ voulez-vous? 2. ________ vous désirez? 3. ________ vous faites? 4. ________ faisons-nous? 5. ________ il y a dans le livre? 6. ________ va arriver? 7. ________ vous écoutez? 8. ________ pensez-vous de mon ami? 9. ________ est sur le papier? 10. ________ il y a dans mon sac? 11. Avec ________ faites-vous le pain? 12. De ________ parlez-vous?

D. Fill in the blank with the correct form of *quel, quels, quelle,* or *quelles:*

1. ________ maison voulez-vous acheter? 2. ________ heure est-il? 3. ________ livres voulez-vous? 4. ________ chapeau désirez-vous? 5. ________ travail faites-vous là? 6. ________ âge avez-vous? 7. ________ gants voulez-vous acheter? 8. ________ voyage allez-vous faire? 9. ________ route (*fem.*) prenez-vous? 10. ________ langues (*fem. pl.*) parlez-vous?

THÈME

—What's the weather like outside?

—It's nice today.

—Let's go out and take a walk.

—Agreed. But take your coat. It is windy. It is not warm.

—My wife writes (*écrit*) that it is cold in (*à*) New York and that it rains every day (*tous les jours*).

—The weather is always bad in (*à*) New York.

—Have you your hat and your gloves? Are you ready? Let's go out.

—It's cold. And there are clouds. Where is the sun?

—After all (*après tout*), it is going to rain perhaps (*peut-être*). If it rains are we going to return home?

—No, then let's go to the movies.

—I agree. But let's get started. I do not want to return too late. Now it is sunny.

Lesson 7

Plural of present indicative of *comprendre* as reciprocal verb

Present indicative of *dire*

Orthographic changes and conjugation of *répéter*

Use and translation of *on*

Use of *on* or reflexive to translate the English passive

Use of *n'est-ce pas*

Uses of *ceci* and *cela*

Substitution of ce for *cela* before *être*

CONVERSATION

Un Malentendu

PAULINE: Dites donc, Guillaume, comment s'appelle ceci en français?

GUILLAUME: Quoi, Pauline?

PAULINE: Ceci.

GUILLAUME: Ça! C'est un cahier.

PAULINE: Ca-hier. Comment écrit-on ça?

GUILLAUME: C-a-h-i-e-r. Cahier. Et maintenant voyons. Qu'est-ce que cela veut dire en anglais?

PAULINE: Cahier? "Newspaper," n'est-ce pas?

GUILLAUME: Pas du tout!

PAULINE: Que voulez-vous dire?

GUILLAUME: Je veux dire tout simplement que "newspaper" n'est pas "cahier" en français. C'est "journal."

PAULINE: Mais voyons. Attendez un instant. Est-ce que nous nous comprenons? Comment dit-on "newspaper" en français?

GUILLAUME: Journal.

PAULINE: Mais je ne parle pas du journal.

GUILLAUME: De quoi parlez-vous alors?

PAULINE: De cela. Qu'est-ce que c'est que cela?

GUILLAUME: Je répète que c'est un cahier. En anglais, on appelle ça un "notebook."

PAULINE: Ah! Enfin, je comprends. Maintenant, nous parlons de la même chose!

VOCABULAIRE ET EXPRESSIONS

le cahier the notebook
le journal (*pl.* **journaux**) the newspaper
la chose the thing
le malentendu the misunderstanding

Pauline Pauline
Guillaume William
tel (*masc.*) such, **telle** (*fem.*) such
même same
large wide

aimer to like, to love
se comprendre to understand each other

dire to say, to tell
répéter (je répète) to repeat

ceci this
on one, people, we, you, they (*indefinite*)

cela (ça) that
tout everything, all

dites donc listen, look here, say!
comment s'appelle ceci en français? what do you call this in French?

de quoi parlez-vous? what are you talking about?
qu'est-ce que c'est que cela? what is that?
voyons let's see
qu'est-ce que cela veut dire? what does that mean?
que voulez-vous dire? what do you mean?
je veux dire I mean
n'est-ce pas? isn't he? didn't they? isn't that so? etc.
comment dit-on . . . en français? how do you say . . . in French?
comment écrit-on cela? how is that spelled?

VERBES

Present Indicative of **se comprendre** (Reciprocal Verb)

nous nous comprenons we understand each other
vous vous comprenez you understand each other
ils se comprennent they understand each other
elles se comprennent they understand each other

→ This is the verb *comprendre* used reciprocally, with two or more subjects acting upon one another. This use can occur only in the plural. The same pronouns are used as in reflexive verbs to translate "each other," "one another": *nous* for the first person, *vous* for the second, *se* for the third.

Present Indicative of **dire** (to say, to tell)

je dis bonjour
tu dis bonjour
il dit bonjour
elle dit bonjour

nous disons bonjour
vous dites bonjour
ils disent bonjour
elles disent bonjour

je veux dire I mean
qu'est-ce que cela veut dire? what does that mean?
que voulez-vous dire? what do you mean?

→ *Vouloir dire* idiomatically translates "to mean." The *vouloir* is conjugated, while the *dire* stays in the infinitive form.

Present Indicative of **répéter** (to repeat)

je répète la phrase
tu répètes la phrase
il répète la phrase
elle répète la phrase
on répète la phrase

nous répétons la phrase
vous répétez la phrase
ils répètent la phrase
elles répètent la phrase

→ Verbs in *er* in which the last vowel of the stem is *é* change *é* to *è* when the ending of the present indicative has an *e* mute.

GRAMMAIRE

Word Order

je parle du livre I am talking about the book
de quoi parlez-vous? what are you talking about?
Parler de means "to talk about" as well as "to speak of."

→ A preposition cannot be placed at the end of the clause or sentence in French as is often done in English, but must precede the word it governs.

On

quand on fait son travail, tout va bien when one does his work, when you do your work, when people do their work, everything goes right

→ *On* is an indefinite pronoun which may be translated: "one," "people," "you," "we."

on dit qu'il est ici people say he is here, they say he is here, it is said that he is here

→ *On* may also translate "somebody" or an indefinite "they," or an English passive. Note that the conjunction "that" (*que*) cannot be omitted in French.

ici on parle français French is spoken here

→ The English passive is often translated in French by *on* with the third person singular of the active verb.

on appelle ça un cahier that is called a notebook
ça s'appelle un cahier that is called a notebook
on ne fait pas cela you don't do that, that isn't done
cela ne se fait pas you don't do that, that isn't done

→ The reflexive is also used, though not so frequently as *on,* to translate the English passive.

N'est-ce pas?

il fait son travail, n'est-ce pas? he does his work, doesn't he?
vous allez voir le médecin, n'est-ce pas? you are going to see the doctor, aren't you?
elle est ici, n'est-ce pas? she is here, isn't she?

→ The abbreviated interrogative repetition of the verb in English is invariably translated in French by *n'est-ce pas?*

This; That (Pronouns)

j'aime ceci I like this
je dis ceci pour amuser les enfants I say this to amuse the children
cela ne veut rien dire that means nothing
qu'est-ce que c'est que cela? what is that?

→ "This" and "that" referring to general situations, statements, and undefined objects are usually translated by *ceci* and *cela,* respectively. *Ceci* and *cela* do sometimes refer to clearly defined objects when you point to them.

je n'aime pas ça I don't like that
qu'est-ce que c'est que ça? what is that?

→ *Cela* is frequently abbreviated to *ça.*

c'est vrai that's true
ce n'est pas tout that's not all

As subject of *être, ce, c'* is used in preference to *cela* or *ceci.*

QUESTIONS

1. Qu'est-ce que c'est qu'un malentendu? 2. Un cahier, est-ce

un journal? 3. Comment écrit-on cahier? 4. Comment écrit-on journal? 5. De quoi parlent Guillaume et Pauline? 6. Pourquoi ne se comprennent-ils pas? 7. Pourquoi Guillaume répète-t-il la réponse (*the answer*)? 8. Quand vous discutez avec des amis, est-ce que vous vous comprenez toujours? 9. Quand dit-on "Que voulez-vous dire?" 10. Racontez la conversation qu'on lit dans cette leçon.

EXERCICES

A. Translate the following:

1. They are saying. 2. He says. 3. They understand each other. 4. We say. 5. You understand each other. 6. You say. 7. She repeats. 8. Mary and Louise understand each other. 9. You are repeating yourself. 10. They are repeating. 11. We are repeating. 12. What do you mean? 13. I mean that we are not going out. 14. What does that mean? 15. What is he talking about? 16. He is talking about the water. 17. Now, what are you talking about? 18. We are talking about the weather. 19. She is talking about her friends. 20. It is said that he does his work. 21. He is here, isn't he? 22. People speak French here. 23. This is not true. 24. What is that?

B. Replace the blank by one of the following: *on, ceci, cela, ça, ce, c', n'est-ce pas.*

1. Où va-t ________ maintenant? 2. ________ est très joli. 3. C'est vrai, ________? 4. Quand fait-________ son lit? 5. ________ est trop grand, ________ est trop petit. 6. Georges est malade, ________? 7. Parle-t-________ anglais, ici? 8. A-t-________ des gâteaux dans ce restaurant? 9. ________, c'est un journal, ________? 10. Qu'est-ce que c'est que ________?

THÈME

—Where are we now?

—We are in (*à*) Paris.

—What is that?

—That is the Seine.

—Is the Seine wide (*large*)?

—Yes, it is very wide.

—What is that over there?

—That is the Louvre.

—Is that Notre-Dame over there?

—No, it is not Notre-Dame.

—Are you going to the Sorbonne (*la Sorbonne*)?

—Yes, I want to see a man (*quelqu'un*) at the Sorbonne.

—Where are we going to eat (*manger*)?

—Is there a restaurant (*un restaurant*) near here?

—Yes, let's go there (*allons-y*).

—What do you want to take?

—I want some ice cream.

—Very good. I want some ice cream, too. Let's call the waiter (*le garçon*).

Lesson 8

Present indicative of *venir* and compounds

Past participle of -er verbs

Past participle of some irregular verbs

Formation of past indefinite with *avoir*

Negative of the past indefinite

Distinction between *matin* and *matinée*, *soir* and *soirée*

CONVERSATION

Au Café

GEORGES: Comment! Vous, ici? D'où venez-vous?

HENRI: Je viens de Bordeaux. J'ai fait le voyage de Bordeaux à Paris en auto.

GEORGES: Avez-vous une auto, maintenant? Pas possible!

HENRI: Si, je vous assure. J'ai acheté une Ford, la semaine dernière.

GEORGES: Cette fois alors, vous n'avez pas pris le train? Avez-vous conduit la nuit?

HENRI: Non, nous avons quitté Bordeaux ce matin à trois heures.

GEORGES: Et vous n'avez pas eu de pannes en route?

HENRI: Non, l'auto a marché merveilleusement bien.

GEORGES: Mais, vous n'avez pas encore commandé. N'avez-vous pas faim?

HENRI: Si, je vais commander dans un instant.

GEORGES: Eh bien, alors, je vais appeler le garçon. Hier on a servi un excellent repas dans ce café-restaurant. J'ai eu un excellent bifteck. J'ai été si content de mon repas que, quand le garçon a rendu la monnaie, j'ai laissé cent francs.

VOCABULAIRE ET EXPRESSIONS

la panne breakdown (*auto*)
le bifteck the (beef) steak
le garçon the waiter
la carte the menu
le repas the meal
le café the café; the coffee
le restaurant the restaurant

la monnaie the change (*money*)
le jour, la journée the day
le matin, la matinée the morning
le soir, la soirée the evening
la nuit the night
content (de) pleased, satisfied (with), glad, happy

quitter to leave (depart from)
laisser to leave, leave behind
conduire to drive, lead
assurer to assure
commander to order

servir to serve, *p.p.* **servi,** served
marcher to go (*lit.* to walk)
rendre to return, give back, *p.p.* **rendu** returned, given back

compris understood, *p.p.* of **comprendre**
pris taken, *p.p.* of **prendre**
voulu wanted, *p.p.* of **vouloir**

eu had, *p.p.* of **avoir**
été been, *p.p.* of **être**
fait done, made, *p.p.* of **faire**
dit said, told, *p.p.* of **dire**

heureusement luckily, happily, fortunately
merveilleusement wonderfully, marvelously
si yes (*in reply to a negative statement or question*)
la semaine dernière last week

VERBES

Present Indicative of **venir** (to come)

je viens de Paris
tu viens de Paris

nous venons de Paris
vous venez de Paris

il vient de Paris	**ils viennent** de Paris
elle vient de Paris	**elles viennent** de Paris

→ Like *venir* are conjugated all its compounds: *devenir,* to become; *convenir,* to agree; *parvenir,* to arrive; to succeed, etc.; also, *tenir,* to hold, and its compounds: *appartenir,* to belong; *contenir,* to contain; *retenir,* to retain, to hold back.

GRAMMAIRE

Past Participle of -er Verbs

parler to speak	**parlé** spoken
acheter to buy	**acheté** bought
visiter to visit	**visité** visited
montrer to show	**montré** shown
appeler to call	**appelé** called

→ The past participle of *-er* verbs is formed by replacing the *er* of the infinitive with *é*.

Some Irregular Past Participles

prendre to take	**pris** taken
comprendre to understand	**compris** understood
vouloir to want	**voulu** wanted
avoir to have	**eu** had
être to be	**été** been
faire to do, to make	**fait** done, made
dire to say, to tell	**dit** said, told

→ The past participle of irregular verbs must be learned separately.

The Past Indefinite

j'ai parlé I have spoken, I spoke
tu as acheté you have bought, you bought
il a visité he has visited, he visited

elle a écouté she has listened, she listened
nous avons pris we have taken, we took
vous avez compris you have understood, you understood
ils ont fait they have done, they did, they have made, they made
elles ont dit they have said, they have told, they said, they told

→ The past participle preceded by the present indicative of ***avoir*** forms a tense called the past indefinite. This tense translates both the English present perfect (*I have spoken*) and the English past (*I spoke*).

je n'ai pas parlé I haven't spoken, I didn't speak

→ With any compound tense used in the negative ***ne*** precedes the auxiliary, while *pas* follows it.

Matin, matinée; Soir, soirée

j'ai étudié à la bibliothèque ce matin I studied in the library this morning
j'ai passé la matinée à la bibliothèque I spent the morning in the library
je vais au cinéma ce soir I'm going to the movies tonight
nous avons passé la soirée au cinéma we spent the evening at the movies

→ Note the distinction between **matin** and **matinée,** and between **soir** and **soirée.** The feminine form stresses the period of time throughout its duration.

QUESTIONS

1. D'où vient Henri? 2. Comment a-t-il fait le voyage de Bordeaux? 3. Qu'est-ce qu'il a acheté la semaine dernière? 4. A-t-il conduit la nuit? 5. A-t-il pris le train? 6. Quand a-t-il quitté Bordeaux? 7. Est-il content de son auto? 8. Est-ce qu'il a fait bon voyage? 9. Pourquoi Georges demande-t-il à Henri s'il n'a pas faim? 10. Où a-t-on servi un excellent repas à Georges? 11. Qu'est-ce qu'il a mangé? 12. Pourquoi est-il content?

EXERCICES

A. Conjugate:

1. Je viens du Louvre.
2. Je sors le matin quand j'ai déjeuné.

B. Put the following sentences into the past indefinite tense:

1. Je parle à mon frère. 2. J'achète une maison. 3. Je visite le musée. 4. Je montre mon chapeau à mon ami. 5. J'appelle le monsieur. 6. Je prends le livre. 7. Je comprends la leçon. 8. Je veux étudier ma leçon. 9. J'ai mon passeport. 10. Je ne suis pas malade. 11. Je fais mon lit.

C. Substitute the past indefinite tense for the present in the following:

1. Il est malade. 2. Il fait froid. 3. Nous faisons notre travail. 4. Il fait du vent. 5. Vous êtes malade, n'est-ce pas? 6. Il ne fait pas chaud. 7. Ils ont leur passeport. 8. Est-ce qu'il fait frais? 9. Nous voulons aller au cinéma. 10. Ils comprennent la leçon. 11. Vous prenez les livres. 12. Il appelle l'étudiant. 13. Il montre ses gants à sa femme. 14. Nous ne visitons pas la ville. 15. Vous achetez des gâteaux, n'est-ce pas? 16. Je parle de ceci, pas de cela.

D. To what questions are the following sentences answers:

1. J'ai pris le train à six heures et demie. 2. J'ai fait mon lit hier soir. 3. J'ai été malade ce matin. 4. Vers huit heures j'ai dit au revoir. 5. J'ai déjeuné près du Louvre. 6. Nous avons bien dîné. 7. Nous avons parlé français. 8. Nous avons été au Louvre de bonne heure. 9. Nous avons visité le musée. 10. Il a écouté l'opéra. 11. J'ai été content. 12. Ils ont fait un voyage.

THÈME

—George! Where are you coming from?
—I am coming from Versailles.
—Did you make the trip by train?

—No, I took the Ford. I drove all night and I assure you (that: *que*) I am tired (*fatigué*).

—Did you have any breakdowns?

—No, luckily, we had no breakdowns. The auto went marvelously well.

—Aren't you hungry?

—Yes, I am very hungry. Let's order. Where is the waiter?

—There is the waiter. Have you had a beefsteak here? They're very good.

—Good, we are going to have a good meal. Did the waiter return the menu? Oh! Here is the menu!

Review Lesson 2

A. *Continuez la conjugaison des verbes suivants:*

1. Je ne comprends pas la leçon. 2. Je dis de répéter la phrase. 3. Je répète ma leçon. 4. Je viens de New York en auto. 5. Je sors à sept heures et demie. 6. J'appelle ma sœur à sept heures. 7. J'ai parlé à mon ami. 8. J'ai acheté trois livres. 9. J'ai passé la journée chez mon ami. 10. J'ai pris deux billets. 11. J'ai voulu être chez Henriette vers cinq heures. 12. J'ai appelé Georges à huit heures. 13. J'ai montré mon chapeau à ma femme.

B. *Traduisez les phrases suivantes:*

1. George is a foreigner. 2. Henry is a physician. 3. Paul is a professor. 4. He is a Protestant. 5. We are Americans. 6. He is French. 7. Mary is my friend. 8. Have you my book and my pen? 9. He has your fountain pen. 10. There is our house. 11. Here is their house. 12. Has he my books? 13. I haven't your books. 14. Where is his friend? 15. Is that their passport? 16. Give me my gloves, please. 17. I want his papers. 18. Show me your tickets.

C. *Employez les mots suivants dans des phrases:*

1. que, qu'est-ce que, qu'est-ce qui, quoi. 2. quel, quels, quelle, quelles.

D. *Remplacez les tirets* (dashes) *par le mot qui convient* (which suits): beau, froid, soleil, faim, soif, chaud, vent.

1. Quand il fait ________, nous avons ________. 2. Après (*after*) le dîner, nous n'avons pas ________. 3. Il fait du ________ en mars (*March*). 4. Vous n'avez pas ________ quand il fait beaucoup de ________. 5. Il ne fait pas ________ quand il pleut.

E. *Employez chacun* (each) *des mots suivants dans deux phrases différentes:*

on, ceci, cela, ça, cet, cette, ce, ces, c'est, n'est-ce pas, temps.

Lecture 2

LE CADEAU

(D'après un conte de Pierre Mille)

Le 29 décembre 1950, M. Lepoupin arrive à la maison quelques minutes avant l'heure du dîner. Sa femme n'est pas encore là. Le dîner va être froid. M. Lepoupin est un homme ponctuel, mais sa femme n'est jamais à l'heure (*on time*). Cependant (*however*), elle n'est pas contente quand son mari est en retard. Elle a d'ailleurs (*besides*) ses raisons:

—C'est parce que tu es exact en général, dit-elle, que je suis anxieuse[1] quand tu n'es pas là; moi, ce n'est pas la même chose.

M. Lepoupin, qui a bon caractère, accepte cette distinction féminine.

En arrivant, il trouve dans le vestibule une grande boîte en carton (*cardboard*) enveloppée de[2] papier multicolore.

—C'est un cadeau de nouvel an[3] (*New Year's present*)! dit-il.

Il va ouvrir le paquet, mais il hésite et replace l'objet sur la petite table du vestibule.

—Ma femme n'est pas contente, pense-t-il, quand on ouvre un paquet en son absence.

M. Lepoupin va donc à son bureau (*his study*), il ouvre son journal et attend sa femme.

Enfin, vers (*at about*) huit heures et demie, elle arrive. M. Lepoupin ne fait pas de reproche. Il dit:

1 anxieuse: *masculine adjectives ending in* -eux *take* -euse *in the feminine:* précieux, précieuse.

2 enveloppée de, *wrapped in or with;* de *used after certain past participles is translated by "with" or "in" in English. Similarly:* couvert de, *covered with;* rempli de, *filled with.*

3 le nouvel an: *this adjective has five forms:* nouvel, *masculine singular before a vowel;* nouveau, *masculine singular before a consonant;* nouvelle, *feminine singular before a vowel or consonant;* nouveaux, *masculine plural;* nouvelles, *feminine plural.*

—Il y a dans le vestibule un paquet qui est arrivé (*has arrived*) en ton absence. Je suppose que c'est un cadeau de nouvel an.

—Probablement, dit Mme Lepoupin, qui a le paquet dans les bras.

Elle pose le paquet sur une table, enlève le papier multicolore, ouvre la boîte et en tire[4] (*takes out of it*) un objet enveloppé de papier de soie (*tissue paper*).

—Qu'est-ce que c'est? (*What is it?*) dit M. Lepoupin, qui éprouve (*experiences*) une certaine curiosité.

Il est impossible de ne pas éprouver[5] une certaine curiosité. Un objet vous arrive. Il va être à vous (*yours*). Il est à vous. On est naturellement intrigué.

C'est un vase de cuivre (*copper*) d'un style très moderne. M. Lepoupin n'aime pas le style moderne.

—C'est affreux! dit-il.

Mme Lepoupin n'aime pas avoir la même opinion que son mari, mais cette fois-ci elle approuve.

—C'est vrai, ce n'est pas joli!

—C'est infect (*awful*)! déclare M. Lepoupin.

Mme Lepoupin regarde dans le vase. Elle en tire une carte.

—C'est le cadeau des Boisvieux.

—Quelle (*what a*) atrocité![6] dit M. Lepoupin.

Il prend le vase qu'il essaye de cacher (*hide*) sous le canapé (*sofa*) de son bureau.

—Qu'est-ce que tu fais? demande sa femme.

—Je le cache. J'aime mieux (*prefer*) ne pas voir[7] ça.

—Mais tu es fou! dit sa femme. Tu oublies que nous avons un cadeau à faire aux Girardon.[8]

—Ça, dit M. Lepoupin, c'est une excellente idée.

Après le dîner, Mme Lepoupin écrit à Mme de Boisvieux le plus aimable billet du monde (*in the world*).

4 en tire: *the pronoun* en, *placed before the verb, is often translated by "from it," "from them," "of it," "of them."*

5 de ne pas éprouver, *not to feel; not to experience. Note that the two parts of the negation* ne pas *come before the infinitive.*

6 quelle atrocité: *note that, in French, in an exclamation the article is omitted. The English would be "What an atrocity!"*

7 *See note 5.*

8 *Note that the French do not add the mark of the plural* s *to proper names.*

"Pourquoi nous gâtez-vous (*spoil us*) ainsi, chère amie? Tout ce qui (*everything that*) vient de vous est toujours charmant; mais, cette fois, comment vous exprimer mon plaisir? . . ."

La lettre continue sur ce ton. Ensuite, Mme Lepoupin replace le vase dans sa boîte, y met[9] (*puts in it*) une carte de M. et Mme Lepoupin, enveloppe la boîte du même papier multicolore, appelle (*calls*) sa femme de chambre (*chambermaid*) et lui dit:

—Demain matin, allez porter ça chez Mme Girardon. Prenez le Métro[10] et descendez à Courcelles.

M. Girardon n'a pas la même patience que M. Lepoupin. Quand le paquet arrive, il tire la boîte du papier multicolore qui l'enveloppe, puis il tire le vase de cuivre de la boîte et il porte le cadeau à sa femme.

—Qu'est-ce que c'est que cet objet ridicule? dit-il. Les Lepoupin se moquent de nous (*are making fun of us*). . . . Qu'est-ce que nous allons faire de cela (*with that*)?

—Malheureusement, dit Mme Girardon, tous nos cadeaux[11] sont envoyés. Ce vase arrive deux jours trop tard.

—Alors, dit M. Girardon, jetons ça dans une armoire (*cupboard*) et attendons l'année prochaine.

Mais après le dîner, Mme Girardon écrit à Mme Lepoupin le plus aimable billet du monde:

"Pourquoi nous gâtez-vous ainsi, chère amie? Tout ce qui vient de vous est toujours charmant; mais, cette fois, comment vous exprimer mon plaisir? . . ."

Pendant les années suivantes le vase de cuivre va faire de nombreux voyages.

En 1914, il arrive chez un ingénieur (*engineer*) de talent qui ne s'intéresse pas aux beaux-arts, mais qui tourne et retourne (*turns over and over*) le fameux vase et remarque (*notices*) qu'il fuit (*leaks*).

9 y met, *puts there, puts in it. The pronoun* y, *placed usually before the verb, may mean "in it," "in them," "there," "on it," "to it," etc.*

10 le métro *is the Paris underground railway.* Courcelles *is one of the stations.*

11 cadeaux: *nouns ending in* -eau *take* -x *in the plural.*

En 1951, il arrive chez le général de cavalerie Lacharge, beau-père (*father-in-law*) de l'ingénieur.

En 1952, le général envoie son vase à un sénateur qu'il désire remercier de sa protection.

En 1953, il arrive chez un journaliste, M. Chauvin, qui va écrire un article sur les exploits du général. Mais Mme Chauvin refuse de voir cet horrible objet dans son salon. Elle déclare que ce vase est parfait (*perfect*) pour un nouveau riche.

En 1954, il arrive donc chez les Corduron. Depuis le début (*from the beginning*) de la guerre d'Indochine M. Corduron vend des tissus (*cloth*) à l'armée française. Sa fortune est récente. Cependant les Corduron n'aiment pas le vase. Ils achètent tout au celèbre (*famous*) magasin Wasserman. C'est cher (*expensive*), mais il est agréable de dire à ses amis: "Nous achetons tout chez Wasserman." Pourtant, les Corduron ont encore des habitudes d'économie.

Voilà pourquoi, le 27 décembre 1955, M. Lepoupin, quand il arrive à la maison, trouve une boîte en carton, enveloppée d'un papier multicolore. Sur le paquet, il y a une enveloppe avec la carte des Corduron. Il est l'heure du dîner; Mme Lepoupin n'est pas là. Mais elle n'est pas contente si on ouvre un paquet en son absence. M. Lepoupin attend donc son retour. Elle arrive enfin et ouvre la boîte.

—Adolphe, s'écrie Mme Lepoupin, c'est le même!

—Le même quoi (*what*)? demande M. Lepoupin.

—Le même vase de cuivre! Le cadeau de nouvel an des Boisvieux pour 1951.

—Mais nous l'avons envoyé à nos amis Girardon! Ah! c'est dégoutant (*disgusting*)! s'écrie M. Lepoupin, qui est scandalisé.

—Écoute (*listen*), Adolphe, dit Mme Lepoupin, nous n'avons pas gardé (*kept*) le vase non plus (*either*).

—Ça, c'est vrai, dit M. Lepoupin. C'est clair, personne ne désire avoir une horreur pareille (*like that*) dans son salon. Il faut vendre ce vase. C'est la seule solution.

M. Lepoupin va donc avec le vase chez un marchand de curiosités.

—C'est moderne! dit le marchand avec dédain.

—C'est vrai, répond M. Lepoupin . . . et combien m'en donnez-vous?

—Mille francs.

—Mille francs! dit M. Lepoupin, qui est très étonné (*astonished*).

—Pas un franc de plus, dit le marchand. C'est le cuivre que je paie, la valeur du cuivre. Il monte tous les jours.

—Et . . . , demande M. Lepoupin, est-ce qu'il va continuer à monter?

—C'est très probable.

Une heure plus tard, M. Lepoupin arrive chez lui (*is back home*).

—Comment! s'écrie Mme Lepoupin, tu rapportes cette monstruosité?

—Eh bien, oui, répond M. Lepoupin, il paraît (*appears*) que c'est une excellente spéculation.

QUESTIONNAIRE

1. Pourquoi M. Lepoupin attend-il sa femme? 2. Pourquoi Mme Lepoupin est-elle anxieuse quand son mari est en retard? 3. Qu'est-ce que M. Lepoupin trouve dans le vestibule? 4. Pourquoi n'ouvre-t-il pas le paquet? 5. Quand sa femme arrive, que lui dit-il? 6. Quand elle ouvre le paquet, que trouve-t-elle? 7. Pourquoi M. et Mme Lepoupin ont-ils cette fois-ci la même opinion? 8. Que font-ils du (*with the*) cadeau? 9. Quel billet Madame Lepoupin envoie-t-elle à Madame Boisvieux? 10. Que dit M. Girardon quand il voit le vase de cuivre? 11. Quels voyages le vase de cuivre fait-il successivement (*in succession*)? 12. Enfin, en 1955, où arrive-t-il? 13. Où M. Lepoupin va-t-il avec son vase? 14. Que lui dit le marchand? 15. Pourquoi Monsieur Lepoupin ne vend-il pas le vase?

Lesson 9

Present indicative of *partir*

Formation of past indefinite with *être*

Agreement of the past participle with subject of intransitive verbs conjugated with *être*

Past indefinite of reflexive verbs

Agreement of past participle with direct object preceding reflexive verbs

Uses of *tout, tous, toute, toutes*

CONVERSATION

PAUL: Qu'est-ce que vous avez fait hier, Marguerite?

MARGUERITE: Eh bien, je vais vous le dire: hier matin, je me suis levée de bonne heure; puis. . . .

PAUL: Pas possible!

MARGUERITE: C'est tout à fait vrai, je vous assure; à huit heures moins le quart.

PAUL: Puis?

MARGUERITE: Puis; je me suis promenée toute la matinée dans ce beau Jardin du Luxembourg. A midi, je suis rentrée à l'hôtel. Robert est venu me voir et nous avons déjeuné ensemble.

PAUL: Et l'après-midi?

MARGUERITE: L'après-midi, je suis allée au musée du Louvre C'est vraiment magnifique. Nous avons passé toute l'après-midi au musée. Nous avons visité toutes les salles. Enfin, Robert est parti. Je suis rentrée, bien fatiguée, vers six heures et demie. Heureusement j'ai trouvé ma sœur prête à sortir quand je suis arrivée. Nous sommes sorties et nous avons dîné d'une façon magnifique au restaurant Marguery.

PAUL: Et hier soir?

MARGUERITE: Le soir, nous sommes allées à un théâtre au Boulevard des Italiens, tout près de la place de l'Opéra. Nous avons passé toute la soirée au théâtre. Nous ne sommes rentrées à l'hôtel que vers minuit.

VOCABULAIRE ET EXPRESSIONS

l'après-midi (*fem.*) the afternoon
l'hôtel (*mas.*) the hotel
la salle the (large) room, hall
la façon the fashion, the way
le théâtre the theatre
l'opéra (*mas.*) the opera
le jardin the garden
le musée the museum
la place the square; the place
la sœur the sister
Marguerite Margaret
magnifique magnificent, wonderful
fatigué tired, weary
tout (toute, tous, toutes) all, whole

se lever (je me lève) to get up
passer to spend (time, not money); to pass
se promener (je me promène) to walk about, to take a walk
venir to come (*p.p.* **venu**)
visiter to visit
trouver to find
dîner to have dinner, to dine
rentrer to return, come back, come home again
déjeuner to have lunch
partir to leave, to depart (*p.p.* **parti**)
arriver to arrive, to get (to)

puis then (especially in the sense of "afterwards")
ensemble together
vers toward; with expressions of time, "at about"
assez fairly, rather, enough

ne . . . que not . . . but; not . . . except; only (the verb is inserted between *ne* and *que: je n'ai passé que deux heures au Louvre,* I spent only two hours at the Louvre). The *que* must precede immediately the word upon which *only* or *except* bears.

hier matin yesterday morning
hier soir last night
ce soir this evening, tonight
l'après-midi (in) the afternoon
le soir (in) the evening
de bonne heure early
vers huit heures at about eight o'clock
(tout) près de (very) near
toute l'après-midi the whole afternoon
toute la matinée the whole morning
toute la soirée the whole evening
toute la journée the whole day
tout à fait altogether, quite
d'une façon magnifique in grand fashion

VERBES

Present Indicative of **partir** (to leave, to depart)

Past Participle: **parti**

je pars ce soir
tu pars ce soir
il part ce soir
elle part ce soir
nous partons ce soir
vous partez ce soir
ils partent ce soir
elles partent ce soir

Note that *partir* is conjugated like *sortir* (Lesson 6).

GRAMMAIRE

Past Indefinite Formed with **être**

je suis allé (*fem.* **je suis allée**) I have gone, I went
tu es allé (*fem.* **tu es allée**) you have gone, you went
il est allé he has gone, he went
elle est allée she has gone, she went

nous sommes allés (*fem.* **nous sommes allées**) we have gone, we went
vous êtes allé (*fem.* **vous êtes allée;** *mas. pl.* **vous êtes allés;** *fem. pl.* **vous êtes allées**) you have gone, you went
ils sont allés they went
elles sont allées they (*fem.*) went

→ Certain intransitive verbs form the past indefinite with the present of *être* instead of "avoir" (compare archaic English "he is come"; modern English "they are gone"). When *être* is used, the past participle fulfills the function of a predicate adjective; it must therefore agree with the subject.

elle est venue à la maison she came to the house
nous sommes sortis ce matin we went out this morning
ils sont partis hier soir they left last night
mes parents sont arrivés à Paris my parents have arrived in Paris
quand êtes-vous rentré? when did you get home?
est-ce qu'ils sont montés à votre chambre? did they go up to your room?
à quelle heure sont-ils descendus déjeuner? at what time did they come down to breakfast?
elle est née en octobre she was born in October
elle est morte hier she died yesterday
ils sont tombés de l'auto they fell out of the car
ils sont restés à la maison they stayed at home
nous sommes entrés au Louvre we went into the Louvre
quand êtes-vous retournés? when did you go back?
ils sont devenus riches they became rich

→ Some of the verbs that take *être* as an auxiliary are: *aller* (to go, p.p. *allé*); *venir* (to come, p.p. *venu*); *sortir* (to go out, p.p. *sorti*); *partir* (to leave, depart, p.p. *parti*); *arriver* (to arrive, p.p. *arrivé*); *rentrer* (to get back, get home, p.p. *rentré*); *monter* (to go up, come up, p.p. *monté*); *descendre* (to go, come down, p.p. *descendu*); *naître* (to be born, p.p. *né*); *mourir* (to die, p.p. *mort*); *tomber* (to fall, p.p. *tombé*); *rester* (to stay, remain, p.p. *resté*); *entrer* (to go in, come in, enter, p.p. *entré*); *retourner* (to return, go back, p.p. *retourné*); *devenir* (to become, p.p. *devenu*).

Past Indefinite of Reflexive Verbs

je me suis levé (*fem.* **je me suis levée**)
tu t'es levé (*fem.* **tu t'es levée**)
il s'est levé
elle s'est levée

nous nous sommes levés (*fem.* **nous nous sommes levées**)
vous vous êtes levé(s) (*fem.* **vous vous êtes levée[s]**)
ils se sont levés
elles se sont levées

→ The past indefinite of reflexive verbs is formed with the auxiliary ***être***. The past participle agrees with the preceding reflexive pronoun when this pronoun is the direct object. The reflexive pronouns are ***me, te, se, nous, vous, se.***

Tout—Toute—Tous—Toutes

tout est prêt everything is ready, all is ready; **je sais tout** I know everything

→ *Tout* without a noun means "everything," or "all" in the sense of "everything."

tous sont prêts all are ready, everybody is ready

→ The mas. pl. *tous* (with final -s pronounced), without a noun, means "all" referring to people, "everyone", "everybody". It requires a plural verb.

tout le jardin the whole garden
tout le travail all the work
toute la matinée the whole morning
toute l'eau all the water

→ *Tout le, toute la,* with a noun following, means "all the," "the whole." In French, the article follows *tout, toute;* it does not precede, as in the English usage: "the whole."

tous les hommes all the men
toutes les femmes all the women

→ *Tous les* (final -s of *tous* silent), *toutes les,* with a plural noun following, mean "all the."

QUESTIONS

1. Que demande Paul à Marguerite? 2. Qu'est-ce que Marguerite a fait hier matin? 3. A quelle heure Marguerite s'est-elle levée? 4. Où s'est-elle promenée? 5. Où est-elle rentrée à midi? 6. Qui est venu la voir et qu'est-ce qu'ils ont fait ensemble? 7. Où est-elle allée l'après-midi? 8. A quelle heure est-elle rentrée? 9. Qui est prêt à sortir? 10. Où sont-elles allées? 11. Où ont-elles dîné? 12. Comment ont-elles dîné?

EXERCICES

A. *Continuez:*

1. Je suis rentré chez moi de bonne heure. Tu es, etc.
2. Je me suis promené dans le jardin toute la matinée.
3. Je suis arrivé à Paris à minuit cinq.
4. Je suis parti du Louvre à midi.
5. Je suis allé chez mon frère vers deux heures.

B. *Traduisez:*

1. She has not died. 2. They have come from Paris. 3. We arrived this morning. 4. We came home at midnight. 5. They left at three o'clock. 6. They went up. 7. She came down. 8. She took a walk in the street. 9. We got up at nine o'clock.

C. *Donnez les questions qui correspondent aux réponses suivantes:*

1. C'est tout à fait vrai. 2. Nous nous sommes levés de bonne heure. 3. Nous avons passé toute l'après-midi au musée. 4. Marie est partie vers six heures et demie. 5. J'ai trouvé ma sœur prête à sortir. 6. Nous ne sommes rentrés qu'à six heures. 7. Il a visité toutes les salles de tous les musées. 8. Le soir, ils sont allés au cinéma. 9. Enfin, elle est partie. 10. Paul et Marguerite sont arrivés ce matin.

D. *Remplacez l'infinitif par la forme correcte du participe passé:*

1. Elle s'est (promener). 2. Nous nous sommes (lever). 3. Ils sont (rentrer). 4. Sont-elles (aller) au théâtre? 5. Elle est (tomber)

de la fenêtre (*window*). 6. Elle s'est (lever) à six heures. 7. Je suis (arriver) ce matin de très bonne heure. 8. Il m'a (assurer) que c'est tout à fait vrai. 9. Il est (venir) me voir à l'hôtel. 10. Nous avons (dîner) ensemble.

E. Use the proper form of *tout, toute, tous, toutes* before the following nouns and use in a sentence:

1. les jours. 2. la matinée. 3. les soirs. 4. le monde. 5. l'eau. 6. la salle. 7. les matins. 8. le théâtre. 9. les jardins. 10. les restaurants. 11. les places. 12. le musée. 13. les opéras. 14. les soirées. 15. le travail. 16. les hôtels. 17. l'après-midi. 18. les femmes. 19. les hommes. 20. les chapeaux.

THÈME

"Do you know (*savez-vous*) that Paul visited Paris yesterday?"

"It's not possible!"

"Yes, he arrived by auto yesterday morning with Henry."

"Where did they go?"

"They came to my house first (*d'abord*). Luckily I got up early yesterday. They had breakfast and then they spent the whole morning in the Museum of the Louvre. We took a walk in the Luxembourg Garden. Then at noon, Mary went back to the hotel. Paul and Henry came to the hotel at about twelve-thirty and we went out together. We had lunch at Marguery's and in the afternoon we went to a movie house on the Boulevard des Italiens."

"How did you spend the evening?"

"Paul bought tickets for the theater. Towards six-thirty we had dinner at a little restaurant quite near the Opera Square. We spent a wonderful evening but I have never been so tired. At midnight, after the theater, we went to dance (*danser*) at Montmartre and we got home only at four o'clock this morning."

Lesson 10

Present indicative of *voir* and *mettre*

Position of *pas* in compound tenses

Direct object pronouns

Position of direct object pronouns in simple and compound tenses

Agreement of past participle in verbs conjugated with *avoir*

Uses of *voici, voilà,* and *il y a*

Use of *il y a* in expressions of time

Position of adjectives of color

CONVERSATION

Une Invitation à Déjeuner

ÉTIENNE: Dites, Yvonne, avez-vous vu mon frère?

YVONNE: Mais, oui, je l'ai vu en classe il y a une heure. Pourquoi? Est-ce que vous ne le trouvez pas?

ÉTIENNE: Je le cherche depuis une heure. Ah, enfin! Le voilà!

FRANÇOIS: Tiens! Étienne! Qu'est-ce que tu fais ici? Bonjour, Yvonne.

YVONNE: Bonjour, François.

ÉTIENNE: François, je te cherche depuis une heure. Où est-ce que tu te caches?

François: Eh bien, me voici maintenant! J'ai été occupé. Où est votre sœur, Yvonne? Je ne l'ai pas vue ce matin.

Yvonne: Elle est toujours en classe, je pense. Ah, mon Dieu! Ma serviette noire! Où est-ce que je l'ai mise? Est-ce que je l'ai oubliée dans la salle de classe?

Étienne: Non, Yvonne, ne vous inquiétez pas. La voici. Je la tiens ici sous ce journal.

Yvonne: Ah, coquin! Est-ce que vous l'avez cachée?

Étienne: Pas du tout. Vous l'avez laissée là-bas sur ce banc, il y a un instant. Je l'ai trouvée et la voici.

Yvonne: Les voilà!

Étienne: Qui?

Yvonne: Ma mère et ma sœur. Je les ai vues ce matin de bonne heure. Puis elles sont sorties ensemble, et je ne les revois qu'à présent.

Étienne: Bonjour, Madame! Bonjour, Rose!

Madame: Bonjour. Est-ce que vous avez fini toutes vos classes?

Étienne: Oui, Madame. Nous les avons toutes finies. Pour aujourd'hui du moins.

Madame: Eh bien, rentrons pour le déjeuner. Je vous invite.

Étienne: Avec plaisir. Nous avons tous faim.

VOCABULAIRE ET EXPRESSIONS

le frère the brother
le père the father
la mère the mother
les parents (*masc. pl.*) the parents
le banc the bench
la serviette the briefcase
la classe the class
la salle de classe the classroom

Madame madam, ma'am, Mrs. (in writing it is often abbreviated to *Mme* [no period]. Where English uses "Mrs." followed by the last name in direct address, French usually has *Madame* without the name.)

le déjeuner the lunch
l'invitation (*fem.*) the invitation
le coquin the rascal

Étienne Stephen
François Frank, Francis
Yvonne Yvonne

rouge red
blanc (*fem.* **blanche**) white
bleu blue
vert green

noir black
jaune yellow
violet purple
occupé busy

voir to see (*p.p.* **vu**)
revoir to see again
chercher to look for (do not translate *for*)
inviter to invite
mettre to put, place (*p.p.* **mis**)
cacher to hide, to conceal

laisser to leave (*leave behind*); to leave in the sense of "to depart" is **partir**
finir to finish (*p.p.* **fini**)
tenir to hold (*p.p.* **tenu**)
s'inquiéter to worry

voilà there is, there are (*points out*)
les voilà there they are
me voici here I am
il y a there is, there are (*statement*); ago (*precedes expression of time:* **il y a deux heures** two hours ago)

que (*relative pronoun*) whom, which, that (only as *object* of verb)
du moins at least
en classe in class
sous under, beneath
ah, coquin! you rascal!

VERBES

Present Indicative of voir (to see) *p.p.* vu

je vois mon frère à l'école
tu vois
il voit
elle voit

nous voyons
vous voyez
ils voient
elles voient

Present Indicative of **mettre** (to put, to place) *p.p.* **mis**

je mets sa serviette sur le banc
tu mets
il met
elle met
nous mettons
vous mettez
ils mettent
elles mettent

je n'ai pas vu votre père I haven't seen your father, I didn't see your father
j'ai mis mon chapeau I put on my hat

→ Remember: In compound tenses, *ne* precedes and *pas* follows the auxiliary (*avoir* or *être*).

GRAMMAIRE

Direct Object Pronouns

elle me voit she sees me
je te vois I see you
tu le vois you see him, you see it
il la voit he sees her, he sees it
vous nous voyez you see us
ils vous voient they see you
nous les voyons we see them
elles les voient they see them

→ The direct object pronouns are:

me me
te you
le him, it
la her, it
nous us
vous you
les them

They are normally placed immediately before the verb.

je ne le vois pas I don't see him, I don't see it
je ne l'ai pas vu I haven't seen him (it), I didn't see him (it)

→ Notice the relative position of *subject pronoun, ne, object pronoun, verb, pas;* and in compound tenses, *subject pronoun, ne, object pronoun, auxiliary, pas, past participle.*

→ *Me, te, se, le, la,* become *m', t', s', l', l',* respectively, *if the next word begins with a vowel.*

Agreement of Past Participle

j'ai vu votre frère I saw your brother **je l'ai vu** I saw him
j'ai vu votre sœur I saw your sister **je l'ai vue** I saw her
j'ai vu vos frères I saw your brothers **je les ai vus** I saw them
j'ai vu vos sœurs I saw your sisters **je les ai vues** I saw them

→ A *past participle* conjugated with *avoir* may change its form if the *direct object* pronoun *precedes* the verb; then the past participle agrees in gender and number with this direct object pronoun.

j'ai vu Louis et Marie I saw Louis and Mary **je les ai vus** I saw them

→ If the *preceding* direct object pronoun covers mixed genders, the agreement is masculine plural.

où est la femme que j'ai vue hier? where is the woman (whom) I saw yesterday?
où sont les femmes que j'ai vues hier? where are the women (whom) I saw yesterday?

→ The *past participle* conjugated with *avoir* also *agrees with a preceding relative pronoun direct object,* the relative pronoun taking the same gender and number as its antecedent.
→ Note that the relative pronoun cannot be omitted in French as it so often is in English: (**les femmes que j'ai vues** the women whom I saw, the women I saw.)

quelle maison avez-vous vue hier? what house did you see yesterday?
quelles maisons avez-vous vues hier? what houses did you see yesterday?

→ In an interrogative sentence, there is also *agreement with a preceding noun direct object.*
→ The rule may be summed up as follows:

A *past participle* conjugated with *avoir agrees with a preceding direct object,* but not with a following direct object.

In the majority of instances, this makes no difference in the *spoken language*, since *vu, vue, vus, vues* are all pronounced alike; note however the change in pronunciation in: *pris, prise; mis, mise; fait, faite; dit, dite; mort, morte; ouvert, ouverte; conduit, conduite; écrit, écrite.*

Voici—Voilà—Il y a

voici mes parents here are my parents **les voici** here they are
voilà ma mère there is my mother **la voilà** there she is

Voici means "here is," "here are," pointing out.
Voilà means "there is," "there are," pointing out.

→ The subject of the English "here is," "here are," "there is," "there are" becomes the direct object of *voici, voilà,* and is placed before them.

Il y a un livre sur la table. Où? **Le voilà.** There is a book on the table. Where? There it is.
Il y a deux hommes dans la rue. Où? **Les voilà.** There are two men in the street. Where? There they are.

→ **Il y a** and **voilà** both mean "there is," "there are." But **voilà** *points out,* while **il y a** *makes a simple statement.*

Je l'ai vu **il y a une heure** I saw him an hour ago

→ **Il y a** also means *ago.* It precedes the expression of time.

Adjectives of Color

un sac-à-main rouge a red purse
un banc vert a green bench
une maison blanche a white house
un crayon jaune a yellow pencil
un crayon bleu a blue pencil
une plume verte a green pen
un stylo blanc a white fountain pen
un encrier noir a black inkwell

→ Adjectives of color regularly follow the noun.

QUESTIONS

1. Qui est François? 2. Qui le cherche depuis une heure? 3. Est-ce que François est venu, finalement? 4. Qu'est-ce qu'il a dit à Étienne? 5. Que dit-il à Yvonne? 6. Depuis combien de temps Étienne cherche-t-il son frère? 7. Où était-il occupé? 8. Qu'est-ce qu'Yvonne a perdu?

9. Qui l'a trouvée? 10. Où l'a-t-il trouvée? 11. Qui arrive? 12. Qui a fini ses classes? 13. Pourquoi va-t-on rentrer?

EXERCICES

A. *Employez la forme correcte du verbe* voir *dans les phrases suivantes:*

1. Elles ________ le professeur tous les jours. 2. Nous ________ notre mère le soir. 3. Vous ________ ce monsieur; il est médecin. 4. Ils ________ que je suis malade. 5. Tu ________ que j'ai sommeil. 6. Je ________ que mon amie n'est pas ici. 7. Il ________ le livre sur la table. 8. Elle ne ________ pas son frère.

B. *Conjuguez:*

Je mets la chaise près de la table.

C. *Mettez les formes suivantes au négatif:*

1. Nous avons vu votre père ce matin. 2. Il a vu l'agent de police dans la rue. 3. Tu as vu ton frère. 4. Vous avez vu le livre que j'ai acheté. 5. Ils ont vu mes amis dans l'auto. 6. J'ai vu son fils.

D. I. *Employez les pronoms compléments directs* le, la, les *dans les phrases suivantes et traduisez-les:*

1. je vois 2. il voit 3. nous voyons 4. vous voyez 5. ils voient

II. *Employez les pronoms compléments directs* le, la, les *avec les verbes suivants et complétez les phrases:*

1. je mets 2. elle met 3. nous mettons 4. vous mettez 5. elles mettent

E. *Remplacez le tiret par* le (l'), la (l') *et* les (*masc. ou fém.*) *et faites accorder le participe passé:*

1. je ________ ai vu 2. il ________ a vu 3. nous ________ avons vu 4. vous ________ avez vu 5. ils ________ ont vu

F. *Remplacez le tiret par* me (m'), te (t'), nous, vous (*sing. ou pl.) et faites accorder le participe passé:*

1. elle ________ a vu 2. il ________ a cherché 3. il ________ a trouvé 4. ils ________ ont caché 5. ils ________ ont quitté

G. *Traduisez en français:*

1. Where is the invitation (which) I left on the table? 2. There is Mary; I saw her in (*à*) Paris yesterday. 3. Here is the house (which) I bought. 4. There are the pens (which) we put on the table. 5. There are five houses on (*dans*) that street. 6. On the table there is a small green pencil, and some yellow paper.

H. *Faites des phrases en employant un verbe au passé indéfini et le vocabulaire suivant:*

le frère, le déjeuner, les parents, le crayon rouge, du moins, un coquin.

THÈME

—Whom (*qui*) are you looking for? Your sister?

—Yes, have you seen her?

—Yes, I saw her in the classroom two hours ago.

—If you find her, tell her (*dites-lui*) that (*que*) you have seen me and that I want to see her.

—There she is with Paul.

—Yvonne! Where's my black briefcase?

—Oh! I put it on a table and I forgot it.

—Go look for it, please. Have you finished your classes?

—Yes, I have finished them all.

—Quickly. I want to go to lunch. Aren't you hungry? Today, I am inviting you.

—Oh, thank you. Put these books in the car.

Lesson 11

Present indicative of *écrire, lire, se sentir,* and *se remettre*

Present indicative of *se rappeler*

Uses of *venir de*

Use and position of indirect object noun and pronoun

Use and omission of article with names of days of the week

CONVERSATION

Lettres de Famille

HENRI: Est-ce que vous avez écrit à votre beau-père, Jean?

JEAN: Oui, je viens de lui écrire aujourd'hui même. Je lui ai écrit une très longue lettre, mais je ne l'ai pas encore mise à la poste. La semaine dernière, il m'a envoyé une carte postale. Je l'ai reçue hier matin de bonne heure. Quand je l'ai lue, je me suis senti tout bouleversé.

HENRI: Pourquoi?

JEAN: Il me dit que ma belle-mère, mon beau-frère et ma belle-sœur ont été très malades.

HENRI: Ah, c'est dommage!

JEAN: Oui, vraiment. Puis, comme j'ai eu hier matin une dépêche de ma tante qui me dit que mon oncle vient de se remettre d'une longue maladie, je pense qu'il y a vraiment eu assez de maladies dans ma famille.

HENRI: En effet. Quand est-ce qu'elle vous a envoyé cette dépêche? Elle vous a écrit une lettre la semaine dernière, n'est-ce pas?

JEAN: Oui, elle m'a écrit mardi et elle a envoyé la dépêche dimanche matin. Quant à mes parents, je leur ai envoyé les paquets que vous m'avez donnés.

HENRI: Quand ça?

JEAN: Je les ai envoyés—voyons—jeudi ou vendredi dernier. Je ne suis pas tout à fait sûr de la date. En tout cas, ils sont arrivés. Ils les ont reçus samedi après-midi.

HENRI: Est-ce que vous avez des nouvelles de votre frère?

JEAN: Non. Je vais lui écrire mardi ou mercredi prochain—enfin, la semaine prochaine. Mais on m'a dit qu'il va beaucoup mieux.

VOCABULAIRE ET EXPRESSIONS

le beau-père the father-in-law
le beau-frère the brother-in-law
la belle-sœur the sister-in-law
la belle-mère the mother-in-law
l'oncle the uncle
la tante the aunt
la famille the family
la lettre the letter
la carte (postale) the (post) card
la dépêche, le télégramme the wire, the telegram
le paquet the package
la maladie the illness
la date the date (*not* a date with someone; use **le rendez-vous** for that)
les nouvelles (*fem. pl.*) the news (**la nouvelle** the piece of news)
(le) **lundi** Monday
(le) **mardi** Tuesday
(le) **mercredi** Wednesday
(le) **jeudi** Thursday
(le) **vendredi** Friday
(le) **samedi** Saturday
(le) **dimanche** Sunday

long (*fem.* **longue**) long
dernier (*fem.* **dernière**) last
bouleversé upset
sûr (*fem.* **sûre**) certain
prochain next

écrire (*p.p.* **écrit**) to write
envoyer (j'envoie) to send
se sentir (*p.p.* **senti**) to feel
se rappeler (je me rappelle) to remember, to recall
recevoir (*p.p.* **reçu**) to receive
lire (*p.p.* **lu**) to read
donner to give
se remettre (*p.p.* **remis**) to recover

comme as, like
en effet indeed, that's right
venir de + *infinitive* to have just + *past participle*
mettre à la poste to mail
en tout cas at any rate, in any case
aujourd'hui même this very day
la semaine dernière (prochaine) last (next) week
il y a eu there was, there were, there has been, there have been
lundi (on) Monday
lundi dernier (prochain) last (next) Monday
lundi matin Monday morning
lundi après-midi Monday afternoon
lundi soir Monday evening, Monday night
tous les lundis every Monday
c'est dommage! that's too bad! what a pity!
avoir des nouvelles de to have heard from, to have news of
on m'a dit somebody told me, I have been told

VERBES

Present Indicative of **écrire** (to write) *p.p.* **écrit**

j'écris une lettre à ma tante
tu écris
il (elle) écrit
nous écrivons
vous écrivez
ils (elles) écrivent

Present Indicative of **lire** (to read) *p.p.* **lu**

je lis une dépêche
tu lis
il (elle) lit
nous lisons
vous lisez
ils (elles) lisent

Present Indicative of **se sentir** (to feel) *p.p.* **senti**

je me sens beaucoup mieux	**nous nous sentons**
tu te sens	**vous vous sentez**
il (elle) se sent	**ils (elles) se sentent**

→Note in the case of *se sentir* that the conjugational scheme is like that of *partir* or *sortir*. Remember that *reflexive verbs take être,* not *avoir,* in the compound tenses (**je me suis senti** I felt). *Sentir,* when not reflexive, means *to smell* or *to feel* something.

Present Indicative of **se remettre** (to recover) *p.p.* **remis**

je me remets bien vite	**nous nous remettons**
tu te remets	**vous vous remettez**
il (elle) se remet	**ils (elles) se remettent**

→Conjugated like *mettre.* The same applies to all other compounds of *mettre* (*promettre,* to promise; *permettre,* to permit, to allow; *soumettre,* to submit; etc.).

Present Indicative of **se rappeler** (to remember)

je me rappelle cette histoire	**nous nous rappelons**
tu te rappelles	**vous vous rappelez**
il (elle) se rappelle	**ils (elles) se rappellent**

Venir de + Infinitive

je viens d'écrire la lettre   I have just written the letter
il vient de parler à mon frère   he has just spoken to my brother
nous venons de le faire   we have just done it

→**Venir de** *followed by the infinitive* translates the English "to have just" followed by a past participle. Note that in French *venir* is conjugated while the infinitive remains unchanged.

GRAMMAIRE

Indirect Object Pronouns

j'ai parlé **à mon frère** I spoke to my brother
il a écrit **à sa mère** he wrote to his mother, he wrote his mother
il a écrit une lettre **à sa mère** he wrote his mother a letter
nous avons envoyé le paquet **à nos parents** we sent our parents the package
ils ont donné le livre **à Henri** they gave Henry the book

→ An indirect object is not merely one before which "to" is used in English, but one before which "to" *can* be used. English omits "to" quite frequently, even when the sentence also contains a direct object. French never omits *à* if the indirect object is a noun. English, when it omits "to," places the indirect object before the direct. French normally places the direct noun object before the indirect noun object.

il m'a écrit he wrote to me, he wrote me
je t'ai parlé I spoke to you
elle lui a donné un livre she gave him a book
tu lui as envoyé le paquet you sent her the package
vous nous avez écrit you wrote to us, you wrote us
ils vous ont dit they said to you, they told you
elles leur ont donné des livres they gave them books
nous leur avons envoyé les paquets we sent them the packages

→ In English, indirect object pronouns have exactly the same form as direct object pronouns (*me, you, him, her, us, you, them*), sometimes with "to," more frequently without.

The French indirect object pronouns are as follows:

me to me, me	**nous** to us, us
te to you, you	**vous** to you, you
lui to him, to her, him, her	**leur** to them, them
se to himself, to herself (reflexive)	**se** to themselves (reflexive)

→ It will be noted that these indirect pronouns are like the direct object pronouns *save in the third person,* where the *direct forms* are *le* (him), *la* (her), *les* (them), while the *indirect forms* are *lui* (to him, to her, him, her), *leur* (to them, them).

The test for an indirect object is to determine whether "to" *can* be used before it in English. If it can, and the object is a noun, *à* must be used in French; if the object is a pronoun, an *indirect,* not a direct *object pronoun* must be used.

Days of the Week

(le) lundi Monday **(le) mardi** Tuesday
(le) mercredi Wednesday **(le) jeudi** Thursday
(le) vendredi Friday **(le) samedi** Saturday
(le) dimanche Sunday

→ Names of the days of the week are all masculine. They are not capitalized in French.

je l'ai vu lundi I saw him on Monday
je vais le voir lundi I am going to see him on Monday

→ "On" is not translated with days of the week.
→ If the article is not used with days of the week "next" or "last" is implied.

je le vois le lundi I see him Mondays, I see him on Mondays
je le vois tous les lundis I see him every Monday

→ The English plural "Mondays" or "on Mondays" is translated by a singular in French: *le lundi.* The English singular "every Monday" is translated by the French plural form: *tous les lundis.*

QUESTIONS

1. A qui Jean vient-il d'écrire? 2. Quelle sorte de (*what kind of*) lettre a-t-il écrite? 3. L'a-t-il mise à la poste? 4. Quand son beau-père lui a-t-il envoyé une carte postale? 5. Quand il l'a lue, comment s'est-il senti? 6. Qu'est-ce que le beau-père a dit sur sa carte? 7. Quand Jean a-t-il eu une dépêche de sa tante? 8. Qu'est-ce que sa tante a dit dans

sa dépêche? 9. Est-ce que sa tante lui a aussi écrit une lettre? 10. Qu'est-ce qu'il a envoyé à ses parents? 11. Quand les a-t-il envoyés? 12. Qui n'a pas de nouvelles de son frère?

EXERCICES

A. *Traduisez les formes suivantes:*

a) j'écris, ils écrivent, nous écrivons, elle a écrit, vous écrivez, you have written, il lit, we have written, I have read, nous lisons, she reads, we feel, ils se sentent, you feel, I am recovering, we are recovering, they recover.

b) Conjuguez les phrases suivantes: 1. j'écris une lettre à ma mère 2. j'ai lu la leçon devant la classe 3. je me sens beaucoup mieux maintenant 4. je me suis remis de cette indisposition après quelques heures de repos 5. je me rappelle le jour de votre mariage 6. je me suis rappelé son nom tout de suite 7. je viens de lire le livre.

B. *Remplacez le tiret par tous les pronoms suivants:* me (m'), te (t'), lui, nous, vous, leur.

1. Il ________ écrit une lettre. 2. Il ________ a parlé de la Révolution française. 3. Il ________ a donné un livre qui vient de paraître (*appear*). 4. Il ________ envoie un paquet tous les samedis.

C. *Traduisez les phrases suivantes:*

1. I saw her Sunday. 2. We are going to write them Tuesday. 3. I give him a new book every Wednesday afternoon. 4. She goes to their house Fridays. 5. I mailed the letter last Monday. 6. What a pity! Monday afternoon I am going to see my mother. 7. I am writing to her, this very day. 8. At any rate I have a telegram from my father. 9. I am still upset by (*par*) the letter which I read in Saturday morning's paper. 10. A telegram from my aunt came last Thursday evening.

THÈME

—I am all upset. I have just received a letter from my father-in-law.

He has just recovered from a long illness. He told me that his wife, my mother-in-law, has been ill too.

—That's too bad. How are they, now?

—I sent them a telegram this morning and I wrote him a letter, but I have not yet mailed it. I am going to send them some packages Thursday. Last Saturday I sent them a package with Saturday's newspaper. He does not say in his letter that he is going to come to Paris. At any rate, I am going to see them next Wednesday or Thursday, I mean (*je veux dire*) Wednesday of next week.

Lesson 12

Present indicative and past participle of *valoir*

Relative position of direct and indirect object pronouns

Review of agreement of past participle with preceding direct object

Use of *quatre-vingt(s)* and *cent(s)*

Use of *mille, million,* and *milliard*

CONVERSATION

L'Oncle riche et le Neveu pauvre

PHILIPPE: Bonsoir, Pierre.
PIERRE: Bonsoir, Philippe. Ça va bien, cher ami?
PHILIPPE: Comme ci comme ça, mon vieux. Des rhumes de temps en temps. Dites-moi, est-ce que vous voyez quelquefois votre neveu Charles?
PIERRE: Oui, même trop souvent. L'autre jour, il est venu m'emprunter six mille francs.
PHILIPPE: Et vous les lui avez prêtés?
PIERRE: Eh bien, oui. Pauvre garçon! Il ne gagne pas grand'chose. Et la vie coûte cher.
PHILIPPE: Il dépense beaucoup d'argent, n'est-ce pas?
PIERRE: Oui, c'est normal quand on a une grande famille—six fils

et quatre filles. Six beaux garçons et quatre bien jolies jeunes filles. Je leur envoie quelquefois des cadeaux—de petits mandats-poste. Je leur ai envoyé un petit mandat-poste avant-hier.

PHILIPPE: Oui, mais revenons à la question d'argent. Vous lui avez donné tout cet argent?

PIERRE: Oui, je le lui ai donné. Bien entendu, il va me le rendre.

PHILIPPE: Quand ça?

PIERRE: Eh bien, vers la fin du mois.

PHILIPPE: Et s'il ne vous le rend pas?

PIERRE: Oh! par exemple! C'est un homme fort honnête.

PHILIPPE: Oui, mais j'ai entendu dire qu'il emprunte de l'argent à tout le monde.

PIERRE: C'est peut-être vrai. Mais il paie toujours ses dettes. L'année dernière, par exemple, il m'a emprunté mille francs. Il me les a rendus le mois dernier.

PHILIPPE: Et puis, il vous a emprunté six mille francs l'autre jour?

PIERRE: Je les lui ai prêtés volontiers. Je suis bien sûr qu'il va me les rendre.

PHILIPPE: Et s'il ne vous les rend pas?

PIERRE: Eh bien, ça m'est égal. Tant pis pour moi.

PHILIPPE: Et les dix mille francs que vous avez donnés à Paul et à Marie?

PIERRE: Je les leur ai donnés comme cadeau. Ce n'est pas un emprunt. Ils sont bien pauvres. Ils ont besoin d'argent. D'ailleurs, j'ai tant d'argent à la banque en ce moment. Je peux bien leur donner dix mille francs.

PHILIPPE: Vous êtes très bon. Mais il est tard. J'ai un rendez-vous.

PIERRE: Eh bien, bonsoir, Philippe.

PHILIPPE: A demain, Pierre.

VOCABULAIRE ET EXPRESSIONS

le neveu the nephew
le garçon the boy
le fils (*-s* pronounced; *pl.* same) the son

la fille the daughter
le rhume the cold (*disease*)
la fin the end
la vie the life
l'emprunt (*mas.*) the loan
la dette the debt
la banque the bank
le dollar the dollar
le mandat-poste (*pl.* **les mandats-poste**) the money-order
le cadeau (*pl.* **cadeaux**) the present, the gift
mille (usually spelt **mil** in dates) 1000
le million (de) the million
le milliard (de) the billion
deux cents 200
Pierre Peter
Philippe Philip
riche rich
pauvre poor
cher (*fem.* **chère**) dear, expensive
fort strong (*used as an adverb*: quite, very)
honnête honest
joli pretty
égal (*masc. pl.* **égaux**) equal
autre other
vieux (use **vieil** before a vowel or h; *fem. sing.* **vieille**; *masc. pl.* **vieux,** *fem. pl.* **vieilles**) old

emprunter (à) to borrow (from)
revenir (conj. like **venir;** *être* in compound tenses; *p.p.* **revenu**) to come back, to get back
prêter to lend
dépenser to spend
coûter to cost
gagner to earn, to gain, to win
payer to pay **(je paie)**

même (*as an adverb*) even
ne . . . pas grand'chose not much
avant-hier day before yesterday
comme ci comme ça so so
l'autre jour the other day
j'ai entendu dire I have heard (people) say
peut-être perhaps, maybe
par exemple! the very idea! I declare!
volontiers gladly, willingly
ça m'est égal it's all the same to me
tant pis so much the worse, too bad
la vie coûte cher the cost of living is high
à demain see you tomorrow
mon vieux old man, my friend
avoir besoin de to need
maintenant now
demain tomorrow
un billet de banque a bank note
bien entendu of course
tout le monde everybody
par exemple for instance
l'année dernière last year
le mois dernier last month
d'ailleurs on the other hand, besides

VERBES

Present Indicative of **valoir** (to be worth) *p.p.* **valu**

je vaux autant que lui I am as good as he
tu vaux autant que lui
il (elle) vaut autant que lui
nous valons autant que lui
vous valez autant que lui
ils (elles) valent autant que lui

GRAMMAIRE

Position of Two Pronouns (Direct and Indirect) Before Verb

Philippe me donne un livre; **il me le donne** Philip gives me a book; he gives it to me
Albert me donne une plume; **il me la donne** Albert gives me a pen; he gives it to me

→ "it to me" is **me le, me la,** according to the French gender of the "it."

Arthur me donne les paquets; **il me les donne** Arthur gives me the packages; he gives them to me

→ "them to me" is **me les.**

Philippe te prête un livre; **il te le prête** Philip lends you a book; he lends it to you
Albert te prête une plume; **il te la prête** Albert lends you a pen; he lends it to you

→ "it to you," when a familiar "you" is used, is **te le, te la,** according to the French gender of the "it."

Arthur te prête les stylos; **il te les prête** Arthur lends you the fountain pens; he lends them to you

→ "them to you" (familiar you) is **te les.**

Philippe nous envoie le paquet; **il nous l'envoie** Philip sends us the package; he sends it to us

Albert nous envoie la lettre; **il nous l'envoie** Albert sends us the letter; he sends it to us

→ "it to us" is **nous le, nous la,** according to the gender of the "it"; note that both **le** and **la** lose their final vowel before a vowel.

Arthur nous envoie les dépêches; **il nous les envoie** Arthur sends us the wires; he sends them to us

→ "them to us" is **nous les.**

Jean vous donne le livre; **il vous le donne** John gives you the book; he gives it to you

Madeleine vous donne la plume; **elle vous la donne** Madeline gives you the pen; she gives it to you

→ "it to you" (polite or plural "you") is **vous le, vous la,** according to the gender of the "it."

François vous envoie les paquets; **il vous les envoie** Frank sends you the packages; he sends them to you

→ "them to you" (polite or plural "you") is **vous les.**

→ If there are two object pronouns in the phrase, put the indirect forms **me, te, nous, vous** *before* the direct forms **le, la, les.**

Philippe a donné un livre à son frère; **il le lui a donné** Philip gave his brother a book; he gave it to him

Philippe a donné une plume à son frère; **il la lui a donnée** Philip gave his brother a pen; he gave it to him

Philippe a donné un livre à sa sœur; **il le lui a donné** Philip gave his sister a book; he gave it to her

Philippe a donné une plume à sa sœur; **il la lui a donnée** Philip gave his sister a pen; he gave it to her

→ "it to him," "it to her" is **le lui, la lui,** according to the French gender of the "it." Note that "to him" and "to her" both appear as **lui.**

Henri a donné les livres à son frère; **il les lui a donnés** Henry gave the books to his brother; he gave them to him

Henri a donné les plumes à sa sœur; **il les lui a données** Henry gave the pens to his sister; he gave them to her

→ "them to him," "them to her" are both rendered by **les lui.**

il a donné les livres à ses frères; **il les leur a donnés** he gave the books to his brothers; he gave them to them
il a donné les plumes à ses sœurs; **il les leur a données** he gave the pens to his sisters; he gave them to them

→ "them to them" is **les leur.**

→ If both object pronouns are third person, put the direct before the indirect, except for the third person reflexive:
ils se les sont donnés they gave them to each other

→ In all the foregoing examples, *note the agreement of the past participle with the preceding direct object,* and the lack of agreement with an indirect object, or with a following direct object.

il a emprunté une valise à son frère; **il la lui a empruntée** he borrowed a valise from his brother; he borrowed it from him
j'ai emprunté six cents francs à mes parents; **je les leur ai empruntés** I borrowed 600 francs from my parents; I borrowed them from them

→ Note the construction used with **emprunter.** English says "to borrow *from* someone," French says "to borrow *to* someone."

Some Irregular Numerals

quatre-vingts hommes eighty men
quatre-vingt-un hommes eighty-one men
deux cents dollars two hundred dollars
deux cent cinq dollars two hundred and five dollars

→ **Quatre-vingts** and plural hundreds are spelt with an *-s* unless they are followed by another numeral.

mille francs one thousand francs
cinq mille francs five thousand francs

→ **Mille** is invariable. Never use **un** with **cent** or **mille** (a hundred, one hundred, a thousand, one thousand), except when it means "mile": *j'ai marché un mille ce matin.*

un million de dollars a million dollars
cinq millions de dollars five million dollars
un milliard de dollars a billion dollars
cinq milliards de dollars five billion dollars

→ **Million** and **milliard** take an *-s* if plural, and require *de* before a following noun.

QUESTIONS

1. Votre oncle, est-il riche? 2. Est-ce que vous lui empruntez de l'argent? 3. Votre oncle, comment se porte-t-il? 4. A-t-il souvent des rhumes? 5. Et vous, avez-vous des rhumes de temps en temps? 6. Prêtez-vous de l'argent à vos amis? 7. Avez-vous jamais emprunté de l'argent? 8. Empruntez-vous à la banque ou à vos amis? 9. Connaissez-vous quelqu'un (*someone*) qui ne gagne pas grand'chose? 10. Est-ce qu'il dépense beaucoup? 11. Est-ce que vous dépensez beaucoup? 12. Est-ce qu'on vous envoie quelquefois des mandats-poste? 13. Envoyez-vous des mandats-poste comme cadeaux? 14. Est-ce que Charles paie toujours ses dettes?

EXERCICES

A. *Placez* me le, me la, me les *correctement dans les phrases suivantes pour en compléter le sens; faites accorder le participe passé.*

1. Il donne. 2. Il prête. 3. Ils ont donné. 4. Ils ont prêté.

B. *Placez* te le, te la, te les *correctement dans les phrases suivantes pour en compléter le sens; faites accorder le participe passé.*

1. Donne-t-il? 2. Prête-t-il? 3. Ont-ils donné? 4. Ont-ils prêté?

C. *Placez* nous le, nous la, nous les *correctement dans les phrases suivantes pour en compléter le sens; faites accorder le participe passé.*

1. Il ne promet pas. 2. Il ne rend pas. 3. Il n'a pas promis. 4. Il n'a pas montré.

D. *Placez* vous le, vous la, vous les *correctement dans les phrases suivantes pour en compléter le sens; faites accorder le participe passé.*

1. Ils vendent. 2. Ils montrent. 3. J'ai emprunté. 4. J'ai écrit.

E. *Placez* le lui, la lui, les lui *correctement dans les phrases suivantes pour en compléter le sens; faites accorder le participe passé.*

1. Nous donnons. 2. Je n'ai pas rendu. 3. Avez-vous demandé? 4. Est-ce que je montre?

F. *Placez* le leur, la leur, les leur *correctement dans les phrases suivantes, pour en compléter le sens; faites accorder le participe passé.*

1. Vous avez promis. 2. Je n'ai pas envoyé. 3. Avez-vous demandé? 4. Est-ce que j'ai emprunté?

G. *Traduisez:*

1. There are eighty professors at our university. 2. Eighty-five men have returned to our town today. 3. Now, I have five hundred dollars. 4. He wants seven hundred and fifty dollars, Wednesday. 5. He has one thousand dollars and his mother has five thousand dollars.

H. *Préparez des questions auxquelles on répondra* (will answer) *en classe en employant les mots et les expressions suivants:*

1. un million 2. un rhume 3. le mandat-poste 4. la jeune fille 5. dépenser 6. de temps en temps 7. ça m'est égal 8. à demain 9. la vie coûte cher 10. bien entendu 11. comme ci comme ça 12. tant pis 13. j'ai entendu dire 14. le mois dernier 15. tout le monde

THÈME

—How are you?

—Oh, just so-so. And how are you? I don't see you very often.

—I have been ill. I have colds very frequently.

—And how is that young man who was (*qui était*) in the bank when I saw you the last time?

—My nephew? He is very well.

—He borrowed a thousand dollars from my bank and he has not paid them back (*rembourser*) yet. They (*on*) say that (*qu'*) he has borrowed money from everybody.

—Poor boy. He is really a very honest fellow but he does not earn much and he has a large family. I often send them gifts. I sent them a gift yesterday. But he always pays his debts. The cost of living is so high now. I am going to send him some money this afternoon. I always say that (*que*) I have lent it to him. His brother is always borrowing. He spends money without thinking (*réfléchir*).

Review Lesson 3

A. *Conjuguez les verbes suivants:*

1. Je pars pour Paris, tu pars, etc. 2. Je suis sorti cette après-midi. 3. Je suis rentré de bonne heure. 4. Je suis allé à l'église. 5. Je suis venu de France. 6. Je vois Yvonne en classe. 7. Je mets la serviette sur la chaise. 8. Je les ai vus ce matin. 9. J'écris une lettre tous les jours. 10. Je lis un livre tous les huit jours. 11. Je ne me sens pas très bien. 12. Je me suis rappelé cette histoire. 13. Je la lui ai écrite. 14. Je les leur ai donnés.

B. *Traduisez les phrases suivantes:*

1. He goes out every day. 2. She wrote all morning. 3. Don't take all the good things. 4. We understand everything. 5. They listened to the whole opera. 6. They are very happy. 7. She stayed home all evening. 8. All the men arrived.

C. *Remplacez tous les noms, compléments directs et indirects, par les pronoms convenables et changez la forme du participe passé, quand c'est nécessaire.*

1. Il a trouvé les deux plumes. 2. Ils ont caché ma serviette. 3. Avez-vous fini vos leçons? 4. Nous avons vu nos cousines ce matin. 5. Il a mis sa serviette sur le banc. 6. Voilà Yvonne! 7. Nous avons vu vos parents hier matin. 8. Elle a envoyé cette dépêche à son frère. 9. Nous avons écrit une lettre à sa tante. 10. Il a donné les livres à ses amis. 11. Vous avez donné les livres à Jean et à moi. 12. Ils ont emprunté mille dollars à son frère.

D. a) *Employez d'abord* me le, me la, me les; *puis* nous le, nous la, nous les *pour compléter le sens des phrases suivantes; faites accorder le participe passé:*

1. Vous avez donné. 2. Elle a envoyé. 3. Ils ont pris. 4. Il n'a pas acheté. 5. Elles ont montré.

b) *Complétez les phrases suivantes par* le lui, la lui, les lui; *puis* le leur, la leur, les leur:

1. Nous avons rendu. 2. Vous avez lu. 3. Avez-vous promis? 4. Nous avons prêté. 5. Vous avez emprunté.

E. *Remplacez l'infinitif par la forme correcte du participe passé:*

1. Avez-vous la plume que j'ai *acheter* hier? 2. Où est la maison que nous avons *voir* il y a huit jours? 3. Quelles chaises avez-vous *prendre?* 4. Quelle robe a-t-elle *faire?* 5. Où sont les deux hommes que nous avons *voir* devant la maison?

F. *Écrivez des phrases avec la première ou la troisième personne du passé composé* (past indefinite) *de chacun des verbes suivants:*

aller, venir, arriver, partir, monter, descendre, rester, tomber, entrer, sortir, devenir, retourner.

G. *Traduisez:*

1. Here is my pen. 2. There it is. 3. Where are your brothers? There they are. 4. Now there are three men in the room. 5. Here he is. 6. There are fifty pages (*la page*) in this book. 7. I write to him on Wednesdays. 8. She told me the news Tuesday. 9. I am going to borrow three hundred dollars. 10. Eighty-one men have come to the bank and they have all borrowed money.

Lecture 3

LES POULES

(D'après *Poil de Carotte* de Jules Renard)

La famille Lepic a trois enfants, Félix, Ernestine et Poil de Carotte. Félix est un grand garçon. C'est le favori de sa mère. Il est très gâté (*spoiled*). Ernestine est aussi très gâtée, mais elle est bonne très gâtée (*spoiled*). Ernestine est aussi très gâtée, mais elle est bonne et assez jolie (*rather pretty*). Poil de Carotte est très laid (*ugly*). Il est petit. Il a les cheveux[1] rouges comme une carotte. Voilà pourquoi (*that's why*) on l'appelle[2] Poil de Carotte. Sa mère ne l'aime pas beaucoup et son frère et sa soeur donnent beaucoup de[3] travail (*work*) au petit garçon parce qu'ils sont paresseux[4] (*lazy*). En général, Poil de Carotte est très docile et accepte ce travail supplémentaire sans se plaindre (*without complaining*).[5]

Un soir madame Lepic remarque que la servante n'a pas enfermé (*shut up*) les poules (*the chickens*). Elle se tourne donc (*therefore*) naturellement vers (*towards*) son fils aîné (*oldest son*), Félix, et dit: "La servante n'a pas enfermé les poules. Félix, va[6] dans la cour (*courtyard*) enfermer les poules."

Il fait froid[7] dehors (*outside*). Il fait du vent. Il fait noir. Félix ne veut pas sortir. Il est content auprès de (*near*) la cheminée

[1] les cheveux: *nouns ending in* -eu, -eau, *form the plural by adding* -x: les cheveux, les couteaux. *Note the use of the article:* il a les cheveux rouges, *he has red hair.*

[2] on l'appelle, *he is called. The indefinite* on, *(one, they) with an active verb often translates the English passive. Similarly:* Ici, on parle français, *French is spoken here.*

[3] beaucoup de, *followed by a noun, means "a lot of." Compare with* assez de, *enough;* peu de, *little, few;* trop de, *too many.* Beaucoup *without* de *is an adverb and means "a great deal, a lot, much."*

[4] paresseux: *note that nouns or adjectives ending in* -s, -x, *or* -z *do not change in the plural.*

[5] sans se plaindre, *without complaining. In French, the infinitive is used after all prepositions except* en: il arrête de parler, *he stops talking;* il se met à courir, *he starts running; but:* en parlant, *while speaking.*

[6] va, *familiar, singular imperative form of* aller.

[7] il fait froid, *it is cold. Weather is described in French by using the verb* il fait: il fait froid *(cold)*, chaud *(hot)*, beau *(fine weather)*, du vent *(windy), etc. Note also that* il a froid, il a peur *mean "he is cold," "he is afraid."*

où il fait chaud. Il répond[8] donc à sa mère: "Je ne suis pas ici pour enfermer les poules. Je ne veux pas sortir. Il fait trop froid dehors."

Alors sa mère demande à Ernestine d'aller enfermer les poules. Ernestine refuse aussi de sortir. "Ô! maman," dit-elle, "il fait trop noir. Il fait trop froid. J'ai peur de sortir. Écoute ce vent.[9] Ne me fais pas (*do not make me*) sortir."

Madame Lepic commence à s'impatienter (*to get impatient*). Mais elle remarque le petit Poil de Carotte qui joue (*is playing*) sous la table.

"Poil de Carotte," dit-elle, "va enfermer les poules; va vite, ou je te bats (*I will beat you*)."

Le pauvre petit garçon n'ose pas (*does not dare*) protester. Il se lève lentement et marche vers la porte. Il tremble un peu. Sa soeur, Ernestine, a pitié de[10] lui. Elle comprend qu'il a peur comme elle. Elle prend une lanterne et l'accompagne jusqu'à la porte qui se trouve (*is*) au bout (*at the end*) du corridor. Quand Poil de Carotte ouvre la porte, le vent éteint la lumière (*puts out the light*). Ernestine a très peur, elle laisse là le petit Poil de Carotte et court retrouver (*to join*) sa mère et son frère Félix. Poil de Carotte aussi voudrait bien (*would like to*) rentrer dans la maison, mais il a plus peur (*is more afraid*) de sa mère que (*than*) de l'obscurité. Il avance donc timidement dans la cour. Les poules qui entendent (*hear*) le bruit de ses petits pas (*steps*) ont peur aussi. Elles commencent à piailler (*screech*). "C'est moi,[11] c'est moi. Taisez-vous (*be quiet*)!" dit Poil de Carotte pour les rassurer. Enfin il ferme la porte du poulailler (*chicken coop*) et se met à (*begins to*) courir vers la maison. Il croit voir des loups (*wolves*) et des renards (*foxes*) dans la nuit (*night*) noire. Il entend des bruits bizarres. Quand enfin il voit la porte de sa maison, il l'ouvre vite et entre. Il est content de voir la lumière et le feu dans la cheminée. Maintenant, il est très fier (*proud*) et il espère recevoir des compliments

[8] Il répond à sa mère, *he answers his mother. The* à *is not translated in English. Similarly:* elle demande à Ernestine, *she asks Ernestine.*

[9] écoute ce vent, *listen to that wind. Note that* écouter *takes a direct object; the English "listen" requires "to" before a noun complement.*

[10] avoir pitié de, *to pity, to have pity on.*

[11] c'est moi, *it is I. The French use the emphatic disjunctive forms of the pronoun:* c'est lui, ce sont eux, *etc.*

de sa mère. Mais sa mère ne lui fait pas de compliments. Elle le regarde un instant sans rien dire, puis elle déclare: "Eh bien! puisque tu n'as pas peur, tu peux enfermer les poules tous les soirs (*every evening*). Le pauvre Poil de Carotte baisse (*hangs*) la[12] tête. Il reprend sa place sous la table. Il ne peut plus (*he can no longer*) jouer. Il a les larmes (*tears*) aux[12] yeux et son frère et sa soeur se moquent de lui.

QUESTIONNAIRE

1. Qui sont les trois enfants de Mme Lepic? 2. Décrivez Félix. 3. Décrivez Poil de Carotte. 4. Pourquoi le frère et la soeur donnent-ils beaucoup de travail à Poil de Carotte? 5. Qu'est-ce que Mme Lepic remarque un soir? 6. Vers qui se tourne-t-elle? 7. Que dit-elle? 8. Quel temps (weather) fait-il dehors? 9. Pourquoi Félix veut-il rester dans la maison? 10. Quand Ernestine et Félix refusent de sortir, qu'est-ce que Mme Lepic dit à Poil de Carotte? 11. Pourquoi Ernestine accompagne-t-elle Poil de Carotte? 12. Qu'est-ce qui éteint la lanterne? 13. Pourquoi les poules ont-elles peur? 14. Qu'est-ce que Poil de Carotte croit voir? 15. Quand il entre dans la maison, qu'est-ce qu'il espère recevoir de sa mère? 16. Pourquoi Poil de Carotte baisse-t-il la tête?

[12] la tête, *his head. Note the use of the definite article with parts of the body. Similarly:* aux yeux, *in his eyes.*

LETTRE DE M. LEPIC À POIL DE CAROTTE

D'après *Poil de Carotte* de Jules Renard)

Mon cher Poil de Carotte,

Ta lettre de ce matin m'étonne beaucoup. Je la relis vainement. Ce n'est pas ton style ordinaire et tu y[1] parles de choses bizarres qui ne me semblent pas de ta compétence.[2]

D'habitude (*as a rule*) tu nous racontes tes petites affaires.[3] Tu nous écris les places[4] que tu obtiens,[5] les qualités et les défauts que tu trouves à (*in*) chaque professeur, les noms de tes nouveaux camarades, l'état (*condition*) de ton linge (*linen*), si tu dors[6] et si tu manges bien.

Voilà ce qui (*what*) m'intéresse. Aujourd'hui, je ne comprends plus.[7] A propos de quoi,[8] s'il te plaît, cette sortie (*outburst*) sur le printemps (*spring*) quand nous sommes en hiver (*winter*) ? Que veux-tu dire ? As-tu besoin d'un[9] cache-nez (*muffler*) ?

Ta lettre n'est pas datée et on ne sait[10] si tu l'adresses à moi ou au chien (*dog*). La forme même de ton écriture (*handwriting*) me semble modifiée, et la disposition des lignes, la quantité de majuscules (*capitals*) me déconcertent (*puzzle me*). Bref, tu as l'air de te moquer de quelqu'un.[11] Je suppose que c'est de toi.[12]

Réponse de Poil de Carotte

Mon cher papa,

Un mot à la hâte (*hastily*) pour t'expliquer ma dernière lettre. Tu n'as pas remarqué (*noticed*) qu'elle était en vers.

[1] y, *in it. The adverbial pronoun* y *often means "there," but it may also have to be translated "to it," "in it," "on it," etc.*
[2] de ta compétence, *in your province.*
[3] tes petites affaires = les petits événements de ta vie, *the insignificant events of your life.*
[4] les places, *the grades. In French schools the pupils are ranked from first to last in the class besides being given a numerical grade.*
[5] tu obtiens, *you get. This is the second-person singular of the present indicative of* obtenir, *to obtain, to get, to receive, which is conjugated like the irregular verb* tenir.
[6] dors, *second-person singular of the present indicative of* dormir, *to sleep.*
[7] ne . . . plus, *no longer, no more.*
[8] à propos de quoi = pour quelle raison. *Literally: about what, in what connection.*
[9] as-tu besoin de, *do you need. Literally: have you need of?*
[10] sait, *third-person singular, present indicative, of the irregular verb* savoir, *to know.*
[11] tu as l'air de te moquer de quelqu'un, *it looks as if you were making fun of somebody. Literally: you have the appearance* (l'air) *of . . .*
[12] c'est de toi (*understood:* que tu te *moques*), *you are making fun of yourself.*

QUESTIONNAIRE

1. Pourquoi monsieur Lepic relit-il la lettre de son fils Poil de Carotte? 2. Qu'y a-t-il dans cette lettre qui étonne monsieur Lepic? 3. De quoi Poil de Carotte parle-t-il d'habitude dans les lettres qu'il écrit à son père? 4. Est-ce que ces détails de sa vie intéressent son père? 5. De quoi Poil de Carotte parle-t-il dans sa dernière lettre? 6. Pourquoi monsieur Lepic pense-t-il qu'il a peut-être (*perhaps*) besoin d'un cache-nez? 7. Qu'est-ce que monsieur Lepic a trouvé déconcertant (*puzzling*) dans la lettre de son fils? 8. A quelle conclusion monsieur Lepic arrive-t-il? 9. Qu'est-ce que Poil de Carotte explique dans sa réponse à son père?

Lesson 13

Present indicative and past participle of *-re* verbs

Comparison of uses of *y* and *là*

Position of *y*

Comparative uses of *y* and indirect object pronouns

Use and position of partitive pronoun *en*

Idiomatic uses of *en*

Relative position of *y* and *en*

CONVERSATION

La Cousine Arrive de la Campagne

PAULETTE: Est-ce que vous allez attendre votre cousine à la gare, Sylvie?

SYLVIE: Oui, je vais l'y attendre. Je vais m'y rendre vers huit heures. Voulez-vous m'y accompagner, Paulette?

PAULETTE: Non, malheureusement. J'ai perdu beaucoup de temps la semaine dernière. Je vais essayer d'en rattraper un peu ce soir.

SYLVIE: Pourtant, vous êtes allée à l'opéra hier soir. Est-ce que vous y avez entendu de bons chanteurs?

PAULETTE: Oui, j'en ai entendu deux vraiment épatants. Avez-vous répondu à la lettre de Georges?

SYLVIE: Non, je n'y ai pas encore répondu. Je vais lui répondre demain soir, si je trouve le temps. Il m'écrit tous les jours, mais je ne lui réponds qu'une fois par semaine.

PAULETTE: Votre cousine, à quel hôtel va-t-elle descendre?

SYLVIE: A l'Hôtel du Nord. Elle y descend chaque fois qu'elle vient à Paris.

PAULETTE: C'est vrai, elle y est descendue la dernière fois qu'elle est venue. C'est là que je lui ai fait visite.

SYLVIE: Vous avez du rouge?

PAULETTE: Mais, oui, chère amie. En voulez-vous?

SYLVIE: S'il vous plaît. J'ai essayé d'en acheter aujourd'hui, mais, au magasin, on n'a pas voulu m'en vendre. C'est embêtant, n'est-ce pas? Et moi, qui en ai besoin à chaque instant!

PAULETTE: C'est vrai! On en trouve très peu à présent. Rappelez-vous, pendant la guerre il n'y en a pas eu du tout.

SYLVIE: Oui, je sais. Mais enfin, nous sommes de vieilles clientes.

PAULETTE: On va nous en vendre demain, j'en suis sûre.

SYLVIE: Oh, il est déjà sept heures et demie! Je pars tout de suite pour la gare. Je ne veux pas être en retard. Au revoir, Paulette.

PAULETTE: A demain, Sylvie. Venez me voir avec votre cousine.

VOCABULAIRE ET EXPRESSIONS

le cousin the cousin (*masc.*)
la cousine the cousin (*fem.*)
le client the customer (*masc.*)
la cliente the customer (*fem.*)
le rouge the rouge
le chanteur the singer
la campagne the country
la gare the station
la guerre the war
le verre the glass
le besoin the need
la fois the time (in the sense of first, last, next, this time; for time in the absolute, use *le temps*)
Sylvie Sylvia
Paulette Paulette
moi I (when used without a verb immediately following)
chaque each
embêtant annoying, exasperating

attendre to wait, to await, to wait for (do not translate "for")
se rendre to betake oneself, to go
perdre to lose
vendre to sell
essayer de to try to **(j'essaie de)**
rattraper to catch up, to regain
entendre to hear
répondre (à) to answer
descendre to put up (***at a hotel***); to go down, to come down (usually conj. with *être*)

là there (*pointing out*)
y there, to it, to them
par by (is also used where English uses the indefinite article with an expression of time in a distributive sense: **trois fois par jour** three times a day)
pourtant however, nevertheless
plusieurs several
en some, any, of it, of them, from it, from them
peu de little, few
déjà already
en retard late

chaque fois each time
une fois par jour once a day
deux fois par semaine twice a week
la première fois the first time
la dernière fois the last time
la prochaine fois the next time
c'est que the fact is that, the reason is that
je suis en retard I am late
tout de suite at once, immediately
tous les jours every day
faire visite à to visit, pay a visit to, make a call on

VERBES

Present Indicative of **perdre** (to lose) *p.p.* **perdu**

je perds
tu perds
il (elle) perd
nous perdons
vous perdez
ils (elles) perdent

→ When verbs have the ending *-re* in the infinitive, this ending is replaced in the present indicative by *-s, -s, -, -ons, -ez, -ent,* and in the past participle by *-u.*

Entendre (to hear), *attendre* (to wait, to wait for), *répondre* (to answer), *vendre* (to sell), *rendre* (to give back), *se rendre* (to betake oneself, to go; to surrender), *descendre* (to put up at a hotel, to go

down, to come down; conjugated with *être*), are all verbs of this type.
Caution: many verbs ending in *-re* are irregular.

GRAMMAIRE

The Pronoun y

je vais à Paris I am going to Paris
j'y vais I am going there
je l'y ai vu I saw him there
je les y attends I am waiting for them there
j'ai vu le livre dans le train I saw the book in the train
je l'y ai vu I saw it there
mettez-la sur la table put it on the table
mettez-l'y put it there
il est chez Louis he is at Louis'
il y est he is there
votre plume est dans la boîte your pen is in the box
elle y est it is there
votre livre est sur la table your book is on the table
il y est it is there

→ *Y* is an adverbial pronoun meaning "there" and referring to a place already mentioned (use *là* for "there," to point out). *Y*, because it means "there," replaces not only *à* + *noun,* but *dans, sur, chez, sous,* etc., + noun. Its position in the sentence is like that of an object pronoun, preceding the verb and following all the other object pronouns, except *en* (**il y en a** there is some).

je le lui ai donné là I gave it to him there

→ *Y* is never used when more than one other pronoun accompanies the verb.

Avez-vous répondu à Jean? **Je lui ai répondu.** Did you answer John? I answered him.
Avez-vous répondu à sa lettre? **J'y ai répondu.** Did you answer his letter? I answered it.

→ *Y* is also used to translate "to it," "to them," referring to things (*lui* means "to him," "to her," and *leur* means "to them" referring to people). Observe that *répondre* in French calls for an indirect personal object.

The Pronoun **en**

Avez-vous de l'eau? **En avez-vous?** Do you have any water? Do you have any?
Avez-vous des livres? **Oui, j'en ai.** Have you any books? Yes, I have.
Avez-vous de l'encre? **En avez-vous?** Have you any ink? Have you any?
A-t-il de bons livres? **Il en a.** Has he any good books? He has.
Il n'a pas d'encre. **Il n'en a pas.** He has no ink. He hasn't any.
Voilà l'eau; **j'en ai pris un verre.** There is the water; I took a glass (*of it*).
Voilà les livres; **j'en ai pris trois.** There are the books; I took three (*of them*).
Combien de sœurs a-t-il? How many sisters has he?
Il en a plusieurs. He has several (*of them*).
Il en a trois. He has three (*of them*).

→ *En* is a pronoun meaning *"some," "any." En* also translates *"of it," "of them."* In English, "some," "any," "of it," "of them" are often left out of such sentences, but *en* must be used in French in order to express the thought fully.
→ Note that there is *no agreement of a past participle* with a preceding *en*.

Avez-vous besoin de ces livres? Oui, j'en ai besoin. Do you need these books? Yes, I need them.

"To need" is *avoir besoin de*. Since *en* replaces *de + a noun or pronoun,* "to need it," "to need them" is *en avoir besoin*.

Venez-vous de Paris? **Oui, j'en viens.** Do you come from Paris? Yes, I come from there.
Il arrive du Canada. **Il en arrive.** He is coming from Canada. He is coming from there.

→ *En* also means *"thence," "from there."*

il nous en a donné he gave us some
je leur en ai donné I gave them some

ne lui en parlez pas don't speak of it to him
il y en a there are some

→ In the sentence, *en* follows all other object pronouns. *Y* and *en* are never found together except in *il y en a* (there is some, there are some), and other tenses of *y avoir.*

Tard—en retard

il est tard it is late
il est arrivé tard he came late; i.e., at a late hour
il est arrivé en retard he came late; i.e., behind schedule
le train est arrivé en retard the train came in late
je suis en retard I am late

Tard and *en retard* both mean "late"; but *tard* calls attention to the lateness of the hour, *en retard* to the lateness of the act.

QUESTIONS

1. Qui est-ce que Sylvie va attendre à la gare? 2. A quelle heure va-t-elle s'y rendre? 3. Est-ce que Paulette va l'y accompagner? 4. Pourquoi Paulette refuse-t-elle? 5. Qu'est-ce qu'elle va essayer de faire ce soir? 6. Où est-elle allée hier soir? 7. Qu'est-ce qu'elle y a entendu? 8. A-t-elle répondu à la lettre de Georges? 9. Combien de fois par semaine écrit-il? 10. Combien de fois par semaine répond-elle? 11. Où est-ce que sa cousine va descendre? 12. Quand est-ce qu'elle y est descendue? 13. Est-ce que Paulette a du rouge? 14. Pourquoi Sylvie n'en a-t-elle pas? 15. Pourquoi Sylvie part-elle tout de suite pour la gare?

EXERCICES

A. *Conjuguez:*

1. J'ai perdu un stylo. 2. Je perds du temps. 3. Je réponds à la lettre. 4. J'y ai répondu. 5. Je descends à cet hôtel. 6. J'y descends. 7. Je ne les y attends pas. 8. Est-ce que j'entends bien?

B. *Remplacez les noms en italique par le pronom* en *ou* y:

1. Je vais *à la maison* immédiatement. 2. Je vous ai vus *au théâtre.* 3. Je vous ai attendu *à la gare.* 4. Je n'ai pas répondu *à la dépêche.* 5. Avez-vous *de la viande* aujourd'hui? 6. Je n'ai plus *de vin.* 7. Mon père m'a dit qu'il avait besoin *d'argent.* 8. Henri vient *de Versailles.* 9. J'ai acheté une douzaine *d'oranges.* 10. Je suis allé en avion *à Paris.* 11. A-t-il dîné *chez Maurice?* 12. Le livre est *sur la table.* 13. Les souliers sont *dans la boîte.* 14. J'ai mis les paquets *sous la table.* 15. Elle est arrivée *à Paris* aujourd'hui.

C. *Traduisez les phrases suivantes:*

1. It is always late when I return home. 2. Why are you always late? 3. The train is late today. 4. It is late, let's go home. 5. My cousin is late, I am leaving.

D. *Employez les mots suivants dans des phrases et traduisez-les en anglais:*

1. chaque fois 2. deux fois par semaine 3. la première fois 4. il a besoin de 5. tout le temps 6. tous les jours 7. pourtant 8. peu de 9. le verre 10. chaque 11. embêtant 12. la gare 13. descendre 14. faire visite 15. du rouge.

THÈME

—Where are you going?

—I am going to the station. I am going to see Mary there and we are going to wait for Sylvia.

—Did I see you at the opera last night?

—Yes, I went there to hear the new singers. There are several that I have not yet heard.

—Are there any good singers?

—There are two. Why don't you ever go (there)?

—The last time I went to the opera I did not have a good time (*s'amuser*).

—Try to buy tickets for tonight. The opera is good, I am sure (of it).

—Do I need an evening suit (*un habit*) to (*pour*) go there tonight?

—No.

—Well, here we are at the station. Wait a minute. I am going to see if the train is late. It is half past eight.

—No, I am going home. I am tired. I went to bed late last night and I want to go to the opera tomorrow (*demain*).

Lesson 14

Present indicative and past participle of *boire*

Present indicative of *manger* and *commencer* and orthographic changes

Present indicative and past participle of regular *-ir* verbs

Uses and position of *ne . . . rien, ne . . . personne, ne . . . jamais*

***Rien de* followed by an adjective**

Uses of *ni . . . ni, ne . . . plus, ne . . . point*

Use of definite article with generic nouns

CONVERSATION

Un Repas à la française

ÉDOUARD: Qu'est-ce que vous choisissez, Ernestine?

ERNESTINE: Du jus de tomate pour commencer, puis un consommé, des œufs au jambon, une salade et du gâteau à la crème. Et vous, qu'est-ce que vous prenez?

ÉDOUARD: Moi, je préfère déjeuner à la française. Vous allez voir. Garçon, s'il vous plaît, des hors-d'œuvre, un potage Julienne, du poulet rôti avec des légumes et des pommes de terre frites, puis du fromage de Brie, et pour finir des fruits.

ERNESTINE: Qu'est-ce que c'est qu'un potage Julienne?

ÉDOUARD: C'est un potage aux légumes: des choux, des carottes, un peu de lard peut-être.

LE GARÇON: C'est tout, Monsieur? Et comme fruit? Que voulez-vous? Nous avons des pommes, des poires, des pêches et du raisin.

ÉDOUARD: Des pêches et du raisin, s'il vous plaît.

ERNESTINE: Il me semble que vous avez bien choisi, parmi tous les plats de ce menu, Édouard. Les Français mangent beaucoup à midi, n'est-ce pas?

ÉDOUARD: Oui, c'est souvent le repas principal de la journée.

ERNESTINE: Ce vin est délicieux. Voulez-vous remplir mon verre?

ÉDOUARD: Avec plaisir. En Amérique je ne bois presque jamais de vin. Mais ici, c'est autre chose. Tout le monde en boit.

ERNESTINE: Vous avez raison. Personne dans ma famille ne boit de vin. A table, nous ne buvons ni vin ni bière.

ÉDOUARD: Qu'est-ce que vous buvez?

ERNESTINE: Nous ne buvons rien. C'est-à-dire, rien d'alcoolique. On prend du café, du thé, du lait, ou tout simplement de l'eau avec ses repas.

ÉDOUARD: Est-ce que vous n'avez jamais bu de vin avant aujourd'hui?

ERNESTINE: Si, j'en ai bu. Mais en général on ne boit pas d'alcool chez nous.

ÉDOUARD: En France, on ne considère ni le vin ni la bière comme des boissons alcooliques. Ce terme est réservé aux boissons fortement alcooliques, comme le rhum, le cognac, le whiskey et les liqueurs. Buvez donc sans crainte ce bon vin de France.

ERNESTINE: A votre santé!

ÉDOUARD: A la vôtre!

VOCABULAIRE ET EXPRESSIONS

le jus the juice
le consommé the consomme
le plat the dish
le jambon the ham

l'œuf (*masc.*) the egg (final *-f* pronounced in the singular but silent in the plural: *œufs*)
la tomate the tomato
la salade the salad
le gâteau the cake (*pl.* **gâteaux**)
la crème the cream
la pomme the apple
la terre the land, the earth, the ground
la pomme de terre the potato
les hors-d'œuvre the hors-d'œuvres
le potage the soup
le lard the bacon
le chou the cabbage (*pl.* **choux**)
le poulet the chicken
le légume the vegetable
le fromage the cheese
le fruit the fruit
le raisin the grapes
la poire the pear
la pêche the peach
le menu the menu
la boisson the beverage, the drink
la bière the beer
l'alcool (*masc.*) the alcohol
le vin the wine
la liqueur the liquor, the liqueur, the cordial
le rhum rum
le cognac cognac
le café the coffee
le thé the tea
le lait the milk
la santé the health
l'histoire (*fem.*) the story, the history
la crainte the fear
le terme the term
l'Amérique (*fem.*) America
Ernestine Ernestine
Édouard Edward

rôti (*adj.*) roasted; (*noun, masc.*) roast
frit fried
délicieux (*fem.* **délicieuse**) delicious, delightful
alcoolique alcoholic
principal (*masc. pl.* **principaux**) chief, principal
général (*masc. pl.* **genéraux**) general

choisir to choose
manger to eat **(nous mangeons)**
boire (*p.p.* **bu**) to drink
rôtir to roast
commencer to begin **(nous commençons)**
préférer to prefer **(je préfère)**
sembler to seem
réserver to reserve
remplir to fill
considérer to consider **(je considère)**

ne . . . jamais never, not ever
ne . . . personne no one, nobody, not anyone, not anybody

ne . . . rien nothing, not anything
ne . . . ni . . . ni neither . . . nor, not . . . either . . . or
ne . . . point not (*emphatic*), not at all (*literary*)
pour in order to, to (use before an infinitive when "to" expresses purpose)
avant before (*preposition*)
fortement strongly
surtout especially, above all
donc, so, then, therefore

les œufs au jambon ham and eggs
le gâteau à la crème cream cake, cream pie, cream tart
à la française French style
il me semble it seems to me
c'est autre chose it's something else, it's a different story
en Amérique in America, to America
en France in France, to France
avoir raison to be right (**vous avez bien raison** you are quite right
avoir tort to be wrong
à table at the table
c'est-à-dire that is to say
en général in general
à votre santé! to your health! (reply: **à la vôtre!** to yours!)

VERBES

Present Indicative of **boire** (to drink) *p.p.* **bu**

je bois une tasse de thé	**nous buvons**
tu bois	**vous buvez**
il (elle) boit	**ils (elles) boivent**

Present Indicative of **manger** (to eat)

je mange des pommes de terre	**nous mangeons**
tu manges	**vous mangez**
il (elle) mange	**ils (elles) mangent**

→ *-er* verbs ending in *-ger* insert *e* after *g* when the ending starts with *a* or *o*. This is done to keep the palatal sound of the *g*, which before *a* or *o* would sound like the *g* of *good*. The inserted *e* is completely silent.

Present Indicative of **commencer** (to begin)

je commence ma lecture	**nous commençons**
tu commences	**vous commencez**
il (elle) commence	**ils (elles) commencent**

→ *-er* verbs ending in *-cer* change the *c* to *ç* when the ending starts with *a* or *o* to keep the same pronunciation of the *c* (*s*).

Present Indicative of **choisir** (to choose) *p.p.* **choisi**

je choisis	**nous choisissons**
tu choisis	**vous choisissez**
il (elle) choisit	**ils (elles) choisissent**

→ Another class of verbs end with *-ir* in the infinitive. This ending is replaced in the present indicative by *-is, -is, -it, -issons, -issez, -issent,* and in the past participle by *-i.*

Like *choisir,* conjugate ***remplir*** (to fill), ***finir*** (to finish), ***rôtir*** (to roast).

→ Caution—not all verbs ending in *-ir* are regular. *Partir, sortir, sentir,* for example, do not follow this scheme.

GRAMMAIRE

Some Negative Locutions

je n'ai rien vu	I saw nothing, I didn't see anything
je ne vois rien	I see nothing, I don't see anything

rien n'est prêt nothing is ready
Qu'avez-vous vu? Rien. What did you see? Nothing.
je vous donne cela pour rien I give you that for nothing

→ "Nothing," "not anything" is *rien,* which requires *ne* before the verb if a verb is used. If *rien* is the object of a verb in a compound tense, it goes between the auxiliary and the past participle.

il n'y a **rien de vrai** dans cette histoire there is nothing true in that story

→ *Rien* followed by an adjective requires *de.*

il n'a **rien à manger** he has nothing to eat

→ *Rien* followed by an infinitive requires *à.*

donnez-moi **quelque chose de bon à manger** give me something good to eat

→ The same prepositions are used under like circumstances with *quelque chose* (something).

je ne vois personne I see no one; I don't see anybody
je n'ai vu personne I saw no one; I didn't see anybody
personne n'est venu no one came; nobody came
Qui avez-vous vu? Personne. Whom did you see? No one.
il n'a parlé à personne he spoke to no one

→ "No one," "nobody," "not anyone," "not anybody" are translated by *personne,* with *ne* before the verb if a verb is used. Unlike *rien, personne* follows the past participle if it is the object of a compound tense.

je ne le vois jamais I never see him
je ne l'ai jamais vu I have never seen him; I haven't ever seen him
Quand est-il venu ici? Jamais. When did he come here? Never.

→ "Never," "not ever" are translated by *jamais,* which precedes the past participle in compound tenses and requires *ne* before the verb if the verb is expressed.

L'avez-vous jamais vu? Have you ever seen him?

→ In interrogative sentences, without *ne, jamais* means "ever."

je ne bois ni vin ni bière I drink neither wine nor beer
je n'ai jamais bu ni vin ni bière I have never drunk either wine or beer

→"Neither . . . nor," "not either . . . or" is *ni . . . ni,* with *ne* before the verb. The partitive "some" or "any" (*du, de l', de la, des*) is generally omitted with *ni . . . ni.*

je ne le vois plus I no longer see him; I don't see him any more
je ne l'ai plus vu I no longer saw him; I didn't see him any more
il n'a plus d'argent he has no more money

→*Ne . . . plus* means "no longer," "no more," "not any longer," "not any more." Its position is the same as that of *ne . . . pas.*

je ne le vois point I *don't* see him; I don't see him at all
je ne l'ai point vu I *haven't* seen him; I haven't seen him at all

→ *Ne . . . point* is a somewhat stronger negative than *ne . . . pas.* It is somewhat archaic and purely literary.

Special Use of Definite Article

le vin est alcoolique wine is an alcoholic beverage
j'aime **le lait** I like milk
la liberté est nécessaire à l'homme liberty is necessary to man

→Nouns used in a general sense and abstract nouns require the definite article in French. However, the article is not used in many idiomatic expressions.

vous avez raison you are right
j'ai eu tort I was or have been wrong

→"to be right" is *avoir raison,* and "to be wrong" is *avoir tort. Avoir* is conjugated; *raison* and *tort* are nouns.

QUESTIONS

1. Aimez-vous le consommé? 2. Préférez-vous un déjeuner à l'américaine ou à la française? 3. Qu'est-ce que c'est qu'un potage Julienne? 4. Aimez-vous le jambon? 5. Qu'est-ce qu'Ernestine a choisi? 6. Est-ce

qu'Édouard a bien choisi? 7. Est-ce qu'on boit du vin en Amérique? 8. Est-ce qu'on boit du vin en France? 9. Que préférez-vous avec votre repas: du café, du thé, du vin, du lait ou de l'eau? 10. Est-ce qu'on boit beaucoup de bière en France? 11. Quelles sont les boissons fortement alcooliques? 12. Quelle est la boisson favorite des Français? 13. En général, qu'est-ce qu'on boit en Amérique?

EXERCICES

A. I. *Remplacez le tiret par la forme correcte du verbe* boire:

1. Est-ce qu'il ———— son thé? 2. Je n'ai pas ———— mon café. 3. Nous ———— de l'eau tous les jours. 4. Est-ce que vous ———— ce verre d'eau? 5. Ils ne ———— pas beaucoup de thé. 6. Je ———— mon lait.

II. *Remplacez le tiret par la forme correcte du verbe* manger:

1. Nous ne ———— pas assez. 2. Vous ———— trop de viande. 3. Je ne ———— pas beaucoup. 4. Ils n'ont rien ————. 5. ———— nous maintenant?

III. *Conjuguez:*

1. Je commence ces leçons de chant demain. 2. Je choisis toujours une chambre au deuxième étage.

B. I. *Employez* ne . . . rien, ne . . . personne, *dans les questions suivantes et répondez-y:*

1. Avez-vous vu? 2. Avez-vous trouvé? 3. Entendent-ils? 4. Choisit-il?

II. *Employez* ne . . . jamais, ne . . . plus *dans les questions suivantes et répondez-y:*

1. Avez-vous revu votre ami? 2. Avez-vous parlé de cet incident? 3. Discute-t-il cette question? 4. Mangeons-nous de la salade?

III. *Employez* ne . . . ni . . . ni *dans les phrases suivantes:*

1. Il a de l'argent et des amis. 2. Nous avons une plume et de l'encre. 3. Vous avez du pain et de l'eau.

C. *Traduisez:*

1. He is always right and I am always wrong. 2. We had nothing

to eat this morning. 3. Who came? Nobody. 4. What do you want? Nothing. 5. You are right, she is wrong once more (*encore une fois*). 6. Is everything ready? Nothing is ready. 7. There is nothing true in this book. 8. Have you nothing good to eat? 9. I want something good to read. 10. He likes bread.

D. *Préparez trois menus différents en vous servant du vocabulaire de cette leçon.*

Lesson 15

Present indicative and past participle of *suivre*

Present indicative and past indefinite of *s'en aller*

Formation of the imperative

Some irregular imperatives

Use of *veuillez*

Position of pronoun objects with the imperative affirmative and negative

Donnes-en, vas-y,* and *va-t-en

Use of *moi* and *toi* after imperative

CONVERSATION

Comment on Trouve son Chemin

LA DEMOISELLE: Pardon, Monsieur. Voulez-vous m'indiquer le chemin pour aller à la Place de la Concorde?

LE MONSIEUR: Avec plaisir, Mademoiselle. Suivez-moi, s'il vous plaît, jusqu'à cette rue que vous voyez là-bas, tout droit devant vous.

LA DEMOISELLE: Merci, Monsieur.

LE MONSIEUR: Attention, Mademoiselle. Les taxis marchent vite dans ces rues étroites. Restez sur le trottoir.

LA DEMOISELLE: Merci encore une fois, Monsieur.

LE MONSIEUR: A présent, Mademoiselle, regardez bien.

LA DEMOISELLE: De quel côté, Monsieur?

LE MONSIEUR: De ce côté-ci. Nous entrons à présent dans la rue de Grenelle, tout près du Boulevard Raspail. Pour arriver à la Place de la Concorde, suivez ce grand boulevard jusqu'au Boulevard St-Germain. Là, tournez à gauche et suivez le Boulevard St-Germain. Suivez-le jusqu'à la Seine. Au bout du boulevard, à votre gauche, il y a un grand bâtiment public. C'est la Chambre des Députés qui est maintenant l'Assemblée Nationale. En face, il y a un pont—le Pont de la Concorde. Traversez-le, et de l'autre côté du pont, sans tourner ni à droite ni à gauche, vous allez vous trouver dans la Place de la Concorde.

LA DEMOISELLE: Merci infiniment, Monsieur. Mais alors, pourquoi m'a-t-on dit de continuer jusqu'à la Seine, de prendre à gauche le long des quais et puis, après cinq minutes de marche, de traverser le fleuve?

LE MONSIEUR: On s'est trompé, Mademoiselle.

LA DEMOISELLE: Merci beaucoup, Monsieur.

LE MONSIEUR: Il n'y a pas de quoi, Mademoiselle. . . . Mademoiselle, attendez un instant.

LA DEMOISELLE: Qu'est-ce qu'il y a?

LE MONSIEUR: Venez ici, s'il vous plaît. Vous allez vous tromper.

LA DEMOISELLE: Pourquoi?

LE MONSIEUR: Vous voulez prendre le chemin qui conduit à la Place de la Concorde, n'est-ce pas?

LA DEMOISELLE: Eh bien?

LE MONSIEUR: Eh bien, allez par ici, pas par là. Ça, c'est la rue de La Chaise.

LA DEMOISELLE: Par où alors?

LE MONSIEUR: Par le boulevard que je vous ai indiqué. Par là, vous allez dans la direction contraire. C'est ce boulevard-ci. Regardez-le bien.

LA DEMOISELLE: Ah, merci, Monsieur! Oui, en effet, je me suis trompée. C'est de ce côté-là. Excusez-moi. Je ne vous ai pas bien écouté.

LE MONSIEUR: Encore une fois, au revoir, Mademoiselle.

VOCABULAIRE ET EXPRESSIONS

le taxi the taxi
le trottoir the sidewalk
la route the way, the road, the highway
l'avenue (*fem.*) the avenue
le boulevard the boulevard
le côté the side, the direction
le chemin the way, the road, the path
la direction the direction
l'endroit (*masc.*) the place, the spot
le moyen the way, the means
le fleuve the river
le pont the bridge
le quai the quay, the wharf
le bâtiment the building
la marche the walk, walking
la chambre the chamber, the room
le député the deputy, the representative
l'attention (*fem.*) the attention, the care
droit right, straight
gauche left, clumsy, awkward
large wide (large is **grand**)
public (*fem.* **publique**) public
contraire contrary, opposite

indiquer to indicate, to show
regarder to look (at) (*use a direct object and do not translate "at"*)
se tromper to make a mistake, to be mistaken
excuser to excuse
tourner to turn
se trouver to find oneself, to be
suivre to follow (*p.p.* **suivi**)
rester to stay, to remain (*être*)
continuer to continue, to go on
traverser to cross
entrer (dans) to enter, to go in (*être*) (**j'entre dans la chambre** I enter the room; **j'y entre** I go in [there])
s'en aller to go away (*être*)

jusqu'à as far as, up to
devant in front of
le long de along
sans without
en face (de) opposite
après after
infiniment infinitely

voulez-vous m'indiquer . . . ? will you show me . . . ?
tout droit straight ahead
encore une fois once again
de ce côté-ci on this side, this way
à gauche to the left
merci infiniment a thousand thanks
par ici this way; **par là** that way
par où? which way?
excusez-moi excuse me
suivez-moi follow me
attention! careful! attention!
de quel côté? on which side? which way?
à droite to the right
de l'autre côté de on the other side of
venez ici come here
en effet in fact, as a matter of fact

VERBES

Present Indicative of **suivre** (to follow) *p.p.* **suivi**

je suis ce chemin I follow this road
tu suis
il (elle) suit
nous suivons
vous suivez
ils (elles) suivent

Present Indicative of **s'en aller** (to go away)

je m'en vais à la maison
tu t'en vas
il (elle) s'en va
nous nous en allons
vous vous en allez
ils (elles) s'en vont

Past Indefinite of s'en aller

je m'en suis allé (*or* **allée**)
tu t'en es allé (allée)
il s'en est allé
elle s'en est allée
nous nous en sommes allés (allées)
vous vous en êtes allé (allée, allés, allées)
ils s'en sont allés
elles s'en sont allées

The Imperative

écoutez	**finissez**	**attendez**
écoutons	**finissons**	**attendons**

→ As stated before (Lesson 6) the polite imperative has normally the same form as the second person plural of the present indicative without the subject pronoun, while the "let us" form is the same as the first person plural of the present indicative without the subject pronoun.

écoute **finis** **attends**

→ The familiar singular imperative (corresponding to the pronoun *tu*) normally has the same form as the second singular of the present indicative, without the subject pronoun. However, verbs in *-er* drop the *-s* of the second singular present indicative.

sois be **soyons** let us be **soyez** be
aie have **ayons** let us have **ayez** have
veuille be willing **veuillons** let us be willing **veuillez** be willing
va go **allons** let us go **allez** go

→ There are very few exceptions to the rules stated above. Note, however, the irregular imperatives of *être, avoir,* and *vouloir,* and the irregular second singular imperative of *aller*.

veuillez le faire please do it; be kind enough to do it

→ The imperative of *vouloir* followed by an infinitive has the meaning of "please," "be kind enough to."

GRAMMAIRE

Object Pronouns with the Imperative

suivons-le let us follow him
rappelons-nous let us remember
prends-le take it
regardez-la look at her
écrivons-lui let us write to him
allons-y let us go there
prenez-en take some
suivez-nous follow us
rappelez-vous remember
prenons-le let us take it
regardez-les look at them
écrivez-leur write to them
allez-y go there
prenons-en let us take some

→ *With the imperative affirmative, object pronouns follow* **the verb** instead of preceding, and are attached to it by a hyphen.

suivez-moi follow me
écrivez-moi write to me
donnez-m'en give me some
donnes-en give some
rappelle-toi remember
donnez-moi give me
va-t'en go away
vas-y go there

→ With the imperative *affirmative, me* and *te* are changed to *moi* and *toi,* save before *y* and *en*. Note that, for the sake of euphony, *donnes* and *vas* are used instead of *donne* and *va*.

donnons-leur-en let us give them some
allons-nous-en let us go away
donne-le-lui give it to him
donnons-les-leur let us give them to them
donnez-m'en give me some
allez-vous-en go away

→ With the imperative affirmative, two object pronouns are attached to each other by hyphens, save for *m'en* and *t'en.*

vendez-les-moi sell them to me
envoyez-la-leur send it to them
donnez-les-nous give them to us

→ In the imperative *affirmative,* the *direct* object pronoun always *precedes* the *indirect*. However, *en* or *y* always comes last.

ne le suivons pas let us not follow him
ne lui écris pas don't write to him
ne m'en donnez pas don't give me any
ne m'y écrivez pas don't write to me there
ne les lui donnez pas don't give them to him
ne me les vends pas don't sell them to me
ne me l'y envoyez pas don't send it to me there
ne vous les écrivez pas don't write them to yourself
ne les prenez pas don't take them
ne me suivez pas don't follow me
ne t'en va pas don't go away
ne leur en donnons pas let us not give them any
ne me l'envoyez pas don't send it to me

→ If the imperative *negative* is used, the general rules apply: 1. the object pronouns precede the verb; 2. no hyphens are used; 3. *me* is used exclusively for me, to me; *te* is used exclusively for you, to you (familiar); 4. the indirect pronouns *me, te, nous, vous* precede the direct *le, la, les*. 5. the indirect pronouns *lui, leur* follow *le, la, les*.

QUESTIONS

1. Quel renseignement la demoiselle demande-t-elle au monsieur? 2. Quelle est la première indication qu'il lui donne? 3. Pourquoi lui dit-il de rester sur le trottoir? 4. Quels boulevards faut-il suivre pour arriver à la Place de la Concorde? 5. Où se trouve la Chambre des Députés? 6. Où se trouve le Pont de la Concorde? 7. Est-ce que la Place de la Concorde est près du Pont de la Concorde? 8. Pourquoi le monsieur dit-il à la demoiselle d'attendre un instant? 9. Quelle rue veut-elle prendre? 10. Est-ce qu'elle prend la bonne direction? 11. Pourquoi s'excuse-t-elle? 12. Comment leur conversation se termine-t-elle (*does it end*)?

EXERCICES

A. *Remplacez le tiret par la forme correcte au présent de l'indicatif de*

I. suivre:

1. Je ———— l'agent de police qui me montre le chemin. 2. Nous ———— vos conseils. 3. Il ———— les indications que le monsieur lui a données. 4. Vous ———— le chemin. 5. Ils ———— le petit enfant.

II. s'en aller:

1. Elle ———— pour une semaine. 2. Nous ———— tous les ans en été (*in the summer*). 3. Elles ———— maintenant. 4. Ils ———— très souvent le matin. 5. Je ———— immédiatement.

B. *Remplacez le tiret par la forme correcte du passé indéfini de* s'en aller *ou* de suivre:

1. Il ________ hier matin. 2. Nous ________. 3. Vous les ________. 4. Quel cours ________ tu ________? 5. Ils ________ en chantant.

C. *Traduisez les phrases suivantes:*

1. Don't send it to me. 2. Don't send it to him. 3. Don't give them to him. 4. Let's follow him. 5. Let's take some. 6. Follow me. 7. Give me some. 8. Will you please come here? 9. Look at them. 10. Let's go there. 11. Send it to me. 12. Give them to us. 13. Give them some. 14. Give it to him. 15. Don't take them. 16. Don't write to him. 17. Don't sell them to her. 18. Send them to them. 19. Go there. 20. Follow them.

D. *Écrivez des phrases en vous servant des expressions et des mots suivants:*

1. tout droit 2. de l'autre côté 3. en effet 4. de quel côté 5. à gauche 6. encore une fois 7. en face de 8. vite 9. par où 10. le trottoir 11. venez ici 12. merci infiniment

THÈME

—Do you want to go to Concord Square?

—Yes, please. I have lost my way.

—If you want to go on foot (*à pied*), cross this street, turn to the left and then continue straight ahead.

—Thank you. I have been walking for three hours and I am very tired. I wanted to go to the Chamber of Deputies, I walked to the Seine and there I got lost (lost myself). I asked a policeman who told me to follow the Seine. I crossed from the left bank (*la rive*) to the right bank on the bridge, but I did not find the Chamber of Deputies. After an hour's walk I found a street which leads into this avenue, but now I am lost again. Please show me again which street I must (*je dois*) follow.

Lesson 16

Present indicative and past participle of *savoir*

Present indicative and past participle of *connaître*

Comparative uses of *savoir* and *connaître*

Present indicative and past participle of *pouvoir*

Uses of *pouvoir*

Use of re- as prefix to verb

Use of ce *qui* and ce *que*

Use of ordinal and cardinal numbers in dates

Use and omission of definite article in expressions of time

The seasons

Distinction between *quand* and *lorsque*

CONVERSATION

Le Grand-père et la Grand'mère Voyagent

THÉRÈSE: Savez-vous ce qui arrive, André?

ANDRÉ: Non, Thérèse, naturellement je ne le sais pas. Racontez-moi ça.

Thérèse: Eh bien, mon grand-père et ma grand'mère sont partis de New-York le vingt-neuf août et ils vont arriver à Paris demain matin.

André: Je suis heureux de l'apprendre. Est-ce que je les connais?

Thérèse: Mais certainement! Vous avez fait leur connaissance au mois de janvier, en Amérique.

André: Ah, oui! je me rappelle. Et dites-moi; à leur âge, est-ce qu'ils peuvent voyager sans difficulté?

Thérèse: Sans aucun doute. En été on voyage facilement. Et puis, ils ne sont pas si âgés, après tout. Grand-père a soixante ans et grand'maman. . . . Je ne vais pas vous dire son âge. On ne révèle jamais l'âge d'une femme, même lorsqu'elle est grand'mère.

André: Vous avez tout à fait raison. D'ailleurs être vieux, cela ne fait rien, lorsqu'on se sent jeune. Quand est-ce que je vais avoir le plaisir de les revoir?

Thérèse: Pouvez-vous venir chez nous demain soir? Ils sont sûrs d'y être.

André: Malheureusement, je ne peux pas. J'ai rendez-vous avec mon chef de bureau.

Thérèse: Quel dommage! Vous êtes bien sûr que c'est avec votre chef de bureau, et pas avec quelque jolie jeune fille que vous avez connue à l'université?

André: Thérèse, je vous assure. . . .

Thérèse: C'était pour rire! Alors, voici ce que nous allons faire. Vous allez venir dîner chez nous après-demain.

André: C'est entendu. J'en prends note. Cela me fait grand plaisir. C'est pour le vendredi, huit septembre, alors.

Thérèse: C'est juste. A vendredi.

André: A vendredi. En attendant, présentez mes respects à vos grands-parents.

Thérèse: Au revoir, André.

André: Au revoir, Thérèse, et n'oubliez pas de présenter mes hommages à madame votre mère.

VOCABULAIRE ET EXPRESSIONS

le grand-père the grand-papa, the grandfather
la grand'mère, la grand'maman the grandmother
le monde the world
le chef the chief, the head (of an office)
le bureau (*pl.* **bureaux**) the office
la connaissance the acquaintance
la difficulté the difficulty
la note the note
les hommages regards, respects (used in the plural when referring to a lady)
les respects regards, respects (referring to old people)
l'Amérique America
en Amérique in America
André Andrew
Thérèse Theresa

janvier January
février February
mars March
avril April
mai May
juin June
juillet July
août August
septembre September
octobre October
novembre November
décembre December
lundi Monday
mardi Tuesday
mercredi Wednesday
jeudi Thursday
vendredi Friday
samedi Saturday
dimanche Sunday
l'hiver (*masc.*) winter
le printemps spring
l'été (*masc.*) summer
l'automne (*masc.*) autumn
en hiver in the winter
au printemps in the spring
en été in the summer
en automne in the fall
juste just, right, correct

savoir to know, to know how
connaître to know, to be acquainted with
arriver (*être*) to happen, to arrive
se passer to happen
raconter to tell, to relate

révéler (je révèle) to reveal
assurer to assure
reconnaître to recognize
pouvoir can, to be able
voyager (nous voyageons) to travel
nager (nous nageons) to swim

ce qui (*subj.*), **ce que** (*obj.*) what
naturellement naturally, of course
assurément certainly, surely
sans aucun doute undoubtedly
quelque some (one or another), any
lorsque when
en attendant meanwhile
si so
avoir tout à fait raison to be absolutely right
après-demain day after tomorrow
au mois de février in February
cela ne fait rien it makes no difference
cela me fait (grand) plaisir that gives me (great) pleasure
faire la connaissance de to make the acquaintance of
je ne (le) sais pas I don't know
être heureux de + ***infinitive*** to be happy to
prendre note de to make a note of
je ne peux pas I can't
puis-je? est-ce que je puis? *or* **est-ce que je peux?** may I?
quel dommage! what a pity! too bad!
présenter ses hommages à to pay one's respects to, offer one's regards to
c'était pour rire I was joking
après tout after all

VERBES

Present Indicative of **savoir** (to know) *p.p.* **su**

je sais ma leçon aujourd'hui
tu sais
il (elle) sait
nous savons
vous savez
ils (elles) savent

Imperative: **sache, sachons, sachez**

je sais ce qui s'est passé I know what happened
je sais ce que vous avez fait I know what you did
je ne sais pas I don't know

→ *Savoir* is to know a fact, a situation, but not a person.

savez-vous nager? Can you swim? Do you know how to swim?
Ce petit enfant sait écrire. This little child can (knows how to) write.

→ *Savoir* translates "can" when "can" means "to know how to."

Present Indicative of **connaître** (to know) *p.p.* **connu**

je connais ce monsieur	**nous connaissons**
tu connais	**vous connaissez**
il (elle) connaît	**ils (elles) connaissent**

reconnaître (to recognize) is conjugated like **connaître**

je connais bien cet homme I know that man well
Est-ce que vous le connaissez? Do you know him?
c'est un endroit qu'il connaît It's a spot he knows

→ *Connaître* means to know a person, to be acquainted with a specific place or thing.

Present Indicative of **pouvoir** (can, to be able) *p.p.* **pu**

je peux (je puis) le faire	**nous pouvons**
tu peux	**vous pouvez**
il (elle) peut	**ils (elles) peuvent**

je ne peux pas le faire I can't do it
Pouvez-vous nager après cette maladie? Can you swim after that illness?

→ *Pouvoir* means "to be able," "can" (provided "can" does not mean "to know how"; use *savoir* for that).

Est-ce que je peux (*or* **Puis-je**) **sortir?** May I go out?
Oui, vous pouvez sortir à présent. Yes, you may go out now.

→ *Pouvoir* also translates "may" in the sense of asking for or granting permission.

Enfin, j'ai pu le voir. Finally, I was able to see him, managed to see him, succeeded in seeing him.

The *past indefinite* of *pouvoir* means "could" in the sense of "managed," "succeeded."

The Prefix re-

appeler to call
voir to see
faire to do, to make
venir to come
partir to start, leave

rappeler to recall
revoir to see again
refaire to do again, make again
revenir to come back
repartir to start off again

→ *Re-* or *R-* prefixed to a verb usually has the sense of "again." Compare English "make," "remake"; "tell," "retell." The use of this prefix is much more common in French than in English.

GRAMMAIRE

Ce qui—ce que

Je ne sais pas **ce qui** est arrivé. I don't know what happened.
Savez-vous **ce que** vous avez fait? Do you know what you did?
Ce qu'il a vu, personne ne le sait. What he saw, no one knows.

→ The relative pronoun "what" is translated by *ce qui* if it is the *subject, ce que* if it is the *object* of the verb.

Dates

Il est arrivé **le premier mai.** He arrived on the first of May (on May 1st).
Il est reparti **le trois juin.** He left again on the third of June (on June the third).

→ Names of the months are not capitalized in French. They are all masculine. For days of the month, do not translate "on" or "of." Use *le premier* for "the first," *cardinal numbers* from the "second" on.

Note that in French the day must precede the month.

Je l'ai vu **vendredi.** I saw him on Friday.
Je l'ai vu **le six juillet.** I saw him on July the sixth.
Je l'ai vu **le vendredi six juillet.** I saw him on Friday, July the sixth.
Je l'ai vu **vendredi, le six juillet.** I saw him on Friday, July the sixth.

→ If the day of the week is stated along with the day of the month, the article precedes either the day of the week or the date.

The Seasons

le printemps Spring	**au printemps** in the Spring
l'été Summer	**en été** in the Summer
l'automne Fall	**en automne** in the Fall
l'hiver Winter	**en hiver** in Winter

→ Names of the seasons are all masculine. They are not capitalized in French. "In" is translated by *au* with printemps, by *en* with the others.

Je l'ai vu **quand** il est parti. I saw him when he left.
Je l'ai vu **lorsqu'**il est parti. I saw him when he left.
Quand est-il parti? When did he leave?
Savez-vous **quand** il est venu? Do you know when he came?

→ *Quand* and *lorsque* both mean "when." They are interchangeable, except *in questions,* direct or indirect, where *quand* alone may be used.

QUESTIONS

1. Est-ce qu'André sait ce qui arrive? 2. Qui va arriver à Paris? 3. Où est-ce qu'André a connu les grands-parents de Thérèse? 4. Quand les a-t-il vus? 5. Est-ce qu'ils voyagent beaucoup? 6. Pourquoi pas? 7. Est-ce qu'André va avoir le plaisir de refaire leur connaissance? 8. Où vont-ils se réunir? 9. Quand vont-ils se réunir? 10. Avec qui André a-t-il un rendez-vous? 11. Pourquoi André proteste-t-il? 12. Quand André va-t-il dîner chez Thérèse? 13. Comment André va-t-il se rappeler cette invitation? 14. Qu'est-ce qu'il présente aux grands-parents de Thérèse?

EXERCICES

A. *Conjuguez au présent de l'indicatif:*

1. Je sais nager maintenant. 2. Je ne sais pas ce qui s'est passé. 3. Je sais ce que vous avez fait. 4. Est-ce que je sais la leçon aujourd'hui? 5. Est-ce que je connais cet homme? 6. C'est un endroit

que je ne connais pas. 7. Paris est une ville que je connais bien. 8. Je ne peux pas le faire maintenant. 9. Je repars tout de suite. 10. Je refais tous les devoirs.

B. *Remplacez le tiret par* ce que *ou* ce qui *selon le sens:*

1. Je sais ________ vous avez fait. 2. Est-ce que vous savez ________ est arrivé? 3. Il n'a dit à personne ________ il a vu. 4. Personne ne veut lui dire ________ est arrivé à son fils. 5. Tout ________ je sais, c'est qu'il est malade. 6. ________ est vrai, c'est qu'il n'est pas arrivé.

C. *Traduisez les expressions en italiques:*

1. Il a quitté Paris *the first of June.* 2. Elle est arrivée en France *the fifth of May.* 3. Je l'ai vu au théâtre *the second of March.* 4. Je l'ai vu à Paris *in the spring.* 5. Il neige beaucoup *in winter.* 6. Je l'ai connu *when* il était enfant. 7. *In summer,* il fait très chaud à New York. 8. Les feuilles tombent des arbres *in autumn.* 9. *When* voulez-vous acheter cette maison? 10. Je l'ai reçu *the sixth of October.*

D. *Faites des phrases avec les expressions suivantes.*

1. Présenter mes hommages à 2. prendre note de 3. après tout 4. faire la connaissance de 5. certainement 6. se passer 7. ce qui 8. ce que 9. cela me fait plaisir 10. je ne peux pas

THÈME

—Do you know that my grandmother and grandfather arrived from America today?

—No, when did they leave America?

—They left New York a week ago and are arriving at Le Havre tomorrow. I am going to Le Havre to wait for them. They are so old. At their age they cannot travel without some difficulty.

—Were they sick?

—Yes, of course, my grandmother was very ill.

—What a shame! At her age. I hope they are well now. Give them my regards. Are you going to invite them to have dinner with me Friday, January 3? I want to see them again. I remember them very well. I met a very pretty girl at their house (*chez eux*) in New York. They invited her for dinner and I made her acquaintance.

—Yes, I know. They know you well. Until Friday, then.

Review Lesson 4

A. *Conjuguez, au même temps, les verbes des phrases suivantes:*

1. Je perds du temps à leur parler. 2. Je bois du café tous les jours. 3. Je mange des fruits à chaque repas. 4. Je commence à comprendre le français. 5. Je choisis ces fleurs pour les donner à des amis. 6. Je finis de dîner avant de sortir. 7. Je suis trois cours par jour. 8. Je m'en vais tout de suite. 9. Je m'en suis allé de bonne heure. 10. Je sais ce qui s'est passé. 11. Je connais la ville de Paris. 12. Je peux vous dire la vérité.

B. *Traduisez les phrases suivantes:*

1. He is at Henry's; George is there, too. 2. He wrote me a letter and I answered it. 3. Did she answer him? 4. He has some milk. Have you any? 5. Here are your pencils, I have two. 6. She speaks of her book and he speaks of it, too. 7. Speak to her about it. 8. They come from New York. Do you come from there? 9. Has he any coffee? He has some. 10. They haven't much. 11. Here is your briefcase. Do you need it? 12. Are there any flowers? There are some in that room. 13. It is late. I am tired. 14. The train arrived late. 15. He came home very late. 16. Please excuse me (*excusez-moi*); I am very late.

C. *Employez les expressions suivantes dans des phrases, en mettant le verbe au présent et au passé composé:*

1. ne . . . rien 2. ne . . . personne 3. ne . . . jamais 4. ni . . . ni 5. ne . . . plus

D. *Changez les phrases suivantes en mettant tous les verbes à l'impératif, à la première et deuxième personnes du pluriel, et employez les mêmes pronoms compléments:*

1. Je le suis. 2. Ils la regardent. 3. Elle lui écrit. 4. Il lui en donne. 5. Ils le lui donnent. 6. Elle les leur vend. 7. Il ne le lui envoie pas. 8. Elle y va. 9. Il les leur vend. 10. Elle lui écrit.

E. *Remplacez le tiret par* ce que *ou* ce qui:

1. J'ai vu ________ il a fait. 2. Nous avons lu ________ il a écrit. 3. Savez-vous ________ est arrivé à Marie? 4. Dites-lui ________ peut arriver. 5. ________ il peut faire, c'est de partir.

F. *Écrivez toutes les dates en français:*

1. Elle est arrivée (*June 5*), et elle est repartie (*September 1*). 2. Je l'ai vu (*Friday, August 5*). 3. L'avez-vous vu (*Saturday*)? 4. J'ai fait sa connaissance (*Monday, May 1*).

Lecture 4

LES PRUNES DE MONSIEUR LE CURÉ

(D'après un conte de Max et Alex. Fischer)

—Bonjour, monsieur l'instituteur.[1]

—Bonjour, monsieur le curé.

—Figurez-vous,[2] monsieur l'instituteur, que je suis, tous les jours, victime d'un vol (*theft*). Mon prunier qui, comme vous le savez, se trouve[3] derrière le presbytère, est chargé de beaux fruits, mais chaque jour des prunes disparaissent.[4] Je ne peux vraiment pas soupçonner (*suspect*) Constance, ma vieille bonne (*maid*), de les manger en cachette.[5]

—C'est évident. Alors, monsieur le curé, vous ne savez pas qui commet ces vols?

—Non, mais j'ai une indication. Hier, caché derrière les volets (*shutters*) de ma chambre à coucher, je regarde mon pauvre prunier et qu'est-ce que je vois?—une ombre enfantine (*a child's shadow*) qui joue autour de l'arbre.

—Et cette ombre, monsieur le curé, à qui appartient-elle?[6]

—Hélas! monsieur l'instituteur, je l'ignore.[7] Ma vue est assez faible. A cette distance je ne vois pas très bien. Puis, à mon âge, je ne peux vraiment pas courir après un gamin; je n'ai plus mes

[1] monsieur l'instituteur: *When addressing people by title, the French usually add* monsieur *or* madame: monsieur le docteur, madame la marquise. *An* instituteur *is a teacher in an elementary school. A* professeur *teaches in the higher schools.*

[2] Figurez-vous = Imaginez, *just imagine.*

[3] se trouve = est. Se trouver *stresses location:* Où se trouve l'opéra? *Where is the opera house?*

[4] disparaissent, *disappear. Third-person plural, present indicative, of the irregular verb* disparaître.

[5] en cachette, *secretly.* Cacher, *to hide;* une *cachette,* a hiding place.

[6] à qui appartient-elle? *whose is it? to whom does it belong?* Appartenir *is conjugated like the irregular verb* tenir.

[7] je l'ignore = je ne le sais pas, *I don't know. Students should be very careful to remember that* ignorer *means* ne pas savoir, *not to know, to be ignorant of.*

jambes de vingt ans.[8]—Mais le coupable est certainement[9] un de vos élèves.

—Vous avez sans doute raison,[10] monsieur le curé. Que faire?[11]

—Monsieur l'instituteur, je ne demande pas une punition exagérée pour le coupable (*culprit*), mais je désire voir finir ces petits vols. Pensez donc,[12] mes belles prunes que j'aime tant! L'autre jour, j'en ai compté plus de cinq cents.[13] Aujourd'hui, il y en a cinquante-cinq, exactement. Quel désastre!

Le lendemain,[14] pendant toute la classe du matin, l'instituteur tâche (*tries to*) de découvrir l'identité du jeune malfaiteur. D'abord, il a l'idée de demander brusquement:

—Quel (*which*) est l'élève qui, chaque soir, vole des prunes dans le jardin de monsieur le curé?

Mais il pense que la peur du châtiment va sans doute laisser sa question sans réponse.

Un élève se lève et vient se placer devant lui (*him*) pour réciter une fable de La Fontaine.[15] Est-ce le petit malfaiteur? L'instituteur le regarde fixement; il tâche de lire dans les yeux de l'enfant la preuve du crime. En vain! Pour être certain, c'est dans les ventres (*bellies*) qu'il faudrait (*one would have to*) regarder.

L'instituteur a alors une autre idée. C'est l'heure de[16] la dictée. Au lieu de[17] lire un passage sur la gloire de Louis XIV ou sur les victoires de Napoléon, il va improviser quelques (*a few*) lignes sur le sujet: "Le goût (*taste*) des prunes de monsieur le curé." Et voici ce qu'il (*what he*) dicte:

8 mes jambes de vingt ans, *the legs I had when I was twenty.*

9 certainement, *certainly. Most adverbs in French are formed by adding* -ment *to the masculine adjective ending in a vowel* (fixe—fixement), *and to the feminine forms of adjectives ending in a consonant* (exact—exactement).

10 Vous avez . . . raison, *you are right. Similarly:* avoir tort, *to be wrong;* avoir faim, *to be hungry;* avoir peur, *to be afraid;* avoir besoin de, *to need.*

11 Que faire? *What is one to do? Similarly:* Que dire? *What is one to say?* Que penser? *What is one to think?*

12 Pensez donc! *Just think!* Donc *is often used to emphasize or to give more force to the preceding word. Similarly:* Venez donc! *Do come, please come.*

13 en . . . cinq cents, *five hundred of them. The French like to express their thoughts fully. Similarly:* il y en a dix, *there are ten (of them).*

14 Le lendemain, *the next day. One should be careful to distinguish this word from* demain, *tomorrow.*

15 La Fontaine: *a famous French writer of fables of the seventeenth century.*

16 l'heure de, *the time for. Similarly:* l'heure du déjeuner, *lunchtime;* l'heure de partir, *time to leave.*

17 au lieu de, *instead of (lit.: in lieu of).*

"Il y a dans un joli petit village de France que vous connaissez[18] tous[19] -virgule-, mes amis -virgule-, un très vilain (*wicked*) petit garçon -point-. Il se conduit[20] comme un voleur -point d'exclamation-! Il entre dans le jardin de monsieur le curé -point-. Il vole une -virgule-, deux -virgule-, dix prunes -point-. Ces prunes lui paraissent[21] délicieuses -point-. Mais le lendemain il a des coliques effroyables (*frightful*) -point d'exclamation-!"

A la fin de la dictée, il déclare que les instituteurs connaissent un remède à (*for*) ce genre de douleurs (*pains*) intestinales et que, si le petit voleur avoue (*confesses*) immédiatement son crime, son maître est prêt à lui venir en aide (*to help him out*).

La dictée est finie. L'instituteur attend. Personne ne se lève pour avouer. Ses cinquante-huit élèves ne semblent pas avoir peur de ces douleurs futures.

La classe continue; elle va bientôt finir. L'instituteur pense alors à (*of*) un autre stratagème.

—Un élève de cette classe, dit-il,—je préfère ne pas le nommer —a volé des prunes dans le jardin de monsieur le curé. Je ne désire pas le punir sévèrement, mais lui infliger l'humiliation qu'il mérite. Après la classe, il va courir au prunier du presbytère, et revenir à l'école cet après-midi, portant (*wearing*) ostensiblement une prune pendue à (*hanging from*) son cou par une ficelle (*string, cord*) rouge. Sa punition sera (*will be*) de porter cette preuve de son crime pendant huit jours.

A l'heure du déjeuner (*lunch*), l'instituteur est très satisfait de son astucieuse (*wily*) initiative. Il pense aussi à (*about*) la gratitude du curé en mangeant (*eating*) ses cinquante-quatre dernières prunes.

A deux heures moins dix, il attend ses élèves dans sa salle de classe. La porte s'ouvre. Le petit Pierre entre. L'instituteur voit qu'il porte autour du cou une ficelle rouge avec quelque chose de noir au bout.

18 connaissez *is the second-person plural, present indicative, of the irregular verb* connaître.

19 tous, *all of you. The final* s *is pronounced.* Tous *is a pronoun here. It might also mean "all of us," "all of them."*

20 Il se conduit, *he behaves (lit.: he conducts himself).*

21 lui paraissent, *seem to him; third person plural, present indicative of the irregular verb* paraître. *See note 4.*

—Ah! Ah!, pense-t-il, c'est donc le petit Pierre qui est le voleur!

Mais il ne dit rien. Il préfère attendre et accuser le petit Pierre devant toute la classe.

Un autre garçon entre. Autour du cou, il semble porter aussi une ficelle rouge, avec quelque chose de noir au bout. L'instituteur ne peut pas en[22] croire ses yeux.

—Mais non,[23] pense-t-il, puisque Pierre est le coupable, le coupable ne peut pas être Paul. Je suis victime d'une illusion d'optique. Je suis myope (*short-sighted*).

Il est deux heures. Tous les élèves sont là. L'instituteur va fermer la porte de sa salle de classe. Mais voilà le curé qui arrive. Il est affolé (*out of his senses*) et s'écrie:

—C'est épouvantable (*frightful*), monsieur l'instituteur. Je viens de regarder[24] mon beau prunier. Il n'y a plus un seul fruit dessus (*on it*). Quel désastre!

L'instituteur est fort (*very*) surpris, mais il est aussi très fier (*proud*) de pouvoir indiquer le voleur à monsieur le curé. Il cherche le petit Pierre parmi les élèves. Ses yeux vont d'un banc à l'autre. Autour de tous les cous pend quelque chose de noir au bout d'une ficelle rouge.

L'instituteur est abasourdi (*dumfounded*) et scandalisé. Pourtant, en regardant (*looking*) bien (*more carefully*) il remarque que trois de ses élèves ne portent pas le collier (*necklace*) d'infamie. Cela le console un peu et il commence un petit discours pour les féliciter. Mais les trois garçons l'interrompent en sanglotant (*sobbing*):

—Ne nous félicitez pas, monsieur l'instituteur. Nous ne sommes pas moins coupables que nos camarades, mais nous courons moins vite. Nous sommes cinquante-huit élèves et il ne restait que[25] cinquante-cinq prunes sur l'arbre. Nous sommes arrivés les derniers.

22 en, *about this*. En *completes the thought.*
23 Mais non! *Certainly not! It can't be!* Mais *often gives more force to the following word. Similarly:* Mais oui! *Certainly!* Mais voyons! *Now, look here!*

24 Je viens de regarder, *I have just looked at.*
25 il ne restait que, *there remained only.* Rester *is often used impersonally:* il reste quelque chose à faire, *something remains to be done. (Lit.: there remains . . .)*

QUESTIONNAIRE

1. De quel vol le curé est-il victime? 2. Où se trouve le prunier du curé? 3. Est-ce que le curé peut soupçonner Constance, sa bonne? 4. Caché derrière les volets et regardant dans son jardin, que voit le curé? 5. L'ombre qu'il voit, à qui appartient-elle? 6. Comment est la vue du curé? Comment sont ses jambes? 7. Comment savez-vous que le curé aime ses prunes? 8. Combien de prunes restent au curé, après le vol? 9. Quelle question l'instituteur pose-t-il à la classe pour découvrir le voleur? 10. Pourquoi regarde-t-il l'élève qui récite la fable de La Fontaine? 11. Quel est le sujet de la dictée qu'il donne à la classe? 12. Quel est le dernier stratagème de l'instituteur? 13. Pourquoi pense-t-il enfin que le petit Pierre est le voleur? 14. Quand le curé revient à l'école, qu'est-ce qu'il annonce à l'instituteur? 15. Pourquoi trois élèves de la classe n'ont-ils pas de prune pendant au bout d'une ficelle rouge?

Lesson 17

Imperfect indicative of *parler, vendre,* and *finir*

Imperfect of some irregular verbs

Uses of the imperfect

Use of imperfect compared with use of past indefinite

Disjunctive personal pronouns and uses

Use of disjunctive pronoun with *présenter,* etc.

Use of disjunctive pronoun with *c'est* and *ce sont*

Use of *qui, qui est-ce qui, qui est-ce que*

CONVERSATION

Les Présentations

M. Brunot: Joseph, voulez-vous me permettre de vous présenter mon gendre Raoul Bernier?

M. Bernier: Enchanté, Monsieur.

Joseph: C'est moi qui suis enchanté de faire votre connaissance. J'ai beaucoup entendu parler de vous.

M. Bernier: Je vous remercie de votre amabilité. Qui est-ce qui vous a parlé de moi?

JOSEPH: Votre beau-père et votre belle-sœur Louise. Elle me disait presque chaque fois qu'elle me rencontrait: "Vous allez faire un de ces jours la connaissance de mon beau-frère. Il va revenir à Paris, et je vais vous présenter à lui."

M. BERNIER: C'est très gentil de sa part. Lorsque nous étions à New-York, elle nous répétait toujours qu'elle allait nous faire connaître ses bons amis parisiens. Bien entendu, nous ne demandions pas mieux, mais il y avait la mer entre nous et eux.

JOSEPH: Eh bien, à présent, nous voici.

(Madeleine entre)

MADELEINE: Pardon, Messieurs. Ah! te voilà, Joseph! On t'attend là-bas.

JOSEPH (avant de partir): Madeleine! Je veux te présenter M. Bernier, le beau-fils de notre hôte, qui vient de rentrer des États-Unis.

M. BERNIER: Enchanté, Madame.

MADELEINE: Enchantée, Monsieur. Alors, Joseph, va voir tes amis. Je me charge de M. Bernier. Voilà ma sœur Henriette. Je vais vous présenter à elle.

VOCABULAIRE ET EXPRESSIONS

le mari the husband
le gendre, le beau-fils the son-in-law
la mer the sea

gentil (*fem.* **gentille**) nice, kind
chéri darling, dear, beloved
parisien (*fem.* **parisienne**), Parisian

présenter to introduce
remercier de to thank for
entendre parler de to hear about (*entendre* is conjugated, *parler* stays in the infinitive)
rencontrer to meet (casually; use **faire la connaissance de** for "to meet socially")
vouloir bien to be willing
se charger de to take charge of, take care of **(nous nous chargeons)**

moi me, I
toi you
lui him, he
elle her, she

nous us, we
vous you
eux them, they
elles them, they

qui est-ce qui? who?

qui est-ce que? whom?

entre between
près de near

loin de far from

enchanté (de faire votre connaissance) pleased to meet you, delighted
c'est moi it is I
il y avait there was, there were

c'est très gentil de sa (votre) part it's very kind of him or her (you)
je ne demande pas mieux I don't ask for anything better

VOCABULAIRE SUPPLÉMENTAIRE

les messieurs the gentlemen (plural of **monsieur**)
l'hôte the host; the guest

la présentation the introduction
la bonté, l'amabilité the kindness
Raoul Ralph

VERBES

The Imperfect Tense

Imperfect Indicative of **parler, vendre,** and **finir**

je parl-ais à mon beau-frère
tu parl-ais
il (elle) parl-ait

nous parl-ions
vous parl-iez
ils (elles) parl-aient

je vend-ais ma bibliothèque
tu vend-ais
il (elle) vend-ait

nous vend-ions
vous vend-iez
ils (elles) vend-aient

je fin-iss-ais mes leçons
tu fin-iss-ais
il (elle) fin-iss-ait

nous fin-iss-ions
vous fin-iss-iez
ils (elles) fin-iss-aient

→ The imperfect indicative has these endings, for all verbs: *-ais, -ais, -ait, -ions, -iez, -aient.*

They are added to the stem. However, regular *-ir* conjugation verbs insert *-iss-* between the stem and the ending.

Some Irregular Imperfects

être to be; **j'étais** I was, used to be
avoir to have; **j'avais** I had, used to have
savoir to know; **je savais** I knew, used to know
connaître to know; **je connaissais** I knew, used to know
dire to say, tell; **je disais** I was saying, telling, used to say, tell
faire to do, make; **je faisais** I was doing, making, used to do, make
prendre to take; **je prenais** I was taking, used to take
vouloir to want; **je voulais** I wanted, used to want
boire to drink; **je buvais** I was drinking, used to drink
lire to read; **je lisais** I was reading, used to read
écrire to write; **j'écrivais** I was writing, used to write
venir to come; **je venais** I was coming, used to come
sortir to go out; **je sortais** I was going out, used to go out
partir to leave; **je partais** I was leaving, used to leave
voir to see; **je voyais** I was seeing, used to see
pouvoir can, to be able; **je pouvais** I could, used to be able

→ Irregular verbs in *-ir, -oir,* generally form the imperfect by dropping the *-ir, oir* of the infinitive and adding the endings given above.

Note that the irregularities in the imperfect of *être, dire, faire, prendre, boire, lire, écrire, voir, connaître* appear in the stem, not in the endings, which are the same for all verbs.

Lorsque j'allais à l'université, je le voyais tous les jours. When I went (used to go) to the university, I saw (used to see) him every day.

→ The imperfect indicates what used to happen, repeatedly or regularly. English expresses this by "used to" or by the simple past. If an English past can be replaced by "used to," use the imperfect in French.

Imperfect and Past Indefinite Compared

Il écrivait quand je suis entré. He was writing when I came in.

→ The imperfect also denotes what was going on when something else took place. English here uses the past progressive (*he was writing*).

j'ai parlé I spoke, I have spoken
je parlais I was speaking, I used to speak

Pauvre Albert! Je le voyais souvent. Poor Albert! I saw him often.
je l'ai vu la semaine dernière I saw him last week

→ Note the contrast between the past indefinite, indicating generally a single past action or event considered as completed (taking place and then ceasing), and the imperfect, indicating an incompleted past action, state, or condition, as to the completion of which no indication is given.

je savais qu'il allait venir I knew (all along) he was going to come
j'ai su qu'il allait venir I learned that he was going to come
je voulais le faire I wanted to (but did not get to) do it
j'ai voulu le faire I wanted to (and decided to) do it; I insisted on doing it
l'année dernière je ne pouvais pas nager Last year I was not able to swim
enfin, j'ai pu le voir finally, I was able to (managed to) see him

→ With verbs like *savoir, vouloir, pouvoir* which by their nature generally indicate a continuing action, it is the imperfect rather than the past indefinite which translates the English past. The past indefinite of these verbs often has a special meaning which denotes a single occurrence at a specific point of time: *j'ai su,* I learned, I found out; *j'ai voulu,* I insisted upon, decided upon (and did); *j'ai pu,* I was able to, succeeded in (and did).

GRAMMAIRE

Disjunctive Pronouns

avec moi with me
sans toi without you
pour lui for him
d'elle from her

entre nous between us
vers vous toward you
près d'eux near them
loin d'elles far from them

→ The disjunctive personal pronouns, *moi, toi, lui, elle, nous, vous, eux, elles,* are used after prepositions.

Qui va là? **Moi.** Who goes there? I.
Qui a-t-il vu? **Toi.** Whom did he see? You.
Qui a parlé? **Lui.** Who spoke? He.

→ These pronouns are also used when the verb is understood.

moi, je vais le faire *I* am going to do it
toi, tu vas le faire? *You*'re going to do it?
je le crois, **moi** *I* believe it
lui peut le faire *He* can do it
eux vont le faire *They* are going to do it
je l'ai vu, **lui** I saw *him*

→ They are also used as stressed subject or object pronouns. As subjects, *moi* and *toi* are often followed by *je* and *tu,* respectively. The others are usually immediately followed by the verb.

moi et toi, nous allons le faire you and I are going to do it
toi et lui, vous pouvez le faire you and he can do it
lui et elle savent le faire he and she know how to do it

→ Two subject pronouns of different persons are expressed by the disjunctives and summed up by *nous* or *vous.* If both are third person, the disjunctives alone are used.

il me présente à lui he introduces me to him
il me le présente he introduces him to me
il t'a présenté à moi he introduced you to me
il te l'a présentée he introduced her to you
il nous a présentés à eux he introduced us to them
il nous les a présentés he introduced them to us
il vous a présenté à nous he introduced you to us
il s'est présenté à eux (à moi, etc.) he introduced himself to them (to me, etc.)

→ If there are two object pronouns both denoting people, and the direct is *me, te, nous,* or *vous,* the indirect pronoun cannot be used, but must be replaced by a disjunctive with *à* after the verb.

c'est moi (it is I) **qui le fais**
c'est toi (it is you)
c'est lui (it is he) **que j'ai vu**
c'est elle (it is she)
c'est nous (it is we)
c'est vous (it is you)
ce sont eux (it is they) *or* **c'est eux**
ce sont elles (it is they) *or* **c'est elles**

→ Disjunctives are used after *c'est* and *ce sont* (it is). Note that *ce sont* is used only with a third person plural, *c'est* can be used in all cases, including the third person plural.

Qui? Qui est-ce qui? Qui est-ce que?

Qui est arrivé? **Qui est-ce qui** est arrivé? Who came?
Qui avez-vous vu? **Qui est-ce que** vous avez vu? Whom did you see?

→ *Qui?* means both *who?* and *whom? Qui est-ce qui* (*who?*) and *qui est-ce que?* (*whom?*) may replace it, but require declarative word-order.

QUESTIONS

1. Qui veut-on présenter à Joseph? 2. Est-ce que Joseph est content de faire la connaissance de M. Bernier? 3. Comment M. Bernier répond-il quand on le présente? 4. De qui Joseph a-t-il entendu parler? 5. Qui avait parlé de M. Bernier? 6. Qui allait revenir à Paris? 7. Que disait Louise quand elle était à New York? 8. Qu'est-ce qui séparait ces futurs amis? 9. Qui interrompt la discussion? 10. Est-elle présentée aux autres? 11. Quelles autres présentations se font ensuite?

EXERCICES

A. *Conjuguez:*
1. Je parlais à mon oncle quand son gendre est entré.
2. Avant la guerre je vendais des dictionnaires.
3. Je finissais mon travail au moment où ces messieurs sont arrivés.

B. *Remplacez les infinitifs par les temps passés qui conviennent et traduisez les phrases en anglais:*

1. Quand nous (*être*) en France nous (*aller*) souvent au café. 2. Il (*avoir*) de bons professeurs mais ne (*savoir*) jamais ses leçons. 3. Elle (*faire*) ses devoirs quand il (*arriver*). 4. Je (*prendre*) des leçons de français tous les samedis quand (*être*) petit. 5. Quand il (*avoir*) dix ans, il (*manger*) du matin au soir. 6. Je (*vouloir*) acheter ce livre, mais on a refusé de me le vendre. 7. Elle (*boire*) toujours de l'eau avec ses repas. 8. Je (*lire*) dans le journal que Georges (*écrire*) un autre roman. 9. Il (*sortir*) de chez lui quand sa sœur (*arriver*). 10. Nous (*partir*) pour l'Afrique du Nord tous les ans à cette époque. 11. Elle (*suivre*) les conseils qu'on lui (*donner*). 12. Mon professeur (*voir*) nos devoirs.

C. *Remplacez le nom propre par le pronom qui convient:*

1. Il est sorti avec Marie mais sa sœur est sortie avec Georges. 2. Nous allons partir avec Georges et Marie. 3. Les enfants sont loin de Madame Dupont. 4. Entre Jean et moi, il n'y a jamais eu de malentendu. 5. C'est Marie qui m'a présenté à M. Duhamel. 6. C'est Georges. 7. C'est Marie. 8. Qui est là? C'est Georges et Philippe. 9. Est-ce que c'est Henri? 10. Est-ce vous? Non, c'est Antoine.

D. *Quelles questions ont pu suggérer les réponses suivantes?*

1. Je pense à mes amis très souvent. 2. Je pense que ce film est très stupide. 3. Lui et moi, nous sortons souvent ensemble. 4. Rien n'est arrivé. 5. Il nous a présentés à eux.

E. *Faites des phrases avec les expressions suivantes:*

1. Qui est-ce qui? 2. se charger de 3. vouloir bien 4. entendre parler de 5. Qui est-ce que? 6. remercier de 7. rencontrer 8. faire la connaissance de

THÈME

—May I present my friend, George Smith.

—I am delighted to make your acquaintance.

—Delighted, sir! My friend has often spoken of you.

—I, too, have heard about you. You met my father-in-law in Paris, I believe?

—Yes, when I was in Paris I saw him often. He was a real Parisian.

—When did you return from Paris?

—I just returned from France last week.

—Oh! here is my sister. May I present her to you? She is going to France soon.

Lesson 18

Present indicative and past participle of *rompre*

Imperfect indicative of *manger* and *commencer*

Penser à* and *penser de

***Demander* with a direct and an indirect object**

Distinction between *gens* and *personnes*

CONVERSATION

La Situation internationale

—Maintenant que nos amis sont partis, nous pouvons reprendre notre conversation interrompue.

—Oui, avec plaisir; qu'est-ce que nous disions?

—Vous me disiez que, lorsque vous étiez à New York, ma belle-sœur vous demandait toujours si vous ne vouliez pas faire la connaissance de leurs amis de Paris.

—Ah, oui, en effet. Elle pensait toujours à vous.

—Ce qui nous flatte énormément.

—Qu'est-ce qu'on pense ici de la situation internationale?

—Eh bien, on est d'avis que les choses vont se remettre petit à petit, surtout en ce qui concerne la France et l'Europe occidentale. Mais on se demande aussi s'il en sera de même partout.

—La situation est donc meilleure en France. J'en suis très heureux.

En Amérique, il y a plusieurs personnes qui s'opposent toujours à l'intervention des États-Unis dans les affaires de l'Europe.

—Ce sont des gens qui ne pensent qu'à eux-mêmes, et qui ne se rendent pas compte des difficultés.

—C'est vrai; ils ont raison et ils ont tort à la fois. Mais, voici ma femme. Nous partons déjà, Jeanne?

—Oui, il est tard. Es-tu prêt?

—Oui. Au revoir, Monsieur. J'espère continuer cette conversation une autre fois.

VOCABULAIRE ET EXPRESSIONS

les gens (*masc.*) the people
le soldat the soldier
la voix (*pl.* **voix**) the voice
la question the question
la situation the situation
haut high
complet (*fem.* **complète**) complete
meilleur better (*adjective*)
mieux better (*adverb*)
demander to ask, ask for
se demander to wonder
poser une question to ask a question
rompre to break
interrompre to interrupt

moi-même (I) myself
toi-même (you) yourself
lui-même (he) himself
elle-même (she) herself
nous-mêmes (we) ourselves
vous-même, vous-mêmes (you) yourself, yourselves
eux-mêmes (they) themselves
elles-mêmes (they) themselves

quelqu'un, quelqu'une someone, anyone
quelques-uns, quelques-unes some, any
quoi? (*interrogative*) what?
j'en suis heureux I'm glad, I'm glad of that
en être de même to be the same
un (une) autre another
au sujet de about, concerning
partout everywhere
se rendre compte (de + *noun or pronoun;* **que** + *verb*) to realize

à haute voix out loud
aux États-Unis in, to the U.S.A.
petit à petit little by little
en ce qui concerne so far as . . . is (are) concerned

VOCABULAIRE SUPPLÉMENTAIRE

l'avis (*masc.*) the opinion (not advice)
la paix peace
la difficulté the difficulty
la conversation the conversation
l'Europe (*fem.*) Europe
international (*masc. pl.* **internationaux**) international
occidental (*masc. pl.* **occidentaux**) western

reprendre to resume, retake
être d'avis to be of the opinion
flatter to flatter
concerner to concern

VERBES

Present Indicative of **rompre** (to break) *p.p.* **rompu**

je **romps** le silence	**nous rompons**
tu romps	**vous rompez**
il (elle) rompt	**ils (elles) rompent**

Like **rompre,** conjugate **interrompre** (to interrupt)

Imperfect Indicative of **manger** and **commencer**

je **mangeais** un fruit quand il est entré	**nous mangions**
tu mangeais	**vous mangiez**
il (elle, on) mangeait	**ils (elles) mangeaient**

je commençais	**nous commencions**
tu commençais	**vous commenciez**
il (elle, on) commençait	**ils (elles) commençaient**

→ In accordance with the rules given in Lesson 14, verbs ending in *-ger* insert *e* before *-ais, -ait, -aient,* while those ending in *-cer* change *c* to *ç* before the same endings.

GRAMMAIRE

Penser—Penser à—Penser de

Il pense partir. He thinks (believes) he will leave.
Pensez-vous vraiment cela? Do you really think (believe) that?
Oui, je le pense. Yes, I do (believe it).

Pensez-vous à lui? Oui, je pense à lui. Are you thinking of him? Yes, I'm thinking of him
Pensez-vous à vos amis? Je pense à eux. Are you thinking of your friends? I'm thinking of them.
Pensez-vous à vos cours? J'y pense. Are you thinking of your courses? I'm thinking of them.
A quoi pensez-vous? What are you thinking of?

→ *Penser à* means *to think of* in the sense of "to direct one's thought toward." The indirect object pronouns are not used in this construction, being replaced by disjunctives. *Y* is, however, used for things or ideas, both singular and plural.

Que pensez-vous de lui? What do you think of him?
Qu'en pensez-vous? What do you think about it?

→ *Penser de* means "to think of" in the sense of *"to have an opinion about." En* is used for things or ideas, *de* with a disjunctive for persons.

Objects Used with **demander**

J'ai demandé à **mon frère** ce qu'il allait faire. I asked my brother what he was going to do.
Je **lui** ai demandé ce qu'il allait faire. I asked him what he was going to do.
J'ai demandé sa plume **à mon frère.** I asked my brother for his pen.
Je **lui** ai demandé sa plume. I asked him for his pen.
Je **l'ai** demandée **à mon frère.** I asked my brother for it.

Je la lui ai demandée. I asked him for it.

→ *The thing* one asks for is a *direct object* in French.
The person one asks is an *indirect object* in French.

Gens—Personnes

Beaucoup de gens sont ici. Many people are here.
Peu de gens comprennent tout ce qu'ils lisent. Few people understand all they read.
Combien de personnes y a-t-il? How many persons are there?
Trois personnes sont venues. Three persons have come.

Gens and *personnes* both mean "people." *Gens,* however, refers to an indefinite number of people, while *personnes* usually refers to a definite number of people.

QUESTIONS

1. Maintenant que nos amis sont partis, que peut-on faire? 2. Lorsqu'on était à New York, que demandait toujours la belle-sœur? 3. A qui pensait-elle? 4. Sur quoi voulait-on poser des questions? 5. De quel avis est-on? 6. Qu'est-ce qu'on se demande? 7. A quoi s'opposent certaines personnes, aux États-Unis? 8. Quelle sorte de gens ne se rendent pas compte des difficultés? 9. Quelle opinion peut-on avoir de ces gens-là? 10. Pourquoi la conversation est-elle interrompue? 11. Comment la conversation se termine-t-elle?

EXERCICES

A. I. *Conjuguez:*

1. Je romps le silence (à l'affirmatif et au négatif).
2. Est-ce que j'ai interrompu la conversation?
3. Je n'ai pas interrompu la conversation.
4. Je mangeais une pomme quand Georges est entré.
5. Je commençais à lire quand la petite Marie est tombée.

II. *Remplacez le tiret par la forme correcte*: moi-même, lui-

même, nous-mêmes, vous-mêmes, eux-mêmes, elles-mêmes:
1. Je veux lire ce livre ________. 2. Le petit garçon s'est lavé ________. 3. Nous avons préparé notre déjeuner ________. 4. Faites ce travail ________, je refuse de le faire. 5. Elles s'en sont chargées ________.

B. *Répondez aux questions suivantes par une phrase:*

1. A qui pensez-vous? 2. Pensez-vous à Marie? 3. Est-ce qu'il pense souvent à ses cours? 4. Pense-t-elle jamais à ses amis? 5. Qu'est-ce qu'il a demandé à son frère? 6. Lui avez-vous demandé son billet? 7. Ne pensons-nous pas toujours à vous? 8. Y pensez-vous encore? 9. Que pensez-vous de cette pièce (*play*)? 10. Que pensez-vous de ce livre qui vient de paraître? 11. Que pensez-vous de ce nouveau journal? 12. Avez-vous répondu à ma lettre? 13. A qui l'avez-vous demandé? 14. En pensez-vous du bien ou du mal? 15. Est-ce que je le lui ai demandé? 16. Est-ce que beaucoup de gens vont en France maintenant? 17. Combien de personnes avez-vous vues au bal? 18. Est-ce qu'il y a plusieurs personnes ici aujourd'hui? 19. Pensez-vous aller en France cet été? 20. Que pensez-vous?

C. *Traduisez:*

1. The soldier asked the policeman a question. 2. I wonder what (*ce que*) it is. 3. She always thinks of herself. 4. I like him because he never thinks of himself; he always thinks of others. 5. I am glad of that. 6. Speak out loud. 7. Someone always interrupts me when I speak. 8. I realize that. 9. Some people have arrived in the United States from France today. 10. What are the people thinking of now?

THÈME

—Hello! How are you? I was thinking about you. Do you want to meet Marie's brother? He is coming to our house tomorrow evening.

—Why! of course. At what time?

—Oh! At 8:30 or 9 o'clock. Marie will be (*sera*) there, too.

—I am glad (*of it*). I was thinking of her yesterday. We used to have lunch together (*ensemble*) every day but I haven't seen her for a month. How is she? I have not been in Boston for three weeks.

—She is quite well. But do you realize that I haven't seen you for several weeks?

—You are right. I was in New York. I was studying (*étudier*) the international situation for my history professor (*professeur d'histoire*). I wonder if things are going to right themselves (*s'arranger*).

—Of course. After a war, there are always difficulties. But may I ask you some questions?

—Yes, but not now. I am going to see Henry in ten minutes. Until tomorrow then. Goodbye.

Lesson 19

Future indicative of *parler, vendre,* and *finir*

Future of some irregular verbs

Use of *aller* plus the infinitive

Uses of the future indicative

Comparison of adjectives

Use of *de* and *que* after the superlative

Use of *aussi . . . que* and *si . . . que*

Plus que, moins que, plus de, moins de

Tant de* and *tant

Autant de* and *autant que

***À* before an infinitive**

Formation of adverbs from adjectives

Comparison of adverbs

Some irregular forms of adverbs

LETTRES

le 3 février, 19—

Cher ami,

Un mot, en hâte, pour vous demander si vous pourriez venir chez nous dimanche soir. On fêtera l'anniversaire de la naissance de ma gentille belle-fille Jeannette.

Je peux vous assurer qu'on s'amusera beaucoup, même plus que l'année dernière. On dansera, on jouera aux cartes; Robert Dubois, qui viendra certainement et qui est un grand artiste, jouera du piano; il y aura d'excellents rafraîchissements. Mon cousin Paul viendra aussi avec son ami Joseph Chénier qui acceptera peut-être de chanter pour nous. Nous attendons plus de trente personnes. Puis-je compter sur vous?

Bien amicalement,

Annette

Le 5 février, 19—

Chère Annette,

Malheureusement, dimanche, je serai occupé toute la soirée. Je regrette infiniment. La chose la plus difficile pour moi, c'est de refuser vos bonnes invitations. Mais je serai très pris. C'est le sort d'un médecin qui se trouve presque seul dans sa petite ville. J'aurai tant de visites à faire, tant de malades à voir! L'année dernière, il y avait ici autant de médecins que dans votre grande ville. A présent, il y en a moins d'une demi-douzaine. Tant pis! Je devrai remettre le plaisir de vous voir à la prochaine fois que vous voudrez bien m'inviter. Les choses iront un peu mieux après la Nouvelle Année, car quelques-uns de mes collègues reviendront à ce moment-là. Je vous prie de souhaiter un heureux et joyeux anniversaire à votre belle-fille que je n'ai pas vue depuis plus de trois mois. Si votre oncle est là, faites-lui mes amitiés. Veuillez accepter mes excuses ainsi que mes hommages respectueux.

Jacques

VOCABULAIRE ET EXPRESSIONS

le monde the world, people
la belle-fille the daughter-in-law
le mot the word
le piano the piano
la carte the card; map
la visite the visit
le (la) malade the patient
l'élève (*masc.* or *fem.*) the pupil
l'amitié (*fem.*) the friendship
la douzaine (de) the dozen
la demi-douzaine (de) the half-dozen
pris (*p.p.* of **prendre**) taken up, busy
difficile hard, difficult
bon kind

s'amuser to have a good time, enjoy oneself
danser to dance
jouer to play (use à for games, de for instruments)
inviter to invite
remettre to put off, postpone; put again, put on again (conj. like *mettre*)
chanter to sing
prier de to beg to
compter to count

à cause de because of, on account of
plus que, plus de more than
peut-être perhaps, maybe (use *que* if a clause follows)
aussi . . . que, si . . . que as . . . as, so . . . as
autant de as much, as many
que than, as
quelques-uns (-unes) some
moins que, moins de less than
tant (de) so much, so many
car for

un mot a (one) word
en hâte in haste
bien à vous, bien amicalement, votre bien cordialement dévoué sincerely yours, cordially yours
souhaiter un heureux anniversaire to wish a happy birthday
faire ses amitiés à to give one's regards to
mes hommages (les plus) respectueux my kindest regards, my respects (usually from a man to a woman)
de cette façon this way, in this fashion
une chose à faire a thing to do (to be done)

VOCABULAIRE SUPPLÉMENTAIRE

l'anniversaire (*masc.*) the anniversary
la naissance the birth
l'anniversaire de naissance the birthday
la fête the feast, celebration
la famille the family
l'échange (*masc.*) the exchange
l'excuse (*fem.*) the excuse, the apology
le souhait the wish (*usually addressed to another person*)
la Nouvelle Année the New Year
le rafraîchissement the refreshment
l'hommage (*masc.*) the respect, the homage
le collègue the colleague
le sort the fate
Annette Annie
Jacques James
nouveau (use **nouvel** before a vowel; *fem.* **nouvelle;** *masc. pl.* **nouveaux**) new
énorme enormous (*adv. irreg.* **énormément**)

cordial (*masc. pl.* **cordiaux**) cordial, heartfelt
respectueux (*fem.* **respectueuse**) respectful
dévoué devoted
meilleur (*adj.*); **mieux** (*adv.*) better
pire (*adj.*); **pis** (*adv.*) worse
je devrais I should, ought to
vouloir bien to be willing to
fêter to celebrate
refuser to refuse
infiniment infinitely, tremendously
à propos de concerning
tant pis so much the worse

VERBES

The Future Tense

Future Indicative of **parler, vendre,** and **finir**

je parler-ai	**nous parler-ons**
tu parler-as	**vous parler-ez**
il (elle, on) parler-a	**ils (elles) parler-ont**
je vendr-ai	**nous vendr-ons**
tu vendr-as	**vous vendr-ez**
il (elle, on) vendr-a	**ils (elles) vendr-ont**
je finir-ai	**nous finir-ons**
tu finir-as	**vous finir-ez**
il (elle, on) finir-a	**ils (elles) finir-ont**

→ The future tense is formed by *adding to the whole infinitive* (not to the stem) the endings *-ai, -as, -a, -ons, -ez, -ont. Infinitives ending in -e drop -e* before adding these endings.

The endings apply to all verbs without exception. Irregular verbs, however, often have irregularities in their stems.

être to be; **je serai** I shall be
avoir to have; **j'aurai** I shall have
savoir to know; **je saurai** I shall know
aller to go; **j'irai** I shall go
faire to do, make; **je ferai** I shall do, make

vouloir to want; **je voudrai** I shall want
valoir to be worth; **je vaudrai** I shall be worth
venir to come; **je viendrai** I shall come
tenir to hold; **je tiendrai** I shall hold
voir to see; **je verrai** I shall see
pouvoir to be able; **je pourrai** I shall be able
envoyer to send; **j'enverrai** I shall send

→ Note the above irregular futures. The endings, however, are invariably *-ai, -as, -a, -ons, -ez, -ont.*

appeler to call; **j'appellerai** I shall call
acheter to buy; **j'achèterai** I shall buy
jeter to throw; **je jetterai** I shall throw
payer to pay; **je paierai** I shall pay

→ In accordance with the rules given in lessons 4 and 5, verbs ending in *-eler* double the *l,* verbs in *-eter* either double the *t* or change *e* to *è* in the future tense, while verbs in *-yer* change *y* to *i.*

je vais le voir demain I am going to see him tomorrow
je le verrai demain I shall see him tomorrow

→ As in English, the future and the construction "to be going to" are often interchangeable. The *aller* + *infinitive form* often expresses a near future.

je le verrai quand il viendra I shall see him when he comes
je viendrai la prochaine fois que vous m'inviterez I shall come the next time you invite me

→ Unlike English, the future must be used in a subordinate clause if future time is implied.

il vous le donnera si vous le lui demandez he will give it to you if you ask him for it

→ The future, however, is not permitted in a clause introduced by *si,* "if."

vous me demandez si je viendrai you are asking me if I shall come

→ But the future must be used to express future time when "if" is equivalent to "whether."

GRAMMAIRE

Comparative—Superlative

un petit livre a small book
un plus petit livre a smaller book
le plus petit livre the smaller book, the smallest book
ma petite plume my little pen
ma plus petite plume my smaller pen, my smallest pen

→ The comparative is formed by prefixing *plus* (more) to the adjective. The superlative is formed by using the comparative with the definite article or a possessive.

→ There is no distinction between the comparative and superlative in French when the adjective precedes the noun.

l'étudiant intelligent the intelligent student
c'est un étudiant plus intelligent he is a more intelligent student
l'étudiant le plus intelligent the most intelligent student
mon élève le plus intelligent my brightest pupil

→ If the adjective follows the noun, the definite article is used before *plus* to mark the superlative, even if the noun already has an article.

l'étudiant le plus intelligent de la classe the brightest student in the class
l'homme le plus riche du monde the richest man in the world

→ "In" after a superlative is rendered by *de*.

il est plus intelligent que vous he is brighter than you
il est moins riche que vous he is less wealthy than you

→ "Than" is translated by *que*.

il est aussi riche que vous he is as rich as you
il n'est pas si (aussi) riche que vous he is not so rich as you

→ "As . . . as" is *aussi . . . que* in affirmative; *aussi . . . que, si . . . que* in negative sentences.

j'en ai plus que vous I have more than you

j'en ai moins que vous I have less (or fewer) than you
j'en ai plus de trente I have more than thirty
j'en ai moins de trente I have less than thirty

→ "More than," "less than" in a comparison are *plus que, moins que*. But in a quantitative expression they are expressed by *plus de, moins de*.

j'ai tant de choses à faire! I have so many things to do!
il a tant d'argent! He has so much money!

→ "So much," "so many," modifying a noun is *tant de*.

il aime tant la musique! He loves music so much!

→ "So much," "so many," used adverbially are translated by *tant*.

j'ai autant de choses à faire que vous I have as many things to do as you
vous avez autant d'argent que lui you have as much money as he

→ "As much," "as many" is *autant de*. In these expressions the second "as" is translated by *que*.

Adverbs

vrai true, real **vraiment** truly, really

→ Adjectives ending in vowels usually form the corresponding adverb by adding *-ment* to the masculine form.

cordial cordial; *fem.* **cordiale**
cordialement cordially
respectueux respectful; *fem.* **respectueuse**
respectueusement respectfully

→ Adjectives ending in consonants generally form the corresponding adverb by *adding -ment to the feminine* form.

ardent—ardemment **suffisant—suffisamment**
intelligent—intelligemment **constant—constamment**

→ To form adverbs from adjectives ending in *-ent* or *-ant* change

-ent to *-emment* and *-ant* to *-amment.* **Lentement** (slowly, from **lent** (slow) is an exception.

énorme—énormément **précis—précisément**
profond—profondément

→ Some adjectives change *e* to *é* before *-ment* to form the adverb.

The Comparative and the Superlative of Adverbs

il m'a écrit **cordialement** he wrote me cordially
il m'a écrit **plus cordialement que vous** he wrote me more cordially than you
il m'a écrit **le plus cordialement de tous** he wrote me most cordially of all
il m'a écrit **très cordialement (de la façon la plus cordiale)** he wrote me most cordially

→ Adverbs form their comparatives and superlatives like adjectives. The article *le* in the superlative is invariable; but unless *de* follows, the superlative form is usually replaced by *très* or by *de la façon la plus* (in the most . . . fashion).

bon good	**meilleur** better	**le meilleur** the best
mauvais bad	**pire** worse	**le pire** the worst
bien well	**mieux** better	**le mieux** the best
mal badly, poorly	**pis** worse	**le pis** the worst

→ As in English, a few adjectives and adverbs have irregular comparative and superlative forms.

QUESTIONS

1. Pourquoi Annette écrit-elle à Jacques? 2. Que va-t-on célébrer? 3. Pourquoi s'amusera-t-on plus que l'année dernière? 4. Qui viendra? 5. Qui chantera? 6. Pourquoi Jacques ne peut-il pas venir? 7. Qu'est-ce qui lui est difficile? 8. Pourquoi Jacques est-il si pris? 9. A quand remettra-t-il l'invitation? 10. Quand aura-t-il plus de temps?

EXERCICES

A. *Lisez à haute voix les phrases suivantes en y introduisant le futur de* parler:

1. Je ________ demain à mon professeur. 2. Il ________ aux membres du corps professoral (*faculty*) samedi prochain. 3. Nous ________de cela une autre fois. 4. Quand vous en ________ à mon père, je suis sûr qu'il vous donnera de bons conseils. 5. Partons, ils ________ jusqu'à minuit.

Lisez à haute voix en employant le futur de vendre: 1. A la fin de l'année je ________ tous mes livres. 2. Si vous voulez acheter cette maison, Georges vous la ________ à bon marché. 3. Nous ________ tout ce que nous possédons avant d'aller en Europe. 4. Quand ________-vous votre auto? 5. Ils ________ leurs meubles quand ils ________ leur maison.

Lisez à haute voix en employant le futur de finir: 1. Je ________ mon travail dans une heure. 2. Il ________ de manger avant vous, j'en suis sûr. 3. Nous ________ nos leçons après dîner. 4. Vous ________ quand vous aurez le temps. 5. Quand ________ ils leurs devoirs?

Employez le futur du verbe qui convient dans chacune des phrases suivantes: être, avoir, savoir, aller, faire, vouloir, valoir, venir, tenir, voir, pouvoir, envoyer, appeler, acheter, jeter, payer: 1. Nous ________ votre lettre par la poste demain. 2. Vous ________ ce que je veux dire quand vous ________ chez moi. 3. Il ________ rester chez nous s'il le veut. 4. Gardez ces tableaux, ils ________ trois fois leur prix dans dix ans. 5. Je ________ votre valise pendant que vous ________ chercher votre billet. 6. Je ________ manger un bon repas quand je reviendrai de ma promenade. 7. Nous ________ à la messe (*mass*) dimanche prochain. 8. Ils ________ si j'ai raison ou non. 9. Nous ________ deux autos l'année prochaine. 10. Vous ________ malade si vous mangez tant de pommes. 11. Je ________ la balle et vous l'attraperez. 12. Il ________ tout ce que vous voulez lui vendre. 13. Nous vous ________ si nous avons besoin de vous. 14. Vous ________ comme c'est beau!

B. *Faites des adverbes des adjectifs suivants:*

1. cordial 2. respectueux 3. constant 4. seul 5. nouveau 6. vrai 7. simple 8. énorme 9. affectueux 10. rapide.

C. *Donnez la forme superlative des adjectifs et des adverbes suivants:*

1. bon 2. mauvais 3. grand 4. petit 5. intelligent 6. bien 7. mal 8. respectueux 9. cordial 10. simple.

D. *Faites des phrases avec chacun des mots suivants et traduisez-les en anglais:*

1. occupé 2. pris 3. s'amuser 4. jouer à 5. jouer de 6. remettre 7. revenir 8. prier de 9. à cause de 10. plus que 11. aussi que 12. autant de 13. tant de 14. moins que 15. car.

THÈME

1. He will see you if you are here. 2. We shall buy the books if we have enough money. 3. I shall go if he invites me. 4. She will go when he invites her. 5. They will sell the house if they need the money. 6. We are asking you if you will come or not. 7. Are you asking me whether I shall sell my house? 8. My pen is the smallest, your pen is the largest. 9. Mary is the most intelligent girl in the class. 10. She is more intelligent than you. 11. He is certainly the richest man in town. 12. No, I think he is less wealthy than Mrs. Dupont. 13. She is as rich as Mary, isn't she? 14. No, she is not as rich as Mary. 15. How many books have they? 16. They have more than you; they have more than twenty. 17. We have so many things to do! 18. You haven't as many things to do as I (have). 19. You have so much money! 20. I haven't as much as he (has); he has less than ten thousand dollars.

Lesson 20

Present conditional of *parler, vendre,* and *finir*

Conditional of some irregular verbs

Uses of the conditional

Conjugation of *falloir* and *pleuvoir*

Uses of the impersonal verb

Use of the definite article when referring to parts of the body

Possessive pronoun and its uses

CONVERSATION

La Toilette — les Vêtements

JULIEN: Arthur, as-tu envie de m'accompagner à la conférence de M. Mornet?

ARTHUR: Je le ferais avec plaisir si j'avais un imperméable. Il pleut à verse.

JULIEN: N'importe. Prends le mien.

ARTHUR: Et toi?

JULIEN: Moi, je mettrai mon vieux pardessus et je prendrai le parapluie.

ARTHUR: Entendu. Où est-ce que j'ai laissé mon rasoir?

JULIEN: Je l'ai vu dans la salle de bain. Est-ce que tu as besoin de te raser? Dépêche-toi, alors, ou nous serons en retard.

ARTHUR: Écoute, mon vieux, si je ne me rasais pas j'aurais l'air d'un hérisson. Est-ce que tu veux te présenter à la conférence en compagnie d'un hérisson?

JULIEN: Eh bien, puisqu'il faut attendre, pendant que tu te raseras je changerai de vêtements et de souliers. As-tu vu mon complet gris?

ARTHUR: Certainement. Il est dans le placard, à côté de mon pardessus brun.

JULIEN: Je ne le vois pas.

ARTHUR: Mais regarde donc! A côté de mon pantalon! En bas et dans le fond!

JULIEN: Zut! Quelle guigne! Il y a un bouton de mon gilet qui manque.

ARTHUR: Eh bien! ne mets pas de gilet, alors! Si j'avais toujours chaud comme toi j'irais en manches de chemise.

JULIEN: Dis donc. Je vais ôter le mien et porter le tien. Ça va?

ARTHUR: Non, mon vieux. Apporte-moi le savon et une serviette, s'il te plaît.

JULIEN: Quoi! Tu vas prendre un bain à présent?

ARTHUR: Non, mais il faut se laver les mains et la figure de temps en temps.

JULIEN: C'est vrai. Deux fois par an au moins. Mais ne te fâche pas. Tiens.

ARTHUR: As-tu vu ma cravate violette?

JULIEN: Mon Dieu! Tu vas porter ça?

ARTHUR: Si je ne la portais pas, on le remarquerait.

JULIEN: Qui le remarquerait?

ARTHUR: Mais! Le professeur . . . les charmantes demoiselles. . . .

JULIEN: C'est la plus laide de tes cravates. Tu n'es pas encore prêt?

ARTHUR: Je le serai bientôt. Donne-moi le peigne et la brosse.

JULIEN: Les miens?

ARTHUR: Les tiens sont les miens, n'est-ce pas?

JULIEN: Tu es fou. Ça y est?

ARTHUR: Oui. Je mets un mouchoir dans ma poche, je prends ma montre et nous voilà prêts.
JULIEN: Enfin! En route!

VOCABULAIRE ET EXPRESSIONS

le parapluie the umbrella
le soulier the shoe
le complet the suit (man's)
le pantalon the pants
le mouchoir the handkerchief
la chemise the shirt
la cravate the tie
la poche the pocket
le pardessus the overcoat

la main the hand
la figure the face
l'air (*masc.*) the air, the appearance
la bague the ring
la montre the watch
le savon the soap
le bain the bath
la demoiselle the young lady

gris gray
brun brown

charmant charming
fou (fol *before a vowel; fem.* **folle)** crazy

mettre to put on (*p.p.* **mis)**
avoir l'air de to look like
changer de to change **(nous changeons)**
porter to wear, to carry
ôter to take off

avoir envie de to feel like (having)
se dépêcher to hurry
falloir must
se laver to wash
se fâcher to get angry

puisque since
à côté de next to, besides
pendant que while
n'importe it doesn't matter, never mind
dépêche-toi, dépêchez-vous hurry up!
zut! heck! darn it!

apporte-moi, apportez-moi bring me
au moins at least
tiens, tenez here! (when handing someone something)
ça y est? ready? O.K.?
en bas down, below, downstairs
dans le fond to the rear

VOCABULAIRE SUPPLÉMENTAIRE

le vêtement the garment (*in the plural,* the clothes)
l'imperméable (*masc.*) the raincoat
le placard the closet
le gilet the vest
la manche the sleeve
la serviette (de toilette) the towel
la salle de bain the bathroom
le rasoir the razor
la brosse the brush
le peigne the comb

le bouton the button
la chaîne the chain
le hérisson the hedgehog
le professeur the professor
la compagnie the company
la conférence the lecture
la guigne the bad luck
l'envie (*fem.*) the desire; the envy
Arthur Arthur
violet (*fem.* **violette**) violet, purple

pleuvoir à verse to pour (rain)
se raser to shave
manquer to lack, to be lacking, to be missing

prendre un bain to bathe
se présenter to appear, to present oneself
remarquer to notice

certainement certainly
en compagnie de in the company of

en manches de chemise in shirt-sleeves

VERBES

The Conditional

Present Conditional of **parler, vendre, finir**

je parler-ais
tu parler-ais
il (elle, on) parler-ait

nous parler-ions
vous parler-iez
ils (elles) parler-aient

je vendr-ais
tu vendr-ais
il (elle, on) vendr-ait

nous vendr-ions
vous vendr-iez
ils (elles) vendr-aient

je finir-ais
tu finir-ais
il (elle, on) finir-ait
nous finir-ions
vous finir-iez
ils (elles) finir-aient

→ The conditional has the *same endings as the imperfect: -ais, -ais, -ait, -ions, -iez, -aient.* These endings, however, are *added on to the infinitive,* not to the stem. Infinitives ending in *-e* drop the *-e* before adding the endings.

Some Irregular Conditionals

être to be; **je serais** I should (would) be
avoir to have; **j'aurais** I should (would) have
savoir to know; **je saurais** I should (would) know (how)
aller to go; **j'irais** I should (would) go
faire to do, make; **je ferais** I should (would) do, make
vouloir to want; **je voudrais** I should (would) want
valoir to be worth; **je vaudrais** I should (would) be worth
venir to come; **je viendrais** I should (would) come
tenir to hold; **je tiendrais** I should (would) hold
voir to see; **je verrais** I should (would) see
pouvoir to be able; **je pourrais** I should (would) be able
envoyer to send; **j'enverrais** I should (would) send

→ Whatever irregularities occur in the stem of the future tense of a given verb will also occur in the conditional. The endings, however, are always regular.

il m'a dit qu'il viendrait demain he told me he would come tomorrow

→ The conditional is generally used in French where English uses the auxiliary "would."

s'il était ici, il s'amuserait bien if he were here, he would have a good time
s'il venait, je lui parlerais avec plaisir if he came (were to come, should come), I would speak to him with pleasure
s'il parlait français, il n'aurait pas de difficulté if he spoke (were to speak, should speak) French, he would have no trouble

→ When the *conditional* appears *in the main clause* of a conditional sentence, the *imperfect* is used *in the "if" clause*. In such sentences, the French imperfect translates the English past (indicative or subjunctive), "came," "were to come," "should come."

Impersonal **falloir** and **pleuvoir**

falloir must
il faut must
il fallait must
il faudra must
fallu *p.p.*

pleuvoir to rain
il pleut it rains, it is raining
il pleuvait it was raining, used to rain
il pleuvra it will rain
plu *p.p.*

→ *Falloir* and *pleuvoir* are impersonal verbs, used only in the third person singular.

il faut attendre one (I, you, he, she, we, they) must wait
il faut le faire one (I, you, he, she, we, they) must do it; it must be done
il fallait le faire it was necessary that it be done, to do it, etc.
il faudra le faire it will have to be done
il a fallu le faire it had to be done

→ *Falloir* followed by the infinitive conveys a general idea of necessity or obligation, translated by the English "must," "have to." The subject is unspecified, but may generally be inferred from the context. An English passive often is the best translation for *il faut* with the infinitive.

il me faut du pain I need some bread
il lui faut de la patience he must have patience

→ In these impersonal constructions, an indirect object pronoun is often introduced, which in English usually becomes the subject of the sentence. If a noun instead of an infinitive follows **falloir**, the meaning is often "need," "need to have," "must have."

GRAMMAIRE

Possessive Pronouns

le mien	**la mienne**	**les miens**	**les miennes**	mine
le tien	**la tienne**	**les tiens**	**les tiennes**	yours
le sien	**la sienne**	**les siens**	**les siennes**	his, hers, its
le nôtre	**la nôtre**	**les nôtres**	**les nôtres**	ours
le vôtre	**la vôtre**	**les vôtres**	**les vôtres**	yours
le leur	**la leur**	**les leurs**	**les leurs**	theirs

→ These are *possessive pronouns,* not to be confused with the possessive adjectives (see lesson 5). The possessive adjectives (*mon, ma, mes, etc.*) accompany the noun. The *possessive pronouns replace the noun.*

voici ta plume; donne-moi la mienne here is your pen; give me mine
il a vu mes crayons, mais il veut les siens he saw my pencils, but he wants his (own)
j'ai vendu ma maison et la leur I sold my house and theirs
ma sœur et la sienne sont allées au cinéma my sister and his (hers) went to the movies

→ *The possessive pronoun takes the gender and number of the noun it replaces.*

je me lave les mains I am washing my hands
sa mère lui a lavé la figure his mother washed his face

→ In referring to parts of the body, the definite article is often used in place of the possessive adjective; a reflexive indirect pronoun or an indirect pronoun clearly indicates the possessor.

QUESTIONS

1. Est-ce qu'Arthur a envie d'aller à la conférence de M. Mornet? 2. Pourquoi ne peut-il pas y aller? 3. Quel temps fait-il? 4. Quelle

proposition lui fait-on? 5. Comment son ami va-t-il se tirer d'affaire (*get out of his difficulties*)? 6. Où est-ce qu'Arthur a laissé son rasoir? 7. Pourquoi lui dit-on de se dépêcher? 8. Pourquoi doit-il (*does he have to*) se raser? 9. Qu'est-ce que son ami va faire en l'attendant? 10. Quel complet cherche-t-il? 11. Où est-il? 12. Près de quel autre vêtement? 13. Qu'est-ce qui manque à son gilet? 14. Pourquoi Arthur veut-il du savon et une serviette? 15. Pourquoi porte-t-il sa cravate violette? 16. Que fait-il encore pour se préparer? 17. Que met-il dans sa poche? 18. Que prend-il à la dernière minute?

EXERCICES

A. I. *Continuez:*

1. Si je voyais mon oncle, je lui parlerais de cela. Si tu . . . etc.
2. Je vendrais ma maison si j'en avais une autre.
3. Je finirais mes leçons si j'avais le temps.
4. Je serais malade si je mangeais tant de bonbons.
5. J'aurais mal à la tête si je lisais sans lunettes.

II. *Traduisez les formes suivantes:*

1. That would be worth two millions.
2. They said that they would come tonight.
3. You would see my friend if you went there.
4. I would be able to see you.
5. We would send the books if (it were) necessary.
6. They would be able to do the work.
7. I would see him Tuesday, if he wished (it).
8. He told me (that) he would come to see me.

B. *Remplacez l'infinitif par la forme convenable du verbe:*

1. S'il était ici, il m'(*acheter*) ce livre.
2. S'il venait à Paris, je le (*voir*) de temps en temps.
3. S'il pleuvait, je n'(*aller*) pas.
4. Il pouvait voir que je ne le (*faire*) pas.

5. S'il (*parler*) français, il pourrait aller à Paris.
6. S'il me donnait l'adresse, j'(*envoyer*) le paquet.
7. S'il réparait la maison, elle (*valoir*) davantage.

C. *Traduisez:*

1. It will rain tomorrow. 2. One must often wait an hour. 3. It will have to be done today or tomorrow. 4. This work (*ce travail*) had to be done before mine. 5. It was raining when I came in. 6. It rained yesterday and it is going to rain again today. 7. Goodbye. I must have some money. 8. Now one must wait for two hours and a half.

D. *Remplacez le mot entre parenthèses par la forme convenable du pronom possessif:*

1. son pardessus et (*mine*) 2. mes livres et (*his*) 3. nos enfants et (*theirs*) 4. sa femme et (*yours*) 5. vos maisons et (*ours*) 6. vos crayons et (*mine*) 7. l'argent de mon père et (*yours*) 8. vos étudiants et (*mine*) 9. ces souliers et (*hers*) 10. mes cravates et (*his*)

E. *Traduisez:*

1. This umbrella is mine; yours is in the dining-room. 2. He doesn't want your shirts; he wants his. 3. He did not put the money in my pocket; he put it in his. 4. She took her handkerchiefs and mine. 5. He says that he likes his watch, but he hasn't seen yours.

THÈME

GEORGE: Where are my raincoat and umbrella? It's pouring.

MOTHER: Here they are in the bathroom. But you haven't finished shaving (*to shave*). Here is your razor.

GEORGE: I have finished shaving but I left my razor there for a minute. I shall get it when I come back. I have to go on a trip when I get back from this lecture. Can you pack (*faire*) my valise?

MOTHER: Yes, if you wish. But what would you like to put in it?

GEORGE: Oh! Just the things that you find on the bed. Goodbye.

. . . . .

George's mother finds his gray suit, an old vest, a pair of pants, some shoes, a shirt, a necktie, a handkerchief, two towels. She opens the valise and puts them in the bottom. Then she looks for the other things. She finds some soap, his razor, a comb and brush and then closes the valise.

When George comes back, he has only to take a bath, put on his gray suit, and go to the station.

Review Lesson 5

A. *Continuez la conjugaison des verbes et faites les changements nécessaires dans chaque phrase:*

1. Je parlais français avec mon professeur quand Jean est entré.
2. Je vendais des stylos dans ce petit magasin.
3. Je finissais mes leçons quand Marie est revenue.
4. Quand je mangeais au restaurant je commençais toujours par la soupe.
5. Je n'interromps jamais mon professeur quand il parle.
6. Je parlerai quand je saurai toute l'histoire.
7. Je l'enverrai chez vous quand il viendra ici.
8. Je voudrais les voir demain.
9. Si je lui donnais la maison, il la vendrait.
10. Si j'avais une auto, j'irais à la campagne.

B. *Remplacez l'infinitif par la forme correcte de l'imparfait ou du passé composé:*

1. Il (*lire*) quand je (*partir*). 2. Quand elle (*aller*) à l'école, elle (*étudier*) tous les jours. 3. Il y a vingt ans, je (*visiter*) Paris. 4. Il (*être*) à Paris quand je suis arrivé. 5. Il (*avoir*) vingt dollars quand il (*arriver*). 6. Elle (*voir*) Henri hier matin. 7. Je (*vouloir*) le voir ce matin, mais il n'était pas chez lui. 8. Nous (*savoir*) qu'il (*être*) malade.

C. *Traduisez les phrases suivantes:*

1. He knew it, I did not. 2. They are our friends, you are not our friends. 3. He and she are going to write to them. 4. Henry introduced me to him yesterday. 5. Mary introduced me to them last night. 6. Who is there? It is he. 7. Who arrived? It is they. 8. Is it you? Yes, it is we.

D. *Remplacez les tirets par* de *or* à; y, en, *or* lui:

1. Je pense qu'il est intelligent. Que pensez-vous ________ lui? 2. Je viens de lire ce roman. Qu'________ pensez-vous? 3. Mon fils est très malade. Je pense ________ lui tout le temps. 4. Qu'est-ce que

vous allez acheter? ________ pensez-vous? 5. Je ne savais pas l'adresse. Je la ________ ai demandée. 6. Je ________ ai demandé ce qu'il voulait faire.

E. *Remplacez l'infinitif par la forme correcte du futur ou du présent:*

1. Il (*arriver*) demain matin. 2. Je lui (*donner*) le livre quand je le (*voir*). 3. Nous lui en (*parler*) s'il (*venir*) nous voir. 4. Vous l'(*inviter*) la prochaine fois qu'il (*venir*). 5. Si nous le lui (*demander*), je sais qu'il (*venir*).

F. *Traduisez les phrases suivantes:*

1. She is the most intelligent girl in the class. 2. She is more intelligent than Mary. 3. George is much less wealthy than Henry. 4. His most intelligent student is now in France. 5. I am going to buy the smaller house. 6. He is as tall as his father. 7. She is now more than forty. 8. He has so much money that he has bought the finest house in town. 9. He has so many things to do that he cannot do them well. 10. They received (*ont reçu*) me at their home most cordially.

G. *Remplacez l'infinitif par le conditionnel ou l'imparfait:*

1. Il (*envoyer*) une lettre, s'il (*avoir*) le temps de l'écrire. 2. S'il (*aller*) en France, il (*apprendre*) à parler français. 3. Il (*s'amuser*) certainement, s'il (*aller*) à la campagne. 4. Si vous (*manger*) moins, vous ne (*être*) pas si souvent malade. 5. Il m'a dit que si je (*vouloir*) être riche, il (*falloir*) travailler beaucoup.

H. *Employez la forme correcte de* falloir:

1. Il ________ travailler pour réussir. 2. Demain il ________ aller chez le dentiste. 3. Quand il venait, il ________ toujours aller au théâtre. 4. S'il vous écrivait, il ________ lui répondre.

I. *Remplacez le pronom possessif par tous les autres pronoms qui conviennent:* le tien, le sien, la mienne, etc.

1. J'ai vendu (*la mienne*). 2. Il avait perdu (*le mien*). 3. J'ai acheté (*les miens*). 4. Je n'ai pas reçu (*les miennes*).

Lecture 5

UNE AVENTURE EN CALABRE

(Adaptation d'un conte de Paul-Louis Courier)

Un jour, je voyageais* en Calabre.[1] C'est un pays perdu dans les montagnes. Les gens y vivent isolés. Ils ne voient* que[2] très peu d'étrangers. Ils ont la réputation de ne pas les aimer.[3] Ils considèrent les Français comme leurs ennemis.

J'avais pour compagnon un jeune homme. Dans ces montagnes, les chemins sont dangereux; nos chevaux marchaient avec beaucoup de peine. Mon jeune compagnon[4] allait devant. Il a choisi un sentier (*path*) qui lui paraissait* (*appeared*) plus praticable (*passable*) et plus court. Malheureusement (*unfortunately*) ce sentier nous a égarés[5] (*led us astray*). Nous avons donc dû* chercher notre chemin à travers (*through*) ces bois toute la journée.[6] Mais plus nous cherchions, plus[7] nous nous perdions. Il faisait nuit noire (*very dark*) quand nous sommes arrivés[8] près d'une maison encore plus noire. Nous sommes entrés, mais pas sans appréhension. Là, nous avons trouvé toute une famille de charbonniers (*charcoal-burners*) à table (*eating*). Immédiatement on nous a invités à manger. Mon jeune compagnon a accepté avec enthousiasme, car (*for*) nous avions faim. Il a commencé à manger

* *Asterisks, which will be found in this and subsequent* Lectures, *are intended to focus the attention of the student on important irregular verb forms which will be found in the Appendix, pages 374-388.*

1 en Calabre: *feminine names of countries use* en *without the article to express "to," "at," or "in."*

2 ne . . . que, *only.*

3 ne pas les aimer: *note the use of* ne *and* pas *together* before *an infinitive. Note also the position of the object pronoun before the infinitive and* after *the negative.*

4 compagnon: *the feminine is irregular:* la compagne.

5 égarés: *the past participle of verbs conjugated with* avoir *agrees with the preceding direct object.*

6 toute la journée, *the whole day long. Note the position of* toute *before the article. Similarly:* tout le monde, *everybody;* tous les soirs, *every evening.*

7 plus . . . plus, *the more . . . the more.*

8 nous sommes arrivés: *the past participle conjugated with* être *agrees with the subject.*

et à boire sans perdre une minute; mais moi, j'examinais la salle et la mine (*looks*) de nos hôtes. Ils ressemblaient (*looked like*) bien (*truly*) à des charbonniers, mais la maison ressemblait à un arsenal. Il n'y avait que des fusils, des pistolets, des sabres et des couteaux. Tout m'a déplu* (*displeased me*) et j'ai bientôt vu* que je déplaisais aussi. Mon camarade, au contraire, s'amusait bien. Il riait, il causait avec tout le monde. Il était de la famille (*one of the family*). Il a dit* d'abord d'où nous venions,* où nous allions, que nous étions des Français. Il disait* cela, imaginez un peu (*just*), à nos plus mortels ennemis. Nous étions seuls, égarés (*lost*), loin de tout secours (*help*) humain! Puis, pour ne rien omettre de ce qui (*that which*) pourrait* (*might*) nous perdre (*ruin*), il a expliqué qu'il était riche, il a promis* à ces gens tout ce qu'[9]ils demandaient pour nous guider le lendemain (*the next day*). Il a parlé de sa valise. Il leur a demandé d'aller la mettre avec grand soin au chevet (*at the head*) de son lit. Ils ont certainement pensé que nous portions les diamants de la couronne.

Le souper fini (*when supper was over*) on nous laisse. Nos hôtes couchaient en bas (*downstairs*); nous, dans une sorte de soupente (*garret*) avec un lit où on montait par une échelle (*ladder*). Au dessus du lit, les solives (*beams*) étaient chargées de provisions pour toute l'année. Mon compagnon s'est couché[10] et s'est endormi, la tête sur sa précieuse valise. Moi, déterminé à veiller (*to stay awake*), j'ai fait un bon feu et je me suis assis* auprès (*near it*). La nuit s'est passée assez tranquillement et je commencais* à me rassurer, quand, à l'aube (*dawn*), j'ai entendu au-dessous de moi mon hôte et sa femme parler et se quereller. Prêtant l'oreille (*listening carefully*) par la cheminée (*fireplace*) qui communiquait avec celle (*the one*) d'en bas, j'ai distingué parfaitement ces mots du mari:

"Enfin, oui ou non, faut-il les tuer tous deux?"

A quoi la femme a répondu: "Oui."

Et je n'ai plus rien entendu. Je suis resté respirant à peine

[9] tout ce que, *all that which, all that.*

[10] s'est couché: *reflexive verbs are conjugated with* être.

(*hardly*), tout mon corps froid comme du marbre. Je ne savais* pas si j'étais mort ou vivant. Nous deux (*the two of us*), presque sans armes, contre eux, douze ou quinze, qui avaient tant de fusils, de pistolets, de sabres et de couteaux. Mon jeune camarade était mort de sommeil et de fatigue. Je n'osais pas l'appeler ou faire du bruit. Je ne pouvais* pas m'échapper tout seul. La fenêtre n'était pas très haute, mais en bas (*down below*) deux gros chiens hurlaient (*were howling*) comme des loups. Imaginez mon anxiété. Au bout d'un quart d'heure j'ai entendu quelqu'un sur l'escalier, et par les fentes (*cracks*) de la porte, j'ai vu* le père, une lampe à la main,[11] et dans l'autre un de ses grands couteaux. Il montait, sa femme après lui. Moi, je me suis caché derrière la porte. Le père l'ouvre; mais avant d'entrer, il donne la lampe à sa femme. Puis il entre, pieds nus, dans la soupente. Elle, du dehors (*from outside*), lui disait* a voix basse: "Doucement (*quietly*), va* doucement." Lui (*he*) avance.[12] Il monte à l'échelle, son couteau entre les dents, et arrive à la hauteur du lit où le pauvre jeune homme étendu (*stretched out*) offrait sa gorge découverte. Alors, d'une main il prend son couteau et de l'autre . . . .il saisit un jambon qui pendait tout près, en coupe une tranche et se retire (*withdraws*) comme il était venu.* La porte se referme, la lampe s'en va* et je reste seul avec mes pensées.

A l'aube, toute la famille à grand bruit (*with lots of noise*), est venue nous éveiller. Puis on nous a servi un déjeuner copieux et excellent. Deux chapons en faisaient* partie. En les voyant,* j'ai compris* enfin le sens de ces terribles mots: "Faut-il les tuer tous deux?"

11 à la main, *in his hand. Note the use of* à, *meaning "in," and of* la, *with parts of the body, to translate the possessive pronoun "his."*

12 lui = il. *Lui* is an emphatic form.

QUESTIONNAIRE

1. Dites ce que vous savez (*know*) de la Calabre. 2. Qui sont les deux personnes qui voyageaient en Calabre? 3. Décrivez la maison des charbonniers où ils sont entrés? 4. Qu'est-ce que le plus jeune des deux a raconté à la famille des charbonniers? 5. Le souper fini, où sont-ils allés dormir? 6. Comment ont-ils passé la nuit? 7. Qu'est-ce que l'hôte a dit à sa femme le matin? 8. De quoi l'homme qui raconte l'histoire avait-il peur? 9. Au bout d'un quart d'heure, qui a monté l'escalier? 10. Qu'est-ce qu'il portait entre les dents? 11. Que fait-il en arrivant dans la soupente? 12. Le lendemain matin, pourquoi a-t-il enfin compris la question qui l'avait troublé pendant la nuit?

Lesson 21

Present indicative and past participle of *s'asseoir*

Present indicative and past participle of *ouvrir*

Demonstrative pronouns: *celui, celle, ceux, celles,* and uses

Use of *celui-ci* and *celui-là*

The relative pronoun *dont* and its uses

Use of *à* in a descriptive phrase

CONVERSATION

Une Villa à louer

—Voici la villa dont je vous parlais hier.

—Celle de M. Reynaud?

—Non, celle que je vous ai montrée l'autre jour, quand nous avons passé par ici en auto.

—Ah, oui, je m'en souviens. La maison au toit rouge, aux murs blancs, et aux volets verts. Qui est-ce qui l'habite en ce moment?

—Personne. Est-ce que vous avez envie d'en voir l'intérieur?

—Pourquoi pas? Mais je vous avoue d'avance que je préfère celles qui sont sur la colline. Est-ce que vous avez la clé de la maison?

—Oui. La porte est toujours fermée à clé. Attendez un instant. Je vais l'ouvrir. Tiens! Elle était ouverte! Entrez, s'il vous plaît.

—Combien de pièces y a-t-il?

—Six: le salon, la salle à manger et la cuisine en bas. En haut, trois chambres à coucher et la salle de bain. Montons d'abord au premier étage. Attention! L'escalier est étroit et obscur.

—La maison est complètement meublée?

—Oui. Il y a ici tous les meubles nécessaires: tables, chaises, fauteuils, lampes, armoires, pendules, et même des oreillers, des couvertures, des draps, et des matelas. Pourquoi ne vous asseyez-vous pas un instant dans ce fauteuil?

—Non, merci, je suis fatigué d'être assis. Je préfère rester debout. Je suis resté trop longtemps dans l'auto.

—Néanmoins, essayons ce fauteuil.

—De quel fauteuil parlez-vous? De celui-ci ou de celui-là?

—Essayons celui-ci.

—Bon! Asseyons-nous. Mais, dites-moi, qui demeure dans la maison d'à côté?

—Un certain M. Rameau, avec sa nièce, son petit-fils et sa petite-fille. Il y demeurait l'année dernière, mais il n'y venait que rarement. Par conséquent, il l'a louée à notre compagnie l'autre jour. A présent, il demeure en ville, tout près d'ici. Voulez-vous descendre à la cave?

—Qu'est-ce qu'on y trouve?

—Le calorifère, la buanderie, un W. C.

—Et là-bas, qu'est-ce qu'il y a?

—Une fenêtre et une porte qui donnent sur le jardin. Voulez-vous y aller?

—Ça n'en vaut pas la peine. Montons et asseyons-nous, et quand nous nous serons reposés nous pourrons nous en aller.

VOCABULAIRE ET EXPRESSIONS

le volet the shutter
le toit the roof
le mur the wall
le salon the parlor
l'étage (*masc.*) the floor
les meubles (*masc.*) the furniture
la fenêtre the window
la clé (or clef) the key

la porte the door
la pièce the room; the piece; the play
la salle à manger the dining-room
la cuisine the kitchen
la chambre à coucher the bedroom
la chaise the chair

la lampe the lamp
l'escalier (*masc.*) the staircase
l'œil (*masc.; pl.* **les yeux**) the eye
l'auto (*fem.*) the automobile, the car
le petit-fils the grandson
la petite-fille the granddaughter
la nièce the niece

certain certain
obscur, noir dark

rare rare
étroit narrow

se souvenir de to remember (conj. like *venir*)
demeurer (dans), habiter to live (in)
fermer to close (**fermer à clé** to lock)

ouvrir (*p.p.* **ouvert**) to open
couvrir (*p.p.* **couvert**) to cover
monter (*être*) to go up, to climb
s'asseoir (*p.p.* **assis**) to sit down
se reposer to rest
louer to rent, to hire

celui, celle the one
ceux, celles the ones
celui-ci, celle-ci this one
celui-là, celle-là that one
ceux-ci, celles-ci these (ones)
ceux-là, celles-là those (ones)

dont whose, of whom, of which
dedans inside
d'avance in advance
en haut upstairs, above
rarement seldom
complètement completely

VOCABULAIRE SUPPLÉMENTAIRE

en auto in an automobile
être assis to be seated
être (rester) debout to be (remain) standing
se tenir debout to stand

ça n'en vaut pas la peine it's not worth while
par conséquent consequently, therefore

la villa the cottage
l'intérieur (*masc.*) the inside
le fauteuil the armchair, the easy chair

l'oreiller (*masc.*) the pillow
le drap the bedsheet
la couverture the blanket
la pendule the clock

le calorifère the heating plant
la cave the cellar
la buanderie the laundry
le W. C. (pronounced *le double vé sé*) the toilet
le matelas the mattress

la barbe the beard
la peine the trouble, the sorrow
la compagnie the company, the firm
la colline the hill

en ville in town, downtown
le premier étage the second floor
meublé furnished
à côté beside, next door

donner sur to face on, open out on
avouer to confess, avow
néanmoins nevertheless

VERBES

Present Indicative of **s'asseoir** (to sit down) *p.p.* **assis**

je m'assieds sur cette chaise
tu t'assieds
il (elle) s'assied

nous nous asseyons
vous vous asseyez
ils (elles) s'asseyent

Note—the future of *s'asseoir* is *je m'assiérai,* or *je m'assoirai.* The imperfect is *je m'asseyais.*

Present Indicative of **ouvrir** (to open) *p.p.* **ouvert**

j'ouvre
tu ouvres
il (elle) ouvre

nous ouvrons
vous ouvrez
ils (elles) ouvrent

Note—*couvrir,* to cover, is conjugated like *ouvrir.*

GRAMMAIRE

Demonstrative Pronouns

Je n'aime pas **ce chapeau-ci;** je préfère **celui-là.** I don't like this hat; I prefer that one.

J'ai besoin d'une plume; donnez-moi **celle-là,** s'il vous plaît. I need a pen; give me that one, please.

Où sont mes livres? **Ceux-là** ne sont pas les miens. Where are my books? Those are not mine.

Ces villas sont jolies, mais **celles-là** sont vraiment belles. These cottages are pretty, but those are really beautiful.

→ Demonstrative adjectives (*ce, cet, cette, ces;* see Lesson 3) precede nouns. *Demonstrative pronouns replace nouns, taking the gender and number of the noun replaced. They are:*

celui-ci, celle-ci	this one	**ceux-ci, celles-ci**	these (ones)
celui-là, celle-là	that one	**ceux-là, celles-là**	those (ones)

Avez-vous vu mon chapeau et **celui** de mon frère? Have you seen my hat and my brother's?

Cette femme et **celle** à qui vous avez parlé sont les tantes du petit garçon qui est là-bas. This woman and the one to whom you spoke are the aunts of the little boy over there.

Prêtez-moi ces livres et **ceux** que vous avez déjà lus. Lend me these books and those you have already read.

Pas **ces jeunes filles-là** mais **celles** qui sont entrées sont mes sœurs. Not those girls but the ones who came in are my sisters.

→ *Celui, celle, ceux, celles* also translate "the one," "the ones," expressed or understood. *-ci* and *-là* are not used if the demonstrative pronoun is followed by a preposition, a relative clause, or any restrictive clause. Otherwise, the use of *-ci* and *-là* with the demonstrative pronouns is compulsory.

Dont

Voici l'homme **dont** je vous ai parlé. Here's the man of whom I spoke to you.

Que pensez-vous de la maison **dont** nous avons vu les pièces? What do you think of the house the rooms of which we saw?

L'étudiant **dont** j'ai pris le livre est parti. The student whose book I took left.

→ **Dont** is a relative pronoun, translating "whose," "of whom," "of which." In English, "whose" is immediately followed by the noun it modifies (the man whose book I saw). In French, the correct word-order is obtained by changing "whose" to "of whom," "of which" (the man of whom I saw the book).

À in Descriptive Locution

L'homme aux yeux gris et à la barbe noire était assis à la table. The gray-eyed, black-bearded man was seated at the table.

Nous avons vu la villa aux volets verts et au toit rouge. We saw the cottage with green shutters and a red roof.

→ In a descriptive phrase, "with" is often rendered by *à* with the definite article. It *introduces an adjective phrase giving the characteristic of the object.* When two nouns are the objects of the same preposition, English usually does not repeat the preposition. French does.

QUESTIONS

1. De quelle villa parlait-on? 2. Où se trouvait-elle? 3. D'où l'avait-on vue? 4. De quelle couleur était le toit? les murs? les volets? 5. Est-ce que c'était la seule villa? 6. Où se trouvaient les autres? 7. Combien de pièces y avait-il? 8. Nommez-les. 9. Pourquoi fallait-il faire attention en montant l'escalier? 10. De quoi la maison était-elle meublée? 11. Pourquoi ne s'est-on pas assis immédiatement? 12. Qui habitait la maison? 13. Où demeurent-ils maintenant? 14. Qu'est-ce qu'il y a à la cave? 15. Pourquoi n'y est-on pas descendu?

EXERCICES

A. *Continuez la conjugaison:*

1. Je m'assieds devant eux. Tu t'assieds, etc.
2. Je m'assiérai à table quand le dîner sera prêt.
3. Pendant l'été je m'asseyais au soleil tous les jours.
4. J'ouvre les fenêtres tous les jours.

B. *Remplacez le tiret par la forme correcte de* celui-ci, celui-là, celle-ci, celle-là, ceux-ci, ceux-là, celles-ci, celles-là.

1. Quel chapeau préférez-vous, ________ ou ________?
2. Voici les pendules que nous venons d'acheter. ________ est la mienne; ________ est à Henri.
3. Si vous avez besoin d'une plume prenez ________. ________ est la mienne.
4. Parmi ces chaises, ________ sont les plus jolies.
5. Montrez-moi vos livres; ________ sont les miens.

C. *Traduisez les phrases suivantes:*

1. Here is my house and there is my brother's.
2. That man and the one to whom you spoke are my uncles.
3. Those books over there and these here will make a good library.
4. Those girls in the car and not those who are talking in the street are my sisters.
5. Do you see that red car? Well, the one which is to the right is mine.

D. *Traduisez les phrases suivantes en employant* dont *comme pronom relatif:*

1. There is the boy of whom I was talking.
2. The boy whose mother is so rich is sitting in the car.
3. The woman whose key I borrowed is his mother.
4. There is the girl whose mother died yesterday.

E. *Traduisez les mots en italique:*

1. L'homme *with the black hat.* 2. Nous avons acheté la villa *with a red roof.* 3. Le vieillard *with the white beard* est mon grand-père. 4. La maison *with the green shutters is my father's.* 5. La femme *with the green hat* est une actrice célèbre.

THÈME

—Here is the house of which we saw the photo (*la photographie*). I prefer this one to the one which is on the hill. Don't you prefer it, too?

—Yes, let's look at the inside.

—Here we are! This living room is larger than the one we saw in that cottage yesterday.

—Wouldn't you prefer a furnished cottage for the summer?

—If my husband likes the house, he will rent it for the year, and we will bring our furniture. Let's go and see the other houses. I don't like this one. Let's look at the one with the red shutters.

—If you rented the house furnished how much furniture would you need?

—Oh! not much: tables, chairs, beds, lamps, and one or two arm-chairs.

—Would you want also mattresses, pillows, sheets, blankets, and dishes?

—Of course! Isn't this the cottage whose owner (*le propriétaire*) is in France now? Let's go in.

Lesson 22

Present indicative and past participle of *recevoir*

Present indicative and past participle of *plaire*

Agreement of past participle with preceding direct object in reflexive and pronominal verbs

Plural of nouns ending in *s, x,* and *z*

Plural of nouns and masculine adjectives ending in *al*

Plural of nouns ending in *au, eu,* and *ou* and masculine adjectives ending in *au*

Plural and feminine of adjectives ending in *x*

Feminine of adjectives ending in *en* and *el*

Feminine of adjectives ending in *er*

Feminine of adjectives ending in *f*

Inversion after a direct quotation

CONVERSATION

Un Conte de Guerre

—Qu'est-ce que c'est que ce livre que vous lisez, Léon?

—C'est un conte de guerre bien intéressant, écrit dans un français à la fois excellent et facile.

—Où l'avez-vous trouvé?

—Dans un des deux livres que mon père m'a envoyés. Je les ai reçus tous les deux hier. Je vais vous en lire des passages si vous avez le temps. En voici un. C'est une description qui se trouve dans une lettre écrite par un soldat à sa mère, reçue par celle-ci après la mort de son fils.

—Je vous écoute avec la plus grande attention.

—Ce matin, notre bataillon est arrivé en première ligne, sous un bombardement effroyable, après avoir fait un long détour. Nous avons marché longtemps. Il y avait sur la route que nous suivions toutes sortes de poteaux indicateurs: "Tenez la droite"; "tenez la gauche"; "défense d'entrer." A plusieurs reprises nous nous sommes arrêtés et éparpillés dans les champs pour éviter le feu de mitrailleuse des avions ennemis. Puis, tout à coup, nous sommes arrivés à notre destination. "Prenez garde!" nous a soufflé le sergent. "Voilà l'entrée des tranchées ennemies!" Un jeune soldat a eu le courage de blaguer. "Est-ce qu'il y a aussi une sortie, sergent?" a-t-il demandé à son supérieur. Tout le monde s'est mis à rire. Plus loin, un colonel parlait à voix basse avec le capitaine. Celui-ci s'est retourné de notre côté. "Défense de fumer, mes enfants!" nous a-t-il annoncé. "Est-ce que nous sommes en avance?" a-t-il demandé au colonel. "Non, vous êtes à l'heure." "Y a-t-il d'autres ordres, mon colonel?" "Rien d'autre." Ils se sont serré la main, et le colonel est reparti.

VOCABULAIRE ET EXPRESSIONS

le champ the field
le feu (*pl.* **feux**) the fire
l'avion the plane, airplane
l'ennemi (*masc.*) the enemy, foe
la mort the death
le sang the blood
l'entrée (*fem.*) the entrance
la sortie the exit
le morceau (*pl.* **morceaux**) the piece
le nez (*pl.* **nez**) the nose
le cheval (*pl.* **chevaux**) the horse

facile easy
bas, basse, bas, basses low
naturel, naturelle natural
sale dirty
heureux, heureuse happy
italien, italienne Italian

se mettre à to begin to, to start to
s'arrêter to stop, to halt
recevoir (*p.p.* **reçu**) to receive
se retourner to turn around
rire to laugh
se serrer la main to shake hands

qu'est-ce que c'est que . . . ? what is . . . ?
celui-ci the latter
celui-là the former
longtemps a long time
à la fois at the same time, both
à l'heure on time
en avance ahead of time
tous les deux both
tout à coup suddenly
toutes sortes de all kinds of
plus loin further on
à plusieurs reprises repeatedly
tenez la droite (la gauche) keep right (left)
de mon côté in my direction
défense d'entrer (de fumer) no entrance (no smoking)
prenez garde! watch out!
à voix basse in a low voice

VOCABULAIRE SUPPLÉMENTAIRE

le conte the tale, the story
le bataillon the battalion
le bombardement the bombardment
la ligne the line
la mitrailleuse the machine gun
le poteau indicateur the signpost
le colonel the colonel
le capitaine the captain
le sergent the sergeant
le supérieur the superior
l'intérêt (*masc.*) the interest
le courage the courage
l'animal (*masc.; pl.* **animaux**) the animal
le bijou (*pl.* **bijoux**) the jewel
le veuf the widower
la veuve the widow
effroyable frightful
égal equal
national national
fameux famous
s'éparpiller to scatter
souffler to breathe, to whisper
éviter to avoid
annoncer to announce. **(nous annonçons)**

VERBES

Present Indicative of **recevoir** (to receive) *p.p.* **reçu**

je reçois	**nous recevons**
tu reçois	**vous recevez**
il (elle) reçoit	**ils (elles) reçoivent**

Imperfect: **je recevais** Future: **je recevrai** Conditional: **je recevrais**

Like *recevoir,* conjugate *apercevoir,* to perceive, to see in the distance; *s'apercevoir de,* to perceive, to realize; *décevoir,* to disappoint; *concevoir,* to conceive.

Present Indicative of **plaire** (to please) *pp.* **plu**

je plais	**nous plaisons**
tu plais	**vous plaisez**
il (elle) plaît	**ils (elles) plaisent**

Like **plaire,** conjugate **déplaire,** to displease.

GRAMMAIRE

Agreement of Past Participles in Reflexive and Pronominal Verbs

elle s'est lavée she washed (herself)
elle s'est lavé les mains she washed her hands
les robes qu'elle s'est achetées étaient chères the dresses she bought herself were expensive
ils se sont vus they saw each other
ils se sont serré la main they shook hands
les cadeaux qu'elles se sont donnés étaient jolis the presents they gave each other were pretty

→ *Reflexive verbs* (see Lesson 7) and *reciprocal verbs* (see Lesson 9) *use* être *in their compound tenses. But the agreement is as though* avoir *were used;* that is, the past participle agrees not with the subject, but only with a direct object if there is one and it precedes the verb. In *ils se sont vus,* where the reflexive pronoun *se* is a preceding direct object, *vus* agrees with it; in *ils se sont serré la main, se* is an indirect object (the direct object is *la main*), consequently there is no agreement; in *les cadeaux qu'elles se sont donnés, etc., donnés* agrees not with *se,* which is an indirect object, nor with the subject *elles,* but with the direct object *que,* which is masculine plural because it refers to *les cadeaux.* This makes little difference in the spoken language, since most past participles have the same pronunciation regardless of their gender and number; note, however, such participles as *écrites* in *les lettres qu'ils se sont écrites.*

Irregular Feminine and Plural of Nouns and Adjectives

le temps the time — **les temps** the times
le nez the nose — **les nez** the noses
la voix the voice — **les voix** the voices

→ Nouns ending in *-s, -z,* and *-x* remain unchanged in the plural. The article, however, marks the distinction between singular and plural.

le cheval the horse — **les chevaux** the horses
l'animal the animal — **les animaux** the animals
égal, égale, égaux, égales equal
national, nationale, nationaux, nationales national

→ Nouns and masculine adjectives ending in *-al,* generally change *-al* to *-aux* in the plural.

le cadeau the present — **les cadeaux** the presents
le poteau the signpost — **les poteaux** the signposts
le feu the fire — **les feux** the fires
le bijou the jewel — **les bijoux** the jewels
beau (bel *before a vowel***), belle, beaux, belles** beautiful, fine
nouveau (nouvel *before a vowel***), nouvelle, nouveaux, nouvelles** new

→ Nouns and masculine adjectives in *-au,* and nouns in *-eu* generally form the plural by adding *-x.* So do several nouns in *-ou.*

heureux, heureuse, heureux, heureuses happy
fameux, fameuse, fameux, fameuses famous

→ Adjectives ending in *-x* remain unchanged in the masculine plural, change *-x* to *-se* in the feminine singular, and to *-ses* in the feminine plural.

italien, italienne, italiens, italiennes Italian
naturel, naturelle, naturels, naturelles natural

→ Adjectives ending in *-en* and *-el* double the final consonant before adding *-e* for the feminine.

cher, chère, chers, chères dear, expensive
léger, légère, légers, légères light
premier, première, premiers, premières first
dernier, dernière, derniers, dernières last

→ Adjectives ending in *-er* change to *-ère* in the feminine forms.

neuf, neuve, neufs, neuves new
veuf, veuve, veufs, veuves widower, widow, widowed

→ Adjectives ending in *-f* change to *-ve* in the feminine forms.

The Latter—The Former

J'ai écrit à ma mère et à ma sœur. **Celle-ci m'a répondu; celle-là n'a pas reçu ma lettre.** I wrote my mother and my sister. The latter answered me; the former did not get my letter.

"The former" is expressed by **celui-là, celle-là, ceux-là, celles-là**
"The latter" is expressed by **celui-ci, celle-ci, ceux-ci, celles-ci**
"The latter" normally precedes "the former" in a French sentence.

Inversion after Direct Quotation

"Est-ce qu'il est ici?" lui a-t-il demandé. "Oui, il vient d'arriver," a répondu mon frère. "Is he here?" he asked him. "Yes, he has just arrived," my brother answered.

→ Following a direct quotation, there is normally inversion of the subject and verb, in the parenthetical use of *dire, répondre, s'écrier, demander,* etc.

QUESTIONS

1. Qu'est-ce que c'est qu'un conte de guerre? 2. Que lisait Léon? 3. Quelle était son opinion du conte qu'il lisait? 4. Où l'avait-il trouvé?

5. Combien en avait-il reçu? 6. Quel passage voulait-il lire à son ami? 7. Par qui le conte avait-il été écrit? 8. Où se passait l'action? 9. Que voulait-on éviter? 10. Enfin, où les soldats sont-ils arrivés? 11. Comment le colonel parlait-il? 12. Quelles restrictions y avait-il à observer?

EXERCICES

A. I. *Employez la forme correcte de* recevoir *dans les phrases suivantes:*

1. Quand elle ________ ses amies, elle sert toujours une tasse de café. 2. Quand je ________ une lettre, j'y réponds immédiatement. 3. Nous ne ________ plus de livres de France. 4. Ils ________ souvent des cadeaux de leurs parents. 5. Si nous ne ________ pas assez de viande, nous aurions faim.

II. *Conjuguez:*

1. Je recevais mes amis dans le salon. 2. Je recevrais une bonne note en français si j'étudiais davantage. 3. J'aperçois mon ami qui s'approche. 4. Je m'aperçois que nous ne nous intéressons pas à ce livre. 5. J'ai reçu un cadeau de mon oncle. 6. Je ris chaque fois que je pense à ce livre.

B. *Remplacez l'infinitif par la forme correcte du participe passé:*

1. Les services qu'ils se sont (*rendre*) sont importants. 2. Elles se sont (*voir*) hier après-midi pour la première fois. 3. Elle s'est (*laver*) la figure et les mains en rentrant de sa promenade. 4. Ils se sont (*serrer*) la main et puis ils sont partis. 5. Nous nous sommes (*laver*) avant de descendre pour le déjeuner.

C. *Employez la forme correcte de l'auxiliaire dans les phrases suivantes:*

1. Elle s'________ lavée ce matin. 2. Ils se ________ lavé les mains. 3. Vous vous ________ serré la main. 4. Nous nous ________ vus. 5. Les robes qu'elle se ________ achetées étaient jolies. 6. Les lettres qu'elles se ________ écrites sont charmantes.

D. *Donnez le pluriel des mots suivants:*

1. le temps 2. le cheval 3. le morceau 4. le feu 5. le nez 6. la voix 7. le bijou 8. le poteau 9. l'animal 10. le cadeau.

E. *Donnez toutes les formes possibles des adjectifs suivants:*

1. beau 2. égal 3. nouveau 4. national 5. heureux 6. italien 7. premier 8. neuf 9. fameux 10. dernier 11. naturel 12. veuf.

F. *Traduisez le mot anglais par la forme correcte de* celui-ci, celui-là, celle-ci, celle-là, ceux-ci, ceux-là, celles-ci, celles-là:

1. J'ai vu madame Dupont et son fils au café, hier; *the former* est veuve maintenant et *the latter* est dans l'armée. 2. J'ai écrit à ma mère et à mes frères, *the latter* n'ont pas encore répondu à ma lettre. 3. J'ai parlé longtemps à ma tante et à sa fille ce matin; *the former* va en Europe, *the latter* va rester ici quelque temps.

THÈME

—What's that short story you are reading?

—It's a very interesting story about the war. My father sent it to me. It's a story based (*basée*) upon a letter from a soldier to his mother.

—Will you read me a passage? I should like to hear what (*ce que*) he says:

—After a fearful bombardment our battalion arrived at the first line of trenches. There were all sorts of signs along the road to help us find our way (*trouver notre chemin*). Some read: keep to the right; others, keep to the left; others, keep out. We could hear the machine guns and the noise of the airplanes. Everyone spoke in a low voice. One of the soldiers began to smoke.

"No smoking," said the captain, "and hurry up, we are not ahead of time."

"Ah! at last here we are at the entrance to the enemy trenches," said the sergeant.

"Are we on time, Colonel?"

"Yes, Captain."

They shook hands and the soldiers entered the trenches.

Lesson 23

Present indicative and past participle of *dormir*

Pluperfect indicative of *parler* and *aller* and its uses

Past conditional of *parler* and *aller* and its uses

***Falloir* with a direct and indirect object**

Formation of an ordinal number from a cardinal number

Use of ordinals and cardinals in dates and titles

Uses of *moitié* and *demi*

Uses of collective numerals ending in *aine*

CONVERSATION

Une jeune Fille fatiguée

PAULINE: Pardonnez-moi si je bâille. Je ne peux pas m'empêcher de le faire. Mon Dieu, que je suis fatiguée!

HENRI: C'est très naturel. Si je m'étais promené autant que vous, je serais fatigué aussi. Pourquoi vous êtes-vous tellement épuisée?

PAULINE: Ce n'est rien; c'était ma première visite dans les grands magasins depuis 1938. Que voulez-vous? Je voulais tout voir.

HENRI: Je me souviens qu'autrefois vous les visitiez chaque année. C'est votre huitième visite en France, n'est-ce pas?

PAULINE: Voyons; mais non, c'est ma dixième. Si j'avais pu, je serais venue aussi en 1939, mais la guerre était sur le point d'éclater. D'ailleurs, c'était impossible cette année-là, faute d'argent. Malgré moi, il a fallu rester en Amérique.

HENRI: A quelle heure est-ce que vous vous êtes réveillée ce matin?

PAULINE: Vers huit heures. Mais j'ai mis quelque temps à m'habiller.

HENRI: Si vous vous étiez reposée hier, comme je vous l'avais conseillé, vous n'auriez pas été fatiguée aujourd'hui.

PAULINE: J'ai dormi sept heures et demie. C'est tout ce qu'il me faut.

HENRI: Ça suffit d'ordinaire. Mais après un tel voyage, il faut quelques heures de plus. Allez vite vous coucher. Vous avez besoin de dormir.

PAULINE: Vous avez raison. Bonne nuit.

HENRI: A demain.

VOCABULAIRE ET EXPRESSIONS

la moitié half
la paire the pair
demi half

second second
un tel, une telle such a

se réveiller to wake up
se coucher to lie down, go to bed
dormir to sleep

s'endormir to fall asleep
s'habiller to dress
empêcher (de) to prevent, hinder (from)

que . . . ! how . . . ! (exclamatory; follow with declarative word-order: *qu'il est bon!*
tellement so, so much, to such an extent
malgré in spite of

autrefois formerly
faute de for lack of
de plus more, furthermore, in addition, besides
d'ordinaire usually
bonne nuit good night (used only on retiring)

que voulez-vous? what would you? what would you expect?
à peu près more or less
ça suffit that's enough
pardonnez-moi pardon me
je ne peux pas m'empêcher de I can't help
ce n'est rien that's nothing

VOCABULAIRE SUPPLÉMENTAIRE

le départ the departure
la vingtaine the score
la centaine about a hundred
éclater to burst out
bâiller to yawn
s'épuiser to get exhausted
conseiller to advise (*conseiller à quelqu'un de faire quelque chose,* to advise someone to do something)
mettre quelque temps à + *inf.* to take some time to

VERBES

Present Indicative of **dormir** (to sleep) *p.p.* **dormi**

je dors
tu dors
il (elle) dort
nous dormons
vous dormez
ils (elles) dorment

Like *dormir* conjugate *s'endormir,* to fall asleep.

The Pluperfect Indicative

j'avais parlé
tu avais parlé
il avait parlé
elle avait parlé
nous avions parlé
vous aviez parlé
ils avaient parlé
elles avaient parlé

j'étais allé(-e)
tu étais allé(-e)
il était allé
elle était allée
nous étions allés(-es)
vous étiez allé(-e, -s, -es)
ils étaient allés
elles étaient allées

je l'avais vu avant son départ I had seen him before his departure
il avait fini son travail he had finished his work
elle m'avait rendu mon livre she had given me back my book

ils étaient sortis avant mon arrivée they had gone out before my arrival
elles s'étaient parlé hier they had spoken to each other yesterday

→ The pluperfect indicative is used generally like the English past perfect.

The Past Conditional

j'aurais parlé	**nous aurions parlé**
tu aurais parlé	**vous auriez parlé**
il aurait parlé	**ils auraient parlé**
elle aurait parlé	**elles auraient parlé**

je serais allé(-e)	**nous serions allés(-es)**
tu serais allé(-e)	**vous seriez allé(-e, -s, -es)**
il serait allé	**ils seraient allés**
elle serait allée	**elles seraient allées**

il m'aurait parlé s'il m'avait vu he would have spoken to me if he had seen me
je serais parti à trois heures, si je m'étais dépêché I would have left at three o'clock if I had hurried
elle m'aurait rendu mon livre, si je l'avais demandé she would have returned my book if I had asked for it

→ The past conditional is used in conditional sentences where English uses "should have," "would have." The pluperfect indicative is used in the "if" clause.

GRAMMAIRE

Objects of **falloir**

il me faut deux dollars I need two dollars
il lui faut du courage he needs courage
il vous faut de l'argent you need money

The impersonal *falloir* may be accompanied by a direct and an indirect object. It may be translated by "to need." The indirect object becomes the subject of the English sentence.

Numerals

un one
deux two
trois three
quatre four
cinq five
six six
sept seven
huit eight
neuf nine
dix ten

premier first
second, deuxième second
troisième third
quatrième fourth
cinquième fifth
sixième sixth
septième seventh
huitième eighth
neuvième ninth
dixième tenth
onzième eleventh
douzième twelfth
treizième thirteenth
quatorzième fourteenth
dix-neuvième nineteenth
vingtième twentieth
vingt et unième twenty-first
vingt-deuxième twenty-second
quatre-vingtième eightieth
centième hundredth

→ To form an ordinal numeral from a cardinal, add *-ième*. If the cardinal ends in *-e*, drop the final *-e* of the cardinal and add *-ième*. Note the change of *f* to *v* in *neuvième*, and the insertion of *u* in *cinquième*.

Napoléon premier Napoleon 1st
Napoléon trois Napoleon 3rd
le premier avril April 1st
le cinq avril April 5th

→ In dates and titles, *premier* is the only ordinal used. *Cardinal numbers are used from second on.*

la moitié de ma classe half of my class
une demi-heure half an hour
une heure et demie an hour and a half

→ "Half" as a noun is *moitié;* as an adjective it is *demi. Demi* is invariable and attached to the noun by a hyphen if it precedes, but agrees with the noun in gender if it follows.

une paire de souliers a pair of shoes
une douzaine d'œufs a dozen eggs
une dizaine de jours about ten days
une vingtaine d'hommes a score of men; about twenty men
une trentaine de femmes about thirty women; some thirty women
une centaine de dollars about a hundred dollars

→ Collective numerals similar to our "dozen" may be formed in some cases by adding the suffix *-aine* to *huit, dix, douze, vingt, trente, quarante,* etc., after dropping the final *-e*.

QUESTIONS

1. Pourquoi Pauline bâille-t-elle? 2. Qu'est-ce qu'elle ne peut pas s'empêcher de faire? 3. Quelle explication Henri donne-t-il de la fatigue de Pauline? 4. Pourquoi Pauline avait-elle visité les grands magasins? 5. Combien de fois Pauline a-t-elle visité la France? 6. Pourquoi n'est-elle pas allée en 1939? 7. A quelle heure Pauline s'est-elle réveillée? 8. Est-ce qu'elle s'est habillée vite? 9. De combien d'heures de repos Pauline a-t-elle besoin? 10. Quand lui faut-il quelques heures de plus?

EXERCICES

A. *Traduisez les verbes suivants en français et employez-les dans des phrases:*

1. they are sleeping 2. she sleeps 3. I sleep 4. we are sleeping 5. are you sleeping? 6. I had spoken 7. she had gone 8. we should have gone 9. they had spoken 10. we should have spoken 11. you would have gone 12. you had gone 13. she would have spoken 14. he had spoken 15. he would have gone 16. I woke up 17. they went to bed 18. she rested.

B. *Traduisez le mot en anglais par son équivalent en français:*

1. Henri *the fourth* 2. Louis *the eleventh* 3. Louis *the fourteenth* 4. Napoléon *the first* 5. Louis *the sixteenth*

C. *Donnez l'équivalent français des dates suivantes:*

1. May 1st 2. April 2 3. May 4 4. June 5 5. July 1st 6. August 10 7. September 12 8. October 26 9. November 6 10. December 1st 11. January 30 12. February 12.

D. *Remplacez le tiret par un des mots suivants et traduisez chaque phrase en anglais:* la moitié, demi, une paire, une douzaine, une demi-douzaine, une vingtaine, une trentaine, une centaine.

1. ________ de la classe est absente. 2. Je vais partir dans une ________ heure. 3. Il y a ________ de livres français dans sa bibliothèque. 4. Il reviendra dans ________ de jours. 5. Donnez-moi ________ d'œufs, s'il vous plaît. 6. Vous avez besoin d'________ de souliers, mon enfant. 7. Six crayons font ________ de crayons. 8. Donnez-moi un ________ litre de lait.

E. *Faites une question avec chacune des expressions suivantes et répondez-y:*

1. se reposer 2. se réveiller 3. se coucher 4. s'habiller 5. dormir 6. d'ordinaire 7. autrefois 8. à peu près 9. bonne nuit 10. pardonnez-moi 11. ça suffit 12. que voulez-vous . . . ?

THÈME

—Oh! you are yawning.

—Excuse me. I could not help myself. I am completely exhausted.

—Why are you so tired? You went to bed early last night.

—Yes, but I walked everywhere today. I wanted to see Paris again.

—If you had rested this afternoon for (*omit*) an hour or two, you would not be so tired. I wanted to go to the theatre tonight.

—If I had known that, I should have come home early.

—Perhaps (*insert:* that) if you lie down you can sleep for (*omit*) an hour or two and we can still go.

—All right. If I had been able to sleep late this morning, I would not be so tired now. Tomorrow I shall stay at home. I wanted to go to some department stores tomorrow morning, but I shall not go until the afternoon.

Lesson 24

Present subjunctive of *parler, vendre,* and *finir*

Formation and general uses of subjunctive

Subjunctive of some irregular verbs

Present indicative of *devoir*

Conjugation of *falloir*

***Il faut* with an infinitive**

***Il faut* followed by the subjunctive**

Uses and meaning of *devoir*

Devoir* compared with *falloir

CONVERSATION

On Déjeune en hâte

PAUL: Je dois dîner chez Louis ce soir.

GEORGES: Ça, c'est chic! Vous refusez mes invitations, mais vous acceptez les siennes!

PAUL: Écoutez! Je lui ai promis d'aller dîner chez lui, il y a deux mois. Il faut absolument que j'y aille!

GEORGES: Chacun son goût! Mais dites-moi, vous qui êtes gourmand, est-ce qu'on dîne bien chez lui?

PAUL: Oh, à merveille! La dernière fois que j'y étais, on nous a servi un repas épatant. Ce qui (*which*) me rappelle que nous n'avons pas encore déjeuné. Voici un restaurant où je mange de temps en temps lorsque je rentre tard le soir. On y mange bien et à bon marché.

GEORGES: Soit, mais alors c'est moi qui vous invite. Il faut que vous me permettiez de le faire.

PAUL: Comme vous voulez. Entrons.

GEORGES: Pas de garçons ici. Il n'y a que des serveuses.

PAUL: Tant mieux. Elles sont plus soigneuses.

LA SERVANTE: Monsieur désire?

GEORGES: Je prendrai du gigot aux haricots.

PAUL: Apportez-moi du veau sauté aux petits pois et une bouteille de vin ordinaire.

LA SERVANTE: Oui, monsieur.

GEORGES: Elle ne nous a pas mis de cuillers, de fourchettes, ou de couteaux.

PAUL: Mais si! Les voilà sous votre serviette.

GEORGES: Qu'est-ce que vous faites à présent?

PAUL: Je devrais préparer mes cours pour demain. Mais j'ai dû tant étudier hier que je n'en ai pas envie. D'ailleurs, il faut bien se reposer de temps en temps.

GEORGES: Vous avez tout à fait raison. Moi aussi, je devais travailler, mais j'ai préféré y renoncer pour venir vous voir.

PAUL: Hélas! il faut que nous soyons à l'université à trois heures. Mademoiselle, l'addition, s'il vous plaît. Qu'est-ce qu'on lui donne comme pourboire?

GEORGES: Une vingtaine de francs.

PAUL: Partons.

VOCABULAIRE ET EXPRESSIONS

les haricots (*masc.*) the beans
le veau the veal
le gigot the leg of lamb
la tranche the slice
la fourchette the fork
les petits pois (*masc.*) the peas
la bouteille the bottle
la cuiller the spoon
le couteau the knife
l'addition (*fem.*) the bill, the check (in a restaurant)

la serveuse the waitress
la servante the maid
le pourboire the tip

devoir to owe, must, have to, be to
promettre (de) to promise (the person promised is an indirect object)
permettre (de) to permit, allow to (the person permitted is an indirect object)
renoncer (à) to give up (something)
apporter to bring

chacun, chacune each one
apportez-moi bring me
à bon marché cheaply (**bon marché** cheap)

VOCABULAIRE SUPPLÉMENTAIRE

le goût the taste
le gourmand the glutton
la hâte the haste
soigneux (*fem.* **soigneuse**) careful, attentive
préparer to prepare
hélas! alas!
offrir (*p.p.* **offert**) to offer, to "treat"
ça, c'est chic! that's fine!; I like that! (*ironical*)
chacun son goût everyone to his tastes
soit so be it, all right

VERBES

The Subjunctive

Present Subjunctive of **parler, vendre, finir**

que je parle that I speak
que tu parles that you speak
qu'il (elle) parle that he (she) speak
que nous parlions that we speak
que vous parliez that you speak
qu'ils (elles) parlent that they speak

que je vende that I sell
que tu vendes that you sell
qu'il (elle) vende that he (she) sell
que nous vendions that we sell
que vous vendiez that you sell
qu'ils (elles) vendent that they sell

que je finisse that I finish
que tu finisses that you finish
qu'il (elle) finisse that he (she) finish
que nous finissions that we finish
que vous finissiez that you finish
qu'ils (elles) finissent that they finish

→ The subjunctive is generally used in subordinate clauses when the main clause implies some measure of doubt or necessity. The cases where the subjunctive is used will be explained in detail further on. The endings of the present subjunctive are: *-e, -es, -e, -ions, -iez, -ent.* These endings are added to the stem of the verb (*parl-, vend-*); but in regular *-ir* verbs, *-iss-* is inserted between the stem and the endings (*fin-iss-*).

Irregular Subjunctives

courir to run; **que je coure** that I run
partir to leave; **que je parte** that I leave
ouvrir to open; **que j'ouvre** that I open
sortir to go out; **que je sorte** that I go out
dormir to sleep; **que je dorme** that I sleep
couvrir to cover; **que je couvre** that I cover
fuir to flee; **que je fuie** that I flee
cueillir to gather; **que je cueille** that I gather

→ Several *-ir* verbs add the regular endings to the stem in the present subjunctive.

dire to say; **que je dise** that I say
pouvoir to be able; **que je puisse** that I be able
faire to do; **que je fasse** that I do
lire to read; **que je lise** that I read
écrire to write; **que j'écrive** that I write
connaître to know; **que je connaisse** that I know
savoir to know; **que je sache** that I know

→ Other irregular verbs make a change in the stem before adding the endings *-e, -es, -e, -ions, -iez, -ent.*

prendre to take: **prenne, prennes, prenne, prenions, preniez, prennent**
vouloir to want: **veuille, veuilles, veuille, voulions, vouliez, veuillent**
valoir to be worth: **vaille, vailles, vaille, valions, valiez, vaillent**
boire to drink: **boive, boives, boive, buvions, buviez, boivent**

voir to see: **voie, voies, voie, voyions, voyiez, voient**
devoir to owe: **doive, doives, doive, devions, deviez, doivent**
recevoir to receive: **reçoive, reçoives, reçoive, recevions, receviez, reçoivent**
aller to go: **aille, ailles, aille, allions, alliez, aillent**
venir to come: **vienne, viennes, vienne, venions, veniez, viennent**
tenir to hold: **tienne, tiennes, tienne, tenions, teniez, tiennent**

→A few irregular verbs use two different stems in the present subjunctive: one for the singular and third plural, the other for the first and second plural; the latter is often the regular stem.

être to be: **sois, sois, soit, soyons, soyez, soient**
avoir to have: **aie, aies, ait, ayons, ayez, aient**

→The present subjunctive of *être* and *avoir* are completely irregular. Note that these are the only two verbs in which the endings are irregular.

GRAMMAIRE

Falloir (must, have to)

Pres. ind. **il faut**; impf. **il fallait**; fut. **il faudra**; pres. subj. **il faille**; p.p. **fallu.**

il faut le faire someone (I, we, you) must do it; it must be done
il me faut le faire I must do it (archaic)
il faut que je le fasse I must do it
il faut que Jean le fasse John must do it

→*Il faut* followed by the infinitive is often translated by "must," with the subject of the "must" unspecified or understood.

→The subject of the "must" may be expressed by an indirect object pronoun, but this usage is somewhat antiquated.

→*Il faut* may also be followed by a subjunctive clause. This occurs especially when there is a noun subject for the English "must."

Devoir

Present Indicative (am to, must, owe)

je dois	**nous devons**
tu dois	**vous devez**
il (elle) doit	**ils (elles) doivent**

Impf. **devais;** fut. **devrai;** pres. subj. **doive—devions;** *p.p.* **dû.**

je dois y aller demain I am to go there tomorrow
Où est Jean? **Il doit être ici.** Where is John? He must be here.
on doit toujours dire la vérité one must always tell the truth

→ The present indicative of *devoir* indicates: (1) mild obligation combined with futurity, as expressed by the English "am to"; (2) "must" when it expresses not compulsion but probability; (3) "must," "should," "ought to" when these terms indicate a general, moral obligation.

je devais y aller hier, mais j'étais malade I was to go there yesterday, but I was ill

→ The imperfect of *devoir* expresses "was to," "were to."

vous devrez étudier plus longtemps you will have to study longer
il vous faudra étudier plus longtemps you will have to study longer
il faudra que vous étudiiez plus longtemps you will have to study longer

→ The future of *devoir* expresses strong future compulsion, like English "will have to." In this tense, it is interchangeable with the future of *falloir*.

je devrais le voir demain I ought to see him tomorrow

→ The conditional of *devoir* expresses "ought to," "should."

j'aurais dû le faire la semaine dernière I ought to have done it last week

→ The past conditional of *devoir* expresses past obligation, like the English "ought to have," "should have."

il a dû le faire he had to do it; he must have done it
il a dû être ici he must have been here

→ The past indefinite of *devoir* denotes (1) "had to"; in this sense it is interchangeable with the past indefinite of *falloir;* (2) "must have," in the sense of inference or belief. Note that in the latter sense it is followed by the infinitive, not by the past participle, as is the case in English.

je lui dois cinq dollars I owe him five dollars
je lui devais dix dollars I owed him ten dollars
je lui devrai mille francs I shall owe him a thousand francs

→ *Devoir* also has the meaning of "to owe" in all its tenses.

QUESTIONS

1. Où Paul va-t-il dîner? 2. Pourquoi Georges est-il fâché? 3. Pourquoi faut-il que Paul aille chez Louis? 4. Est-ce qu'on dîne bien chez Georges? 5. Où Paul mange-t-il quand il rentre tard le soir? 6. Qui sert à table dans ce restaurant? 7. Pourquoi Paul est-il content de cela? 8. Qu'est-ce que Georges choisit? 9. Que choisit Paul? 10. Pourquoi Paul demande-t-il l'addition immédiatement après le repas?

EXERCICES

A. *Continuez la conjugaison:*

1. Il faut que je parle à cet homme, il faut que tu . . . , etc. 2. Il faut que je vende ce livre. 3. Il faut que je finisse cette leçon. 4. Il faut que je mette la nappe. 5. Il faut que je parte tout de suite. 6. Il faut que j'ouvre la porte. 7. Il faut que je sorte. 8. Je devrais les inviter à venir. 9. Il faut que je suive cet homme. 10. J'ai dû partir. 11. Il faut que je couvre la table. 12. Je dois de l'argent à Monsieur Georges.

B. *Remplacez l'infinitif par la forme correcte du subjonctif:*

1. Il faut que vous le (*dire*). 2. Il faut que nous (*pouvoir*) partir tout à l'heure. 3. Il faut qu'elles (*faire*) leur lit maintenant. 4. Faut-il que je (*lire*) ce livre tout de suite? 5. Il faut que mon frère (*écrire*)

cette lettre immédiatement. 6. Il faut que vous (*connaître*) ma tante. 7. Il faut absolument que vous (*savoir*) votre rôle ce soir. 8. Pourquoi ne faut-il pas que je (*prendre*) ce journal? 9. Il ne faut pas qu'ils (*venir*). 10. Il faut que vous (*dormir*) mieux.

C. *Dans chacune des phrases suivantes, remplacez l'infinitif par trois formes du subjonctif, la première personne du singulier et du pluriel et la troisième personne du pluriel:*

1. Il faut que (*recevoir*) bientôt une réponse. 2. Faut-il que (*boire*) cette eau chaude? 3. Il faut que (*voir*) Charles. 4. Faut-il que (*lire*) ce livre tout de suite? 5. Il faut que (*payer*) cet homme. 6. Il faut que (*aller*) au musée aujourd'hui. 7. Il faut que (*venir*) ce soir. 8. Il ne faut pas que (*être*) en retard. 9. Il faut (*avoir*) deux crayons à l'examen. 10. Il faut que (*se reposer*) maintenant.

D. *Traduisez en français:*

1. We must do it. 2. He is to go there next week. 3. She must be here now. 4. One should always see one's friends. 5. We were to go to the movies, but Mary was ill. 6. You must study longer if you want to learn your lesson. 7. He must have been here, he has left this letter. 8. Excuse me, but I had to do it. 9. I owed him twenty dollars but I paid him last week. 10. Let us see! I owe you ten dollars, don't I?

THÈME

—Will you have dinner (*dine*) with me this evening?

—I am very sorry but I must go to dinner with Henry.

—Perhaps some other (*another*) time, then. But here we are in front of the restaurant. Let's see what is (*what there is*) on the menu. Roast lamb with string beans. Braised veal with peas. There is not much choice. But I shall go in anyway.

—Well, goodbye then. I must hurry or I shall be late.

(The other enters the restaurant and sits down. There are waitresses instead of waiters.)

—Miss, will you bring the menu, please?

—Here is a napkin, too, sir.

—But you have forgotten to give me a fork and knife. There is only a spoon here and a glass.

—Excuse me a moment. I must go get (*chercher*) that gentleman's roast lamb. I shall return in a minute for your order (*votre commande*).

—Please hurry. I must be back at my house at 7:30. Bring the check as soon as you (*will*) bring my order, please.

—Very well, sir.

Review Lesson 6

A. *Traduisez les phrases suivantes:*

1. He is sitting down in the armchair. 2. We are sitting down near the lamp. 3. She was sitting down when I came in. 4. I shall sit down when I am tired. 5. They are opening the door. 6. Open the window, please. 7. She opened the door. 8. He received the book. 9. I am receiving letters from her every day. 10. Do you receive many books from France? 11. I used to receive letters from England every day. 12. He will receive his valise tomorrow. 13. They were laughing. 14. You were laughing. 15. I shall laugh. 16. He smiled. 17. They are sleeping. 18. We are not sleeping. 19. He is sleeping now. 20. They will fall asleep. 21. You slept well. 22. We must speak to you at once. 23. He must sell the house. 24. They must finish their work today. 25. I must leave this afternoon.

B. I. *Remplacez le tiret par la forme convenable du pronom démonstratif:*

1. Avez-vous besoin de ce chapeau-ci ou de ————? 2. Quelle chaise préférez-vous, ———— ou ————? 3. J'aime ces cravates-ci; voulez-vous ————? 4. J'ai fait mon choix; ceux-ci sont les miens, ———— sont les vôtres.

II. *Traduisez les expressions en italique dans les phrases suivantes:*

1. La dame *to whom* je parlais est la mère de Jean. 2. La dame *with the green hat* est la sœur de Marie. 3. L'homme *with the black beard* est son père. 4. La maison *of which* nous avons vu le toit tout à l'heure est la nôtre. 5. Il a écrit à sa tante et à son oncle; *the former* a répondu par lettre, *the latter* a répondu par téléphone.

III. *Remplacez l'infinitif par la forme correcte du participe passé:*

1. Elles se sont (*laver*) les mains. 2. Elles se sont (*voir*) hier soir. 3. Les chapeaux qu'elle s'est (*acheter*) sont très jolis. 4. Ils se sont (*laver*).

IV. *Donnez le pluriel des noms suivants:*

le temps	le nez	le cheval	le cadeau	le bijou
le feu	l'animal	la voix	le poteau	le chapeau

V. *Donnez le féminin et le masculin pluriel des adjectifs suivants:*

égal	national	beau	nouveau	heureux	italien
cher	neuf	premier	dernier	veuf	fameux

VI. *Écrivez en toutes lettres les chiffres en italique:*

Napoléon *I*	Henri *IV*	le *6* avril
une *½* heure	le *15* mai	Louis *XV*
une heure et *½*	le *10* août	le *25* octobre
le *4* juillet		

VII. *Remplacez l'infinitif par la forme correcte du verbe:*

1. Il faut que Jean (*venir*). 2. Il faut que je (*vendre*) cette maison. 3. Il faudra qu'il (*étudier*) s'il veut réussir. 4. Il faut que vous (*savoir*) toute la leçon. 5. Il faudra que nous (*lire*) ce livre ce soir.

VIII. *Traduisez les phrases suivantes:*

1. I was to read that book yesterday. 2. He should have done it last week. 3. We had to write that letter. 4. She must have arrived this morning. 5. They owe me ten dollars.

Lecture 6

LE POISSON ROUGE

(D'après un conte de Tristan Dérème)

Un soir, comme je me rendais (*was going*) chez mon ami Carco, je me suis arrêté près de sa maison devant une boutique où on vendait des poissons rouges. Après quelque temps, j'ai choisi un petit poisson qui me plaisait.* J'ai acheté aussi un vase que j'ai rempli d'eau, et je suis parti chez Carco. Offrir un poisson rouge à un ami me paraissait* à la fois (*at the same time*) singulier, ridicule et charmant, et d'un goût assez rare. Carco habitait au troisième étage (*fourth floor*). Je suis monté[1] et j'ai sonné (*I rang*) à la porte. J'ai attendu un instant mais personne ne m'a répondu.[2] J'ai sonné de nouveau (*again*). En vain. Sans poser le vase, je suis allé consulter la concierge (*doorkeeper*). Elle ne savait* pas où était mon ami. J'ai remonté l'escalier,[1] j'ai encore sonné plusieurs fois, puis je suis descendu de nouveau, me promettant de revenir le lendemain (*the next day*). Mais, qu'allais-je faire de mon poisson?

Laisser le vase et le poisson chez la concierge? Il n'y fallait* pas songer (*that was unthinkable*). Je suis donc parti[3] dîner. Mon poisson dans sa prison de cristal, sur la table du restaurant, me regardait. Le garçon m'a recommandé des soles, mais par une sorte de scrupule je n'ai pas osé dévorer un autre poisson sous les yeux de mon prisonnier.

Vers minuit, après avoir promené (*having taken along*) mon poisson au café, dans le métro, dans un tramway, au milieu de la gaieté curieuse des personnes que je rencontrais et qui se de-

1 je suis monté, *I went up*. Monter *is usually conjugated with* être, *but when followed by an object, as in* j'ai remonté l'escalier, *it takes* avoir.

2 personne ne m'a répondu: *note that except when it stands alone in a sentence* personne *requires* ne. *Note also that the object* ne . . . personne *becomes* personne (. . .) ne *when it is the subject of the verb.*

3 je suis donc parti: donc *is usually placed before the past participle.*

mandaient (*wondered*) comment un homme d'aspect raisonnable pouvait* de la sorte (*in that manner*) transporter un poisson rouge, je suis rentré chez moi. Je n'ai pas pu empêcher (*prevent*) un jeune enfant au (*with*) coeur tendre,[4] de mettre dans mon vase la moitié d'un bâton (*bar*) de chocolat qu'il mangeait* et qu'il voulait* partager (*share*) avec mon poisson.

Le lendemain, j'ai pris* mon vase et je suis parti chez mon ami Carco. J'ai pris un taxi afin de ne pas m'offrir en (*as a*) spectacle comme la veille (*the night before*), et nous voilà (*there we were*) le poisson et moi, emportés vers le logis de mon ami. Je ne sais* si[5] vous avez jamais (*ever*) transporté un poisson rouge, dans une auto. C'est chose périlleuse.[6] Nous n'avions pas fait* (*gone*) deux cents mètres, que j'avais (*before I had*) les mains trempées. Mais, ce n'était encore rien. Tout à coup, à un tournant brusque, l'eau du vase s'est répandue dans mon gilet et le pauvre poisson a roulé sur la banquette (*cushion seat*) du taxi. Je me suis mis* à[7] crier si fort (*loud*) que la voiture s'est arrêtée. Le chauffeur a sans doute pensé qu'il avait affaire à un fou[8] car, brusquement, nu-tête (*bareheaded*), le poisson rouge fourré (*stuck*) dans le vase vide, je me suis précipité (*rushed*) dans la première maison venue,[9] en criant: "de l'eau! de l'eau!" Il m'a fallu* (*It took me*) longtemps pour trouver de l'eau. J'aurais bien pleuré dans le vase, mais les larmes sont salées (*salty*). Ah! quelle joie lorsque j'ai vu* mon petit poisson donner un coup de queue dans son vase de nouveau plein d'eau!

J'ai payé le taxi[10] et je me suis décidé à[11] continuer ma route à pied. Les vêtements encore mouillés, je suis enfin arrivé chez mon ami Carco. Cette fois il était chez lui. Je lui ai fait un petit

[4] au coeur tendre: *note the use of* au, *meaning "with." Similarly: l'homme* aux yeux bleus, *with blue eyes;* la dame au chapeau vert, *with the green hat.*

[5] je ne sais si: *note the omission of* pas. *With* oser, savoir, pouvoir, *the* pas *is often omitted in the negative.*

[6] C'est chose périlleuse: *the indefinite article is often omitted after* c'est *followed by* chose.

[7] je mes suis mis à, *I began to, I started to.*

[8] il avait affaire à un fou, *he was dealing with a mad man.*

[9] la première maison venue, *the first house I came to.*

[10] j'ai payé le taxi: *in French* payer *takes a direct object; in English it is followed by "for."*

[11] je me suis décidé à, *I decided. Literally: I made up my mind. Note that the reflexive form of this verb is followed by* à, *the active verb by* de: j'ai décidé de.

discours et je lui ai offert* mon cadeau. Vous ne pouvez* pas vous imaginer l'importance que ce poisson rouge a pris* dans ma vie à partir de (*beginning with*) ce moment. Carco était mon meilleur ami. Les saisons ont passé, il est toujours mon ami. Le poisson rouge me semblait le symbole de cette amitié. Après bien des années, je continuais de m'attacher à ce poisson, n'ayant que la crainte de le voir mourir un jour.

Il y avait plus de vingt ans qu'il vivait chez Carco. D'après le proverbe: "Petit poisson deviendra* grand." Mais non, mon poisson avait toujours la même dimension.

Un jour que (*when*) Carco était à Tournay, j'ai reçu* un télégramme qui m'invitait à venir le voir. En entrant dans sa maisonnette, quelle surprise m'attendait! Sur la table était mon poisson qui vivait toujours.

—Tu vois, je l'ai amené.

Nous passions les journées les plus agréables du monde à ne rien faire[12] ou à pêcher à la ligne. Mais voilà qu'un soir, après dîner, comme nous rentrions de promenade je pousse un cri. Le vase était vide.

—Où est le poisson? ai-je demandé.

—Où est le poisson? a demandé Carco.

Mon ami interroge Mariette, sa vieille servante, qui lui répond bien calmement:

—Que Monsieur se figure . . . (*Imagine, Sir*); tout à l'heure, pendant que je mettais le couvert,[13] le chat, avec sa patte, l'a pêché. Il y a longtemps qu'il rôdait (*was prowling*) autour. Pourtant le poisson avait échappé à son ennemi et sautillait (*was hopping*) sur la table. J'ai chassé le chat, puis j'ai pensé qu'un jour ou l'autre il finirait par l'attraper . . .

—Et alors?

—Alors, je l'ai ajouté, ce soir, à la friture.

—Ce soir?

—Cela a fait un petit poisson de plus, et bien frais; il était encore vivant quand je l'ai pris.

12 à ne rien faire: *like* ne pas, ne rien *is placed before the infinitive.*

13 mettre le couvert, *to set the table.* Couvert *stands for plates, forks, knives.*

Nous l'avions mangé! Du moins l'un de nous deux l'avait mangé. J'en étais tout mélancolique. Mais mon ami m'a avoué alors:

—Ce poisson, tu penses bien que ce n'était pas le même après vingt ans. Chaque fois que j'allais en voyage, qu'en aurais-je fait?* Quand je revenais* à Paris, j'en achetais un autre, pour toi. Je savais que tu y tenais* (*you were very fond of it*). . . . En vingt ans . . . j'en ai acheté des poissons rouges! . . .

QUESTIONNAIRE

1. Qu'est-ce que l'auteur (*author*) a acheté un soir avant de monter chez son ami Carco? 2. Pourquoi a-t-il fini par consulter la concierge? 3. Quand il s'est promis de revenir le lendemain, quel était son problème? 4. Pourquoi n'a-t-il pas voulu manger des soles au restaurant? 5. Pourquoi était-on surpris en le regardant dans le tramway et dans le métro? 6. Qu'est-ce qu'un jeune enfant a mis dans son vase? 7. Pourquoi a-t-il pris un taxi le lendemain? 8. Pourquoi est-ce que c'est chose périlleuse de transporter un poisson rouge dans une auto? 9. Qu'est-ce qu'il a fait pour trouver de l'eau? 10. Comment le poisson rouge est-il devenu le symbole de son amitié pour Carco? 11. Quand il est allé voir Carco à Tournay quelle surprise l'attendait? 12. Un soir, après dîner, pourquoi a-t-il trouvé le vase vide? 13. Pour quelle raison était-il tout mélancolique? 14. Comment Carco l'a-t-il consolé?

Lesson 25

Future anterior of *parler* and *aller*

Use of the future anterior

Conjunctions requiring the future anterior under certain conditions

Formation of the present participle

Use of the French infinitive instead of the English gerund

CONVERSATION

Le Départ de nos Amis

JEAN: Voici la Gare du Nord!

MARIANNE: Encore une gare!

JEAN: Oui, il y en a une demi-douzaine à Paris. Tous les chemins de fer de l'Europe se rencontrent ici.

MARIANNE: Allons voir si nous trouverons Geneviève et Maurice sur le quai.

LE PORTEUR: Attention, Mademoiselle! Laissez passer, s'il vous plaît.

MARIANNE: Je trouve ces porteurs bien grossiers et bruyants! On les rencontre partout. Ils bousculent tout le monde avec leurs valises et leurs malles!

JEAN: Pas plus qu'ailleurs. Il faut bien que quelqu'un porte les bagages; et s'ils n'étaient pas là pour vous aider, vous le remarqueriez bien davantage.

MARIANNE: A quelle heure partent nos amis?

JEAN: Regardons cette affiche. Non, ce n'est pas l'horaire des trains; ce n'est qu'un avis au public.

MARIANNE: Ah, enfin, les voilà! Geneviève!

GENEVIÈVE: Marianne! Quelle joie! Vous êtes seule?

MARIANNE: Non, Jean est avec moi. Il est en train de lire une affiche. Nous sommes venus vous dire adieu et vous souhaiter bon voyage.

GENEVIÈVE: Que c'est gentil à vous d'être venus! C'est nous qui aurions dû aller prendre congé de vous et de votre famille. Vous avez été tous si aimables pour nous. Mais passons sur le quai. Notre train part dans dix minutes. Voilà notre voiture.

MARIANNE: Vous voyagez en première?

GENEVIÈVE: Non, en wagon-lit.

MARIANNE: Quel chic! Et il y a un wagon-restaurant tout à côté de votre voiture. Ça sera très commode!

GENEVIÈVE: Ma foi, oui! Nous avons pris le petit déjeuner assez tard ce matin. Nous dînerons dans le train avant d'arriver.

MARIANNE: Vous nous donnerez de vos nouvelles dès que vous serez arrivés à Amsterdam, n'est-ce pas?

GENEVIÈVE: Bien entendu! Nous vous enverrons une dépêche aussitôt que nous serons descendus du train. Allons, ne soyez pas triste! Après tout, on se dit au revoir et pas adieu. Nous reviendrons le plus tôt possible.

MARIANNE: C'est vrai. Amsterdam n'est pas tellement loin.

LE CONDUCTEUR: En voiture!

GENEVIÈVE: Encore une fois, au revoir!

MARIANNE: Au revoir, Geneviève! Bon voyage!

VOCABULAIRE ET EXPRESSIONS

le nord the north

le sud, le midi the south

l'est (*masc.*) the east

l'ouest (*masc.*) the west

le train the train
l'horaire (*masc.*) **des trains** the timetable
la voiture the railroad coach
le compartiment the compartment
le wagon-lit the sleeping-car
le wagon-restaurant the dining car
le fer the iron
le chemin de fer the railroad
le quai the platform
le porteur the porter
les bagages (*masc.*) the baggage
la malle the trunk
la valise the suitcase
l'affiche (*fem.*) the notice, the poster
l'avis (*masc.*) the notice
le petit déjeuner the breakfast
le chien the dog
la joie the joy

gros (*fem.* **grosse**) big, large
dur hard
triste sad
propre clean
commode comfortable
aimable kind

réussir à to succeed in
travailler to work
remarquer to notice
causer to talk, chat
aider to help
souhaiter to wish

un (une) autre another (a different one)
encore un (une) another (one more)
bon (pour) kind (to)
loin far, far away
après (que) after
adieu farewell
dès que, aussitôt que as soon as
tant que as long as
bien davantage much more

être en train de faire to be (in the act of) doing
laissez passer gangway!
avis (au public) public notice
dire adieu à, faire ses adieux à to say goodbye to
que c'est gentil à vous how kind it is of you
prendre congé de to take leave of
donnez-moi de vos nouvelles let me hear from you
le plus tôt possible, au plus tôt as soon as possible
en voiture! all aboard!
bon voyage! have a good trip!

VOCABULAIRE SUPPLÉMENTAIRE

le public the public
l'art (*masc.*) the art
grossier (*fem.* **grossière**) rude
bruyant noisy
bousculer to push, to shove
tellement so

VERBES

The Future Anterior

j'aurai parlé I shall have spoken
tu auras parlé you will have spoken
il (elle) aura parlé he (she) will have spoken
nous aurons parlé we shall have spoken
vous aurez parlé you will have spoken
ils (elles) auront parlé they will have spoken

je serai allé(e) I shall have gone
tu seras allé(e) you will have gone
il sera allé he will have gone
elle sera allée she will have gone
nous serons allés(es) we shall have gone
vous serez allé(e)(s)(es) you will have gone
ils seront allés they will have gone
elles seront allées they will have gone

aussitôt qu'il m'aura écrit, je partirai as soon as he has written me, I shall leave
après que je serai arrivé, je vous écrirai After I have arrived, I shall write you
dès qu'ils se seront rencontrés, ils rentreront dans leur pays as soon as they have met, they will return to their countries

→ The future anterior corresponds in form to the English future perfect. In English, the latter is seldom used, being replaced by the present perfect ("after I have arrived" rather than "after I shall have arrived"). In French, the future anterior must be used after certain conjunctions if future perfect time is implied; that is, to indicate an action which is future to the present, but past with respect to another future action.

The most frequently used conjunctions requiring the future anterior under these circumstances are: *quand, lorsque* (when); *aussitôt que, dès que* (as soon as); *après que* (after); *tant que* (as long as).

je le verrai quand il viendra I shall see him when he comes
tant qu'il restera ici, je resterai avec lui as long as he stays here, I shall stay with him

→ The same conjunctions take the future where English uses the present to indicate future time.

The Present Participle

parler to speak Imperfect **parlais** Present Participle **parlant**
vendre to sell Imperfect **vendais** Present Participle **vendant**
finir to finish Imperfect **finissais** Present Participle **finissant**
voir to see Imperfect **voyais** Present Participle **voyant**
prendre to take Imperfect **prenais** Present Participle **prenant**
dire to say Imperfect **disais** Present Participle **disant**
devoir to owe Imperfect **devais** Present Participle **devant**
boire to drink Imperfect **buvais** Present Participle **buvant**
lire to read Imperfect **lisais** Present Participle **lisant**
écrire to write Imperfect **écrivais** Present Participle **écrivant**
faire to do Imperfect **faisais** Present Participle **faisant**
s'asseoir to sit down Imperfect **m'asseyais** Present Participle **s'asseyant**
rire to laugh Imperfect **riais** Present Participle **riant**
connaître to know Imperfect **connaissais** Present Participle **connaissant**
être to be Imperfect **étais** Present Participle **étant**

→ To form the present participle of any verb, regular or irregular, drop the *-ais* of the imperfect and add *-ant*.

Exceptions: **savoir** to know Impf. **savais** Pres. part. **sachant**
avoir to have Impf. **avais** Pres. part. **ayant**

en causant, nous sommes sortis while talking, we went out
il a réussi **en travaillant** comme un esclave he succeeded by working like a slave

il a répondu en riant he answered laughing
elle est partie en courant she left running
voilà un étudiant **faisant** (qui fait) ses devoirs there is a student doing his homework
j'ai vu une femme **portant** (qui portait) un grand paquet I saw a woman carrying a large package

→ The French present participle is translated by the English participle in *-ing,* but has a limited use.

Preceded by the preposition *en,* it often translates the English gerund with or without "by" or "while," but in that case must always qualify the subject.

voilà des animaux vivants there are some living animals

→ It is occasionally used as an adjective, like the English participle, in which case it agrees.

elle est charmante she is charming
quelle histoire amusante! what an amusing story!

→ It often becomes a real adjective.

je parle I am speaking
nous travaillons we are working

→ It is *never* used with the verb "to be" to form a progressive conjugation.

The Infinitive after Prepositions

l'art de parler the art of speaking
il m'a regardé sans parler he looked at me without speaking
elle était en train de lire she was (in the act of) reading

→ After all prepositions *except en,* the part of the verb used in French is the infinitive, not the present participle.

parler est un art speaking is an art
écrire en français est difficile writing in French is difficult

→ The infinitive is used in French where a gerund is used in English as the subject of a sentence.

QUESTIONS

1. Y a-t-il beaucoup de gares à Paris? 2. Pourquoi? 3. Quelle opinion Marianne a-t-elle des porteurs? 4. Quelle réponse Jean lui fait-il? 5. Pourquoi Jean et Marianne sont-ils venus à la gare? 6. Est-ce que leurs amis sont contents? 7. Comment vont-ils voyager? 8. Qu'est-ce qui se trouve tout à côté de leur voiture? 9. Quelle est leur destination? 10. Que feront-ils quand ils arriveront à destination?

EXERCICES

A. *Continuez la conjugaison:*

1. Aussitôt que j'aurai écrit ces lettres je partirai. 2. Après que je serai arrivé, je vous écrirai. 3. Lorsque je lui aurai parlé, j'irai chez vous. 4. Dès que j'aurai acheté ce livre, je vous le passerai. 5. Je le verrai quand il viendra.

B. *Donnez le participe présent de chacun des verbes suivants:*

parler, prendre, finir, voir, vendre, dire, devoir, boire, lire, écrire, faire, s'asseoir, rire, connaître, être, avoir, savoir, servir, donner, rendre.

C. *Remplacez le tiret par un participe présent:*

1. En ________ il m'a dit qu'il allait en France. 2. En ________ ces livres à bon marché, vous perdrez beaucoup. 3. En ________ son travail, il a eu le temps de fumer une pipe. 4. En ________ un taxi, vous arriverez plus tôt. 5. En ________ vos devoirs tous les jours, vous apprendrez mieux. 6. En ________ ce livre vous trouverez que l'auteur écrit très bien. 7. En ________ du lait tous les jours vous deviendrez plus fort. 8. En ________ cela, il m'a quitté brusquement. 9. En ________ son amie pour la dernière fois, elle a pleuré. 10. En ________, il a remarqué qu'il occupait la dernière place.

D. *Remplacez le mot en italique par le participe présent ou l'infinitif:*

1. Il m'a regardé sans *speaking*. 2. *Speaking* est un art. 3. *Answering* n'est pas difficile. 4. *Seeing*, c'est croire. 5. *Knowing* la répu-

tation de l'homme, il a refusé d'aller le voir. 6. Tout en *laughing,* il a accepté le cadeau. 7. *Being* amis, ils se sont souvent écrit. 8. *Having* trop d'argent, il en donnait aux pauvres. 9. *Owing* tant d'argent lui semblait dangereux. 10. *Eating* est souvent un plaisir.

THÈME

MARIANNE: At what time does the train leave? Have you looked at the timetable? From what platform does the train leave?

PAUL: Don't ask me so many questions. Go get a porter to (*pour*) help us cross the tracks (*les voies*) with our luggage. That must be the train over there.

MARIANNE: Well! Here's a porter! Do you know what compartment we have? Did you reserve our seats?

PAUL: Yes, here are the tickets. We are traveling first class in the sleeper. Porter, will you please take us there?

PORTER: Where are you going? To Marseilles? The train for Marseilles is an hour late. Do you want to wait on the platform?

PAUL: Take my baggage to the platform and we shall go to the waiting room (*la salle d'attente*) later.

MARIANNE: This train for Marseilles is always late. Why didn't you get tickets for a different train? I am exhausted. I want to sit down. I'll go to the waiting room.

Lesson 26

Present indicative, past participle, and imperfect of *conduire*

Use of *en* with the present participle

Past infinitive with *après*

Other uses of past infinitive

Use of *pour* before an infinitive

***De* with an infinitive depending upon a noun**

***À* or *de* with an infinitive depending upon an adjective**

Verbs requiring *à*, *de*, or no preposition before an infinitive

Il est facile de, ce travail est facile à . . .

CONVERSATION

En Auto

ANNA: Emmeline, je suis fatiguée. Ayez la bonté de conduire.

EMMELINE: Avec plaisir. Je vais vous remplacer au volant.

ANNA: Vous allez bien lentement.

EMMELINE: C'est que je ne peux m'empêcher d'avoir un peu peur sur ces routes de campagne. Elles sont si étroites! De plus, elles sont souvent mouillées, ou bien couvertes de poussière. Et les autos américaines sont si larges!

ANNA: Est-ce que vous auriez préféré aller par le train?

EMMELINE: Non, je préfère aller en automobile. Je reconnais que j'ai tort de m'énerver. Ici, à la campagne, il n'y a ni tramways ni autobus pour me déranger, comme en ville.

ANNA: Tenez la droite un peu plus. Et attention aux vaches! Servez-vous de vos freins dans les descentes.

EMMELINE: Je vais essayer. Oh, regardez ce petit village là-bas, dans les champs, au pied de la montagne!

ANNA: Ce n'est pas une montagne. Ce n'est qu'une colline.

EMMELINE: Je ne vais pas discuter la géographie du pays. Que c'est joli! Cette herbe verte, ces fleurs, ce petit lac, la forêt à notre gauche, pleine d'oiseaux, les arbres, les rochers! Quel charme!

ANNA: Oui, mais n'oubliez pas le chemin. Il faut prendre la route à droite après avoir passé ce carrefour qui est là-bas devant nous. Et faites attention à cette charrette à foin qui encombre la route. Ainsi nous n'aurons rien à regretter.

EMMELINE: Savez-vous ce qu'on vous appellerait en Amérique? Un "back-seat driver." Au lieu de jouir des beautés de la nature, les "back-seat drivers" ne songent qu'à critiquer ceux qui conduisent. Mais, dites-moi, est-ce que nous sommes encore très loin de Bourges?

ANNA: Non, la ville est là-bas, sur cette colline qui domine ces petites rivières. Regardez ces arbres tout autour de la ville. Parmi ces maisons nous trouverons celle de nos amis. Dans quelques minutes nous serons chez eux. Après avoir déjeuné, nous repartirons pour Paris. Ainsi nous serons rentrées avant la tombée de la nuit.

VOCABULAIRE ET EXPRESSIONS

le tramway the streetcar
l'autobus (*masc.*) the bus
le frein the brake
le carrefour the intersection
le village the village
le pays the country, countryside

la montagne the mountain
la colline the hill
l'arbre (*masc.*) the tree
l'oiseau (*masc.; pl.* **oiseaux**) the bird
l'herbe (*fem.*) the grass
la fleur the flower
la forêt, le bois the wood
la rivière the (small) river, stream
la poussière the dust
le pied the foot
la tombée de la nuit nightfall

agité nervous, upset
mouillé wet
plein (de) full (of), filled (with)
couvert (de) covered (with)
rond round

espérer to hope **(j'espère)**
s'énerver to be (to get) nervous
traduire to translate
frapper to strike, knock
défendre (de) to forbid (to)
apprendre (à) to learn (to), to teach (to)
cesser (de) to stop (doing something), to cease
se servir de to use, make use of

à travers across, through
derrière behind, back of
parmi among
ainsi thus, so, that way
au lieu de instead of
autour de around
ou bien or else

ayez la bonté de have the kindness to, please
critiquer quelqu'un to criticize somebody
attention à careful with
faites attention à pay attention to, watch out for
aller (par le train, à pied, à cheval, en auto, en bateau, en voiture) to go (by train, on foot, on horseback, by car, by boat, by carriage)

VOCABULAIRE SUPPLEMENTAIRE

le volant the steering-wheel
le lac the lake
le rocher the rock
le charme the charm
la beauté the beauty
la bonté the kindness
la géographie the geography
la descente the down-grade
le conducteur the driver
la charrette the wagon
le foin the hay
la vache the cow

remplacer to replace **(nous remplaçons)**
jouir de to enjoy
discuter to discuss
regretter to regret

déranger to trouble, disturb, bother **(nous dérangeons)**
songer (à) to think of **(nous songeons)**
encombrer to fill up, to encumber

possible possible

impossible impossible

VERBES

Present Indicative of **conduire** (to lead, to drive)

je conduis
tu conduis
il (elle) conduit
nous conduisons
vous conduisez
ils (elles) conduisent

Past participle: **conduit** Imperfect: **conduisais**

Like *conduire,* conjugate all verbs ending in *-duire,* such as *traduire,* to translate; *produire,* to produce; *déduire,* to deduce, etc.

GRAMMAIRE

Infinitive and Past Infinitive after Prepositions

je suis fatigué de conduire I am tired of driving
il est entré sans frapper he came in without knocking
il est prêt à partir he is ready to leave
avant d'entrer, il faut frapper before coming in, you must knock

→ The form of the verb regularly used after prepositions in French is the infinitive.

il est sorti en parlant he went out talking

→ The preposition *en,* meaning "by" or "while," requires the present participle.

après avoir mangé, il s'est couché after eating, he lay down
après être sorti, il est rentré after going out, he came in again

→ The preposition *après,* meaning "after," requires the past infinitive. This consists of the infinitive of *avoir* (or *être*) plus the past participle of the verb.

il est parti **sans avoir mangé** he left without eating
elle est sortie **avant d'avoir répondu** she went out before answering

→ The past infinitive is also used after other prepositions when past time is implied.

il faut travailler pour réussir you must work in order to succeed

→ *Pour* is used to translate "in order to" or "to" in the sense of "in order to" before an infinitive.

ayez la bonté de me dire have the kindness to tell me

→ An infinitive depending on a noun with the definite article is usually preceded by *de.*

je suis prêt à partir I am ready to leave
je serai très content de le faire I shall be very happy to do it

→ An infinitive depending on an adjective is preceded by a preposition, usually *à* or *de.*

cet exercice est **facile à traduire** this exercise is easy to translate
il (c')est difficile de traduire cet exercice it is hard to translate this exercise
ce travail **est impossible à faire** this work is impossible to do
il (c')est possible de faire ce travail it is possible to do this work

→ With *facile, difficile, possible, impossible, and other adjectives,* use *à* before the infinitive if there is a real subject. If the subject is an impersonal "it," use *de.*

Theoretically, *il* is used for an impersonal "it" and *ce* for a specific subject. Colloquially, however, the impersonal *il* is often replaced by *ce.*

il m'a permis de le faire he allowed me to do it
je lui ai promis de le faire I promised him to do it
il s'est dépêché de le faire he hurried to do it
je lui ai demandé de le faire I asked him to do it

je lui ai défendu de le faire I forbade him to do it
j'ai essayé de le faire I tried to do it
j'ai oublié de le faire I forgot to do it
j'ai fini de le faire I finished doing it
cessez de le faire stop doing it
j'accepte de le faire I accept to do it
je refuse de le faire I refuse to do it
j'ai offert de le faire I offered to do it
je lui ai dit de le faire I told him to do it
je l'ai prié de le faire I begged him to do it

→ *Permettre, promettre, se dépêcher, demander, défendre, essayer, oublier, finir, cesser, accepter, refuser, offrir, dire, prier,* and many other verbs, require *de* before a following infinitive.

il demande à le faire he asks to do it
j'aime à le faire I like to do it
j'ai appris à le faire I learned to do it
je lui ai appris à le faire I taught him to do it
je l'ai aidé à le faire I helped him to do it
j'ai cherché à le faire I tried to do it
je me suis mis à le faire I began to do it
il continue à le faire he goes on doing it
j'ai réussi à le faire I managed to do it, I succeeded in doing it

→ *Demander* (when you are asking to do something yourself), *aimer, apprendre, aider, chercher, se mettre, continuer, réussir* require *à* before a following infinitive.

Verbs Followed by Infinitive without Preposition

je dois le faire I should, must, have to do it
je sais le faire I know how to do it
je veux le faire I want to do it
je peux le faire I am able to do it
je désire le faire I desire to do it
je préfère le faire I prefer to do it
je vais le faire I am going to do it
j'espère le faire I hope to do it

→*Devoir, savoir, pouvoir, vouloir, désirer, préférer, aller, espérer* take the infinitive directly, without a preposition.

QUESTIONS

1. Pourquoi Anna ne veut-elle plus conduire? 2. Qui la remplace au volant? 3. Pourquoi Emmeline conduit-elle lentement? 4. Quels sont les dangers quand on conduit en ville? 5. Quels sont les dangers quand on conduit à la campagne? 6. Pourquoi une promenade en auto à la campagne est-elle charmante? 7. De quelle ville les amies approchent-elles? 8. Pendant combien de temps vont-elles rester chez leurs amis? 9. Où iront-elles ensuite? 10. Quand espèrent-elles rentrer chez elles?

EXERCICES

A. *Conjuguez les verbes dans les phrases suivantes:*

1. Je conduis mon père à la gare tous les jours. 2. Je conduisais mon auto à toute vitesse quand l'agent de police m'a arrêté. 3. Je traduirai mon devoir. 4. J'ai produit les preuves demandées. 5. Si j'avais le temps, je les conduirais chez eux.

B. *Traduisez les mots anglais:*

1. Avant de *going out,* il faut dire au revoir à tout le monde. 2. Nous avons travaillé sans *stopping.* 3. Il ne faut jamais entrer sans *knocking.* 4. N'êtes-vous pas fatigué de *driving?* 5. Après *knocking,* elle est entrée. 6. Après *coming in,* elle s'est assise. 7. Avant de *going out,* il a dit bonsoir.

C. *Remplacez le tiret par la préposition qui convient:*

1. Il faut manger ———— vivre. 2. Veuillez avoir la bonté ———— me passer le pain. 3. Elle sera prête ———— partir dans dix minutes. 4. Je suis très content ———— vous voir. 5. Il me promet ———— venir tous les jours. 6. Le médecin me permet ———— sortir maintenant tous les jours. 7. Dépêchez-vous ———— descendre. 8. Ne me demandez pas ———— vous accompagner. 9. Il a appris ———— étudier. 10. Il a offert ———— m'aider. 11. Il m'a aidé ———— monter la malle. 12. Il n'a pas réussi

———— le faire. 13. Je refuse ———— vous donner cet argent. 14. Cessez ———— me tourmenter. 15. Avez-vous vraiment cherché ———— faire votre devoir?

D. *Complétez les phrases en ajoutant un infinitif ou une préposition avec l'infinitif:*

1. Je l'ai prié ————. 2. Il continue ————. 3. Je sais ————. 4. Je désire ————. 5. Il a fini ————. 6. Il lui a appris ————. 7. Nous lui avons dit ————. 8. Avez-vous essayé ————. 9. Il peut ————. 10. Il s'est mis————. 11. Pourquoi lui avez-vous défendu ————. 12. Je préfère ————. 13. Il est difficile ————. 14. Tout ceci est impossible ————. 15. Ce livre est amusant ————.

THÈME

—Won't you please drive the car? I'm exhausted.

—Of course. Get up and give me the wheel. I shall drive slowly.

—Yes, please. I am very nervous, today. I am afraid on these narrow mountain roads. In the morning they are quite wet.

—Perhaps you prefer to travel by autobus or by train?

—Oh, no! But be careful. Keep to the left. Use your brakes more often.

—What pretty flowers on that hill!

—Don't look at the flowers and the trees. Look at the road. A chauffeur drives his car; he doesn't look at the beauties of nature.

—How nervous you are! I am going to stop and you can take the wheel again.

—Oh! Excuse me. Continue to drive, please. I shall say nothing more.

Lesson 27

Present indicative and past participle of *vivre*

Present indicative and past participle of *mourir*

Use of definite article with parts of the body

Use of possessive adjective or indirect object pronoun with parts of the body

Use of *faire mal à, se faire mal, avoir mal à*

CONVERSATION

La Visite du Médecin

LE MÉDECIN: Qu'avez-vous, mon garçon?

GASTON: J'ai mal à la tête, Monsieur le docteur, puis j'ai des douleurs dans le dos et dans la poitrine.

LE MÉDECIN: Voyons d'abord si vous avez de la fièvre. Non, votre pouls est normal. Ôtez votre veston et écoutons un peu le cœur et les poumons.

GASTON: Oui, Monsieur le docteur.

LE MÉDECIN: Tiens! Où avez-vous reçu cette blessure?

GASTON: J'ai été blessé pendant la guerre. Un fragment d'obus dans l'épaule, un autre à la jambe droite au-dessus du genou, un troisième dans le cou. Rien de sérieux. . . . J'ai passé un mois à l'hôpital à bavarder avec les infirmières et à avaler des médicaments. Après, je suis retourné au régiment, mais je suis tombé malade tout de suite et il a fallu me renvoyer à l'hôpital.

LE MÉDECIN: Et cette brûlure au menton et à la lèvre?

GASTON: Ça, je l'ai attrapée aux États-Unis dans une collision d'autos. Ça aussi m'a valu un mois à l'hôpital. J'avais le visage complètement couvert de pansements. Je me regardais dans le miroir, et je ne voyais plus ni front, ni bouche, ni cheveux, ni oreilles, ni joues, ni gorge. Un de ces jours, je vais laisser pousser ma moustache et ma barbe, et ça cachera les cicatrices. D'ailleurs, elles ne sont pas très profondes.

LE MÉDECIN: Toussez un peu, s'il vous plaît.

GASTON: Je tousse toujours un peu. Ce sont ces sacrées cigarettes que je fume sans arrêt.

LE MÉDECIN: Essayez le cigare. C'est moins mauvais pour la santé. Est-ce que vous avez mal au bras gauche? Vous avez de la difficulté à le remuer.

GASTON: Ça, c'est encore une petite blessure de guerre. Une balle allemande qui m'a traversé le bras un peu au-dessous du coude, mais sans briser l'os. Pendant un mois j'ai eu de la difficulté à remuer les doigts, mais à présent ça va assez bien.

LE MÉDECIN: La peau est toujours un peu enflée au dessous du poignet. Pas de maux d'estomac? Jamais mal aux dents? Montrez la langue.

GASTON: Voilà, Docteur.

LE MÉDECIN: Eh bien! Ce n'est qu'un petit rhume. Voici une ordonnance qu'on vous préparera à la pharmacie qui se trouve en face de mon bureau. Une pilule toutes les trois heures. Vous ne serez pas vraiment malade cette fois. Ne vous fatiguez pas trop. Faites attention de ne pas trop fumer.

GASTON: Merci bien, Monsieur le docteur. Au revoir.

LE MÉDECIN: Au revoir, mon garçon.

VOCABULAIRE ET EXPRESSIONS

le cœur the heart
la tête the head
le dos the back
la dent the tooth
le cou the neck
le genou (*pl*- **genoux**) the knee

la poitrine the chest, breast
le coude the elbow
le doigt the finger
l'ongle (*masc.*) the nail
le menton the chin
le visage the face
les cheveux (*masc.*) the hair
la lèvre the lip
la bouche the mouth
l'oreille (*fem.*) the ear
la gorge the throat
la joue the cheek
la moustache the mustache
l'épaule (*fem.*) the shoulder
la jambe the leg
le bras the arm
le poignet the wrist
la barbe the beard
le corps the body
la peau the skin
l'estomac (*masc.*) the stomach
la langue the tongue
l'os (*masc.*) the bone (pronounce the *s* in the sing., but not in the plural, **les os**)
la cicatrice the scar
la toux the cough
la fièvre the fever
la brûlure the burn
l'infirmière (*fem.*) the nurse
le médicament the medicine
le pansement the bandage
l'ordonnance (*fem.*) the prescription
l'hôpital (*masc.*) the hospital
le cigare the cigar
le tabac the tobacco
la cigarette the cigarette

profond deep
sacré (*slang*) confounded, darned

tomber (*être*) to fall
fumer to smoke
attraper to catch
pousser to push, grow
renvoyer to send back (**je renvoie;** fut. **je renverrai**)

qu'avez-vous? what is the matter with you?
au cours de, pendant during
au dessus de above
au dessous de below, beneath
à tout instant at every moment
faites-moi voir show me
avoir soin de to take care of
avoir mal à to have a —ache
faire mal à to hurt

VOCABULAIRE SUPPLÉMENTAIRE

le pouls the pulse
le poumon the lung
le front the forehead
le veston the coat, the jacket

le miroir the mirror
la balle the bullet
l'obus (*masc.*) the shell (cannon)
le fragment the fragment
le régiment the regiment
la pharmacie the drug store
la pilule the pill
la collision the collision

sérieux (*fem.* **sérieuse**) serious
enflé swollen
dangereux (*fem.* **dangereuse**) dangerous
blesser to wound
tousser to cough
avaler to swallow
traverser to pierce, cross
remuer to move, stir
bavarder to chat, "chew the rag"

VERBES

Present Indicative of **vivre** (to live) *p.p.* **vécu**

je vis	**nous vivons**
tu vis	**vous vivez**
il (elle) vit	**ils (elles) vivent**

Present Indicative of **mourir** (to die) *p.p.* **mort**

je meurs	**nous mourons**
tu meurs	**vous mourez**
il (elle) meurt	**ils (elles) meurent**

Future: **je mourrai** Conditional: **je mourrais. Mourir** is conjugated with *être* in the compound tenses **(il est mort; ils sont morts).**

GRAMMAIRE

Idiomatic Possessive Forms

donnez-moi la main give me your hand
montrez-moi la langue show me your tongue

→ With parts of the body, the definite article is generally used instead of the possessive when there is no doubt as to the possessor.

la balle a traversé son bras the bullet pierced his arm
la balle lui a traversé le bras the bullet pierced his arm
il s'est cassé le bras he broke his arm

→ If the possessor of the part of the body must be indicated, use either the possessive adjective or an indirect object pronoun (which may be a reflexive) before the verb.

Faire mal (à)—Se faire mal (à)—Avoir mal (à)

il m'a fait mal he hurt me
il m'a fait mal au doigt he hurt my finger
je me suis fait mal au pied I hurt my foot

→ "To hurt" is *faire mal à* (*lit.* to do harm to). "To hurt oneself" is *se faire mal* (to do harm to oneself). The part of the body that is hurt takes *à* with the definite article.

j'ai mal à la tête I have a headache
j'ai mal aux dents. I have a toothache
j'ai mal à l'épaule I have a pain in the shoulder

→ "To have a —ache" is *avoir mal à.*

QUESTIONS

1. Où Gaston a-t-il mal? 2. Comment le médecin découvre-t-il que Gaston n'a pas de fièvre? 3. Gaston a-t-il été blessé à la guerre? 4. Quand il est retourné au régiment, qu'est-ce qui lui est arrivé? 5. Quelle expérience Gaston a-t-il eue en auto? 6. Comment Gaston va-t-il cacher la cicatrice qu'il a à la figure? 7. Pourquoi tousse-t-il? 8. Quel conseil le médecin lui donne-t-il? 9. Quelles blessures Gaston a-t-il au bras? 10. Quand le médecin découvre que Gaston a un rhume, comment le soigne-t-il?

EXERCICES

A. *Continuez la conjugaison:*

1. Je vis seule avec mon père. 2. J'ai vécu loin de la ville. 3. Je vivrai jusqu'à cent ans. 4. Je vivais à la campagne.

B. *Traduisez les formes suivantes:*

1. he dies 2. we are dying 3. I am dying 4. I shall die 5. they

died 6. you are dying 7. she died 8. they would die 9. they will die 10. they are dying

C. *Traduisez les phrases suivantes:*

1. Have you a toothache? 2. Yes, I have a toothache. 3. John hurt my finger. 4. Stop! You're hurting me. 5. Her shoulder hurts, help her. 6. Show me your hand. 7. Shake hands with me. 8. A bullet pierced his shoulder. 9. She hurt her foot. 10. I hurt his finger. 11. Show me your tongue. 12. Have you a headache? 13. Does your head hurt? 14. His back hurts.

D. *Faites la description d'un ami en vous servant des mots suivants:*

le dos, le cou, le menton, le visage, les cheveux, la tête, les dents, les lèvres, la joue, le nez, la peau, la bouche, l'épaule, la poitrine, les os.

THÈME

—What's the matter? You seem to be sick?

—I have a headache!

—Why don't you go to the doctor? Perhaps you have a fever.

—I must have a cold. I have pains in the back and chest.

—Let me see if your pulse is normal. I think I ought to call the doctor.

(An hour later when the doctor arrives)

—Show me your tongue. Let me see your throat. It is quite red. Are you coughing very much? Come, let me feel your pulse. You have a little fever. You will have to go to bed. Your cheek seems to be swollen, too. Does it hurt?

—Yes. Perhaps I have a small abscess (*un abcès*). I wanted to go to the dentist's today but I felt too ill. How long do you think I shall be sick?

—About a week. I shall give you a prescription. Send someone to the drug store near my office. Do not smoke for a week and drink lots of water. When you get this prescription, take one of these pills every hour. Are your war wounds hurting you much these days?

—No, only the bullet in my arm above the elbow. I cannot move my wrist. I don't know why.

—That's strange. I'll examine you again when your cold is better. Meanwhile, rest as much as you can.

Lesson 28

Present indicative, past participle, and imperfect of *convaincre*

Present indicative, past participle, and imperfect of *joindre*

Formation of the passive

Use of the passive with *par* and *de*

Use of *on* with an active verb as a substitute for the passive

Use of the reflexive as a substitute for the passive

Noun with *de* instead of noun used as adjective in English

Use of *à* with noun to indicate purpose

Use of definite article with abstract and generic nouns

CONVERSATION

Un Roman policier

FRÉDÉRIQUE: Qu'est-ce que vous lisez, Paul?

PAUL: Un roman policier, intitulé *Arsène Lupin,* et écrit par Maurice Leblanc. C'est vraiment épatant.

FRÉDÉRIQUE: Vraiment? Est-ce aussi passionnant que notre *Dick Tracy* ou que *Sherlock Holmes?*

PAUL: Mais oui. Je suis arrivé au point où la maison de pierre où se sont réfugiés les voleurs est assiégée par les agents de police, dirigés par Arsène. Celui-ci, qui est soupçonné d'être lui-même un bandit, avait été arrêté auparavant par les agents. Mais il a finalement réussi à convaincre l'inspecteur de police, qui se laisse conduire à la maison des voleurs.

FRÉDÉRIQUE: Tout seul?

PAUL: Non; il est accompagné d'un grand nombre de ses hommes, et suivi à distance par un peloton de gendarmes. Il le faut, car les voleurs sont nombreux et bien armés.

FRÉDÉRIQUE: Et alors?

PAUL: Dès que l'édifice a été complètement entouré par les agents, Arsène y pénètre au moyen d'une échelle de corde. Il manque d'être tué par le chef de la bande, qui fait feu sur lui. Il se sauve et rejoint les agents, qui viennent à son secours. Puis on fait sauter la porte à la dynamite. Les agents et les gendarmes entrent. Il y a un échange de coups de feu entre les bandits et les agents. Le chef des voleurs et la plupart de ses copains sont tués. Les autres se rendent. Arsène Lupin et la loi triomphent encore une fois.

FRÉDÉRIQUE: Magnifique!

PAUL: Il faut le lire pour l'apprécier. Ça prouve, pour emprunter une phrase à nos romans policiers d'Amérique, que "le crime est toujours puni."

VOCABULAIRE ET EXPRESSIONS

le voleur the thief
la loi the law
le gendarme the trooper (similar to our State police)
le copain the pal
le secours the help, aid
la tasse the cup
le nombre the number (use **numéro** for a specific number, as "number 6")
l'échange (*masc.*) the exchange
la pierre the stone
l'échelle (*fem.*) the ladder
la corde the rope

vaincre to win, conquer
convaincre to convince
manquer to miss
manquer de + *inf.*, to fail to . . . , to miss . . .

joindre to join, unite
rejoindre to join again
entourer to surround
tuer to kill

cependant nevertheless, however
au moyen de by means of

contre against
à distance at a distance
auparavant previously

se laisser conduire to let oneself be led
faire sauter to blow up
faire feu to fire (shoot)

faire feu sur to shoot at
au secours! help!
au secours de to the help of
mais oui of course it is

VOCABULAIRE SUPPLÉMENTAIRE

le roman the novel
le bandit the bandit
l'inspecteur (*masc.*) the inspector
le chef the chief
la compagnie the company
la bande the band
la dynamite the dynamite
le peloton the platoon

le coup de feu the shot
le crime the crime
la machine the machine
la machine à écrire the typewriter
l'édifice (*masc.*) the building, the structure
le thé the tea

policier (*fem.* **policière**) police, detective (as an adjective)
passionnant exciting

nombreux (*fem.* **nombreuse**) numerous
fidèle faithful

intituler to entitle
assiéger to besiege **(j'assiège, nous assiégeons)**
soupçonner to suspect
armer to arm
se réfugier to take shelter

arrêter to arrest
pénétrer to penetrate **(je pénètre)**
se sauver to escape
apprécier to appreciate
triompher to triumph
diriger to direct **(nous dirigeons)**

VERBES

Present Indicative of **convaincre** (to convince)

je convaincs	**nous convainquons**
tu convaincs	**vous convainquez**
il (elle) convainc	**ils (elles) convainquent**

Imperfect: **je convainquais** Past participle: **convaincu.**
Like *convaincre,* conjugate ***vaincre,*** to win, conquer, overcome.

Present Indicative of **joindre** (to join, unite)

je joins	**nous joignons**
tu joins	**vous joignez**
il joint	**ils joignent**

Imperfect: **je joignais** Past participle: **joint.**
Like *joindre,* conjugate ***rejoindre,*** to rejoin; ***peindre,*** to paint.

The Passive Voice

je suis invité I am invited
j'étais invité I was invited
je serai invité I shall be invited
je serais invité I would be invited
j'ai été invité I have been invited, I was invited
j'avais été invité I had been invited
j'aurai été invité I shall have been invited
j'aurais été invité I would have been invited

→ The passive is formed in French, as in English, by using the auxiliary "to be" with the past participle. The latter agrees with the subject (***il a été invité,*** *elle a été invitée, ils ont été invités, elles ont **été invitées***).

le voleur a été arrêté par les agents the thief was arrested by the police
le garçon sera puni par son père the boy will be punished by his father
les enfants sont aimés de leurs parents children are loved by their parents

→ The passive is used in French as in English. "By" is translated by *par* if the action is definite, special, or indicates an unusual relation; by *de* if the action is vague or habitual. *Par* is used in most cases.

la maison est entourée d'arbres the house is surrounded by trees
la maison a été entourée par les agents the house was surrounded by the police
il était suivi de (or **par**) **ses hommes** he was followed by his men
il a été suivi par son père he was followed by his father
il est accompagné de (or **par**) **sa mère** he is accompanied by his mother
il sera accompagné par ses sœurs he will be accompanied by his sisters

→ With some verbs, either preposition may be used; in these cases, *par* tends to indicate a true passive action, *de* a static condition or a description.

Use of **on**

on m'a donné le livre I was given the book
on m'a dit cela I was told that

→ English often uses a passive construction such as "I was given," "I was told," when it is clear that the past participle (given, told) cannot logically qualify the subject (the logical construction being "the book was given to me," "that was told to me"). This is impossible in French and an *active* construction must be used with the subject *on* (one gave me, one told me). *On* may translate the English one, people, we, you, they used in a general sense.

Use of the Reflexive

le beurre se vendait quatre cents francs le kilo butter was sold at four hundred francs a kilogram

→ The reflexive is also used frequently to replace the passive when "by" is not expressed. The reflexive construction is more frequently used when the subject is an inanimate object.

GRAMMAIRE

Adjective Phrases

une maison de pierre, une maison en pierre a stone house
une échelle de corde a rope ladder

une montre d'or, une montre en or a gold watch
une robe de soie a silk dress

→ To indicate the material of which a thing is made, French never uses a noun as an adjective to modify another noun. The noun of material follows the other noun, with the preposition *de,* sometimes replaced by *en.* This same principle (*de* + *noun*) is extended to many adjective clauses such as *un jour d'été; un jour de pluie; un compagnon de voyage,* etc.

une tasse à thé a teacup
un verre à vin a wine-glass
du papier à écrire writing paper
une machine à écrire a typewriter

→ The preposition *à* indicates the purpose for which a noun is used. Where English uses the gerund, French uses the infinitive with *à.*

QUESTIONS

1. Que lit Paul? 2. A quoi peut-on comparer l'histoire d'Arsène Lupin? 3. Où se sont réfugiés les voleurs? 4. Que font les agents de police? 5. De quoi Arsène Lupin est-il soupçonné? 6. Est-ce que les voleurs sont bien armés? 7. Comment Arsène entre-t-il dans l'édifice? 8. Par qui est-il attaqué et par qui est-il sauvé? 9. Qui est obligé de se rendre? 10. Pourquoi faut-il lire ce roman de Maurice Leblanc?

EXERCICES

A. *Conjuguez:*

1. Je le convaincs de la nécessité de travailler. 2. Je l'ai convaincu de sa faute. 3. J'ai rejoint mon ami au coin de la rue. 4. Je me joins à eux pour finir ce travail. 5. J'ai été arrêté par la police hier soir. 6. Je serais arrêté si je faisais une telle chose. 7. J'ai été arrêté par la sentinelle. 8. J'aurais été arrêté si j'avais fait cela.

B. *Faites une série de phrases au passif en employant les mots suivants:*

1. le voleur, arrêter, les agents de police. 2. la petite fille, punir, sa

mère. 3. la maison, détruire, le feu. 4. le roi, accompagner, les soldats. 5. les enfants, aller à l'école, accompagner, leurs parents. 6. la ville, entourer, d'arbres. 7. les voleurs, suivre, l'homme.

C. *Traduisez:*

1. Eggs sell at fifty cents a dozen. 2. Did you buy a stone house? 3. She just bought a silk dress. 4. His brother gave him a gold watch. 5. There is a rope ladder near that window. 6. We want to buy a half-dozen teacups. 7. What a pretty wine-glass! 8. Haven't you any more writing paper? 9. When I have my new typewriter, I shall write you a letter. 10. Freedom is desired by most men.

THÈME

Everyone was seated in the living room and talking. Suddenly there was a rifle shot (*coup de fusil*) and Henry fell dead. His sister ran to the telephone and called the police. The police questioned everyone present (all those who were) in the building. They suspect a thief who had been arrested a week before and freed without trial (*procès*). He lived in a stone house in the mountains. They laid siege to the house. The police and the thief exchanged several shots. The inspector thought that the bandit was about to (*sur le point de*) surrender when the thief blew up (*a fait sauter*) the door with dynamite. The inspector, sure that the bandit was dead, went into the house to find him. When he entered he found that the thief had escaped by a rope ladder which was attached to a window, back of the house.

Review Lesson 7

EXAMEN

A. *TRADUCTION*

I. Le voyageur va au guichet et demande un billet aller et retour pour Amsterdam. Quand il a son billet il fait enregistrer ses bagages, passe sur le quai et cherche le compartiment de première où il a une place réservée. Il le trouve. Le porteur met ses valises dans le filet. "En voiture," crie le contrôleur. Le train part. Un garçon passe dans les couloirs, criant "Wagon-restaurant. Retenez vos places." "Une place, s'il vous plaît, pour le premier service."

II. C'est un train rapide qui ne s'arrête que rarement. On traverse des villes, des villages, la campagne verte et fertile. Les champs sont très beaux. Sur les collines il y a des vaches qui lèvent un œil étonné en voyant passer le train. Le voyageur consulte un indicateur pour voir si le train est à l'heure. Après deux heures de marche il n'a que dix minutes de retard. "Il les rattrapera avant l'arrivée à Amsterdam, s'il n'y a pas d'accidents," pense le voyageur. En effet, le train arrive en gare sans une minute de retard. Le voyageur en est bien content.

25 points

B. *THÈME*

GEORGE: There has been an auto accident. Let's call the doctor. He lives next door.

PETER: Oh! There he is now. Let's follow and see what has happened. There is a man who has been hurt. He seems to have pains in the back.

GEORGE: Yes. The doctor is examining him. He has a wound above the elbow. The doctor is asking the nurse for his bag. He is going to put on a dressing (*un bandage*).

PETER: Look, how his wrist is swollen! Now the doctor is looking at his knee. I hope (that) the poor man has not broken the bone of his leg. It must be serious. The doctor is going to take him to the hospital. He seems to have pains in his chest, too.

25 points

C. *COMPOSITION*

Écrivez une conversation qui se passe pendant une promenade en auto. (250 mots)

25 points

D. *VERBES*

Continuez la conjugaison:

1. Je ne conduis pas l'auto.
2. Je vis tout seul dans une petite maison.

10 points

E. *GRAMMAIRE*

Traduisez:

1. As soon as you have gone, I shall tell him what you asked me. 2. She is (in the act of) writing a charming and amusing story. 3. After hurrying he had to wait an hour. 4. I began to write the letter for (*car*) he refused to do it. 5. He was accompanied by his mother wearing a black silk dress.

15 points

Lecture 7

LE BAPTÊME

(D'après un conte de Guy de Maupassant)

Devant la porte de la ferme, les hommes attendaient. Le soleil de mai versait sa claire lumière sur les pommiers[1] ronds comme d'immenses bouquets blancs, roses et parfumés, et qui mettaient sur la cour entière[2] un toit de fleurs.

Tout à coup, derrière les arbres des fermes, la cloche de l'église tinta[3] (*rang*). Sa voix de fer jetait dans le ciel joyeux son appel faible et lointain. Une odeur d'étable (*stable*) passait parfois, mêlée au souffle (*aroma*) doux et sucré des pommiers.

Un des hommes, debout devant la porte, se tourna vers la maison et cria:

—Allons, allons, Mélina, v'là que ça sonne![4]

Il avait peut-être trente ans. C'était un grand paysan, que les longs travaux des champs n'avaient pas encore courbé (*stooped*) ni déformé. Un vieux,[5] son père, noueux (*knotty*) comme un tronc de chêne, déclara:

—Les femmes, c'est jamais prêt.

Les deux autres fils du vieux se mirent* à rire, et l'un, se tournant vers le frère aîné, qui avait appelé le premier, lui dit:

—Va les chercher, Polyte. Elles ne viendront* pas avant midi.[6]

Et le jeune homme entra dans sa demeure (*dwelling*).

[1] les pommiers, *apple trees. In like manner,* cerise *(cherry) gives* cerisier; poire *(pear),* poirier; abricot *(apricot),* abricotier.

[2] entière: *note that the feminine of adjectives ending in* -ier *becomes* -ière.

[3] tinta: *note the ending* -a. *This is the third-person singular of the past definite of a verb of the first conjugation. It is equivalent to the preterite in English. In this story, we also have the first-conjugation verbs* se tourna, cria, baptisa, *etc. The third plural ends in* -èrent, *as in* se levèrent. *Second conjugation* -ir *verbs and* -re *verbs and some irregular verbs give* -it *in the singular and* -irent *in the plural as in* il prit, ils partirent. -Oir *verbs and some irregular verbs give* -ut *in the singular and* -urent *in the plural;* il fut, il furent; il vint *and* ils vinrent *are irregular forms.*

[4] v'là que ça sonne, *Listen! The church bells are ringing.* v'là *is a popular abbreviation for voilà.*

[5] un vieux = un vieil homme, *an old man.*

[6] midi: *note that* midi *without capitals means "noon," but* le Midi, *capitalized, means "the South of France."*

Une bande de canards (*ducks*), arrêtée près des paysans, se mit à crier en battant des ailes; puis ils partirent de leur pas (*step, gait*) lent et balancé (*swinging*).

Alors, sur la porte demeurée ouverte, une grosse femme parut* qui portait une enfant de deux mois. C'était la garde-malade (*nurse*). Puis la mère, grande et forte, sortit à son tour, à peine âgée de dix-huit ans, fraîche et souriante, tenant* le bras de son homme.[7] Et les deux grand'mères vinrent* ensuite, fanées (*shriveled*) comme de vieilles pommes, avec une fatigue évidente dans leurs reins (*backs*). Une d'elles était veuve (*a widow*); elle prit* le bras du grand-père, demeuré devant la porte, et ils partirent en tête du cortège (*procession*), derrière l'enfant et la garde-malade. Et le reste de la famille se mit en route.[8] Les plus jeunes portaient des sacs de papiers pleins de dragées (*sugar-coated almonds*).[9]

Là-bas la petite cloche sonnait sans repos, appelant le petit enfant. Des gamins (*young boys*) montaient sur les talus (*road embankments*); des gens apparaissaient* aux barrières (*farm gates*); des filles de ferme restaient debout entre deux seaux pleins de lait qu'elles posaient à terre pour regarder passer le cortège.

La garde, triomphante (*as proud as a peacock*), portait l'enfant, évitant les flaques d'eau (*puddles*) dans le chemin. Les vieux venaient* ensuite, marchant avec difficulté; et les jeunes avaient envie de[10] danser et ils regardaient les filles qui venaient les voir passer; et le père et la mère allaient gravement (*solemnly*), suivant cet enfant qui les remplacerait plus tard dans la vie, qui continuerait dans le pays leur nom. Ils traversèrent les champs pour éviter le long détour de la route.

On apercevait* l'église maintenant, avec son clocher pointu. La cloche sonnait toujours, criant au nouveau-né (*newly born child*) de venir pour la première fois à l'église. Un chien s'était mis* à suivre. On lui jetait des dragées.

[7] son homme: *popular usage in place of* mari *among the peasants and lower middle class.*

[8] se mit en route, *started. Literally, got on the way.*

[9] dragées: *sugar-coated almonds are often distributed in this way at marriages and baptisms, especially in the country.*

[10] avaient envie de, *felt like.*

La porte de l'église était ouverte. Le prêtre, un grand garçon (*young man*) à cheveux rouges, maigre et fort, oncle du petit, un frère du père, attendait devant l'autel (*altar*). Et il baptisa suivant les rites son neveu.

Quand la cérémonie fut achevée,[11] la famille demeura sur le seuil (*doorsteps*) pendant que l'abbé quittait son surplis;[12] puis on se remit* en route. On allait vite maintenant, car (*for*) on pensait au dîner. Beaucoup d'enfants suivaient, et chaque fois qu'on jetait une poignée (*handful*) de bonbons, c'était une mêlée furieuse, des cheveux arrachés (*yanked out*); et le chien aussi se jetait dans le tas (*scramble*) pour ramasser les sucreries.

La garde, un peu lasse, dit* à l'abbé qui marchait près d'elle:

—Dites* donc, m'sieu[13] le curé, si ça ne vous ennuyait pas de me (*for me*) tenir un peu votre neveu. . . . J'ai une crampe dans les estomacs.

Le prêtre prit* l'enfant, dont la robe blanche faisait* une grande tache éclatante (*glaring spot*) sur sa soutane (*cassock*) noire, et il l'embrassa (*kissed*), gêné, ne sachant* comment le tenir, comment le poser (*place*). Tout le monde se mit* à rire. Une des grand'mères demanda de loin:

—Ça ne te fait-il pas de la peine (*make you feel sad*) que tu n'en auras* jamais comme ça?

Le prêtre ne répondit pas. Il allait (*went on*) à grandes enjambées (*with long strides*), regardant fixement l'enfant aux yeux bleus, dont il avait envie d'embrasser encore les joues rondes; et le levant jusqu'à son visage, il l'embrassa longuement.

Le père cria:

—Dis donc, curé, si tu en veux* un, tu n'ais qu'à le dire.

Et on se mit à plaisanter, comme plaisantent les gens des champs.

Dès qu'on fut* à table, la lourde gaieté campagnarde éclata comme une tempête. Les deux autres fils allaient aussi se marier;

[11] fut achevée, *was ended. This is a passive tense; the past definite of the auxiliary,* fut, *stresses what happened.*

[12] surplis, *surplice, a white lace vestment, worn by the priest over his robe while performing a marriage or a baptism.*

[13] m'sieu, *a popular abbreviation for* monsieur.

leurs fiancées étaient là, arrivées seulement pour le repas; et les invités ne cessaient de faire des allusions à toutes les générations futures que promettaient ces unions. C'étaient des gros mots (*coarse words*), fortement salés (*very spicy*), qui faisaient* ricaner (*chuckle*) les filles rougissantes et se tordre (*split their sides laughing*) les hommes. Ils tapaient du poing (*banged*) sur la table, poussaient des cris.

Le curé, habitué à ces débauches paysannes, restait tranquille, assis à côté de la garde-malade qui avait l'enfant sur les genoux, agaçant (*tickling*) du doigt la petite bouche de son neveu pour le faire rire. Il semblait surpris par la vue de cet enfant, comme s'il n'en avait jamais aperçu.* Il le considérait avec une attention réfléchie (*thoughtful*), avec une tendresse (*deep affection*) éveillée au fond de lui, une tendresse inconnue, singulière, vive et un peu triste, pour ce petit être (*being*) fragile qui était le fils de son frère.

Il n'entendait rien, il ne voyait rien, il contemplait l'enfant. Il avait envie de le prendre encore sur ses genoux, car il gardait dans son coeur la sensation douce de l'avoir porté tout à l'heure, en revenant* de l'église. Il restait ému (*stirred*) devant le grand mystère de la vie qui commence, de l'amour qui s'éveille, de la race qui se continue.

La garde-malade mangeait, la face rouge, gênée par le petit.

L'abbé lui dit:

—Donnez-le-moi. Je n'ai pas faim.

Et il reprit* l'enfant. Alors tout disparut* (*disappeared*) autour de lui; et il restait les yeux fixés sur cette figure (*face*) rose; et peu à peu la chaleur du petit corps, à travers les langes (*swaddling clothes*) et le drap de la soutane, le pénétrait comme une caresse très légère, très bonne; une caresse délicieuse (*wonderful*) qui lui mettait les larmes aux yeux.

Le bruit des mangeurs devenait* effrayant. L'enfant, agacé (*irritated*), se mit* à pleurer.

Une voix s'écria:

—Dis donc, l'abbé, donne-lui à têter (*suckle him*).

Et une explosion de rires secoua la salle. Mais la mère s'était levée; elle prit* son fils et l'emporta dans la chambre voisine. Elle revint* au bout de quelques minutes en déclarant qu'il dormait tranquillement dans son berceau.

Et le repas continua. Hommes et femmes sortaient de temps en temps dans la cour, puis rentraient se mettre à table. Les viandes, les légumes, le cidre et le vin s'engouffraient (*were swallowed up*) dans les bouches, gonflaient les ventres (*stomachs*), allumaient (*lighted up*) les yeux, faisaient* délirer (*rave*) les esprits.

La nuit tombait quand on prit* le café. Depuis longtemps le prêtre avait disparu,* mais personne ne s'étonnait de son absence.

La jeune mère enfin se leva pour aller voir si le petit dormait toujours (*still*). Il faisait sombre à présent. Elle pénétra dans la chambre à tâtons (*feeling her way*) et elle avançait, les bras étendus pour ne point heurter[14] (*hit against*) de meuble. Mais un bruit singulier l'arrêta net (*short*); et elle ressortit effarée (*scared*), sûre d'avoir entendu remuer quelqu'un. Elle rentra dans la salle, fort pâle, tremblante, et raconta la chose. Tous les hommes se levèrent en tumulte, gris (*tipsy*) et menaçants; le père, une lampe à la main, s'élança (*rushed forward*).

L'abbé, à genoux près du berceau, sanglotait (*was sobbing*), le front sur l'oreiller où reposait la tête de l'enfant.

QUESTIONNAIRE

1. Où attendaient les hommes? 2. Quel temps faisait-il? 3. Qu'est-ce qui appelait cette famille au baptême? 4. Quelle différence y avait-il entre les jeunes et les vieux paysans? 5. Qu'est-ce que les hommes disaient des femmes? 6. Décrivez le cortège. 7. Qui portait les dragées? 8. Qui regardait passer le cortège? 9. Pourquoi le père et la mère étaient-ils graves? 10. Qui attendait devant l'autel de l'église? 11. Qu'est-ce que la garde-malade a demandé au curé? 12. Pourquoi est-ce que tout le monde s'est mis à rire? 13. Qu'est-ce que le père a dit

[14] ne point heurter: *note the use of* ne point, *a very strong negative, before the infinitive.*

au curé quand il a embrassé l'enfant? 14. Décrivez la conversation à table. 15. Comment le curé passait-il son temps? 16. Quelle sensation a-t-il eue (*did he have*) quand il a pris l'enfant à (*from*) la garde-malade? 17. Qu'a-t-on fait de l'enfant quand il s'est mis à pleurer? 18. Quand la mère est allée voir son enfant, par quoi a-t-elle été effrayée? 19. Quand les hommes se sont élancés dans la chambre, qu'ont-ils vu (*did they see*)?

Lesson 29

Past definite of *parler, vendre,* and *finir*

Formation of the past definite

Past definite of some irregular verbs

Use of the past definite

Use of the past definite or the imperfect

Past definite passive

CONFÉRENCE HISTORIQUE—LA RÉSISTANCE EN FRANCE

Quand les troupes allemandes *occupèrent* la France, en 1940, un mouvement de résistance *se développa* parmi les populations du pays occupé. *Il y eut* de nombreux actes de sabotage. On *fit sauter* des lignes de chemin de fer, des ponts, des gares, des usines, au moyen d'explosifs qui arrivaient on ne savait jamais d'où. Des sentinelles *furent assassinées* à leurs postes. Des signaux *furent donnés* mystérieusement aux avions anglais qui *venaient* bombarder les usines qui *travaillaient* pour les Allemands. La Gestapo *fit* de son mieux pour découvrir les auteurs de ces "crimes." En vain. On *prit* des otages, on les *mit* en prison, on les *fusilla,* mais, pour chaque saboteur qui *mourait* sous les balles allemandes, *il en surgit* dix, cent, mille. *Il y eut* des cas où la population d'un village *fut massacrée* tout entière pour punir les habitants d'avoir abrité les saboteurs. La résistance *continua* dans tous les villages de France, dans chaque ville, dans chaque endroit, dans les campagnes et dans les fermes, dans les usines et dans les bureaux. Et les actes de sabotage *continuèrent* sans cesse.

Il se forma ainsi, à l'intérieur de la France, une armée secrète. Elle *combattit* avec des armes mystérieuses; elle *donna* des renseignements précieux aux alliés; elle *collabora* avec ce qui *restait* de l'armée française régulière dans l'Afrique du Nord; et elle *réussit* à échapper à toutes les recherches des ennemis de la liberté. Sans canons, presque sans munitions et sans vivres, les soldats des F.F.I. (Forces Françaises de l'Intérieur), *remportèrent* des victoires qui, sans être éclatantes, *furent* nombreuses et importantes.

Ainsi, le jour où les troupes américaines et anglaises *débarquèrent* sur les plages de Normandie, elles *trouvèrent,* derrière les lignes allemandes, une véritable armée française, prête à leur servir de guide, à les aider de toutes les façons possibles, à rendre plus brève cette bataille finale qui *devait* mener à la libération complète du pays.

VOCABULAIRE ET EXPRESSIONS

le poste the post
le signal (*pl.* **signaux**) the signal
le renseignement the piece of information (use the plural for "information")
la recherche the search, research, investigation

l'allié (*masc.*) the ally
la ligne the line
l'arme (*fem.*) the arm, the weapon
l'usine (*fem.*) the factory
l'habitant (*masc.*) the inhabitant
la ferme the farm

entier (*fem.* **entière**) entire, whole
secret (*fem.* **secrète**) secret

bref (*fem.* **brève**) brief, short
nombreux (*fem.* **nombreuse**) numerous

combattre to fight (**je combats, tu combats, il combat**)
échapper à to escape
s'échapper de to escape from
débarquer to land

servir to serve (like **dormir: je sers, tu sers, il sert**)
remporter to gain, win
punir to punish

en vain in vain
sans cesse unceasingly
à l'insu de without the knowledge of

servir de guide à . . . to serve . . . as a guide
il y eut, il y a eu there was, there were

VOCABULAIRE SUPPLÉMENTAIRE

le mouvement the movement
la résistance the resistance
l'acte (*masc.*) the act
l'intérieur (*masc.*) the interior
le cas the case
la sentinelle the sentinel, the sentry
l'autorité (*fem.*) the authority
l'auteur (*masc.*) the author
le guide the guide
l'otage (*masc.*) the hostage
la prison the prison, jail
la liberté liberty, freedom
l'explosif (*masc.*) the explosive
les munitions (*fem.*) ammunition
le canon the cannon
les vivres (*masc.*) the food
le sabotage sabotage
le saboteur the saboteur
la victoire the victory
la libération the liberation
la bataille the battle
la conférence the lecture

mystérieux (-euse) mysterious
important important
complet (-ète) complete
régulier (-ière) regular
éclatant brilliant
véritable veritable
final (*masc. pl.* **finals**) final
précieux (-euse) precious

faire sauter to blow up
fusiller to shoot (by military execution)
massacrer to massacre, slaughter
assassiner to murder, assassinate
surgir to rise, arise
collaborer to collaborate
occuper to occupy
abriter to shelter
former to form
dessiner to draw, outline

VERBES

The Past Definite

je parlai	**nous parlâmes**
tu parlas	**vous parlâtes**
il parla	**ils parlèrent**
je vendis	**nous vendîmes**
tu vendis	**vous vendîtes**
il vendit	**ils vendirent**

je finis	**nous finîmes**
tu finis	**vous finîtes**
il finit	**ils finirent**

→ The endings of the past definite of *-er* verbs are: *-ai, -as, -a, -âmes, -âtes, -èrent.* Verbs ending in *-cer* change *c* to *ç* in the singular and first and second plural (*je commençai, etc.*). Verbs ending in *-ger* insert *e* in the singular and first and second plural (*je mangeai, etc.*).

The endings of the past definite of *-re* and *-ir* verbs are: *-is, -is, -it, -îmes, -îtes, -irent.*

Some Irregular Past Definites

faire: je fis, tu fis, il fit, nous fîmes, vous fîtes, ils firent
mettre: je mis, tu mis, il mit, nous mîmes, vous mîtes, ils mirent
prendre: je pris, tu pris, il prit, nous prîmes, vous prîtes, ils prirent
voir: je vis, tu vis, il vit, nous vîmes, vous vîtes, ils virent
écrire: j'écrivis, tu écrivis, il écrivit, nous écrivîmes, vous écrivîtes, ils écrivirent
craindre: je craignis, tu craignis, il craignit, nous craignîmes, vous craignîtes, ils craignirent
conduire: je conduisis, tu conduisis, il conduisit, nous conduisîmes, vous conduisîtes, ils conduisirent
dire: je dis, tu dis, il dit, nous dîmes, vous dîtes, ils dirent
rire: je ris, etc.
s'asseoir: je m'assis, etc.

→ Several irregular verbs use the same endings as *-re* and *-ir* verbs, but with changes in the stem.

boire: je bus, tu bus, il but, nous bûmes, vous bûtes, ils burent
avoir: j'eus, tu eus, il eut, nous eûmes, vous eûtes, ils eurent
être: je fus, tu fus, il fut, nous fûmes, vous fûtes, ils furent
lire: je lus, tu lus, il lut, nous lûmes, vous lûtes, ils lurent
courir: je courus, etc.
mourir: je mourus, etc.
connaître: je connus, etc.
croire: je crus, etc.
vivre: je vécus, etc.
devoir: je dus, etc.

recevoir: je reçus, etc.
falloir: il fallut
pleuvoir: il plut
pouvoir: je pus, etc.
savoir: je sus, etc.
vouloir: je voulus, etc.
valoir: je valus, etc.

→ Other irregular verbs make use of this set of endings: *-us, -us, -ut, -ûmes, -ûtes, -urent,* with or without a change in the stem.

venir: je vins, tu vins, il vint, nous vînmes, vous vîntes, ils vinrent
tenir: je tins, tu tins, il tint, nous tînmes, vous tîntes, ils tinrent

→ *Venir, tenir,* and their compounds are completely irregular.

The Passive Form

Wellington battit Napoléon à Waterloo Wellington defeated Napoleon at Waterloo
Napoléon fut battu par Wellington à Waterloo Napoleon was defeated by Wellington at Waterloo

→ This form is often used in narrating. Although it is a passive form, it stresses the event (what happened) as does the past definite.

GRAMMAIRE

les troupes prirent la ville the troops seized the town
Louis XVI régna au dix-huitième siècle Louis XVI reigned in the 18th century

→ The past definite is translated by the English past. It is not used in ordinary conversation, but only in books (occasionally in lectures of a historical nature) to narrate what took place.

le mouvement commença the movement began
le mouvement a commencé the movement began, has begun
le mouvement commençait the movement was beginning

→The past definite is purely historical and narrative. The past indefinite is also narrative, but conversational. Both past definite and past indefinite are translated by the English past, but the past indefinite may also be translated by the English present perfect, which is never the case with the past definite. Both past definite and past indefinite state what happened at a given point of time. The imperfect is a descriptive tense, stating what was happening, continued to happen or to exist, happened regularly, repeatedly, or habitually.

j'écrivais quand il est entré I was writing when he came in
Napoléon écrivait quand Joséphine entra Napoleon was writing when Josephine came in

→The imperfect may be used (to state what was happening) in connection with either past definite or past indefinite (both of which state what happened).

QUESTIONS

N'employez pas le passé défini, mais le passé indéfini, comme dans les questions:

1. Quand le mouvement de résistance a-t-il commencé en France? 2. Comment les Français ont-ils résisté? 3. Qui venait bombarder les usines qui travaillaient pour les Allemands? 4. Qui a fait de son mieux pour découvrir les membres de la Résistance? 5. Qui a fait prendre des otages? 6. Pourquoi? 7. Quelle sorte d'armée a été formée? 8. Avec qui travaillait-elle? 9. Qu'est-ce que les troupes américaines et anglaises ont trouvé quand elles ont débarqué? 10. Quel a été le résultat de cette collaboration?

EXERCICE

Expliquez le temps de chaque verbe en italique dans le texte.

Lesson 30

Present indicative, imperfect, and past participle of *croire*

Present indicative, imperfect, and past participle of *coudre*

Use of indicative or subjunctive with *penser*, *croire*, and other verbs of thinking and believing

Use of the subjunctive or infinitive with verbs of wanting, desiring, etc.

Use of the subjunctive or infinitive with verbs of emotion

Use of the interrogative pronouns

Lequel, laquelle, lesquels, lesquelles

Use of the interrogative adjectives

quel, quelle, quels, quelles

CONVERSATION

Un Jour d'Hiver

YVONNE: Croyez-vous qu'il pleuve, Caroline?

CAROLINE: Non, je crois plutôt qu'il va neiger. Il fait trop froid pour qu'il pleuve.

YVONNE: Quel dommage! Hier soir, la lune et les étoiles brillaient dans le ciel. Aujourd'hui, le temps est couvert et très humide. Quel sale climat, n'est-ce pas? Il est regrettable qu'il y ait tant de brouillard, de glace, de boue et de neige, l'hiver.

CAROLINE: Vous allez sortir quand même?

YVONNE: Oui, il faut que j'aille à la poste.

CAROLINE: Il y a une boîte aux lettres ici dans l'hôtel. Vous pourriez envoyer vos lettres sans sortir.

YVONNE: Oui, mais il faut aussi que j'achète des timbres-poste, et il faut que je fasse des emplettes. J'ai besoin d'enveloppes, d'encre, et de papier à lettres. Puis, il faut que je me procure des allumettes, des épingles, des aiguilles, du fil, et une revue.

CAROLINE: Laquelle?

YVONNE: "La France Illustrée" ou "Le Monde Nouveau."

CAROLINE: Voulez-vous que je vous accompagne?

YVONNE: Non, je préfère que vous restiez ici, où il fait bien chaud, surtout s'il va neiger. Vous êtes restée très faible depuis votre maladie.

CAROLINE: C'est vrai, on est vraiment bien ici, et c'est agréable d'être à l'abri du mauvais temps. Il n'y a pas assez de lumière pour lire, mais je vais regarder par la fenêtre. Quelle chaleur! Voulez-vous ouvrir la fenêtre un peu avant de sortir?

YVONNE: Avec plaisir. Et je suis bien contente que vous restiez ici. Je regrette que vous soyez sortie hier, malgré le mauvais temps qu'il faisait.

CAROLINE: Lequel de ces livres désirez-vous que je lise?

YVONNE: Celui que je vous ai prêté l'autre jour. Il vaut la peine d'être lu.

CAROLINE: Fort bien. Je vous attendrai donc ici.

VOCABULAIRE ET EXPRESSIONS

le ciel the sky, heaven
la pluie the rain
la neige the snow
le brouillard the fog, mist
la lune the moon
l'étoile (*fem.*) the star

la glace the ice (note that this word also means "mirror" and "ice cream")
la boue the mud
la lumière the light
la poste the post office
le fil the thread
le timbre-poste (*pl.* **timbres-poste**) the stamp
l'enveloppe (*fem.*) the envelope
le papier à lettres the writing-paper
la boîte aux lettres the letter-box
l'encre (*fem.*) the ink
l'allumette (*fem.*) the match
l'aiguille (*fem.*) the needle (pronounce the *u*)
l'épingle (*fem.*) the pin
la revue the magazine
l'emplette (*fem.*) the purchase

clair clear, bright
faible weak, feeble
sale nasty; dirty
agréable pleasant, agreeable
désagréable unpleasant, disagreeable

croire to believe, to think
se procurer to get
neiger to snow (*impf.* **il neigeait**)
coudre to sew
obtenir to get, obtain (conjugate like **tenir**)

lequel (laquelle, lesquels, lesquelles) which, which one, which ones

cela vaut la peine (de) it's worth while (to)
faire des emplettes to go shopping
à l'abri under cover
quand même just the same, all the same

VOCABULAIRE SUPPLÉMENTAIRE

la chaleur the warmth, heat
couvert cloudy
humide damp
briller to shine, gleam

VERBES

Present Indicative of **croire** (to believe, to think)

je crois	**nous croyons**
tu crois	**vous croyez**
il (elle) croit	**ils (elles) croient**

Imperfect: **je croyais** Past participle: **cru**

Present Indicative of **coudre** (to sew)

je couds	**nous cousons**
tu couds	**vous cousez**
il (elle) coud	**ils (elles) cousent**

Imperfect: **je cousais** Past participle: **cousu**

GRAMMAIRE

The Subjunctive (Continued)

je crois qu'il viendra I think he will come
je ne crois pas qu'il vienne I don't think he will come
Croyez-vous qu'il vienne? Do you think he will come?
Ne croyez-vous pas qu'il viendra? Don't you think he will come?

→ After *croire, penser,* and other verbs of thinking or believing, as well as after *dire* and other verbs of saying, the subjunctive is used if the main verb is negative or interrogative; but the indicative appears if the main verb is affirmative, or both interrogative and negative.

je veux (désire, préfère) le faire I want (wish, prefer) to do it
je veux (désire, préfère) que vous le fassiez I want (wish, prefer) you to do it

→ Verbs of wanting, desiring, preferring, and the like, take the infinitive, just as in English, if the same person is involved. But if one person wants another person to do something, a subjunctive clause is used, with the construction literally translated: I want that you do it.

je suis content d'être ici I am glad to be here; I am glad I am here
je suis content que vous soyez ici I am glad you are here
je regrette de l'avoir fait I am sorry I did it
je regrette que vous l'ayez fait I am sorry you did it
je suis surpris de le voir I am surprised to see him
je suis surpris qu'il m'ait vu I am surprised that he saw me

→ With verbs and expressions of joy, sorrow, surprise, or other emotions, the infinitive is used if the identical person is involved. But if there are different subjects, a subjunctive clause is used.

Interrogative Pronouns

Lequel de ces livres voulez-vous? Which (one) of these books do you want?
Laquelle des deux est arrivée? Which (one) of the two came?
Lesquels des frères sont partis? Which (ones) of the brothers left?
Avec lesquelles de vos sœurs allez-vous dîner? With which (ones) of your sisters are you going to dine?

→ **Lequel**; *fem.* **laquelle**; *masc. pl.* **lesquels**; *fem. pl.* **lesquelles** are interrogative pronouns, meaning: which, which one, which ones.

Interrogative Adjectives

Quels livres avez-vous lus? Which books have you read?
Lesquels des livres avez-vous lus? Which of the books have you read?
Quels sont les livres que vous avez lus? Which are the books that you read?

→ **Quel, quelle, quels, quelles** are adjectives. **Lequel, laquelle, lesquels, lesquelles** are pronouns. Use **lequel,** etc., whenever "one" or "ones" can logically be added to English "which."

QUESTIONS

1. Qu'est-ce qu'Yvonne demande à Caroline? 2. Pourquoi Caroline croit-elle qu'il va neiger? 3. Quand il fait beau la nuit, que voit-on dans le ciel? 4. Qu'est-ce qu'Yvonne pense du temps? 5. Pourquoi n'aime-t-elle pas l'hiver? 6. Où Yvonne va-t-elle? 7. Comment peut-elle envoyer ses lettres de l'hôtel? 8. De quoi a-t-elle besoin? 9. Quelle revue veut-elle acheter?

EXERCICES

A. *Conjuguez, en faisant tous les changements que le sens exige:*

1. Je crois que vous êtes malade. 2. Je croyais qu'il était à la campagne. 3. J'ai cru être spirituel (*witty*). 4. Je ne crois pas qu'il soit arrivé.

B. *Traduisez:*

1. I sewed my dress today. 2. What are you sewing, Mary? 3. I was sewing when she came into the room. 4. She would sew your coat if you would help her to study her French.

C. I. *Mettez l'infinitif en italique au temps qui convient:*

1. Georges croit qu'elle *venir.* 2. Croyez-vous qu'il *voir* sa mère? 3. Il ne croit pas que vous *être* sincère. 4. Ne croient-ils pas que leur ami *venir?* 5. Il préfère que vous *rester* assis. 6. Je veux que vous *venir* me voir. 7. Je suis content qu'ils vous *voir.* 8. Nous regrettons que vous ne *être* pas américain. 9. N'êtes-vous pas surpris qu'il *avoir* tant d'argent?

II. *Complétez par un verbe de votre choix:*

1. Nous sommes heureux que vous ________. 2. Je suis content qu'il ________. 3. Il est surpris de nous ________. 4. Est-ce que vous ne regrettez pas que je ________? 5. Il désire ________. 6. Nous préférons ________.

D. *Remplacez le tiret par la forme correcte d'un des mots suivants:*
lequel, laquelle, lesquelles, quels, quelle, lesquels, quel.

1. ________ de ces machines à écrire voulez-vous? 2. ________ de vos amies vont rester? 3. Chez ________ de vos sœurs allez-vous dîner? 4. ________ chambre préférez-vous? 5. ________ sont les stylos que vous avez choisis? 6. ________ des professeurs est le plus intelligent? 7. A ________ professeur avez-vous parlé? 8. ________ des trois est arrivée? 9. ________ de vos frères sont en Europe? 10. ________ de ces réponses vous a surpris le plus?

THÈME

—What a nasty day! When it doesn't rain, it snows in this country.

—Why! last night it was beautiful.

—Yes, but today it is damp, cloudy, and cold. I don't like this weather at all.

—Well, you will have to be content with the weather that is given you. Why have you put on your raincoat? Where are you going?

—I must buy some writing paper and envelopes, some ink and some stamps.

—When you go out, would you please get (buy) me some pins and needles? And if you pass (before) a newspaper stand (*un kiosque*) get me a magazine, will you? And some matches, too.

—What's the matter? Aren't you going out today?

—No, I am not going out today. I am very tired. I went out yesterday. I am afraid that I am still pretty weak.

—Very well. Stay in and rest. What do you want me to bring you? Another book or only a magazine and a newspaper?

—Oh! bring me another book, too. The one I read last week was really very interesting. I want another.

Lesson 31

Present indicative, imperfect, present subjunctive, and past participle of *craindre*

Use of the subjunctive after some impersonal expressions

Expressions of probability and certainty with the subjunctive if negative or interrogative

Use of the subjunctive with *douter*

Use of the subjunctive with verbs of fearing

Use of redundant *ne*

Position and spelling of adjectives of religion and nationality

Use of article with feminine names of countries except after *en* and often *de*

Use of *à* and *de* plus the article with masculine names of countries and feminine plurals

Use of *dans* plus the article with modified names of countries

CONVERSATION

Un Interview

LE REPORTER: M. Richard, vous êtes revenu de l'Europe centrale il y a quelques jours. Voulez-vous nous donner vos impressions pour la presse franco-américaine?

M. Richard: Avec plaisir. Il me semble que la situation est en train de s'améliorer, mais assez lentement. Au moment où j'ai quitté le port de Trieste, j'ai voulu réfléchir sur tout ce que j'avais vu. Eh bien, il semble que la situation en Pologne et en Hongrie du moins ne se soit pas beaucoup améliorée. La Russie a beaucoup de difficultés également. Comme toujours, plusieurs grands pays européens cherchent à dicter leur politique étrangère aux petits pays, mais c'est inévitable. Ça a toujours été ainsi.

Le Reporter: Vous ne craignez donc pas que l'Union Soviétique veuille réglementer les affaires de l'Europe continentale?

M. Richard: Si. Mais on peut craindre aussi qu'elle veuille dominer toute l'Asie; et, dans ce cas, la situation pourrait être encore plus difficile.

Le Reporter: Et pour l'Europe occidentale, pensez-vous qu'il soit possible d'établir un bloc de puissances?

M. Richard: Au point de vue purement politique, je doute qu'on réussisse à réunir des pays aussi différents que la France, l'Espagne, l'Italie, la Suisse, le Portugal, la Belgique, la Hollande, la Suède, la Norvège, et le Danemark. Mais je ne doute pas qu'on puisse former un bloc économique.

Le Reporter: Craignez-vous qu'il y ait des difficultés permanentes dans les Balkans?

M. Richard: Il y existe certainement des difficultés d'ordre religieux aussi bien que politique. Il ne faut pas oublier qu'en Yougoslavie, par exemple, il y a des Croates catholiques, des Serbes orthodoxes et des Bosniens musulmans. Et toutes les églises se mêlent de politique dans tous ces états balkaniques.

Le Reporter: Alors, vous craignez. . . .

M. Richard: Je crains qu'il ne soit pas possible pour le moment de se débarrasser de toutes les questions gênantes créées par la guerre. Le progrès vers une paix permanente ne peut pas être très rapide. Pourtant, il est nécessaire avant tout qu'on ne soit ni timide ni peureux. Il faut, au contraire, être courageux, calme, et plein d'espoir. Il est possible qu'il y ait des difficultés au cours des années prochaines, mais il est évident aussi que toutes les nations ne désirent que la paix.

VOCABULAIRE ET EXPRESSIONS

le lieu (*pl.* **lieux**) the place, spot
l'église (*fem.*) the church
le reporter reporter
l'Asie (*fem.*) Asia
la Hongrie Hungary
l'Union Soviétique the Soviet Union
la Russie Russia
la Yougoslavie Yugoslavia
l'Italie (*fem.*) Italy
la Hollande Holland
la Belgique Belgium
l'Espagne (*fem.*) Spain
la Suisse Switzerland
la Norvège Norway
la Suède Sweden
le Danemark Denmark
l'Angleterre (*fem.*) England
le Canada Canada
le Mexique Mexico
le Brésil Brazil
le Pérou Peru
le Japon Japan
la Chine China

pénible troublesome
gênant annoying
lâche cowardly
peureux (*fem.* **peureuse**) timid, fearful
inévitable inevitable

retourner (*être*) to return, go back
s'améliorer to improve
craindre to fear
se plaindre to complain
se débarrasser de to get rid of
douter de to doubt
tâcher de to try to

au point de vue from the point of view
à mon avis in my opinion

VOCABULAIRE SUPPLÉMENTAIRE

le port the port, the harbor
l'avis (*masc.*) the opinion (not advice; use *conseil* for latter)
l'impression (*fem.*) the impression
le danger the danger
le cas the case
la presse the press
la politique the politics, the policy

le bloc the block
le mouvement the movement, the gesture, the motion
la puissance the power
l'affaire (*fem.*) the affair, the business
les Balkans (*masc.*) the Balkans
le Portugal Portugal
la Grèce Greece
la Pologne Poland
la Turquie Turkey
la Roumanie Romania

militaire military
politique political
naturel (*fem.* **naturelle**) natural
économique economic
probable probable
certain certain
possible possible
divers different, diverse
étranger (*fem.* **étrangère**) foreign
permanent permanent
brave brave
calme calm
rapide rapid
courageux (*fem.* **courageuse**) courageous
tranquille tranquil, peaceful
religieux (*fem.* **religieuse**) religious
catholique Catholic
orthodoxe Orthodox
protestant Protestant
musulman Mohammedan
serbe Serb, Serbian
croate Croat, Croatian
bosnien (*fem.* **bosnienne**) Bosnian
balkanique Balkan

s'emparer de to take possession of
régler to rule, regulate (**je règle**)
dicter to dictate
s'intéresser à to take interest in
dominer to dominate, to control
établir to establish
créer to create
se mêler de to meddle with

VERBES

Present Indicative of **craindre** (to fear)

je crains
tu crains
il (elle) craint
nous craignons
vous craignez
ils (elles) craignent

Imperfect: **je craignais** Present Subjunctive: **que je craigne** Past Participle: **craint**

Like *craindre,* conjugate ***plaindre,*** to bemoan, be sorry for; ***se plaindre,*** to complain.

GRAMMAIRE

The Subjunctive (Continued)

il est possible qu'il soit ici it is possible that he is (or will be) here
il est probable qu'il sera ici it is probable that he will be here
il est certain qu'il viendra it is certain that he will come
il me semble qu'il sera ici it seems to me he will be here
il est naturel qu'il vienne it is natural that he will come
il semble qu'il soit ici it seems he is here

→ Impersonal expressions are generally followed by the subjunctive, unless certainty or probability is implied. Note that "it seems" takes the subjunctive, but "it seems to me" takes the indicative.

est-il probable qu'il vienne? is it probable that he will come?
il n'est pas certain qu'il vienne it is not certain that he will come

→ Expressions of probability and certainty are naturally followed by the subjunctive if negative or interrogative, because uncertainty is then implied.

je doute qu'il vienne I doubt that he will come

→ *Douter* regularly takes the subjunctive.

je crains qu'il (ne) vienne I am afraid he is coming
je ne crains pas qu'il vienne I am not afraid he is coming
je crains qu'il ne vienne pas I am afraid he is not coming
je ne crains pas qu'il ne vienne pas I am not afraid he is not coming

→ Verbs of fearing (*craindre, avoir peur*) always take the subjunctive. If both the verb of fearing and the following verb are affirmative, the second verb is preceded by *ne,* but only in literary usage.

The Definite Article and Prepositions with Names of Countries

j'ai visité la Belgique (la France) I have visited Belgium (France)
il demeure en Belgique (en France) he lives in Belgium (in France)
il est allé en Belgique (en France) he went to Belgium (to France)
il est revenu de France he came back from France
nous avons du vin de France we have some wine from France (French wine)

→ With feminine names of countries, the article is used, save after *en* ("in" or "to"). With *de* ("from") the article is often omitted, especially when *de* plus the country's name is equivalent to an adjective.

j'ai visité **le Japon (les États-Unis)** I visited Japan (the United States)
il demeure **au Japon (aux États-Unis)** he lives in Japan (in the United States)
il est rentré **du Japon (des États-Unis)** he came back from Japan (from the United States)
nous avons du riz **du Japon** we have some rice from Japan (Japanese rice)
nous venons **des Indes** we come from India

→ With masculine names of countries and feminine plurals, the article is always used, even after *à* ("in" or "to") and *de* ("of" or "from").

il a visité l'Amérique centrale he visited Central America
il demeure dans l'Amérique centrale he lives in Central America
il est revenu de l'Amérique centrale he came back from Central America
j'ai reçu des bananes de l'Amérique centrale I got some bananas from Central America

→ If a feminine name of a country is modified, the article is always used. With a modified feminine name of a country, *dans* replaces *en* in the sense of "to" or "in."

QUESTIONS

1. Que demande le reporter à M. Richard? 2. Que pense-t-il de la situation en Pologne et en Hongrie? 3. Que font les grands pays? 4. Quelle est la situation en Russie? 5. Quel rôle craint-on que la

Russie veuille jouer? 6. Quelles sont les difficultés qui se présentent pour les Balkans? 7. Comment ces questions gênantes se sont-elles développées? 8. Quel devrait être le but des nations? 9. Quelle sorte d'action faut-il éviter? 10. Quel est certainement le désir de toutes les nations?

EXERCICES

A. *Conjuguez:*

1. Je crains les chiens. 2. Je craignais la nuit, quand j'étais petit. 3. J'ai craint de ne pas les voir. 4. Je plains ceux qui sont pauvres. 5. J'ai toujours plaint Marguerite. 6. Je me suis plaint trop souvent.

B. *Employez les verbes en italique à la troisième personne du singulier:*

1. Il est possible *arriver.* 2. Il est naturel *lire* le livre. 3. Il semble *comprendre.* 4. Il est possible *suivre* ce cours. 5. Il est naturel *venir* me voir. 6. Il semble *avoir* fini. 7. Il est probable *venir.* 8. Il est certain *faire* ses devoirs. 9. Il me semble *avoir* le temps de le faire. 10. Il n'est pas certain *revenir* cette semaine. 11. Est-il probable que le bal *être remis?* 12. Il n'est pas probable *être* chez elle.

C. *Finissez chaque phrase en mettant le verbe en italique à la troisième personne du pluriel:*

1. Je doute *descendre.* 2. Je doute *vouloir* venir. 3. Je crains *décider* en sa faveur. 4. Je ne crains pas *aller* à la campagne. 5. Il craint *ne pas partir* demain. 6. Nous ne craignons pas *ne pas revenir.* 7. Avez-vous peur *tomber?* 8. Est-ce que vous craignez *s'endormir?*

D. *Complétez les phrases suivantes:*

1. Nous avons visité ________ Amérique du Sud et ________ Amérique centrale. 2. Mon père est allé ________ France. 3. Avez-vous jamais voyagé ________ Japon? 4. Il demeure ________ Canada. 5. Mon oncle n'est pas encore revenu ________ France. 6. Nous voulons du vin ________ France. 7. Nous n'avons plus de riz ________ Japon. 8. Quand reviendra-t-il ________ Suisse? 9.

Est-ce que votre ami demeure ________ l'Amérique du Nord?
10. Est-ce que vous demeurez ________ États-Unis?

THÈME

—I should like to have your impressions of Europe, Mr. Smith. I have been told that you have visited the Balkans. What is the situation in Yugoslavia?

—It is difficult to analyze, but most of the difficulties seem to come from the great number of political and religious differences that exist there.

—Have you visited the rest of Europe? Russia, Poland, Hungary, Norway, Holland, and Belgium? Have you traveled in the Latin countries like France, Spain, and Italy?

—Yes, I have visited them all.

—Do you think that a political block can be formed as after the last war?

—No, I do not believe so. There are too many embarrassing situations which have been created by the Second Great War. But if we all remain courageous and calm and try to maintain (*maintenir*) peace, we shall certainly succeed.

Lesson 32

Past subjunctive of *parler* and *aller* as model for all past subjunctives

Use of the past subjunctive

Use of the subjunctive as an imperative

Use of the subjunctive after the conjunctions: *avant que, jusqu'à ce que, bien que, quoique, pourvu que, afin que, pour que, sans que*

Use of *à moins que* with *ne*

Use of *avant de, afin de, pour,* and *sans* with the infinitive

CONVERSATION

Une Déclaration d'Amour

LOUIS: Voulez-vous que nous nous asseyions ici sur l'herbe, Charlotte?

CHARLOTTE: Non, Louis, j'ai peur des fourmis. Asseyons-nous plutôt sur cette belle pierre carrée et plate, là-bas.

LOUIS: Ce n'est pas très tendre, mais je suis prêt à tous les sacrifices pourvu que vous soyez satisfaite.

CHARLOTTE: Apportez le panier et ouvrez-le. Voyons ce qu'il y a dedans. Ah! Du sel, du poivre, du sucre. Puis du beurre, des petits pains. Ah! De la viande froide! Même un morceau du jambon d'hier soir dans ce sac de papier. Quelle idée magnifique vous avez eue de faire un pique-nique à la campagne! Après avoir mangé, nous pourrions jouer à la balle, ou bien aller là-bas sur la plage tremper nos pieds dans l'eau. Mais qu'est-ce que vous avez? Vous ne mangez pas. Est-ce que la viande est trop salée ou le café trop amer?

LOUIS: Non, Charlotte. C'est que je suis un peu . . . comment dirais-je? un peu ému, et même bouleversé.

CHARLOTTE: Par exemple! Et pourquoi?

LOUIS: Eh bien! Avant que vous soyez arrivée dans cette ville, j'étais tout à fait satisfait, bien que ma vie ait été bien vide pendant ces dernières années. Puis, un jour, vous êtes entrée dans mon existence et quelque chose de très doux a rempli mon âme.

CHARLOTTE: Attendez, Louis! Vous ne vous moquez pas de moi?

LOUIS: Pourquoi est-ce que je me moquerais de vous? C'est plutôt vous qui avez le droit de rire de moi. J'ai attendu pour parler jusqu'à ce que je vous aie mieux connue. J'avais peur de me tromper.

CHARLOTTE: Il est même possible que vous vous trompiez encore.

LOUIS: Non, je suis bien sûr de mes sentiments. Vous me permettez de continuer?

CHARLOTTE: Pourvu que vous ne disiez pas de sottises.

LOUIS: Croyez-moi, Charlotte, ce que je désire vous dire n'est pas frivole; c'est profondément sincère. Je veux vous avouer tout simplement que je suis tombé amoureux de vous, et je voudrais vous demander si vous accepteriez de m'épouser. Est-ce que c'est drôle?

CHARLOTTE: Non, pas du tout. Mais avant que je vous épouse. . . .

LOUIS: Quoi?

CHARLOTTE: Il faudra faire des visites.

LOUIS: A qui?

CHARLOTTE: A mes parents, pour qu'ils puissent vous connaître.

LOUIS: Alors, vous consentez?

CHARLOTTE: Oui, je consens. Vous avez été franc. Je serai aussi franche que vous. Moi aussi, je vous aime.

LOUIS: Ah, chérie! (Il l'embrasse) Tu me rends le plus heureux des hommes!

CHARLOTTE: Tu?

LOUIS: Nous sommes fiancés à présent, et ça me donne bien le droit de te tutoyer, en te disant que je t'aime!

VOCABULAIRE ET EXPRESSIONS

l'amour (*masc.*) love
l'âme (*fem.*) the soul
le fiancé, la fiancée the sweetheart
le droit the right
le panier the basket
le sel the salt
le poivre the pepper
le sucre the sugar
le petit pain the roll
la viande the meat
le beurre the butter
le sac the bag
la balle the ball
la plage the beach
le jambon the ham

plat flat
salé salty
amer (*fem.* **amère**) bitter
aigre sour
mou (**mol** *before a vowel; fem.* **molle**; *masc. pl.* **mous**; *fem. pl.* **molles**) soft
carré square
vide empty
ému moved, upset
doux (*fem.* **douce**) sweet
sot (*fem.* **sotte**) foolish
drôle funny
faux (*fem.* **fausse**) false

embrasser to kiss
se moquer de, se rire de to laugh at, make fun of
épouser, se marier avec to marry
tomber amoureux de (**amoureuse de**) to fall in love with

avant que, avant de before
jusqu'à, jusqu'à ce que until
pourvu que provided
pour, afin de in order to
pour que, afin que in order that, so that
bien que, quoique although
à moins que unless

disposé à disposed to
faire une visite to pay a visit
je suis sûr de mon affaire I know what I'm talking about

n'importe quoi anything at all, no matter what
tout de même, quand même just the same, all the same
à moi mine (only after the verb *être;* likewise **à toi, à lui, à elle, à nous, à vous, à eux, à elles** yours, his, hers, ours, yours, theirs; in this construction, *être* may be translated by "to belong to")

VOCABULAIRE SUPPLÉMENTAIRE

le pique-nique the picnic
la fourmi the ant
l'araignée (*fem.*) the spider
la sottise the foolishness
la déclaration the declaration, proposal
la volonté the will
franc (*fem.* **franche**) frank

avouer to confess
consentir à to consent to (conjugate like *sentir*)
tutoyer to address familiarly, to "thou and thee"
tremper to dip, soak

VERBES

The Past Subjunctive

que j'aie parlé
que tu aies parlé
qu'il ait parlé
qu'elle ait parlé
que nous ayons parlé
que vous ayez parlé
qu'ils aient parlé
qu'elles aient parlé

que je sois allé(e)
que tu sois allé(e)
qu'il soit allé
qu'elle soit allée
que nous soyons allés(es)
que vous soyez allé(e)(s)(es)
qu'ils soient allés
qu'elles soient allées

All past subjunctives are formed after this pattern.

je ne crois pas qu'il soit venu I don't believe he came
je crains qu'il (ne) l'ait fait I am afraid he did it
il est impossible qu'il ait fait cela It's impossible that he did that

→ The past subjunctive is used when the action of the subordinate clause is past in relation to the action of the main clause.

GRAMMAIRE

The Subjunctive as a Third-Person Imperative

Qu'on fasse cela immédiatement! Let that be done at once!
Dieu vous bénisse! God bless you!
Qu'il vienne me voir demain! Let him come to see me tomorrow!

→ The subjunctive with *que* (which is occasionally omitted) expresses an indirect command (let him, let them), or a wish (may he, may they). As such, it is the third person form of the imperative.

The Subjunctive after Certain Conjunctions

avant que j'aie fait sa connaissance, il était à l'armée before I met him, he was in the army
attendez (jusqu'à ce) qu'il soit parti wait until he has left
bien qu'il ait écrit cette lettre, je l'excuse although he wrote that letter, I excuse him
quoiqu'il ne soit pas venu, nous avons joué although he did not come, we played
j'irai là-bas, **pourvu que vous m'y accompagniez** I shall go there, provided you come with me
je lui ai prêté cet argent **afin qu'il puisse payer ses dettes** I lent him that money so that he might pay his debts
faites tout ce que vous pourrez **pour qu'il vienne** do anything you can in order that he may come
j'ai mis la lettre à la poste **sans qu'il s'en soit aperçu** I mailed the letter without his noticing it

→ The subjunctive must be used in clauses introduced by the following conjunctions: *avant que* (before); *jusqu'à ce que* (until); *bien que, quoique* (although); *pourvu que* (provided); *afin que, pour que* (in order that, so that); *sans que* (without).

à moins que vous (ne) veniez, on ne pourra pas jouer unless you come, we shall not be able to play

→ *A moins que* (unless) requires not only the subjunctive, but also a redundant *ne* in the affirmative (*ne . . . pas* in the negative); this use of *ne,* however, is literary.

Avoiding the Subjunctive

avant de lui parler, je lui ai écrit before I spoke to him, I wrote to him
j'ai attendu **afin de le voir** I waited so that I might see him
j'ai fait de mon mieux **pour venir** I did my best so that I could come
j'ai tout vu **sans sortir** I saw everything without going out

→ If the subject of the subordinate clause is the same person as the subject of the main clause, some of the foregoing conjunctions with the subjunctive are replaced by prepositions with the infinitive. The replaceable ones are: *avant que* (*avant de*); *afin que* (*afin de*); *pour que* (*pour*); *sans que* (*sans*). The following conjunctions are not replaceable by prepositions, and must be used even if the subjects are the same: *bien que, quoique; pourvu que.*

QUESTIONS

1. Où Louis veut-il s'asseoir? 2. Pourquoi Charlotte ne veut-elle pas s'asseoir sur l'herbe? 3. Pourquoi Louis accepte-t-il de s'asseoir sur la pierre? 4. Qu'est-ce qu'ils ont apporté à manger? 5. Qu'est-ce que Charlotte veut faire après avoir mangé? 6. Pourquoi Louis ne veut-il pas manger? 7. Quel sentiment exprime-t-il à Charlotte? 8. Quelle déclaration finit-il par lui faire? 9. Quelle réponse obtient-il de Charlotte? 10. Comment sait-on qu'il est content de sa réponse?

EXERCICES

A. *Conjuguez le verbe au subjonctif:*

1. Georges n'est pas arrivé avant que je sois parti. 2. Henri a mis la lettre à la poste sans que je m'en sois aperçu. 3. Bien que j'aie écrit la lettre, je ne l'ai pas envoyée.

B. *Faites des phrases en employant le passé du subjonctif après les conjonctions:* quoique; avant que; pourvu que; afin que; sans que.

C. *Traduisez:*

1. Do you think we came early? 2. He is afraid that she wrote the letter. 3. Before we met him he had been in China. 4. Don't wait

until (qu') she has left. 5. Although we wrote the letter together, he refuses to admit it. 6. Although you did not come on time (*à l'heure*), we waited for you before starting. 7. I shall write the letter now, provided that you mail it. 8. They lent him the money in order that he might pay his debts. 9. He said he would do anything (*n'importe quoi*) in order that he might see her again. 10. He came into the room without anyone's noticing it. 11. Before writing to him, I remembered everything that he had told me. 12. They waited until ten o'clock so that they might see him once more. 13. Didn't he tell you that I would do my best to come? 14. Don't you know that you can mail your letter without leaving the hotel?

THÈME

—Let's sit down there on the grass near the river.

—Not there, please. There are ants there, and I am afraid of them. Isn't there a flat rock near here, where we might put our basket and eat?

—Yes, over there. Let's see what is in the basket. Cold meat, ham, butter and rolls. After lunch we can go swimming. We can perhaps hire a boat this afternoon.

—May I prepare the lunch? I hope the ham is not too salty? What is there in this paper bag? Oh! matches and coffee.

—Before we came here the weather was so hot. Now it is quite cool. Why did you make fun of me when I said I wanted to come to the river's bank for a picnic?

—I wasn't making fun of you. I was just being silly (*plaisanter*). There have been a good many young ladies who have become engaged here.

—Oh! don't be afraid. I don't intend (*avoir l'intention de*) to propose (*faire une déclaration*). Not today.

Lesson 33

Present indicative, imperfect, future, and past participle of *courir*

Subjunctive after an indefinite antecedent

Subjunctive after *seul, premier, dernier, ne . . . que,* and a superlative

Contraction of *lequel, laquelle, lesquels,* and *lesquelles* with *de and à*

Uses of *lequel,* etc.

Use of *qui* after a preposition

Use of *dont*

Use of *duquel* to replace *dont*

CONVERSATION

Le Professeur de Chimie

ANDRÉ: Ne courez pas si vite, Antoine.

ANTOINE: Il faut courir si nous voulons arriver à l'université avant que le professeur ne s'en aille.

ANDRÉ: Auquel des professeurs est-ce que vous voulez parler?

ANTOINE: A M. Firmin, le professeur de chimie, dont je vous ai si souvent parlé. Je cherche de nouvelles méthodes pour extraire l'essence du pétrole. Je voudrais que ce professeur m'indique un procédé qui ne soit pas trop compliqué, et que je puisse appliquer dans le pays où je travaille. M. Firmin est le seul qui les connaisse tous. De plus, il n'y a que lui qui sache enseigner d'une façon parfaite les dernières méthodes d'extraction de l'argent, du cuivre et du plomb.

ANDRÉ: Vous le connaissez bien?

ANTOINE: Je lui ai fait visite, il y a un mois, dans sa maison de campagne. Il habite une vieille ferme. Il a une vache, des cochons, des moutons. Quand j'ai frappé, la bonne, qui ne m'attendait pas, ne voulait pas me laisser entrer, mais j'ai insisté. Elle l'a appelé. Il s'est levé de sa chaise où il lisait dans un coin de la cour, entouré de coqs et de poules. Je l'ai salué, il m'a reconnu et m'a reçu très cordialement. Nous avons causé un peu et il n'a pas eu de difficulté à me renseigner sur ce que je voulais savoir. Il m'a même emmené dans son laboratoire et il m'a fait voir son nouveau procédé pour la production de la laine artificielle. Il obtient une étoffe magnifique.

ANDRÉ: C'est sans doute une laine plus légère que la laine naturelle?

ANTOINE: Pas du tout. Il produit une étoffe épaisse, sèche et lourde, dans le fil de laquelle se trouve une matière grasse qui rend le drap imperméable.

ANDRÉ: Mais nous voici à l'université. Dans lequel des bâtiments se trouve votre professeur?

ANTOINE: Dans le bâtiment de l'École des Mines en face duquel se trouve la statue du Marteleur. Nous avons de la chance. M. Firmin est encore là. Je le vois à sa fenêtre avec sa haute taille et ses grosses lunettes. Mon Dieu, qu'il est mince! Je n'avais jamais remarqué cela. Il a dû maigrir.

ANDRÉ: Je vais vous attendre sous ces arbres, à l'ombre desquels je me reposerai de la course que vous m'avez fait faire.

ANTOINE: Entendu. Ce ne sera pas long. A tout à l'heure.

VOCABULAIRE ET EXPRESSIONS

le pétrole petroleum oil
l'acier (*masc.*) steel
l'argent (*masc.*) silver, money
le cuivre copper
le fer-blanc tin
l'essence (*fem.*) gasoline
la vache the cow
le mouton the sheep
le cochon the pig
le coq the rooster

la poule the hen
la cour the courtyard
la bonne the maid, the servant
le coin the corner
l'étoffe (*fem.*) the cloth
le drap the cloth
le fil the thread
la laine the wool
la taille the figure
les lunettes (*fem.*) the eyeglasses

léger (*fem.* **légère**) light (in weight; use **clair** for color)
épais (*fem.* **épaisse**) thick

gras (*fem.* **grasse**) fat
mince thin, slender
sec (*fem.* **sèche**) dry

courir to run
renseigner to inform
mener to lead, take (to a place)
emmener to lead, take a person from a place, take out or away

amener to lead, take a person to a place, to bring
saluer to greet
enseigner to teach

imperméable waterproof
à l'ombre de in the shade of

avoir de la chance to be lucky
en face de facing, opposite

VOCABULAIRE SUPPLÉMENTAIRE

le procédé the process
le laboratoire the laboratory
la méthode the method
la matière the matter
la chimie chemistry
l'application (*fem.*) the application

l'extraction (*fem.*) the extraction
la mine the mine
la philosophie philosophy
la statue the statue
le marteleur the hammerer
la course the run, the race, the errand

parfait perfect
naturel (*fem.* **naturelle**) natural
allemand German
russe Russian
chinois Chinese
japonais Japanese

extraire to extract
appliquer to apply
taper à la machine to type

VERBES

Present Indicative of **courir** (to run)

je cours
tu cours
il (elle) court
nous courons
vous courez
ils (elles) courent

Imperfect: **je courais** Future: **je courrai** Past participle: **couru**

GRAMMAIRE

The Subjunctive (Continued)

je cherche un homme qui sache l'allemand I am looking for a man who knows German
je ne connais personne qui sache le russe I don't know anyone who knows Russian
Est-ce que vous connaissez une jeune fille qui sache bien le chinois? Do you know a girl who knows Chinese well?

→ The subjunctive is used in a relative adjective clause when the antecedent is not definitely known; that is, does not, or may not, exist.

je connais une dame qui sait le japonais I know a lady who knows Japanese
j'ai trouvé une jeune fille qui sait taper à la machine I have found a girl who knows how to type

→ But if the antecedent is definitely known (does exist), the indicative is used in the relative adjective clause.

c'est le seul qui la connaisse he is the only one who knows her
c'est la dernière chose que je fasse it is the last thing I'll (ever) do

il n'y a que lui qui sache cette langue there is no one but he who knows that language

c'est le plus beau cheval que j'aie jamais vu it's the finest horse I have ever seen

→ The subjunctive is often used in relative clauses following: (a) the expressions *seul, premier, dernier, ne . . . que;* (b) *a superlative.*

The subjunctive is used when it is felt that the statement is exaggerated, the indicative when it is literally true: **c'est la plus jolie jeune fille que j'ai vue dans cette classe** she is the prettiest girl I've seen in this class.

Some Relative Pronouns

le tableau auquel je pense the picture I'm thinking of

voici le crayon avec lequel j'ai écrit la lettre here is the pencil with which I wrote the letter

voilà la table sous laquelle est tombée la serviette there is the table under which the napkin fell

l'homme pour lequel j'ai fait ce sacrifice the man for whom I made this sacrifice

→ *Lequel,* etc., are also used as relative pronouns, after prepositions. They combine with *de* and *à* in the following forms:

duquel	de laquelle	**desquels**	**desquelles**
auquel	à laquelle	**auxquels**	**auxquelles**

voilà l'homme avec qui je suis sorti there is the man with whom I went out

→ *Qui* may be used as a relative pronoun after prepositions to refer to persons, when the antecedent is unmistakable.

voilà l'homme dont je parle there's the man I'm speaking of

voici le livre dont je parle here's the book I'm speaking of

voilà l'homme dont j'ai vu la fille hier there is the man whose daughter I saw yesterday

→ The relative "whose," "of whom," "of which" is usually translated by *dont.* Note (a) that English often omits "whom" and transfers "of" to the end of the clause (the man I'm speaking of—the man of whom I'm speaking); (b) after *dont* meaning "whose," the order of words is the normal order: subject, verb, object (*la femme dont j'ai vu le mari*). No inversion occurs as in English (the woman whose husband I saw), and the definite article is used before the noun connected with *dont* (*le mari*).

voilà la femme au fils de laquelle j'ai donné le livre there is the woman to whose son I gave the book

ce sont les hommes aux filles desquels nous avons parlé they are the men to whose daughters we spoke

→ *Dont* is replaced by *duquel,* etc., if the noun to which "whose" refers is the object of a preposition.

Some Interrogative Pronouns

Auquel de ces hommes allez-vous parler? To which of these men are you going to speak?

De laquelle de ces femmes parlez-vous? Of which of these women are you talking?

→ The interrogative pronouns *lequel,* etc., are used exactly as the relative pronouns.

QUESTIONS

1. Où court Antoine? 2. Qui est son professeur de chimie? 3. Pourquoi Antoine veut-il voir le professeur de chimie? 4. Qu'est-ce qu'il a découvert? 5. Comment savez-vous qu'il est bon professeur? 6. Qu'est-ce qu'Antoine a vu quand il est allé à la maison de campagne de son professeur? 7. Que faisait-il dans son laboratoire? 8. Dans quel bâtiment de l'université fait-il ses cours? 9. Faites la description de M. Firmin. 10. Où André attend-il son ami?

EXERCICES

A. *Conjuguez:*

1. Si je cours, je me ferai mal. 2. Si je courais, je me ferais mal. 3. Quand Marie courra, je courrai après elle. 4. J'ai couru pour arriver à temps à la gare. 5. Il faut que je coure aussi vite que Georges.

B. *Traduisez:*

I. 1. Are you looking for a man who knows how to drive a car? 2. Well, I know a man who can drive very well. 3. Do you know a professor who can teach Russian (*le russe*)? 4. Yes, I have a friend who knows Russian and can teach it very well. 5. Are you still looking for a girl who knows how to type? 6. No, I have found a young man who types very well.

II. 1. This is the best book that was ever published. 2. He is the only one who really knows Chinese (*le chinois*). 3. Pasteur is the first who made that discovery. 4. She is the only one who knows them. 5. It's the last book he has written.

III. 1. Is that the man to whom you gave the book? 2. Isn't that the girl from whom you received the letter? 3. Are those the friends (*fem.*) to whom you sent the flowers? 4. Why don't you give the money to the men from whom you received the auto? 5. To which of the men are you going to give gasoline? 6. Give me the pen with which I signed that check. 7. Do you know the girl with whom I went out? 8. There is the book under which I put the letter.

IV. 1. There is the woman I was speaking of yesterday. 2. Can't you find the pencil I was talking about? 3. The girl whose father you saw yesterday is leaving for Paris. 4. The man whose son you met at the station is a lawyer. 5. The professor whose students have passed their exams so well is a very modest (*modeste*) man.

THÈME

—Where are you running?

—I am late for (*à*) an appointment with my chemistry professor.

—What building is he in?

—His laboratory is in the Chemistry Building (*le bâtiment de Chimie*) but he lectures (*fait ses conférences*) at the School of Mines.

—Isn't that strange?

—Yes, they have a larger lecture hall (*salle de conférence*) at the School of Mines, which used to be the Science Building (*le bâtiment des sciences*).

—Has your professor ever discovered anything important?

—Yes, the Firmin method for the production of artificial wool.

—Is that all?

—No, he works in his laboratory on the extraction of silver and copper from lead.

—He must be quite remarkable (*remarquable*). I should like very much to meet him.

—Wait here in the shade, and if he is not busy, I shall ask him if you can see him after my interview is over.

—Thank you, I shall be here on this bench.

Review Lesson 8

A. *Traduisez les expressions idiomatiques suivantes en anglais:*

1. être en train de 2. faire ses adieux à 3. prendre congé de 4. en voiture! 5. donnez-moi de vos nouvelles. 6. ayez la bonté de m'écrire 7. au cours de 8. ayez soin de mon chat 9. avez-vous mal à la tête? 10. il m'a fait mal hier 11. il a fait sauter la maison 12. au secours! 13. il se laisse conduire par sa femme 14. les soldats ont fait feu 15. une maison entourée de gendarmes

(20 points)

B. *Employez les expressions suivantes dans des phrases que vous traduirez ensuite:*

1. cela vaut la peine 2. être à l'abri 3. faire des emplettes 4. mettre à la poste 5. du papier à lettres 6. à mon avis 7. se débarrasser de 8. se plaindre 9. au point de vue 10. être gênant 11. être disposé à 12. n'importe quoi 13. tout de même 14. se tromper 15. tomber amoureux de 16. à l'ombre de 17. avoir de la chance 18. renseigner 19. l'essence 20. le pétrole

(40 points)

C. *Remplacez l'infinitif en italique par la forme correcte du verbe:*

1. Tant qu'il *être* ici, je ne *partir* pas.
2. Elles sont *sortir* en *causer*.
3. Quand je la *voir*, je lui *dire* combien je la trouve charmante.
4. Après *manger*, elle est *partir* en ville.
5. Je ne crois pas qu'il *être* à la maison.
6. Je suis content qu'elle *avoir* une jolie auto.
7. Je regrette que nous *avoir* dit cela.
8. Il n'est pas naturel que vous *avoir* tant mangé au dîner.
9. Il est certain qu'elle *venir* demain.
10. Je ne crains pas qu'il *prendre* ce livre.
11. Je doute qu'il *savoir* la vérité.
12. Attendez jusqu'à ce qu'elle *être* arrivée.
13. Bien qu'il m'*avoir* rendu tous mes livres je ne lui en prêterai plus.

14. J'ai mis la lettre dans ma poche sans qu'elle s'en *être* aperçue.
15. Je cherche un domestique qui *savoir* le français.

(20 points)

D. *Remplacez le tiret par* de *ou* à:

1. Je suis fatigué ———— entendre parler de la sorte. 2. Êtes-vous enfin prêt ———— partir? 3. Il m'a permis ———— lire la lettre. 4. Il ne m'a pas demandé ———— le faire. 5. Elle m'a appris ———— lire. 6. Il nous ont aidé ———— le faire. 7. Je lui ai dit ———— le finir. 8. Il n'a pas cessé ———— manger. 9. Il est difficile ———— lire son écriture. 10. Ce livre est impossible ———— traduire. 11. Avez-vous une machine ———— écrire? 12. Il était accompagné ———— sa mère. 13. La maison est entourée ———— arbres. 14. C'est une grande maison ———— pierre. 15. Il est toujours suivi ———— ses hommes quand il sort. 16. Quelle jolie robe ———— soie! 17. Je veux du papier ———— lettres. 18. N'avez-vous pas mal ———— la tête? 19. Il s'est mis ———— lire. 20. Il m'a prié ———— lui écrire.

(20 points)

Lecture 8

LE JONGLEUR DE NOTRE DAME

(D'après un conte d' Anatole France)

Au temps de Saint Louis,[1] il y avait en France un pauvre jongleur nomme Barnabé. Les jours de foire[2] il étendait sur la place publique un vieux tapis, et après avoir attiré[3] les enfants et les passants, il mettait une assiette en équilibre sur son nez pour étonner les gens. On le regardait d'abord avec indifférence.

Mais quand, se tenant sur les mains, la tête en bas, il jetait en l'air et rattrapait avec ses pieds six boules de cuivre, ou quand il donnait à son corps la forme d'une roue (*wheel*) parfaite et jonglait, dans cette posture, avec douze couteaux, un murmure d'admiration s'élevait et l'argent pleuvait (*rained, fell*) sur le tapis.

Pourtant, Barnabé avait grand'peine[4] à vivre car, en hiver, il ne pouvait* guère travailler en plein air (*outdoors*). Alors il souffrait du froid et de la faim, mais il était doux et patient. Il ne blasphémait (*cursed*) jamais et il était très dévot (*devoted*) à la sainte Vierge. Quand il entrait dans une église, il s'agenouillait (*knelt*) toujours devant l'image de la Mère de Dieu et lui adressait cette prière.

"Madame, prenez soin de ma vie jusqu'à ce que je meure[5]* et quand je serai* mort, faites*-moi avoir les joies du paradis."

Un certain soir, après une journée de pluie, triste et découragé,

[1] Saint Louis: *Louis IX, king of France from 1226 to 1270 was a saintly and most popular monarch. He was canonized in 1297.*

[2] la foire: *in most European towns there are, during the good seasons, town fairs at regular intervals. In addition to merchants selling goods at these fairs there are many entertainers, singers, acrobats, jugglers, and so on.*

[3] après avoir attiré: *note the use of the past infinitive after* après.

[4] grand'peine, *much trouble. Many feminine nouns in French accompanied by* grand *use* grand *with the apostrophe instead of the customary feminine form. This is true of* grand'mère, grand'messe, grand'-rue.

[5] jusqu'à ce que *requires the subjunctive when referring to a future action.*

cherchant une grange pour s'y coucher (*lie down*) sans souper, il vit sur la route un moine (*monk*) qui suivait le même chemin.

"Compagnon, dit le moine, d'où vient* que[6] vous êtes habillé tout de vert[7]? Êtes-vous acteur?"

"Oh non, mon père, répondit Barnabé, je suis jongleur. Et ce serait le plus beau métier du monde, si on y mangeait tous les jours."

"Mon ami, dit le moine, prenez garde à (*be careful*) ce que vous dites.* Il n'y a pas de plus beau métier (*calling*) que la vie monastique. La vie du religieux (*monk*) est un perpétuel cantique (*hymn*) à Dieu et à la Vierge."

Barnabé répondit: "Mon frère, je confesse que j'ai parlé comme un ignorant. Je voudrais* bien, comme vous, chanter tous les jours les louanges (*praises*) de Dieu et spécialement celles[8] (*those*) de la très sainte Vierge. Je renoncerai bien volontiers (*gladly*) à ma vie de jongleur pour embrasser (*take up*) la vie monastique."

Le moine reconnut* en Barnabé un homme de bonté et de vertu. "Mon ami," dit-il, "venez* avec moi et je vous ferai* entrer dans le même monastère que moi." C'est ainsi que Barnabé devint* moine. Dans ce monastère les religieux célébraient tous[9] le culte de la sainte Vierge et chacun employait à la servir tout le savoir (*knowledge*) et l'habileté que Dieu lui avait donnés.

Le prieur (*Prior*) composait des livres qui traitaient des vertus de la Mère de Dieu. Le Frère Alexandre peignait[10] de fines miniatures. Le Frère Marbode sculptait des images de pierre, surtout celle de la sainte Vierge. Il y avait aussi des frères qui composaient en latin des poèmes en l'honneur de la Vierge Marie. Mais Barnabé n'était pas heureux, il regrettait son ignorance.

6 d'où vient que, *how does it happen that, how does it come about that.*

7 tout de vert: *an idiomatic way of saying "all in green." In like manner we have* tout de blanc vêtu. *In the Middle Ages the members of the brotherhood of actors were dressed in green.*

8 celles: *this demonstrative pronoun has four forms,* celui, celle, ceux, *and* celles; *it is translated by "this" or "the one" in the singular and by "these," "those," or "the ones" in the plural.*

9 tous: *when this form is a pronoun the* s *is pronounced.*

10 peignait: *third-person singular of the imperfect of* peindre, *to paint, conjugated like* craindre.

"Hélas! hélas! soupirait-il, je suis un homme rude et sans art, et je n'ai, pour le service de la Vierge, ni poèmes, ni livres, ni peintures, ni statues.[11] Je n'ai rien, hélas!"

Un soir que les moines parlaient ensemble, il entendit l'un d'eux raconter l'histoire d'un religieux qui ne savait réciter qu'Ave Maria. C'était le plus ignorant de tous les moines de son monastère, mais il était dévot et sincère et, à sa mort, il lui sortit de la bouche[12] cinq roses en l'honneur des cinq lettres du nom de Marie.

En écoutant ce récit, Barnabé admira une fois de plus la bonté de la Vierge et il voulut[13] la servir aussi, car son coeur était plein de zèle. Il courut* à la chapelle et y demeura seul pendant plus d'une heure. Il y retourna l'après-midi; et à partir de ce moment (*from that time on*), il allait chaque jour à la chapelle, à l'heure où (*when*) elle était déserte et il y passait une grande partie du temps que les autres moines consacraient (*devoted*) à la poésie, la sculpture et la peinture. Il n'était plus triste maintenant. Mais cette conduite éveilla la curiosité des moines. Ils se demandaient pourquoi le frère Barnabé faisait* des prières si fréquentes. Un jour donc que Barnabé s'était retiré comme d'habitude dans la chapelle, le prieur, accompagné de deux autres moines, vint* observer par un trou (*hole*) de la porte ce qu'il faisait.

Ils virent* Barnabé devant l'autel de la Vierge, la tête en bas (*standing on his head*), les pieds en l'air, jonglant avec six boules de cuivre et douze couteaux. Cet homme simple (*unpretending*) mettait ainsi tout son talent et tout son savoir (*knowledge*) au service de la sainte Vierge.

Le prieur et les deux frères croyaient* que Barnabé était devenu* fou. Ils étaient sur le point d'aller le tirer (*pull*) rudement de la chapelle, quand ils virent* la sainte Vierge descendre de l'autel pour venir essuyer (*wipe*) d'un coin (*corner*) de sa robe bleue la sueur (*sweat*) de son front. Puis elle retourna à sa place.

Alors le prieur répéta tout haut (*aloud*) ces paroles (*words*)

[11] n'ai ni poèmes, ni livres, *etc.*: *"neither" "nor" in French takes* ne *before the verb and* ni *without any article before the nouns.*

[12] il lui sortit de la bouche, *there came out of his mouth. Note the impersonal* il *(there) and the use of the indirect object* lui *to indicate the possessor.*

[13] il voulut, *he decided to (literally: he willed). The past definite of* vouloir *stresses volition rather than wishing.*

de la Bible: "Heureux les simples (*pure in heart*), car ils verront Dieu!"

"Amen!" répondirent les deux frères en baisant (*kissing*) la terre.

QUESTIONNAIRE

1. Comment Barnabé amusait-il son public? 2. Que faisait-il pour attirer l'admiration des gens? 3. Pourquoi Barnabé souffrait-il? 4. Comment savez-vous que Barnabé était dévot? 5. Qui vit-il un soir sur la route? 6. Que pense-t-il du métier de jongleur? 7. Qu'est-ce que le moine lui répond? 8. A quoi Barnabé est-il prêt à renoncer? 9. Comment le moine offre-t-il de l'aider? 10. Comment les Frères passaient-ils leur temps au monastère? 11. Pourquoi Barnabé n'était-il pas heureux? 12. Quelle histoire un des moines a-t-il racontée? 13. Après ce récit, qu'est-ce que Barnabé s'est décidé à faire? 14. Qu'est-ce que les moines se demandaient au sujet de Barnabé? 15. Qu'est-ce qu'ils ont vu un jour? 16. Quelle a été leur première pensée? 17. Pendant qu'ils regardaient Barnabé, qu'est-ce qu'ils ont vu? 18. Qu'est-ce que le prieur et les deux frères ont fait?

Lesson 34

Review of *faire* in imperfect, future, conditional, and past participle

Idiomatic uses of *faire*

Use of *faire* followed by an infinitive

Direct and indirect objects with causative *faire*

Position of pronoun and noun objects with *faire*

Use of *voir* and *entendre* followed by an infinitive

Relative clause replacing infinitive in this construction

Il ne faut pas compared with *il n'est pas nécessaire*

CONVERSATION

Suzanne A Fait des Courses

RENÉE: Si nous faisions allumer le feu, Suzanne?

SUZANNE: C'est une bonne idée. Il fait froid. Je vais sonner le domestique, et je vais lui faire apporter du charbon et du bois. Puis, nous allumerons nous-mêmes.

LE DOMESTIQUE: Mademoiselle a sonné?

SUZANNE: Oui. Je voudrais que vous apportiez du bois et du charbon.

LE DOMESTIQUE: A l'instant, mademoiselle.

SUZANNE: Il faut que je vous raconte. J'ai été aujourd'hui dans une banque pour faire changer en francs un de mes chèques sur une banque américaine. Quelle histoire! Il a fallu que je répète au moins cent fois mon nom et mon adresse; puis il a fallu que je donne le nom de tous mes amis français; on m'a posé un tas de questions; enfin, on m'a donné l'argent, mais je suis sûre qu'on m'a volé sur le change. De plus, je trouve qu'ils sont bien impolis dans ces bureaux de province. Ils parlent presque toutes les langues, c'est vrai, mais de quelle façon! N'importe! Ils font de leur mieux. Ah, voici le domestique. Avez-vous quelque chose à lui donner? Moi, je n'ai pas de petite monnaie.

RENÉE: Vous en trouverez dans mon porte-monnaie.

LE DOMESTIQUE: Mademoiselle désire que j'allume le feu?

SUZANNE: Non, laissez. Merci bien.

LE DOMESTIQUE: Bien, Mademoiselle.

RENÉE: Et après être allée au bureau de change?

SUZANNE: Ensuite, je suis allée à un magasin chercher des ciseaux et des chaussettes.

RENÉE: Des chaussettes?

SUZANNE: Oui, des bas courts, qui dépassent à peine la cheville. Vous savez; ce qu'on appelle "bobby-sox" en Amérique. On n'avait que des chaussettes d'homme. Je les ai prises, quoique ça ait fait rire le vendeur. Mais enfin, j'avais besoin de chaussettes neuves, et cela m'a amusée autant que lui.

RENÉE: Et le prix?

SUZANNE: Oh, c'était très raisonnable. Cent francs la paire. Et j'ai trouvé des ciseaux. A présent, pour notre collection d'articles intéressants, nous pourrons découper les journaux au lieu de les déchirer. Et je vous ai acheté une boîte de bonbons.

RENÉE: Ah, que vous êtes gentille!

SUZANNE: Dites, voulez-vous que je fasse venir le médecin mercredi?

RENÉE: Non, ce n'est plus nécessaire. N'importe quel jour. Je me sens beaucoup mieux.

VOCABULAIRE ET EXPRESSIONS

le (la) domestique the servant
le charbon the coal
le bois the wood
la course the errand
l'histoire (*fem.*) the history; story; fuss
la monnaie the coin
la petite monnaie the (small) change
le change the exchange
le bureau de change the exchange office
le porte-monnaie the change purse
le nom the name
la langue the language, tongue
le prix (*pl.* **prix**) the price; the prize
les ciseaux (*masc.*) the scissors
la chaussette the sock
la cheville the ankle
le bas the stocking
l'adresse (*fem.*) the address
la boîte the box
le bonbon the piece of candy; (use plural, **les bonbons,** in the English collective sense)

court short
gai gay, merry, jolly
poli polite
impoli impolite
neuf (*fem.* **neuve**) new
convenable suitable
raisonnable reasonable, fair, sensible

découper to cut out, to cut up
changer to change, exchange (*nous changeons*)
voler to steal, rob
dépasser to go beyond
sonner to ring, ring for

à peine barely, hardly, scarcely
n'importe quel . . . any . . . whatsoever
à l'instant at once
faire venir to send for
je n'ai pas de petite monnaie I have no change
de leur mieux the best they can

VOCABULAIRE SUPPLÉMENTAIRE

le tas the heap
nécessaire necessary
allumer to light
la province the province; France outside of Paris
déchirer to tear

VERBES

Review the Present Indicative of **faire** (Lesson 6)

Imperfect: **je faisais** Future: **je ferai** Conditional: **je ferais** P.p. **fait**

GRAMMAIRE

Idiomatic Uses of **faire**

nous avons fait une promenade we took a walk
il a fait un voyage en France he took a trip to France
il fait beau (mauvais) it's fine (bad) weather
il fait chaud (froid) it's warm (cold)
faites attention! pay attention! be careful!
les soldats ont fait feu the soldiers fired
il a fait le sourd he acted like a deaf man
si nous faisions une partie de cartes? how about a game of cards?
ma femme a fait des emplettes my wife did some shopping (**aller faire des emplettes** to go shopping)
nous avons fait la bombe hier soir we had a grand time last night
ça me fait plaisir that pleases me
faites voir votre langue show your tongue
il leur a fait savoir qu'il ne pouvait pas venir he informed them that he could not come

→ Observe the above idiomatic uses of *faire* (which by no means exhaust the list), and note how many English verbs are translated by *faire*, with or without a following verb.

Use of **faire** + Infinitive

j'ai fait parler le garçon I made (had) the boy speak
j'ai fait écrire la lettre I had the letter written

→ *Faire* followed by an infinitive often means: (a) to have or make someone do; (b) to have something done.

je l'ai fait parler I made (had) him speak (*l'* = *le garçon*)
je l'ai fait écrire I had it written (*l'* = *la lettre*)
faites-le écrire have him write (*le* = *le garçon*)
faites-la écrire have it written (*la* = *la lettre*)

→ If an object pronoun is used in this construction, it assumes the position of an object of *faire,* even if it is the object of the following verb. In compound tenses there is no agreement of the participle of *faire* with the preceding direct object.

j'ai fait comprendre la situation à mon frère I made my brother understand the situation.
j'ai fait lire le journal par les élèves I had the students read the paper

→ In the sense of "to have someone do something," "to make someone do something," "to have something done by somebody," the thing is a direct object, the person an indirect object or an object introduced by *par.*

je l'ai fait comprendre à mon frère I made my brother understand it
je lui ai fait comprendre la situation I made him understand the situation
je la lui ai fait comprendre I made him understand it
faites-lui passer l'examen make him take the examination
faites-le passer à l'élève make the pupil take it
faites-le-lui passer make him take it

→ If there are two objects, person and thing, pronoun objects go with *faire,* noun objects follow the second verb.

j'ai fait venir le médecin I had the doctor come
je l'ai fait venir I had him come

→ *Faire venir* means to cause to come, to have someone come.

Voir, entendre, laisser + Infinitive

je l'ai vue jouer Phèdre I saw her play Phaedra
je l'ai vu sortir I saw him go out
je les ai entendus chanter I heard them sing
nous avons laissé détruire la maison we let the house be destroyed
nous l'avons laissé détruire we let it be destroyed

→ Constructions similar to that of the causative *faire* may be used with *voir* and *entendre* (to see someone do something, to hear someone do something). With these verbs the normal agreement of the past participle with the direct object of the conjugated verb occurs. In the last two examples, *l'* is the direct object of détruire, not of *laisser.*

je l'ai vu qui sortait I saw him go out
je l'ai entendu qui chantait I heard him sing

→ An alternative construction is formed with a relative clause.

Il ne faut pas—Il n'est pas nécessaire

il ne faut pas le faire it must not be done
il n'est pas nécessaire de le faire it is not necessary to do it

→ *Il ne faut pas* means "must not." For "it is not necessary" use ***il n'est pas nécessaire.***

QUESTIONS

1. Qu'est-ce que Renée demande à Suzanne? 2. Pourquoi Suzanne sonne-t-elle le domestique? 3. Pourquoi est-elle allée au bureau de change? 4. Pourquoi se plaint-elle du bureau de change? 5. Où trouve-t-elle de la petite monnaie? 6. Est-ce que le domestique va allumer le feu? 7. Pourquoi est-elle allée à un magasin après être allée au bureau de change? 8. Est-elle contente du prix des chaussettes? 9. Pourquoi achète-t-elle des ciseaux? 10. Est-ce que Renée a encore besoin d'un médecin?

EXERCICES

A. *Conjuguez les verbes dans les phrases suivantes:*

1. Je fais une promenade tous les jours. 2. J'ai fait un voyage en France. 3. Si je faisais une partie de cartes, je n'aurais pas le temps d'aller en ville. 4. Je ferai mes devoirs ce soir. 5. Si j'en avais le droit, je ferais écrire cette lettre tout de suite.

B. *Remplacez le verbe en italique par la forme correcte du verbe* faire *suivi du même infinitif:*

1. Il va *write* la lettre. 2. Nous *speak* la jeune fille. 3. Je *dance* la jeune dame. 4. Ils *go out* le chien. 5. Ils *come* le médecin.

C. *Traduisez les phrases suivantes:*

1. We will make him come tomorrow. 2. They made the pupils go out. 3. He made the doctor come. 4. Have the letter written now.

5. Make him write. 6. Make her talk. 7. We made the boy speak. 8. We saw him go out. 9. I heard her singing this morning. 10. They made him study all afternoon.

D. *Remplacez tous les noms dans les phrases suivantes par des pronoms:*

1. Jean a fait comprendre la situation à sa sœur. 2. Marie a fait venir le médecin. 3. Georges a fait faire son complet hier. 4. Pourquoi ne pas faire passer l'examen aux élèves? 5. Marie et sa mère ont entendu chanter Mlle Pons. 6. Il ne faut pas faire ce travail immédiatement. 7. Est-ce que Mme Dupont a vu sortir sa fille? 8. Les parents ont laissé sortir leurs enfants.

E. *Traduisez:*

1. They took a walk in the garden. 2. When I go shopping I always have change in my purse. 3. I am happy to know that he gave you that box of candies. 4. She had her servant bring the stockings. 5. You must not light the fire; really, it is not necessary.

THÈME

—Aren't you cold?

—Yes, tell the servant to bring in some wood and coal, and to light a fire.

—Where is he?

—Ring (for) him. He will come at once.

—Did you go to the department stores today?

—Yes, I had to buy some socks and some scissors.

—Where did you get (*trouver*) the money? You had none this morning.

—I changed one of my checks at the bank (Bureau of Exchange).

—Did you have to answer many questions before receiving the money?

—Yes, and I think I was robbed on the exchange. The clerk was very impolite when I questioned him.

—What is the matter with your knee?

—I cut (*couper*) it a little. That is why I bought socks, they are shorter than stockings and reach just above the ankle.

—Must I get a doctor?

—Oh no! it is nothing. You would make him laugh if you called him for such a thing.

—Well! you know. He comes for anything at all.

Lesson 35

The past anterior and its use

Imperfect subjunctive of *parler, vendre,* and *finir*

Imperfect subjunctive of some irregular verbs

Pluperfect subjunctive of *parler* and *aller*

Use of the imperfect subjunctive

Use of the pluperfect subjunctive

Substitution of the present subjunctive for the imperfect subjunctive

Colloquial substitution of the imperfect indicative for the imperfect subjunctive

LA BATAILLE FINALE (CONFÉRENCE)

Dès que l'armée américaine *eut débarqué* en Normandie, le commandant en chef des armées alliées, craignant que les Allemands *n'eussent réussi* à détruire toutes les lignes de communication par lesquelles *il comptait* avancer, *fut obligé* de déployer ses forces avec une prudence extrême, car *il s'agissait* du succès de tous ses plans d'invasion. Comme il ne *croyait* pas que l'ennemi *pût* s'échapper du côté de la Loire, il *envoya* trois de ses divisions motorisées vers la frontière belge. Leur mission *était* d'empêcher les renforts allemands de venir au secours de leurs camarades pris dans le piège de la péninsule normande. Mais la destinée *en* disposa autrement. Cinq divisions allemandes, doutant que les Américains *fussent* déjà *arrivés* jusqu'à la Seine, *se plongèrent* dans l'ouverture créée par le mouvement allié vers le nord. A peine *eurent-elles achevé* cette manœuvre que les Canadiens, tenus en réserve jusque là, *s'avancèrent* sur le flanc droit de l'armée allemande. Le piège *se serra,* puis *se referma* complètement. Les divisions motorisées *firent* un demi-tour à droite, *brisèrent* la résistance de quelques brigades allemandes restées sur leur chemin, puis *se joignirent* aux forces qui *s'avançaient* du sud.

VOCABULAIRE ET EXPRESSIONS

le camarade the comrad
le piège the trap
le roi the king
le palais the palace
la force the strength (*pl.* the forces)
la frontière the frontier, border
la destinée fate
normand Norman
canadien (*fem.* **canadienne**) Canadian
espéré hoped for
inespéré unhoped for
inattendu unexpected

détruire (conj. like **conduire**) to destroy
avancer to advance (**nous avançons**)
se joindre à to join
céder to yield (**je cède**)
compter to expect
lancer to hurl, throw (**nous lançons**)
refermer to close tight
s'agir de to be a matter of (**il s'agit de,** etc.)

VOCABULAIRE SUPPLÉMENTAIRE

le commandant the major (**le commandant en chef** the commander-in-chief)
le succès the success
les renforts (*masc.*) the reinforcements
le flanc the flank, the side
la communication the communication
la prudence prudence
le demi-tour the half-turn
faire demi-tour to turn around
l'ouverture (*fem.*) the opening
la réserve the reserve
la brigade the brigade
la péninsule the peninsula
l'occasion (*fem.*) the opportunity
le ministre the minister
l'invasion (*fem.*) the invasion

extrême extreme

motorisé motorized, mechanized

déployer to deploy **(je déploie)**

plonger to plunge **(nous plongeons)**

se plonger to rush

disposer to dispose

VERBES

The Past Anterior

j'eus parlé	**nous eûmes parlé**
tu eus parlé	**vous eûtes parlé**
il eut parlé	**ils eurent parlé**
elle eut parlé	**elles eurent parlé**

je fus allé(e)	**nous fûmes allés(e)**
tu fus allé(e)	**vous fûtes allé(e)(s)(es)**
il fut allé	**ils furent allés**
elle fut allée	**elles furent allées**

→ The past anterior is formed by combining the past definite of the auxiliary (*avoir* or *être*) with the past participle.

Imperfect Subjunctive of **parler, vendre, finir**

je parlasse	**nous parlassions**
tu parlasses	**vous parlassiez**
il (elle) parlât	**ils (elles) parlassent**

je vendisse	**nous vendissions**
tu vendisses	**vous vendissiez**
il (elle) vendît	**ils (elles) vendissent**

je finisse	**nous finissions**
tu finisses	**vous finissiez**
il (elle) finît	**ils (elles) finissent**

→ To form the imperfect subjunctive, drop the final *-i* of the past definite of *-er* verbs (*je parlai*), or the final *-s* of the past definite of all other verbs (*je vendis, je finis*); then add the following endings: ***-sse, -sses, ˆ-t, -ssions, -ssiez, -ssent.***

Infinitive	Past Definite	Imperfect Subjunctive
faire:	**je fis**	**je fisse**
mettre:	**je mis**	**je misse**
prendre:	**je pris**	**je prisse**
voir:	**je vis**	**je visse**
dire:	**je dis**	**je disse**
boire:	**je bus**	**je busse**
être:	**je fus**	**je fusse**
avoir:	**j'eus**	**j'eusse**
vivre:	**je vécus**	**je vécusse**
pleuvoir:	**il plut**	**il plût**
venir:	**je vins**	**je vinsse**
tenir:	**je tins**	**je tinsse**

→ The rule given above for the formation of the imperfect subjunctive works for all irregular verbs without exception.

Pluperfect Subjunctive of **parler, aller**

j'eusse parlé	**nous eussions parlé**
tu eusses parlé	**vous eussiez parlé**
il eût parlé	**ils eussent parlé**
elle eût parlé	**elles eussent parlé**
je fusse allé(e)	**nous fussions allés(-ées)**
tu fusses allé(e)	**vous fussiez allé (-ée, -és, -ées)**
il fût allé	**ils fussent allés**
elle fût allée	**elles fussent allées**

→ The pluperfect subjunctive is formed by combining the imperfect subjunctive of the auxiliary (*avoir* or *être*) with the past participle.

GRAMMAIRE

à peine fut-il entré que Louis le vit hardly had he come in when Louis saw him

dès que Napoléon fut rentré en France, la guerre recommença as soon as Napoleon had come back to France, the war began once more

quand il eut perdu cette bataille, il se retira jusqu'en France when he had lost that battle, he retreated to France

→ The past anterior is used to relate what happened immediately before something else took place. It generally appears in subordinate clauses of time, after *quand, lorsque, dès que, aussitôt que, à peine, après que.*

When *à peine* (hardly) begins the sentence an interrogative construction is used, and *que* translates the English "when" in the following clause.

il avait déjà fini son travail quand je l'ai vu he had already finished his work when I saw him

dès qu'il fut entré, je lui ai expliqué la difficulté as soon as he entered, I explained the difficulty to him

→ Note that the pluperfect (*avait fini*) is used in the first sentence to express something which happened some time (but not immediately) before something else took place (*je l'ai vu*).—But in the second sentence the past anterior is used because *fut entré* expresses an act which took place immediately before the next (*j'ai expliqué*).

Le roi craignit que son ministre ne voulût le faire assassiner. The king feared that his minister wanted to have him murdered.

C'était le seul qui pût réussir. He was the only one who might succeed.

→ The imperfect subjunctive is used chiefly in the historical style (books, lectures of a historical nature, etc.), seldom conversationally. It follows a past tense of the indicative in the main clause, and is usually translated by an English past.

Jeanne d'Arc douta que les Anglais eussent déjà traversé la Manche. Joan of Arc doubted that the English had already crossed the Channel.

Avant que le roi eût cédé le trône, son fils mourut. Before the king had given up his throne, his son died.

→ The pluperfect subjunctive is also used chiefly in the historical style (books, lectures, etc.). It follows a past tense of the indicative in the main clause, and is usually translated by an English past perfect.

Il a demandé que vous lui répondissiez (or **répondiez**) **le plus tôt possible.** He asked that you answer as soon as possible.

Il attendait que vous eussiez (or **ayez**) **fini.** He was waiting until you had finished.

Le roi ne croyait pas que son ministre fût dans le palais. The king did not think his minister was in the palace.

Je suis parti, avant qu'il n'eût eu le temps de me répondre. I left before he had the time to answer me. (literary form)

Je suis parti, avant qu'il n'ait eu le temps de me répondre. I left before he had the time to answer me. (conversational form)

→ The imperfect indicative, which is used both in conversation and in the historical style, and the past indefinite, which is commonly used in conversation, are followed by the present or past subjunctive if the style is historical. However, the present subjunctive can replace the imperfect subjunctive, and the perfect subjunctive can replace the pluperfect subjunctive, only when it is clear that the time of the subordinate clause is future to the time of the main clause.

Je ne croyais pas qu'il fût si malade. I did not think that he was so sick.

Je ne croyais pas qu'il était si malade. I did not think that he was so sick.

→ The imperfect indicative is sometimes used colloquially to replace the imperfect subjunctive when the time expressed by the verb in the subordinate clause is clearly past, happening at the same time in the past as the action of the verb in the main clause and not later.

QUESTIONS

N'employez pas le passé défini, mais le passé indéfini, comme dans les questions:

1. Pourquoi le commandant en chef des armées alliées a-t-il été obligé de déployer ses forces avec prudence? 2. Pourquoi a-t-il envoyé ses divisions motorisées vers la frontière belge plutôt que du côté de la Loire? 3. Qui a été pris dans le piège de la péninsule normande? 4. Quelle erreur les Allemands ont-ils commise en voyant le mouvement des alliés vers le nord? 5. Pourquoi les Alliés ont-ils été contents de l'action allemande? 6. Quelles troupes se sont avancées sur le flanc droit de l'armée allemande? 7. Quelles sortes de troupes ont brisé la résistance allemande? 8. Quelle a été la conclusion de cette bataille?

EXERCICE

Expliquez le temps de chaque verbe en italique dans le texte.

Review Lesson 9

A. *Faites des phrases avec les expressions suivantes:*

1. laisser partir 2. faire voir 3. voir écrire 4. entendre parler 5. faire faire 6. laisser jouer

(25 points)

B. *Traduisez en français:*

1. He hurt his finger. 2. It is warm. 3. He made him write the letter. 4. He made him write it. 5. He made his brother write it. 6. He took a walk. 7. Are you going to do some shopping? 8. Let me know what you are going to do.

(25 points)

C. *Remplacez le tiret par le mot qui convient:* quel, dont, laquelle, que, qui, cet, cette, celle, ce que, en:

1. La femme ——— je parlais n'est pas encore arrivée. 2. C'est lui ——— est malade. 3. ——— homme-là est mon cousin. 4. ——— qui m'a parlé ce matin n'est pas venue en classe. 5. Le livre ——— Jean m'a donné est un chef d'œuvre. 6. ——— de ces jeunes filles est votre sœur? 7. ——— livre voulez-vous que je vous donne? 8. ——— femme n'est certainement pas sa cousine? 9. ——— je vous dis là, c'est la vérité. 10. J'avais déjà trois sous. Il me ——— a donné deux autres.

(20 points)

D. *Faites des phrases avec les expressions suivantes:*

1. en haut 2. en bas 3. au secours 4. faire sauter 5. avoir mal à la gorge 6. faire mal à quelqu'un 7. aller à pied 8. le plus tôt possible 9. à tout à l'heure 10. fermer à clé

(10 points)

E. *THÈME*

(Peter and Mary are getting into an auto.)

PETER: Do you want to drive, Mary?

MARY: No, (you) take the wheel. I prefer to look at the scenery.

Peter: Would you like to go to (*dans*) the mountains or to the seashore? Both are about ten miles from here.

Mary: Let's go to the mountains. I like to see the trees and the lakes, and it is usually cool.

Peter: That's true, but it rains heavily (*à verse*) in the mountains, especially in summer.

Mary: Isn't the weather ever bad at the seashore?

Peter: Not often. Sometimes it is windy and it is damp but it is usually sunny.

(20 points)

Lecture 9

LA COMÉDIE DE CELUI QUI ÉPOUSA UNE FEMME MUETTE

Anatole France

(Adaptation)

PERSONNAGES

MONSIEUR LÉONARD BOTAL, *juge*
MAÎTRE ADAM FUMÉE, *avocat*
MAÎTRE SIMON COLLINE, *médecin*
MAÎTRE JEAN MAUGIER, *chirurgien*
MAÎTRE SÉRAPHIN DULAURIER, *apothicaire*
LE SIEUR GILLES BOISCOURTIER, *secrétaire de M. Léonard Botal*
UN AVEUGLE, *qui joue de la musette*
CATHERINE, *femme de M. Léonard Botal*
ALIZON, *servante de M. Léonard Botal*
MADEMOISELLE DE LA GARANDIÈRE

ÉPOQUE : LE XVIE SIÈCLE

Une salle du rez-de-chaussée, dans la maison de M. Léonard Botal. A droite une porte donnant sur la cuisine. Au fond un escalier de bois mène aux chambres du premier étage. Aux murs, des portraits de magistrats, puis de vastes armoires remplies de livres, de papiers et de parchemins. Une échelle double permet d'atteindre au haut des armoires. Une table à écrire, des chaises et des fauteuils, un rouet.

ACTE PREMIER

SCÈNE PREMIÈRE

Gilles Boiscourtier, Alizon, *puis* Maître[1] Adam Fumée *et* M. Léonard Botal

[GILLES BOISCOURTIER *est occupé à écrire et à bâiller lorsque entre la servante* ALIZON, *un grand panier sous*[2] *chaque bras. Dès qu'il la voit,* GILLES BOISCOURTIER *saute sur elle.*]

ALIZON: Sainte Vierge,[3] est-il permis* de se jeter ainsi sur les créatures?[4]

GILLES [*Il tire de l'un des paniers une bouteille de vin.*]: Ne crie donc pas ainsi, petite oie.

ALIZON: Veux-tu bien laisser[5] le vin de monsieur[6] le juge, voleur! [*Elle pose ses paniers à terre, reprend sa bouteille, gifle*[7] *le secrétaire, et s'en va à la cuisine. Entre maître* ADAM FUMÉE.]

MAÎTRE ADAM: N'est-ce pas ici que demeure monsieur le juge Léonard Botal?

1 *The title* Maître *was given before the French Revolution to lawyers, physicians, surgeons, pharmacists, etc.*
2 sous chaque bras, *on each arm (lit: under, hanging from each arm).*
3 Sainte Vierge, *Good heavens! In French such words as* Dieu, Vierge, Diable, *are used frequently in exclamations.*
4 créatures = gens, *people.*
5 Veux-tu bien laisser, *Will you please leave alone.* Bien *emphasizes the preceding verb.*
6 Monsieur le juge. *In polite conversation titles are usually accompanied by "monsieur," "madame." Examples:* monsieur le professeur; madame la comtesse.
7 gifle, *boxes the ears of.*

GILLES: C'est ici, monsieur, et vous parlez à son secrétaire, Gilles Boiscourtier, pour vous servir.[8]

MAÎTRE ADAM: Eh! bien, mon garçon, va lui dire que son ancien condisciple,[9] maître Adam Fumée, avocat, vient lui parler d'une affaire.

GILLES: Monsieur, le voici lui-même. [LÉONARD BOTAL *descend l'escalier.* GILLES *s'en va à la cuisine.*]

MAÎTRE ADAM: Bonjour, monsieur Léonard Botal, je suis heureux de vous revoir.

LÉONARD: Bonjour, maître Adam Fumée, comment vous portez-vous depuis le long temps que je n'ai eu le plaisir de vous voir?

MAÎTRE ADAM: Fort bien! Et vous aussi, j'espère, monsieur le juge.

LÉONARD: Quel bon vent vous amène, maître Adam Fumée?

MAÎTRE ADAM: Je viens tout exprès[10] de Chartres[11] pour vous présenter un mémoire[12] en faveur d'une jeune orpheline.

LÉONARD: Vous souvenez-vous, maître Adam Fumée, du temps où nous étudiions le droit[13] à l'université d'Orléans?[14]

MAÎTRE ADAM: Oui, nous jouions de la flûte et nous dansions du matin au soir . . . Je viens,* monsieur le juge et cher condisciple, vous présenter un mémoire en faveur d'une jeune orpheline dont vous avez à juger la cause.[15]

LÉONARD: Donne-t-elle des épices?[16]

MAÎTRE ADAM: C'est une jeune orpheline . . .

LÉONARD: Je sais,* je sais. Mais donne-t-elle des épices?

8 pour vous servir = à votre service.
9 ancien condisciple, *former schoolmate.*
10 tout exprès, *especially, purposely.*
11 Chartres: *a city 55 miles southwest of Paris, famous for its cathedral, which is a masterpiece of Gothic architecture.*
12 un mémoire, *a bill of complaint; here a legal term, not to be confused with the feminine* la mémoire, *memory.*
13 le droit, *law.*
14 Orléans: *an old city 75 miles south of Paris. It is no longer the seat of a university.*
15 la cause = le procès, *the lawsuit.*
16 des épices, *presents, gifts. In the old days litigants would give the judge a gift in the hope of influencing his decision or in gratitude for a decision in their favor.*

MAÎTRE ADAM: C'est une jeune orpheline dépouillée par son tuteur,[17] qui ne lui a laissé que les yeux pour pleurer. Si elle gagne son procès, elle redeviendra* riche et donnera de grandes marques de sa reconnaissance.

LÉONARD [*prenant le mémoire*]: Nous examinerons son affaire.

MAÎTRE ADAM: Je vous remercie, monsieur le juge et cher ancien condisciple.

LÉONARD: Nous l'examinerons sans haine ni faveur.

MAÎTRE ADAM: Vous n'avez pas besoin de le dire . . . Mais répondez-moi. Tout va-t-il bien comme vous voulez? Vous paraissez* soucieux.[18] Pourtant vous avez une bonne charge?[19]

LÉONARD: Je l'ai payée comme bonne[20] et n'ai pas été trompé.

MAÎTRE ADAM: Peut-être êtes-vous las[21] de vivre seul. Ne songez-vous pas à vous marier?

LÉONARD: Eh! quoi? maître Adam, ne savez-vous pas que je suis marié? J'ai épousé, le mois dernier, une jeune fille de bonne famille et fort belle, Catherine Momichel, la septième fille d'un procureur.[22] Malheureusement elle est muette. C'est ce qui m'afflige.

MAÎTRE ADAM: Votre femme est muette?

LÉONARD: Hélas!

MAÎTRE ADAM: Tout à fait muette?

LÉONARD: Comme un poisson.

MAÎTRE ADAM: Ne vous en étiez-vous pas aperçu[23] avant de l'épouser?

17 tuteur, *guardian.*
18 soucieux, *worried.*
19 charge = position.
20 Je l'ai payée comme bonne, *I paid for a good one. Before the Revolution in France, it was possible to buy certain official positions such as judgeships.*
21 las = fatigué, *tired.*
22 procureur, *public prosecutor.*
23 s'apercevoir de (*p.p.* aperçu), *to notice, to perceive.*

LÉONARD: Il était bien impossible de ne pas le remarquer. Mais je ne m'en[24] sentais pas affecté alors comme aujourd'hui. Je considérais qu'elle était belle, qu'elle était riche, et je ne pensais qu'aux avantages qu'elle m'apportait et au plaisir de l'avoir près de moi. Mais maintenant ces considérations ne me frappent pas autant et je serais heureux si elle pouvait parler; j'y[25] trouverais un plaisir pour mon esprit et un avantage pour ma maison. Que faut-il[26] dans la demeure d'un juge? Une jolie femme, qui reçoive*[27] obligeamment les plaideurs[28] et, par une conversation subtile, les amène à[29] faire des présents pour qu'on s'occupe de leur affaire avec plus de soin. Les gens ne donnent que lorsqu'ils y[30] sont encouragés. Une femme qui parle adroitement tire de l'un un jambon, de l'autre une pièce de drap; d'un troisième, du vin ou de la volaille. Mais cette pauvre Catherine est muette, et ne m'aide en rien. Vous voyez, maître Adam Fumée, comme cela me fait du tort[31] d'avoir une femme muette . . . Cela me rend mélancolique.[32]

MAÎTRE ADAM: Vous avez tort, monsieur le juge. On peut trouver dans votre cas des avantages qui ne sont pas à dédaigner.

LÉONARD: Vous ne savez pas ce que c'est, maître Adam. Quand je prends ma femme dans mes bras, elle est aussi belle que la plus belle statue. Puis, il me semble avoir affaire à[33] une idole, à un automate, à une poupée magique, plutôt qu'à une créature du bon Dieu.[34]

MAÎTRE ADAM: Quelle imagination!

LÉONARD: Ce n'est pas tout. A vivre[35] près d'une muette, j'en[36]

24 en, *by this, because of this.*
25 y, *in this (in her being able to speak).*
26 Que faut-il, *What is needed.*
27 qui reçoive (*infin.* recevoir), *who might receive, entertain. The subjunctive is used because there is no certainty that such a wife could be found.*
28 plaideurs, *litigants.*
29 les amène à, *might encourage them to (lit.: might bring them to the point of).*
30 y = à cela, *in this, in giving.*
31 comme cela me fait du tort, *how bad it is for me* (faire du tort, *to harm, to wrong*).
32 me rend mélancolique, *makes me sad.* Rendre *is often used with the meaning "to make" when followed by an adjective.*
33 avoir affaire à, *to be dealing with, to be in front of.*
34 une créature du bon Dieu, *a human being (God's creation).*
35 à vivre, *by living.*
36 en, *as a result of this.*

deviens* muet moi-mème. Parfois, je me mets à m'exprimer, comme elle, par signes. L'autre jour, au tribunal, il m'est arrivé de rendre une sentence[37] au seul moyen du geste et de la mimique.

MAÎTRE ADAM: Vous n'avez pas besoin d'en dire davantage, et je vous plains.* Évidemment, on n'aime pas à parler, quand on ne reçoit jamais de réponse.

LÉONARD: Vous savez maintenant quelle est la cause de ma tristesse.

MAÎTRE ADAM: Sans doute. Mais peut-être existe-t-il[38] un moyen de la faire cesser. Dites-moi: votre femme est-elle sourde comme elle est muette?

LÉONARD: Catherine n'est pas plus sourde que vous et moi; elle l'est même moins, si j'ose dire; elle entendrait l'herbe pousser.

MAÎTRE ADAM: En ce cas, il faut avoir bon espoir. Les médecins et chirurgiens ne guérissent jamais totalement un sourd-muet. Mais il en va tout autrement des[39] muets qui entendent. C'est très facile, pour un médecin, de les guérir. L'opération coûte si peu qu'on la fait journellement sur les petits chiens qui tardent à[40] aboyer. Ne savez-vous pas qu'un fameux médecin demeure à quelques pas de votre logis? C'est maître Simon Colline, qui a opéré plusieurs dames de Paris. Croyez-moi, en un tournemain, il fera sortir de la bouche de madame votre épouse un flot clair de paroles charmantes.

LÉONARD: Est-ce vrai, maître Adam? Vous ne me trompez point? vous ne plaidez pas?[41]

MAÎTRE ADAM: Je vous parle en[42] ami et vous dis la vérité pure.

LÉONARD: Je ferai* donc venir ce célèbre médecin. Et sans tarder d'un instant.

37 rendre une sentence, *render a verdict.*
38 peut-être existe-t-il = il existe peut-être, *there exists, there is. The inverted order is due to the fact that* peut-être *precedes the verb.*
39 il en va tout autrement des, *it's entirely different in the case of.*
40 qui tardent à, *who are slow in being able to.*
41 vous ne plaidez pas, *you are not pleading, this is not the talk of a lawyer.*
42 en ami, *as a friend.*

MAÎTRE ADAM: Bien! Mais avant de l'appeler, vous réfléchirez sur ce qu'il convient de faire.[43] Car, tout bien considéré, si une femme muette a ses inconvénients, elle a aussi ses avantages. Bonsoir, monsieur le juge et ancien condisciple. Croyez-moi bien votre ami et lisez* mon mémoire, je vous prie. Si vous exercez votre justice en faveur d'une jeune orpheline dépouillée par un tuteur avide, vous n'aurez pas à vous en[44] repentir.

LÉONARD: Revenez tantôt, maître Adam Fumée; j'aurai* préparé mon arrêt.[45] [MAÎTRE ADAM *sort.*]

SCÈNE II

LÉONARD, *puis* GILLES, *puis* CATHERINE

LÉONARD [*appelant*]: Gilles! Gilles! . . . Le vaurien ne m'entend pas; il est dans la cuisine en train de boire mon vin et de faire la cour à[1] la servante. Gilles! . . . Gilles! . . .

GILLES: Me voici, monsieur le juge.

LÉONARD: Va tout de suite chez ce fameux médecin qui demeure près d'ici, maître Simon Colline, et dis-lui de venir donner ses soins à une femme muette.

GILLES: Oui, monsieur le juge. [*Il sort.*]

LÉONARD [*assis devant sa table, couverte de documents*]: J'ai quatorze arrêts à rendre aujourd'hui, sans compter la sentence relative à la pupille de maître Adam Fumée. Et cela est un grand travail, car une sentence ne fait pas honneur à un juge quand elle n'est pas bien rédigée[2] et garnie de tous les ornements du style et de la pensée. [CATHERINE, *qui est descendue par l'escalier intérieur, vient s'asseoir devant son rouet, tout*

[43] ce qu'il convient de faire, *what is the right thing to do.*
[44] en, *because of it.*
[45] mon arrêt, *my verdict.*
[1] faire la court à, *make love to.*
[2] rédigée = écrite.

près de la table. Elle sourit à son mari et se prépare à filer.
LÉONARD, *s'interrompant d'écrire*]: Bonjour, mon amour ... Je ne vous avais pas entendue. Vous êtes comme ces songes que les dieux, selon les poètes, envoient aux heureux mortels. Vous êtes une merveille de la nature; il ne vous manque que[3] la parole. Ne seriez*-vous pas bien contente de l'acquérir? Ne seriez-vous pas heureuse de pouvoir exprimer toutes les jolies pensées qu'on devine dans vos yeux? Ne vous serait-il pas agréable de dire à votre époux que vous l'aimez? Oui, sans doute! ... Eh! bien, je vous annonce une bonne nouvelle. Il va venir tantôt ici un bon médecin[4] qui vous fera parler ... [CATHERINE *donne des marques de satisfaction.*] Il vous guérira sans vous faire de mal. [CATHERINE *exprime sa joie par une gracieuse impatience de la tête et des bras.*] Mon amour, depuis que vous êtes descendue près de moi, je n'ai pas perdu mon temps; j'ai envoyé en prison quatorze hommes et six femmes; j'ai distribué ... [*Il additionne.*] Six ... vingt-quatre ... trente-deux ... quarante-quatre ... quarante-sept et neuf, cinquante-six, et onze, soixante-sept, et dix, soixante-dix-sept, et huit, quatre-vingt-cinq, et vingt, cent cinq. Cent cinq ans de prison. Cela ne donne-t-il pas une haute idée du pouvoir d'un juge, et puis-je m'empêcher d'en être fier? [CATHERINE *ne file plus. Elle regarde son mari en souriant. Puis elle s'assied sur la table couverte de documents.* LÉONARD *et* CATHERINE *s'embrassent par-dessus la table. Mais voyant venir les médecins,* CATHERINE *se sauve par l'escalier intérieur.*]

SCÈNE III

Léonard, Gilles, Maître Simon Colline, Maître Séraphin Dulaurier, *puis* Maître Jean Maugier, *puis* Alizon

GILLES: Monsieur le juge, voici ce grand docteur que vous désirez voir.

[3] il ne vous manque que, *you only lack.*
[4] il va venir un bon médecin = un bon médecin va venir. *Lit.: there is going to come ...*

MAÎTRE SIMON: Oui, je suis maître Simon Colline en personne... Et voici maître Jean Maugier, chirurgien. Vous avez besoin de nos services?

LÉONARD: Oui, monsieur, pour donner la parole à une femme muette.

MAÎTRE SIMON: Fort bien. Nous attendons maître Séraphin Dulaurier, apothicaire. Dès qu'il sera venu, nous opérerons selon notre science.

LÉONARD: Ah! vraiment il faut un apothicaire pour faire parler une muette?

MAÎTRE SIMON: Oui, monsieur, et quiconque[1] en doute ignore totalement[2] les relations des organes du corps humain entre eux. Maître Séraphin Dulaurier ne tardera pas à venir.

MAÎTRE JEAN MAUGIER [*se met soudain à crier*]: Oh! qu'il faut être reconnaissant aux savants médecins qui, tels que maître Simon Colline, travaillent à nous conserver la santé[3] et nous soignent dans nos maladies. Oh! qu'ils sont dignes de bénédictions, ces bons médecins qui suivent les règles d'une savante physique et d'une longue expérience.

MAÎTRE SIMON [*s'inclinant légèrement*]: Vous êtes trop aimable, maître Jean Maugier.

LÉONARD: En attendant monsieur l'apothicaire, voulez-vous vous rafraîchir,[4] messieurs?

MAÎTRE SIMON: Volontiers.

MAÎTRE JEAN: Avec plaisir.

LÉONARD: Ainsi donc, vous ferez, maître Simon Colline, une petite opération qui fera parler ma femme?

MAÎTRE SIMON: C'est-à-dire que je dirigerai l'opération. J'ordonne,

[1] quiconque, *whoever.*
[2] ignore complètement, *is completely ignorant of, fails completely to understand.*
[3] nous conserver la santé, *keep us in good health.*
[4] vous rafraîchir, *have something to drink.*

maître Jean Maugier exécute . . . Avez-vous vos instruments, maître Jean?

MAÎTRE JEAN: Oui, maître. [*Il montre une scie de trois pieds de long, des couteaux, des ciseaux, une gigantesque vrille, etc. Entre* ALIZON, *avec le vin.*]

LÉONARD: J'espère, messieurs, que vous n'allez pas vous servir de tout cela?

MAÎTRE SIMON: On ne sait jamais.

LÉONARD: Buvez,* messieurs.

MAÎTRE SIMON: Ce vin n'est pas mauvais.

LÉONARD: Il vient* de mes vignes.

MAÎTRE SIMON: Vous m'en enverrez* une barrique.

LÉONARD [*à* GILLES *qui se verse un grand verre de vin*]: Je ne t'ai pas dit de boire, vaurien.

MAÎTRE JEAN [*regardant par la fenêtre dans la rue*]: Voici maître Séraphin Dulaurier, apothicaire! [*Entre* MAÎTRE SÉRAPHIN.]

MAÎTRE SIMON: Et voici sa mule! . . . Non, vraiment: C'est maître Séraphin Dulaurier lui-même. On s'y trompe toujours.[5] Buvez* maître Séraphin. Il est frais.[6]

MAÎTRE SÉRAPHIN: A votre santé, mes maîtres!

MAÎTRE SIMON [*à* ALIZON]: Versez, ma belle enfant. Versez à droite, versez à gauche, versez ici, versez là. N'êtes-vous pas fière d'être si jolie?

ALIZON: Je n'ai pas de raison d'être fière. On n'apprécie pas la beauté quand elle n'est pas couverte de soie et de brocart.

MAÎTRE SÉRAPHIN: A votre santé, mes maîtres! [*Ils boivent tous et font boire* ALIZON.]

[5] on s'y trompe toujours, *one always gets them mixed up (Maître Dulaurier and his mule).*

[6] il est frais, *it (the wine) is nice and cool.*

MAÎTRE SIMON: Maintenant que nous sommes au complet[7] nous pouvons monter auprès de la malade.

LÉONARD: Je vais vous y conduire, messieurs. [*Il monte par l'escalier intérieur.*]

MAÎTRE SIMON: Après vous, maître Maugier.

MAÎTRE MAUGIER [*son verre à la main*]: Je passe, sachant bien que l'honneur est de marcher derrière.

MAÎTRE SIMON: Passez, maître Séraphin Dulaurier. [MAÎTRE SÉRAPHIN *monte, une bouteille à la main.*]

MAÎTRE SIMON [*ayant fourré*[8] *une bouteille dans chaque poche de sa robe*[9] *et embrassé la servante* ALIZON, *monte en chantant*]:

A boire! à boire! à boire!
Nous quitt'rons-nous sans boire?
Les bons amis ne sont pas si fous
Que d'se quitter sans boire un coup.[10]

ALIZON, *après avoir giflé* GILLES *qui voulait l'embrasser, monte la dernière. On les entend qui chantent:*

A boire! à boire! à boire!

ACTE DEUXIÉME

SCÈNE PREMIÈRE

LÉONARD, MAÎTRE ADAM

MAÎTRE ADAM: Bonsoir, monsieur le juge. Comment vous portez-vous?

LÉONARD: Assez bien. Et vous?

[7] *au complet* = *tous ici.*
[8] fourré = mis, *stuck.*
[9] sa robe, *his gown. Doctors used to wear black gowns.*
[10] boire un coup, *having a drink together.*

Maître Adam: On ne peut* mieux. Excusez-moi de vous déranger,[1] monsieur le juge et cher ancien condisciple. Avez-vous examiné l'affaire[2] de ma jeune pupille dépouillée par son tuteur?

Léonard: Pas encore, maître Adam Fumée... Mais que me dites-* vous là? Vous avez dépouillé votre pupille?...[3]

Maître Adam: Mais non,[4] monsieur. Je dis « ma pupille » par amitié pure. Je ne suis pas son tuteur, Dieu merci! Je suis son avocat. Et si on lui rend sa fortune, qui est grande, je l'épouserai. Elle éprouve[5] déjà de l'amour pour moi. C'est pourquoi je vous serai reconnaissant d'examiner son affaire le plus promptement possible. Vous n'avez, pour cela, qu'à lire mon mémoire: il contient* tout ce qu'il faut savoir.

Léonard: Votre mémoire, maître Adam, est là, sur ma table. Je l'aurais étudié, si je n'avais pas eu d'autres affaires. J'ai reçu chez moi la fleur de la Faculté de médecine, et c'est à cause de votre conseil que m'est venu ce tracas.[6]

Maître Adam: Que voulez-vous dire?

Léonard: J'ai fait venir le fameux médecin dont vous m'aviez parlé, maître Simon Colline. Il est venu avec un chirurgien et un apothicaire; il a examiné Catherine, ma femme, des pieds à la tête, pour savoir si elle était muette. Puis, le chirurgien a opéré ma chère Catherine, l'apothicaire lui a donné un remède et elle a parlé.

Maître Adam: Elle a parlé? Lui fallait-il[7] un remède pour cela?

Léonard: Oui, à cause de la relation entre les organes.

Maître Adam: Ah! . . . Enfin,[8] l'essentiel est qu'elle a parlé. Qu'a-t-elle dit?

1 déranger, *to disturb.*
2 l'affaire, *the case.*
3 pupille, *ward.*
4 Mais non, *certainly not.* Mais *adds emphasis. Similarly:* mais oui, *yes, of course.*
5 elle éprouve, *she feels.*
6 ce tracas = cet ennui, *this trouble.*
7 lui fallait-il = avait-elle besoin de.
8 Enfin, *Oh, well!*

LÉONARD: Elle a dit « Apportez-moi le miroir! » Et, me voyant tout[9] ému, elle a ajouté: « Mon chéri, vous me donnerez pour ma fête[10] une robe de satin et un manteau de velours. »

MAÎTRE ADAM: Et elle a continué de parler?

LÉONARD: Elle ne s'est plus arrêtée.

MAÎTRE ADAM: Et vous ne me remerciez pas du conseil que je vous ai donné; vous ne me remerciez pas de vous avoir fait connaître ce grand médecin? N'êtes-vous pas bien content[11] d'entendre parler madame votre épouse?

LÉONARD: Ah, oui! je vous remercie de tout mon cœur, maître Adam Fumée, et je suis bien content d'entendre parler mon épouse.

MAÎTRE ADAM: Non! vous ne montrez pas autant de satisfaction qu'il faudrait.* [12] Il y a quelque chose que vous ne dites* pas et qui vous chagrine.

LÉONARD: Qu'est-ce qui vous fait dire cela?

MAÎTRE ADAM: Je le vois sur votre visage . . . Qu'est-ce qui vous fâche? Madame votre épouse ne parle-t-elle pas bien?

LÉONARD: Elle parle bien et beaucoup. Je vous avoue que cela m'ennuierait beaucoup si elle devait continuer[13] à parler ainsi bien longtemps.

MAÎTRE ADAM: Je comprends. Mais il ne faut pas désespérer si vite. Ce flux de paroles décroîtra peut-être. C'est l'expression d'un premier enthousiasme . . . Tous mes compliments, monsieur le juge. Ma pupille se nomme Ermeline de la Garandière. N'oubliez pas son nom; soyez-lui[14]* favorable et vous n'aurez* pas à le regretter. Je reviendrai ce soir.

LÉONARD: Maître Adam Fumée, je vais tout de suite étudier votre affaire. [MAÎTRE ADAM FUMÉE *sort.*]

9 tout, *very, deeply.*
10 ma fête, *my anniversary. (The same word can refer to one's Saint's day, which French people celebrate).*
11 bien content = très content.
12 qu'il faudrait, *as you should.*
13 devait continuer, *was to go on.*
14 soyez, *be* (*imperative of* être).

SCÈNE II

LÉONARD *puis* CATHERINE

LÉONARD [*à sa table, lisant**]: Mémoire pour la demoiselle Ermeline-Jacinthe-Marthe de la Garandière.

CATHERINE [*qui est venue* s'asseoir à son rouet,*[1] *contre la table, avec volubilité*]: Qu'est-ce que vous faites-là, mon ami? Vous paraissez* occupé. Vous travaillez beaucoup. Ne craignez*-vous pas que cela vous fasse* du mal[2]? Il faut se reposer quelquefois. Mais vous ne me dites pas ce que vous faites-là, mon ami?

LÉONARD: Mon amour, je . . .

CATHERINE: Est-ce donc un si grand secret? et dois*-je l'ignorer?[3]

LÉONARD: Mon amour, je . . .

CATHERINE: Si c'est un secret ne me le dites pas.

LÉONARD: Laissez-moi du moins le temps de vous répondre. J'étudie une affaire et je me prépare à rendre une sentence.[4]

CATHERINE: C'est important de rendre une sentence.

LÉONARD: Sans doute. Non seulement l'honneur, la liberté et parfois la vie des personnes en[5] dépendent, mais encore[6] le juge y montre la profondeur de son esprit et l'élégance de son langage.

CATHERINE: Alors étudiez votre affaire et préparez votre sentence, mon ami. Je ne dirai rien.

LÉONARD: C'est cela[7] . . . La demoiselle Ermeline-Jacinthe-Marthe de la Garandière . . .

1 son rouet, *her spinning-wheel.*
2 vous fasse du mal, *may be harmful to you. The subjunctive is used after a verb of emotion:* craindre.
3 l'ignorer, *not know about it. Note carefully that* ignorer *means "not to know," "to be ignorant of."*
4 à rendre une sentence, *to render a verdict.*
5 en, *on it.*
6 encore = de plus, *moreover.*
7 C'est cela, *Fine! That's it!*

CATHERINE: Mon ami, que croyez-vous qui me sera le plus séant,[8] une robe de damas ou de velours?

LÉONARD: Je ne sais*, je . . .

CATHERINE: Il me semble que le satin à fleurs[9] conviendrait* mieux à mon âge, surtout s'il est clair[10] et les fleurs petites . . .

LÉONARD: Peut-être! mais . . .

CATHERINE: Et ne pensez-vous pas, mon ami, qu'on aurait* tort[11] d'exagérer l'ampleur du vertugadin? Je suis sûre que cette mode tombera[12]; il viendra* un jour[13] où les dames de la noblesse l'abandonneront, et les bourgeoises suivront cet exemple. Vous ne croyez pas?

LÉONARD: Si! mais . . .

CATHERINE: Quant aux mules[14] il faut bien les choisir. C'est au pied qu'on juge une femme, et la vraie élégante[15] se distingue par la chaussure. N'est-ce pas votre avis, mon ami?

LÉONARD: Oui mais . . .

CATHERINE: Écrivez votre sentence. Je ne dirai plus rien.

LÉONARD: C'est cela! [*Lisant* et prenant* des notes.*] Or le tuteur de la dite demoiselle,[16] Hugues Thomassin seigneur de Piédeloup a dérobé à la dite demoiselle son . . .

CATHERINE: Mon ami, s'il en[17] faut croire madame de Montbadon, le monde est bien corrompu; il court à sa perte,[18] les jeunes gens[19] d'aujourd'hui préfèrent à de charmantes jeunes filles

[8] qui me sera le plus séant = qui m'ira le mieux, *will be most becoming to me.*
[9] à fleurs, *with a flower design.*
[10] clair, *light (in color).*
[11] qu'on aurait tort, *that it would be wrong.*
[12] tombera, *is going to decline.*
[13] il viendra un jour = un jour viendra. *Lit.: there will come a day.*
[14] mules, *slippers, shoes.*
[15] élégante = femme élégante.
[16] la dite demoiselle, *the aforesaid young lady.*
[17] en, *about this, in this connection.*
[18] sa perte, *its ruin, its destruction.*
[19] les jeunes gens, *young men. Although* jeunes gens *may refer to girls and boys, the expression usually refers only to young men and is the masculine form of* jeunes filles, *girls.*

de vieilles dames fort[20] riches; et pendant ce temps-là, les filles honnêtes ne se marient pas. Est-ce possible? répondez-moi, mon ami.

LÉONARD: Ma bonne amie, consentez à vous taire un moment ou bien allez parler ailleurs. Je ne sais où j'en suis.[21]

CATHERINE: Soyez* tranquille,[22] mon ami. Je ne dirai plus un mot.

LÉONARD: A la bonne heure.[23] [*Écrivant.*] « Ledit seigneur de Piédeloup, ayant acquis* frauduleusement[24] des prés, des quantités de pommes. . . . »

CATHERINE: Mon ami, nous avons aujourd'hui pour souper un hachis de mouton avec le reste de l'oie[25] qu'un plaideur[26] nous a donnée. Est-ce assez, dites-moi; cela vous suffit-il? Je déteste l'avarice, mais à quoi sert[27] de faire servir des plats qu'on remporte tout garnis[28] à la cuisine. La vie est devenue fort coûteuse. Au marché de la volaille,[29] au marché aux légumes, chez le boucher, chez le fruitier, tout a tellement augmenté qu'il sera* vraiment moins cher de commander les repas chez le traiteur.[30]

LÉONARD: Je vous prie . . . [*Écrivant.*] « Orpheline de naissance. »

CATHERINE: Vous verrez* qu'on y viendra.[31] C'est[32] qu'un chapon, une perdrix, un lièvre, coûtent moins, lardés et rôtis, qu'en les achetant au marché. Cela vient de ce que[33] les rôtisseurs, qui les achètent en gros,[34] les ont à bas prix et peuvent* les revendre très avantageusement. Je ne dis pas de faire venir tous nos repas de chez le traiteur. Mais quand on invite des

20 fort = très.
21 où j'en suis, *where I am.*
22 soyez tranquille, *don't worry.*
23 à la bonne heure = C'est parfait, *That's fine.*
24 acquis frauduleusement, *acquired fraudulently* (*infin.:* acquérir).
25 le reste de l'oie, *what's left of the goose.*
26 un plaideur, *a litigant.*
27 à quoi sert, *what's the use, what's the good of.*
28 tout garnis = presque pleins, *almost full.*
29 marché de la volaille, *poultry market.*
30 chez le traiteur, *from the caterer.*
31 on y viendra = on en arrivera à cela, *it will come to that.*
32 C'est qu' = La raison est qu'.
33 de ce que, *from the fact* (ce, *this*) *that.*
34 en gros, *wholesale* (*the opposite:* au détail, *retail*).

amis, le mieux et le moins cher est de faire venir le dîner du dehors. Les traiteurs en moins d'une heure vous préparent un dîner pour douze, pour vingt, pour cinquante personnes; le rôtisseur vous donne la viande et la volaille; le cuisinier, les sauces, les ragoûts; le pâtissier, les pâtes, les desserts. C'est bien commode.[35] Vous n'êtes pas de cet avis, Léonard?

LÉONARD: De grâce![36]

CATHERINE: Ce n'est pas étonnant que tout enchérisse.[37] Le luxe de la table devient chaque jour plus insolent. Quand on invite quelqu'un, on veut* avoir des viandes de cinq ou six façons différentes. Vous ne jugez pas cela excessif, mon ami? Moi, je ne conçois* pas[38] le plaisir qu'on trouve à s'empiffrer[39] de tant de viandes. Ce n'est pas que je dédaigne les bons plats, je suis friande.[40] Il me faut peu mais fin. J'aime surtout les rognons de coq et les fonds d'artichaut. Et vous, Léonard, n'avez-vous pas un faible[41] pour les tripes et les andouilles? Fi! fi! peut-on aimer les andouilles?

LÉONARD [*se prenant la tête dans les mains*]: Je vais devenir fou! Je sens que je vais devenir fou.

CATHERINE: Mon ami, je ne vais plus rien dire, parce qu'en parlant, je pourrais vous déranger de[42] votre travail.

LÉONARD: Puissiez*-vous faire[43] ce que vous dites!

CATHERINE: Je n'ouvrirai pas la bouche.

LÉONARD: A merveille.

CATHERINE: Vous voyez, mon ami; je ne dis plus rien.

LÉONARD: Oui.

[35] commode, *convenient.*
[36] De grâce, *For pity's sake.*
[37] que tout enchérisse = que tout devienne plus cher.
[38] je ne conçois pas, *I can't imagine (infin.:* concevoir, *to conceive).*
[39] s'empiffrer de, *fill oneself up with.*
[40] friande, *fond of good food.*
[41] un faible, *weakness, predilection.*
[42] vous déranger de, *take your attention away from.*
[43] Puissiez-vous faire, *I certainly hope you are going to do . . . (lit.: may you do . . .).*

CATHERINE: Je vous laisse travailler bien tranquillement.

LÉONARD: Oui.

CATHERINE: Et écrire en paix votre sentence. Est-elle bientôt faite?

LÉONARD: Elle ne le sera jamais si vous ne vous taisez* pas. [*Écrivant.*] « Puis, cent vingt livres de rentes[44] que cet indigne tuteur a volées à la pauvre orpheline . . . »

CATHERINE: Écoutez! Chut! Écoutez! Est-ce qu'on ne crie pas au feu? Il m'a semblé l'entendre. Mais peut-être me serai*-je trompée.[45] Y a-t-il rien d'effrayant comme un incendie? Le feu est plus terrible encore que l'inondation. J'ai vu* brûler l'année dernière les maisons du Pont-au-Change.[46] Quel désordre![47] Quels dégâts! Les habitants jetaient leurs meubles dans la rivière et se jetaient eux-mêmes par les fenêtres. Ils ne savaient pas ce qu'ils faisaient*; la peur leur ôtait la raison.[48]

LÉONARD: Seigneur, ayez* pitié de moi!

CATHERINE: Pourquoi gémissez-vous, mon ami? Dites-moi ce qui vous importune.

LÉONARD: Je n'en puis* plus.[49]

CATHERINE: Reposez-vous, Léonard. Il ne faut pas[50] vous fatiguer ainsi. Ce n'est pas raisonnable, et vous auriez* tort de . . .

LÉONARD: Ne vous tairez-vous donc jamais?

CATHERINE: Ne vous fâchez pas, mon ami. Je ne dis plus rien.

LÉONARD: Le ciel le veuille!* [51]

44 cent vingt livres de rentes, *an income of 120 francs.*
45 peut-être me serai-je trompée = je me serai peut-être trompée. *The inverted word order is used when* peut-être *begins the sentence.*
46 Pont-au-change: *one of the old bridges of Paris, crossing the Seine to the* Île de la Cité. *Like other old Paris bridges, it used to be bordered with houses.*
47 Quel désordre! *What a mess!*
48 leur ôtait la raison = les rendait fous. *Lit.: took away from them the reasoning power.*
49 Je n'en puis plus, *I can't stand it any more.*
50 Il ne faut pas, *You must not. Note carefully that "it is not necessary" would be translated by* il n'est pas nécessaire.
51 Le ciel le veuille! *With God's help! (lit.: May God be willing!).* Veuille *is a third-person subjunctive of* vouloir, *used as an imperative.*

CATHERINE [*regardant par la fenêtre*]: Oh! voici madame de la Bruine, la femme du procureur,[52] qui approche; elle porte un grand manteau brun pardessus sa robe de soie. Elle est suivie d'un laquais.[53] Léonard, elle regarde de ce côté[54]: elle a l'air de venir nous faire visite. Dépêchez-vous de mettre en place les fauteuils pour la recevoir. Elle va s'arrêter à notre porte. Non, elle passe; elle est passée. Peut-être me suis-je trompée. Peut-être n'est-ce pas elle. On ne reconnaît pas toujours les personnes. Mais si ce n'est pas elle, c'est quelqu'un qui lui ressemble, et même qui lui ressemble beaucoup. Quand j'y songe, je suis sûre que c'était elle, il ne peut se trouver[55] à Paris une seule femme aussi semblable à madame de la Bruine. Mon ami . . . mon ami . . . est-ce que vous auriez été content de recevoir la visite de madame de la Bruine? [*Elle s'assied* sur la table.*] Vous qui n'aimez pas les femmes bavardes, il est heureux pour vous que vous ne l'ayez* pas épousée; elle ne fait que parler[56] du matin au soir. Quelle bavarde! [LÉONARD, *excédé,*[57] *monte à une haute échelle; il s'assied sur un échelon du milieu, où il tâche d'écrire.*] D'abord elle énumère tous les présents que son mari reçoit. [*Elle monte de l'autre côté de l'échelle double et s'assied en face de* LÉONARD.] En quoi cela nous intéresse-t-il que le procureur de la Bruine reçoive du gibier, de la farine, du poisson? Mais madame de la Bruine a bien soin de[58] ne pas dire que son mari a reçu un jour un grand pâté d'Amiens,[59] et que, à l'intérieur, il a trouvé deux grandes cornes.[60]

LÉONARD: Ma tête éclate! [*Il va s'asseoir sur l'armoire avec ses papiers.*]

CATHERINE [*au plus haut*[61] *de l'échelle*]: Avez-vous vu cette femme

52 procureur, *public prosecutor.*
53 laquais, *manservant, lackey.*
54 de ce côté, *this way, in this direction.*
55 il ne peut se trouver = il ne peut pas y avoir, *there cannot be.*
56 elle ne fait que parler, *she does nothing but speak.*
57 excédé, *fed up.*
58 a bien soin de, *is very careful to.*
59 Amiens: *an important city in the northwest of France.*
60 *Catherine is now casting suspicion on the fidelity of Madame de la Bruine.*
61 au plus haut, *at the top.*

de procureur? Elle porte une robe de princesse. Ne trouvez-vous pas cela ridicule? Mais aujourd'hui tout le monde s'habille au-dessus de sa condition, les hommes comme les femmes. Les jeunes clercs du palais[62] veulent passer pour des gentilshommes; ils portent des chaînes d'or, des chapeaux à plumes; malgré cela on voit bien ce qu'ils sont.

LÉONARD [*sur son armoire*]: C'est trop! Je me sens capable de commettre un crime. [*Appelant.*] Gilles! Gilles! Gilles! le fripon! Gilles! Alizon! Gilles! Gilles! [*Entre* GILLES.] Va vite trouver le célèbre médecin, maître Simon Colline, et dis-lui qu'il revienne* tout de suite pour une affaire bien plus nécessaire et pressante que la première.

GILLES: Oui, monsieur le juge. [*Il sort.*]

CATHERINE: Qu'avez-vous, mon ami? Vous êtes tout rouge.[63] C'est peut-être le temps qui est lourd. Non? . . . C'est le vent d'Est, ne croyez-*vous pas? ou le poisson que vous avez mangé à dîner.

LÉONARD [*donne sur son armoire des signes de frénésie,*[64] *puis il éclate*]: Oh! que je me repens* de t'avoir fait opérer![65] Mais, sois tranquille,[66] ce grand médecin va bientôt te rendre plus muette qu'auparavant. [*Il prend tous ses papiers et les jette à la tête de Catherine qui descend de l'échelle et se sauve, par l'escalier intérieur, en criant*]: Au secours,[67] au meurtre! Mon mari est devenu fou! Au secours!

LÉONARD: Alizon! Alizon! [*Entre* ALIZON.]

ALIZON: Quelle vie! monsieur, vous êtes donc devenu meurtrier?

LÉONARD: Alizon, suivez-la, restez auprès d'elle et ne la laissez pas descendre. Sur votre vie, Alizon, ne la laissez pas descendre. Car si je l'entends encore je deviendrai enragé et Dieu sait

62 clercs du palais, *employees at the Palace of Justice, court assistants.*
63 rouge, *flushed, red in the face.*
64 frénésie, *frenzy, raving madness.*
65 de t'avoir fait opérer, *to have had you operated upon.*
66 sois tranquille *(ironical), don't worry, never mind.*
67 Au secours! *Help!*

quels crimes je serais* capable de commettre! [ALIZON *monte l'escalier.*]

SCÈNE III

LÉONARD, MAÎTRE ADAM, MADEMOISELLE DE LA GARANDIÈRE
suivis d'un laquais portant un panier

MAÎTRE ADAM: Permettez, monsieur le juge, que, pour attendrir votre cœur, je vous présente cette jeune orpheline qui, dépouillée par un tuteur avide, implore votre justice. Ses yeux parleront mieux que ma voix. Mademoiselle de la Garandière vous apporte ses prières et ses larmes; elle y joint[1] un jambon, une oie et deux barbots.[2] Elle ose espérer en échange, une sentence favorable.

LÉONARD: Mademoiselle, vous m'intéressez . . . Avez-vous quelque chose à ajouter pour la défense de votre cause?

MADEMOISELLE DE LA GARANDIÈRE: Vous êtes trop bon, monsieur; je m'en[3] réfère à ce que vient de dire mon avocat.

LÉONARD: C'est tout?

MADEMOISELLE DE LA GARANDIÈRE: Oui monsieur.

LÉONARD: Elle parle bien, elle parle peu. Cette orpheline est touchante. [*Au laquais.*] Portez ce paquet à la cuisine. [*Le laquais sort. A maître* ADAM.] Maître Adam, quand vous êtes entré j'écrivais le jugement[4] que je rendrai tantôt dans l'affaire de cette demoiselle. [*Il descend de son armoire.*]

MAÎTRE ADAM: Quoi, sur cette armoire?

LÉONARD: Je ne sais où j'en suis. Voulez-vous entendre le jugement? J'ai moi-même besoin de le relire. [*Lisant.**] « Attendu que[5] la demoiselle de la Garandière, orpheline de naissance, a

[1] elle y joint = elle y ajoute, *she adds to this.*
[2] barbots, *burbots (rather common fresh-water fish).*
[3] en, *about this, in this connection.*
[4] le jugement, *the verdict.*
[5] Attendu que *(a legal term), whereas.*

volé frauduleusement au sieur Piédeloup son tuteur, des prés, des quantités de pommes, attendu qu'il n'y a rien d'effrayant comme un incendie, attendu que monsieur le Procureur a reçu* un pâté d'Amiens dans lequel il y avait deux cornes . . .

MAÎTRE ADAM: Ciel! Que lisez*-vous là?

LÉONARD: Ne me le demandez pas; je n'en sais rien moi-même. Je suis devenu* idiot . . . Et c'est par votre faute, maître Adam Fumée . . . Si ce bon médecin n'avait pas rendu la parole[6] à ma femme. . . .

MAÎTRE ADAM: Ne m'accusez pas, monsieur Léonard. Je vous avais prévenu. Je vous avais bien dit qu'il fallait longuement réfléchir avant de délier[7] la langue d'une femme.

LÉONARD: Ah! maître Adam Fumée, combien je regrette le temps où[8] Catherine était muette. Non! la nature n'a pas de calamité plus terrible qu'une femme bavarde . . . Mais je compte bien que les médecins vont remédier à cela. Je les ai fait appeler et voici justement le chirurgien.

SCÈNE IV

LES MÊMES, MAÎTRE JEAN MAUGIER, *puis* MAÎTRE SIMON COLLINE *et* MAÎTRE SÉRAPHIN DULAURIER *suivi de deux petits garçons apothicaires*

MAÎTRE JEAN MAUGIER: Monsieur le juge, j'ai l'honneur de vous saluer. Voici maître Simon Colline qui arrive sur sa mule, suivi de maître Séraphin Dulaurier, apothicaire. Il est entouré d'un peuple idolâtre. [*Entre maître Simon Colline et sa suite.*] Oh! C'est avec justice que maître Simon Colline fait l'admiration du peuple. Oh! il faut être reconnaissant à ces bons médecins qui travaillent à nous conserver la santé[1] et à nous soigner . . .

[6] n'avait pas rendu la parole, *had not given back the power of speech.*
[7] délier, *untie, loosen.*
[8] où, *when (in which).*
[1] nous conserver la santé = conserver notre santé, *to protect our health.*

MAÎTRE SIMON [*à maître* JEAN MAUGIER]: Cela suffit . . .

LÉONARD: Maître Simon Colline, j'avais hâte[2] de vous voir. Je réclame instamment[3] votre intervention.

MAÎTRE SIMON: Pour vous, monsieur? Où souffrez-vous?

LÉONARD: Non! pour ma femme: celle qui était muette.

MAÎTRE SIMON: Éprouve-t-elle quelque incommodité?[4]

LÉONARD: Aucune. C'est moi qui suis incommodé.

MAÎTRE SIMON: Quoi! C'est vous qui êtes incommodé et c'est votre femme que vous voulez guérir?

LÉONARD: Maître Simon Colline, elle parle trop. Il fallait* [5] lui donner la parole,[6] mais ne pas tant[7] la lui donner. Depuis que vous l'avez guérie de son mutisme, elle me rend fou. Je ne puis l'entendre davantage. Je vous ai appelé pour la faire redevenir muette.

MAÎTRE SIMON: C'est impossible!

LÉONARD: Que dites-vous? Vous ne pouvez lui ôter[8] la parole que vous lui avez donnée?

MAÎTRE SIMON: Non! je ne le puis.* Mon art est grand, mais il ne va pas jusque-là.[9]

MAÎTRE JEAN MAUGIER: Cela nous est impossible.

MAÎTRE SÉRAPHIN: Tous nos soins n'y feraient* rien.[10]

MAÎTRE SIMON: Nous avons des remèdes pour faire parler les femmes; nous n'en avons pas pour les faire taire.

LÉONARD: Vous n'en avez pas? Que me dites-vous là? Vous me désespérez.

[2] j'avais hâte de = j'étais pressé de, je désirais beaucoup, *I was eager to.*
[3] je réclame instamment, *I urgently beseech.*
[4] incommodité, *little trouble.*
[5] il fallait, *it was all right to.*
[6] la parole, *the power of speech.*
[7] tant, *so much as that.*
[8] lui ôter, *take away from her.*
[9] jusque-là, *that far.*
[10] n'y feraient rien, *would be useless, would have no effect* (rien) *in such a case* (y).

MAÎTRE SIMON: Hélas! monsieur le juge, il n'y a ni élixir, ni baume, ni aucun remède pour guérir chez la femme l'intempérance de la glotte.[11]

LÉONARD: Est-ce vrai?

MAÎTRE SIMON: Vous m'offenseriez, monsieur, d'en douter.

LÉONARD: En ce cas, je suis un homme perdu.[12] Je n'ai plus qu'à[13] me jeter dans la Seine, une pierre au cou. Je ne peux pas vivre dans ce vacarme.[14] Si vous ne voulez pas que je me noie tout de suite, il faut, messieurs les docteurs, que vous me trouviez un remède.

MAÎTRE SIMON: Il n'y en a pas, vous ai-je dit, pour votre femme. Mais il y en aurait un pour vous, si vous consentiez à le prendre.

LÉONARD: Vous me rendez quelque espoir. Expliquez-vous, je vous prie.

MAÎTRE SIMON: Au bavardage d'une femme, il existe un remède unique. C'est la surdité[15] du mari.

LÉONARD: Que voulez-vous dire?

MAÎTRE SIMON: Je veux dire ce que je dis.

MAÎTRE ADAM: Ne le comprenez-vous pas? C'est la plus belle invention du monde. Ne pouvant rendre votre femme muette, ce grand médecin vous offre de vous rendre sourd.

LÉONARD: Me rendre vraiment sourd?

MAÎTRE SIMON: Sans doute. Je vous guérirai subitement et radicalement du bavardage excessif de madame votre épouse par la cophose.[16]

LÉONARD: Par la cophose? Qu'est-ce que c'est que la cophose?

11 l'intempérance de la glotte, *the excessive use of the glottis.*
12 un homme perdu, *done for.*
13 je n'ai plus qu'à, *the only thing left for me to do is to.*
14 ce vacarme, *this constant hubbub.*
15 surdité, *deafness.*
16 cophose, *cophosis, total deafness.*

MAÎTRE SIMON: C'est ce qu'on appelle vulgairement la surdité. Voyez-vous quelque inconvénient[17] à devenir sourd?

LÉONARD: Oui, j'en vois; car vraiment il y en a.

MAÎTRE JEAN MAUGIER: Croyez-vous?

MAÎTRE SÉRAPHIN: Lesquels?

MAÎTRE SIMON: Vous êtes juge. Quel inconvénient y a-t-il à ce qu'un juge soit[18] sourd.

MAÎTRE ADAM: Aucun. On peut m'en croire: je suis avocat. Il n'y en a aucun.

MAÎTRE SIMON: Quel dommage en résulterait-il pour la justice?

MAÎTRE ADAM: Il n'en résulterait nul dommage. Au contraire, monsieur Léonard Botal n'entendrait ni les avocats, ni les plaignants,[19] et il ne risquerait plus d'être trompé par des mensonges.

LÉONARD: C'est vrai.

MAÎTRE ADAM: Il n'en jugera que mieux.[20]

LÉONARD: C'est possible.

MAÎTRE ADAM: N'en doutez pas.

LÉONARD: Mais comment s'opère[21] cette . . .

MAÎTRE JEAN MAUGIER: Cette guérison.

MAÎTRE SIMON: La cophose ou surdité peut être obtenue de plusieurs manières. On la produit soit par la sclérose de l'oreille, soit[22] par l'otite. Mais ces moyens sont longs et douloureux.

LÉONARD: Je les repousse[23]! . . . Je les repousse de toutes mes forces.

17 inconvénient, *disadvantage, objection.*
18 à ce qu'un juge soit, *for a judge to be.*
19 plaignants, *plantiffs.*
20 Il n'en jugera que mieux, *He will judge all the better* (en, *because of this*).
21 comment s'opère, *how does one perform.*
22 soit . . . soit, *either . . . or.*
23 repousser, *to reject.*

MAÎTRE SIMON: Vous avez raison. Il vaut* bien mieux[24] obtenir la surdité par une certaine poudre blanche que j'ai dans ma trousse[25] et dont une pincée, introduite dans l'oreille, suffit pour vous rendre aussi sourd qu'un pot.[26]

LÉONARD: Merci beaucoup, maître Simon Colline; gardez votre poudre. Je ne veux pas être sourd.

MAÎTRE SIMON: Quoi, vous ne voulez pas être sourd? Quoi, vous rejetez la cophose? Vous fuyez[27] la guérison que vous imploriez tout à l'heure? C'est un spectacle trop fréquent que celui du malade indocile qui repousse le remède salutaire . . .

MAÎTRE JEAN MAUGIER: . . . Qui se dérobe aux[28] soins qui soulageraient ses souffrances . . .

MAÎTRE SÉRAPHIN: . . .Et refuse d'être guéri.

MAÎTRE ADAM: Ne vous décidez pas[29] si vite, monsieur Léonard Botal. Réfléchissez!

LÉONARD: Non! je ne veux pas être sourd; je ne veux pas de cette poudre.

SCÈNE V

LES MÊMES, ALIZON, *puis* CATHERINE

ALIZON [*descendant l'escalier, en se bouchant les oreilles*]: Je n'y puis* tenir.[1] Ma tête éclate. Il n'est pas humainement possible d'entendre bourdonner[2] de cette sorte. Elle n'arrête pas. Il me semble que je suis depuis deux heures dans la roue d'un moulin.

LÉONARD: Ne la laissez pas descendre! Alizon! Gilles! Enfermez-la!

24 Il vaut bien mieux, *It is much better.*
25 trousse, *doctor's case or bag.*
26 aussi sourd qu'un pot, *as deaf as a post.*
27 vous fuyez, *you shrink from (lit.: you run away from).*
28 qui se dérobe aux . . . , *who tries to escape the . . .*
29 ne vous décidez pas, *do not make up your mind.*
1 Je n'y puis tenir, *I can't stand this any more.*
2 bourdonner, *buzzing.*

MAÎTRE ADAM: Oh! monsieur!

MADEMOISELLE DE LA GARANDIÈRE: Oh! monsieur, pouvez-vous avoir la cruauté de vouloir emprisonner cette pauvre dame?

CATHERINE [*qui est descendue*]: Quelle belle et nombreuse compagnie. Je suis votre servante, messieurs. [*Elle fait la révérence.*[3]]

MAÎTRE SIMON COLLINE: Eh! bien, madame? N'êtes-vous pas contente de nous, et ne vous avons-nous pas bien délié la langue?

CATHERINE: Assez bien, messieurs, et je vous en suis fort obligée; dans les premiers moments, je ne pouvais pas articuler beaucoup de mots. Mais maintenant, j'ai assez de facilité à parler; j'en use modérément, car une femme bavarde est une calamité domestique. Messieurs, je serais désolée si vous pouviez me soupçonner de loquacité. C'est pourquoi je vous demande la permission de me justifier. Mon mari, je ne sais pourquoi, s'est imaginé que mes paroles l'empêchaient d'écrire une sentence. C'était une sentence en faveur d'une jeune orpheline . . . Mais cela n'a pas d'importance. J'étais assise auprès de lui et je ne lui parlais pour ainsi dire pas. Mon seul discours était ma présence. Un mari peut-il s'en plaindre? Peut-il trouver mauvais qu'une épouse reste auprès de lui, comme elle le doit?* [*A son mari.*] Plus j'y pense et moins je puis comprendre votre impatience. Quelle en est la cause? Cessez de donner le prétexte de mon bavardage. Il n'est pas soutenable. Mon ami, vous devez avoir contre moi quelque grief que je ne connais pas, je vous prie de me le dire. Vous me devez[4] une explication, et quand je saurai* ce qui vous a fâché, je tâcherai de vous éviter tout sujet de mécontentement. Ma mère disait: « Entre époux, on ne doit* pas avoir de secrets. » Elle avait bien raison. Souvent un mari ou une femme, pour ne pas s'être confiés[5] l'un à l'autre, ont attiré sur leur maison et sur eux-mêmes des catastrophes terribles. C'est

[3] la révérence, *a curtsy.*
[4] vous me devez, *you owe me.*
[5] pour ne pas s'être confiés, *for not having confided.*

ce qui est arrivé à madame de Beaupréau. Pour surprendre agréablement son mari, elle avait enfermé dans un coffre de sa chambre un petit cochon de lait.[6] Le mari l'entendit crier et, croyant que c'était un amant,[7] il tira son épée et perça le cœur de son épouse avant même d'entendre les explications de sa malheureuse femme. Quand il ouvrit le coffre, jugez de sa surprise et de son désespoir. C'est pourquoi il ne faut jamais rien cacher. Vous pouvez vous expliquer devant ces messieurs. Je ne suis pas coupable, et tout ce que vous pourrez* dire fera* éclater mon innocence.

LÉONARD [*qui depuis quelques instants essaie vainement par ses gestes et ses cris d'arrêter les paroles de* CATHERINE *et qui a déjà donné les signes d'une extrême impatience*]: La poudre! La poudre! Maître Simon Colline, votre poudre, votre poudre blanche, par pitié!

MAÎTRE SIMON: Jamais poudre à rendre sourd n'a été en effet plus nécessaire. Veuillez* vous asseoir[8] monsieur le juge. Maître Séraphin Dulaurier va vous insuffler[9] la poudre assourdissante dans les oreilles.

MAÎTRE SÉRAPHIN: Bien volontiers, monsieur.

MAÎTRE SIMON: Voilà qui est fait.

CATHERINE [*à maître* ADAM FUMÉE]: Faites* entendre raison à mon mari,[10] monsieur l'avocat. Dites-lui qu'il faut qu'il m'écoute, qu'on n'a jamais condamné une épouse sans l'entendre, dites-lui qu'on ne jette pas des papiers à la tête d'une femme (car il m'a jeté ses papiers à la tête). . . . Mais non! je vais lui parler moi-même. [*A* LÉONARD.] Mon ami, répondez, vous ai-je offensé? Suis-je une méchante femme? Suis-je une mauvaise épouse? J'ai été fidèle à mon devoir; je vous dirai même que je l'ai aimé . . .

6 cochon de lait, *suckling pig.*
7 un amant, *a lover.*
8 Veuillez vous asseoir, *Please sit down.*
9 insuffler, *to blow.*
10 Faites entendre raison à mon mari, *Make my husband listen to reason.*

LÉONARD [*son visage exprime un calme parfait*]: Cela est délicieux. Je n'entends plus rien.

CATHERINE: Écoutez-moi, Léonard, je vous aime tendrement. Je vais vous ouvrir mon cœur. Je ne suis pas une de ces femmes légères et frivoles qu'un rien[11] afflige, qu'un rien console. J'ai besoin d'amitié. Je suis née ainsi: dès l'âge de sept ans j'avais un petit chien, un petit chien jaune . . . Vous ne m'écoutez pas . . .

MAÎTRE SIMON: Madame, il ne saurait* vous écouter, vous ou tout autre. Il n'entend plus.

CATHERINE: Comment il n'entend plus?

MAÎTRE SIMON: Non, il n'entend plus grâce à un médicament qu'il vient de prendre.

MAÎTRE SÉRAPHIN: Et qui a produit* en lui une douce et riante cophose.

CATHERINE: Je le ferai bien entendre, moi.

MAÎTRE SIMON: Vous n'en ferez rien,[12] madame; c'est impossible.

CATHERINE: Vous allez voir . . . [*A son mari.*] Mon ami, mon chéri, mon amour, mon cœur, ma moitié . . . Vous n'entendez pas. [*Elle le secoue.*] Barbe-Bleue, monstre!

LÉONARD: Je ne l'entends plus par les oreilles. Mais je ne l'entends que trop[13] par les bras, par les épaules ou par le dos.

MAÎTRE SIMON: Elle devient enragée.

LÉONARD: Où fuir?[14] Elle m'a mordu, et je me sens devenir enragé[15] comme elle.

[*On entend un aveugle au dehors. Il entre dans la salle en chantant.*]

11 un rien, *a trifle.*
12 vous n'en ferez rien, *you will do nothing of the sort* (en).
13 ne . . . que trop, *only too well.*
14 Où fuir, *Where can one escape?*
15 enragé, *mad, insane (but also affected by rabies).*

Passant vers la rivière,
Nous donnant le bras,
La déra;
Passant vers la rivière,
Nous donnant le bras,
Trouvons la meunière,
Avec nous dansa,
La déra;
Trouvons la meunière,
Avec nous dansa.

[CATHERINE ET LÉONARD *vont en dansant et en chantant mordre tous les assistants,*[16] *qui devenus enragés, dansent et chantent furieusement et ne s'arrêtent que pour dire, par la bouche de* M. LÉONARD BOTAL] : Mesdames et messieurs, excusez les fautes de l'auteur.

FIN

16 les assistants, *those present.*

QUESTIONS

Acte Premier, Scène Première

1. Où se passe cette comédie? A quelle époque? 2. Qui est Alizon? 3. Qui est Gilles? 4. Quelle est la profession de monsieur Léonard Botal? 5. Quelle est la profession de maître Adam Fumée? 6. De qui et de quoi s'agit-il dans le mémoire que maître Adam vient présenter au juge? 7. Qu'est-ce qui intéresse surtout le juge? 8. Qu'est-ce que maître Adam promet? 9. Qui le juge a-t-il épousée? Que dit-il de sa jeune femme? 10. Pourquoi regrette-t-il maintenant que sa femme soit muette? 11. A quoi compare-t-il sa femme? 12. Qu'est-ce qu'il lui arrive de faire au tribunal? 13. Pourquoi maître Adam est-il content d'apprendre que la femme du juge n'est pas sourde? 14. Quel espoir donne-t-il au juge? 15. Pourquoi dit-il au juge de réfléchir avant de faire venir le médecin?

Scène II

1. Que fait le juge en attendant l'arrivée du médecin? 2. Qui vient s'asseoir près de lui? Que fait-elle? 3. De quoi Léonard parle-t-il à sa femme? 4. Comment Catherine manifeste-t-elle sa joie? 5. De quoi le juge est-il fier? 6. Catherine a-t-elle beaucoup de respect pour les travaux de son mari? 7. Pourquoi Catherine se sauve-t-elle en voyant entrer les médecins?

Scène III

1. Qui sont les nouveaux personnages? 2. D'après maître Simon, pourquoi un apothicaire est-il nécessaire? 3. Maître Jean Maugier montre-t-il de l'enthousiasme pour la profession de médecin? 4. Comment l'opération se fera-t-elle? 5. Quels instruments le chirurgien a-t-il apportés? 6. Qu'est-ce que le juge fait servir aux médecins? 7. Ceux-ci apprécient-ils le vin du juge Léonard? 8. Quel effet le bon vin du juge a-t-il eu sur eux?

Acte Deuxième, Scène Première

1. Que s'est-il passé pendant le temps qui sépare le deuxième acte du premier? 2. Pourquoi l'avocat est-il revenu voir le juge? 3. Pourquoi le juge a-t-il mal compris ce que disait maître Adam? 4. Pourquoi le juge n'a-t-il pas eu le temps d'étudier le mémoire de maître Adam? 5. L'opération avait-elle réussi? 6. Pourquoi le juge n'est-il pas enchanté du succès de l'opération? 7. Qu'est-ce que maître Adam lui fait espérer? 8. Qu'est-ce que le juge promet de faire?

Scène II

1. Le juge se met-il à l'étude du mémoire de maître Adam? 2. Qui vient l'interrompre? 3. De quoi parle-t-elle? 4. Qu'est-ce qu'elle promet de temps en temps? 5. Quels autres sujets de conversation trouve-t-elle? 6. Quel effet ce bavardage a-t-il sur le mari? 7. Quel incendie Catherine se rappelle-t-elle? 8. Qui est madame de la Bruine? Qu'est-ce que Catherine espère? 9. Où le juge se réfugie-t-il pour tâcher d'échapper au bavardage de sa femme? 10. Que fait Catherine, alors? 11. Qu'est-ce que Catherine dit de madame de la Bruine quand elle voit que celle-ci ne vient pas lui faire visite? 12. Pourquoi le juge envoie-t-il Gilles chez le médecin? Qu'est-ce qu'il espère? 13. Que fait-il de tous ses papiers? 14. Où Catherine se sauve-t-elle? Pourquoi?

Scène III

1. Pourquoi mademoiselle de la Garandière est-elle venue voir le juge? 2. Est-ce qu'elle plaît au juge? 3. Quelle sorte de jugement le juge a-t-il rédigé? Pourquoi? 4. Qu'est-ce qu'il regrette amèrement?

Scène IV

1. Qui entre en scène de nouveau? 2. Maître Jean Maugier est-il toujours aussi enthousiaste? 3. Qu'est-ce que le juge désire que les médecins fassent? 4. Est-ce possible? 5. Le juge apprend-il ceci avec calme? 6. Quel est le seul remède aux ennuis du juge? 7. La surdité empêcherait-elle monsieur Léonard Botal d'être un bon juge? Qu'en

pense maître Adam? Qu'en pense le juge lui-même? 8. De quelles façons peut-on rendre un homme sourd? 9. Les médecins encouragent-ils le juge? 10. Celui-ci accepte-t-il qu'on le rende sourd?

Scène V

1. Pourquoi Alizon a-t-elle cessé de surveiller sa maîtresse? 2. Catherine est-elle satisfaite des médecins? 3. De qui se plaint-elle? Quelles explications donne-t-elle sur les rapports qui doivent exister entre époux? 4. Est-il possible d'arrêter son bavardage? 5. Quelle décision le juge prend-il? 6. Que fait Catherine pendant qu'on insuffle la poudre bienfaisante dans les oreilles de son mari? 7. Quel est l'effet immédiat de la poudre sur le juge? 8. Qu'est-ce qui arrive à Catherine quand elle apprend que son mari ne peut pas l'entendre? Que fait-elle? 9. Qui entre en scène en chantant? 10. Qu'est-ce qui arrive alors? 11. Pourquoi l'auteur termine-t-il la pièce de cette façon?

Appendix

THE VERB

REGULAR VERBS

INFINITIVE MOOD

PRESENT	PRESENT	PRESENT
donn er, ***to give***	**fin ir,** ***to finish***	**vend re,** ***to sell***

PARTICIPLES

PRESENT	PRESENT	PRESENT
donn ant, ***giving***	**fin iss ant,** ***finishing***	**vend ant,** ***selling***
PAST	**PAST**	**PAST**
donn é, ***given***	**fin i,** ***finished***	**vend u,** ***sold***

INDICATIVE MOOD

PRESENT	PRESENT	PRESENT
I give, am giving, do give, etc.	***I finish, am finishing, do finish, etc.***	***I sell, am selling, do sell, etc.***
je donn e	je fin is	je vend s
tu donn es	tu fin is	tu vend s
il donn e	il fin it	il vend
nous donn ons	nous fin iss ons	nous vend ons
vous donn ez	vous fin iss ez	vous vend ez
ils donn ent	ils fin iss ent	ils vend ent
IMPERFECT	**IMPERFECT**	**IMPERFECT**
I was giving, used to give, etc.	***I was finishing, used to finish, etc.***	***I was selling, used to sell, etc.***
je donn ais	je fin iss ais	je vend ais
tu donn ais	tu fin iss ais	tu vend ais
il donn ait	il fin iss ait	il vend ait
nous donn ions	nous fin iss ions	nous vend ions
vous donn iez	vous fin iss iez	vous vend iez
ils donn aient	ils fin iss aient	ils vend aient

PAST DEFINITE	PAST DEFINITE	PAST DEFINITE
I gave, etc.	*I finished, etc.*	*I sold, etc.*
je donn **ai**	je fin **is**	je vend **is**
tu donn **as**	tu fin **is**	tu vend **is**
il donn **a**	il fin **it**	il vend **it**
nous donn **âmes**	nous fin **îmes**	nous vend **îmes**
vous donn **âtes**	vous fin **îtes**	vous vend **îtes**
ils donn **èrent**	ils fin **irent**	ils vend **irent**

FUTURE	FUTURE	FUTURE
I shall give, etc.	*I shall finish, etc.*	*I shall sell, etc.*
je donner **ai**	je finir **ai**	je vendr **ai**
tu donner **as**	tu finir **as**	tu vendr **as**
il donner **a**	il finir **a**	il vendr **a**
nous donner **ons**	nous finir **ons**	nous vendr **ons**
vous donner **ez**	vous finir **ez**	vous vendr **ez**
ils donner **ont**	ils finir **ont**	ils vendr **ont**

CONDITIONAL	CONDITIONAL	CONDITIONAL
I should give, etc.	*I should finish, etc.*	*I should sell, etc.*
je donner **ais**	je finir **ais**	je vendr **ais**
tu donner **ais**	tu finir **ais**	tu vendr **ais**
il donner **ait**	il finir **ait**	il vendr **ait**
nous donner **ions**	nous finir **ions**	nous vendr **ions**
vous donner **iez**	vous finir **iez**	vous vendr **iez**
ils donner **aient**	ils finir **aient**	ils vendr **aient**

IMPERATIVE MOOD

PRESENT	PRESENT	PRESENT
Give, etc.	*Finish, etc.*	*Sell, etc..*
donn **e**	fin **is**	vend **s**
(qu'il donn **e**)	(qu'il fin iss **e**)	vend **e**)
donn **ons**	fin iss **ons**	(qu'il vend **ons**
donn **ez**	fin iss **ez**	vend **ez**
(qu'ils donn **ent**)	(qu'ils fin iss **ent**)	(qu'ils vend **ent**)

SUBJUNCTIVE MOOD

PRESENT	PRESENT	PRESENT
That I may give, etc.	*That I may finish, etc.*	*That I may sell, etc.*
que je donn e	que je fin iss e	que je vend e
que tu donn es	que tu fin iss es	que tu vend es
qu'il donn e	qu'il fin iss e	qu'il vend e
que nous donn ions	que nous fin iss ions	que nous vend ions
que vous donn iez	que vous fin iss iez	que vous vend iez
qu'ils donn ent	qu'ils fin iss ent	qu'ils vend ent

IMPERFECT	IMPERFECT	IMPERFECT
That I might give, etc.	*That I might finish, etc.*	*That I might sell, etc.*
que je donn asse	que je fin isse	que je vend isse
que tu donn asses	que tu fin isses	que tu vend isses
qu'il donn ât	qu'il fin ît	qu'il vend ît
que nous donn assions	que nous fin issions	que nous vend issions
que vous donn assiez	que vous fin issiez	que vous vend issiez
qu'ils donn assent	qu'ils fin issent	qu'ils vend issent

AUXILIARY VERBS

INFINITIVE MOOD

PRES. avoir, *to have* PRES. être. *to be*

PARTICIPLES

PRES. ayant, *having* PRES. étant, *being*
PAST eu, *had* PAST été, *been*

INDICATIVE MOOD

PRESENT		PRESENT	
I have, am having, do have, etc.		*I am, am being, etc.*	
j'ai	nous avons	je suis	nous sommes
tu as	vous avez	tu es	vous êtes
il a	ils ont	il est	ils sont

IMPERFECT		IMPERFECT	
I had, used to have, was having, etc.		*I was, used to be, was being, etc.*	
j'avais	nous avions	j'étais	nous étions
tu avais	vous aviez	tu étais	vous étiez
il avait	ils avaient	il était	ils étaient

PAST DEFINITE		PAST DEFINITE	
I had, etc.		*I was, etc.*	
j'eus	nous eûmes	je fus	nous fûmes
tu eus	vous eûtes	tu fus	vous fûtes
il eut	ils eurent	il fut	ils furent

FUTURE		FUTURE	
I shall have, etc.		*I shall be, etc.*	
j'aurai	nous aurons	je serai	nous serons
tu auras	vous aurez	tu seras	vous serez
il aura	ils auront	il sera	ils seront

CONDITIONAL		CONDITIONAL	
I should have, etc.		*I should be, etc.*	
j'aurais	nous aurions	je serais	nous serions
tu aurais	vous auriez	tu serais	vous seriez
il aurait	ils auraient	il serait	ils seraient

IMPERATIVE MOOD

PRESENT		PRESENT	
Have, etc.		*Be, etc.*	
	ayons		soyons
aie	ayez	sois	soyez
(qu'il ait)	(qu'ils aient)	(qu'il soit)	(qu'ils soient)

SUBJUNCTIVE MOOD

PRESENT		PRESENT	
That I may have, etc.		*That I may be, etc.*	
que j'aie	que nous ayons	que je sois	que nous soyons
que tu aies	que vous ayez	que tu sois	que vous soyez
qu'il ait	qu'ils aient	qu'il soit	qu'ils soient

IMPERFECT		IMPERFECT	
That I might have, etc.		*That I might be, etc.*	
que j'eusse	que nous eussions	que je fusse	que nous fussions
que tu eusses	que vous eussiez	que tu fusses	que vous fussiez
qu'il eût	qu'ils eussent	qu'il fût	qu'ils fussent

COMPOUND TENSES

Compound tenses are formed by combining the past participle of the principal verb with an auxiliary verb.

Avoir or **Être**

INFINITIVE MOOD

PERFECT	PERFECT
To have given, sold, finished	*To have arrived*
avoir donné, vendu, fini	être arrivé(e) (s) (es)

PARTICIPLES

PERFECT	PERFECT
Having given, sold, finished	*Having arrived*
ayant donné, vendu, fini	étant arrivé(e) (s) (es)

INDICATIVE MOOD

PAST INDEFINITE	PAST INDEFINITE
I have given, did give, gave, etc.	*I have arrived, did arrive, arrived, etc.*
j'ai donné, vendu, fini	je suis arrivé(e)
tu as donné, vendu, fini	tu es arrivé(e)
etc.	etc.

PLUPERFECT	PLUPERFECT
I had given, etc.	*I had arrived, etc.*
j'avais donné, vendu, fini	j'étais arrivé(e)
etc.	etc.

PAST ANTERIOR	PAST ANTERIOR
I had given, etc.	*I had arrived, etc.*
j'eus donné, vendu, fini	je fus arrivé(e)
etc.	etc.

FUTURE PERFECT

I shall have given, etc.
j'aurai donné, vendu, fini
etc.

FUTURE PERFECT

I shall have arrived, etc.
je serai arrivé(e)
etc.

CONDITIONAL PAST

I should have given, etc.
j'aurais donné, vendu, fini
etc.

CONDITIONAL PAST

I should have arrived, etc.
je serais arrivé(e)
etc.

SUBJUNCTIVE MOOD

PERFECT

That I may have given, etc.
que j'aie donné, vendu, fini
etc.

PERFECT

That I may have arrived, etc.
que je sois arrivé(e)
etc.

PLUPERFECT

That I might have given, etc.
que j'eusse donné, vendu, fini
etc.

PLUPERFECT

That I might have arrived, etc.
que je fusse arrivé(e)
etc.

ORTHOGRAPHIC CHANGES IN SOME VERBS

Verbs in –cer and –ger

1. Verbs in **–cer**, e.g., **avancer**, *to advance*, require the s-sound of **c** throughout their conjugation, and hence **c** becomes **ç** before **a** or **o** of an ending:

Pres. Part.	*Pres. Indic.*	*Impf. Indic.*	*Past Def.*	*Impf. Subj.*
avançant	avance	avançais	avançai	avançasse
	avances	avançais	avanças	avançasses
	avance	avançait	avança	avançât
	avançons	avancions	avançâmes	avançassions
	avancez	avanciez	avançâtes	avançassiez
	avancent	avançaient	avancèrent	avançassent

2. Verbs in **–ger**, e.g., **manger**, *to eat*, require the sound of **g** soft throughout their conjugation, and hence **g** becomes **ge** before **a** or **o**:

Pres. Part.	*Pres. Indic.*	*Impf. Indic.*	*Past Def.*	*Impf. Subj.*
mangeant	mange	mangeais	mangeai	mangeasse
	manges	mangeais	mangeas	mangeasses
	mange	mangeait	mangea	mangeât
	mangeons	mangions	mangeâmes	mangeassions
	mangez	mangiez	mangeâtes	mangeassiez
	mangent	mangeaient	mangèrent	mangeassent

Verbs in –yer

Verbs in **–oyer** and **–uyer** change **y** to **i** whenever it comes before **e** mute in conjugation, but not elsewhere; verbs in **–ayer** may either retain **y** throughout, or change it to **i** before **e** mute:

Pres. Indic.	*Pres. Subj.*	*Fut.*	*Condl.*
ennuie, etc.	ennuie, etc.	ennuierai, etc.	ennuierais, etc.
paye, } etc.	paye, } etc.	payerai } etc.	payerais, } etc.
paie, }	paie, }	paierai, }	paierais, }

Verbs with Stem-Vowel e or é

Verbs with stem-vowel **e** require the sound of **è** whenever, in conjugation, the next syllable contains **e** mute; so also verbs with the stem-vowel **é**, shown orthographically as follows:

1. By changing **e** or **é** to **è**, e.g., **mener**, *to lead;* **préférer**, *to prefer:*

Pres. Indic.	*Pres. Subj.*	*Fut.*	*Condl.*
mène	mène	mènerai	mènerais
mènes	mènes	mèneras	mènerais
mène	mène	mènera	mènerait
menons	menions	mènerons	mènerions
menez	meniez	mènerez	mèneriez
mènent	mènent	mèneront	mèneraient

But **préférer** with the stem-vowel **é**:

préfère, etc.	préfère, etc.	préférerai, etc.	préférerais, etc.

Like **mener**: Verbs with stem-vowel **e** (for exceptions in **–eler** and **–eter**, see below).

Like **préférer**: Verbs with stem-vowel **é** + consonant, e.g., **espérer**, *to hope,* etc.

2. Most verbs in **–eler, –eter,** however, indicate the **è**-sound by doubling **l** or **t,** e.g., **appeler,** *to call;* **jeter,** *to throw:*

Pres. Indic.	*Pres. Subj.*	*Fut.*	*Condl.*
appelle	appelle	appellerai	appellerais
appelles	appelles	appelleras	appellerais
appelle	appelle	appellera	appellerait
appelons	appelions	appellerons	appellerions
appelez	appeliez	appellerez	appelleriez
appellent	appellent	appelleront	appelleraient

So also **jeter:**

jette, etc.	jette, etc.	jetterai, etc.	jetterais, etc.

A few verbs in **–eler, –eter** take the grave accent precisely like **mener,** e.g., **acheter,** *to buy:*

achète, etc.	achète, etc.	achèterai, etc.	achèterais, etc.

IRREGULAR VERBS

PRINCIPAL IRREGULAR VERBS IN –ER

Aller, *to go*

1. *Infinitive* **aller;** *fut.* irai, iras, ira, etc.; *condl.* irais, etc.
2. *Pres. Part.* **allant;** *impf. indic.* allais, etc.; *pres. subj.* aille, ailles, aille, allions, alliez, aillent.
3. *Past Part.* **allé;** *past indef.* je suis allé, etc.
4. *Pres. Indic.* vais, vas, va, allons, allez, vont; *impve.* va, allons, allez.
5. *Past Def.* **allai,** allas, alla, allâmes, allâtes, allèrent; *impf. subj.* allasse, allasses, allât, allassions, allassiez, allassent.

Like aller:

s'en aller, *to go away.*

Envoyer, *to send*

1. *Infinitive* **envoyer;** *fut.* enverrai, etc.; *condl.* enverrais, etc.
2. *Pres. Part.* **envoyant;** *impf. indic.* envoyais, envoyais, envoyait; envoyions, envoyiez, envoyaient; *pres. subj.* envoie, envoies, envoie; envoyions, envoyiez, envoient.
3. *Past Part.* **envoyé;** *past indef.* j'ai envoyé, etc.
4. *Pres. Indic.* envoie, envoies, envoie, envoyons, envoyez, envoient; *impve.* envoie, envoyons, envoyez.

5. *Past Def.* envoyai, envoyas, envoya, envoyâmes, envoyâtes, envoyèrent; *impf. subj.* envoyasse, envoyasses, envoyât, envoyassions, envoyassiez, envoyassent.

Like envoyer:

renvoyer, *to send away, dismiss.*

PRINCIPAL IRREGULAR VERBS IN -IR

Acquérir, *to acquire*

1. *Infinitive* acquérir; *fut.* acquerrai, acquerras, etc.; *condl.* acquerrais, etc.
2. *Pres. Part.* acquérant; *impf. indic.* acquérais, etc.; *pres. subj.* acquière, acquières, acquière, acquérions, acquériez, acquièrent.
3. *Past Part.* acquis; *past indef.* j'ai acquis, etc.
4. *Pres. Indic.* acquiers, acquiers, acquiert, acquérons, acquérez, acquièrent; *impve.* acquiers, acquérons, acquérez.
5. *Past Def.* acquis, acquis, acquit, acquîmes, acquîtes, acquirent; *impf. subj.* acquisse, acquisses, acquît, acquissions, acquissiez, acquissent.

Like acquérir:

conquérir, *to conquer.*

Courir, *to run*

1. *Infinitive* courir; *fut.* courrai, courras, etc.; *condl.* courrais, etc.
2. *Pres. Part.* courant; *impf. indic.* courais, etc.; *pres. subj.* coure, coures, coure, courions, couriez, courent.
3. *Past Part.* couru; *past indef.* j'ai couru, etc.
4. *Pres. Indic.* cours, cours, court, courons, courez, courent; *impve.* cours, courons, courez.
5. *Past Def.* courus, courus, courut, courûmes, courûtes, coururent; *impf. subj.* courusse, courusses, courût, courussions, courussiez, courussent.

Like courir are its compounds:

accourir, *to run up, hasten*
secourir, *to succor, help*
parcourir, *to run over, pass through, glance over*

Cueillir, *to gather, pick*

1. *Infinitive* cueillir; *fut.* cueillerai, etc.; *condl.* cueillerais, etc.
2. *Pres. Part.* cueillant; *impf. indic.* cueillais, etc.; *pres. subj.* cueille, cueilles, cueille, cueillions, cueilliez, cueillent.
3. *Past Part.* cueilli; *past indef.* j'ai cueilli, etc.
4. *Pres. Indic.* cueille, cueilles, cueille, cueillons, cueillez, cueillent; *impve.* cueille, cueillons, cueillez.

5. *Past Def.* **cueillis,** cueillis, cueillit, cueillîmes, cueillîtes, cueillirent; *impf. subj.* cueillisse, cueillisses, cueillît, cueillissions, cueillissiez, cueillissent.

Like cueillir:

accueillir, *to welcome*
assaillir, *to assail (regular in future and conditional)*
recueillir, *to gather, collect*
se recueillir, *to collect one's thoughts, reflect*

Dormir, *to sleep*

1. *Infinitive* **dormir;** *fut.* dormirai, etc.; *condl.* dormirais, etc.
2. *Pres. Part.* **dormant;** *impf. indic.* dormais, etc.; *pres. subj.* dorme, dormes, dorme, dormions, dormiez, dorment.
3. *Past Part.* **dormi;** *past indef.* j'ai dormi, etc.
4. *Pres. Indic.* **dors,** dors, dort, dormons, dormez, dorment; *impve.* dors, dormons, dormez.
5. *Past Def.* **dormis,** dormis, dormit, dormîmes, dormîtes, dormirent; *impf. subj.* dormisse, dormisses, dormît, dormissions, dormissiez, dormissent.

Like dormir:

endormir, *to put to sleep*
s'endormir, *to fall asleep*
mentir, *to lie*
démentir, *to contradict, belie*
partir, *to set out, leave, go away*
repartir, *to set out again, reply*
se repentir de, *to repent*
sentir, *to feel, smell*
se sentir + *adj.* or *adv., to feel*
consentir à, *to consent*
servir, *to serve*
se servir de, *to make use of*
desservir, *to clear the table*
sortir, *to go out, come out*

Observe the present indicative of the following types, which are represented in the above list:

mentir: mens, mens, ment, mentons, mentez, mentent
partir: pars, pars, part, partons, partez, partent
se repentir: repens, repens, repent, repentons, repentez, repentent
sentir: sens, sens, sent, sentons, sentez, sentent
servir: sers, sers, sert, servons, servez, servent
sortir: sors, sors, sort, sortons, sortez, sortent
bouillir: bous, bous, bout, bouillons, bouillez, bouillent

Fuir, *to flee, fly*

1. *Infinitive* **fuir;** *fut.* fuirai, etc.; *condl.* fuirais, etc.
2. *Pres. Part.* **fuyant;** *impf. indic.* fuyais, etc.; *pres. subj.* fuie, fuies, fuie, fuyions, fuyiez, fuient.
3. *Past Part.* **fui;** *past indef.* j'ai fui, etc.

4. *Pres. Indic.* **fuis,** fuis, fuit, fuyons, fuyez, fuient; *impve.* fuis, fuyons, fuyez.

5. *Past Def.* **fuis,** fuis, fuit, fuîmes, fuîtes, fuirent; *impf. subj.* fuisse, fuisses, fuît, fuissions, fuissiez, fuissent.

Mourir, *to die*

1. *Infinitive* **mourir;** *fut.* mourrai, mourras, etc.; *condl.* mourrais, etc.

2. *Pres. Part.* **mourant;** *impf. indic.* mourais, etc.; *pres. subj.* meure, meures, meure, mourions, mouriez, meurent.

3. *Past Part.* **mort;** *past indef.* je suis mort, etc.

4. *Pres. Indic.* **meurs,** meurs, meurt, mourons, mourez, meurent; *impve.* meurs, mourons, mourez.

5. *Past Def.* **mourus,** mourus, mourut, mourûmes, mourûtes, moururent; *impf. subj.* mourusse, mourusses, mourût, mourussions, mourussiez, mourussent.

Ouvrir, *to open*

1. *Infinitive* **ouvrir;** *fut.* ouvrirai, etc.; *condl.* ouvrirais, etc.

2. *Pres. Part.* **ouvrant;** *impf. indic.* ouvrais, etc.; *pres. subj.* ouvre, ouvres, ouvre, ouvrions, ouvriez, ouvrent.

3. *Past Part.* **ouvert;** *past indef.* j'ai ouvert, etc.

4. *Pres. Indic.* **ouvre,** ouvres, ouvre, ouvrons, ouvrez, ouvrent; *impve.* ouvre, ouvrons, ouvrez.

5. *Past Def.* **ouvris,** ouvris, ouvrit, ouvrîmes, ouvrîtes, ouvrirent; *impf. subj.* ouvrisse, ouvrisses, ouvrît, ouvrissions, ouvrissiez, ouvrissent.

Like **ouvrir:**

entr'ouvrir, *to open slightly*
couvrir, *to cover*
découvrir, *to discover, uncover*
offrir, *to offer*
souffrir, *to suffer*

Tenir, *to hold*

1. *Infinitive* **tenir;** *fut.* tiendrai, tiendras, etc.; *condl.* tiendrais, etc.

2. *Pres. Part.* **tenant;** *impf. indic.* tenais, etc.; *pres. subj.* tienne, tiennes, tienne, tenions, teniez, tiennent.

3. *Past Part.* **tenu;** *past indef.* j'ai tenu, etc.

4. *Pres. Indic.* **tiens,** tiens, tient, tenons, tenez, tiennent; *impve.* tiens, tenons, tenez.

5. *Past Def.* **tins,** tins, tint, tînmes, tîntes, tinrent; *impf. subj.* tinsse, tinsses, tînt, tinssions, tinssiez, tinssent.

Like tenir are its compounds:

appartenir à, *to belong to*
contenir, *to restrain*
maintenir, *to maintain*
obtenir, *to obtain*
retenir, *to detain, engage, keep back*
soutenir, *to sustain*

Venir, *to come*

1. *Infinitive* **venir;** *fut.* viendrai, viendras, etc.; *condl.* viendrais, etc.
2. *Pres. Part.* **venant;** *impf. indic.* venais, etc.; *pres. subj.* vienne, viennes, vienne, venions, veniez, viennent.
3. *Past Part.* **venu;** *past indef.* je suis venu, etc.
4. *Pres. Indic.* **viens,** viens, vient, venons, venez, viennent; *impve.* viens, venons, venez.
5. *Past Def.* **vins,** vins, vint, vînmes, vîntes, vinrent; *impf. subj.* vinsse, vinsses, vînt, vinssions, vinssiez, vinssent.

Like **venir** are its compounds:

convenir, *to agree, suit* (conjugated with **avoir** or **être**)
devenir, *to become*
parvenir, *to attain, reach*
prévenir (conjugated with **avoir**), *to notify, warn*
revenir, *to come back, return*
se souvenir de, *to recollect, remember*

Vêtir, *to clothe*

1. *Infinitive* **vêtir;** *fut.* vêtirai, etc.; *condl.* vêtirais, etc.
2. *Pres. Part.* **vêtant;** *impf. indic.* vêtais, etc.; *pres. subj.* vête, vêtes, vête, vêtions, vêtiez, vêtent.
3. *Past Part.* **vêtu;** *past indef.* j'ai vêtu, etc.
4. *Pres. Indic.* **vêts,** vêts, vêt, vêtons, vêtez, vêtent; *impve.* vêts, vêtons, vêtez.
5. *Past Def.* **vêtis,** vêtis, vêtit, vêtîmes, vêtîtes, vêtirent; *impf. subj.* vêtisse vêtisses, vêtît, vêtissions, vêtissiez, vêtissent.

PRINCIPAL IRREGULAR VERBS IN –RE

Battre, *to beat*

Loses one **t** in the present indicative singular: **bats, bats, bat.**

Like battre:

se battre, *to fight*
abattre, *to fell*
combattre, *to fight, oppose*
débattre, *to debate*
se débattre, *to struggle*
rabattre, *to beat down*

Boire, *to drink*

1. *Infinitive* boire; *fut.* boirai, etc.; *condl.* boirais, etc.
2. *Pres. Part.* buvant; *impf. indic.* buvais, etc.; *pres. subj.* boive, boives, boive, buvions, buviez, boivent.
3. *Past Part.* bu; *past indef.* j'ai bu, etc.
4. *Pres. Indic.* bois, bois, boit, buvons, buvez, boivent; *impve.* bois, buvons, buvez.
5. *Past Def.* bus, bus, but, bûmes, bûtes, burent; *impf. subj.* busse, busses, bût, bussions, bussiez, bussent.

Conclure, *to conclude*

1. *Infinitive* conclure; *fut.* conclurai, etc.; *condl.* conclurais, etc.
2. *Pres. Part.* concluant; *impf. indic.* concluais, etc.; *pres. subj.* conclue, conclues, conclue, concluions, concluiez, concluent.
3. *Past Part.* conclu; *past indef.* j'ai conclu, etc.
4. *Pres. Indic.* conclus, conclus, conclut, concluons, concluez, concluent; *impve.* conclus, concluons, concluez.
5. *Past Def.* conclus, conclus, conclut, conclûmes, conclûtes, conclurent; *impf. subj.* conclusse, conclusses, conclût, conclussions, conclussiez, conclussent.

Conduire, *to conduct, take, lead, etc.*

1. *Infinitive* conduire; *fut.* conduirai, etc.; *condl.* conduirais, etc.
2. *Pres. Part.* conduisant; *impf. indic.* conduisais, etc.; *pres. subj.* conduise, conduises, conduise, conduisions, conduisiez, conduisent.
3. *Past Part.* conduit; *past indef.* j'ai conduit, etc.
4. *Pres. Indic.* conduis, conduis, conduit, conduisons, conduisez, conduisent; *impve.* conduis, conduisons, conduisez.
5. *Past Def.* conduisis, conduisis, conduisit, conduisîmes, conduisîtes, conduisirent; *impf. subj.* conduisisse, conduisisses, conduisît, conduisissions, conduisissiez, conduisissent.

Like conduire:

se conduire, *to conduct oneself, behave*
introduire, *to introduce, bring into*
produire, *to produce*
réduire, *to reduce*
reproduire, *to reproduce*
séduire, *to charm, seduce*
traduire, *to translate*
construire, *to construct*
instruire, *to instruct*
détruire, *to destroy*
cuire, *to cook*
luire,[1] *to shine*
reluire,[1] *to glisten*

[1] *Past part.* lui and relui respectively. No past def. or impf. subj.

Connaître, *to know, etc.*

1. *Infinitive* connaître; *fut.* connaîtrai, etc.; *condl.* connaîtrais, etc.
2. *Pres. Part.* connaissant; *impf. indic.* connaissais, etc.; *pres. subj.* connaisse, connaisses, connaisse, connaissions, connaissiez, connaissent.
3. *Past Part.* connu; *past indef.* j'ai connu, etc.
4. *Pres. Indic.* connais, connais, connaît, connaissons, connaissez, connaissent; *impve.* connais, connaissons, connaissez.
5. *Past Def.* connus, connus, connut, connûmes, connûtes, connurent; *impf. subj.* connusse, connusses, connût, connussions, connussiez, connussent.

Like connaître:

reconnaître, *to recognize*
paraître, *to appear*
apparaître, *to appear*
disparaître, *to disappear*

Coudre, *to sew*

1. *Infinitive* coudre; *fut.* coudrai, etc.; *condl.* coudrais, etc.
2. *Pres. Part.* cousant; *impf. indic.* cousais, etc.; *pres. subj.* couse, couses, couse, cousions, cousiez, cousent.
3. *Past Part.* cousu; *past indef.* j'ai cousu, etc.
4. *Pres. Indic.* couds, couds, coud, cousons, cousez, cousent; *impve.* couds, cousons, cousez.
5. *Past Def.* cousis, cousis, cousit, cousîmes, cousîtes, cousirent; *impf. subj.* cousisse, cousisses, cousît, cousissions, cousissiez, cousissent.

Craindre, *to fear*

1. *Infinitive* craindre; *fut.* craindrai, etc.; *condl.* craindrais, etc.
2. *Pres. Part.* craignant; *impf. indic.* craignais, etc.; *pres. subj.* craigne, craignes, craigne, craignions, craigniez, craignent.
3. *Past Part.* craint; *past indef.* j'ai craint, etc.
4. *Pres. Indic.* crains, crains, craint, craignons, craignez, craignent; *impve.* crains, craignons, craignez.
5. *Past Def.* craignis, craignis, craignit, craignîmes, craignîtes, craignirent; *impf. subj.* craignisse, craignisses, craignît, craignissions, craignissiez, craignissent.

Like craindre:

in –aindre:
contraindre, *to constrain*
plaindre, *to pity*
se plaindre de, *to complain*

in –eindre:
atteindre, *to attain*
éteindre, *to extinguish*
peindre, *to paint*
teindre, *to dye*

in –oindre:
se joindre à, *to join*
rejoindre, *to rejoin, overtake*

Croire, *to believe*

1. *Infinitive* **croire;** *fut.* croirai, etc.; *condl.* croirais, etc.
2. *Pres. Part.* **croyant;** *impf. indic.* croyais, etc.; *pres. subj.* croie, croies, croie, croyions, croyiez, croient.
3. *Past Part.* **cru:** *past indef.* j'ai cru, etc.
4. *Pres. Indic.* **crois,** crois, croit, croyons, croyez, croient; *impve.* crois, croyons, croyez.
5. *Past Def.* **crus,** crus, crut, crûmes, crûtes, crurent; *impf. subj.* crusse, crusses, crût, crussions, crussiez, crussent.

Croître, *to grow*

1. *Infinitive* **croître;** *fut,* croîtrai, etc.; *condl.* croîtrais, etc.
2. *Pres. Part.* **croissant;** *impf. indic.* croissais, etc.; *pres. subj.* croisse, croisses, croisse, croissions, croissiez, croissent.
3. *Past Part.* **crû** (*f.* crue); *past indef.* j'ai crû, etc.
4. *Pres. Indic.* **croîs,** croîs, croît, croissons, croissez, croissent; *impve.* croîs, croissons, croissez.
5. *Past Def.* **crûs,** crûs, crût, crûmes, crûtes, crûrent; *impf. subj.* crûsse, crûsses, crût, crûssions, crûssiez, crûssent.

Dire, *to say, tell*

1. *Infinitive* **dire;** *fut.* dirai, etc.; *condl.* dirais, etc.
2. *Pres. Part.* **disant;** *impf. indic.* disais, etc.; *pres. subj.* dise, dises, dise, disions, disiez, disent.
3. *Past Part.* **dit;** *past indef.* j'ai dit, etc.
4. *Pres. Indic.* **dis,** dis, dit, disons, dites, disent; *impve.* dis, disons, dites.
5. *Past Def.* **dis,** dis, dit, dîmes, dîtes, dirent; *impf. subj.* disse, disses, dît, dissions, dissiez, dissent.

Like dire:

contredire, *to contradict*	**médire (de),** *to slander*
se dédire, *to retract, deny*	**prédire,** *to predict*
interdire, *to forbid*	**redire,** *to say again*

Note. The 2nd plur. pres. indic. and impve. is: **Contredisez, dédisez, interdisez, médisez, prédisez.** But: **redites.**

Écrire, *to write*

1. *Infinitive* **écrire;** *fut.* écrirai, etc.; *condl.* écrirais, etc.
2. *Pres. Part.* **écrivant;** *impf. indic.* écrivais, etc.; *pres. subj.* écrive, écrives, écrive, écrivions, écriviez, écrivent.

3. *Past Part.* écrit; *past indef.* j'ai écrit, etc.

4. *Pres. Indic.* écris, écris, écrit, écrivons, écrivez, écrivent; *impve.* écris, écrivons, écrivez.

5. *Past Def.* écrivis, écrivis, écrivit, écrivîmes, écrivîtes, écrivirent; *impf. subj.* écrivisse, écrivisses, écrivît, écrivissions, écrivissiez, écrivissent.

Like écrire are all verbs in –(s)crire:

décrire, *to describe*
inscrire, *to inscribe, enroll, register*
prescrire, *to prescribe*
récrire, *to rewrite*—

Faire, *to do, make*

1. *Infinitive* faire; *fut.* ferai, etc.; *condl.* ferais, etc.

2. *Pres. Part.* faisant; *impf. indic.* faisais, etc.; *pres. subj.* fasse, fasses, fasse, fassions, fassiez, fassent.

3. *Past Part.* fait; *past indef.* j'ai fait, etc.

4. *Pres. Indic.* fais, fais, fait, faisons, faites, font; *impve.* fais, faisons, faites.

5. *Past Def.* fis, fis, fit, fîmes, fîtes, firent; *impf. subj.* fisse, fisses, fît, fissions, fissiez, fissent.

Like faire:

défaire, *to undo, untie*
se défaire de, *to get rid of*
satisfaire, *to satisfy*

Lire, *to read*

1. *Infinitive* lire; *fut.* lirai, etc.; *condl.* lirais, etc.

2. *Pres. Part.* lisant; *impf. indic.* lisais, etc.; *pres. subj.* lise, lises, lise, lisions, lisiez, lisent.

3. *Past Part.* lu; *past indef.* j'ai lu, etc.

4. *Pres. Indic.* lis, lis, lit, lisons, lisez, lisent; *impve.* lis, lisons, lisez.

5. *Past Def.* lus, lus, lut, lûmes, lûtes, lurent; *impf. subj.* lusse, lusses, lût, lussions, lussiez, lussent.

Like lire:

élire, *to elect*
relire, *to re-read*

Mettre, *to place, put*

1. *Infinitive* mettre; *fut.* mettrai, etc.; *condl.* mettrais, etc.

2. *Pres. Part.* mettant; *impf. indic.* mettais, etc.; *pres. subj.* mette, mettes, mette, mettions, mettiez, mettent.

3. *Past Part.* mis; *past indef.* j'ai mis, etc.

4. *Pres. Indic.* **mets,** mets, met, mettons, mettez, mettent; *impve.* mets, mettons, mettez.
5. *Past Def.* **mis,** mis, mit, mîmes, mîtes, mirent; *impf. subj.* misse, misses, mît, missions, missiez, missent.

Like mettre:

se mettre à, *to begin*
admettre, *to admit*
commettre, *to commit*
omettre, *to omit*
permettre, *to permit*
promettre, *to promise*
remettre, *to put back, hand to, defer*
soumettre, *to submit*
transmettre, *to transmit*

Naître, *to be born, spring forth, etc.*

1. *Infinitive* **naître;** *fut.* naîtrai, etc.; *condl.* naîtrais, etc.
2. *Pres. Part.* **naissant;** *impf. indic.* naissais, etc.; *pres. subj.* naisse, naisses, naisse, naissions, naissiez, naissent.
3. *Past Part.* **né;** *past indef.* je suis né, etc.
4. *Pres. Indic.* **nais,** nais, naît, naissons, naissez, naissent; *impve.* nais, naissons, naissez.
5. *Past Def.* **naquis,** naquis, naquit, naquîmes, naquîtes, naquirent; *impf. subj.* naquisse, naquisses, naquît, naquissions, naquissiez, naquissent.

Like naître:

renaître, *to be born again, spring forth again.*

Plaire, *to please*

1. *Infinitive* **plaire;** *fut.* plairai, etc.; *condl.* plairais, etc.
2. *Pres. Part.* **plaisant;** *impf. indic.* plaisais, etc.; *pres. subj.* plaise, plaises, plaise, plaisions, plaisiez, plaisent.
3. *Past Part.* **plu;** *past indef.* j'ai plu, etc.
4. *Pres. Indic.* **plais,** plais, plaît, plaisons, plaisez, plaisent; *impve.* plais, plaisons, plaisez.
5. *Past Def.* **plus,** plus, plut, plûmes, plûtes, plurent; *impf. subj.* plusse, plusses, plût, plussions, plussiez, plussent.

Like plaire:

se taire, *to be silent, become silent*
(Il se tait has no circumflex.)
se plaire à, *to like, enjoy*

Prendre, *to take*

1. *Infinitive* **prendre;** *fut.* prendrai, etc.; *condl.* prendrais, etc.
2. *Pres. Part.* **prenant;** *impf. indic.* prenais, etc.; *pres. subj.* prenne, prennes, prenne, prenions, preniez, prennent.

3. *Past Part.* **pris**; *past indef.* j'ai pris, etc.
4. *Pres. Indic.* **prends**, prends, prend, prenons, prenez, prennent; *impve.* prends, prenons, prenez.
5. *Past Def.* **pris**, pris, prit, prîmes, prîtes, prirent; *impf. subj.* prisse, prisses, prît, prissions, prissiez, prissent.

Like prendre are its compounds:

apprendre, *to learn*
comprendre, *to understand, to include*
entreprendre, *to undertake*
reprendre, *to take back*
surprendre, *to surprise*

Résoudre, *to resolve*

1. *Infinitive* **résoudre**; *fut.* résoudrai, etc.; *condl.* résoudrais, etc.
2. *Pres. Part.* **résolvant**; *impf. indic.* résolvais, etc.; *pres. subj.* résolve, résolves, résolve, résolvions, résolviez, résolvent.
3. *Past Part.* **résolu**; *past indef.* j'ai résolu, etc.
4. *Pres. Indic.* **résous**, résous, résout, résolvons, résolvez, résolvent; *impve.* résous, résolvons, résolvez.
5. *Past. Def.* **résolus**, résolus, résolut, résolûmes, résolûtes, résolurent; *impf. subj.* résolusse, résolusses, résolût, résolussions, résolussiez, résolussent.

Rire, *to laugh*

1. *Infinitive* **rire**; *fut.* rirai, etc.; *condl.* rirais, etc.
2. *Pres. Part.* **riant**; *impf. indic.* riais, etc.; *pres. subj.* rie, ries, rie, riions, riiez, rient.
3. *Past Part.* **ri**; *past indef.* j'ai ri, etc.
4. *Pres. Indic.* **ris**, ris, rit, rions, riez, rient; *impve.* ris, rions, riez.
5. *Past Def.* **ris**, ris, rit, rîmes, rîtes, rirent; *impf. subj.* risse, risses, rît rissions, rissiez, rissent.

Like rire:

se rire de, *to make sport of*
sourire, *to smile*

Soustraire, *to subtract*

1. *Infinitive* **soustraire**; *fut.* soustrairai, etc.; *condl.* soustrairais, etc.
2. *Pres. Part.* **soustrayant**; *impf. indic.* soustrayais, etc.; *pres. subj.* soustraie, soustraies, soustraie, soustrayions, soustrayiez, soustraient.
3. *Past Part.* **soustrait**; *past indef.* j'ai soustrait, etc.
4. *Pres. Indic.* **soustrais**, soustrais, soustrait, soustrayons, soustrayez, soustraient; *impve.* soustrais, soustrayons, soustrayez.
5. *No Past Def. or impf. subj.*

Suivre, *to follow*

1. *Infinitive* suivre; *fut.* suivrai, etc.; *condl.* suivrais, etc.
2. *Pres. Part.* suivant; *impf. indic.* suivais, etc.; *pres. subj.* suive, suives, suive, suivions, suiviez, suivent.
3. *Past Part.* suivi; *past indef.* j'ai suivi, etc.
4. *Pres. Indic.* suis, suis, suit, suivons, suivez, suivent; *impve.* suis, suivons, suivez.
5. *Past Def.* suivis, suivis, suivit, suivîmes, suivîtes, suivirent; *impf. subj.* suivisse, suivisses, suivît, suivissions, suivissiez, suivissent.

Like suivre:

poursuivre, *to pursue, chase*

Vaincre, *to conquer*

1. *Infinitive* vaincre; *fut.* vaincrai, etc.; *condl.* vaincrais, etc.
2. *Pres. Part.* vainquant; *impf. indic.* vainquais, etc.; *pres. subj.* vainque, vainques, vainque, vainquions, vainquiez, vainquent.
3. *Past Part.* vaincu; *past indef.* j'ai vaincu, etc.
4. *Pres. Indic.* vaincs, vaincs, vainc, vainquons, vainquez, vainquent; *impve.* vaincs, vainquons, vainquez.
5. *Past Def.* vainquis, vainquis, vainquit, vainquîmes, vainquîtes, vainquirent; *impf. subj.* vainquisse, vainquisses, vainquît, vainquissions, vainquissiez, vainquissent.

Note: Stem **c** becomes **qu** before any vowel except **u**.

Like vaincre:

convaincre, *to convince*

Vivre, *to live*

1. *Infinitive* vivre; *fut.* vivrai, etc.; *condl.* vivrais, etc.
2. *Pres. Part.* vivant; *impf. indic.* vivais, etc.; *pres. subj.* vive, vives, vive, vivions, viviez, vivent.
3. *Past Part.* vécu; *past indef.* j'ai vécu, etc.
4. *Pres. Indic.* vis, vis, vit, vivons, vivez, vivent; *impve.* vis, vivons, vivez.
5. *Past Def.* vécus, vécus, vécut, vécûmes, vécûtes, vécurent; *impf. subj.* vécusse, vécusses, vécût, vécussions, vécussiez, vécussent.

Like vivre:

survivre, *to survive*

PRINCIPAL IRREGULAR VERBS IN –OIR

Asseoir, *to seat*

1. *Infinitive* **asseoir;** *fut.* assiérai, etc., *or* asseyerai, etc., *or* assoirai, etc.; *condl.* assiérais, etc., *or* asseyerais, etc., *or* assoirais, etc.

2. *Pres. Part.* **asseyant** *or* **assoyant;** *impf. indic.* asseyais, etc., *or* assoyais, etc.; *pres. subj.* asseye, asseyes, asseye, asseyions, asseyiez, asseyent, *or* asssoie, assoies, assoie, assoyions, assoyiez, assoient.

3. *Past Part.* **assis;** *past indef.* j'ai assis, etc.

4. *Pres. Indic.* **assieds,** assieds, assied, asseyons, asseyez, asseyent, *or* **assois,** assois, assoit, assoyons, assoyez, assoient; *impve.* assieds, asseyons, asseyez, *or* assois, assoyons, assoyez.

5. *Past Def.* **assis,** assis, assit, assîmes, assîtes, assirent; *impf. subj.* assisse, assisses, assît, assissions, assissiez, assissent.

Like **asseoir:**

s'asseoir, *to sit down*

Devoir, *to owe, have to, must*

1. *Infinitive* **devoir;** *fut.* devrai, etc.; *condl.* devrais, etc.

2. *Pres. Part.* **devant;** *impf. indic.* devais, etc.; *pres. subj.* doive, doives, doive, devions, deviez, doivent.

3. *Past Part.* **dû** (*f.* due, *pl.* du(e)s); *past indef.* j'ai dû, etc.

4. *Pres. Indic.* **dois,** dois, doit, devons, devez, doivent; *no impve.*

5. *Past Def.* **dus,** dus, dut, dûmes, dûtes, durent; *impf. subj.* dusse, dusses, dût, dussions, dussiez, dussent.

Falloir, *must, etc.* (impers.)

1. *Infinitive* **falloir;** *fut.* il faudra; *condl.* il faudrait.

2. *No Pres. Part.; impf. indic.* il fallait; *pres. subj.* il faille.

3. *Past Part.* **fallu;** *past indef.* il a fallu.

4. *Pres. Indic.* **il faut;** *no impve.*

5. *Past Def.* **il fallut;** *impf. subj.* il fallût.

Pleuvoir, *to rain* (impers.)

1. *Infinitive* **pleuvoir;** *fut.* il pleuvra; *condl.* il pleuvrait.

2. *Pres. Part.* **pleuvant;** *impf. indic.* il pleuvait; *pres. subj.* il pleuve.

3. *Past Part.* **plu;** *past indef.* il a plu.

4. *Pres. Indic.* **il pleut;** *no impve.*

5. *Past Def.* **il plut;** *impf. subj.* il plût.

Pouvoir, *to be able, etc.*

1. *Infinitive* **pouvoir;** *fut.* pourrai, etc.; *condl.* pourrais, etc.

2. *Pres. Part.* **pouvant;** *impf. indic.* pouvais, etc.; *pres. subj.* puisse, puisses, puisse, puissions, puissiez, puissent.

3. *Past Part.* **pu;** *past indef.* j'ai pu, etc.

4. *Pres. Indic.* **puis** *or* **peux,** peux, peut, pouvons, pouvez, peuvent; *no impve.*

5. *Past Def.* **pus,** pus, put, pûmes, pûtes, purent; *impf. subj.* pusse, pusses, pût, pussions, pussiez, pussent.

Note: The first sing. pres. indic. in negation is usually **je ne peux pas** *or* **je ne puis;** in questions, only **puis-je?;** otherwise **puis** *or* **peux.**

Recevoir, *to receive*

1. *Infinitive* **recevoir;** *fut.* recevrai, etc.; *condl.* recevrais, etc.

2. *Pres. Part.* **recevant;** *impf. indic.* recevais, etc.; *pres. subj.* reçoive, reçoives, reçoive, recevions, receviez, reçoivent.

3. *Past Part.* **reçu;** *past indef.* j'ai reçu, etc.

4. *Pres. Indic.* **reçois,** reçois, reçoit, recevons, recevez, reçoivent; *impve.* reçois, recevons, recevez.

5. *Past Def.* **reçus,** reçus, reçut, reçûmes, reçûtes, reçurent; *impf. subj.* reçusse, reçusses, reçût, reçussions, reçussiez, reçussent.

Like **recevoir:**

s'apercevoir de, *to realize, become aware of*
apercevoir, *to perceive*
concevoir, *to conceive*
décevoir, *to disappoint, to deceive*
percevoir, *to collect (taxes, etc.)*

Savoir, *to know, etc.*

1. *Infinitive* **savoir;** *fut.* saurai, etc.; *condl.* saurais, etc.

2. *Past Part.* **sachant;** *impf. indic.* savais, etc.; *pres. subj.* sache, saches, sache, sachions, sachiez, sachent.

3. *Past Part.* **su;** *past indef.* j'ai su, etc.

4. *Pres. Indic.* **sais,** sais, sait, savons, savez, savent; *impve.* sache, sachons, sachez.

5. *Past Def.* **sus,** sus, sut, sûmes, sûtes, surent; *impf. subj.* susse, susses, sût, sussions, sussiez, sussent.

Valoir, *to be worth, bring upon*

1. *Infinitive* **valoir;** *fut.* vaudrai, etc.; *condl.* vaudrais, etc.

2. *Pres. Part.* **valant;** *impf. indic.* valais, etc.; *pres. subj.* vaille, vailles, vaille, valions, valiez, vaillent.

3. *Past Part.* **valu;** *past indef.* j'ai valu, etc.

4. *Pres. Indic.* **vaux,** vaux, vaut, valons, valez, valent; *impve.* vaux, valons, valez.

5. *Past Def.* **valus,** valus, valut, valûmes, valûtes, valurent; *impf. subj.* valusse, valusses, valût, valussions, valussiez, valussent.

Voir, *to see*

1. *Infinitive* **voir;** *fut.* verrai, etc.; *condl.* verrais, etc.

2. *Pres. Part.* **voyant** *impf. indic.* voyais, etc.; *pres. subj.* voie, voies, voie, voyions, voyiez, voient.

3. *Past Part.* **vu;** *past indef.* j'ai vu, etc.

4. *Pres. Indic.* **vois,** vois, voit, voyons, voyez, voient; *impve.* vois, voyons, voyez.

5. *Past Def.* **vis,** vis, vit, vîmes, vîtes, virent; *impf. subj.* visse, visses, vît, vissions, vissiez, vissent.

Like **voir:**

entrevoir, *to catch a glimpse of* **revoir,** *to see again*

Vouloir, *to will, etc.*

1. *Infinitive* **vouloir;** *fut.* voudrai, etc.; *condl.* voudrais, etc.

2. *Pres. Part.* **voulant;** *impf. indic.* voulais, etc.; *pres. subj.* veuille, veuilles, veuille, voulions, vouliez, veuillent.

3. *Past Part.* **voulu;** *past indef.* j'ai voulu, etc.

4. *Pres. Indic.* **veux,** veux, veut, voulons, voulez, veulent; *impve.* **veux,** voulons, voulez.

5. *Past Def.* **voulus,** voulus, voulut, voulûmes, voulûtes, voulurent; *impf. subj.* voulusse, voulusses, voulût, voulussions, voulussiez, voulussent.

Note: The regular imperative **veux, voulons, voulez** is rare; **veuille, veuillons, veuillez** generally serve as imperatives.

Reference List of Verbs Requiring the Infinitive with de

s'absenter, *absent o. s. (from)*
s'absoudre, *absolve o. s. (from)*
s'abstenir, *abstain (from)*
accorder, *grant*
accuser (s'), *accuse (of)*
achever, *finish*
admirer, *wonder (at)*
affecter, *affect*
s'affliger, *grieve (at, over)*
ambitionner, *aspire*
s'apercevoir, *perceive*
s'applaudir, *congratulate o. s. (on)*
appréhender, *fear*
arrêter, *prevent (from), determine*
s'attrister, *become sad (at)*
avertir, *notify, warn*
s'aviser, *think (of)*
blâmer, *blame (for)*
brûler, *be eager to*
censurer, *censure (for)*

cesser, *cease*
se chagriner, *grieve (at, over)*
charger, *charge*
se charger, *undertake*
choisir, *choose*
commander, *command*
commencer,[1] *begin*
conjurer, *beseech*
conseiller, *advise*
consoler, *console (for)*
se contenter, *be satisfied*
continuer,[1] *continue*
contraindre,[1] *constrain*
convaincre, *convict (of)*
convenir, *agree*
craindre, *fear*
crier, *cry*
décider,[3] *decide, resolve*
décourager (se), *discourage (from)*
dédaigner, *disdain*
défendre, *forbid*
se défendre, *forbear, excuse o. s.*
défier, *defy*
se défier, *distrust*
dégoûter, *disgust (with)*
délibérer, *deliberate (about)*
demander,[1] *ask*
se dépêcher, *make haste*
désaccoutumer (se), *disaccustom (from)*
désespérer, *despair (of)*
déshabituer (se), *disaccustom (from)*
déterminer,[3] *resolve*
détester, *detest*
détourner, *dissuade (from)*
dire,[4] *tell*
discontinuer, *cease*
disconvenir, *deny*
se disculper, *excuse o. s. (for)*
dispenser, *dispense (from)*
dissuader, *dissuade (from)*
douter, *hesitate*
se douter, *suspect*
écrire, *write*
s'efforcer,[1] *try*
s'effrayer, *be afraid*
empêcher, *prevent*
s'empêcher, *abstain (from)*
s'empresser,[3] *hasten*
s'empresser,[1] *be eager*
enjoindre, *enjoin*
s'ennuyer,[2,3] *be tired (of)*
s'enorgueillir, *be proud*
enrager, *be enraged (at)*
entreprendre, *undertake*
épargner, *spare*
essayer,[1] *try*
s'étonner, *be astonished*
être à . . . ,[2,3] *be duty (or office) (of)*
éviter, *avoid*
excuser (s'), *excuse (from)*
exempter, *exempt (from)*
faire bien, *do well*
se fatiguer,[3] *be tired (of)*
feindre, *feign*
féliciter (se), *congratulate (on)*
finir,[3] *finish*
se flatter, *flatter o. s.*
forcer,[1] *force*
frémir, *shudder*
gager, *wager*
garder (se), *forbear*
gémir, *groan*
gêner, *incommode*
se glorifier, *boast (of)*
gronder, *scold (for)*
hasarder, *venture*
se hâter, *hasten*
imaginer, *imagine*
s'impatienter, *be impatient*
imputer, *impute*
s'indigner, *be indignant*
s'ingérer, *meddle (with)*

[1] Or à.
[2] Sometimes à.
[3] See also list of verbs requiring à.
[4] See also list of verbs requiring direct infinitive.

inspirer, *inspire*
interdire, *interdict (from)*
jouir, *enjoy*
juger bon, *think fit*
jurer,[4] *promise (on oath)*
ne pas laisser,[3, 4] *not to cease*
se lasser,[3] *be weary (of)*
louer, *praise (for)*
mander, *bid*
manquer,[3] *fail, be on point of*
méditer, *meditate*
se mêler, *meddle (with)*
menacer, *threaten*
mériter, *deserve*
se moquer, *make sport (of)*
mourir, *die, long*
négliger, *neglect*
notifier, *notify*
obliger,[1] *oblige, force*
obliger,[3] *do favor*
obtenir, *obtain*
s'occuper,[3] *be intent (on)*
offrir, *offer*
omettre, *omit*
ordonner, *order*
oublier,[2] *forget*
pardonner, *forgive*
parier, *bet*
parler, *speak*
se passer, *do without*
permettre (se), *permit*
persuader, *persuade*
se piquer, *pride o. s. (on)*
plaindre, *pity*
se plaindre, *complain (of)*
prendre garde,[3] *take care not, beware (of)*
prendre soin, *take care*
prescrire, *prescribe*
presser, *urge*
se presser, *hasten*
présumer, *presume*
prier,[3] *beg, pray*
priver (se), *deprive (of)*
projeter, *intend*
promettre (se), *promise*
proposer, *propose*
se proposer, *intend*
protester, *protest*
punir, *punish (for)*
recommander, *recommend*
recommencer,[1] *begin again*
refuser,[3] *refuse*
regretter, *regret*
se réjouir, *rejoice*
remercier, *thank (for)*
se repentir, *repent (of)*
reprendre, *reprove (for)*
réprimander, *reprimand (for)*
reprocher (se), *reproach (with)*
résoudre,[3] *resolve*
se ressouvenir, *remember*
rire (se), *laugh*
risquer, *risk*
rougir, *blush*
sommer, *summon*
se soucier, *care*
souffrir,[1] *suffer*
soupçonner, *suspect*
sourire, *smile*
se souvenir, *recollect*
suggérer, *suggest*
supplier, *beseech*
tâcher,[2] *try*
tenter,[2] *attempt*
trembler,[3] *tremble, fear*
trouver bon, *think fit*
se vanter, *boast (of)*
venir,[3, 4] *have just*

[1] Or **à.**
[2] Sometimes **à.**
[3] See also list of verbs requiring **à.**
[4] See also list of verbs requiring direct infinitive.

Reference List of Verbs Requiring the Infinitive without any Preposition

accourir, *hasten*
affirmer, *affirm*
aimer (condl.),[3] *should like*
aimer autant, *like as well*
aimer mieux, *prefer*
aller, *go*
apercevoir, *perceive*
assurer, *assure*
avoir beau, *no matter how . . .*
avouer, *avow*
compter,[1] *intend*
confesser, *confess*
courir, *run*
croire, *think*
daigner, *deign*
déclarer, *declare*
déposer, *testify*
descendre,[3] *come (go) down*
désirer,[1] *desire, wish*
devoir, *ought, to be, etc.*
dire,[4] *say*
écouter, *listen to*
entendre, *hear, intend*
envoyer, *send*
espérer,[1] *hope*
être, *be*
être censé, *be supposed*
faillir,[2] *be on the point of, nearly to do something*
faire, *make, cause*
il fait (impers.), *it is*
falloir, *be necessary*
se figurer, *imagine*
s'imaginer, *fancy*
juger, *consider*
jurer,[4] *swear, attest by oath*
justifier, *justify*
laisser,[3, 4] *let, allow*
mener, *lead, bring*
mettre, *set, put at*
monter, *go up*
nier,[1] *deny*
oser, *dare*
ouïr, *hear*
paraître, *appear*
penser,[3] *intend, be near*
pouvoir, *can, may*
préférer, *prefer*
prétendre,[3] *assert, claim*
se rappeler,[1] *recollect*
reconnaître, *acknowledge*
regarder, *look at*
rentrer, *go in again, return home*
retourner, *go back*
revenir, *come back*
savoir, *know how to, can*
sembler, *seem*
sentir, *hear, feel*
souhaiter,[1] *wish*
soutenir, *maintain*
supposer, *suppose*
être supposé, *be supposed*
témoigner, *testify*
se trouver, *be*
valoir autant, *be as good*
valoir mieux, *be better*
venir,[3, 4] *come*
voir, *see*
voler, *fly*
vouloir, *will, wish*

[1] Sometimes takes **de.**
[2] Sometimes takes **à** or **de.**
[3] See also list of verbs requiring **à.**
[4] See also list of verbs requiring **de.**

REFERENCE LIST OF VERBS REQUIRING THE INFINITIVE WITH À

s'abaisser, *stoop*
abandonner (s'), *give up*
aboutir, *end (in), tend*
s'abuser, *be mistaken (in)*
s'accorder,[2] *agree (in)*
être d'accord, *agree (in)*
accoutumer (s'),[2] *accustom*
s'acharner, *be bent (on)*
admettre, *admit*
s'adonner, *become addicted to*
aguerrir (s'), *inure*
aider, *help*
aimer,[2, 4] *like*
amener, *lead*
amuser (s'), *amuse (in, by)*
animer (s'), *excite*
appeler, *call*
appliquer (s'), *apply*
apprendre, *learn, teach*
apprêter (s'), *get ready*
s'arrêter, *stop*
aspirer, *aspire*
assujettir (s'), *subject*
astreindre, *compel*
s'astreindre, *bind o. s.*
attacher, *attach*
s'attacher, *be intent (on)*
attendre (s'), *expect*
autoriser, *authorize*
s'avilir, *stoop*
avoir, *have, must*
avoir (de la) peine, *have difficulty (in)*
balancer, *hesitate*
se borner, *limit o. s.*
chercher, *seek, try*
commencer,[2] *begin*
se complaire, *take pleasure (in)*
concourir, *coöperate (in)*
condamner (se), *condemn*
condescendre, *condescend*
conduire, *lead*
consacrer (se), *devote*
consentir,[2] *consent*
consister, *consist (in)*
conspirer, *conspire*
consumer (se), *consume (in)*
continuer,[1] *continue*
contraindre,[1] *constrain*
contribuer, *contribute*
convier,[2] *invite*
coûter, *cost*
décider,[3] *induce*
se décider, *resolve*
défier,[3] *challenge, incite*
demander,[1] *ask*
demeurer, *remain*
dépenser, *spend (in)*
désapprendre, *forget*
descendre,[4] *stoop, abase o. s.*
destiner, *destine*
déterminer,[3] *induce*
se déterminer, *resolve*
dévouer (se), *devote*
différer,[2] *delay*
disposer (se), *dispose*
divertir (se), *amuse*
donner, *give*
dresser, *train*
s'efforcer,[1] *try*
s'égayer, *divert o. s. (by)*
employer (s'), *employ (in)*
s'empresser,[1, 3] *be eager*
encourager, *encourage*
engager (s'),[2] *engage, advise*
enhardir,[2] *embolden*
s'enhardir,[2] *venture*
s'ennuyer,[2, 3] *tire o. s. (in)*

[1] Or **de.**
[2] Sometimes takes **de.**
[3] See also list of verbs requiring **de.**
[4] See also list of verbs requiring direct infinitive.

enseigner, *teach*
s'entendre, *know well how*
entrainer, *allure*
essayer,[1] *try*
s'essayer, *try o. s. (in)*
être,[3] *to be occupied (in, at)*
être à,[3] *be one's turn*
s'étudier, *apply o. s.*
s'évertuer, *exert o. s., try*
exceller, *excel (in)*
exciter (s'), *excite*
exercer (s'), *exercise (in)*
exhorter, *exhort*
exposer (s'), *expose*
se fatiguer,[3] *tire o. s. (in, at)*
finir (neg.),[3] *have done*
forcer,[1] *force*
gagner, *gain (by)*
habituer,[2] *accustom*
s'habituer, *accustom o. s.*
haïr, *hate*
se hasarder,[2] *venture*
hésiter,[2] *hesitate*
inciter, *incite*
incliner, *incline*
induire, *induce*
instruire, *instruct*
intéresser (s'), *interest (in)*
inviter, *invite*
jouer, *play (at)*
laisser,[3, 4] *leave*
se lasser,[3] *tire o. s. (in)*
manquer,[3] *be remiss (in)*
mettre, *put, set*
se mettre, *set about*
montrer, *show how*
obliger,[1, 3] *oblige, force*
s'obliger,[2] *bind o. s.*
s'obstiner, *persist (in)*
occuper (s'),[3] *employ (in)*
s'offrir,[2] *offer*
s'opiniâtrer, *persist (in)*
parvenir, *succeed (in)*
passer, *spend (in)*
pencher, *incline*
penser,[4] *think (of)*
perdre, *lose (in, by)*
persévérer, *persevere (in)*
persister, *persist (in)*
se plaire, *delight (in)*
se plier, *submit*
porter, *induce*
pousser, *urge, incite*
prendre garde,[3] *take care*
prendre plaisir, *delight (in)*
se prendre, *begin*
préparer (se), *prepare*
prétendre,[4] *aspire*
prier,[3] *invite (formally)*
procéder, *proceed*
provoquer, *incite*
recommencer,[1] *begin again*
réduire, *reduce*
se réduire, *confine o. s.*
refuser,[3] *refuse to give*
se refuser, *refuse*
renoncer, *renounce*
répugner, *be reluctant*
se résigner, *resign o. s.*
résoudre,[3] *induce*
se résoudre, *resolve*
rester, *remain*
réussir *succeed (in)*
servir, *serve*
songer, *think (of)*
souffrir,[1] *suffer*
suffire, *suffice*
surprendre, *discover*
tarder, *be long, delay (in)*
tendre, *tend*
tenir, *be anxious*
travailler, *work*

[1] Or **de.**
[2] Sometimes takes **de.**
[3] See also list of verbs requiring **de.**
[4] See also list of verbs requiring direct infinitive.

trembler,[3] *tremble (at, on)*
trouver, *find*
venir,[3, 4] *happen*
viser, *aim*
vouer (se), *devote*

Cardinal Numbers

1 un, une
2 deux
3 trois
4 quatre
5 cinq
6 six
7 sept
8 huit
9 neuf
10 dix
11 onze
12 douze
13 treize
14 quatorze
15 quinze
16 seize
17 dix-sept
18 dix-huit
19 dix-neuf
20 vingt
21 vingt et un
22 vingt-deux
23 vingt-trois
30 trente
31 trente et un
32 trente-deux
40 quarante
50 cinquante
60 soixante
70 soixante-dix
71 soixante et onze
72 soixante-douze
73 soixante-treize
74 soixante-quatorze
75 soixante-quinze
76 soixante-seize
77 soixante-dix-sept
78 soixante-dix-huit
79 soixante-dix-neuf
80 quatre-vingts
81 quatre-vingt-un
82 quatre-vingt-deux
90 quatre-vingt-dix
91 quatre-vingt-onze
92 quatre-vingt-douze
93 quatre-vingt-treize
99 quatre-vingt-dix-neuf
100 cent
101 cent un
102 cent deux
200 deux cents
210 deux cent dix
1000 mille
1001 mille un
1500 mille cinq cents *or* quinze cents
2000 deux mille
40,350 quarante mille trois cent cinquante
1,000,000 un million

Note 1: All compound numbers under 100 are connected by a hyphen, except when **et** occurs (in 21, 31, 41, 51, 61, 71).

Note 2: Vingt and **cent** take **s** in the plural when multiplied, *if not followed by another number.* **Mille** *never* takes **s.**

trois cents, 300
trois cent trente, 330
quatre-vingts, 80
quatre-vingt-dix, 90
quatre mille, 4000

Note 3: Un million and **un milliard,** *a billion,* are nouns of quantity, and take **de** when immediately followed by a noun.

deux millions d'hommes, *two million men*

But: deux millions deux cent mille hommes, *two million two hundred thousand men.*

Note 4: The indefinite article may never be used with **cent** and **mille.**

cent hommes, ***a hundred men***
mille hommes, ***a thousand men***

Note 5: Pronunciation of Numerals. The final consonants of 5, 6, 7, 8, 9, 10, 17, 18, 19, are pronounced except before a word ***multiplied*** by them, beginning with a consonant or **h** aspirate. The **t** of **vingt** is pronounced from 21 to 29, but is silent from 81 to 99. The **t** of **cent** is silent in **cent un.** There is no elision before **huit** and **onze.** (**le huit, le onze**)

Vocabularies

VOCABULAIRE FRANÇAIS-ANGLAIS

The following abbreviations have been used in this vocabulary: *abbrev.* abbreviation; *adj.* adjective; *adv.* adverb; *art.* article; *conj.* conjunction; *conjug.* conjugated; *dem.* demonstrative; *exclam.* exclamatory; *f.* feminine; *fam.* familiar; *fut.* future; *imperf.* imperfect; *infin.* infinitive; *interr.* interrogative; *m.* masculine; *neg.* negative; *obj.* object; *pl.* plural; *p.p.* past participle; *prep.* preposition; *pron.* pronoun; *rel.* relative; *s.* singular; *subj.* subjunctive.

A

à [a] to, at, in, for, with, of
abasourdi [abazurdi] dumfounded
abbé *m.* [abe] abbé, priest, clergyman
abnégation *f.* [abnegasjɔ̃] self-sacrifice
abord: d'— [dabɔːr] first, at first, in the first place
aboyer [abwaje] to bark
abri *m.* [abri] shelter; **à l'— de** free from
abriter [abrite] to shelter
absolument [apsɔlymɑ̃] absolutely
accabler [akɑble] to overwhelm, overcome
accepter [aksɛpte] to accept
accès *m.* [aksɛ] attack, fit, paroxysm
accident *m.* [aksidɑ̃] accident
accommoder (s'en) [sɑ̃nakɔmɔde] to agree, to come to terms
accompagner [akɔ̃paɲe] to accompany, come with, go with
accord *m.* [akɔːr] agreement; **d'—** agreed; **se mettre d'—** to come to an agreement
accorder [akɔrde] to grant; **s'—** to agree
accourir [akuriːr] to rush in
accrocher [akrɔʃe] to catch (*as of automobile motor*); **s'—** to hang on to
achat *m.* [aʃa] purchase
acheter [aʃte] to buy, purchase
achever [aʃve] to finish, achieve
acier *m.* [asje] steel
acompte *m.* [akɔ̃ːt] down payment
acquérir [akeriːr] to acquire
acte *m.* [akt] act
acteur *m.* [aktœːr] actor
actrice *f.* [aktris] actress
adieu *m.* [adjø] farewell; (*pl.*) **faire ses —x à** to say good-by to
adjectif *m.* [adʒɛktif] adjective
admettre [admɛtr] to admit
admirable [admirabl] admirable
admiration *f.* [admirasjɔ̃] admiration
admirer [admire] to admire
adorer [adɔre] to adore
adresse *f.* [adrɛs] address
adresser [adrɛse] to address; **s'— à** to speak to
adroitement [adrwatmɑ̃] cleverly, adroitly
adverbe *m.* [advɛrb] adverb
aérodrome *m.* [aerɔdrɔːm] airport
affaire *f.* [afɛːr] affair; **je suis sûr de mon —** I know what I'm talking about; **avoir — à** to have to deal with, to deal with; (*pl.*) **les —s** business
affecter [afɛkte] to affect
affiche *f.* [afiʃ] notice, timetable
affligé [afliʒe] afflicted
affliger [afliʒe] to afflict
affolé [afɔle] frantic, bewildered, out of his senses
affreux [afrø] frightful, horrible
affronter [afrɔ̃te] to face
afin de [afɛ̃ də] in order to
afin que [afɛ̃ kə] in order that, so that
agacer [agase] to tease, tickle
âge *m.* [ɑːʒ] age
âgé [ɑʒe] old
agenouiller (s') [saʒnuje] to kneel
agent *m.* [aʒɑ̃] agent; **— de police** [dəpɔlis] policeman, officer
agile [aʒil] agile
agir [aʒiːr] to act; **s'— de** to be a matter of
agité [aʒite] nervous, upset
agréable [agreabl] agreeable, pleasant
agréablement [agreabləmɑ̃] agreeably, pleasantly
agriculture *f.* [agrikyltyːr] agriculture

aide *f.* [ɛːd]. help, aid, assistance; **venir en —** to help out
aide de camp *m.* [ɛddəkɑ̃] aide, aide-de-camp
aider [ɛde] to help, assist, aid
aigre [ɛːgr] sour
aiguille *f.* [ɛgɥiːj] needle
aile *f.* [ɛl] wing
ailleurs [ajœːr] elsewhere; **d'—** besides, on the other hand
aimable [ɛmabl] kind; **— pour** [pur] kind to, friendly to
aimer [ɛme] to like, love; **— mieux** prefer
aîné [ɛne] elder, elder brother or sister
ainsi [ɛ̃si] so, that way, thus; **— que** as well as
air *m.* [ɛːr] air, appearance; **avoir l'— de** to look like, appear, seem; **en plein —** outdoors, in the open air
aise *f.* [ɛːz] ease
aisément [ɛzemɑ̃] easily
ajouter [aʒute] to add
ajuster [aʒyste] to adjust
alcool *m.* [alkɔl] alcohol
alcoolique [alkɔlik] alcoholic
aliéné *m.* [aljene] demented person
Allemagne *f.* [almaɲ] Germany
allemand [almɑ̃] German
aller [ale] to go, be going to, fit, suit, be becoming; **— (par le train, à pied, à cheval, en auto, en bateau, en voiture)** to go (by train, on foot, on horseback, by car, by boat, by carriage); **— à merveille** (*of clothing*) be extremely becoming; **— mieux** be better (in health); **s'en —** go away; **allons donc!** come, come! come now!
allié *m.* [alje] ally
allô! [alo] hello! (*telephone*)
allonger [alɔ̃ʒe] to stretch; **s'—** to lie, stretch out
allumer [alyme] to light, light up
allumette *f.* [alymɛt] match
alors [alɔːr] then
amabilité *f.* [amabilite] kindness
amant *m.* [amɑ̃] lover
amasser [amɑse] to amass
âme *f.* [ɑːm] soul
améliorer [ameljɔre] to improve
amener [amne] to lead, take a person to a place, bring
amer (*f.* **amère**) [amɛːr] bitter
amèrement [amɛrmɑ̃] bitterly
américain [amerikɛ̃] American; **je suis —** I am an American
Amérique *f.* [amerik] America; **en —** in, to America
ami *m.* (*f.* **amie**) [ami] friend, dear
amicalement [amikalmɑ̃] cordially; **bien —** cordially yours
amitié *f.* [amitje] friendship; **faire ses —s à** to give one's regards to
amour *m.* [amuːr] love
amoureux (*f.* **amoureuse**) [amurø, amurøːz] loving; **tomber — de** to fall in love with
amour-propre *m.* [amurprɔpr] pride, self-respect
ampleur *f.* [ɑ̃plœːr] fullness, width
amuser [amyze] to amuse; **s'—** to have a good time, enjoy oneself
an *m.* [ɑ̃] year; **avoir (dix) —s** to be (ten) years old
ancien (*f.* **ancienne**) [ɑ̃sjɛ̃, ɑ̃sjɛn] former
ancre *f.* [ɑ̃kr] anchor
andouille *f.* [ɑ̃duːj] chitterlings, sausage
André [ɑ̃dre] Andrew
anesthésier [anɛstezje] to anesthetize
anglais [ɑ̃glɛ] English
angle *m.* [ɑ̃ːgl] angle
Angleterre *f.* [ɑ̃glətɛːr] England
animal *m.* (*pl.* **animaux**) [animal, animo] animal
année *f.* [ane] year; **Nouvelle Année** New Year
Annette [anɛt] Annie, Annette
anniversaire *m.* [anivɛrsɛːr] anniversary; **— de naissance** birthday; **souhaiter un heureux —** to wish a happy birthday
annoncer [anɔ̃se] to announce
annonceur *m.* [anɔ̃sœːr] announcer
antécédent [ɑ̃tesedɑ̃] previous
antenne *f.* [ɑ̃tɛn] antenna
anxieux (*f.* **anxieuse**) [ɑ̃ksjø, ɑ̃ksjøːz] anxious, worried
août *m.* [u] August
apercevoir [apɛrsəvwaːr] to see, perceive; **s'—** to notice
apéritif *m.* [aperitif] drink before meals, cocktail
aplomb *m.* [aplɔ̃] poise
apostropher [apɔstrɔfe] to address

apothicaire *m.* [apɔtikɛːr] apothecary, dispenser
apparaître [aparɛːtr] to appear
appareil *m.* [aparɛːj] outfit, apparatus
apparemment [aparamɑ̃] apparently
apparence *f.* [aparɑ̃ːs] appearance
appartement *m.* [apartəmɑ̃] apartment
appartenir [apartəniːr] to belong to
appel *m.* [apɛl] call, appeal, roll call
appeler [aple] to call, name; **s'—** to call oneself, be called, be named; **je m'appelle** my name is
appétit *m.* [apeti] appetite
application *f.* [aplikasjɔ̃] application
appliquer [aplike] to apply
apporter [apɔrte] to bring
apprécier [apresje] to appreciate
appréhension *f.* [apreɑ̃sjɔ̃] apprehension, fear, dread
apprendre (**à**) [aprɑ̃ːdra] to learn (to), teach (to)
apprentissage *m.* [aprɑ̃tisaːʒ] apprenticeship
approbation *f.* [aprɔbasjɔ̃] approval, assent
approcher (**s'**) [saprɔʃe] to approach, draw near
approuver [apruve] to approve
après [aprɛ] after; **d'—** according to, taken from; **— que** after
après-demain [aprɛdmɛ̃] day after tomorrow
après-midi *m.* or *f.* [aprɛmidi] afternoon; **l'—** in the afternoon
aquarelle *f.* [akwarɛl] water color
araignée *f.* [arɛɲe] spider
arbre *m.* [arbr] tree
ardeur *f.* [ardœːr] ardor
argent *m.* [arʒɑ̃] silver, money
argot *m.* [argo] slang
argumenter [argymɑ̃te] to argue
arithmétique *f.* [aritmetik] arithmetic
arme *f.* [arm] arm, weapon
armée *f.* [arme] army
armer [arme] to arm
armoire *f.* [armwaːr] closet, cabinet, cupboard; **— à glace** *f.* wardrobe with mirror
arracher [araʃe] to pull out
arranger (**s'**) [sarɑ̃ʒe] to be arranged
arrêt *m.* [arɛ] arrest, stopping, verdict
arrêter [arɛte] to arrest; **s'—** to halt, stop
arrière *m.* [arjɛːr] back, rear
arrivée *f.* [arive] arrival
arriver [arive] to arrive
art *m.* [aːr] art
artichaut *m.* [artiʃo] artichoke
articuler [artikyle] to articulate, pronounce
artificiel [artifisjɛl] artificial
artillerie *f.* [artijri] artillery
aspect *m.* [aspɛ] appearance, look
asperge *f.* [aspɛrʒ] asparagus
assassin *m.* [asasɛ̃] assassin, murderer
assassiner [asasine] to assassinate, murder
assaut *m.* [aso] assault
asseoir (**s'**) (*p.p.* **assis**) [saswaːr] to sit down
assez (**de**) [ase de] quite, rather, enough; **— bien** well enough, fairly well
assidûment [asidymɑ̃] assiduously
assiéger [asjeʒe] to besiege
assiette *f.* [asjɛt] plate; **— à soupe** soup plate
assis [asi] seated, sitting
assister à [asiste] to attend, be present at
assorti [asɔrti] assorted
assoupir (**s'**) [sasupiːr] to doze off
assourdissant [asurdisɑ̃] deafening
assurance *f.* [asyrɑ̃s] assurance
assuré [asyre] insured
assurer [asyre] to assure
assurément [asyremɑ̃] certainly, surely
astucieux (*f.* **astucieuse**) [astysjø, astysjøːz] wily
atroce [atrɔs] atrocious
atrocité *f.* [atrɔsite] atrocity
attacher [ataʃe] to attach, tie up; **s'—** to attach oneself to, cling
atteindre [atɛ̃dr] to reach, attain
attendant: en — [ɑ̃natɑ̃dɑ̃] meanwhile
attendre [atɑ̃dr] to wait for, expect, await, wait; **s'— à** to expect
attendrir [atɑ̃driːr] to make tender, soften, move to pity
attendu [atɑ̃dy] considering; **— que** whereas, since, inasmuch
attente *f.* [atɑ̃t] waiting, wait; **salle d'—** waiting room

attention! [atɑ̃sjɔ̃] careful! attention! look out!
attention *f.* [atɑ̃sjɔ̃] attention, care; **— à** careful with
attentivement [atɑ̃tivmɑ̃] attentively
atterrir [atɛriːr] to land
attirer [atire] to attract, draw
attitude *f.* [atityd] attitude
attraper [atrape] to catch
aube *f.* [oːb] dawn, daybreak
aubergine *f.* [obɛrʒin] eggplant
aucun [okœ̃] any, anyone; no, none, not one, not any
audace *f.* [odas] daring
augmenter [ɔgmɑ̃te] to increase
augure *m.* [ɔgyːr] augury, prophecy
aujourd'hui [oʒurdɥi] today; **— même** this very day
auparavant [oparavɑ̃] previously
auprès (de) [oprɛ] near
auquel [okɛl] to which, to whom
aussi [osi] also, too, and so, therefore; **— . . . que** as . . . as
aussitôt [osito] immediately, at once; **— que** as soon as
autant [otɑ̃] as much; **— de** as many, as much; **— que** as much as
autel *m.* [otɛl] altar
auteur *m.* [otœːr] author
auto, automobile *f.* [otɔmɔbil] automobile, car; **canot-—** *m.* motorboat; **en —** in an automobile, by car
autobus *m.* [otɔbyːs] bus
automate *m.* [otɔmat] automaton
automne *m.* [otɔn] fall, autumn
autorité *f.* [otɔrite] authority
autour (de) [oturdə] around
autre [oːtr] other; **c'est — chose** it's a different story; **nous —s** we (*emphatic*)
autrefois [otrəfwa] formerly
autrement [otrəmɑ̃] otherwise
Autriche *f.* [otriʃ] Austria
autrui [otrɥi] others
auxiliaire *m.* or *f.* [ɔksiljɛːr] auxiliary, assistant
auxquelles [okɛl] (*see* **auquel**)
avaler [avale] to swallow
avance *f.* [avɑ̃ːs] advance; **à l'—** beforehand, in advance; **d'—** in advance; **en —** ahead of time
avancer [avɑ̃se] to advance
avant [avɑ̃] before; **à l'—** in front; **en —** ahead; **— de** before; **— que** before; **—-hier** day before yesterday
avantage *m.* [avɑ̃taʒ] advantage, benefit
avantageusement [avɑ̃taʒøzmɑ̃] advantageously
avant-poste *m.* [avɑ̃pɔst] outpost
avare *m.* [avar] miser
avarice *f.* [avaris] avarice, stinginess
avec [avɛk] with
aventure *f.* [avɑ̃tyr] adventure
avenue *f.* [avny] avenue
avertir [avɛrtiːr] to warn
aveugle *m.* [avœgl] blind man
aviation *f.* [avjasjɔ̃] aviation
avide [avid] avid, greedy
avion *m.* [avjɔ̃] airplane
avis *m.* [avi] opinion; **à mon —** in my opinion; **— au public** public notice; **être d'—** to be of the opinion; **être de votre —** to agree with you
aviser (s') (de) [savizedə] to decide (to)
avocat *m.* [avɔka] lawyer
avoir [avwar] to have; **il y a** there is, there are, ago; **— (dix) ans** be (ten) years old; **— besoin de** to need; **— chaud** to be warm; **— de la chance** to be lucky; **— des nouvelles de** to have heard from, have had news of; **— envie de** to feel like; **— faim** to be hungry; **— froid** to be cold; **— honte** to be ashamed; **— l'air de** to look like, appear, seem; **— mal à** to have a . . . ache; **— peur** to be afraid; **— raison** to be right; **— soif** to be thirsty; **— soin de** to take care of; **— sommeil** to be sleepy; **— tort** to be wrong
avouer [avwe] to avow, confess
avril *m.* [avril] April

B

baccalauréat *m.* [bakalɔrea] B.A. degree
bagages *m. pl.* [bagaːʒ] baggage; **bulletin de —s** baggage check
bague *f.* [bag] ring
baigner (se) [səbɛɲe] to bathe
baignoire *f.* [bɛɲwaːr] bathtub
bâiller [bɑje] to yawn

bain *m.* [bɛ̃] bath; **caleçon de —** bathing trunks; **prendre un —** to bathe; **salle de —** *f.* bathroom
baïonnette *f.* [bajɔnɛt] bayonet
baiser [bɛze] to kiss
baisser [bɛse] to hang down, to lower; **se —** to lower oneself, be lowered
bal *m.* [bal] dance, ball
balancer [balɑ̃se] to tilt, sway, swing
balbutier [balbysje] to stammer
balkanique [balkanik] Balkan
Balkans *m. pl.* [balkɑ̃] Balkans
balle *f.* [bal] ball, bullet
banal [banal] banal, trifling
banc *m.* [bɑ̃] bench
bande *f.* [bɑ̃d] band
bandit *m.* [bɑ̃di] bandit
banlieue *f.* [bɑ̃ljø] suburbs
banque *f.* [bɑ̃k] bank; **billet de —** *m.* bank note
banquette *f.* [bɑ̃kɛt] bench, seat
banquier *m.* [bɑ̃kje] banker
baptiser [batize] to baptise
barbe *f.* [barb] beard; **— en pointe** pointed beard; **savon à —** shaving soap; **Barbe Bleue** *m.* Bluebeard
barbot *m.* [barbo] burbot (*fish*)
barre *f.* [bɑːr] bar
barrière *f.* [barjɛr] farm gate, fence
barrique *f.* [barik] cask
bas *m.* [bɑ] stocking
bas (*f.* **basse**) [bɑ, bɑːs] low; **à voix basse** in a low voice; **en —** below, down, downstairs; **là-—** over there
baser [bɑze] to base
bast! [bast] pooh! nonsense!
bataille *f.* [batɑːj] battle
bataillon *m.* [batajɔ̃] batallion
bateau *m.* [bato] boat; **— à voile** sailboat
bâtiment *m.* [bɑtimɑ̃] building
bâton *m.* [bɑtɔ̃] stick, bar; **— de rouge pour les lèvres** lipstick
battement *m.* [batmɑ̃] beating, thumping
batterie *f.* [batri] battery
battre [batr] to beat; **se —** to fight; **— la diane** to sound reveille
baume *m.* [boːm] balm, ointment
bavard *m.* [bavar] chatterbox, gossip, prattler
bavardage *m.* [bavardaʒ] prattling, talking, babbling
bavarder [bavarde] to chat, "chew the rag"
béant [beɑ̃] wide open
beau (**bel** *before vowel or mute h*; *f. sing.* **belle**; *m. pl.* **beaux**; *f. pl.* **belles**) [bo, bɛl, bo, bɛl] handsome, beautiful, fine; **faire —** be fine weather
beaucoup (**de**) [boku] much, many, lots of, a great deal
beau-fils *m.* [bofis] son-in-law
beau-frère *m.* [bofrɛːr] brother-in-law
beau-père *m.* [bopɛːr] father-in-law
beauté *f.* [bote] beauty; **c'est de toute —** it's very beautiful
beaux-arts *m. pl.* [bozaːr] fine arts
Belgique *f.* [bɛlʒik] Belgium
belle-fille *f.* [bɛlfij] daughter-in-law
belle-mère *f.* [bɛlmɛːr] mother-in-law
belle-sœur *f.* [bɛlsœːr] sister-in-law
bénédiction *f.* [benediksjɔ̃] blessing
béquille *f.* [bekij] crutch
berceau *m.* [bɛrso] cradle
besoin *m.* [bəzwɛ̃] need; **avoir — de** to need
bête [bɛt] stupid
beurre *m.* [bœːr] butter
bibliothèque *f.* [bibliɔtɛk] library
bicoque *f.* [bikɔk] shack
bicyclette *f.* [bisiklɛt] bicycle
bien *m.* [bjɛ̃] welfare, well-being; property, fortune
bien *adv.* [bjɛ̃] well, very, quite; **— à vous** sincerely yours; **— amicalement** cordially yours; **— de** (**du, de la, des**) much, many; **— entendu** of course; **— que** although; **assez —** well enough, fairly well; **c'est —** all right, O.K.; **eh —!** well! **merci —** thank you very much; **ou —** or else; **votre — cordialement dévoué** cordially yours; **vouloir —** to be willing
bientôt [bjɛ̃to] soon; **à —** I'll see you later, so long
bienveillant [bjɛ̃vejɑ̃] kind, polite, benevolent
bière *f.* [bjɛːr] beer
bifteck *m.* [biftɛk] beefsteak
bijou *m.* [biʒu] jewel
bilieux (*f.* **bilieuse**) [biljø, biljøːz] bilious

billet *m.* [bijɛ] ticket; **— de banque** bank note
biologie *f.* [biɔlɔʒi] biology
bivouac *m.* [bivwak] bivouac, camp
bizarre [biza:r] odd, strange
blaguer [blage] to joke
blâmer [blɑme] to blame
blanc (*f.* **blanche**) [blɑ̃, blɑ̃ʃ] white
blasphémer [blasfeme] to curse
blessé *m.* [blɛse] wounded man
blesser [blɛse] to wound
blessure *f.* [blɛsy:r] wound, injury
bleu [blø] blue; **— foncé** dark blue
bleuâtre [bløɑ:tr] bluish, blue-tinged
bloc *m.* [blɔk] block
bock *m.* [bɔk] small glass of beer
boire (*p.p.* **bu**) [bwa:r, by] to drink
bois *m.* [bwɑ] wood
boisson *f.* [bwasɔ̃] beverage, drink
boîte *f.* [bwat] box; **— aux lettres** letter box
bombardement *m.* [bɔ̃bardəmɑ̃] bombardment
bombe *f.* [bɔ̃b] fling (*slang*)
bon (*f.* **bonne**) [bɔ̃, bɔn] good, kind; **— marché** cheap; **—ne nuit** good night (used only on retiring); **— pour** kind to; **— voyage!** have a good trip!; **à — marché** cheaply; **à quoi —** what's the use (of); **de —ne heure** early
bonbon *m.* [bɔ̃bɔ̃] piece of candy
bonheur *m.* [bɔnœ:r] happiness, good fortune
bonjour [bɔ̃ʒu:r] good day, good morning, good afternoon
bonne *f.* [bɔn] maid
bonsoir [bɔ̃swar] good night, good evening
bonté *f.* [bɔ̃te] kindness, goodness; **ayez la — de** please have the kindness to
bord *m.* [bɔ:r] edge, shore, bank; **à — de** on board; **au — de** on the shore of; **— de la mer** *m.* seashore
bordé [bɔrde] edged, bordered
bosnien (*f.* **bosnienne**) [bɔsnjɛ̃, bɔsnjɛn] Bosnian
bouche *f.* [buʃ] mouth
boucher (se) [səbuʃe] to stop up, be stopped up
boue *f.* [bu] mud
bouger [buʒe] to move, budge
bougie *f.* [buʒi] candle
boule *f.* [bul] ball
boulet *m.* [bulɛ] cannon ball
boulevard *m.* [bulva:r] boulevard
bouleversé [bulvɛrse] upset
bouleverser [bulvɛrse] to overthrow, overwhelm
bouquet *m.* [bukɛ] bouquet
bouquiner [bukine] to book-hunt
bourgeois *m.* [burʒwa] bourgeois, member of the middle class; (*slang*) "boss"
bourse *f.* [burs] pocketbook
bousculer [buskyle] to push, shove
bout *m.* [bu] end, piece; **au — de** at the end of
bouteille *f.* [butɛ:j] bottle
boutique *f.* [butik] shop
bouton *m.* [butɔ̃] button, door knob, bud (*of a flower*); **— de manchette** cuff link
braisé [brɛze] braised
bras *m.* [bra] arm
brave [brav] brave, fine
bravo! [bravo] bravo!
brebis *f.* [brəbi] sheep
bref (*f.* **brève**) [brɛf, brɛv] brief, short
Brésil *m.* [brezil] Brazil
brigade *f.* [brigad] brigade
brigand *m.* [brigɑ̃] brigand, bandit
briller [brije] to gleam, shine, be outstanding
briser [brize] to break
brocart *m.* [brɔca:r] brocade
brosse *f.* [brɔs] brush; **— à dents** toothbrush
brosser [brɔse] to brush
brouillard *m.* [bruja:r] fog, mist
broyer [brwaje] to smash
bruit *m.* [brɥi] noise
brûlé *m.* [bryle] something burning, burned, scorched
brûler [bryle] to burn
brûlure *f.* [bryly:r] burn
brun [brœ̃] brown, dark, brunette
brusque [brysk] unexpected, sharp, sudden
brusquement [bryskəmɑ̃] brusquely, abruptly
bruyant [brɥijɑ̃] noisy
bu [by] *p.p.* of **boire**
buanderie *f.* [bɥɑ̃dri] laundry

buffet *m.* [byfɛ] buffet
bulletin *m.* [byltɛ̃] bulletin, circular; **— de bagages** baggage check
bureau *m.* (*pl.* **bureaux**) [byro] study, office, desk; **— de change** exchange office

C

ça (*abbrev. of* **cela**) [sa, səla] **—, c'est chic!** I like that (*ironical*); **— m'est égal** it's all the same to me; **— n'en vaut pas la peine** it's not worth while; **— suffit** that's enough; **— se fait** that (it) is done; **— va ?** all right? O.K.?; **— y est ?** ready? O.K.?
cabine *f.* [kabin] stateroom, cabin
cabinet *m.* [kabinɛ] office
cache-nez *m.* [kaʃne] muffler
cacher [kaʃe] to hide, conceal
cachette *f.* [kaʃɛt] hiding place; **en —** on the sly, slyly, secretly
cadavre *m.* [kadɑːvr] corpse
cadeau *m.* (*pl.* **cadeaux**) [kado] present, gift
café *m.* [kafe] coffee, café
cahier *m.* [kaje] notebook
caisse *f.* [kɛs] cash register
caisson *m.* [kɛsɔ̃] caisson, ammunition truck or wagon
calamité *f.* [kalamite] calamity, disaster
caleçon *m.* [kalsɔ̃] shorts; **— de bain** bathing trunks
calme [kalm] calm
calmement [kalməmɑ̃] calmly
calmer [kalme] to calm
calorifère *m.* [kalɔrifɛr] heating plant
camarade *m.* [kamarad] comrade
camionette *f.* [kamjɔnɛt] hand truck
campagnard [kɑ̃paɲaːr] rustic, countrified person
campagne *f.* [kɑ̃paɲ] country, campaign
Canada *m.* [kanada] Canada
canadien (*f.* **canadienne**) [kanadjɛ̃, kanadjɛn] Canadian
canapé *m.* [kanape] sofa
canard *m.* [kanaːr] duck
canne *f.* [kan] cane
canon *m.* [kanɔ̃] cannon
canot-automobile *m.* [kano-otɔmɔbil] motorboat
cantique *m.* [kɑ̃tik] hymn, canticle
caoutchouc *m.* [kautʃu] rubber
capable [kapabl] capable
capitaine *m.* [kapitɛn] captain
car [kar] for, because
caractère *m.* [karaktɛːr] nature, character
carafe *f.* [karaf] bottle, decanter, pitcher
cardiaque: crise — *f.* [kriːz kardjak] heart attack
caresse *f.* [karɛs] caress
carnage *m.* [karnaʒ] carnage, mass murder
carnet *m.* [karnɛ] notebook
carotte *f.* [karɔt] carrot
carré [kɑre] square
carrefour *m.* [karfuːr] intersection
carrière *f.* [karjɛːr] career
carte *f.* [kart] card, map, menu; **— postale** post card; **— d'identité** identification card
carton *m.* [kartɔ̃] cardboard
cas *m.* [kɑ] case, matter; **en tout —** at any rate, in any case
case *f.* [kɑːz] compartment
casser [kɑse] to break
catastrophe *f.* [katastrɔf] catastrophe
catholique [katɔlik] Catholic
cause *f.* [koːz] case, cause, lawsuit; **à — de** because of, on account of
cavalerie *f.* [kavalri] cavalry
cave *f.* [kav] cellar
ce (*m. sing.*; **cet** *before vowel or h*; *f. sing.* **cette**; *m. pl.* **ces**; *f. pl.* **ces**) [sə, sɛt, sɛt, se] this, that; **— que** (*obj.*) what; **— qui** (*subj.*) what; **c'est que** the fact is, the reason is
ceci [səsi] this
céder [sede] to yield
cela (*contracted form,* **ça**) [səla, sa] that; **— me fait grand plaisir** that gives me great pleasure; **— ne fait rien** it makes no difference; **— vaut la peine** (**de**) it's worth while (to)
célèbre [selɛbr] famous
célébrer [selebre] to celebrate, praise, glorify
celle [sɛl] (*see* **celui**)
celui (**celle, ceux, celles**) [səlɥi, sɛl, sø, sɛl] he, she, the one, the ones; **—-ci** this one, the latter; **—-là** that one, the former

cendre *f.* [sɑ̃dr] ashes
cent [sɑ̃] one hundred
centaine *f.* [sɑ̃tɛn] about a hundred
centimètre *m.* [sɑ̃timɛtr] centimeter (*French measure*)
cependant [səpɑ̃dɑ̃] nevertheless
cérémonie *f.* [seremɔni] ceremony; **sans —** informal, informally
cerise *f.* [s(ə)riːz] cherry
certain [sɛrtɛ̃] certain
certainement [sɛrtɛnmɑ̃] certainly, surely
certes [sɛrt] certainly
cerveau *m.* [sɛrvo] brain
cervelle *f.* [sɛrvɛl] brain
ces [se] these, those
cesse: sans — [sɑ̃ sɛs] unceasingly, constantly
cesser (**de**) [sɛse] to stop (doing something), cease
ceux [sø] they, those; **—-ci** these, the latter; **—-là** those, the former
chacun (*f.* **chacune**) [ʃakœ̃, ʃakyn] each one; **— à son goût** everyone to his taste
chagriner [ʃagrine] to grieve, afflict, trouble
chaîne *f.* [ʃɛn] chain
chaise *f.* [ʃɛːz] chair; **— longue** lounging chair or couch
châle *m.* [ʃɑl] shawl
chaleur *f.* [ʃalœːr] heat, warmth
chambre *f.* [ʃɑ̃br] chamber, room; **— à coucher** bedroom; **robe de —** *f.* dressing gown
champ *m.* [ʃɑ̃] field
champignon *m.* [ʃɑ̃piɲɔ̃] mushroom
chance *f.* [ʃɑ̃s] luck; **avoir de la —** to be lucky
change *m.* [ʃɑ̃ʒ] exchange; **bureau de —** exchange office
changer (**de**) [ʃɑ̃ʒe] to change, exchange
chanson *f.* [ʃɑ̃sɔ̃] song
chanter [ʃɑ̃te] to sing
chanteur *m.* [ʃɑ̃tœːr] singer
chapeau *m.* [ʃapo] hat
chapelle *f.* [ʃapɛl] chapel
chapon *m.* [ʃapɔ̃] capon
chaque [ʃak] each; **— fois** each time
charbon *m.* [ʃarbɔ̃] coal
charbonnier *m.* [ʃarbɔnje] charcoal burner
charcuterie *f.* [ʃarkytri] cold cuts
charge *f.* [ʃarʒ] caricature, public office, practice
chargé de [ʃarʒe də] given job of, commissioned, charged with
charger [ʃarʒe] to load (*of a gun*); **se — de** to take charge of, take care of
chariot *m.* [ʃarjo] wagon
charmant [ʃarmɑ̃] charming
charme *m.* [ʃarm] charm
charrette *f.* [ʃarɛt] wagon
chasser [ʃase] to dismiss, chase
chat *m.* [ʃa] cat
châteaubriant *m.* [ʃɑtobriɑ̃] tenderloin steak, thick steak
châtiment *m.* [ʃɑtimɑ̃] punishment, chastisement
chatouillement *m.* [ʃatujmɑ̃] tickling
chaud [ʃo] warm, hot; **avoir —** to be warm; **faire —** to be warm (weather)
chauffer [ʃofe] to warm up, heat
chauffeur *m.* [ʃofœːr] chauffeur, driver
chausser [ʃose] to fit
chaussette *f.* [ʃosɛt] sock
chaussure *f.* [ʃosyːr] shoe
chef *m.* [ʃɛf] chief, head (of an office); **commandant en —** *m.* commander-in-chief
chemin *m.* [ʃmɛ̃] road, way; **— de fer** railroad
cheminée *f.* [ʃmine] mantel, fireplace
chemise *f.* [ʃmiːz] shirt; **— de nuit** nightgown; **en manches de —** in shirt sleeves
chêne *m.* [ʃɛn] oak tree
chèque *m.* [ʃɛk] check; **faire un —** to make out a check
cher (*f.* **chère**) [ʃɛr] dear, expensive; **la vie coûte —** the cost of living is high
chercher [ʃɛrʃe] to look for
chéri [ʃeri] darling, dear, beloved
cheval *m.* (*pl.* **chevaux**) [ʃəval, ʃəvo] horse; **à —** on horseback
chevet *m.* [ʃəvɛ] head of a bed, bedside, bolster
cheveux *m. pl.* [ʃəvø] hair
cheville *f.* [ʃəviːj] ankle
chez [ʃe] to (at) home, office, place of business of; **— moi** (at) my house
chic [ʃik] elegant, stylish; **ça c'est —!** I like that (*ironical*)
chien *m.* [ʃjɛ̃] dog

chiffre *m.* [ʃifr] number
chimie *f.* [ʃimi] chemistry
Chine *f.* [ʃin] China
chinois [ʃinwa] Chinese
chirurgien *m.* [ʃiryrʒjɛ̃] surgeon
chocolat *m.* [ʃɔkɔla] chocolate
choisir [ʃwazi:r] to choose
choix *m.* [ʃwa] choice, selection, variety
chose *f.* [ʃo:z] thing; **c'est autre —** it's something else, it's a different story; **ne . . . pas grand' —** not much
chou *m.* (*pl.* **choux**) [ʃu] cabbage
chou-fleur *m.* [ʃuflœ:r] cauliflower
chut! [ʃyt] shh! hush!
cicatrice *f.* [sikatris] scar
cidre *m.* [sidr] cider
ciel *m.* [sjɛl] heaven, sky
cigare *m.* [siga:r] cigar
cigarette *f.* [sigarɛt] cigarette
cinéma *m.* [sinema] movie house
cinq [sɛ̃k] five
cinquante [sɛ̃kɑ̃t] fifty
cinquième [sɛ̃kjɛm] fifth
cirage *m.* [sira:ʒ] wax, polish
circonstance *f.* [sirkɔ̃stɑ̃s] circumstance
cirer [sire] to wax, polish
ciseaux *m. pl.* [sizo] scissors
clair [klɛ:r] clear, bright; **un ton —** a light color
clair de lune *m.* [klɛrdəlyn] moonlight
clameur *f.* [klamœ:r] noise, clamor
claquer [klake] to clatter
classe *f.* [klɑ:s] class; **en —** in class; **salle de —** classroom
clé, clef *f.* [kle] key; **fermer à —** to lock
clerc *m.* [klɛ:r] clerk
client *m.* (*f.* **cliente**) [kliɑ̃, kliɑ̃:t] customer
cloche *f.* [klɔʃ] bell
cocher *m.* [kɔʃe] coachman, driver
cochon *m.* [kɔʃɔ̃] pig
cœur *m.* [kœ:r] heart
coffre *m.* [kɔfr] chest, trunk
cognac *m.* [kɔɲak] cognac
coin *m.* [kwɛ̃] corner
coincé [kwɛ̃se] wedged
colère *f.* [kɔlɛ:r] anger; **se mettre en —** to become (get) angry
colique *f.* [kɔlik] colic, stomach ache
colis *m.* [kɔli] piece of baggage, parcel; (*postal*) parcel-post package
collaborer [kɔlabɔre] to collaborate
collège *m.* [kɔlɛ:ʒ] boarding school
collègue *m.* [kɔlɛg] colleague
collerette *f.* [kɔlrɛt] little collar
collier *m.* [kɔlje] necklace
colline *f.* [kɔlin] hill
collision *f.* [kɔlizjɔ̃] collision
colonel *m.* [kɔlɔnɛl] colonel
colonne (**vertébrale**) *f.* [kɔlɔn vɛrtebral] back, spinal cord
colorer (**se**) [səkɔlɔre] to flush
combattre [kɔ̃batr] to fight
combien (**de**) [kɔ̃bjɛ̃də] how much, how many; **— de temps** how long
combinaison *f.* [kɔ̃binɛzɔ̃] suit of underwear
comédie *f.* [kɔmedi] comedy
comique [kɔmik] comic
commandant *m.* [kɔmɑ̃dɑ̃] major; **— en chef** commander in chief
commande *f.* [kɔmɑ̃:d] order
commander [kɔmɑ̃de] to order, command
comme [kɔm] as, like
comme ci, comme ça [kɔmsi kɔmsa] so-so
commencer [kɔmɑ̃se] to begin; **— par** to begin with
comment [kɔmɑ̃] how; **— allez-vous?** how are you? how do you do? **— ça va?** how are you? how are things? how goes it? **— dit-on . . . en français?** how do you say . . . in French? **— s'appelle ceci en français?** what do you call this in French? **— écrit-on cela?** how is that spelled? **— vous appelez-vous?** what's your name? **— vous portez-vous?** how are you? how do you do?
commerce *m.* [kɔmɛrs] business, trade, commerce
commettre (*p.p.* **commis**) [kɔmetr, kɔmi] to commit
commis *m.* [kɔmi] clerk
commis [kɔmi] *p.p.* of **commettre**
commissaire (**de police**) *m.* [kɔmisɛr də pɔlis] police commissioner
commode [kɔmɔd] comfortable
commode *f.* [kɔmɔd] chest of drawers
communauté *f.* [kɔmynote] community

communication *f.* [kɔmynikasjɔ̃] communication
communiquer [kɔmynike] communicate, lead
compagnie *f.* [kɔ̃paɲi] company; **en — de** in the company of; **tenir — à** to accompany, stay with
compagnon *m.* [kɔ̃paɲɔ̃] companion
comparaison *f.* [kɔ̃parɛzɔ̃] comparison
compartiment *m.* [kɔ̃partimɑ̃] compartment
compatissant [kɔ̃patisɑ̃] sympathetic
compensation *f.* [kɔ̃pɑ̃sasjɔ̃] compensation
compétence *f.* [kɔ̃petɑ̃s] province, sphere
compétiteur *m.* [kɔ̃petitœːr] competitor
complément *m.* [kɔ̃plemɑ̃] object (*grammatical*)
complet (*f.* **complète**) [kɔ̃plɛ, kɔ̃plɛt] complete
complètement [kɔ̃plɛtmɑ̃] completely
compléter [kɔ̃plete] to complete
compliment *m.* [kɔ̃plimɑ̃] compliment
compliquer [kɔ̃plike] to complicate
complot *m.* [kɔ̃plo] plot
composé: passé — *m.* [pɑsekɔ̃poze] past indefinite (tense)
composer [kɔ̃poze] to compose; **se —** be composed
composition *f.* [kɔ̃pozisjɔ̃] composition
comprendre [kɔ̃prɑ̃ːdr] to understand; **se —** understand each other
compris [kɔ̃pri] *p.p.* of **comprendre**
comptant: payer — [pɛjekɔ̃tɑ̃] to pay cash
compte *m.* [kɔ̃ːt] account; **se rendre — de** to realize
compter [kɔ̃te] to count, expect
concerner [kɔ̃sɛrne] to concern; **en ce qui concerne** for what concerns, as for
concert *m.* [kɔ̃sɛːr] concert
concierge *m.* [kɔ̃sjɛrʒ] doorman, doorkeeper
conclure [kɔ̃klyːr] to conclude
conclusion *f.* [kɔ̃klyzjɔ̃] conclusion
concombre *m.* [kɔ̃kɔ̃br] cucumber
condamner [kɔ̃dane] to condemn
condisciple *m.* [kɔ̃disipl] schoolmate
condition *f.* [kɔ̃disjɔ̃] condition, rank, station
conditionnel *m.* [kɔ̃disjɔnɛl] conditional (tense)
conducteur *m.* [kɔ̃dyktœːr] driver
conduire [kɔ̃dɥiːr] to drive, lead; **se —** to behave, conduct oneself; **se laisser —** to let oneself be led; **permis de —** *m.* driving permit
conduite *f.* [kɔ̃dɥit] conduct
conférence *f.* [kɔ̃ferɑ̃s] lecture
confiance *f.* [kɔ̃fjɑ̃ːs] confidence, trust
confidence *f.* [kɔ̃fidɑ̃ːs] confidence
confier [kɔ̃fje] to entrust
confiture *f.* [kɔ̃fityːr] preserves, jam
conformer [kɔ̃fɔrme] to conform
confus [kɔ̃fy] confused, mixed up, abashed
congé *m.* [kɔ̃ʒe] leave, departure; **donner —** to dismiss; **prendre — de** to take leave of
conjugaison *f.* [kɔ̃ʒygɛzɔ̃] conjugation
conjugal [kɔ̃ʒygal] marital
conjuguer [kɔ̃ʒyge] to conjugate
connaissance *f.* [kɔnɛsɑ̃ːs] acquaintance; **faire la — de** to make the acquaintance of
connaître [kɔnɛːtr] to know, be acquainted with
conquis [kɔ̃ki] conquered
consacrer [kɔ̃sakre] to consecrate, devote
conscience *f.* [kɔ̃sjɑ̃ːs] conscience
conscrit *m.* [kɔ̃skri] recruit
conseil *m.* [kɔ̃sɛːj] advice
conseiller [kɔ̃sɛje] to advise
consentement *m.* [kɔ̃sɑ̃tmɑ̃] consent
consentir (**à**) [kɔ̃sɑ̃tiːra] to consent (to)
conséquent: par — [parkɔ̃sekɑ̃] consequently, therefore
conservé [kɔ̃sɛrve] preserved
considérable [kɔ̃siderabl] considerable
considérer [kɔ̃sidere] to consider
consister [kɔ̃siste] to consist
consolation *f.* [kɔ̃sɔlasjɔ̃] consolation
consoler [kɔ̃sɔle] to console
consolider [kɔ̃sɔlide] to consolidate
consommateur *m.* [kɔ̃sɔmatœːr] customer
consommé *m.* [kɔ̃sɔme] consommé, broth

conspirateur *m.* [kɔ̃spiratœ:r] conspirator, plotter
constater [kɔ̃state] to verify
consultation *f.* [kɔ̃syltasjɔ̃] appointment
contact *m.* [kɔ̃takt] contact
conte *m.* [kɔ̃:t] tale, story
contempler [kɔ̃tɑ̃ple] to contemplate
contenir [kɔ̃tni:r] to contain; **se —** to restrain oneself
content (**de**) [kɔ̃tɑ̃də] glad, happy, pleased, satisfied (with)
contenter (**se**) [səkɔ̃tɑ̃te] to be contented
contenu *m.* [kɔ̃tny] contents
conter [kɔ̃te] to relate, tell about
continuer [kɔ̃tinɥe] to continue, go on
contraire [kɔ̃trɛ:r] contrary, opposite
contraster [kɔ̃traste] to contrast
contre [kɔ̃:tr] against; **par —** on the other hand
contre-maître *m.* [kɔ̃trəmɛ:tr] foreman
contribuer [kɔ̃tribɥe] to contribute
contrôler [kɔ̃trole] to check
contrôleur *m.* [kɔ̃trolœ:r] conductor
convaincre [kɔ̃vɛ̃:kr] to convince
convalescence *f.* [kɔ̃valɛsɑ̃s] convalescence
convalescent *m.* [kɔ̃valɛsɑ̃] convalescent
convenable [kɔ̃vnabl] suitable, proper
convenir [kɔ̃vni:r] to be appropriate
conversation *f.* [kɔ̃vɛrsasjɔ̃] conversation
copain *m.* [kɔpɛ̃] pal
copieux (*f.* **copieuse**) [kɔpjø, kɔpjø:ʒ] copious, (*of meals*) hearty
coq *m.* [kɔk] rooster
coquin *m.* [kɔkɛ̃] rascal; **Ah, —!** you rascal!
cor *m.* [kɔ:r] corn (*on foot*)
corde *f.* [kɔrd] rope
cordial (*m.pl.* **cordiaux**) [kɔrdjal, kɔrdjo] cordial, heartfelt
cordialement [kɔrdjalmɑ̃] cordially; **votre bien — dévoué** cordially yours
cordonnier *m.* [kɔrdɔnje] shoemaker
corne *f.* [kɔrn] horn
corporel [kɔrpɔrɛl] bodily
corps *m.* [kɔ:r] body; **— à —** hand to hand, man to man; **— professoral** faculty
correct [kɔrɛkt] correct
correctement [kɔrɛktəmɑ̃] correctly
correspondre [kɔrɛspɔ̃dr] to correspond
corridor *m.* [kɔridɔ:r] corridor, hall
corrompre [kɔrɔ̃pr] to corrupt, deprave
cortège *m.* [kɔrtɛ:ʒ] procession
côte: — à — [kotako:t] side by side
côté *m.* [kote] side, direction; **à — de** beside, next to, next door; **de ce —** on this side, this way; **de l'autre —** on the other side; **de mon —** in my direction; **de quel —** on which side, which way; **du — de** from the direction of
côtelette *f.* [kotlɛt] cutlet, chop
cotillon *m.* [kɔtijɔ̃] cotillion
coton *m.* [kɔtɔ̃] cotton
cou *m.* [ku] neck
coucher [kuʃe] to put to bed; **se —** to go to bed, lie down; **chambre à —** bedroom
couchette *f.* [kuʃɛt] berth
coude *m.* [kud] elbow
coudre [kudr] to sew
couler [kule] to run (*as water*)
couleur *f.* [kulœ:r] color
couloir *m.* [kulwa:r] aisle, corridor
coup *m.* [ku] stroke, flick; **— de feu** shot; **— de soleil** sunburn; **tenir le —** to hold out; **tout à —** suddenly
coupable [kupabl] guilty; **le —** culprit, guilty one
coupé *m.* [kupe] coupé, carriage
couper [kupe] to cut
couple *m.* [kupl] couple
cour *f.* [ku:r] courtyard
courage *m.* [kura:ʒ] courage
courageux (*f.* **courageuse**) [kuraʒø, kuraʒø:z] courageous
courant *m.* [kurɑ̃] current
courbé [kurbe] bent, stooped
courir [kuri:r] to run
couronne *f.* [kurɔn] crown
courrier *m.* [kurje] mail
cours *m.* [ku:r] course; **au — de** during
course *f.* [kurs] run, race, errand, running
court [ku:r] short
cousin *m.* (*f.* **cousine**) [kuzɛ̃, kuzin] cousin

couteau *m.* [kuto] knife
coûter [kute] to cost; **la vie coûte cher** the cost of living is high
couteux (*f.* **couteuse**) [kutø, kutø:z] expensive, costly
couvert *m.* [kuvɛ:r] (table) place setting, cover; **mettre le —** to set the table
couvert [kuvɛ:r] covered, cloudy, overcast; **— de** covered with
couverture *f.* [kuvɛrtyr] blanket
couvrir (*p.p.* **couvert**) [kuvri:r, kuvɛ:r] to cover
craindre [krɛ̃dr] to fear
crainte *f.* [krɛ̃t] fear; **de — de** for fear of; **de — que** for fear that
cravate *f.* [kravat] tie
crayon *m.* [krɛjɔ̃] pencil
créancier *m.* [kreɑ̃sje] creditor
créer [kree] to create
crème *f.* [krɛm] cream; **gâteau à la —** cream cake, cream pie, cream tart
crétin *m.* [kretɛ̃] idiot, dunce
creux *m.* [krø] hollow
crevaison *f.* [krəvɛzɔ̃] blowout
crevé [krəve] burst, broken
cri *m.* [kri] cry
criblé [krible] riddled
crier [krie] to cry, shout
crime *m.* [krim] crime
crise *f.* [kri:z] crisis, fit; **— cardiaque** heart attack
critiquer [kritike] to criticize
croate [krɔat] Croat, Croatian
croire [krwa:r] to believe
croisé [krwaze] double-breasted
croix *f.* [krwɑ] cross
croûte *f.* [krut] crust
cruauté *f.* [kryote] cruelty
cruellement [kryɛlmɑ̃] cruelly
cuiller *f.* [kɥijɛ:r] spoon
cuir *m.* [kɥi:r] leather
cuirasse *f.* [kɥiras] armor
cuisine *f.* [kɥizin] cooking, kitchen; **faire une excellente —** to prepare excellent food, cook extremely well
cuisinier *m.* (*f.* **cuisinière**) [kɥizinje, kɥizinjɛ:r] cook
cuivre *m.* [kɥivr] copper
culbuter [kylbyte] to overturn
culte *m.* [kylt] worship, veneration, adoration
cultiver [kyltive] to cultivate
cupidité *f.* [kypidite] covetousness
curé *m.* [kyre] parish priest, parson, vicar
cure *f.* [ky:r] cure
curieux (*f.* **curieuse**) [kyrjø, kyrjø:z] curious
curiosité *f.* [kyrjɔzite] curiosity

D

dais *m.* [dɛ] platform, dais
damas *m.* [damɑ] damask
dame *f.* [dam] lady
Danemark *m.* [danmark] Denmark
danger *m.* [dɑ̃ʒe] danger
dangereux (*f.* **dangereuse**) [dɑ̃ʒərø, dɑ̃ʒərø:z] dangerous
dans [dɑ̃] in, into, within; **— le fond** to the rear
danse *f.* [dɑ̃s] dance
danser [dɑ̃se] to dance
date *f.* [dat] date
dater [date] to date
davantage [davɑ̃ta:ʒ] more
de (**d'**) [də] of, from, by, with, in, to, for, than, concerning, during, on
débâcle *f.* [debɑkl] break-up, thaw, downfall, crash
débarquer [debarke] to land
débarrasser [debarase] to free; **se — de** to get rid of
débauche *f.* [deboʃ] exuberance, revel
débordé [debɔrde] overwhelmed
debout [dəbu] standing; **se tenir —** to stand
débrayer [debrɛje] to start the car
début *m.* [deby] debut, introduction, beginning
décembre *m.* [desɑ̃br] December
décharge *f.* [deʃarʒ] discharge
déchirer [deʃire] to tear
décidément [desidemɑ̃] decidedly
décider [deside] to decide
déclaration *f.* [deklarasjɔ̃] declaration, proposal
déclarer [deklare] to declare
décoller [dekɔle] to take off (*as an airplane*)
déconcerter [dekɔ̃sɛrte] to puzzle, disconcert
décorer [dekɔre] to decorate

découper [dekupe] to cut out, cut up
découragé [dekuraʒe] discouraged
découvert [dekuvɛːr] uncovered, bare
découvrir [dekuvriːr] to discover
décrire [dekriːr] to describe
décroître [dekrwɑtr] to decrease
dédaigner [dedɛɲe] to disdain
dédaigneusement [dedɛɲøzmɑ̃] disdainfully, contemptuously
dédain *m.* [dedɛ̃] disdain, scorn
dedans [dədɑ̃] inside
défaut *m.* [defo] defect, fault
défendre [defɑ̃ːdr] to defend; **— de** to forbid to
défense [defɑ̃ːs] **— d'entrer** no admittance; **— de fumer** no smoking
défini [defini] **passé —** past definite (tense)
défunt *m.* [defœ̃] dead man
dégagé [degaʒe] unembarrassed
dégât *m.* [degɑ] damage, havoc, devastation
dégoûtant [degutɑ̃] disgusting
dégoûter (**s'en**) [sɑ̃degute] to become disgusted with
dehors [dəɔːr] outside
déjà [deʒa] already
déjeuner *m.* [deʒœne] lunch
déjeuner [deʒœne] to have lunch
delà: au — de [odladə] beyond, yonder
délicat *m.* [delika] delicate person, dainty person
délicatement [delikatmɑ̃] delicately, carefully
délicatesse *f.* [delikatɛs] delicacy
délicieux (*f.* **délicieuse**) [delisjø, delisjøːz] delicious, delightful
délier [delje] to untie
délire *m.* [deliːr] delirium
délirer [delire] to rave, become delirious
délivrer [delivre] to free, save
demain [dəmɛ̃] tomorrow; **à —** see you tomorrow
demander [dəmɑ̃de] to ask, ask for; **se —** to wonder
démarche *f.* [demarʃ] step
démarrage *m.* [demaraːʒ] start
démarreur *m.* [demarœːr] clutch (*of auto*)
démêler [demɛle] to distinguish
demeure *f.* [dəmœːr] dwelling
demeurer (**dans** or **à**) [dəmœre dɑ̃, a] to live (in), remain (in)
demi *m.* [dəmi] large glass of beer
demi [dəmi] half; **à —** halfway
demi-douzaine *f.* [dəmiduzɛn] half-dozen
demi-heure *f.* [dəmiœːr] half-hour
démission *f.* [demisjɔ̃] resignation
demi-tour *m.* [dəmituːr] half-turn; **faire —** to turn around
demoiselle *f.* [dəmwazɛl] young lady
démonstratif [demɔ̃stratif] demonstrative
dénouement *m.* [denumɑ̃] outcome, ending, conclusion
dent *f.* [dɑ̃] tooth; **brosse à —s** *f.* toothbrush
dentelle *f.* [dɑ̃tɛl] lace
dentifrice [dɑ̃tifris] dentifrice; **pâte —** *f.* toothpaste
dentiste *m.* [dɑ̃tist] dentist
denture *f.* [dɑ̃tyːr] set of teeth
départ *m.* [depaːr] departure
dépasser [depɑse] to go beyond
dépayser [depeize] to put in new surroundings, bewilder
dépêche *f.* [depɛʃ] wire, telegram
dépêcher (**se**) [sədepɛʃe] to hurry
dépendre [depɑ̃ːdr] to depend
dépense *f.* [depɑ̃ːs] expenditure
dépenser [depɑ̃se] to spend
déplacer [deplase] to move, displace; **se —** to go out of one's way, change one's abode
déplaire [deplɛːr] to displease
déployer [deplwaje] to deploy
déposer [depoze] to place
dépouiller [depuje] to plunder, despoil
depuis [dəpɥi] since; **— quand** (**combien de temps**) **êtes-vous ici ?** how long have you been here? **— que** since, ever since
député *m.* [depyte] deputy, representative
déraisonner [derɛzɔne] to be out of one's mind, be unbalanced
déranger [derɑ̃ʒe] to trouble, disturb, bother
déraper [derape] to skid
dernier (*f.* **dernière**) [dɛrnje, dɛrnjɛːr] last
dérober [derɔbe] to steal, rob

derrière [dɛrjɛːr] back of, behind
dès que [dɛkə] as soon as
désagréable [dezagreabl] unpleasant, disagreeable
descendre [desɑ̃ːdr] to put up (*as at a hotel*), go down, come down (*usually with* **être**), get off
descente *f.* [desɑ̃t] down-slope, descent
désert [dezɛːr] deserted, solitary
désespérer [dezɛspere] to despair, give up hope
désespoir *m.* [dezɛspwaːr] despair, desperation, grief
désintéresser: se — de [sədezɛ̃terɛsedə] to lose interest in
désirer [dezire] to wish, desire
désolé [dezɔle] desolated, distressed, annoyed; **j'en suis —** I'm very sorry
dessert *m.* [desɛːr] dessert
desservir [desɛrviːr] to clear the table
dessiner [desine] to draw, outline
dessous [dəsu] **au — de** below, beneath; **au — de tout** beyond words, completely despicable
dessus [dəsy] over, above; **au — de** above
destinataire *m.* [dɛstinatɛːr] addressee
destinée *f.* [dɛstine] fate
détacher [detaʃe] to unfasten; **se —** detach oneself, stand out clearly
détour *m.* [detuːr] roundabout way
détourner (**se**) [sədeturne] to turn aside
détraqué [detrake] out of order
détruire [detrɥiːr] to destroy
dette *f.* [dɛt] debt
deux [dø] two; **— fois** twice; **les —** both; **tous les —** both; **tous —** both
deuxième [døzjɛm] second
devant *m.* [dəvɑ̃] the front
devant [dəvɑ̃] in front of
devenir (*p.p.* **devenu**) [dəvənir, dəvəny] to become
deviner [dəvine] to guess, divine
devoir *m.* [dəvwaːr] duty
devoir (*p.p.* **dû**) [dəvwaːr, dy] to owe, have to, be to, ought, must
dévorer [devɔre] to eat with relish, devour
dévot [devo] devout, godly, devoted
dévoué [devwe] devoted
dévouement *m.* [devumɑ̃] devotion
diable *m.* [djaːbl] devil; **du —** the devil of
dialogue *m.* [djalɔg] dialogue
diamant *m.* [djamɑ̃] diamond, jewel
diane *f.* [djan] reveille; **battre la —** to sound reveille
dictée *f.* [dikte] dictation
dicter [dikte] to dictate
Dieu *m.* [djø] God; **mon —!** good heavens!
difficile [difisil] difficult, hard, hard to please
difficilement [difisilmɑ̃] with difficulty
difficulté *f.* [difikylte] difficulty
difforme [difɔrm] deformed
digérer [diʒere] to digest
digne [diɲ] worthy
dignité *f.* [diɲite] dignity
dilater [dilate] to dilate
dimanche *m.* [dimɑ̃ʃ] Sunday
diminuer [diminɥe] to diminish, lessen, decrease
dîner *m.* [dine] dinner
dîner [dine] to have dinner, dine
dire [diːr] (*p.p.* **dit**) to say, tell; **c'est à —** that is to say; **dites!** say! **dites donc** listen, look here, say! **on m'a dit** I have been told; **vouloir —** to mean
direct [dirɛkt] direct
directement [dirɛktəmɑ̃] directly
directeur *m.* [dirɛktœːr] director
direction *f.* [dirɛksjɔ̃] direction
diriger [diriʒe] to direct
discours *m.* [diskuːr] speech
discrétion *f.* [diskresjɔ̃] **à —** as much as desired
discuter [diskyte] to discuss
disparaître [disparɛːtr] to disappear
disposer [dispoze] to dispose, place; **disposé à** disposed to
disposition *f.* [dispozisjɔ̃] arrangement, order
disque *m.* [disk] disc, record, recording
distance *f.* [distɑ̃ːs] distance; **à —** at a distance
distinct [distɛ̃] distinct, clear
distinction *f.* [distɛ̃ksjɔ̃] distinction
distinguer [distɛ̃ge] to distinguish, discern
distraire [distrɛːr] to distract
distrait [distrɛ] absent-minded

distribuer [distribɥe] to distribute
dit [di] *p.p.* of **dire**
divagation *f.* [divagasjɔ̃] rambling
divan *m.* [divɑ̃] divan, sofa
divers [divɛ:r] different, diverse
divertissement *m.* [divɛrtismɑ̃] diversion
dix [dis] ten
dix-huit [dizɥit] eighteen
dix-neuf [diznœf] nineteen
dix-sept [disɛt] seventeen
dizaine *f.* [dizɛn] about ten
docile [dɔsil] docile, obedient
docteur *m.* [dɔktœ:r] doctor
doigt *m.* [dwa] finger; **— de pied** toe
dollar *m.* [dɔlar] dollar
domestique *m.* or *f.* [dɔmɛstik] servant
dommage *m.* [dɔma:ʒ] damage, harm, injury; **c'est —** it's too bad
donc [dɔ̃k] so, then, therefore; **dites —** listen, look here, say; **allons —** come now! come, come!
donner [dɔne] to give; **— à souper** to take to supper; **— sur** to face on, to open out on; **donnant sur** overlooking; **se — rendez-vous** to set a date; **— tort à** to put in the wrong, to consider wrong; **donnez-moi de vos nouvelles** let me hear from you
dont [dɔ̃] whose, of whom, of which
dormeur *m.* [dɔrmœ:r] sleeper
dormir [dɔrmi:r] to sleep
dos *m.* [do] back
douane *f.* [dwan] customs
doublé [duble] lined
douce [dus] (*see* **doux**)
doucement [dusmɑ̃] softly, gently, sweetly
douceur *f.* [dusœ:r] gentleness
douche *f.* [duʃ] shower
douleur *f.* [dulœ:r] pain
douloureux (*f.* **douloureuse**) [dulurø, dulurø:z] painful
doute *m.* [dut] doubt; **sans —** no doubt, to be sure, probably
douter (**de**) [dute de] to doubt; **se —** to suspect
douteux (*f.* **douteuse**) [dutø, dutø:z] doubtful, in doubt
doux (*f.* **douce**) [du, dus] sweet
douzaine (**de**) *f.* [duzɛn də] dozen
douze [du:z] twelve
dragée *f.* [draʒe] sugar-coated almonds, sugarplums
drap *m.* [dra] bed sheet, cloth
dresser (**se**) [sədrɛse] to stand upright
droit *m.* [drwa] law, law studies; **faire son —** to study law
droit [drwa] right, straight, straight forward; **tout —** straight ahead
droite *f.* [drwat] right (hand); **à —** to the right; **tenir la —** to keep to the right
drôle [drol] funny
dû [dy] *p.p.* of **devoir**
duquel [dykɛl] of whom, of which, whose
dur [dy:r] hard
durant [dyrɑ̃] during
durer [dyre] to last, endure
dynamite *f.* [dinamit] dynamite

E

eau *f.* [o] water; **— de quinine** quinine hair tonic
échange *m.* [eʃɑ̃ʒ] exchange
échangé [eʃɑ̃ʒe] exchanged
échapper (**à**) [eʃape a] to escape
échelle *f.* [eʃɛl] ladder
échelon *m.* [eʃlɔ̃] step, rung
échouer [eʃwe] to fail
éclaircir (**s'**) [seklɛrsi:r] to lighten, brighten
éclat *m.* [ekla] fragment, burst; **— de rire** burst of laughter
éclatant [eklatɑ̃] brilliant, glaring
éclater [eklate] to burst out, shine forth
école *f.* [ekɔl] school
économe [ekɔnɔm] economical
économie *f.* [ekɔnɔmi] economy, thrift, saving
économique [ekɔnɔmik] economic
écouter [ekute] to listen, listen to
écrevisse *f.* [ekrəvis] crayfish
écrier (**s'**) [sekrie] to cry, cry out
écrire (*p.p.* **écrit**) [ekri:r, ekri] to write; **comment écrit-on cela ?** how is that spelled? **machine à —** typewriter
écriture *f.* [ekrity:r] handwriting
édifice *m.* [edifis] building
édition *f.* [edisjɔ̃] edition
Édouard [edwa:r] Edward

effaré [efare] frightened, scared
effectivement [efɛktivmɑ̃] indeed, as a matter of fact, that's a fact, in fact
effet *m.* [efɛ] effect; **en —** indeed, in fact, as a matter of fact, that's right
effrayant [efrɛjɑ̃] frightening
effroyable [efrwajabl] frightful
égal (*m. pl.* **égaux**) [egal, ego] equal; **ça m'est —** it's all the same to me
égarer [egare] to lead astray
église *f.* [egli:z] church
égratignure *f.* [egratiɲy:r] scratch
eh bien! [ebjɛ̃] well!
élancer (**s'**) [selɑ̃se] to throw oneself forward
élastique *f.* [elastik] elastic
électrique [elɛktrik] electric; **sonnerie —** electric bell
élève *m.* or *f.* [elɛv] pupil
élever [elve] to lift, raise; **s' —** to rise
elle [ɛl] she, it, her; **à —** hers; **— -même** herself
elles [ɛl] they; **à —** theirs; **—-mêmes** themselves
éloigner (**s'**) [selwaɲe] to go away
emballage *m.* [ɑ̃bala:ʒ] packing
embarrasser (ɑ̃barase] to embarrass
embêtant [ɑ̃bɛtɑ̃] exasperating, maddening
embrasser [ɑ̃brase] to kiss, hug, embrace, take up
embrasure *f.* [ɑ̃brazy:r] recess
émission: poste d'— *m.* [pɔstədemisjɔ̃] radio station
emmener [ɑ̃mne] to lead, take a person from a place; take out or away
emparer: s'— de [sɑ̃paredə] to take possession of
empêcher (**de**) [ɑ̃pɛʃedə] to hinder, prevent; **ne pas pouvoir s'— de** to be unable to, (cannot) help
emplette *f.* [ɑ̃plɛt] purchase; **faire des —s** to go shopping
emplir [ɑ̃pli:r] to fill, to pile
emploi *m.* [ɑ̃plwa] use
employé *m.* [ɑ̃plwaje] clerk
employer [ɑ̃plwaje] to use
emporter [ɑ̃pɔrte] to carry off, carry away
empresser (**s'**) [sɑ̃prɛse] to hasten, hurry
emprisonner [ɑ̃prizɔne] to imprison
emprunter (**à**) [ɑ̃prœ̃te a] to borrow from
Ems [ɛms] German watering place
ému [emy] moved, upset, stirred
en (*pron.*) [ɑ̃] some, any, of it, of them, from it, from them
en (*prep.*) [ɑ̃] in, by, within, to, into, while, when, at
enchanté (**de faire votre connaissance**) [ɑ̃ʃɑ̃te də fɛr vɔtrə kɔnɛsɑ̃s] delighted (pleased) to meet you
encombrement *m.* [ɑ̃kɔ̃brəmɑ̃] jam, crowd
encombrer [ɑ̃kɔ̃bre] to encumber, fill up
encore [ɑ̃kɔ:r] still, yet, again; **— un** another; **— une fois** once again
encourager [ɑ̃kuraʒe] to encourage
encre *f.* [ɑ̃kr] ink
encrier *m.* [ɑ̃krie] inkwell
endormi [ɑ̃dɔrmi] asleep
endormir [ɑ̃dɔrmi:r] to go to sleep, to put to sleep; **s'—** to fall asleep
endosser [ɑ̃dose] to endorse
endroit *m.* [ɑ̃drwa] place, spot
endurci [ɑ̃dyrsi] hardened
endurer [ɑ̃dyre] to endure
énergiquement [enɛrʒikmɑ̃] energetically
énerver (**s'**) [senɛrve] to be (become) nervous
enfance *f.* [ɑ̃fɑ̃s] childhood
enfant *m.* or *f.* [ɑ̃fɑ̃] child
enfantin [ɑ̃fɑ̃tɛ̃] childish
enfermer [ɑ̃fɛrme] to lock up, shut in
enfin [ɑ̃fɛ̃] at last, after all, finally
enflé [ɑ̃fle] swollen
enfoncer [ɑ̃fɔ̃se] to smash in
engagé [ɑ̃gaʒe] involved, obligated
engagement *m.* [ɑ̃gaʒmɑ̃] engagement
engouffrer (**s'**) [sɑ̃gufre] to be swallowed up
enjambée *f.* [ɑ̃ʒɑ̃be] stride
enlèvement *m.* [ɑ̃lɛvmɑ̃] taking away, carrying away, elopement, capture
enlever [ɑ̃lve] to carry away, remove
ennemi *m.* [ɛnmi] enemy, foe
ennuyer [ɑ̃nɥije] to tire, annoy; **s'—** to become tired, to become bored
énorme [enɔ:rm] enormous
énormément [enɔrmemɑ̃] enormously

enquête *f.* [ãkɛt] inquiry
enragé [ãraʒe] mad, enraged, raving
enregistrer [ãrəʒistre] to check
enroué [ãrwe] hoarse
enseigner [ãsɛɲe] to teach
ensemble *m.* [ãsãbl] unity, conformity, harmonious combination
ensemble [ãsãbl] together
ensuite [ãsɥit] following, afterward
entendre [ãtãdr] to hear; **— dire** to hear; **— parler de** to hear about
entendu! [ãtãdy] agreed, O.K.; **bien —** of course
enterrer [ãtɛre] to bury
entêter (s') [sãtɛte] to persist
entier (*f.* **entière**) [ãtje, ãtjɛːr] entire, whole
entourer [ãture] to surround
entraîné [ãtrɛne] trained
entraver [ãtrave] to hinder
entre [ãːtr] between, among
entrecôte *f.* [ãtrəkot] steak
entrée *f.* [ãtre] entrance
entrer (dans) [ãtre dã] to enter, go in (*conj. with* **être**)
énumérer [enymere] to enumerate
enveloppe *f.* [ãvlɔp] envelope
envelopper [ãvlɔpe] to wrap
envers [ãvɛːr] toward
envie *f.* [ãvi] desire, envy; **avoir — de** to feel like
environ [ãvirɔ̃] about
environs *m. pl.* [ãvirɔ̃] neighborhood
envisager [ãvizaʒe] to envisage
envoyer [ãvwaje] to send
épais (*f.* **épaisse**) [epɛ, epɛs] thick
éparpiller (s') [separpije] to scatter
épatant [epatã] wonderful, swell
épaule *f.* [epoːl] shoulder; **large des —s** wide in the shoulders
épaulement *m.* [epolmã] breastwork
épaulette *f.* [epolɛt] epaulette, shoulder strap
épée *f.* [epe] sword
éperdu [epɛrdy] dismayed
épice *f.* [epis] **les —s** (*obsolete*) gifts, presents, court fees
épingle *f.* [epɛ̃gl] pin
époque *f.* [epɔk] period, time
épouse *f.* [epuːz] wife
épouser [epuze] to marry
épouvantable [epuvãtabl] frightful
épouvante *f.* [epuvãt] fright, terror
épouvanté [epuvãte] terrified
époux *m.* [epu] husband; *pl.* married couple, husband and wife
éprendre: s'— de [seprãdr də] to fall in love with
épreuve *f.* [eprœːv] test
épris [epri] in love
éprouver [epruve] to feel, experience
épuisé [epɥize] worn out
épuiser (s') [sepɥize] to become exhausted
équilibre *m.* [ekilibr] balance, poise
équivalent *m.* [ekivalã] equivalent
escalier *m.* [ɛskalje] staircase
escroc *m.* [ɛskro] thief
escroquer [ɛskrɔke] to steal
Espagne *f.* [ɛspaɲ] Spain
espagnol [ɛspaɲɔl] Spanish
espèce *f.* [ɛspɛs] kind, sort
espérance *f.* [ɛsperãs] hope
espéré [ɛspere] hoped for
espérer [ɛspere] to hope
espoir *m.* [ɛspwar] hope
esprit *m.* [ɛspri] mind, spirit, wit
Esquirol [ɛskirɔl] French alienist (1772–1840)
essayer (de) [esɛje də] to try to, try on
essence *f.* [esãːs] gasoline
essuyer [esɥije] to wipe
est *m.* [ɛst] east
estimer [ɛstime] to estimate
estomac *m.* [ɛstɔma] stomach
et [e] and
étable *f.* [etabl] stable, cowshed
établir [etablir] to establish, set down
étage *m.* [etaːʒ] floor, story; **le premier —** one flight up, second floor
état *m.* [eta] state, condition
États-Unis *m. pl.* [etazyni] United States; **aux —** to (in) the United States
été *m.* [ete] summer
été [ete] *p.p.* of **être**
éteindre (s') [setɛ̃ːdr] to go out, be extinguished
étendre [etãːdr] to stretch out
Étienne [etjɛn] Stephen
étiquette *f.* [etikɛt] baggage label
étoffe *f.* [etɔf] cloth, material
étoile *f.* [etwal] star
étonnant [etɔnã] astonishing

étonnement *m.* [etɔnmɑ̃] astonishment
étonner [etɔne] to astonish; **s'—** to be astonished
étrange [etrɑ̃:ʒ] strange, odd
étranger *m.* [etrɑ̃ʒe] stranger, foreigner
étranger (*f.* **étrangère**) [etrɑ̃ʒe, etrɑ̃ʒɛ:r] foreign
étrangler [etrɑ̃gle] to strangle
être (*p.p.* **été**) [ɛ:tr, ete] to be; **où en suis-je de...?** where have I got with...? **n'est-ce pas?** isn't he, didn't they? etc. (*use where English repeats the verb*); **en — de même** to be the same
être *m.* [ɛ:tr] being, creature
étrenne *f.* [etrɛn] New Year's gift
étroit [etrwɑ] narrow, tight
étudiant *m.* [etydjɑ̃] student
étudiante *f.* [etydjɑ̃t] student, co-ed; **Maison des Étudiantes** girls' dormitory
eu [y] *p.p.* of **avoir**
Europe *f.* [ørɔp] Europe
eux [ø] them, they; **à —** theirs; **—-mêmes** themselves
évanouir (s') [sevanwi:r] to faint
évanouissement *m.* [evanwismɑ̃] fainting spell
éveiller [evɛje] to waken, wake up, awaken
événement *m.* [evenmɑ̃] event
évidemment [evidamɑ̃] evidently
évier *m.* [evje] sink
éviter [evite] to avoid, spare
évoquer [evɔke] to call forth, evoke
exact [ɛgzakt] exact, precise
exalter (s') [sɛgzalte] to become excited
examen *m.* [ɛgzamɛ̃] examination
examiner [ɛgzamine] to examine, study
exaspéré [ɛgzaspere] exasperated
excellent [ɛksɛlɑ̃] excellent
exception *f.* [ɛksɛpsjɔ̃] exception
excès *m.* [ɛksɛ] excess
excessif (*f.* **excessive**) [ɛksɛsif, ɛksɛsi:v] extreme, excessive
excuse *f.* [ɛksky:z] excuse, apology
excuser [ɛkskyze] to excuse; **excusez-moi** excuse me
exemple *m.* [ɛgzɑ̃:pl] example; **par —** for instance; **par —!** indeed! the idea! upon my word!
exercice *m.* [egzɛrsis] exercise
exiger [egziʒe] to demand, require, insist
expédier [ɛkspedje] to send
expérience *f.* [ɛksperjɑ̃:s] experience
explication *f.* [ɛksplikasjɔ̃] explanation
expliquer [ɛksplike] to explain
explorer [ɛksplɔre] to explore, search
explosif *m.* [ɛksplozif] explosive
exposer [ɛkspoze] to explain
exprès [ɛksprɛ] on purpose
expressif (*f.* **expressive**) [ɛksprɛsif, ɛksprɛsi:v] expressive
expression *f.* [ɛksprɛsjɔ̃] expression
exprimer [ɛksprime] to express
exquis [ɛkski] delicious, exquisite
extraction *f.* [ɛkstraksjɔ̃] extraction
extraire [ɛkstrɛ:r] to extract
extraordinaire [ɛkstraɔrdinɛ:r] extraordinary
extrême [ɛkstrɛm] extreme
extrêmement [ɛkstrɛməmɑ̃] extremely
extrémité *f.* [ɛkstremite] end, extremity

F

fabricant *m.* [fabrikɑ̃] manufacturer
fabriquer [fabrike] to make, build, manufacture
face *f.* [fas] front, face; **en — de** opposite; **d'en —** across the way; **faire — à** to face
fâcher [fɑʃe] to make angry, to vex; **se —** to get angry
facile [fasil] easy
facilement [fasilmɑ̃] easily
facilité *f.* [fasilite] fluency, ease, facility
façon *f.* [fasɔ̃] fashion, way; **de cette —** in this fashion, this way; **d'une — magnifique** in grand fashion
facture *f.* [fakty:r] bill
faible [fɛbl] weak, feeble
faiblement [fɛbləmɑ̃] feebly, weakly
faiblesse *f.* [fɛblɛs] weakness
faim *f.* [fɛ̃] hunger; **avoir —** to be hungry
faire (*p.p.* **fait**) [fɛ:r, fɛ] to do, make; **— beau** to be fine (weather); **— chaud** to be warm (weather); **— des emplettes** to go shopping; **— du soleil**

faire (*cont.*) to be sunny; **— du vent** to be windy; **— face à** face; **— faire** have (someone) do, have (something) done; **— feu** to fire, shoot; **— feu sur** to shoot at; **— froid** to be cold (weather); **— honneur** to honor; **— la connaissance de** to make the acquaintance of; **— la queue** to stand in line; **— (sa) toilette** to wash and dress; **— sa valise** to pack a bag (suitcase); **— mal à** to hurt; **— mauvais (temps)** to be bad (weather); **— plaisir** to please (**cela me fait grand plaisir** that gives me great pleasure); **— (notre) possible** to do (our) best; **— semblant (de)** to pretend (to); **— ses adieux à** to say good-by to; **— ses amitiés à** to give one's regards to; **— sauter** to blow up; **— signe à** to signal, motion to; **— un chèque** to make out a check; **— un petit tour** to take a short walk; **— une promenade** to take a walk; **— une visite** to pay a visit; **— un voyage** to take a trip; **— venir** to send for; **— visite à** to visit; **— voir** to show (**faites-moi voir** show me): **ça se fait** that (it) is done; **cela ne fait rien** it makes no difference

faisceau *m.* [fɛso] stack

fait *m.* [fɛ] fact

fait [fɛ] *p.p.* of **faire**; **tout à —** quite, altogether

falloir [falwar] must, should, to be necessary

fameux (*f.* **fameuse**) [famø, famø:z] famous, (*ironical*) precious

familial [familjal] home, domestic

familiarisé [familjarize] accustomed, familiar

famille *f.* [fami:j] family; **pension de —** *f.* boardinghouse

fané [fane] shriveled, faded

farce *f.* [fars] prank, practical joke

farci [farsi] stuffed

fardé [farde] made up

farder (se) [sə farde] to make up

farine *f.* [farin] flour, meal

farouche [faruʃ] timid

fatalité *f.* [fatalite] fatal mistake

fatigue *f.* [fatig] fatigue

fatigué [fatige] tired, weary

fatiguer [fatige] to tire

fauché [foʃe] cut off

faute *f.* [fo:t] fault, mistake, error; **— de** for lack of

fauteuil *m.* [fotœ:j] armchair, easy chair

faux (*f.* **fausse**) [fo, fo:s] false, off key

faveur *f.* [favœ:r] favor; **en — de** in behalf of

favori *m.* [favɔri] whisker; **—s** (*pl.*) sideburns

favori (*f.* **favorite**) [favɔri, favɔrit] favorite

fébrile [febril] feverish

féliciter [felisite] to congratulate

féminin [feminɛ̃] feminine

femme *f.* [fam] woman, wife; **— de chambre** chambermaid

fenêtre *f.* [fənɛ:tr] window

fente *f.* [fɑ̃t] crack, slit

fer *m.* [fɛ:r] iron; **chemin de —** *m.* railroad

fer-blanc *m.* [fɛrblɑ̃] tin

ferme *f.* [fɛrm] farm

fermer [fɛrme] to close; **— à clé** to lock

fête *f.* [fɛ:t] celebration, feast, birthday

fêter [fɛte] to celebrate

feu *m.* [fø] fire, firing (*guns*); **coup de —** *m.* shot; **faire —** to fire, shoot

feuille *f.* [fœ:j] leaf, sheet of paper

février *m.* [fevrie] February

fiacre *m.* [fja:kr] cab

fiancé *m.* [fjɑ̃se] betrothed, sweetheart

fiancé [fjɑ̃se] engaged

fiancée *f.* [fjɑ̃se] betrothed, sweetheart

ficelle *f.* [fisɛl] string, cord

fiche *f.* [fiʃ] blank

fidèle [fidɛl] faithful

fier: se — à [səfje a] to have confidence in, trust

fier (*f.* **fière**) [fjɛ:r] proud

fièrement [fjɛrmɑ̃] proudly

fièvre *f.* [fjɛvr] fever

fiévreux *m.* [fjevrø] fever victim

figure *f.* [figy:r] face

figurer [figyre] to imagine, consider

fil *m.* [fil] thread

filer [file] to spin

filet *m.* [filɛ] rack

fille *f.* [fi:j] daughter; **jeune —** girl, young girl
fillette *f.* [fijɛt] little girl
film *m.* [film] film, motion picture, movie
filou *m.* [filu] cheat, thief
fils *m.* [fis] son
fin *f.* [fɛ̃] end; **— de semaine** week-end
fin [fɛ̃] fine, delicate, exquisite
final [final] final
financier (*f.* **financière**) [finɑ̃sje, finɑ̃sjɛ:r] financial
finir [finir] to finish; **— par** end up by
fixement [fiksəmɑ̃] fixedly, in the face
fixer [fikse] to fasten
fixité *f.* [fiksite] stubbornness
flan *m.* [flɑ̃] custard
flanc *m.* [flɑ̃] flank, side
flanelle *f.* [flanɛl] flannel
flaque *f.* [flak] puddle, pool
flatter [flate] to flatter
fleur *f.* [flœ:r] flower
fleuriste *m.* [flœrist] florist
fleuve *m.* [flœ:v] river
flot *m.* [flo] stream, torrent
flotter [flɔte] to float
flux *m.* [fly] flow, stream, flood
foi *f.* [fwa] faith; **ma —!** goodness! my word!
foie *m.* [fwa] liver; **pâté de — gras** *m.* goose-liver paste
foin *m.* [fwɛ̃] hay
foire *f.* [fwa:r] fair
fois *f.* [fwa] time, occasion (*repetition*); **à la —** at the same time; **chaque —** each time; **encore une —** once again; **une — par semaine** once a week
folie *f.* [fɔli] madness, insanity
foncé [fɔ̃se] deep; **bleu —** dark blue
fonctionner [fɔ̃ksjɔne] to work, function
fond *m.* [fɔ̃] back, background, heart; **à —** thoroughly; **dans le —** to the rear; **au —** at bottom
force *f.* [fɔrs] strength, (*pl.*) forces; **en —** in full force, strong
forêt *f.* [fɔrɛ] wood, forest
forme *f.* [fɔrm] form
former [fɔrme] to form
fort [fɔ:r] strong, loud; (*adv.*) quite, very; **c'est un peu —** that's going too far
fortement [fɔrtəmɑ̃] strongly
fortifier [fɔrtifje] to fortify, reinforce
fortune *f.* [fɔrtyn] fortune
fou *m.* [fu] lunatic
fou (**fol** *before vowel*; *f.* **folle**) [fu, fɔl] mad, foolish, crazy
fougère *f.* [fuʒɛ:r] fern
fouiller [fuje] to search
foule *f.* [ful] crowd
four *m.* [fu:r] oven
fourchette *f.* [furʃɛt] fork
fourmi *f.* [furmi] ant
fourneau *m.* [furno] stove
fournir [furnir] to furnish
fourré [fure] thrust, stuck
fourrure *f.* [furyr] fur
foyer *m.* [fwaje] hearth, fireside
fracas *m.* [frakɑ] crash, noise, din
fragment *m.* [fragmɑ̃] fragment, splinter
frais *m. pl.* [frɛ] expense, expenses
frais (*f.* **fraîche**) [frɛ, frɛʃ] cool, blooming, fresh-colored
franc *m.* [frɑ̃] franc
franc (*f.* **franche**) [frɑ̃, frɑ̃ʃ] frank
français [frɑ̃sɛ] French; **à la française** French style
France *f.* [frɑ̃:s] France; **en —** in France, to France
franchement [frɑ̃ʃmɑ̃] frankly
François [frɑ̃swa] Francis, Frank
frapper [frape] to knock, strike
frauduleusement [frodyløzmɑ̃] fraudulently
frein *m.* [frɛ̃] brake
frêle [frɛl] frail, fragile
frénésie *f.* [frenezi] frenzy, madness
frère *m.* [frɛ:r] brother
frigidaire *m.* [friʒidɛ:r] frigidaire, ice-box
fripon *m.* (*f.* **friponne**) [fripɔ̃, fripɔn] knave, rogue, rascal
frissonner [frisɔne] to shudder
frit [fri] fried; **les frites** *f. pl.* French fried potatoes
friture *f.* [frity:r] fried dish, fried fish
frivole [frivɔl] frivolous
froid [frwa] cold; **faire —** to be cold (*weather*); **avoir —** to be cold (*physical sensation*)
froideur *f.* [frwadœ:r] coldness
fromage *m.* [frɔma:ʒ] cheese

front *m.* [frɔ̃] forehead
frontière *f.* [frɔ̃tjɛ:r] frontier, border, boundary
frotter (se) [səfrɔte] to rub, scratch
frousse *f.* [frus] fear, fright
fruit *m.* [frɥi] fruit
fuir [fɥi:r] to flee, leak
fuite *f.* [fɥit] flight
fumée *f.* [fyme] smoke
fumer [fyme] to smoke
fumeur *m.* [fymœ:r] smoker
furie *f.* [fyri] fury, enthusiasm, ardor
furieux (*f.* **furieuse**) [fyrjø, fyrjø:z] furious
furieusement [fyrjøzmɑ̃] furiously
fusil *m.* [fyzi] gun
fusiller [fyzije] to shoot (*military execution*)
futur [fyty:r] future

G

gages *m. pl.* [ga:ʒ] wages
gagner [gaɲe] to earn, gain, win
gai [ge] gay, merry
gaiement [gɛmɑ̃] gaily
gaieté *f.* [gɛte] gaiety
gaillard *m.* [gaja:r] fellow
galerie *f.* [galri] gallery
galop *m.* [galo] gallop
gamin *m.* [gamɛ̃] scamp, little blackguard, young boy
gant *m.* [gɑ̃] glove
ganté [gɑ̃te] gloved
garage *m.* [gara:ʒ] garage
garantir [garɑ̃ti:r] to guarantee
garçon *m.* [garsɔ̃] boy, waiter, bachelor
garçonnet *m.* [garsɔnɛ] little boy
garde *f.* [gard] guard; **prenez —!** look out! watch out!
garde-malade *f.* [gardmalad] nurse
garder [garde] to keep
gare *f.* [ga:r] station
garer [gare] to park, garage
garnir [garnir] to adorn, decorate
garrotter [garɔte] to tie up
gâteau *m.* (*pl.* **gâteaux**) [gɑto] cake; **— à la crème** cream cake, cream pie, cream tart
gâter [gɑte] to spoil
gauche *f.* [go:ʃ] left (hand); **à —** to the left; **tenir la —** to keep to the left
gémir [ʒemi:r] to groan, moan
gémissement *m.* [ʒemismɑ̃] groan
gênant [ʒɛnɑ̃] annoying
gencive *f.* [ʒɑ̃si:v] gum
gendarme *m.* [ʒɑ̃darm] police trooper (*similar to our state police*)
gendre *m.* [ʒɑ̃dr] son-in-law
gêne *f.* [ʒɛn] distress, embarrassment, awkwardness
gêner [ʒɛne] to disturb, embarrass
général *m.* (*pl.* **généraux**) [ʒeneral, ʒenero] general; **en —** in general
généreux (*f.* **généreuse**) [ʒenerø, ʒenerø:z] generous
générosité *f.* [ʒenerozite] generosity
génie *m.* [ʒeni] genius
genou *m.* (*pl.* **genoux**) [ʒənu] knee
genre *m.* [ʒɑ̃:r] sort, kind
gens *m. pl.* [ʒɑ̃] people; **jeunes —** young people, young men
gentil (*f.* **gentille**) [ʒɑ̃ti, ʒɑ̃ti:j] nice, kind; **— comme tout** nice as anything; **c'est très — de (votre) part** it's very kind of you
gentilhomme *m.* [ʒɑ̃tijɔm] gentleman, nobleman
gentillesse *f.* [ʒɑ̃tijɛs] kindness
géographie *f.* [ʒeɔgrafi] geography
géométrie *f.* [ʒeɔmetri] geometry
Georges [ʒɔrʒ] George
gérant *m.* [ʒerɑ̃] manager
geste *m.* [ʒɛst] gesture, sign
gibier *m.* [ʒibje] game, venison
gifler [ʒifle] to box the ears
gigantesque [ʒigɑ̃tɛsk] gigantic
gigot *m.* [ʒigo] leg of lamb; **— de pré-salé** choice leg of lamb
gilet *m.* [ʒilɛ] vest
glace *f.* [glas] ice, ice cream, mirror; **armoire à —** *f.* wardrobe with mirror
glaçon *m.* [glasɔ̃] icicle, piece of ice
glisser [glise] to slip
gloire *f.* [glwa:r] glory
glorieusement [glɔrjøzmɑ̃] gloriously
glotte *f.* [glɔt] glottis
gonflé [gɔ̃fle] inflated, full of air
gonfler [gɔ̃fle] to swell
gorge *f.* [gɔrʒ] throat, gorge
gourmand *m.* [gurmɑ̃] glutton
goût *m.* [gu] taste; **chacun à son —** everyone to his taste

goûter *m.* [gute] snack, light afternoon meal
goûter [gute] to taste
grâce *f.* [grɑːs] grace; **— à** thanks to
gracieuseté *f.* [grasjøzte] courtesy, favor
gracieux (*f.* **gracieuse**) [grasjø, grasjøːz] graceful
grade *m.* [grad] rank
grammaire *f.* [gramɛːr] grammar
grand [grɑ̃] tall, great, large, big
grandeur *f.* [grɑ̃dœːr] largeness, grandeur, size
grandir [grɑ̃diːr] to grow, become larger
grandissant [grɑ̃disɑ̃] growing
grand'maman *f.* [grɑ̃mamɑ̃] grandma
grand'mère *f.* [grɑ̃mɛːr] grandmother
grand-papa *m.* [grɑ̃papa] grandpa
grand-père *m.* [grɑ̃pɛːr] grandfather
grange *f.* [grɑ̃ːʒ] barn
grappe *f.* [grap] bunch
gras (*f.* **grasse**) [grɑ, grɑːs] fat, thick; **pâté de foie —** *m.* goose-liver paste
grave [grav] serious, grave
gravement [gravmɑ̃] seriously, solemnly
gravir [gravir] to climb, clamber up
grec (*f.* **grecque**) [grɛk] Greek
Grèce *f.* [grɛs] Greece
grenadier *m.* [grənadje] grenadier
grève *f.* [grɛv] strike
grief *m.* [griɛf] grievance, complaint
grièvement [griɛvmɑ̃] gravely, seriously
grille *f.* [griːj] iron gate
grillé [grije] burnt out
grimace *f.* [grimas] grimace, wry face
gris [gri] gray, tipsy, drunk
gros (*f.* **grosse**) [gro, groːs] big, large, coarse
grossier (*f.* **grossière**) [grosje, grosjɛːr] rude
groupe *m.* [grup] group
grouper [grupe] to group
guère [gɛːr] **ne...—** hardly, scarcely
guérir [geriːr] to cure; **se —** to recover one's health
guérison *f.* [gerizɔ̃] cure, recovery
guerre *f.* [gɛːr] war
guichet *m.* [giʃɛ] (ticket) window
guide *m.* [gid] guide; **servir de — à** to serve one as a guide
guider [gide] to steer, guide
guidon *m.* [gidɔ̃] handle bars, steering gear
guigne *f.* [giɲ] bad luck
Guillaume [gijoːm] William

H

(†*h indicates aspirate h*)

habile [abil] skillful, clever
habileté *f.* [abilte] ability, skill, talent
habiller (s') [sabije] to dress
habit *m.* [abi] coat; (*pl.*) clothes
habitant *m.* [abitɑ̃] inhabitant
habitation *f.* [abitasjɔ̃] habitation, dwelling
habiter [abite] to live in, occupy, dwell
habitude *f.* [abityd] habit, custom; **d'—** as a rule, usually
habitué [abitɥe] accustomed, used
†**hachis** *m.* [aʃi] hash
†**haine** *f.* [ɛːn] hatred, grudge
halluciné [alysine] mad, suffering from hallucinations
†**hardiment** [ardimɑ̃] boldly
†**haricots** *m. pl.* [ariko] beans
†**hasard** *m.* [azar] chance, accident; **au —** at random
†**hâte** *f.* [ɑːt] haste; **en —** in haste; **à la —** hastily; **avoir — de** to be in a hurry
†**hâter (se)** [sə ɑte] to hasten, hurry
†**hausser** [ose] to shrug
†**haut** [o] high; **en —** above, upstairs; **à —e voix** out loud; **tout —** aloud
†**hauteur** *f.* [otœːr] height
hélas [elɑːs] alas
Hélène [elɛn] Helen
Henri [ɑ̃ri] Henry
Henriette [ɑ̃rjɛt] Henrietta
herbe *f.* [ɛrb] grass
héréditaire [ereditɛːr] hereditary
†**hérisson** *m.* [erisɔ̃] porcupine
hériter [erite] to inherit
héritier *m.* [eritje] heir
héroïque [erɔik] heroic
hésiter [ezite] to hesitate
heure *f.* [œːr] hour; **à l'—** on time; **à quelle —** at what time? **à tout à**

heure (*cont.*) **l'—** I'll see you presently; **de bonne —** early; **tout à l'—** presently, a little while ago
heureusement [œrøzmɑ̃] luckily, happily, fortunately
heureux (*f.* **heureuse**) [œrø, œrøːz] glad, happy, blessed; **en être —** to be glad (of it)
†**heurter** [œrte] to stumble upon, run into or against
hier [iɛːr (jɛːr)] yesterday; **— matin** yesterday morning; **— soir** last night
†**hisser** [ise] to hoist
histoire *f.* [istwaːr] story, history, fuss
hiver *m.* [ivɛr] winter
†**Hollande** *f.* [ɔlɑ̃ːd] Holland
†**homard** *m.* [ɔmaːr] lobster
homéopathe *m.* [ɔmeɔpat] homeopath
hommage *m.* [ɔmaːʒ] respect, homage; **les —s** regards, respects (*used in plural when referring to a lady*); **mes —s les plus respectueux** my kindest regards (*usually from man to woman*); **présenter ses —s à** to pay one's respects to, offer one's regards to
homme *m.* [ɔm] man
†**Hongrie** *f.* [ɔ̃gri] Hungary
honnête [ɔnɛːt] honest
honnêteté *f.* [ɔnɛtte] honesty
honneur *m.* [ɔnœːr] honor; **faire —** to honor
†**honte** *f.* [ɔ̃t] shame; **avoir —** to be ashamed
†**honteux** (*f.* **honteuse**) [ɔ̃tø, ɔ̃tøːz] ashamed, shameful
hôpital *m.* [ɔpital] hospital
horaire (**des trains**) *m.* [ɔrɛːr (de trɛ̃)] timetable (*railroad*)
horriblement [ɔribləmɑ̃] horribly
†**hors** (**de**) [ɔr də] out of
†**hors d'œuvre** *m. pl.* [ɔrdœːvr] appetizers
hospitalité *f.* [ɔspitalite] hospitality
hôte *m.* [oːt] host, guest
hôtel *m.* [ɔtɛl] hotel; **maître d'—** steward, major-domo, headwaiter
†**hourra** *m.* [ura] hurrah, hurray
huile *f.* [ɥil] oil
†**huit** [ɥit] eight; (**jeudi**) **en —** a week from (Thursday)
huître *f.* [ɥitr] oyster
humain [ymɛ̃] human
humanité *f.* [ymanite] humanity
humble [œ̃bl] humble, lowly
humeur *f.* [ymœːr] humor, disposition
humide [ymid] damp
humiliant [ymiljɑ̃] humiliating
†**hurler** [yrle] to howl

I

ici [isi] here; **jusqu'—** until now; **par —** this way
idée *f.* [ide] idea
identité: carte d'— *f.* [kartədidɑ̃tite] identification card
idiomatique [idjɔmatik] idiomatic
idolâtre [idɔlɑːtr] idolizing
idole *f.* [idɔl] idol; (*jest*) doll, statue
Iéna [jena] Jena
ignorant [iɲɔrɑ̃] ignorant
ignorer [iɲɔre] to know nothing about
il [il] he, it
illettré [illɛtre] without education, illiterate
illusion *f.* [illyzjɔ̃] illusion
ils [il] they
image *f.* [imaːʒ] image
imaginé: bien — [bjɛ̃nimaʒine] clever
imaginer [imaʒine] to imagine
immense [immɑ̃ːs] immense
immobile [immɔbil] motionless
imparfait *m.* [ɛ̃parfɛ] imperfect (tense)
impatience *f.* [ɛ̃pasjɑ̃ːs] impatience
impatienter (**s'**) [sɛ̃pasjɑ̃te] to become impatient
impératif *m.* [ɛ̃peratif] imperative (verb mood)
imperceptible [ɛ̃pɛrsɛptibl] imperceptible
imperméable *m.* [ɛ̃pɛrmeabl] waterproof, raincoat
implorer [ɛ̃plɔre] to implore, beg
impoli [ɛ̃pɔli] impolite
important [ɛ̃pɔrtɑ̃] important
importer [ɛ̃pɔrte] to be important or necessary, matter; **n'importe** it doesn't matter, never mind; **n'importe quel** any whatsoever; **n'importe quoi** anything at all, no matter what; **qu'importe?** what does it matter?

importuner [ɛ̃pɔrtyne] to annoy, trouble
imposant [ɛ̃pozɑ̃] imposing
impossible [ɛ̃pɔsibl] impossible
impression *f.* [ɛ̃prɛsjɔ̃] impression
imprimé [ɛ̃prime] printed
improviser [ɛ̃prɔvize] to improvise, make up
inattendu [inatɑ̃dy] unexpected
incendie *m.* [ɛ̃sɑ̃di] fire
incliner (s') [sɛ̃kline] to bow
incommodé [ɛ̃kɔmɔde] indisposed, in distress
incommodité *f.* [ɛ̃kɔmɔdite] discomfort, ailment, indisposition
inconnu *m.* [ɛ̃kɔny] stranger, unknown one
inconnu [ɛ̃kɔny] unknown
inconvenance *f.* [ɛ̃kɔ̃vnɑ̃:s] impropriety
inconvénient *m.* [ɛ̃kɔ̃venjɑ̃] inconvenience, disadvantage
incroyable [ɛ̃krwajabl] unbelievable
incurable [ɛ̃kyrabl] incurable
indéfini [ɛ̃defini] indefinite
indemnité *f.* [ɛ̃dɛmnite] indemnity
indicateur *m.* [ɛ̃dikatœ:r] timetable
indifférent [ɛ̃diferɑ̃] indifferent
indigne [ɛ̃diɲ] unworthy, worthless
indiquer [ɛ̃dike] to indicate, show
individu *m.* [ɛ̃dividy] individual
industrie *f.* [ɛ̃dystri] industry
inespéré [inɛspere] unhoped for
infamie *f.* [ɛ̃fami] infamy
infatigable [ɛ̃fatigabl] tireless
infect [ɛ̃fɛkt] awful
infiniment [ɛ̃finimɑ̃] infinitely; **merci —** a million thanks
infinitif *m.* [ɛ̃finitif] infinitive
infirme *m.* [ɛ̃firm] invalid
infirmier *m.* [ɛ̃firmje] hospital attendant, male nurse
infirmière *f.* [ɛ̃firmjɛ:r] nurse
infliger [ɛ̃fliʒe] to inflict
ingénieur *m.* [ɛ̃ʒenjœ:r] engineer
initier [inisje] to initiate
injure *f.* [ɛ̃ʒy:r] insult
inné [inne] innate, inherent, inner
innocemment [inɔsamɑ̃] innocently
inoffensif (*f.* **inoffensive**) [inɔfɑ̃sif, inɔfɑ̃si:v] inoffensive, harmless
inondation *f.* [inɔ̃dasjɔ̃] inundation
inquiet [ɛ̃kjɛ] worried, anxious
inquiéter [ɛ̃kjete] to disturb, to bother; **s'—** to worry
inquiétude *f.* [ɛ̃kjetyd] anxiety
insaisissable [ɛ̃sɛzisabl] intangible
inscription *f.* [ɛ̃skripsjɔ̃] inscription
inscrire [ɛ̃skri:r] to enroll
insensiblement [ɛ̃sɑ̃sibləmɑ̃] unconsciously, gradually
insinuant [ɛ̃sinɥɑ̃] insinuating
insister [ɛ̃siste] to insist
insolation *f.* [ɛ̃sɔlasjɔ̃] sunstroke
insolent [ɛ̃sɔlɑ̃] unheard of, extraordinary, impudent
inspecteur *m.* [ɛ̃spɛktœ:r] inspector
installé [ɛ̃stale] settled (firmly)
installer (s') [sɛ̃stale] to install oneself, settle oneself
instamment [ɛ̃stamɑ̃] earnestly, urgently
instant *m.* [ɛ̃stɑ̃] instant; **à l'—** at once; **un —** just a moment
instituteur *m.* [ɛ̃stitytœ:r] teacher (*elementary*)
instruction *f.* [ɛ̃stryksjɔ̃] instruction, education
insu: à l'— de [alɛ̃syda] without the knowledge of
insuffler [ɛ̃syfle] to blow
insurgé *m.* [ɛ̃syrʒe] insurgent
insurrection *f.* [ɛ̃syrɛksjɔ̃] insurrection
intelligent [ɛ̃tɛliʒɑ̃] intelligent, bright, smart, clever
intelligible [ɛ̃tɛliʒibl] intelligible, understandable
intention *f.* [ɛ̃tɑ̃sjɔ̃] intention
interdit [ɛ̃tɛrdi] forbidden
intéresser (s') à [sɛ̃terɛse a] to take an interest in
intérêt *m.* [ɛ̃terɛ] interest
intérieur *m.* [ɛ̃terjœ:r] inside, interior
intérieurement [ɛ̃terjœrmɑ̃] internally
international (*m. pl.* **internationaux**) [ɛ̃tɛrnasjɔnal, ɛ̃tɛrnasjɔno] international
interrogatoire *m.* [ɛ̃tɛrɔgatwa:r] interrogation
interroger [ɛ̃tɛrɔʒe] to question
interrompre [ɛ̃tɛrɔ̃:pr] to interrupt
interruption *f.* [ɛ̃tɛrypsjɔ̃] interruption
intituler [ɛ̃tityle] to entitle
intrigué [ɛ̃trige] intrigued

introduire [ɛ̃trɔdɥir] to introduce, usher in; **s'—** to get in, present oneself
inutilisé [inytilize] unused
invasion *f.* [ɛ̃vazjɔ̃] invasion
invitation *f.* [ɛ̃vitasjɔ̃] invitation
invité *m.* [ɛ̃vite] invited guest
inviter [ɛ̃vite] to invite
irrésistible [irezistibl] irresistible
irriter [irite] to irritate, annoy
isolé [izɔle] isolated
Italie *f.* [itali] Italy
italien (*f.* **italienne**) [italjɛ̃, italjɛn] Italian

J

Jacques [ʒɑk] James
jalousie *f.* [ʒaluzi] jealousy
jaloux (*f.* **jalouse**) [ʒalu, ʒaluːz] jealous
jamais [ʒamɛ] ever, never; (*with* **ne** *before verb*) never
jambe *f.* [ʒɑ̃ːb] leg
jambon *m.* [ʒɑ̃bɔ̃] ham; **œufs au —** ham and eggs
janvier *m.* [ʒɑ̃vje] January
Japon *m.* [ʒapɔ̃] Japan
japonais [ʒapɔnɛ] Japanese
jaquette *f.* [ʒakɛt] coat, jacket
jardin *m.* [ʒardɛ̃] garden; **Jardin des Plantes** Botanical Gardens
jaune [ʒoːn] yellow
je, j' [ʒə] I
jeter [ʒəte] to throw; **se —** to jump
jeu *m.* [ʒø] play, game
jeudi *m.* [ʒødi] Thursday
jeune [ʒœn] young; **— fille** *f.* girl; **—s gens** *m. pl.* young men, young people
jeûner [ʒøne] to fast
joie *f.* [ʒwa] joy
joindre [ʒwɛ̃dr] to join, unite; **se — à** to join
joli [ʒɔli] pretty
jongler [ʒɔ̃gle] to juggle
jongleur *m.* [ʒɔ̃glœːr] juggler
joue *f.* [ʒu] cheek
jouer [ʒwe] to play; **— à** to play (a game); **— de** to play (an instrument)
jouet *m.* [ʒwɛ] toy
jouir de [ʒwiːr də] to enjoy
jour *m.* [ʒuːr] day; **en plein —** in broad daylight; **tous les —s** every day; **quinze —s** fortnight
journal *m.* (*pl.* **journaux**) [ʒurnal, ʒurno] newspaper
journaliste *m.* [ʒurnalist] journalist
journée *f.* [ʒurne] day
journellement [ʒurnɛlmɑ̃] daily, every day
juge *m.* [ʒyʒ] judge
jugement *m.* [ʒyʒmɑ̃] opinion, judgment
juger [ʒyʒe] to judge
juillet *m.* [ʒɥijɛ] July
juin *m.* [ʒyɛ̃] June
jupon *m.* [ʒypɔ̃] skirt, petticoat
juré [ʒyre] sworn
jurer [ʒyre] to swear
jus *m.* [ʒy] juice
jusqu'à [ʒyska] as far as, up to, until; **jusqu'ici** until now; **jusqu'à ce que** until
juste [ʒyst] just, right, correct
justement [ʒystəmɑ̃] just, precisely, simply
justifier [ʒystifje] to vindicate, clear, justify

K

kilomètre *m.* [kilɔmɛtr] kilometer
klaxon *m.* [klaksɔ̃] horn (*automobile*)

L

là [la] there (*pointing out*); **par —** that way
là-bas [labɑ] over there, down there
laboratoire *m.* [labɔratwaːr] laboratory
laborieux (*f.* **laborieuse**) [labɔrjø, labɔrjøːz] industrious, hard-working
lac *m.* [lak] lake
lâche *m.* [lɑːʃ] coward
lâche [lɑːʃ] cowardly
là-dedans [ladədɑ̃] therein
là-haut [lao] up there
laid [lɛ] ugly
laine *f.* [lɛn] wool
laisser [lɛse] to leave (behind); **se — conduire** to let oneself be led
laissez-passer *m* [lɛsepɑse] permit
laissez passer! [lɛsepɑse] gangway!
lait *m.* [lɛ] milk
laitue *f.* [lɛty] lettuce

lame *f.* [lam] blade; **— de rasoir** razor blade
lampe *f.* [lɑ̃p] lamp, tube (of radio)
lance à feu *f.* [lɑ̃safø] slow match
lancer [lɑ̃se] to hurl, throw
langage *m.* [lɑ̃ga:z] language
lange *m.* [lɑ̃ʒ] **les —s** swaddling clothes
langue *f.* [lɑ̃g] language, tongue
lanterne *f.* [lɑ̃tɛrn] lantern
laquais *m.* [lakɛ] footman, lackey
laquelle [lakɛl] (*see* **lequel**)
lard *m.* [la:r] bacon
larder [larde] to lard
large [larʒ] wide (*not* large); **— des épaules** wide in the shoulders
larme *f.* [larm] tear
las (*f.* **lasse**) [lɑ, lɑ:s] tired, weary
lassitude *f.* [lɑsityd] lassitude
latin *m.* [latɛ̃] Latin
lavabo *m.* [lavabo] lavatory, wash-basin
laver [lave] to wash; **se —** to wash
Laurent [lɔrɑ̃] Lawrence
le, l', la, les [lə, l, la, le] the
le [lə] him, it
lecture *f.* [lɛkty:r] reading
ledit [lədi] the said, the same
léger (*f.* **légère**) [leʒe, leʒɛ:r) light (in weight), giddy
légèrement [leʒɛrmɑ̃] lightly, slightly
légume *m.* [legym] vegetable
lendemain *m.* [lɑ̃dmɛ̃] next day
lent [lɑ̃] slow
lentement [lɑ̃tmɑ̃] slowly
lequel (**laquelle, lesquels, lesquelles**) [ləkɛl, lakɛl, lekɛl, lekɛl] which, which one, which ones, who, whom
lestement [lɛstəmɑ̃] quickly
lettre *f.* [lɛtr] letter; **boîte aux —s** *f.* letter box; **papier à —s** *m.* writing paper
leur(**s**) [lœ:r] their
leur [lœ:r] to them
lever *m.* [ləve] rising
lever [ləve] to lift, raise; **se —** to get up
lèvre *f.* [lɛvr] lip; **bâton de rouge pour les —s** *m.* lipstick
libération *f.* [liberasjɔ̃] liberation
liberté *f.* [libɛrte] freedom, liberty
libre [libr] free
lier [lje] to tie
lieu *m.* (*pl.* **lieux**) [ljø] place, spot; **au — de** instead of
lieutenant *m.* [ljøtnɑ̃] lieutenant
lièvre *m.* [ljɛ:vr] hare
ligne *f.* [liɲ] line
linge *m.* [lɛ̃ʒ] linen
liqueur *f.* [likœ:r] liquor, liqueur, cordial
lire (*p.p.* **lu**) [li:r, ly] to read
lit *m.* [li] bed
litre *m.* [litr] liter (*about one quart*)
littérature *f.* [literaty:r] literature
livraison *f.* [livrɛzɔ̃] delivery
livre *m.* [li:vr] book
livrer [livre] to deliver
loge *m.* [lɔʒ] apartment, box (at theater)
logis *m.* [lɔʒi] lodging
loi *f.* [lwa] law
loin [lwɛ̃] far, far away; **— de** far from; **plus —** farther on
lointain [lwɛ̃tɛ̃] distant, remote
loisir *m.* [lwazi:r] leisure
Londres [lɔ̃:dr] London
long: le — de [ləlɔ̃də] along
long (*f.* **longue**) [lɔ̃, lɔ̃g] long; **chaise-longue** *f.* lounging chair or couch
longtemps [lɔ̃tɑ̃] a long time
longuement [lɔ̃gmɑ̃] at length, a long time
loquacité *f.* [lɔkwasite] talkativeness, loquacity
lorgner [lɔrɲe] to eye
lors de [lɔrdə] at the time of
lorsque [lɔrskə] when
louange *f.* [lwɑ̃:ʒ] praise
louer [lwe] to hire, rent
loup *m.* [lu] wolf
lourd [lu:r] heavy, clumsy, gross; (*of weather*) muggy
lourdement [lurdəmɑ̃] heavily
lu [ly] *p.p.* of **lire**
lugubre [lygy:br] dismal, gloomy, pessimistic
lui [lɥi] he, him, himself; **à —** his
lui-même [lɥimɛ:m] he, himself
lumière *f.* [lymjɛ:r] light
lundi *m.* [lœ̃di] Monday, on Monday
lune *f.* [lyn] moon; **clair de —** *m.* moonlight
lunettes *f. pl.* [lynɛt] eyeglasses
lutter [lyte] to struggle, combat
luxe *m.* [lyks] luxury, magnificence

M

ma [ma] my
machinalement [maʃinalmɑ̃] mechanically
machine *f.* [maʃin] machine; **— à écrire** typewriter; **taper à la —** to type
Madame *f.* (*abbrev.* **Mme**) [madam] Madam, Ma'am, Mrs.
mademoiselle *f.* (*abbrev.* **Mlle**) [madmwazɛl] Miss
magasin *m.* [magazɛ̃] store
magique [maʒik] magic
magistrat *m.* [maʒistra] magistrate
magnifique [maɲifik] magnificent
mai *m.* [mɛ] May
maigre [mɛːgr] meager, slim
maigreur *f.* [mɛgrœːr] leanness
main *f.* [mɛ̃] hand; **sac à —** *m.* handbag; **se serrer la —** to shake hands
maintenant [mɛ̃tnɑ̃] now
maintenir [mɛ̃tniːr] to maintain
mais [mɛ] but; (*exclam.*) why!
maison *f.* [mɛzɔ̃] house; **Maison des Étudiantes** girls' dormitory; **— de santé** *f.* sanitarium
maisonnette *f.* [mɛzɔnɛt] cottage, lodge
maître *m.* [mɛːtr] master; **— d'hôtel** steward, major-domo, headwaiter
majeur [maʒœːr] of age
majuscule *f.* [maʒyskyl] capital letter
mal *m.* (*pl.* **maux**) [mal, mo] harm, evil, trouble, illness; **avoir — à...** to have a ...ache; **faire — à** to hurt
mal [mal] badly, poorly, ill
malade *m.*, *f.* [malad] patient
malade [malad] ill, sick
maladie *f.* [maladi] illness
malédiction *f.* [malediksjɔ̃] curse
malentendu *m.* [malɑ̃tɑ̃dy] misunderstanding
malfaiteur *m.* [malfɛtœːr] evildoer, malefactor
malgré [malgre] in spite of
malheur *m.* [malœːr] misfortune
malheureux *m.* [malœrø] unfortunate one
malheureux (*f.* **malheureuse**) [malœrø, malœrøːz] unfortunate
malheureusement [malœrøzmɑ̃] unfortunately
malle *f.* [mal] trunk
manche *f.* [mɑ̃ʃ] sleeve; **en —s de chemise** in shirt sleeves
manchette *f.* [mɑ̃ʃɛt] cuff; **bouton de —** cuff link
mandat-poste *m.* (*pl.* **mandats-poste**) [mɑ̃dapɔst] money order
manger [mɑ̃ʒe] to eat; **salle à —** dining room
mangeur *m.* [mɑ̃ʒœːr] eater
manière *f.* [manjɛːr] manner, way, fashion
manquer [mɑ̃ke] to lack, be lacking, miss, be missing; **— de** +*infin.* to fail to do, miss doing, almost
manteau *m.* [mɑ̃to] woman's coat, man's cloak
manuel (*f.* **manuelle**) [manɥɛl] manual
maquillage *m.* [makijaːʒ] make-up
maquiller (se) [səmakije] to paint, make up
marbre *m.* [marbr] marble
marchand *m.* [marʃɑ̃] merchant
marche *f.* [marʃ] walking
marché *m.* [marʃe] market, marketing; **bon —** cheap; **à bon —** cheaply
marchepied *m.* [marʃəpje] step, running board
marcher [marʃe] to go, walk
mardi *m.* [mardi] Tuesday
Marguerite [margərit] Marguerite, Margaret
mari *m.* [mari] husband
mariage *m.* [marjaːʒ] marriage
marier [marje] to marry; **se — (avec)** to marry
marin *m.* [marɛ̃] sailor
marque *f.* [mark] trademark, style, sign, proof, token
marron [mɑrɔ̃] brown
mars *m.* [mars] March
Marseillaise *f.* [marsɛjɛːz] Marseillaise
marteleur *m.* [martəlœːr] hammerer
martyr *m.* [martiːr] martyr
masculin [maskylɛ̃] masculine
massacrer [masakre] to massacre, slaughter
matelas *m.* [matlɑ] mattress
matelot *m.* [matlo] seaman
maternel (*f.* **maternelle**) [matɛrnɛl] maternal
matière *f.* [matjɛːr] matter

matin *m.* [matɛ̃] morning; **le —** in the morning; **du —** in the morning
matinée *f.* [matine] morning
mauvais [mɔvɛ] bad; **faire — (temps)** to be bad (weather)
mayonnaise *f.* [majɔnɛːz] mayonnaise
mécanicien *m.* [mekanisjɛ̃] mechanic
méchant [meʃɑ̃] bad, wicked
mécontentement *m.* [mekɔ̃tɑ̃tmɑ̃] discontent, displeasure, vexation
médecin *m.* [mɛtsɛ̃] physician, doctor
médecine *f.* [mɛtsin] medicine
médicament *m.* [medikamɑ̃] medicine
médiocre [medjɔkr] mediocre
meilleur [mɛjœːr] better, best
mélancolie *f.* [melɑ̃kɔli] melancholy
mélancolique [melɑ̃kɔlik] melancholy
mélange *m.* [melɑ̃ːʒ] mixture, combination
mêlée *f.* [mɛle] scramble, scuffle, confused fight
mêler [mɛle] to mix; **se — de** to meddle with
même (*adj.*) [mɛm] same, self; (*adv.*) even; **aujourd'hui —** this very day; **en être de —** to be the same; **quand —** just the same; **tout de —** just the same, all the same
mémoire *m.* [memwaːr] memorandum, bill of complaint
mémoire *f.* [memwaːr] memory
menaçant [mənasɑ̃] threatening
menace *f.* [mənas] threat, menace
ménagement *m.* [menaʒmɑ̃] care, consideration
mener [məne] to lead, take (a person)
meneur *m.* [mənœːr] leader
mensonge *m.* [mɑ̃sɔ̃ʒ] lie
mental [mɑ̃tal] mental
menthe *f.* [mɑ̃t] mint
mentir [mɑ̃tir] to lie, tell a lie
menton *m.* [mɑ̃tɔ̃] chin
menu *m.* [məny] menu; (*adj.*) little
mépris *m.* [mepri] contempt
mépriser [meprize] to despise
mer *f.* [mɛːr] sea; **bord de la —** *m.* seashore
merci [mɛrsi] thanks, thank you; **— bien** thank you very much; **— infiniment** a million thanks
mercredi *m.* [mɛrkrədi] Wednesday
mère *f.* [mɛːr] mother
mériter [merite] to deserve
merveille *f.* [mɛrvɛːj] wonder, marvel; **à —** wonderfully; **aller à —** to be extremely becoming
merveilleusement [mɛrvɛjøzmɑ̃] marvelously, wonderfully
mes [me] my
messe *f.* [mɛs] mass
messieurs *m. pl.* [mesjø] gentlemen
mesure *f.* [məzyːr] measure; **à — que** in proportion as
mesurer [məzyre] to measure
métamorphose *f.* [mɛtamɔrfoːz] metamorphosis
méthode *f.* [metɔd] method
méticuleux (*f.* **méticuleuse**) [metikylø, metikyløːz] meticulous, scrupulous
métier *m.* [metje] trade, occupation, profession
mètre *m.* [mɛtr] meter (*39 inches*)
Métro *m.* [metro] Paris subway
mettre (*p.p.* **mis**) [mɛtr, mi] to put, place, put on; **— à la porte** to put out; **— à la poste** to mail; **— quelque temps à** +*infinitive* to take some time to; **se —** to put, begin, sit down; **se — à** to begin to, start to; **se — d'accord** to come to an understanding; **se — en colère** to get angry; **se — en route** to start out, set out
meuble *m.* [mœbl] piece of furniture; (*pl.*) furniture
meublé [mœble] furnished
meunière *f.* [mønjɛːr] miller's wife
meurtre *m.* [mœrtr] murder; **au —!** murder!
meurtrier *m.* (*f.* **meurtrière**) [mœrtrie, mœrtriɛr] murderer, murderess
Mexique *m.* [mɛksik] Mexico
midi *m.* [midi] 12 o'clock noon
Midi *m.* [midi] the south (of France)
mien (*f.* **mienne**) [mjɛ̃, mjɛn] mine
mieux (*adv.*) [mjø] better, best; **aimer —** to prefer; **aller —** to be better (in health); **de leur —** to the best of their ability; **tant —** so much the better; **valoir —** to be better
milieu *m.* [miljø] middle, midst; **au — de** in the middle of
militaire *m.* [militɛr] military man
militaire [militɛr] military

mille (**mil** *in dates*) [mil] thousand
milliard (**de**) *m.* [miljaːr də] billion
millier (**de**) *m.* [milje də] thousand
million (**de**) *m.* [miljɔ̃ də] million
mimique *f.* [mimik] mimicry
mince [mɛ̃s] slender, thin
mine *f.* [min] appearance, looks
mine *f.* [min] mine, pit
minime (*adj.*) [minim] very small
ministère *m.* [ministɛːr] ministry, department
ministre *m.* [ministr] minister
minuit *m.* [minɥi] 12 o'clock midnight
minute *f.* [minyt] minute
miroir *m.* [mirwaːr] mirror
mis [mi] *p.p.* of **mettre**
mission *f.* [misjɔ̃] mission
mitrailleuse *f.* [mitrajøːz] machine gun
mocha *m.* [mɔka] coffee sauce
mode *f.* [mɔd] style; **à la —** stylish, popular
modérément [mɔderemɑ̃] moderately, in moderation
moderne [mɔdɛrn] modern
modifier [mɔdifje] to modify, alter
moi [mwa] me, I; **à —** mine; **c'est —** it is I; **chez —** (at) my house
moi-même [mwamɛm] I, myself
moindre [mwɛ̃dr] least
moine *m.* [mwan] monk
moins [mwɛ̃] less, least; **— de** less than; **— que** less than; **à — que** unless; **au —** at least; **du —** at least
mois *m.* [mwɑ] month; **au — de** (**février**) in (February)
moitié *f.* [mwatje] half, better half, helpmate
moment *m.* [mɔmɑ̃] moment
mon (**ma, mes**) [mɔ̃, ma, me] my; **mon vieux** old man, my friend
monastère *m.* [mɔnastɛːr] monastery
monastique [mɔnastik] monastic
monde *m.* [mɔ̃d] people, world; **du —** in the world; **tout le —** everybody
monnaie *f.* [mɔnɛ] change (*money*), coin; **la petite —** small change
monomanie *f.* [mɔnɔmani] monomania
monsieur *m.* (*abbrev.* **M.**) [məsjø] sir, gentleman, Mr.
monstre *m.* [mɔ̃str] monster
monstruosité *f.* [mɔ̃stryozite] monstrosity
montagne *f.* [mɔ̃taɲ] mountain
monter [mɔ̃te] (*conjug. with* **être**) to go up, climb, get in, mount
montre *f.* [mɔ̃tr] watch
montrer [mɔ̃tre] to show; **se —** to appear
moquer (**se**) **de** [sə mɔke də] to laugh at, make fun of
morceau (*pl.* **morceaux**) [mɔrso] piece
mordre [mɔrdr] to bite
mort *m.* [mɔːr] dead person
mort [mɔːr] *p.p.* of **mourir**; (*adj.*) dead
morue *f.* [mɔry] codfish
mot *m.* [mo] word
moteur *m.* [mɔtœːr] motor
motif *m.* [mɔtif] motive, reason
moto *f.* [mɔto] motorcycle
motocyclette *f.* [mɔtɔsiklɛt] motorcycle
motorisé [mɔtɔrize] motorized, mechanized
mou (**mol** *before a vowel*; *f.* **molle**; *m. pl.* **mous**; *f. pl.* **molles**) [mu, mɔl, mɔl, mu, mɔl] soft
mouchoir *m.* [muʃwaːr] handkerchief
mouillé [muje] wet
mouiller [muje] to anchor, wet
moulin *m.* [mulɛ̃] mill
mourant [murɑ̃] *pres. p.* of **mourir** dying
mourir (*p.p.* **mort**; *pres. p.* **mourant**) [muriːr, mɔːr, murɑ̃] to die
mousqueterie *f.* [muskətri] musketry
moustache *f.* [mustaʃ] mustache
moustachu [mustaʃy] with a mustache
mouton *m.* [mutɔ̃] mutton
mouvement *m.* [muvmɑ̃] gesture, motion, movement
moyen *m.* [mwajɛ̃] way, means; **au — de** by means of
moyenne *f.* [mwajɛn] average
muet [mɥɛ] dumb, speechless, mute
multicolore [myltikɔlɔr] multicolored
munitions *f. pl.* [mynisjɔ̃] ammunition
mur *m.* [myːr] wall
mûr [myːr] mature, ripe
murmurer [myrmyre] to murmur
musée *m.* [myze] museum
Musulman [myzylmɑ̃] Mohammedan

mutilé [mytile] mutilated
mutisme *m.* [mytism] dumbness, speechlessness
myope [mjɔp] near-sighted
mystère *m.* [mistɛːr] mystery
mystérieux (*f.* **mystérieuse**) [misterjø, misterjøːz] mysterious

N

nage: être en — [ɛtrɑ̃naːʒ] to be dripping with perspiration
nager [naʒe] to swim
naïf (*f.* **naïve**) [naif, naiːv] simple, guileless
naissance *f.* [nɛsɑ̃ːs] birth; **anniversaire de —** birthday
naître (*p.p.* **né**) [nɛːtr, ne] to be born
nappe *f.* [nap] tablecloth
natation *f.* [natasjɔ̃] swimming
nation *f.* [nasjɔ̃] nation
national (*pl.* **nationaux**) [nasjɔnal, nasjɔno] national (of a country)
nature *f.* [natyːr] nature
naturel (*f.* **naturelle**) [natyrɛl] natural
naturellement [natyrɛlmɑ̃] naturally, of course
né [ne] *p.p.* of **naître** born
ne [nə] no, not; **—...jamais** never, not ever; **—...ni...ni** neither...nor, not...either...or; **— (n')...pas** not; **—...pas grand' chose** not much; **—...personne** no one, nobody, not anyone, not anybody; **—...point** not (*emphatic*), not at all; **—...que** not...but, not...except, only; **—...rien** nothing, not anything
néanmoins [neɑ̃mwɛ̃] nevertheless
nécessaire [necɛsɛːr] necessary
négatif *m.* [negatif] negative
négliger [negliʒe] to neglect
neige *f.* [nɛːʒ] snow
neiger [neʒe] to snow
nerf *m.* [nɛːr] nerve
net (*f.* **nette**) [nɛt, nɛt] clear, short
nettement [nɛtmɑ̃] clearly
neuf (*f.* **neuve**) [nœf, nœːv] new
neuf [nœf] nine
neveu *m.* [nəvø] nephew
nez *m.* [ne] nose
ni [ni] neither, nor
nièce *f.* [njɛs] niece
nier [nie] to deny
noble [nɔbl] noble
noblesse *f.* [nɔblɛs] nobility, rank
Noël *f.* or *m.* [nɔɛl] Christmas
noir [nwaːr] dark, black
noix *f.* [nwa] nut, walnut, kernel
nom *m.* [nɔ̃] name, noun
nombre *m.* [nɔ̃ːbr] number
nombreux (*f.* **nombreuse**) [nɔ̃brø, nɔ̃brøːz] numerous
nommer [nɔme] to name
non [nɔ̃] no
non plus [nɔ̃ ply] either, neither
nord *m.* [nɔr] north
normand [nɔrmɑ̃] Norman
Normandie *f.* [nɔrmɑ̃di] Normandy
norme *f.* [nɔrm] standard
Norvège *f.* [nɔrvɛʒ] Norway
nos *pl.* [no] our
notable *m.* [nɔtabl] prominent citizen
notaire *m.* [nɔtɛr] notary
note *f.* [nɔt] note; **une — suffisante** passing mark; **prendre — de** to make note of
noter [nɔte] to notice
notion *f.* [nosjɔ̃] notion
notre (*pl.* **nos**) [nɔtr, no] our
nôtre [noːtr] ours
noueux (*f.* **noueuse**) [nuø, nuøːz] knotty, gnarled
nourriture *f.* [nurityːr] nourishment, food
nous [nu] we, us, (to) us, (to) ourselves; **— autres** we (*emphatic*); **—-mêmes** (we) ourselves
nouveau (**nouvel** *before a vowel*; *f.* **nouvelle**; *m. pl.* **nouveaux**; *f. pl.* **nouvelles**) [nuvo, nuvɛl, nuvɛl, nuvo, nuvɛl] new; **de —** again; **c'est du —** that's new
nouveau-né [nuvone] newborn child, newborn
nouvelle *f.* [nuvɛl] a piece of news; **nouvelles** *f. pl.* news; **avoir des — de** to have heard from, have news of; **donnez-moi de vos —s** let me hear from you
Nouvelle Année *f.* [nuvɛlane] New Year
novembre *m.* [nɔvɑ̃ːbr] November
noyer *m.* [nwaje] walnut
noyer [nwaje] to drown

nu [ny] bare; **—-tête** bare-headed
nuage *m.* [nɥa:ʒ] cloud
nuit *f.* [nɥi] night; **bonne —** good night; **chemise de —** *f.* nightgown; **la —** at night; **tombée de la —** *f.* nightfall
nul (*f.* **nulle**) [nyl] no, none at all
numéro *m.* [nymero] number

O

obéir (**à**) [ɔbeira] to obey
objet *m.* [ɔbʒɛ] object
obligeamment [ɔbliʒamɑ̃] kindly, obligingly
obligeant [ɔbliʒɑ̃] obliging, agreeable
obliger [ɔbliʒe] to oblige, force, compel
obscur [ɔpsky:r] dark
obscurité *f.* [ɔpskyrite] darkness
observer [ɔpsɛrve] to observe, look at
obstiné [ɔpstine] obstinate, stubborn
obtenir [ɔptənir] to get, obtain
obus *m.* [ɔby] shell (*cannon*)
occasion *f.* [ɔkazjɔ̃] opportunity
occident *m.* [ɔksidɑ̃] west
occidental (*m. pl.* **occidentaux**) [ɔksidɑ̃tal, ɔksidɑ̃to] western
occupé [ɔkype] busy
occuper [ɔkype] to occupy; **s'— de** to be busy with, apply oneself to, attend to
octobre *m.* [ɔktɔbr] October
œil *m.* (*pl.* **yeux**) [œ:j, jø] eye
œillet *m.* [œjɛ] carnation
œuf *m.* [œf] *pl.* [ø] egg; **des —s au jambon** ham and eggs
œuvre *f.* [œ:vr] work, piece of work
offenser [ɔfɑ̃se] to offend, insult
offert [ɔfɛr] *p.p.* of **offrir**
officiellement [ɔfisjɛlmɑ̃] officially
officier *m.* [ɔfisje] officer
offrir (*p.p.* **offert**) [ɔfri:r, ɔfɛr] to offer, treat
oie *f.* [wa] goose
oignon *m.* [ɔɲɔ̃] onion
oiseau *m.* (*pl.* **oiseaux**) [wazo] bird
ombre *f.* [ɔ̃:br] shadow, shade; **à l'— de** in the shade of
omettre [ɔmɛtr] to omit
omnibus *m.* [ɔmnibys] local (train)
on [ɔ̃] one, they, people, we, you, they (*indefinite*); **— m'a dit** somebody told me, I have been told
oncle *m.* [ɔ̃:kl] uncle
onde *f.* [ɔ̃:d] wave
ongle *m.* [ɔ̃:gl] nail (*finger*)
onze [ɔ̃:z] eleven
opéra *m.* [ɔpera] opera
opérer [ɔpere] to operate
opinion *f.* [ɔpinjɔ̃] opinion
or *m.* [ɔr] gold
or [ɔr] now
orange [ɔrɑ̃:ʒ] orange-colored
orchidée *f.* [ɔrkide] orchid
ordinaire [ɔrdinɛ:r] ordinary, usual; **d'—** usually
ordonnance *f.* [ɔrdɔnɑ̃:s] prescription
ordonner [ɔrdɔne] to order, command
ordre *m.* [ɔrdr] order, command
oreille *f.* [ɔrɛj] ear
oreiller *m.* [ɔrɛje] pillow
organiser (**s'**) [sɔrganize] to organize
orgueil *m.* [ɔrgœ:j] pride
orient *m.* [ɔrjɑ̃] east
orpheline *f.* [ɔrfəlin] orphaned, orphan girl
orthodoxe [ɔrtɔdɔks] orthodox, Orthodox
os *m.* [ɔs] bone
oser [oze] to dare
ôtage *m.* [ɔta:ʒ] hostage
ôter [ote] to take off, to take away
otite *f.* [ɔtit] otitis (*medical*)
où [u] where; **— en suis-je de** where have I got with? **par —** which way?
ou [u] or; **—...—** either...or; **— bien** or else
oubli *m.* [ubli] omission, forgetfulness
oublier [ublie] to forget
ouest *m.* [wɛst] west
oui [wi] yes; **mais —** why, yes
ouvert [uvɛr] (*p.p.* of **ouvrir**) open, opened
ouverture *f.* [uvɛrty:r] opening
ouvrage *m.* [uvra:ʒ] work
ouvrier *m.* [uvrie] laborer, workman
ouvrir (*p.p.* **ouvert**) [uvri:r, uvɛr] to open

P

pacifique [pasifik] peaceful
pain *m.* [pɛ̃] bread
paire *f.* [pɛ:r] pair
paix *f.* [pɛ] peace
palais *m.* [palɛ] palace

pâle [pɑl] pale
pâlir [pɑliːr] to grow pale
palissade *f.* [palisad] palisade
panier *m.* [panje] basket
panne *f.* [pan] breakdown (*auto*)
pansement *m.* [pɑ̃smɑ̃] bandage
pantalon *m.* [pɑ̃talɔ̃] pants, trousers
pantoufle *f.* [pɑ̃tufl] slipper
papeterie *f.* [papətri] stationery store
papier *m.* [papje] paper; **— à lettres** writing paper; **— de soie** tissue paper
paquet *m.* [pakɛ] package
par [par] by, by means of, through, via, across, per, each, in, on, around, with, for, during, at, about, out of; **— conséquent** consequently; **— exemple** for instance; **— exemple!** the very idea! I declare! **— ici** this way; **— jour** per day; **— là** that way; **— où?** which way? **— terre** on the (ground) floor; **— tous les temps** in all sorts of weather; **commencer —** to begin with
parade *f.* [parad] parade
paragraphe *m.* [paragraf] paragraph
paraître [parɛːtr] to appear, seem
parapet *m.* [parapɛ] parapet
parapluie *m.* [paraplɥi] umbrella
parc *m.* [park] park
parce que (qu') [pars(ə)kə] because
pardessus *m.* [pardəsy] overcoat
pardon *m.* [pardɔ̃] pardon; pardon! pardon me!
pareil (*f.* **pareille**) [parɛj] such, similar
parent *m.* [parɑ̃] relative; *pl.* parents, relatives
paresseux (*f.* **paresseuse**) [parɛsø, parɛsøːz] lazy
parfait [parfɛ] perfect; **parfait!** that's perfect!
parfaitement [parfɛtmɑ̃] perfectly
parfois [parfwa] at times
parfum *m.* [parfœ̃] perfume
parfumé [parfyme] perfumed
parier [parje] to bet
parisien (*f.* **parisienne**) [parizjɛ̃, parizjɛn] Parisian
parler [parle] to speak
parmi [parmi] among
parole *f.* [parɔl] word, speech, language
part *f.* [paːr] part; **à —** aside; **c'est très gentil de** (**votre**) **—** it's very kind of (you); **de la — de** from; **quelque —** somewhere
partager [partaʒe] to share
parti *m.* [parti] resolution, side, match; **prendre son —** to make up one's mind
participe *m.* [partisip] participle
particulier [partikylje] particular, peculiar, private (room)
partie *f.* [parti] part; **faire — de** to form or be part of
partir [partiːr] to leave, depart; **— en tournée** to go on the road; **à — de** beginning with
partout [partu] everywhere
parvenir [parvəniːr] to succeed
pas *m.* [pɑ] step, pace
pas [pɑ] no, not any, not; **ne...—** not; **— du tout** not at all; **— encore** not yet; **— possible!** impossible! you don't say so!
passablement [pɑsabləmɑ̃] passably
passage *m.* [pɑsaːʒ] passage
passant *m.* [pɑsɑ̃] passer-by
passé *m.* [pɑse] past; **— composé** past indefinite (*tense*); **— défini** past definite (*tense*)
passeport *m.* [pɑspɔːr] passport
passer [pɑse] to spend (time), to pass; **se —** to happen
passerelle *f.* [pɑsrɛl] gangplank
passionnant [pɑsjɔnɑ̃] exciting
pâte *f.* [pɑːt] paste, dough; **— dentifrice** toothpaste
pâté *m.* [pɑte] pie, pasty
pâté de foie gras *m.* [pɑte də fwa grɑ] goose-liver paste
paternel (*f.* **paternelle**) [patɛrnɛl] paternal
patience *f.* [pasjɑ̃ːs] patience
pâtissier *m.* [pɑtisje] pastry cook
patron *m.* [patrɔ̃] boss
patte *f.* [pat] paw
pauvre [poːvr] poor
pavé *m.* [pave] pavement
pavillon *m.* [pavijɔ̃] wing (*of building*)
payer [pɛje] to pay, pay for; **— comptant** to pay cash
pays *m.* [pei] country, countryside
paysage *m.* [peizaːʒ] landscape

paysan *m.* [peizɑ̃] peasant
peau *f.* [po] skin
pêche *f.* [pɛːʃ] peach
pêcher [pɛʃe] to fish; **— à la ligne** to angle
peigne *m.* [pɛɲ] comb
peindre (*p.p.* **peint**) [pɛ̃dr, pɛ̃] to paint
peine *f.* [pɛn] trouble, sorrow, difficulty; **à —** barely, hardly, scarcely; **ça n'en vaut pas la —** it is not worth while; **valoir la —** to be worth while
peint [pɛ̃] *p.p.* of **peindre** painted
peinture *f.* [pɛ̃tyːr] painting, picture
peloton *m.* [plɔtɔ̃] platoon
pelouse *f.* [pluːz] lawn
pendant [pɑ̃dɑ̃] during
pendant que [pɑ̃dɑ̃kə] while
pendre [pɑ̃ːdr] to hang
pendule *f.* [pɑ̃dyl] clock
pénétrer [penetre] to penetrate
pénible [penibl] troublesome, painful
péniblement [peniblәmɑ̃] painfully
péninsule *f.* [penɛ̃syl] peninsula
pensée *f.* [pɑ̃se] thought
penser [pɑ̃se] to think; **— à** to think of; **— de** to have an opinion about
pension *f.* [pɑ̃sjɔ̃] board; **— de famille** boardinghouse
pensionnaire *m.* [pɑ̃sjɔnɛːr] boarder, patient
percer [pɛrse] to pierce, show, appear
perdre [pɛrdr] to lose, ruin; **se —** to lose one's way
perdrix *f.* [pɛrdri] partridge
père *m.* [pɛr] father
perfection *f.* [pɛrfɛksjɔ̃] perfection
périlleux (*f.* **périlleuse**) [perijø, perijøːz] dangerous, perilous
permanent [pɛrmanɑ̃] permanent
permettre (de) (*p.p.* **permis**) [pɛrmɛtr dә, pɛrmi] to permit, allow to
permis [pɛrmi] *p.p.* of **permettre**
permis *m.* [pɛrmi] permit, license; **— de conduire** driving permit
Pérou *m.* [peru] Peru
persil *m.* [pɛrsi] parsley
persister [pɛrsiste] to persist
personnage *m.* [pɛrsɔnaːʒ] personage, character
personne *f.* [pɛrsɔn] person, nobody; **—** (*with* **ne**) nobody
personnel (*f.* **personnelle**) [pɛrsɔnɛl] personal
persuader [pɛrsɥade] to persuade
perte *f.* [pɛrt] loss
petit *m.* [pәti] little one
petit [pәti] little small; **— à —** little by little
petit-fils *m.* [pәtifis] grandson
petit-four *m.* [pәtifur] small cake
petit pain *m.* [pәtipɛ̃] roll (*bread*)
petite-fille *f.* [pәtitfij] granddaughter
petits pois *m. pl.* [pәtipwɑ] peas (*green*)
pétrole *m.* [petrɔl] petroleum oil
peu *m.* [pø] a little, a while; **— à —** little by little
peu (de) (*adv.*) [pø dә] little (of), few (of); **à — près** more or less
peuple *m.* [pœːpl] crowd, multitude
peur *f.* [pœːr] fear; **avoir —** to be afraid; **de — de** for fear of; **de — que** for fear that
peureux (*f.* **peureuse**) [pœrø, pœrøːz] timid, fearful
peut-être [pøtɛːtr] maybe, perhaps
phare *m.* [faːr] headlight
pharmacie *f.* [farmasi] drugstore
pharmacien *m.* [farmasjɛ̃] pharmacist
Philippe [filip] Philip
phrase *f.* [frɑːz] sentence
physionomie *f.* [fizjɔnɔmi] facial features, physiognomy
physique *f.* [fizik] physical science
piailler [pjɑje] to screech, bawl, rant, scold
piano *m.* [pjano] piano
pièce *f.* [pjɛs] room, piece, play (*theatrical*)
pied *m.* [pje] foot; **à —** on foot; **doigt de —** toe
piège *m.* [pjɛːʒ] trap
pierre *f.* [pjɛːr] stone
Pierre [pjɛːr] Peter
pilon *m.* [pilɔ̃] stump
pilote *m.* [pilɔt] pilot
pilule *f.* [pilyl] pill
pin *m.* [pɛ̃] pine
pincée *f.* [pɛ̃se] pinch
pion *m.* [pjɔ̃] monitor
pipe *f.* [pip] pipe
piquant [pikɑ̃] sharp
pique-nique *m.* [piknik] picnic

pire (*adj.*) [pir] worse, worst
pis (*adv.*) [pi] worse, worst; **tant —** so much the worse
piscine *f.* [pisin] pool
pistolet *m.* [pistɔlɛ] pistol
pitié *f.* [pitje] pity
pittoresque [pitɔrɛsk] picturesque
placard *m.* [plakar] closet
place *f.* [plas] place, square, grades (*school*)
placer [plase] to place, put, set
plage *f.* [pla:ʒ] beach
plaider [plɛde] to plead
plaideur *m.* [plɛdœ:r] litigant
plaignant *m.* [plɛɲɑ̃] plaintiff
plaindre [plɛ̃dr] to pity; **se —** to complain
plaine *f.* [plɛn] plain
plaire (*p.p.* **plu**) [plɛr, ply] to please; **se —** like, enjoy oneself; **s'il vous plaît** please, if you please
plaisanter [plɛzɑ̃te] to joke, make fun of
plaisanterie *f.* [plɛzɑ̃tri] joke
plaisir *m.* [plɛzi:r] pleasure; **faire —** to please, do a favor; **cela me fait grand —** that gives me great pleasure
plan *m.* [plɑ̃] plan
plancher *m.* [plɑ̃ʃe] floor
planchette *f.* [plɑ̃ʃɛt] shelf
Plantes: Jardin des — *m.* [ʒardɛ̃ de plɑ̃t] Botanical Gardens
plat *m.* [pla] dish
plat [pla] flat; **être à —** to have a flat tire
plein (**de**) [plɛ̃də] full (of), filled (with); **en — air** outdoors, in the open air; **en — jour** in broad daylight
pleurer [plœre] to weep, cry
pleuvoir [plœvwa:r] to rain; **— à verse** to pour (rain)
pli *m.* [pli] hollow, fold
plombage *m.* [plɔ̃ba:ʒ] filling (*tooth*)
plomber [plɔ̃be] to fill
plongeon *m.* [plɔ̃ʒɔ̃] dive
plonger [plɔ̃ʒe] to plunge, dive; **se —** to rush
plu [ply] *p.p.* of **plaire**
pluie *f.* [plɥi] rain
plume *f.* [plym] pen, feather, plume
plupart: la — *f.* [laplypa:r] the most, majority
pluriel *m.* [plyrjɛl] plural
plus (**de**) [plydə] more; **— loin** further on; **— que** (or **de**) more than; **au — tôt** as soon as possible; **de —** more, furthermore, in addition, besides; **tout au —** at the very most
plusieurs [plyzjœ:r] several; **à — reprises** repeatedly
plutôt [plyto] rather
pneu *m.* [pnø] tire; **— de rechange** spare tire
pneumonie *f.* [pnømɔni] pneumonia
poche *f.* [pɔʃ] pocket
poème *m.* [pɔɛm] poem
poésie *f.* [pɔezi] poetry
poignée *f.* [pwaɲe] handle, handful
poignet *m.* [pwaɲɛ) wrist
poil *m.* [pwal] hair
point: ne — [nə pwɛ̃] not at all
point *m.* [pwɛ̃] point, period (*grammatical*); **au — de vue** from the point of view
pointe *f.* [pwɛ̃t] **barbe en —** *f.* pointed beard
pointu [pwɛ̃ty] pointed, peaked
pointure *f.* [pwɛ̃ty:r] size
poire *f.* [pwa:r] pear
pois *m. pl.* [pwa] peas; **— de senteur** sweet peas; **petits —** peas
poisson *m.* [pwasɔ̃] fish
poitrine *f.* [pwatrin] breast, chest
poivre *m.* [pwa:vr] pepper
poli [pɔli] polite
police *f.* [pɔlis] police; **commissaire de —** *m.* police commissioner
policier (*adj.*) (*f.* **policière**) [pɔlisje, pɔlisjɛr] police, detective; **roman —** *m.* detective story
politesse *f.* [pɔlitɛs] politeness, courtesy, favor
politique *f.* [pɔlitik] politics, policy
politique [pɔlitik] political
Pologne *f.* [pɔlɔɲ] Poland
pomme *f.* [pɔm] apple; **— de terre** potato
pommier *m.* [pɔmje] apple tree
ponctuel (*f.* **ponctuelle**) [pɔ̃ktɥɛl] punctual
pont *m.* [pɔ̃] bridge, deck
population *f.* [pɔpylasjɔ̃] population
porcelaine *f.* [pɔrsəlɛn] porcelain
port *m.* [pɔ:r] port, harbor

porte *f.* [pɔrt] door; **mettre à la —** to put out
porte-allumette *m.* [pɔrtalymɛt] match holder
portée *f.* [pɔrte] range, shot (*of weapon*)
portefeuille *m.* [pɔrtəfœːj] wallet
portemanteau *m.* [pɔrtmɑ̃to] coat rack
porte-mine *m.* [pɔrtəmin] automatic pencil
porte-monnaie *m.* [pɔrtmɔnɛ] change purse
porter [pɔrte] to carry, wear; **se —** to be (*health*)
porteur *m.* [pɔrtœːr] porter
portière *f.* [pɔrtjɛr] compartment door, cab door
portion *f.* [porsjɔ̃] portion
Portugal *m.* [pɔrtygal] Portugal
poser [poze] to place, put down; **— une question** to ask a question
position *f.* [pozisjɔ̃] position
posséder [pɔsede] to own, possess
possessif (*f.* **possessive**) [pɔsɛsif, pɔsɛsiːv] possessive
possession *f.* [pɔsɛsjɔ̃] possession
possible [pɔsibl] possible; **faire (son) —** to do (his) best; **le plus tôt —** as soon as possible
postal [pɔstal] postal; **carte —e** *f.* post card
poste *m.* [pɔst] post; **— de radio** radio set; **— d'émission** radio station
poste *f.* [pɔst] post office; **— restante** general delivery; **mettre à la —** to mail
poster [pɔste] to post
posté [pɔste] posted
pot *m.* [po] pot, jar
potage *m.* [pɔtaːʒ] soup
poteau indicateur *m.* [pɔto ɛ̃dikatœːr] signpost
pouce *m.* [pus] thumb
poudre *f.* [pudr] powder
poulailler *m.* [pulaje] chicken coop
poule *f.* [pul] hen
poulet *m.* [pulɛ] chicken
pouls *m.* [pu] pulse; **tâter le —** to feel the pulse
poumon *m.* [pumɔ̃] lung
poupée *f.* [pupe] doll
pour [pur] for, in order to, to; **bon —** kind to; **— que** in order that, so that
pourboire *m.* [purbwaːr] tip
pourquoi ? [purkwa] why?
pourri [puri] rotten
poursuivre [pursɥivr] to pursue
pourtant [purtɑ̃] however, nevertheless
pourvu que [purvykə] provided
pousser [puse] to grow, push, utter
poussière *f.* [pusjɛr] dust
pouvoir (*p.p.* **pu**) [puvwaːr, py] can, be able; **cela se peut** that may be; **puis-je ?** may I?
praticable [pratikabl] passable, accessible
pré *m.* [pre] field, meadow
précéder [presede] to precede
précieux (*f.* **précieuse**) [presjø, presjøːz] precious
précipiter [presipite] to rush, dash, plunge
précisément [presizemɑ̃] precisely, just
préférence *f.* [preferɑ̃ːs] preference
préférer [prefere] to prefer
préliminaire [preliminɛːr] preliminary
premier (*f.* **première**) [prəmje, prəmjɛːr] first; **le — étage** one flight up, second floor
prémunir [premynir] to forewarn, fortify, secure
prendre (*p.p.* **pris**) [prɑ̃dr, pri] to take; **s'y —** to go about it; **y être pris** to be taken in; **— congé de** to take leave of; **— note de** to make a note of; **— son parti** to make up one's mind; **— un bain** to bathe; **— un billet** to buy a ticket; **prenez garde!** watch out! **je le prends** I'll take it
préoccuper (se) [səpreɔkype] to worry
préparer [prepare] to prepare
près de [prɛdə] near; **à peu —** more or less; **tout —** very near, very close
présager [prezaʒe] to bode
pré-salé: gigot de — *m.* [ʒigo də presale] choice leg of lamb
presbytère *m.* [prɛzbitɛːr] parsonage, vicarage
présence *f.* [prezɑ̃ːs] presence
présent *m.* [prezɑ̃] present
présentation *f.* [prezɑ̃tasjɔ̃] introduction

présenter [prezɑ̃te] to introduce; **— ses hommages à** to pay one's respects to, offer one's regards to; **se —** to appear, present oneself
presque [prɛskə] almost, nearly
pressant [prɛsɑ̃] urgent, pressing
presse *f.* [prɛs] press, write-up in the newspapers
pressé [prɛse] hurried, in haste, in a hurry
pression *f.* [prɛsjɔ̃] pressure (*air pressure of tires*)
prêt [prɛ] ready
prétendre [pretɑ̃:dr] to claim
prêter [prete] to lend
prêtre *m.* [prɛ:tr] priest
preuve *f.* [prœ:v] proof
prévenir [prevnir] to warn
prévoir [prevwa:r] to foresee
prier (de) [prie də] to beg (to)
prière *f.* [priɛ:r] prayer
prieur *m.* [priœ:r] prior
principal (*m. pl.* **principaux**) [prɛ̃sipal, prɛ̃sipo] chief, principal
printemps *m.* [prɛ̃tɑ̃] spring; **au —** in the spring
pris [pri] *p.p.* of **prendre**
prise *f.* [pri:z] capture, taking
prison *f.* [prizɔ̃] prison, jail
prisonnier *m.* [prizɔnje] prisoner
privation *f.* [privasjɔ̃] privation, want
privilège *m.* [privilɛ:ʒ] privilege, power, possibility
prix *m.* [pri] price, prize
probable [prɔbabl] probable
probablement [prɔbabləmɑ̃] probably
probité *f.* [prɔbite] honesty
problème *m.* [prɔblɛm] problem
procédé *m.* [prosede] process
procès *m.* [prɔsɛ] lawsuit
prochain [prɔʃɛ̃] next, coming, approaching
prochainement [prɔʃɛnmɑ̃] very soon
procurer (se) [səprɔkyre] to get, obtain
procureur *m.* [prɔkyrœ:r] attorney, public prosecutor
prodige *m.* [prɔdiʒ] miracle
production *f.* [prɔdyksjɔ̃] production
produire [prɔdɥi:r] to produce
professeur *m.* [prɔfɛsœ:r] professor
professoral: corps — *m.* [kɔrprɔfɛsɔral] faculty
profiter [prɔfite] to gain, profit; **— de** to make use of, take advantage of
profond [prɔfɔ̃] deep
profondément [prɔfɔ̃demɑ̃] deeply
profondeur *f.* [prɔfɔ̃dœ:r] depth
profusion *f.* prɔfyzjɔ̃] profusion; **à —** in profusion
programme *m.* [prɔgram] program
progrès *m.* [prɔgrɛ] progress
projet *m.* [prɔʒɛ] plan
prolongé [prɔlɔ̃ʒe] prolonged
promenade *f.* [prɔmnad] walk, pleasure trip; **faire une —** to take a walk
promener [prɔmne] to take for a walk or ride; **se —** to walk about, take a walk
promesse *f.* [prɔmɛs] promise
promettre (**de** +*infin.*) (**à** *with person*) [prɔmɛtr] to promise
promptement [prɔ̃tmɑ̃] promptly
pronom *m.* [prɔnɔ̃] pronoun
prononcer [prɔnɔ̃se] to pronounce
propos *m.* [prɔpo] conversation, line of talk; **à — de** concerning; **à —** by the way, opportunely; **à ce —** in this connection
proposer [prɔpoze] to propose
propre [prɔpr] neat, clean, own, proper
protection *f.* [prɔtɛksjɔ̃] protection
protéger [prɔteʒe] to protect
protestant [prɔtɛstɑ̃] Protestant
protester [prɔtɛste] to protest
prouver [pruve] to prove
province *f.* [prɔvɛ̃:s] province, France outside of Paris
proviseur *m.* [prɔvizœ:r] director
prudence *f.* [prydɑ̃:s] prudence
prune *f.* [pryn] plum
prunier *m.* [prynje] plum tree
pu [py] *p.p.* of **pouvoir**
public *m.* [pyblik] public; **avis au —** public notice
public (*f.* **publique**) (*adj.*) [pyblik] public
puis [pɥi] then, afterwards, after that
puis-je [pɥiʒ] (*see* **pouvoir**)
puisque [pɥiskə] since
puissance *f.* [pɥisɑ̃:s] power
punir [pynir] to punish
punition *f.* [pynisjɔ̃] punishment
pupille *m.* or *f.* [pypil] ward, pupil
pupitre *m.* [pypi:tr] desk
pyjama *m.* [piʒama] pajamas

Q

quai *m.* [ke] quay, wharf, station, platform

qualité *f.* [kalite] quality, accomplishment, qualification

quand [kɑ̃] when; **— même** just the same

quant à [kɑ̃ta] as for

quantité *f.* [kɑ̃tite] quantity, amount

quarante [karɑ̃t] forty

quart *m.* [kaːr] quarter, fourth, small glass

quartier *m.* [kartje] quarter

quartier-maître *m.* [kartjemɛːtr] quartermaster (*petty officer*)

quatorze [katɔrz] fourteen

quatre [katr̥] four

quatre-vingt-dix [katrəvɛ̃dis] ninety

quatre-vingts [katrəvɛ̃] eighty

quatrième [katriɛm] fourth

que (*conj.*) [kə] that, when, as, than, but, except, in order that; **ne —** only; **bien —** although; **tant —** as long as; **c'est —** the fact is that

que (*exclam.*) [kə] how, why; **— de** how many! **— c'est gentil à vous!** how kind it is of you

que (*pron.*) (**qu'** *before vowel*) [kə] which, what, that, whom; **ce —** what; **— est-ce — ?** what? **— est-ce — c'est que ?** what is? **— est-ce — c'est que cela ?** what is that? **— est-ce — cela veut dire ?** what does that mean? **— est-ce qu'il y a ?** what's the matter? **— est-ce qui ?** what? (*as subject*); **— avez-vous ?** what is the matter with you? **— importe ?** what does it matter? **— sais-je ?** I don't know what all; **— voulez-vous ?** what would you expect? **— y a-t-il ?** what's the matter?

quel (*f.* **quelle**; *m. pl.* **quels**; *f. pl.* **quelles**) [kɛl] what? which? **— âge avez-vous ?** how old are you? **— dommage!** what a pity! **—...que** whatever; **— temps fait-il ?** how is the weather?

quelconque [kɛlkɔ̃k] any whatsoever; some...or other

quelque [kɛlkə] some, any, a few; **— chose (de)** something; **—...que** however

quelquefois [kɛlkəfwa] sometimes

quelqu'un (**une**) [kɛlkœ̃, kɛlkyn] someone, anyone; *pl.* **quelques-uns (unes)** some, any

quereller (se) [səkərɛle] to quarrel, wrangle

question *f.* [kɛstjɔ̃] question; **poser une —** to ask a question

queue *f.* [kø] line, tail; **faire la —** to stand in line

qui [ki] who, which, that; **ce —** what; **— est-ce que ?** whom? **— est-ce — ?** who?

quinine *f.* [kinin] quinine; **eau de —** *f.* quinine hair tonic

quinze [kɛ̃z] fifteen; **— jours** two weeks, a fortnight

quitte [kit] even

quitter [kite] to leave (a person or a place), to take off

quoi [kwa] what; **à — bon** what's the use? **de — (manger)** something (to eat); **il n'y a pas de —** don't mention it

quoique [kwakə] although

quotidien (*f.* **quotidienne**) [kɔtidjɛ̃, kɔtidjɛn] daily

R

raccommoder [rakɔmɔde] to repair

raconter [rakɔ̃te] to tell, relate

radiateur *m.* [radjatœːr] radiator

radicalement [radikalmɑ̃] radically

radieux (*f.* **radieuse**) [radjø, radjøːz] radiant

radio: poste de — *m.* [pɔstə də radjo] radio set

radiographier [radjɔgrafje] to X-ray

rafraîchir [rafrɛʃiːr] to cool

rafraîchissement *m.* [rafrɛʃismɑ̃] refreshment

rage *f.* [raːʒ] rage

raisin *m.* [rɛzɛ̃] grape, grapes

raison *f.* [rɛzɔ̃] reason, sanity; **avoir —** to be right

raisonnable [rɛzɔnabl] reasonable, fair

raisonnant [rɛzɔnɑ̃] reasoning

raisonner [rɛzɔne] to reason, think

ralentir [ralɑ̃tiːr] to slow down

ramasser [ramase] to pick up

rampe *f.* [rɑ̃p] slope

rang *m.* [rɑ̃] place, rank

Raoul [raul] Ralph
rapide [rapid] rapid
rapidement [rapidmɑ̃] rapidly
rapidité *f.* [rapidite] rapidity, speed
rappeler (**se**) [səraple] to remember, recall to mind
rapporter [rapɔrte] to bring back; **s'en — à** to leave it to, refer it to
rapprocher [raprɔʃe] to draw near
rare [rɑːr] rare
rarement [rɑrmɑ̃] seldom
raser [rɑze] to shave; **se —** to shave oneself
rasoir *m.* [rɑzwaːr] razor; **lame de —** *f.* razor blade
rassurer [rasyre] to reassure; **se —** to take confidence, to put one's mind at rest
rater [rate] to miss, misfire, miscarry
rattraper [ratrape] to catch up, regain
ravi [ravi] overjoyed, delighted
rayé [rɛje] striped
rayure *f.* [rɛjyːr] stripe
réaliste [realist] realistic
récapitulation *f.* [rekapitylasjɔ̃] review
récemment [resamɑ̃] recently
récepteur *m.* [resɛptœːr] receiver
recette *f.* [rəsɛt] cash receipt
recevoir (*p.p.* **reçu**) [rəsəvwar, rəsy] to receive
rechange: pneu de — *m.* [pnødrəʃɑ̃ːʒ] spare tire
recherche *f.* [rəʃɛrʃ] search, research, investigation
rechute *f.* [rəʃyt] relapse
récit *m.* [resi] recital, tale
réciter [resite] to recite
réclame: article de — *m.* [artiklə də reklam] bargain
réclamer [reklame] to demand, implore, claim, entreat
recommandation *f.* [rəkɔmɑ̃dasjɔ̃] recommendation
recommander [rəkɔmɑ̃de] to recommend
recommencer [rəkɔmɑ̃se] to begin again
reconnaissance *f.* [rəkɔnɛsɑ̃ːs] gratitude
reconnaissant [rəkɔnɛsɑ̃] grateful
reconnaître [rəkɔnɛːtr] to recognize
recouvrir [rəkuvriːr] to recover
récréation *f.* [rekreasjɔ̃] recess
reçu [rəsy] *p.p.* of **recevoir**
recueil *m.* [rəkœːj] collection, selection, miscellany
reculer [rəkyle] to recoil
redevenir [rədəvniːr] to become again
rédiger [rediʒe] to draw up, write
redoutable [rədutabl] formidable
redoute *f.* [rədut] redoubt
réduire [redɥiːr] to reduce
réel (*f.* **réelle**) [reɛl] real
refaire [rəfɛr] to do over
réfectoire *m.* [refɛktwar] dining hall
refermer [rəfɛrme] to close again
référer [refere] to refer; **s'en — à** to leave it to, to trust
réfléchir [refleʃiːr] to reflect, think over
réfugier (**se**) [sə refyʒje] to take shelter
refus *m.* [rəfy] refusal
refuser [rəfyze] to refuse
regard *m.* [rəgaːr] glance
regarder [rəgarde] to look, look at
régime *m.* [reʒim] regime, diet
régiment *m.* [reʒimɑ̃] regiment
réglage *m.* [reglaːʒ] adjusting of wave length, tuning (of radio)
règle *f.* [rɛgl] rule, regulation; **en —** in order
régler [regle] to regulate, rule
régner [reɲe] to rule, reign
regret *m.* [rəgrɛ] regret
regretter [rəgrɛte] to regret
régulier (*f.* **régulière**) [regylje, regyljɛːr] regular
régulièrement [regyljɛrmɑ̃] regularly
rein *m.* [rɛ̃] kidney (*anatomy*); *pl.* **—s** back
rejeter [rəʒəte] to throw back
rejoindre [rəʒwɛ̃dr] to join again
relèvement *m.* [rəlɛvmɑ̃] arising, raising
religieuse *f.* [rəliʒjøːz] nun, sister
religieux (*f.* **religieuse**) [rəliʒjø, rəliʒjøːz] religious
religieux *m.* [rəliʒjø] monk, friar, brother
relire [rəliːr] to read again
remarquable [rəmarkabl] remarkable
remarquer [rəmarke] to notice
rembourser [rɑ̃burse] to reimburse
remède *m.* [rəmɛd] remedy

remédier [rəmedje] to remedy, cure
remercier (**de**) [rəmɛrsje də] to thank (for)
remettre [rəmɛtr] to put off, postpone, put again, put on again; **se —** to recover
remonter [rəmɔ̃te] to go back, to go up again; **— à** to date from
remplacer [rɑ̃plase] to replace
remplir [rɑ̃pliːr] to fill
remporter [rɑ̃pɔrte] to gain, win
remuer [rəmɥe] to move, stir
renard *m.* [rənar] fox
rencontrer [rɑ̃kɔ̃tre] to meet
rendez-vous *m.* [rɑ̃devu] appointment, date; **se donner —** to set a date, arrange to meet
rendre (*p.p.* **rendu**) [rɑ̃dr, rɑ̃dy] to return, give back, make, render; **se —** to surrender, betake oneself, go; **se — compte de** to realize
rendu [rɑ̃dy] *p.p.* of **rendre**
renfermer [rɑ̃fɛrme] to close tight
renforts *m. pl.* [rɑ̃fɔr] reinforcements
renoncement *m.* [rənɔ̃smɑ̃] renunciation
renoncer (**à**) [rənɔ̃se a] to give up
renseignement *m.* [rɑ̃sɛɲmɑ̃] piece of information; **—s** *m. pl.* information
renseigner [rɑ̃sɛɲe] to inform
rente *f.* [rɑ̃t] income, yearly income
rentrer [rɑ̃tre] to come back, come home, go home
renverser [rɑ̃vɛrse] to upset, overturn
renvoyer [rɑ̃vwaje] to send back
répandre [repɑ̃ːdr] to scatter, spread about, spill
reparaître [rəparɛːtr] to reappear
réparation *f.* [reparasjɔ̃] reparation, damage, repair
réparer [repare] to repair
repas *m.* [rəpɑ] meal
repentir (**se**) [sərəpɑ̃tiːr] to repent
répéter [repete] to repeat
replacer [rəplase] to replace, put back
replier (**se**) [sərəplie] to withdraw
répondre (**à**) [repɔ̃dr a] to answer
réponse *f.* [repɔ̃s] answer, response
reportage *m.* [rəpɔrtaːʒ] reporting
repos *m.* [rəpo] repose, rest
reposé [rəpoze] well rested
reposer (**se**) [sərəpoze] to rest
repousser [rəpuse] to repulse, push back
reprendre [rəprɑ̃ːdr] to resume, retake; **— le dessus** to take control
reprise *f.*: **à plusieurs —s** [aplyzjœːr rəpriz] several times, repeatedly
reproche *m.* [rəprɔʃ] reproach
reprocher [rəprɔʃe] to reproach, find fault with
républicain [repyblikɛ̃] Republican, republican
répugnance *f.* [repyɲɑ̃ːs] repugnance, dislike
réputation *f.* [repytasjɔ̃] reputation
réserver [rezɛrve] to reserve
résignation *f.* [reziɲasjɔ̃] resignation
résigné [reziɲe] resigned
résistance *f.* [rezistɑ̃ːs] resistance
résolu [rezɔly] determined
résoudre [rezuːdr] to solve
respect *m.* [rɛspɛ] decency, respect; **les —s** respects, regards
respectueux (*f.* **respectueuse**) [rɛspɛktɥø, rɛspɛktɥøːz] respectful
respirer [rɛspire] to breathe
ressembler [rəsɑ̃ble] to resemble, look like
ressemeler [rəsəmle] to resole
ressortir [rəsɔrtir] to go out again
restante: poste — *f.* [pɔstrɛstɑ̃t] general delivery
restaurant *m.* [rɛstɔrɑ̃] restaurant
reste [rɛst]: **au —** besides; **du —** besides, moreover
rester [rɛste] to stay, remain
résultat *m.* [rezylta] result
résumé *m.* [rezyme] summary
retard *m.* [rətaːr] delay; **en —** late
retenir [rətniːr] to reserve, restrain, hold back
retentir [rətɑ̃tiːr] to resound
retirer (**se**) [sərətire] to withdraw
retomber [rətɔ̃be] to fall back (again)
retour *m.* [rətur] return; **être de —** to be back
retourner [rəturne] to go back, turn over, return; **se —** to turn around
retrouvèr [rətruve] to find again, rejoin
réussir (**à**) [reysiːr a] to succeed (in)
rêvasserie *f.* [rɛvasri] unconnected, broken dreams
rêve *m.* [rɛːv] dream

réveil *m.* [revɛ:j] awakening
réveiller [revɛje] to awaken; **se —** to wake up
révéler [revele] to reveal
revendication *f.* [rəvɑ̃dikasjɔ̃] claim
revendre [rəvɑ̃:dr] to resell, sell again
revenir [rəvni:r] to come back, get back
revenu *m.* [rəvny] income
rêver [rɛve] to dream
revêtir [rəvɛti:r] to dress, clothe
revoir (*p.p.* **revu**) [rəvwa:r, rəvy] to see again; **au —** good-by
révolte *f.* [revɔlt] revolt
révolter [revɔlte] to revolt
révolu [revɔly] former, past
revu [rəvy] *p.p.* of **revoir**
revue *f.* [rəvy] magazine
rez-de-chaussée *m.* [redʃose] ground floor
rhum *m.* [rɔm] rum
rhume *m.* [rym] cold (*disease*)
riant [rijɑ̃] cheerful, pleasing
ricaner [rikane] to chuckle
riche [riʃ] rich
ridé [ride] wrinkled
rideau *m.* [rido] curtain
ridicule [ridikyl] ridiculous
rien (**ne**) [rjɛ̃] nothing; **cela ne fait —** it makes no difference; **— d'autre?** anything else? nothing else? **ce n'est —** that's nothing; **ne servir à —** to do no good; **— que** nothing but
rigolo (*f.* **rigolote**) [rigɔlo, rigɔlɔt] funny
riposter [ripɔste] to reply
rire *m.* [ri:r] laughter, laughing
rire [ri:r] to laugh; **c'était pour —** I was joking; **éclat de —** *m.* burst of laughter; **— de** to laugh at, make fun of
risquer [riske] to risk
rival *m.* [rival] competitor
rivalité *f.* [rivalite] rivalry, competition
rivière *f.* [rivjɛ:r] stream, (small) river
riz *m.* [ri] rice
robe *f.* [rɔb] dress, gown; **— de chambre** dressing gown
rocher *m.* [rɔʃe] rock
rôder [rode] to prowl
rognon *m.* [rɔɲɔ̃] kidney
roi *m.* [rwɑ] king
rôle *m.* [ro:l] role
roman *m.* [rɔmɑ̃] novel; **— policier** detective story
romancier *m.* [rɔmɑ̃sje] novelist
rompre [rɔ̃pr] to break
rond [rɔ̃] round
ronfler [rɔ̃fle] to snore
rose *f.* [ro:z] rose, rose-colored
rôti [roti] roasted
rôtir [roti:r] to roast
rôtisseur *m.* [rotisœ:r] cook-shop keeper; owner of a rôtisserie
rouage *m.* [rwa:ʒ] wheel-work, wheels, machinery
roue *f.* [ru] wheel
rouet *m.* [rwɛ] spinning wheel
rouge *m.* [ru:ʒ] rouge; **bâton de — pour les lèvres** *m.* lipstick
rouge [ru:ʒ] red
rougir [ruʒi:r] to blush
roulement *m.* [rulmɑ̃] rolling
rouler [rule] to roll
rousse [rus] (*see* **roux**)
route *f.* [rut] way, road, highway; **en —** let's go, on the way; **se mettre en —** to start out, set out
rouvrir [ruvri:r] to reopen
roux (*f.* **rousse**) [ru, rus] reddish
ruban *m.* [rybɑ̃] ribbon
rude [ryd] harsh, stern, rough
rudement [rydmɑ̃] harshly, sternly
rue *f.* [ry] street
ruine *f.* [rɥin] ruin
ruiner [rɥine] to ruin
ruisseau *m.* [rɥiso] brook
Russe *m.* [rys] Russian
russe [rys] Russian
Russie *f.* [rysi] Russia

S

sa [sa] his, her, its
sable *m.* [sɑ:bl] sand
sabotage *m.* [sabɔta:ʒ] sabotage
saboteur *m.* [sabɔtœ:r] saboteur
sabre *m.* [sɑ:br] saber, sword
sac *m.* [sak] bag, woman's bag; **— à main** handbag
sacré [sakre] confounded, darned
sacrifice *m.* [sakrifis] sacrifice
sage *m.* [sa:ʒ] well-balanced person, wise person
sage [sa:ʒ] good, well-behaved

sagesse *f.* [saʒɛs] wisdom
sain [sɛ̃] sane, healthy, sound
sainement [sɛnmɑ̃] intelligently
saint [sɛ̃] holy
saisir [sɛziːr] to seize
saison *f.* [sɛzɔ̃] season
salade *f.* [salad] salad
salé [sale] salty
sale [sal] dirty
salissant [salisɑ̃] easy to soil
salle *f.* [sal] room (*large*), hall; **— à manger** dining room; **— d'attente** waiting room; **— de bain** bathroom; **— de classe** classroom
salon *m.* [salɔ̃] parlor, drawing room, living room
saluer [salɥe] to greet, to bow
salut *m.* [saly] bow, greeting
salutaire [salytɛːr] wholesome, beneficial
samedi *m.* [samdi] Saturday
sandwich *m.* [sɑ̃dwiʃ] sandwich
sang *m.* [sɑ̃] blood
sanglant [sɑ̃glɑ̃] bloody, covered with blood
sangloter [sɑ̃glɔte] to sob
sans [sɑ̃] without; **— que** without
santé *f.* [sɑ̃te] health; **à votre —!** to your health! **maison de —** *f.* sanitarium
satisfaction *f.* [satisfaksjɔ̃] satisfaction
satisfaire [satisfɛːr] to satisfy
saucisse *f.* [sosis] sausage
saucisson *m.* [sosisɔ̃] smoked sausage
saumon *m.* [somɔ̃] salmon
sauter [sote] to jump; **faire —** to blow up
sautiller [sotije] to jump about, frisk
sauver [sove] to save; **se —** to escape
savant [savɑ̃] learned
savoir *m.* [savwaːr] knowledge, wisdom
savoir (*p.p.* **su**) [savwaːr, sy] to know, know how to
savon *m.* [savɔ̃] soap; **— à barbe** shaving soap
scandalisé [skɑ̃dalize] scandalized
scène *f.* [sɛn] scene, stage
schako *m.* [ʃako] cap (*military*)
scie *f.* [si] saw
science *f.* [sjɑ̃ːs] science
scientifique [sjɑ̃tifik] scientific
sclérose *f.* [skleroːz] sclerosis (*medical*)
sculpter [skylte] to sculpture, carve
se [sə] oneself, himself, herself, itself, themselves
seau *m.* [so] pail, bucket
sec (*f.* **sèche**) [sɛk, sɛʃ] dry
second [səgɔ̃] second
seconde *f.* [səgɔ̃ːd] second
secoué [səkwe] shaken
secouer [səkwe] to shake
secours *m.* [səkuːr] aid, help; **au —!** help! **au — de** to the help of
secousse *f.* [səkus] jolt, shock
secret *m.* [səkrɛ] secret
secret (*f.* **secrète**) [səkrɛ, səkrɛt] secret
secrétaire *m.* [səkretɛːr] secretary, clerk
Seigneur *m.* [sɛɲœːr] the Lord
seize [sɛːz] sixteen
sel *m.* [sɛl] salt
selon [səlɔ̃] according to
semaine *f.* [səmɛn] week; **la — dernière** last week; **la — prochaine** next week; **fin de semaine** *f.* weekend
semblable [sɑ̃blabl] similar
semblant: faire — de [sɑ̃blɑ̃] to pretend to
sembler [sɑ̃ble] to seem
sénateur *m.* [senatœːr] senator
sens *m.* [sɑ̃ːs] sense, meaning
sensation *f.* [sɑ̃sasjɔ̃] feeling, sensation
sensiblement [sɑ̃sibləmɑ̃] appreciably
sentence *f.* [sɑ̃tɑ̃ːs] verdict, judgment
senteur: pois de — *m. pl.* [pwadsɑ̃tœːr] sweet peas
sentier *m.* [sɑ̃tje] path
sentiment *m.* [sɑ̃timɑ̃] feeling, sentiment
sentinelle *f.* [sɑ̃tinɛl] sentinel
sentir [sɑ̃tiːr] to feel, to sense; **se —** to feel
sept [sɛt] seven
septembre *m.* [sɛptɑ̃br] September
serbe [sɛrb] Serb, Serbian
sergent *m.* [sɛrʒɑ̃] sergeant
série *f.* [seri] series
sérieux (*f.* **sérieuse**) [serjø, serjøːz] serious
serré [sɛre] pressed together, tightly rolled
serrer [sɛre] to press, to grasp; **se — la main** to shake hands

servante *f.* [sɛrvɑ̃t] maid
serveuse *f.* [sɛrvøːz] waitress
servi [sɛrvi] served
service *m.* [sɛrvis] set of dishes
serviette *f.* [sɛrvjɛt] brief case, napkin; **— de toilette** towel
servir [sɛrviːr] to serve; **ne — à rien** to do no good; **— de guide à** to serve one as a guide; **se — de** to use, to make use of
serviteur *m.* [sɛrvitœːr] servant
ses [se] his, her, its
seuil *m.* [sœːj] doorstep, sill
seul [sœːl] alone
seulement [sœlmɑ̃] only
si [si] if; **s'il vous plaît** please, if you please
si . . . que [si . . . kə] so . . . as
si [si] yes (*in reply to negative statement or question*)
siècle *m.* [sjɛkl] century, age
siège *m.* [sjɛʒ] seat
sien, sienne (*with article*) [sjɛ̃, sjɛn] his, her, its
sieur *m.* [sjœːr] Mr., Mister (*in law*)
sifflement *m.* [sifləmɑ̃] whistling, whistle
siffler [sifle] to whistle
signal (*pl.* **signaux**) *m.* [siɲal, siɲo] signal
signe *m.* [siɲ] omen, sign; **faire — à** to signal somebody, let someone know
silence *m.* [silɑ̃ːs] silence
simple [sɛ̃pl] simple
simplement [sɛ̃pləmɑ̃] simply
simplicité *f.* [sɛ̃plisite] simplicity
sincèrement [sɛ̃sɛrmɑ̃] sincerely
singulier (*f.* **singulière**) [sɛ̃gylje, sɛ̃gyljɛːr] odd, singular
singulièrement [sɛ̃gyljɛrmɑ̃] oddly
sinistre *m.* [sinistr] loss, disaster
sinistre (*adj.*) [sinistr] drab, ugly, sinister
sinon [sinɔ̃] if not, otherwise
situation *f.* [sitɥasjɔ̃] situation
situé [sitɥe] situated
six [sis] six
sœur *f.* [sœːr] sister
soi [swa] oneself; **—-même** ones
soie *f.* [swa] silk
soif *f.* [swaf] thirst; **avoir —** to be thirsty
soigner [swaɲe] to care for, look after, take care of
soigneusement [swaɲøzmɑ̃] carefully
soigneux (*f.* **soigneuse**) [swaɲø, swaɲøːz] careful, attentive
soin *m.* [swɛ̃] care; **avoir — de** to take care of
soir *m.* [swaːr] evening; **hier —** last night; **ce —** this evening, tonight; **le —** in the evening; **à ce —** see you tonight
soirée *f.* [sware] evening
soit [swa(t)] so be it, all right (*subjunctive of* **être**)
soixante [swasɑ̃t] sixty
soixante-dix [swasɑ̃t dis] seventy
sol *m.* [sɔl] ground
soldat *m.* [sɔlda] soldier
sole *f.* [sɔl] sole (*fish*)
soleil *m.* [sɔlɛj] sun; **coup de —** *m.* sunburn, sunstroke; **faire du —** to be sunny
solennellement [sɔlanɛlmɑ̃] solemnly
solidarité *f.* [sɔlidarite] solidarity
solive *f.* [sɔliv] beam, rafter
solution *f.* [sɔlysjɔ̃] solution, answer
sombre [sɔ̃br] grave, serious
somme *m.* [sɔm] nap
sommeil *m.* [sɔmɛj] sleep, sleepiness; **avoir —** to be sleepy
son, sa, ses [sɔ̃, sa, se] his, her, its
sonate *f.* [sɔnat] sonata
songe *m.* [sɔ̃ːʒ] dream
songer (**à**) [sɔ̃ʒe a] to think (of)
sonner [sɔne] to ring, ring for
sonnerie (**électrique**) *f.* [sɔnrielɛktrik] electric bell
sonnette *f.* [sɔnɛt] bell
sort *m.* [sɔr] fate
sorte *f.* [sɔrt] sort, kind; **de la —** in that manner
sortie *f.* [sɔrti] exit, outburst
sortir [sɔrtir] to go out, take out
sot (*f.* **sotte**) [so, sɔt] foolish, stupid
sottise *f.* [sɔtiːz] foolishness, piece of foolishness
sou *m.* [su] penny
souci *m.* [susi] care
soucieux (*f.* **soucieuse**) [susjø, susjøːz] worried
soudain [sudɛ̃] sudden, suddenly
souffle *m.* [sufl] breath, aroma

souffler [sufle] to breathe, whisper, blow
souffrance *f.* [sufrɑ̃:s] suffering
souffrir [sufrir] to suffer
souhait *m.* [swɛ] wish (to a person)
souhaiter [swɛte] to wish (someone something); **— un heureux anniversaire** to wish a happy birthday
soulager [sulaʒe] to relieve, ease, alleviate
soulever [sulve] to lift, to bring to one's feet
soulier *m.* [sulje] shoe
souligner [suliɲe] to underline
soumettre [sumɛtr] to submit
soupçonner [supsɔne] to suspect
soupe *f.* [sup] soup; **assiette à —** *f.* soup plate
soupente *f.* [supɑ̃t] loft, garret
souper *m.* [supe] supper; **donner à —** to take to supper
sourd [su:r] deaf
sourire [suri:r] to smile
sous [su] beneath, under
sous-entendu [suzɑ̃tɑ̃dy] understood
soutane *f.* [sutan] cassock
soutenable [sutnabl] sustainable, tenable
soutenir [sutni:r] to support, sustain, defend
souterrain *m.* [sutɛrɛ̃] underpass
souvenir *m.* [suvnir] memory, regards
souvenir (se) (de) [səsuvnirdə] to remember
souvent [suvɑ̃] often
spécialité *f.* [spesjalite] specialty
spectacle *m.* [spɛktɑkl] sight, show, spectacle
spéculation *f.* [spekylasjɔ̃] speculation
squelette *m.* [skəlɛt] skeleton
station *f.* [stasjɔ̃] station
stationner [stasjɔne] to park
statue *f.* [staty] statue
stature *f.* [staty:r] stature
stupeur *f.* [stypœ:r] stupor
style *m.* [stil] style, manner
stylo *m.* [stilo] fountain pen
su [sy] *p.p.* of **savoir**
subit [sybi] sudden
subitement [sybitmɑ̃] suddenly
subjonctif *m.* [sybʒɔ̃ktif] subjunctive
substituer [sybstitɥe] to substitute
subtil [syptil] subtle, artful
succéder [syksede] to follow
succès *m.* [syksɛ] success
succession *f.* [syksɛsjɔ̃] inheritance
sucre *m.* [sykr] sugar
sucré [sykre] sugary, sweet
sucrerie *f.* [sykrəri] sweetmeat, sweet
sud *m.* [syd] south
Suède *f.* [sɥɛd] Sweden
sueur *f.* [sɥœ:r] sweat
suffire [syfi:r] to suffice, to be enough
suffisant [syfizɑ̃] sufficient; **une note —e** a passing mark
suffoqué [syfɔke] suffocated
suggérer [sygʒere] to suggest
Suisse *f.* [sɥis] Switzerland
suite *f.* [sɥit] continuation; retinue, attendants; **tout de —** at once, immediately
suivant [sɥivɑ̃] following
suivre [sɥi:vr] to follow, to take (a course)
sujet *m.* [syʒɛ] subject; **au — de** on the subject of, concerning
superbe [sypɛrb] superb
supérieur *m.* [syperjœ:r] superior
superlatif (*f.* **superlative**) [sypɛrlatif, sypɛrlati:v] superlative
superstitieux (*f.* **superstitieuse**) [sypɛrstisjø, sypɛrstisjø:z] superstitious
supplémentaire [syplemɑ̃tɛr] supplementary
supplice *m.* [syplis] torture
supplier [syplie] to beg
supporter [sypɔrte] to bear, support
supposition *f.* [sypozisjɔ̃] supposition
sûr [syr] sure, certain; **je suis — de mon affaire** I know what I'm talking about
sur [syr] on, upon, with (*e.g., have money with one*); **deux jours — trois** two days out of three
surdité *f.* [syrdite] deafness
sûreté *f.* [syrte] safety
surgir [syrʒi:r] to rise, arise
surlendemain *m.* [syrlɑ̃dmɛ̃] two days later
surnommé [syrnɔme] nicknamed
surplis *m.* [syrpli] surplice
surprendre (*p.p.* **surpris**) [syrprɑ̃:dr, syrpri] to surprise
surpris [syrpri] *p.p.* of **surprendre**

surtout [syrtu] especially, above all
surveillant *m.* [syrvɛjɑ̃] supervisor, monitor
survivant *m.* [syrvivɑ̃] survivor
survivre [syrvivr] to survive
suspendre [syspɑ̃:dr] to suspend
Sylvie [silvi] Sylvia
sympathie *f.* [sɛ̃pati] sympathy
symptôme *m.* [sɛ̃pto:m] symptom

T

tabac *m.* [taba] tobacco
table *f.* [tabl] table; **— de toilette** dressing table; **à —** at the table
tableau *m.* [tablo] picture
tabletier *m.* [tablətje] dealer in game boards
tabulateur *m.* [tabylatœ:r] dial
tache *f.* [taʃ] spot, stain
tâche *f.* [tɑʃ] task
tâcher (de) [tɑʃedə] to try (to)
Tacite [tasit] Tacitus
taille *f.* [tɑ:j] figure
taire (se) [sətɛr] to be silent
talent *m.* [talɑ̃] talent; **de —** talented
talon *m.* [talɔ̃] heel
talus *m.* [taly] slope, embankment
tambour *m.* [tɑ̃bur] drum
tamponner [tɑ̃pɔne] to hit, stamp
tandis que [tɑ̃dikə] while
tant (de) [tɑ̃ də] so many, so much, so greatly; **— mieux** so much the better; **— pis** so much the worse, too bad; **— que** as long as
tante *f.* [tɑ̃t] aunt
tantôt [tɑ̃to] now
tapage *m.* [tapa:ʒ] noise
taper (à la machine) [tape a la maʃin] to type
tapis *m.* [tapi] carpet
tard [tar] late
tarder [tarde] to delay, hesitate
tarif *m.* [tarif] rate
tas *m.* [tɑ] heap
tasse *f.* [tas] cup
tâter [tɑte] to feel, try, taste; **— le pouls** feel the pulse
tâtons: à — (*adv.*) [atɑtɔ̃] groping, feeling one's way
taxi *m.* [taksi] taxi
teinte *f.* [tɛ̃t] tinge, tint
tel (*f.* **telle**) [tɛl] such; **un —** such a; **— que** such as, such a one as
télégramme *m.* [telegram] telegram
téléphone *m.* [telefɔn] telephone, phone
téléphoner [telefɔne] to telephone
tellement [tɛlmɑ̃] so, so much, to such an extent
témoin *m.* [temwɛ̃] witness
tempête *f.* [tɑ̃pɛt] storm, tempest
temps *m.* [tɑ̃] time, weather, tense (*of verb*); **de — en —** from time to time; **mettre quelque — à** to take some time to; **par tous les —** in all sorts of weather
ténacité *f.* [tenasite] tenacity
tendre [tɑ̃:dr] to extend
tendrement [tɑ̃drəmɑ̃] tenderly
tendresse *f.* [tɑ̃drɛs] deep affection
tenir [tənir] to hold; **— le coup** to hold out; **— compagnie à** to accompany; **s'en — à** to limit oneself to, restrict oneself to; **se — debout** to stand; **tenez! (tiens!)** here! (*when handing someone something*); **tenez la droite (gauche)** keep to the right (left); **y —** to care about, be fond of
tension *f.* [tɑ̃sjɔ̃] tension
terme *m.* [tɛrm] term
terminer (se) [tɛrmine] to end, terminate
terrain *m.* [tɛrɛ̃] terrain, ground
terrasse *f.* [tɛras] terrace; **à la — de** in front of
terre *f.* [tɛr] land, earth, ground; **par —** on the ground, floor; **pomme de —** *f.* potato
terrible [tɛribl] terrible
tête *f.* [tɛ:t] head
téter [tete] to suckle
thé *m.* [te] tea
théâtre *m.* [teɑ:tr] theatre
thème *m.* [tɛm] theme, translation (into a foreign language)
Thérèse [terɛ:z] Teresa
thermomètre *m.* [tɛrmɔmɛtr] thermometer
thon *m.* [tɔ̃] tuna fish
tiens! [tjɛ̃] why! look here!
timbre-poste *m.* (*pl.* **les timbres-poste**) [tɛ̃brəpɔst] stamp, postage stamp
timide [timid] timid

timidement [timidmɑ̃] timidly
timidité *f.* [timidite] timidity
tinter [tɛ̃te] to ring, toll
tirailleur *m.* [tirajœːr] sharpshooter
tirer [tire] to fire, pull, draw; **se — d'affaire** to get out of a difficulty
tiret *m.* [tirɛ] dash
tiroir *m.* [tirwaːr] drawer
tissu *m.* [tisy] cloth, fabric; **les —s** dry goods
toi [twa] you; **—-même** you, yourself; **à —** yours
toile *f.* [twal] canvas
toilette *f.* [twalɛt] toilet, dress, attire; **faire la —** to wash and dress; **serviette de —** *f.* towel; **table de —** *f.* dressing table
toit *m.* [twa] roof
tolérer [tɔlere] to tolerate
tomate *f.* [tɔmat] tomato
tombée *f.* [tɔ̃be] fall; **— de la nuit** nightfall
tomber [tɔ̃be] to fall; **— amoureux de** to fall in love with
ton *m.* [tɔ̃] tone, shade, color; **un — clair** a light color
ton (ta, tes) [tɔ̃, ta, te] your (*familiar*)
tonner [tɔne] to resound, thunder
tordre (se) [sə tɔrdr] to be convulsed with laughter
tort *m.* [tɔr] error, fault; **avoir —** to be wrong; **donner — à** to put in the wrong, to consider wrong; **faire du — à** to injure, to harm
torturé [tɔrtyre] tortured
tôt [to] soon; **au plus —** as soon as possible; **le plus — possible** as soon as possible
totalement [tɔtalmɑ̃] totally
toucher [tuʃe] to touch, cash (a check)
toujours [tuʒur] always, still
tour *m.* [tur] turn; **faire un petit —** to take a short walk
tournant *m.* [turnɑ̃] corner, bend, turn
tournée *f.* [turne] road, tour; **partir en —** to go on the road
tournemain *m.* [turnəmɛ̃] trice, instant
tourner [turne] to turn
tousser [tuse] to cough
tout (*pron.*) [tu] everything, all, whole, every, any; **gentil comme —** nice as anything; **pas du —** not at all
tout (toute, tous, toutes) [tu, tut, tu, tut] all, whole; **— à coup** suddenly; **— à fait** altogether, quite; **— à l'heure** presently, just now, a while ago; **— au plus** at the very most; **— de même** all the same, just the same; **— de suite** at once, immediately; **— droit** straight ahead; **—e l'après-midi** the whole afternoon; **—e la journée** the whole day; **—e la matinée** the whole morning; **—e la soirée** the whole evening; **— le monde** everybody; **— simplement** simply; **tous deux** both; **tous les deux** both; **tous les jours** every day; **tous les lundis** every Monday; **à — à l'heure** I'll see you presently; **à — instant** every moment; **au-dessus de —** beyond words; **du —** at all; **en — cas** at any rate; **c'est —** that's all
toux *f.* [tu] cough
traduction *f.* [tradyksjɔ̃] translation
traduire [tradɥir] to translate
tragique [traʒik] tragic
trahir [trair] to betray
trahison *f.* [traizɔ̃] treachery
train *m.* [trɛ̃] train; **être en — de** to be in the act of
trait *m.* [trɛ] trait, act
traité *m.* [trɛte] treatise
traiter [trɛte] to treat
traiteur *m.* [trɛtœːr] eating-house keeper, caterer
traître *m.* [trɛːtr] traitor
trajet *m.* [traʒɛ] journey, trip
tramway *m.* [tramwe] streetcar
tranche *f.* [trɑ̃ʃ] slice
tranchée *f.* [trɑ̃ʃe] trench
tranquille [trɑ̃kil] peaceful, tranquil
tranquillement [trɑ̃kilmɑ̃] calmly, tranquilly
transférer [trɑ̃sfere] to transfer
transpirer [trɑ̃spire] to perspire
transporter [trɑ̃spɔrte] to carry, transport
travail *m.* (*pl.* **travaux**) [travaj, travo] work
travailler [travaje] to work
travers: à — [a travɛr] across, through
traverse *f.* [travɛrs] crossbar
traversée *f.* [travɛrse] crossing

traverser [traverse] to cross, pierce
treize [trɛːz] thirteen
tremblant [trɑ̃blɑ̃] trembling
trembloter [trɑ̃blɔte] to tremble, shiver, shake
tremper [trɑ̃pe] to dip, soak
trente [trɑ̃t] thirty
très [trɛ] very
trésor *m.* [trezɔːr] treasure
tressaillir [trɛsajiːr] to be startled
tribunal *m.* [tribynal] court
triomphant [triɔ̃ːfɑ̃] triumphant
triomphe *m.* [triɔ̃ːf] triumph
triompher [triɔ̃fe] to triumph
tripe *f.* [trip] tripe
triste [trist] sad
tristement [tristəmɑ̃] sadly
tristesse *f.* [tristɛs] sadness
trois [trwɑ] three
troisième [trwɑzjɛm] third
trombe *f.* [trɔ̃b] whirlwind
tromper [trɔ̃pe] to deceive; **se —** to make a mistake, be mistaken
tronc *m.* [trɔ̃] trunk
trop (**de**) [tro də] too, too much, too many
trotter [trɔte] to run about
trottoir *m.* [trɔtwaːr] sidewalk
trou *m.* [tru] hole
troubler [truble] to trouble, disturb
trousse *f.* [trus] case (of surgical instruments)
trouvaille *f.* [truvaj] discovery
trouver [truve] to find; **se —** to find oneself, to be
truite *f.* [trɥit] trout
tu [ty] you (*familiar*)
tuer [tɥe] to kill
tumulte *m.* [tymylt] tumult, uproar
tumultueux (*f.* **tumultueuse**) [tymyltɥø, tymyltɥøːz] tumultuous
tunnel *m.* [tynɛl] tunnel
Turquie *f.* [tyrki] Turkey
tuteur *m.* [tytœːr] guardian
tutoyer [tytwaje] to address familiarly, to "thou" and "thee"
tuyauterie *f.* [tɥijotri] pipes

U

un (**une**) [œ̃, yn] a, an, one
uniforme *m.* [yniform] uniform
Union Soviétique *f.* [ynjɔ̃ sɔvjetik] Soviet Union
unique [ynik] only, sole
uniquement [ynikmɑ̃] solely
université *f.* [yniversite] university, college
user [yze] to wear out
usine *f.* [yzin] factory

V

vacarme *m.* [vakarm] tumult, uproar
vache *f.* [vaʃ] cow
vague *m.* [vag] vagueness
vague *f.* [vag] wave
vaguement [vagmɑ̃] vaguely
vain: en — [ɑ̃vɛ̃] in vain
vaincre [vɛ̃kr] to conquer, win
vainement [vɛnmɑ̃] in vain
vaisselle *f.* [vɛsɛl] dishes
valeur *f.* [valœːr] value
valise *f.* [valiːz] suitcase; **faire sa —** to pack a bag (suitcase)
valoir [valwaːr] to be worth; **— la peine** to be worth the trouble; **— mieux** to be better
vanille *f.* [vaniːj] vanilla
vapeur *f.* [vapœːr] smoke, steam
vas [va] *imperative of* **aller**
vase *m.* [vɑːz] vase
vaurien *m.* [vorjɛ̃] good-for-nothing
veau *m.* [vo] veal
vécu [veky] *p.p.* of **vivre**
veille *f.* [vɛːj] day (or night) before
veiller [vɛje] to stay awake
vendeur *m.* [vɑ̃dœːr] salesman, clerk
vendre [vɑ̃ːdr] to sell
vendredi *m.* [vɑ̃drədi] Friday
venir [vənir] to come; **— de** +*infinitive* to have just; **faire —** to send for
vent *m.* [vɑ̃] wind; **faire du —** to be windy
ventre *m.* [vɑ̃ːtr] stomach
verbe *m.* [vɛrb] verb
vérifier [verifje] to verify
véritable [veritabl] veritable
vérité *f.* [verite] truth
verni [vɛrni] varnished
verre *m.* [vɛr] glass
vers *m.* [vɛr] verse
vers [vɛr] toward; (*with expressions of time*) at about

verse: pleuvoir à — [plœvwa:r a vɛrs] to pour (rain)
verser [vɛrse] to pour
version *f.* [vɛrsjɔ̃] translation (from foreign language)
vert [vɛr] green
vertu *f.* [vɛrty] virtue
vertugadin *m.* [vɛrtygadɛ̃] farthingale
vestiaire *m.* [vɛstjɛ:r] cloakroom
vestibule *m.* [vɛstibyl] vestibule
veston *m.* [vɛstɔ̃] coat, jacket
vêtement *m.* [vɛtmɑ̃] garment; **les vêtements** clothes; **vêtements de dessous** underwear
veuf *m.* [vœf] widower
veuve *f.* [vœ:v] widow
viande *f.* [vjɑ̃d] meat
victoire *f.* [viktwa:r] victory
vide [vid] empty
vider [vide] to empty
vie *f.* [vi] life, living, livelihood; **la — coûte cher** the cost of living is high
vieillard *m.* [vjɛja:r] old man
vierge *f.* [vjɛrʒ] virgin
vieux (**vieil** *before a vowel or h*; *f. s.* **vieille**; *m. pl.* **vieux**; *f. pl.* **vieilles**) [vjø, vjɛj, vjɛj, vjø, vjɛj] old; **mon —** old man, my friend; **un —** an old man
vif (*f.* **vive**) [vif, vi:v] lively
vigne *f.* [viɲ] vine, vineyard
vilain [vilɛ̃] wicked
villa *f.* [villa] cottage
village *m.* [vila:ʒ] village
ville *f.* [vil] city, town; **en —** in town, downtown
vin *m.* [vɛ̃] wine
vingt [vɛ̃] twenty
vingtaine *f.* [vɛ̃tɛn] score
violemment [vjɔlamɑ̃] violently
violet (*f.* **violette**) [vjɔlɛ, vjɔlɛt] violet colored, purple
violette *f.* [vjɔlɛt] violet
virgule *f.* [virgyl] comma
visage *m.* [viza:ʒ] face
viser [vize] to aim
visite *f.* [vizit] visit; **faire une —** to pay a visit; **faire — à** visit, pay a visit to, make a call on
visiter [vizite] to visit
vite [vit] fast, quickly
vitesse *f.* [vitɛs] speed
vitre *f.* [vitr] windowpane
vivacité *f.* [vivasite] vivacity, liveliness
vivant [vivɑ̃] living, alive
vive [vi:v] (*see* **vif**)
vivement [vivmɑ̃] quickly
vivre (*p.p.* **vécu**) [vivr, veky] to live; **Vive (l'empereur)!** Long live (the emperor)!
vivres *m. pl.* [vivr] food
vocabulaire *m.* [vɔkabylɛ:r] vocabulary
vogue *f.* [vɔg] vogue, fashion; **en —** popular
voici [vwasi] here is, here are; **me —** here I am
voie *f.* [vwa] track
voilà [vwala] there is, there are (*pointing out*); **— tout** that's all; **les —** there they are; **— que** lo and behold!
voile *f.* [vwal] sail; **bateau à —** *m.* sailboat
voir (*p.p.* **vu**) [vwa:r, vy] to see; **faire —** to show; **faites-moi —** show me; **voyons** let's see
voisin *m.* [vwazɛ̃] neighbor; (*adj.*) neighboring, adjoining
voiture *f.* [vwaty:r] railroad coach, carriage, car, vehicle; **en —!** all aboard!
voix *f.* [vwa] voice; **à haute —** aloud; **à — basse** in a low voice
volaille *f.* [vɔla:j] fowl, poultry
volant *m.* [vɔlɑ̃] steering wheel
voler [vɔle] to steal, fly, rob
volet *m.* [vɔlɛ] shutter
voleur *m.* [vɔlœ:r] thief
volonté *f.* [vɔlɔ̃te] will
volontiers [vɔlɔ̃tje] gladly, willingly
votre (*pl.* **vos**) [vɔtr, vo] your
vôtre (le, la) [votr (lə, la)] yours
vouloir (*p.p.* **voulu**) [vulwa:r, vuly] to want, wish; **— bien** be willing; **— dire** to mean; **voulez-vous?** do you want? will you? will you have? **voulez-vous m'indiquer?** will you show me?
voulu [vuly] *p.p.* of **vouloir**
vous [vu] you, to you (*polite, plural*); (to) yourself, (to) yourselves; **—-même** yourself; **—-mêmes** yourselves; **à —** yours; **bien à —** sincerely yours

voyage *m.* [vwaja:ʒ] journey, trip, voyage; **bon —** have a good trip; **faire un —** to take a trip
voyager [vwajaʒe] to travel
voyageur *m.* [vwajaʒœ:r] traveler
voyant [vwajɑ̃] loud (*of colors*)
voyons! [vwajɔ̃] let's see!
vrai [vrɛ] true, real
vraiment [vrɛmɑ̃] really, truly
vraisemblance *f.* [vrɛsɑ̃blɑ̃:s] plausibility
vrille *f.* [vri:j] gimlet
vu [vy] *p.p.* of **voir**
vue *f.* [vy] view; **au point de — de** from the point of view of
vulgaire [vylgɛ:r] ordinary, commonplace
vulgairement [vylgɛrmɑ̃] vulgarly, commonly, generally

W

wagon *m.* [vagɔ̃] coach; **—-lit** sleeping car; **—-restaurant** dining car
W.C. (le) *m.* [watɛrklɔzɛ] toilet
week-end *m.* [wikɛnd] weekend

Y

y [i] there, to it, to them, on it, on them, etc.
yeux (les) *m. pl.* (*s.* **œil**) [lezjø, œ:j] eyes
Yougoslavie *f.* [jugɔslavi] Yugoslavia

Z

zèle *m.* [zɛl] zeal, warmth, ardor
zut! [zyt] darn it! heck!

ENGLISH-FRENCH VOCABULARY

A

a un, -e; (*per*) par
able: be — pouvoir
aboard: all — ! en voiture!
about (*almost*) à peu près; (*concerning*) de, au sujet de; (*toward*) vers; **what are you talking —** de quoi parlez-vous?; **walk —** se promener
above en haut, au-dessus de; **— all** surtout
accompany accompagner
ache: have an — avoir mal à
acquaintance connaissance *f.*; **make the — of** faire la connaissance de
acquainted: be — with connaître; **become — with** faire la connaissance de
across à travers; **— the way** d'en face
act acte *m.*
actor acteur *m.*
address adresse *f.*
address familiarly tutoyer
advance avancer (nous avançons)
advance: in — d'avance
adverb adverbe *m.*
advise conseiller; **— someone to do something** conseiller à quelqu'un de faire quelque chose
affair affaire *f.*
afraid be — of or **to** avoir peur (de), craindre (de)
after *conj.* après que
after *prep.* après; **— all** enfin, après tout
afternoon après-midi *f.*; **in the —** l'après-midi; **good —** bonjour; **the whole —** toute l'après-midi
afterward ensuite
again encore, encore une fois, de nouveau
against contre
age âge *m.*
ago il y a . . .
agree accorder; **to make —** faire accorder; **— with (you)** être de (votre) avis
agreeable agréable, aimable
agreed d'accord; **agreed!** entendu, convenu
ahead: — (*of time*) en avance; **straight —** tout droit
aid secours *m.*
air air *m.*
airplane avion *m.*
Albert Albert
alcohol alcool *m.*
all *pro.* tout, tous
all *adj.* tout, -e; **— aboard!** en voiture!; **— kinds of** toutes sortes de; **— right** c'est bien, soit; **— right?** ça va?; **— the same** tout de même, quand même; **anything at —** n'importe quoi; **not at —** pas du tout, du tout; (*emphatic*) ne . . . point
allow permettre (de) (*p. p.* permis)
ally allié *m.*
almost presque
alone seul
along le long de; **come —** accompagner
aloud à haute voix
already déjà
also aussi
although bien que, quoique
altogether tout à fait
always toujours
America Amérique *f.*; **in, to —** en Amérique
American américain; **I am an —** je suis Américain
ammunition munitions *f. pl.*
among parmi
an un, une
and et
and so aussi
Andrew André
angry: to get — se fâcher
animal animal *m.* (*pl.* animaux)
ankle cheville *f.*
Annie Annette
anniversary anniversaire *m.*
announce annoncer (nous annonçons)
another un autre, encore un

annoying gênant
answer répondre (à)
ant fourmi *f.*
any quelque, quelques-uns, quelques-unes, en (*pro.*)
anyone quelqu'un, quelqu'une
anything at all n'importe quoi
anything else? rien d'autre?
any . . . whatsoever n'importe quel . . .
apology excuse *f.*
appear se présenter
appear to avoir l'air de
appearance air *m.*
appetizers hors-d'oeuvre *m. pl.*
apple pomme *f.*
application application *f.*
apply appliquer
appointment rendez-vous *m.*
appreciate apprécier
appropriate: to be — convenir
April avril *m.*
are there? est-ce qu'il y a?, y a-t-il?
arise surgir
arm bras *m.*
arm (*weapon*) arme *f.*
arm armer
arm-chair fauteuil *m.*
around autour de; **turn —** se retourner, faire demi-tour
arrest arrêter
arrive arriver
art art *m.*
Arthur Arthur
artificial artificiel (*f.* -elle)
as comme, que; **— . . . —** aussi . . . que; **— far —** jusqu'à, jusqu'à ce que; **— for** quant à; **— long —** tant que; **— many** autant de; **— much** autant de; **— soon —** aussitôt que, dès que
ask demander, prier; **— a question** poser une question; **— for** demander; **I don't — for anything better** je ne demande pas mieux
assassinate assassiner
assure assurer
at à, dans, chez; **— first** d'abord; **— home** chez (moi, toi, lui *etc.*); **— least** au moins, du moins; **— once** à l'instant, immédiatement, tout de suite
attention attention *f.*; **attention!** attention!
attentive soigneux (*f.* soigneuse)
August août *m.*
aunt tante *f.*
Austria Autriche *f.*
author auteur *m.*
authority autorité *f.*
automatic pencil porte-mine *m.*
automobile auto, automobile *f.*
avenue avenue *f.*
avoid éviter
avow avouer
await attendre
away: go — s'en aller; **take —** emmener
awkward gauche

B

bachelor garçon *m.*
back dos *m.*
back: be *or* **get —** être de retour; **come —** revenir, rentrer; **give —** rendre; **go —** retourner, rentrer
back of derrière
bacon lard (anglais) *m.*
bad mauvais, -e; **that's too —** c'est dommage; **— luck** guigne *f.*
badly mal
bag valise *f.*; **woman's hand —** sac *m.*; **pack a —** faire sa valise
baggage bagages *m. pl.*
Balkans Balkans *m. pl.*
ball (*dance*) bal *m.*; (*bullet*) balle *f.*
band bande *f.*
bandage pansement *m.*
bandit bandit *m.*
bank banque *f.*; **— note** billet de banque *m.*
banker banquier *m.*
barely à peine
bars: handle- — guidon *m.*
base baser
basket panier *m.*
batallion bataillon *m.*
bath bain *m.*
bathe prendre un bain
bathroom salle de bain *f.*

battle bataille *f.*
be être, se trouver; (*of business or health*) aller; **— in the act of (doing)** être en train de (faire); **so — it** soit; **— to** devoir
beach plage *f.*
beans haricots *m. pl.*
beard barbe *f.*
beautiful beau (bel *before vowel or h,* belle *f. s.,* beaux *m. pl.,* belles *f. pl.*)
beauty beauté *f.*
because parce que; **— of** à cause de
become devenir; **— acquainted with** faire la connaissance de
becoming: be — to aller bien à; **be extremely —** aller à merveille
bed lit *m.;* **go to —** se coucher; **—sheet** drap *m.*
bedroom chambre à coucher *f.*
beefsteak bifteck *m.*
been été (p. p. *of* être)
beer bière *f.;* **large glass of —** demi *m.;* **small glass of —** bock *m.*
before *adv.* avant, auparavant; **day —** veille *f.*
before *conj.* avant que (. . . ne) (+ *subj.*)
before *prep.* (*position*) devant; (*time*) avant; (*before inf.*) avant de; **— that** auparavant
beg prier de
begin commencer (à); se mettre (à); **— with** commencer par
behind derrière
Belgium Belgique *f.*
believe croire
beloved chéri *m.*
below en bas, au-dessous de
belt ceinture *f.*
bench banc *m.*
beneath sous, au-dessous de
beside à côté, à côté de
besides d'ailleurs, de plus
besiege assiéger (nous assiégeons)
best *adj.* le meilleur, la meilleure
best *adv.* le mieux; **the — they can** de leur mieux; **do one's —** faire son possible
betake oneself se rendre
better *adj.* meilleur, -e
better *adv.* mieux; **I don't ask for anything —** je ne demande pas mieux
between entre
beverage boisson *f.*
beyond: go — dépasser
bicycle bicyclette *f.*
big gros, -se; grand
bill addition *f.*
billion milliard (de) *m.*
biology biologie *f.*
bird oiseau *m.* (*pl.* -x)
birth naissance *f.*
birthday anniversaire de naissance *m.*
bitter amer (*f.* amère)
black noir
blade lame *f.;* **razor —** lame de rasoir *f.*
block bloc *m.*
blood sang *m.*
blow up faire sauter
blue bleu
body corps *m.*
bombardment bombardement *m.*
bone os *m.* (*pronounce the* s *in the sing., but not in the plural,* les os)
book livre *m.*
book-hunt bouquiner
border frontière *f.*
bordered bordé
borrow (from) emprunter (à)
Bosnian bosnien (*f.* bosnienne)
Botanical Gardens Jardin des Plantes, *m.*
both tous les deux, les deux
bother déranger (nous dérangeons)
bottle bouteille *f.*
boulevard boulevard *m.*
boundary frontière *f.*
bow saluer
box boîte *f.;* **letter —** boîte aux lettres
boy garçon *m.*
brake frein *m.*
brave brave
Brazil Brésil *m.*
bread pain *m.*
break rompre, casser, briser
breakfast petit déjeuner *m.*

breakdown (*auto*) panne *f.*
breast poitrine *f.*
breasted: double — croisé
breathe souffler
bridge pont *m.*
brief bref (*f.* brève)
brief case serviette *f.*
brigade brigade *f.*
bright intelligent, clair
brilliant éclatant
bring amener, apporter
broad: in — daylight en plein jour
brook ruisseau *m.*
brother frère *m.*
brother-in-law beau-frère *m.*
brown marron, brun
brunette brun, -e
brush brosse *f.*; **tooth —** brosse à dents
bud (*of a flower*) bouton *m.*
building édifice *m.*, bâtiment *m.*
bullet balle *f.*
burn brûler
burn brûlure *f.*
burst out éclater
bus autobus *m.*
business affaire *f.*
busy occupé, pris
busy with: to be — s'occuper de
but mais; **not . . . —** ne . . . que
butter beurre *m.*
button bouton *m.*
buy acheter (j'achète)
by par; **— the way** à propos

C

cabbage chou *m.* (*pl.* choux)
cake gâteau (*pl.* gâteaux); **cream —** gâteau à la crème; **small —** petit-four *m.*
call appeler (j'appelle); **— oneself** s'appeler; **be called** s'appeler; **— on** faire visite à; **what do you — this in French?** comment s'appelle ceci en français?
calm calme
campaign campagne *f.*
can pouvoir, savoir; **— I** puis-je? **I can't** je ne peux pas; **I can't help** je ne peux pas m'empêcher de
Canada Canada *m.*
Canadian canadien (*f.* -ne)
candy (*piece of*) bonbon *m.* (*use plural,* les bonbons, *for English collective candy*)
cannon canon *m.*
canvas toile *f.*
captain capitaine *m.*
car auto, automobile *f.*; **by —** en auto; **dining- —** wagon-restaurant *m.*; **sleeping- —** wagon-lit *m.*; **street —** tramway *m.*
card carte *f.*
care souci *m.*
care attention *f.*; **to take — of** se charger de, avoir soin de
careful soigneux (*f.* soigneuse)
careful! attention!
careful with attention à
carriage voiture *f.*
carry porter
case cas *m.*
cat chat *m.*
catch attraper
catch up rattraper
Catholic catholique
cause causer
cease cesser (de)
celebrate fêter
celebration fête *f.*
cellar cave *f.*
centime centime *m.*
certain sûr, certain
certainly certainement, assurément
chain chaîne *f.*
chair chaise *f.*; **arm- —, easy —** fauteuil *m.*
chamber chambre *f.*
change (*money*) monnaie *f.*; **small —** la petite monnaie *f.*; **I have no —** je n'ai pas de petite monnaie
change changer (de) (nous changeons)
change purse porte-monnaie *m.*
charge: to take . . . of se charger de (nous nous chargeons de)
charm charme *m.*
charming charmant
chat causer, bavarder

cheap bon marché
cheaply à bon marché
check chèque *m.;* **to make out a —** faire un chèque
check (bill) addition *f.*
check contrôler
cheek joue *f.*
cheese fromage *m.*
chemistry chimie *f.*
chest poitrine *f.*
"chew the rag" bavarder
chicken poulet *m.*
chief principal (*m. pl.* principaux)
chief chef *m.*
child enfant *m. or f.*
chin menton *m.*
China Chine *f.*
Chinese chinois
choose choisir
Christmas Noël *m. or f.*
church église *f.*
cigar cigare *m.*
cigarette cigarette *f.*
city ville *f.*
claim prétendre
class classe *f.;* **in —** en classe
classroom salle de classe *f.*
clean propre
clear clair
clear the table desservir
clerk vendeur *m.*
clever intelligent
climb monter (à) (être)
clock pendule *f.*
close to près de; **very close to** tout près de
close fermer
close tight renfermer
closet placard *m.*
cloth étoffe *f.*, drap *m.;* **table —** nappe *f.*
cloud nuage *m.*
cloudy couvert
coal charbon *m.*
coat veston *m.*, jaquette *f.*
coat (*woman's*) manteau *m.*
coffee café *m.*
coffee shop café *m.*
cognac cognac *m.*
coin monnaie *f.*, pièce *f.*
cold rhume *m.*
cold froid; **be —** (*weather*) faire froid; **be —** (*physical sensation*) avoir froid
collaborate collaborer
colleague collègue *m.*
college université *f.*
collision collision *f.*
colonel colonel *m.*
color ton *m.*, couleur *f.;* **a light —** un ton clair
comb peigne *m.*
come venir (*p. p.* venu) (*with* être)
come along accompagner; **come along, come with me** accompagnez-moi; **— back** revenir, rentrer; **— here** venez ici; **— home** rentrer; **come, come!** allons donc!; **come now!** allons donc!; **come, come now, come on** allons; **— down** descendre (être); **— to an understanding** se mettre d'accord; **let's — to an understanding** mettons-nous d'accord; **— with** accompagner
comfortable commode
commissioner (*police*) commissaire de police *m.*
communication communication *f.*
company compagnie *f.;* **in — of** en compagnie de
compartment compartiment *m.*
competitor compétiteur *m.*
complain se plaindre
complete compléter (je complète)
complete complet (*f.* complète)
completely complètement
composition composition *f.*
comrade camarade *m.*
conceal cacher
concern concerner; **for what concerns** en ce qui concerne
concerning au sujet de, à propos de
conditional conditionnel *m.*
conductor contrôleur *m.*
confess avouer
confounded sacré
conjugate conjuguer
conjugation conjugaison *f.*
conquer vaincre
consent consentir (à)
consequently par conséquent

consider considérer (je considère)
consommé consommé *m.*
constantly sans cesse
contents contenu *m.*
continue continuer (à *or* de)
contrary contraire
conversation conversation *f.*
convince convaincre
cook cuisinière *f.*
cooking cuisine *f.*
cool frais (*f.* fraîche)
copper cuivre *m.*
cordial liqueur *f.*
cordial cordial (*m. pl.* cordiaux)
cordially yours bien à vous, bien amicalement, votre bien cordialement dévoué
corn (*foot*) cor *m.*
corner coin *m.*
correct correct, juste
correctly correctement
correspond correspondre
cost coûter; **the — of living is high** la vie coûte cher
cottage villa *f.*
cough toux *f.*
cough tousser
count compter
country campagne *f.*, pays *m.*
countryside pays *m.*, paysage *m.*
couple couple *m.*
courage courage *m.*
courageous courageux (*f.* -se)
course: of — bien entendu, naturellement
courtyard cour *f.*
cousin cousin *m.*, cousine *f.*
cover couvrir
covered couvert; **— with** couvert de
cow vache *f.*
cowardly lâche
crazy fou (fol *before vowel or h*), folle
cream crème *f.*; **— cake (pie, tart)** gâteau à la crème; **ice —** glace *f.*
create créer
creditor créancier *m.*
crime crime *m.*
criticize critiquer
Croat, Croatian croate
cross traverser
cry crier, s'écrier
cuff manchette *f.*; **— link** bouton de manchette
cup tasse *f.*
customer client *m.*, cliente *f.*
cut: — out, — up découper

D

damp humide
dance bal *m.*
dance danser
danger danger *m.*
dangerous dangereux (*f.* -se)
dark noir, obscur; (*of color*) foncé
darling chéri
darn: — it! Zut!
darned sacré
dash tiret *m.*
date date *f.*; rendez-vous *m.*; **to set a —** se donner rendez-vous
daughter fille *f.*; **— in-law** belle-fille *f.*
day jour *m.*, journée *f.*; **— after tomorrow** après-demain; **— before yesterday** avant-hier; **a —** par jour; **all —** toute la journée; **every —** tous les jours; **good —** bonjour; **the whole —** toute la journée; **this very —** aujourd'hui même
daylight: in broad — en plein jour
dead mort
deal: a great — beaucoup (de)
dear cher, chère; chéri
dearest chéri
death mort *f.*
debt dette *f.*
December décembre *m.*
deck pont *m.*
declaration déclaration *f.*
declare déclarer; **I declare!** par exemple!
deep profond; foncé (*color*)
delicious délicieux (*f.* délicieuse)
delighted enchanté
delightful délicieux (*f.* délicieuse)
deliver livrer
delivery livraison *f.*
demand exiger (nous exigeons)

Denmark Danemark *m.*
dentifrice dentifrice
depart partir (*p. p.* parti) (*with* être)
departure départ *m.*
deploy déployer (je déploie)
deputy député *m.*
desire envie *f.;* désir *m.*
desire désirer
desk bureau *m.* (*pl.* bureaux)
dessert dessert *m.*
destroy détruire (*like* conduire)
detective policier (*adj.*) (*f.* policière)
detective story roman policier
devoted dévoué
dialogue dialogue *m.*
dictate dicter
dictation dictée *f.*
die mourir (*p. p.* mort) (*with* être)
diet régime *m.*
difference: it makes no — cela ne fait rien
different divers
difficult difficile
difficulty difficulté *f.*
dine dîner
dining car wagon-restaurant *m.*
dining room salle à manger *f.*
dinner dîner *m*; **to have —** dîner
dip tremper
direct direct
direct diriger (nous dirigeons)
direction direction *f.*, côté *m.*; **in my —** de mon côté
dirty sale
disagreeable désagréable
discuss discuter
dish plat *m.*
dishes: set of — service *m.*
dispose disposer; **disposed to** disposé à
distance: at a — à distance
disturb déranger (nous dérangeons)
diverse divers
diversion divertissement *m.*
do faire; **— our best** faire notre possible; **— no good** ne servir à rien
doctor docteur *m.*
dog chien *m.*
dollar dollar *m.*
done fait, -e
door porte *f.*
door-knob bouton *m.*
double-breasted croisé
doubt douter (de)
down en bas; **come (go) —** descendre; **lie —** se coucher; **set —** établir; **sit —** s'asseoir; **— there** là-bas; **—town** en ville
down-slope descente *f.*
downstairs en bas
dozen douzaine (de) *f.*; **half- —** demi-douzaine *f.*
draw dessiner
drawer tiroir *m.*
drawing-room salon *m.*
dress robe *f.*
dress s'habiller
dressing gown robe de chambre *f.*
drink boisson *f.*
drink boire (*p. p.* bu)
dripping with perspiration (to be) être en nage
drive conduire
driver conducteur *m.*
driving permit permis de conduire *m.*
drug store pharmacie *f.*
dry sec (*f.* sèche)
during pendant, au cours de
dust poussière *f.*
dynamite dynamite *f.*

E

each chaque; **— one** chacun (*f.* chacune); **— other** se, l'un l'autre; **— time** chaque fois
ear oreille *f.*
early de bonne heure, tôt
earn gagner
earth terre *f.*
east orient *m.*, est *m.*
easy facile; **— to soil** salissant
eat manger (nous mangeons)
economic économique
edged bordé
education instruction *f.*
Edward Edouard

egg œuf *m.* (*final f pronounced in singular but silent in plural* œufs); **ham and eggs** des œufs au jambon
eight huit
eighteen dix-huit
eighty quatre-vingts
elbow coude *m.*
electric électrique
elegant chic
eleven onze
else: anything —? rien d'autre?; **it's something —** c'est autre chose
empty vide
encumber encombrer
end fin *f.*
end finir, terminer; **— by** finir par
endorse endosser
enemy ennemi *m.*
England Angleterre *f.*
English anglais
enjoy jouir (de)
enjoy oneself s'amuser (bien)
enormous énorme
enormously énormément
enough assez (de); **that's —** ça suffit
enter entrer (dans) (*with* être)
entire entier (*f.* entière)
entitle intituler
entrance entrée *f.*; **no —** défense d'entrer
envelope enveloppe *f.*
envisage envisager (nous envisageons)
envy envie *f.*
equal égal (*m. pl.* égaux)
Ernestine Ernestine
errand course *f.*
escape se sauver, échapper (à)
especially surtout
establish établir
Europe Europe *f.*
even même (*adv.*)
evening soir *m.*, soirée *f.*; **in the —** le soir; **this —** ce soir; **the whole —** toute la soirée
ever jamais; **not —** ne . . . jamais
every chaque, tout, -e; **— day** tous les jours; **— Monday** tous les lundis
everybody tout le monde
every one chacun, -e; **— to his taste** chacun son goût
everything tout
everywhere partout
exasperating embêtant
excellent excellent
except: not . . . — ne . . . que
exchange change *m.*, échange *m.*
exchange changer (de) (nous changeons)
exchange office bureau de change *m.*
exciting passionnant
excuse excuse *f.*
excuse excuser; **— me** excusez-moi, pardon
exercise exercice *m.*
exhausted: to get — s'épuiser
exit sortie *f.*
expect attendre, compter, s'attendre à; **what would you —?** que voulez-vous?
expenses frais *m. pl.*
expensive cher (*f.* chère)
experience expérience *f.*
explain expliquer
explosive explosif *m.*
expression expression *f.*
extent: to such an — tellement
extract extraire
extraction extraction *f.*
extreme extrême
eye œil *m.* (*pl.* yeux)
eye-glasses lunettes *f. pl.*

F

face visage *m.*, figure *f.*
face faire face à
fact: as a matter of — effectivement, en effet; **in —** effectivement, en effet; **the — is that** c'est que
factory usine *f.*
faculty corps professoral *m.*
fail échouer; **— to do** manquer (de + *inf.*)
faint s'évanouir
fair raisonnable
faithful fidèle
fall tomber (*with* être); **— asleep** s'endormir; **— in love with** tomber amoureux (amoureuse) de

fall automne *m.*
false faux (*f.* fausse)
familiarly: address — tutoyer
family famille *f.*
famous fameux (*f.* -se)
far, far away loin; **far from** loin de; **that's going too far** c'est un peu fort
farewell adieu *m.*
farm ferme *f.*
fashion façon *f.;* **in this —** de cette façon; **in grand —** d'une façon magnifique
fast vite
fat gras (*f.* grasse)
fate destinée *f.*, sort *m.*
father père *m.*
father-in-law beau-père *m.*
fear peur *f.*, crainte *f.;* **for — of** de crainte de, de peur de; **for — that** de crainte que
fear craindre; avoir peur de
fearful peureux (*f.* -se)
feast fête *f.*
February février *m.;* **in —** au mois de février, en février
feeble faible
feel se sentir (*p. p.* senti); **— like** avoir envie de
fever fièvre *f.*
few peu (de), quelques, quelques-uns
field champ *m.*
fifteen quinze
fifty cinquante
fight combattre
figure taille *f.*
fill remplir
filled with plein de
fill up encombrer
film film *m.*
final final (*m. pl.* finals)
find trouver; **— oneself** se trouver
fine beau (bel *before vowel or h, f. s.* belle, *m. pl.* beaux, *f. pl.* belles); excellent, brave; **that's —** très bien; **the weather is —** il fait beau temps
finger doigt *m.*
finish finir (de) (*p. p.* fini); terminer
fire feu *m.*
fire faire feu
firing (*of guns*) feu *m.*
first premier (*f.* première); **at —** d'abord
fish poisson *m.*
fit aller (bien), chausser
five cinq
flank flanc *m.*
flannel flanelle *f.*
flat plat
flatter flatter
flight: one — up au premier étage
"fling" (*slang*) "bombe" *f.*
floor étage *m.;* **on the third —** au second étage
flower fleur *f.*
fly voler
foe ennemi *m.*
fog brouillard *m.*
follow suivre (*p. p.* suivi); **— me** suivez-moi
following suivant, ensuite
food vivres *m. pl.*
foolish sot (*f.* sotte)
foolishness: piece of — sottise *f.*
foot pied *m.*
for pour (*prep.*), car (*conj.*); **as —** quant à; **send —** faire venir
forbid défendre
forehead front *m.*
foreign étranger (*f.* étrangère)
forget oublier (de)
fork fourchette *f.*
form former
former: the — celui-là
formerly autrefois
fortnight quinze jours
fortunately heureusement
forty quarante
fountain pen stylo *m.*
four quatre
fourteen quatorze
fourth quart *m.;* quatrième
fragment fragment *m.*
franc franc *m.*
France France *f.;* **to —, in —** en France
frank franc (*f.* franche)
Frank, Francis François
free libre; **— from** à l'abri de
freedom liberté *f.*
French français; **— style** à la

française; — **fried potatoes** frites *f. pl.*
Friday vendredi *m.*
fried frit; **French — potatoes** frites *f. pl.*
friend ami *m.*, amie *f.*; **girl —** amie *f.*; **my —** mon vieux
friendship amitié *f.*
frightful effroyable
from de (d'), dans; **— me** de ma part; **— it, — them** en
front devant *m.*
front: in — of devant
frontier frontière *f.*
fruit fruit *m.*
full (of) plein (de)
funny drôle
fur fourrure *f.*
furnish fournir
furnished meublé
furniture meubles *m. pl.*
further: — on plus loin
furthermore de plus
fuss histoire *f.*

G

gain gagner, remporter
gangway! laissez passer!
garden jardin *m.*; **Botanical —s** Jardin des Plantes *m.*
garment vêtement *m.*
gasoline essence *f.*
gay gai
gear: steering — guidon *m.*
general général; **in —** en général
gentleman monsieur *m.*; **gentlemen** messieurs *m. pl.*
geography géographie *f.*
George Georges
German allemand
Germany Allemagne *f.*
gesture mouvement *m.*, geste *m.*
get obtenir, prendre, se procurer; **— along** s'entendre, (*manage*) se tirer d'affaire; **— back** revenir, être de retour; **— impatient** s'impatienter; **— in** monter (à) (dans); **— rid of** se débarrasser de; **— to** (*reach*) arriver à; **— up** se lever
gift cadeau *m.*
girl jeune fille *f.*
give donner; **— back** rendre; **— up** (*something*) renoncer à
glad content, heureu-x, -se; **be — to** vouloir bien; **I'm —, I'm — of that** j'en suis heureux
gladly volontiers
glass verre *m.*; **eye- —s** lunettes *f. pl.*; **large — of beer** demi *m.*; **small — of beer** bock *m.*
gleam briller
glove gant *m.*
glutton gourmand *m.*
go aller, partir, marcher, se rendre; **— (by train, on foot, on horseback, by car, by boat, by carriage)** aller (par le train, à pied, à cheval, en auto, en bateau, en voiture); **— away** s'en aller; **— back** retourner, rentrer; **— beyond** dépasser; **— down** descendre; **— for a walk** faire une promenade; **— home** rentrer; **— in** entrer (dans); **— on** continuer; **— on the road** partir en tournée; **— out** sortir; **— to bed** se coucher; **— too far (that's going too far)** c'est un peu fort; **— up (to)** monter (à); **— with** accompagner; **let's —** en route
good bon, -ne, brave; **a — deal** beaucoup; **do no —** ne servir à rien; **have a — time** s'amuser bien
good afternoon (day, morning) bonjour
goodbye au revoir; **say —** faire (ses) adieux (à)
goodness! mon Dieu! ma foi!
good night bonne nuit
gown robe *f.*; **dressing- —** robe de chambre *f.*
gracious! mon Dieu!
grammar grammaire *f.*
granddaughter petite-fille *f.*
grandfather grand-père *m.*
grandmother grand'mère *f.*, grand' maman *f.*
grand-papa grand-père *m.*
grandson petit-fils *m.*
grapes raisin *m.*

grass herbe *f.*
gray gris
great grand; a **— deal** beaucoup
Greece Grèce *f.*
green vert
greet saluer
ground terre *f.*; **on the —** par terre
grow pousser
guest hôte *m.*; **invited —** invité *m.*
guide guide *m.*; **serve as a —** servir de guide (à)
gun: machine — mitrailleuse *f.*

H

had eu (*p. p. of* avoir)
hair cheveux *m. pl.*
half moitié *f.*, demi *m.*
half (*adj.*) demi, -e; **— dozen** demi-douzaine *f.*; **— an hour** demi-heure *f.*; **an hour and a —** une heure et demie *f.*; **— turn** demi-tour *m.*
hall salle *f.*
halt s'arrêter
ham jambon *m.*; **— and eggs** des œufs au jambon
hammerer marteleur *m.*
hand main *f.*; **on the other —** d'ailleurs, par contre; **on the right — side of** à droite de; **to shake —s** se serrer la main
handbag sac à main *m.*
handkerchief mouchoir *m.*
handle bars guidon *m.*
handsome beau (bel *before vowel or mute*, h, *f. s.* belle, *m. pl.* beaux, *f. pl.* belles)
happen arriver, se passer
happily heureusement
happy content (de), heureux (*f.* -se), joyeux (*f.* -se); **be — to** être heureux de + *infinitive*
harbor port *m.*
hard (*adj.*) difficile
hard (*adv.*) fort, dur, ferme
hardly à peine
haste hâte *f.* (*use* la); **in —** en hâte
hat chapeau *m.*
have avoir; **— just** venir de + *infinitive;* **— (*someone*) do** faire faire à; **— (*something*) done** faire faire; **— to** devoir
hay foin *m.*
he il, lui
head tête *f.*; (*of an office*) chef *m.*
headlight phare *m.*
health santé *f.*; **to your —** à votre santé (*reply:* à la vôtre, **to yours**)
heap tas *m.*
hear entendre; **— about** entendre parler de (*conjug.* entendre *only*); **— from (let me hear from you)** donnez-moi de vos nouvelles
heard: I have heard (*people*) say j'ai entendu dire; **to have — from** avoir des nouvelles de
heart cœur *m.*
heartfelt cordial (*m. pl.* cordiaux)
heat chaleur *f.*
heating plant calorifère *m.*
heaven ciel *m.*
heck! Zut!
hedgehog hérisson *m.* (*use* le)
heel talon *m.*
Helen Hélène
hello! allô! (*telephone*)
help aider
help secours *m.*; **help!** au secours!; **to the — of** au secours de
hen poule *f.*
Henrietta Henriette
Henry Henri
her elle, la, lui (*pro.*); son, sa, ses (*adj.*)
here ici; **here!** (*when handing somebody something*) tenez! tiens!
here is (are) voici; **— I am** me voici
hers le sien, *etc.*; à elle
herself elle-même
hide cacher
high haut; (*expensive*) cher; **the cost of living is —** la vie coûte cher
highway route *f.*
hill colline *f.*
him lui, le
himself lui-même
hinder empêcher (de)
hire louer

his son, sa, ses; le sien, *etc.;* à lui
history histoire *f.*
hit tamponner, frapper
hold tenir (*p. p.* tenu)
hold out tenir le coup
Holland Hollande *f.* (*use* la)
homage hommage *m.*
home: at — chez moi, *etc.,* **come, go —** rentrer
honest honnête
honor faire honneur à
hope espérer (j'espère)
hoped for espéré
horse cheval *m.* (*pl.* chevaux)
hospital hôpital *m.*
hospitality hospitalité *f.*
host hôte *m.*
hostage ôtage *m.*
hot chaud
hotel hôtel *m.*
hour heure *f.*
house maison *f.;* **at (my) house** chez (moi)
how! que! (*exclamatory; follow with declarative word order*); **— kind it is of you** que c'est gentil à vous
how comment; **— are things?** comment ça va?; **— are you?** comment ça va?, comment allez-vous?, comment vous portez-vous? **— do you do?** comment allez-vous, comment vous portez-vous?; **— do you say?** comment dit-on (en français)? **— goes it?** comment ça va?; **— is the weather?** quel temps fait-il?; **— long have you been here?** depuis quand (combien de temps) êtes-vous ici?; **— old are you?** quel âge avez-vous?; **— many** *or* **much** combien (de)
however pourtant, cependant, néanmoins
hundred cent; **two —** deux cents; **about a —** une centaine *f.*
Hungary Hongrie *f.* (*use* la)
hunger faim *f.*
hungry: be — avoir faim
hunt: book- — bouquiner
hurl lancer (nous lançons)
hurried pressé
hurry se dépêcher; **be in a —** être pressé; **— up!** dépêche-toi, dépêchez-vous
hurt faire mal à
husband mari *m.*

I

I je, j', moi
ice glace *f.*
ice cream glace *f.*
idea: the very —! par exemple!
if si (s' *before* il, ils)
ill malade (*adj.*), mal (*adv.*)
illness maladie *f.*
illusion illusion *f.*
immediately tout de suite
impatient: to get — s'impatienter
imperative impératif *m.*
imperfect imparfait *m.* (*verb tense*)
impolite impoli
important important
impossible impossible; **impossible!** pas possible!
impression impression *f.*
in en, dans, à; (*after superlative*) de; **go —** entrer (dans) (*with* être)
indeed en effet, effectivement
indefinite indéfini; **past —** passé composé (*verb tense*)
indicate indiquer
infinitely infiniment
infinitive infinitif *m.*
inform renseigner
informal sans cérémonie
information: a piece of — renseignement *m.;* (*collective*) les renseignements *m. pl.*
inhabitant habitant *m.*
ink encre *f.*
inkwell encrier *m.*
inside intérieur *m.;* dedans (*adv.*); dans (*prep.*)
insist exiger, insister
inspector inspecteur *m.*
instance: for — par exemple
instant instant *m.*
instead of au lieu de
instruction instruction *f.*

intelligent intelligent
interest intérêt *m.;* **take — in** s'intéresser à
interior intérieur *m.*
international international (*pl.* internationaux)
interrupt interrompre
intersection carrefour *m.*
introduce présenter
introduction présentation *f.*
invasion invasion *f.*
invitation invitation *f.*
invite inviter
iron fer *m.*
is it? est-ce?
is (are) there? est-ce qu'il y a?, y a-t-il?
isn't he? (didn't they, *etc.***)** n'est-ce pas? (*use where English repeats the verb*)
it il, elle, le, la, se; **— is** c'est; **— is I** c'est moi; **— is done** (*one does it*) ça se fait
Italian italien (*f.* italienne)
Italy Italie *f.*
its son, sa, ses; le sien (la sienne, *etc.*)

J

jacket veston *m.*, jaquette *f.*
jail prison *f.*
James Jacques
January janvier *m.*
Japan Japon *m.*
Japanese japonais
jewel bijou *m.* (*pl.* bijoux)
join joindre, se joindre à
join again rejoindre
joke blaguer, plaisanter; **I was joking** c'était pour rire
Joseph Joseph
journey voyage *m.*
joy joie *f.*
juice jus *m.*
July juillet *m.*
June juin *m.*
just précisément, juste; **— a second** un instant; **— now** tout à l'heure; **— the same** tout de même, quand même

K

keep right (left)! tenez la droite (gauche)!
key clé, clef *f.;* **off —** faux (*f.* fausse)
kill tuer
kind sorte *f.;* **all —s of** toutes sortes de
kind bon, (*f.* bonne), gentil (*f.* gentille), aimable; **— to** aimable pour, bon pour; **it's very — of him (her, you)** c'est très gentil de sa (votre) part; **how — it is of you!** que c'est gentil à vous
kindness amabilité *f.*, bonté *f.;* **please have the — to** ayez la bonté de
king roi *m.*
kiss embrasser
kitchen cuisine *f.*
knee genou *m.* (*pl.* genoux)
knife couteau *m.* (*pl.* couteaux)
knock frapper
know connaître, savoir; **— how** savoir; **I — what I'm talking about** je suis sûr de mon affaire; **I don't —** je ne (le) sais pas; **— nothing about** ignorer
knowledge: without the — of à l'insu de

L

laboratory laboratoire *m.*
lace dentelle *f.*
lack (be lacking) manquer (de)
lack: for — of faute de
ladder échelle *f.*
lady dame *f.;* **young —** demoiselle *f.*
lake lac *m.*
lamb: leg of — gigot *m.*
lamp lampe *f.*
land terre *f.*, pays *m.*
land débarquer
language langue *f.*
large gros, (*f.* grosse), grand; **— glass of beer** demi *m.*
last dernier (*f.* dernière); **at —** enfin; **the — time** la dernière fois; **— night** hier soir

late tard, en retard; **I am —** je suis en retard
later: I'll see you — à plus tard, à bientôt
latter celui-ci, *etc.*
laugh rire; **— at** rire de, se moquer de
laundry (*room*) buanderie *f.*
law loi *f.*, droit *m.; **study —*** faire son droit
lead conduire, mener, amener, emmener
learn apprendre (à)
least: at — au moins
leave congé *m.;* **take — of** prendre congé de
leave laisser, partir, quitter
lecture conférence *f.*
left gauche; **to the —** à gauche; **keep to the —** tenir la gauche
leg jambe *f.;* **— of lamb** gigot *m.*
lend prêter
less moins; **— than** moins de, moins que; **more or —** à peu près
lesson leçon *f.*
let laisser, permettre (de); **— oneself be led** se laisser conduire; **—'s get started (—'s get going)** mettons-nous en route; **—'s go** en route
letter lettre *f.*
letter box boîte aux lettres *f.*
liberation libération *f.*
liberty liberté *f.*
lie down se coucher
life vie *f.*
light lumière *f.*
light allumer
light léger (*f.* légère), (*in color*) clair
like comme; **feel —** avoir envie de; **look —** avoir l'air de
like aimer (à); **I'd — to** je voudrais (+ *inf.*); **I — that!** (*ironical*) ça c'est chic!
line ligne *f.*, queue *f.;* **stand in —** faire la queue
lined doublé
link: cuff- — bouton de manchette *m.*
lip lèvre *f.*
lipstick bâton de rouge pour les lèvres *m.*
liqueur, liquor liqueur *f.*
listen, listen to écouter; **—!** dites donc!
little (*adj.*) petit
little (*adv.*) peu (de)
little peu *m.*
live vivre; **— in** habiter, demeurer dans *or* à
livelihood, living vie *f.;* **the cost of living is high** la vie coûte cher
living room salon *m.*
loan emprunt *m.*
lobster homard *m.* (use *le*)
lock fermer à clé
long long (*f.* longue); **as — as** tant que; **how —** depuis quand, depuis combien de temps: **so —** à bientôt; **a — time** longtemps
look regarder; **— at** regarder, contempler; **— for** chercher; **— here!** dites donc!; **— like** avoir l'air de, ressembler à
lose perdre; **— interest in** se désintéresser de
lots (of) beaucoup (de)
loud (*of a color*) voyant; **out —** à haute voix
love aimer
love amour *m.;* **in —** amoureux (*f.* -se)
low bas (*f.* basse, *m. pl.* bas, *f. pl.* basses)
luck chance *f.;* **bad —** guigne *f.*
luckily heureusement
lucky: to be — avoir de la chance
lunch déjeuner *m.*
lunch: have — déjeuner
lung poumon *m.*

M

Ma'am Madame (*abbrev.* Mme—*no period*)
machine machine *f.*
machine-gun mitrailleuse *f.*
Madam Madame (*abbrev.* Mme—*no period*)
maddening embêtant
made fait (*p. p. of* faire)

Madeleine Madeleine
magazine revue *f.*
magnificent magnifique
maid servante *f.*, bonne *f.*
mail mettre à la poste
major commandant *m.*
make faire; **— a mistake** se tromper; **— no difference** ne faire rien (**it makes no difference** cela ne fait rien); **— a note of** prendre note de; **— oneself understood** se faire comprendre; **— out a check** faire un chèque **— use of** se servir de
make-up maquillage *m.*
make up se maquiller, se farder
ueui homme *m.*; **old —** mon vieux
many beaucoup (de), bien de+*art;* **as — as** autant que; **how —** combien (de); **so —** tant (de); **too —** trop (de)
March mars *m.*
Margaret Marguerite
Marie Marie
mark: a passing — une note suffisante *f.*
marry épouser, se marier (avec); **— off** marier
marvelously merveilleusement
Mary **Marie**
mass messe *f.*
massacre massacrer
match allumette *f.*
material étoffe *f.*
matter matière *f.*; **as a — of fact** effectivement, en effet; **be a — of** s'agir de; **what's the —** qu'y a-t-il?, qu'est-ce qu'il y a?; **what's the — with you?** qu'avez-vous?; **it doesn't —** n'importe
mattress matelas *m.*
May mai *m.*
may pouvoir; **— I?** puis-je?, est-ce que je puis?
maybe peut-être
me moi, me
meal repas *m.*
mean vouloir dire; **what does that —?** qu'est-ce que cela veut dire?; **what do you —?** que voulez-vous dire?
means moyen m.; **by — of** au moyen de
meanwhile en attendant
meat viande *f.*
mechanically machinalement
mechanized motorisé
meddle with se mêler de
medicine médicament *m.*
meet rencontrer, (*socially*) faire la connaissance de
mention: don't — it il n'y a pas de quoi
menu carte *f.*, menu *m.*
merchant marchand *m.*
merry gai
method methode *f.*
Mexico Mexique *m.*
midnight minuit *m.*
military militaire
milk lait *m.*
million million (de) *m.*
mind: never — n'importe
mine mine *f.*
mine à moi; le mien, *etc.*
minister ministre *m.*
ministry ministère *m.*
mint menthe *f.*
minute minute *f.*
mirror miroir *m.*, glace *f.*
Miss mademoiselle (*abbrev.* Mlle)
miss manquer; **—** + *gerund* manquer de+*infinitive*
missing: be — manquer
mission mission *f.*
mist brouillard *m.*
mistake: make a — se tromper
mistaken: be — se tromper
Mister Monsieur (*abbrev.* M.)
misunderstanding malentendu *m.*
Mohammedan musulman
moment: every — à tout instant
Monday lundi *m.*; **on —** lundi; **last (next) —** lundi dernier (prochain)
money argent *m.*
money-order mandat-poste *m.* (*pl.* les mandats-poste)
month mois m.; **last —** le mois dernier
moon lune *f.*
more plus (de), de plus; **— than**

plus de, plus que; **— or less** à peu près, plus ou moins
morning matin *m.*, matinée *f.*; **good —** bonjour; **in the —** le matin; **the whole —** toute la matinée
mother mère *f.*
mother-in-law belle-mère *f.*
motion mouvement *m.*
motion picture film *m.*
motor moteur *m.*
motorcycle motocyclette *f.*, moto *f.*
motorized motorisé
mount monter (à)
mountain montagne *f.*
mouth bouche *f.*
move remuer
moved ému
movement mouvement *m.*
movie film *m.*
movie-house cinéma *m.*
Mr. Monsieur (*abbrev.* M.)
Mrs. Madame (*abbrev.* Mme—*no period*)
much beaucoup (de); **as — as** autant que; **how —** combien (de); **not —** ne . . . pas grand' chose; **not —** tant (de); **so — the worse** tant pis; **too —** trop (de); **very —** beaucoup
mud boue *f.*
murder assassiner
museum musée *m.*
must falloir, devoir
mustache moustache *f.*
my mon, ma, mes
myself moi-même
mysterious mystérieux (*f.* -se)

N

nail ongle *m.*
name nom *m.*; **one's — to be** s'appeler; **my — is** je m'appelle; **what's your —?** comment vous appelez-vous?
napkin serviette *f.*
narrow étroit
nation nation *f.*
national national (*m. pl.* -aux)
natural naturel (*f.* naturelle)
naturally naturellement
nature nature *f.*
near près (de); **very near** tout près (de)
nearly presque
necessary nécessaire
neck cou *m.*
need besoin *m.*
need avoir besoin de
needle aiguille *f.* (*pronounce* the *u*)
negative négatif (*f.* -ve)
neither . . . nor ne . . . ni . . . ni
nephew neveu *m.*
nervous: be — s'énerver
nervous agité
never ne . . . jamais; **— mind** n'importe
nevertheless cependant, néanmoins, pourtant
new nouveau (nouvel *before a vowel or h, f. s.* nouvelle, *m. pl.* nouveaux, *f. pl.* nouvelles); neuf (*f.* neuve); **that's —** c'est du nouveau
news nouvelles *f. pl.*; **a piece of —** nouvelle *f.*; **have — of** avoir des nouvelles de
newspaper journal *m.* (*pl.* journaux)
New Year Nouvelle Année
New York New-York
next prochain; **— door** à côté; **— to** à côté de
nice gentil (*f.* -le)
niece nièce *f.*
night nuit *f.*; **at —** la nuit; **good —** bonne nuit; **last —** hier soir; **tonight** ce soir
nightfall tombée de la nuit *f.*
nightgown chemise de nuit *f.*
nine neuf
nineteen dix-neuf
ninety quatre-vingt-dix
no non, pas; (*adj.*) aucun (*f.* -e); **— entrance** défense d'entrer; **— matter what** n'importe quoi; **— one** personne; **— smoking** défense de fumer
nobody ne . . . personne
noisy bruyant
noon midi *m.*
no one ne . . . personne
nor ni

Norman normand
Normandy Normandie *f.*
north nord *m.*
Norway Norvège *f.*
nose nez *m.*
not ne . . . pas; — **anybody (any one)** ne . . . personne; — **anything** ne . . . rien; — **at all** pas du tout, du tout; (*emphatic*) ne . . . point; — **but** ne . . . que; — **ever** ne . . . jamais; — **except** ne . . . que; — **much** ne . . . pas grand' chose; — **so** ne . . . pas si; — **yet** pas encore
note note *f.;* **bank** — billet de banque *m.;* **make a — of** prendre note de
notebook cahier *m.*
nothing ne . . . rien; **that's** — ce n'est rien; **know — about** ignorer
notice affiche *f.;* **(public)** — avis (au public) *m.*
notice remarquer
noun nom *m.*
novel roman *m.*
novelist romancier *m.*
November novembre *m.*
now maintenant; **come** — allons, allons donc!; **just** — tout à l'heure
number nombre *m.;* (*specific, as 6*) numéro *m.*
numerous nombreux, -se
nurse infirmière *f.*

O

object complément *m.*
obtain obtenir, se procurer
occupy occuper
October octobre *m.*
of de; — **it, them** en; — **course** naturellement
off: — **key** faux (*f.* fausse); **put** — remettre; **take** — ôter
offer offrir (de); — **one's regards to** présenter ses hommages à
office bureau *m.;* **at the — of** chez; **post** — poste *f.*
often souvent
oil: **petroleum** — pétrole *m.*
O. K. c'est bien; —? ça va?, ça y est?; —! entendu!
old vieux *or* vieil, vieille; — **man** mon vieux; **I am (ten) years** — j'ai (dix) ans
on sur, (*with present participle*) en; **go** — continuer; **put** — **again** remettre; — **account of** à cause de
once une fois; — **a day** une fois par jour; — **again** encore une fois; — **a week** une fois par semaine; **at** — à l'instant
one un, -e; (*someone*) on; **each** — chacun, -e; **the** — celui, celle; **the —s** ceux, celles; **which** — lequel, laquelle
oneself se, soi, soi-même
only seulement; ne . . . que
open ouvrir
open, opened ouvert
opening ouverture *f.*
opera opéra *m.*
opinion avis *m.;* **be of the** — être d'avis; **be of your** — être de votre avis; **in my** — à mon avis
opportunity occasion *f.*
opposite contraire, en face de
or ou; — **else** ou bien
order commande *f.;* **money-** — mandat-poste *m.* (*pl.* les mandats-poste)
order commander
order: **in** — en règle; **in — that** pour que, afin que (+ *subj.*); **in — to** afin de, pour
orthodox orthodoxe
other autre; **on the — side of** de l'autre côté de
otherwise autrement
ought devoir; **I — to** je devrais
our notre, nos
ours le nôtre, *etc.*
ourselves nous-mêmes
out dehors; **cut** — découper; **go** — sortir; **put** — mettre à la porte; **set** — se mettre en route; **take** — sortir, emmener; — **loud** à haute voix
outline dessiner
outside dehors

over: — there là-bas
overcast couvert
overcoat pardessus *m.*
overlooking donnant sur
owe devoir
own (*adj.*) propre

P

pack: — a bag faire sa valise
package paquet *m.*
packing emballage *m.*
paint se maquiller
pair paire *f.*
pajamas pyjama *m.*
pal copain *m.*
palace palais *m.*
pants pantalon *m.*
paper papier *m.*; **news—** journal *m.*; **writing —** papier à lettres *m.*
pardon: — me! pardon!
parents parents *m. pl.*
Parisian parisien *m.* (*f.* -ne)
park parc *m.*
parlor salon *m.*
participle participe *m.*
pass passer
passing: a — mark une note suffisante *f.*
passport passeport *m.*
past passé *m.*; **— indefinite** passé composé
paste pâte *f.*; **tooth —** pâte dentifrice *f.*
patient malade *m., f.*
Paul Paul
Paulette Paulette
Pauline Pauline
pay payer (je paie *or* je paye); **— for** payer; **— a visit (to)** faire une visite (à)
peace paix *f.*
peaceful tranquille
peach pêche *f.*
pear poire *f.*
peas petits pois *m. pl.*
pen plume *f.*; **fountain —** stylo *m.*
pencil crayon *m.*; **automatic —** port-mine *m.*
penetrate pénétrer (je pénètre)
peninsula péninsule *f.*
penny sou *m.*
people gens *m. pl.*, monde *m.*, on
pepper poivre *m.*
perfect parfait; **that's —!** parfait!
perfume parfum *m.*
perhaps peut-être
permanent permanent
permit permettre
permit: driving — permis de conduire *m.*
persist persister
personal personnel (*f.* -le)
perspiration: be dripping with — être en nage
perspire transpirer
Peru Pérou *m.*
Peter Pierre
petroleum oil pétrole *m.*
Philip Philippe
phone téléphone *m.*
physician médecin *m.*
piano piano *m.*
picnic pique-nique *m.*
picture tableau *m.* (*pl.* tableaux); **motion —** film *m.*
pie: cream — gâteau à la crème *m.*
piece pièce *f.*, morceau *m.* (*pl.* morceaux); **— of foolishness** sottise *f.*; **— of information** renseignement *m.*
pierce traverser
pig cochon *m.*
pill pilule *f.*
pillow oreiller *m.*
pin épingle *f.*
pity: what a —! c'est dommage!, quel dommage!
place lieu *m.* (*pl.* -x), place *f.*, endroit *m.*
place mettre (*p. p.* mis)
plane avion *m.*
plant: heating — calorifère *m.*
plate assiette *f.*; **soup —** assiette à soupe *f.*
platform: station — quai *m.*
platoon peloton *m.*
play pièce *f.* (*theater*)
pleasant agréable
please faire plaisir (à)
please: (if you) — s'il vous plaît; ayez la bonté de

pleased content (de); **— to meet you** enchanté de faire votre connaissance
pleasure plaisir *m.; **that gives me great —*** cela me fait grand plaisir
plunge plonger (nous plongeons)
plural pluriel *m.*
pocket poche *f.*
point of view: from the — au point de vue
Poland Pologne *f.*
police police *f.; **— commissioner*** commissaire de police *m.; **—man*** agent de police *m.*
police (*adj.*) policier (*f.* policière)
policy politique *f.*
polish cirage *m.*
polish cirer
polite poli
political politique
politics politique *f.*
poor pauvre
poorly mal
population population *f.*
port port *m.*
porter porteur *m.*
Portugal Portugal *m.*
possession: take — of s'emparer de
possessive possessif (*f.* -ve)
possible possible
post poste *m.; **sign —*** poteau indicateur *m.*
postcard carte postale *f.*
post-office poste *f.*
postpone remettre
potato pomme de terre *f.; **French fried —s*** frites *f. pl.*
pour: — rain pleuvoir à verse
powder poudre *f.*
power puissance *f.*
precious précieux (*f.* précieuse); (*ironical*) fameux (*f.* fameuse)
precisely précisément
prefer préférer (je préfère)
prepare préparer
prescription ordonnance *f.*
present oneself se présenter
present (*gift*) cadeau *m.*
present (*time*) présent *m.*
presently tout à l'heure; **I'll see you —** à tout à l'heure
press presse *f.*
pretty joli
prevent empêcher (de)
previously auparavant
price prix *m.* (*pl.* prix)
principal principal (*pl.* principaux)
prison prison *f.*
prize prix *m.* (*pl.* prix)
probable probable
process procédé *m.*
production production *f.*
professor professeur *m.*
promise promesse *f.*
promise promettre (de)
pronoun pronom *m.*
proper convenable; propre
proposal déclaration *f.*
Protestant protestant
provided pourvu que
province province *f.*
prudence prudence *f.*
public public *m.*
public public (*f.* publique); **— notice** avis au public
publicity publicité *f.*, réclame *f.*, annonce *f.*
pulse pouls *m.*
punish punir
pupil élève *m.*, *f.*
purchase emplette *f.*, achat *m.*
push pousser, bousculer
put mettre (*p. p.* mis); **— off** remettre (*p. p.* remis); **— on again** remettre (*p. p.* remis); **— out** mettre à la porte; **— up** (*at a hotel*) descendre (*with* être)

Q

quarter quart *m.*
quay quai *m.*
question question *f.; **ask a —*** poser une question; **be a — of** s'agir de
quickly vite
quinine quinine *f.; **— hair tonic*** eau de quinine *f.*
quite tout à fait, assez, bien; **— well** assez bien

R

rag: "chew the —" bavarder
railroad chemin de fer *m.*
rain pluie *f.*
rain pleuvoir; **pour —** pleuvoir à verse
raincoat imperméable *m.*
Ralph Raoul
rapid rapide
rare rare
rascal coquin *m.;* **you — !** ah, coquin!
rate: at any — en tout cas
rather assez, plutôt
razor rasoir *m.;* **— blade** lame de rasoir *f.*
reach arriver à
read lire (*p. p.* lu)
ready prêt
real vrai
realize se rendre compte de
really vraiment
rear: to the — dans le fond
reason raison *f.;* **the — is that** c'est que
reasonable raisonnable
recall se rappeler (je me rappelle)
receive recevoir (*p. p.* reçu)
recognize reconnaître
recover se remettre (*p. p.* remis)
red rouge
refreshment rafraîchissement *m.*
refuse refuser (de)
regain rattraper
regards respects *m. pl.*, hommages *m. pl.;* **my kindest —** mes hommages les plus respectueux; **give one's — to** faire ses amitiés à; **offer one's — to** présenter ses hommages à
regime régime *m.*
regiment régiment *m.*
regular régulier (*f.* régulière)
regulate régler (je règle)
reinforcements renforts *m. pl.*
relate raconter
religious religieux (*f.* -se)
remain rester (*with* être), demeurer; **— standing** rester debout
remember se rappeler (je me rappelle), se souvenir de
René René
rent louer
repair réparer
repeat répéter
repeatedly à plusieurs reprises
replace remplacer (nous remplaçons)
reporting reportage *m.*
representative député *m.*
require exiger (nous exigeons)
research recherche *f.*
reserve réserver
resistance résistance *f.*
resole ressemeler
respect hommage *m.*
respectful respectueux (*f.* -se)
respects (*referring to old people*) respects *m. pl.;* (*referring to a lady*) hommages *m. pl.;* **my —** (*usually from a man to a woman*) mes hommages (les plus) respectueux
rest se reposer
restaurant restaurant *m.*
resume reprendre
retake reprendre
return rendre, retourner (retourner *with* être)
returned rendu (*p. p. of* rendre)
reveal révéler (je révèle)
rich riche
rid: get — of se débarrasser de
ride promenade (en auto, à cheval, *etc.*) *f.*
right juste, droit; **all —** très bien; **be —** avoir raison (**you are quite —** vous avez bien raison); **be absolutely —** avoir tout à fait raison; **keep to the —** tenir la droite; **on the — hand side of** à droite de; **to the —** à droite; **that's —** en effet, c'est ça
ring bague *f.*
ring, ring for sonner
rise surgir
river rivière *f.*, fleuve *m.*
road tournée *f.*, route *f.*, chemin *m.;* **go on the —** partir en tournée
roast rôtir
roast rôti *m.*

roasted rôti
rob voler
Robert Robert
rock rocher *m.*
roll petit pain *m.*
roof toit *m.*
room chambre *f.*, (*large*) salle *f.*; **class—** salle de classe *f.*; **dining —** salle à manger; **drawing** (*living*) **—** salon *m.*
rope corde *f.*
Rose Rose
rouge rouge *m.*
round rond
rubber caoutchouc *m.*
rude grossier (*f.* grossière)
rum rhum *m.*
run couler (*of water*); courir
rush se plonger (plongeons)
Russia Russie *f.*
Russian russe

S

sabotage sabotage *m.*
saboteur saboteur *m.*
sad triste
salesman vendeur *m.*
said dit (*p. p. of* dire)
salad salade *f.*
salt sel *m.*
salty **salé**
same même; **at the — time** à la fois; **all the —, just the —** tout de même, quand même; **it's all the — to me** ça m'est égal; **to be the —** en être de même
satisfied (with) content (de)
Saturday samedi *m.*
saving économie *f.*
say dire; **say!** dites!, dites donc!; **that is to —** c'est-à-dire; **you don't — so!** pas possible!; **— goodbye to** dire adieu à
scar cicatrice *f.*
scarcely à peine
scatter éparpiller
school école *f.*
scissors ciseaux *m. pl.*
score vingtaine *f.*
sea mer *f.*
season saison *f.*
seated assis; **be —** être assis
second second, deuxième; **just a —** un instant
secret secret (*f.* secrète)
see voir (*p. p.* vu) (*fut.* verrai); **let's —** voyons; **I'll — you later** à bientôt; **— you tomorrow** à demain; **— you tonight** à ce soir
see again revoir
seem sembler, avoir l'air de; **it seems to me** il me semble
seldom rarement
sell vendre
send envoyer (j'envoie); (*fut.* j'enverrai)
send back renvoyer (je renvoie); (*fut.* je renverrai)
send for envoyer chercher, faire venir
sentence phrase *f.*
sentinel sentinelle *f.*
September septembre *m.*
Serb, Serbian serbe
sergeant sergent *m.*
serious sérieux (*f.* sérieuse)
servant domestique *m.*, *f.*, bonne *f.*
serve servir (*like* dormir- je sers, tu sers, *etc.*); **— as a guide** (servir de guide (à)
served servi (*p. p. of* servir)
set a date se donner rendez-vous
set down établir
set out se mettre en route
seven sept
seventeen dix-sept
seventy soixante-dix
several plusieurs
sew coudre
shack bicoque *f.*
shade: window — store *m.*
shade: a light or clear — un ton clair
shade: in the — of à l'ombre de
shake hands se serrer la main
shave se raser
shaving soap savon à barbe *m.*
she elle, elle-même (*herself*)
sheep brebis *f.*
shell obus *m.* (*cannon*)
shelter abri *m.*

shelter abriter
shelter: take — se réfugier
shine briller
shirt chemise *f.*
shirt: in — sleeves en manches de chemise
shoe soulier *m.*, chaussure *f.*
shoemaker cordonnier *m.*
shoot fusiller (*military execution*), faire feu; **— at** faire feu sur
shop boutique *f.*; **coffee —** café *m.*
shop, go shopping faire des emplettes
short court, bref (*f.* brève)
short: in — enfin, bref
shorts caleçon *m.*
shot coup de feu *m.*
should: I — je devrais
shoulder épaule *f.*
shove bousculer
show indiquer, montrer; **— me** montrez-moi, faites-moi voir
shutter volet *m.*
sick malade
side flanc *m.*, côté *m.*; **on this —** de ce côté; **on the other — of** de l'autre côté de; **on which —?** de quel côté?; **on the right — of** à droite de
sideburns favoris *m. pl.*
sidewalk trottoir *m.*
signal signal *m.* (*pl.* signaux)
sign-post poteau indicateur *m.*
silk soie *f.*
silver argent *m.*
similar semblable
simply tout simplement
since puisque (*conj.*), depuis (*prep.*)
sincerely: — yours bien à vous, bien amicalement, votre bien cordialement dévoué
sing chanter
singer chanteur *m.*, chanteuse *f.*
sister sœur *f.*; **— in-law** belle-sœur *f.*
sit down s'asseoir (*p. p.* assis)
sitting assis
situation situation *f.*
six six
sixteen seize
sixty soixante
size pointure *f.*
skin peau *f.*
skirt jupon *m.*
sky ciel *m.* (*pl.* cieux)
slaughter massacrer
sleep dormir
sleep, sleepiness sommeil *m.*
sleeping-car wagon-lit *m.*
sleepy: be — avoir sommeil
sleeve manche *f.*; **in shirt —s** en manches de chemise
slender mince
slice tranche *f.*
slope: down — descente *f.*
slow lent
slowly lentement
small petit; **— glass of beer** bock *m.*, quart *m.*; **— cake** petit-four *m.*
smart intelligent
smoke fumer
smoking: no — défense de fumer
snow neige *f.*
snow neiger (*imperf.* il neigeait)
so donc, ainsi, si, tellement; **— be it** soit, **— long** à bientôt; **— many** tant de; **— much** tellement, tant de; **— much the worse** tant pis; **— so** comme ci comme ça; **— . . . that** si — que; **— that** pour que, afin que
soak tremper
soap savon *m.*; **shaving —** savon à barbe *m.*
sock chaussette *f.*
soft mou (mol *before vowel*, *f.* molle, *m. pl.* mous, *f. pl.* molles)
soil: easy to — salissant
soldier soldat *m.*
some (*partitive*) du, de l', de la, des, de, d'; (*adj.*) quelque; (*pro.*) en, quelques-uns, quelques-unes
somebody quelqu'un, on
someone quelqu'un, quelqu'une, on
something quelque chose (de); **— to eat** de quoi manger; **it's — else** c'est autre chose
sometimes quelquefois
son fils *m.* (*s pronounced*); **— -in-law** beau-fils *m.*, gendre *m.*
sonata sonate *f.*
song chanson *f.*

soon bientôt, tôt; **as — as** aussitôt que, dès que; **as — as possible** au plus tôt, le plus tôt possible
sorrow peine *f.*
sorry fâché; **be —** regretter, être fâché; **I'm —** je le regrette; **I'm very —** j'en suis désolé
soul âme *f.*
soup potage *m.*
soup-plate assiette à soupe *f.*
sour aigre
south sud *m.*, midi *m.*
Soviet Union Union Soviétique *f.*
Spain Espagne *f.*
Spanish espagnol
speak parler; **speak slowly** parlez lentement
spell (how is that spelled?) comment écrit-on cela?
spend dépenser, (*time*) passer
spite: in — of malgré
splinter fragment *m.*
spoon cuiller *f.*
spot endroit *m.*, lieu *m.* (*pl.* lieux)
spring printemps *m.*; **in —** au printemps
square place *f.*
square carré
staircase escalier *m.*
stairs: down — en bas; **up —** en haut
stamp timbre-poste *m.* (*pl.* les timbres-poste)
stamp tamponner
stand se tenir debout
stand in line faire la queue
standing debout; **be —** être debout; **remain —** rester debout
star étoile *f.*
start out se mettre en route
start to se mettre à
station gare *f.*
station platform quai *m.*
stationery store papeterie *f.*
statue statue *f.*
stay rester (*with* être)
steak bifteck *m.*
steal voler
steel acier *m.*
steer guider
steering-gear (handle-bars) guidon *m.*
steering-wheel volant *m.*
Stephen Étienne
still encore, toujours
stocking bas *m.*
stomach estomac *m.*
stone pierre *f.*
stop s'arrêter, cesser (de)
store magasin *m.*; **drug —** pharmacie *f.*; **stationery —** papeterie *f.*
story (*floor*) étage *m.*
story conte *m.*, histoire *f.*; **detective —** roman policier *m.*; **it's a different —** c'est autre chose
stove fourneau *m.*
straight droit
straight ahead tout droit
straightforward droit
stream rivière *f.*
street rue *f.*
streetcar tramway *m.*
strength force *f.*
strike frapper
stripe rayure *f.*
striped rayé
strong fort
strongly fortement
student étudiant *m.*, étudiante *f.*
study étudier; **— law** faire son droit
stuffed farci
stupid sot (*f.* sotte)
style style *m.*; **French —** à la française
stylish chic
suburbs banlieue *f.*
subway Métro *m.*
succeed (in) réussir (à)
success succès *m.*
such tel (*f.* telle); **— a** un tel, une telle; **to — an extent** tellement
suddenly tout à coup
sugar sucre *m.*
suggest suggérer
suit (man's suit) complet *m.*; **— of underwear** combinaison *f.*
suitable convenable
suitcase valise *f.*
summer été *m.*
sun soleil *m.*

Sunday dimanche *m.*
sunny: it's — il fait du soleil
superior supérieur *m.*
superlative superlatif (*f.* -ve)
supplementary supplémentaire
sure sûr, certain
surely certainement, assurément
surrender se rendre
surround entourer
survive survivre
suspect soupçonner
swallow avaler
Sweden Suède *f.*
sweet doux (*f.* douce)
sweetheart fiancé *m.*, fiancée *f.*
"swell" épatant
swim nager (nous nageons)
Switzerland Suisse *f.*
swollen enflé
Sylvia Sylvie
symptom symptôme *m.*

T

table table *f.; **at the —** à table; **clear the —** desservir
table cloth nappe *f.*
take prendre; **— a person** mener; **— a person from a place** emmener; **— a person to a place** amener; **— a walk** se promener (je me promène); **— leave of** prendre congé de; **— off ôter**; **— out** sortir; **— out** *or* **away** emmener; **— possession of** s'emparer de; **— shelter** se réfugier; **— some time to** mettre quelque temps à + *inf.;* **I'll — it** je le prends
taken, taken up pris (*p. p. of* prendre)
tale conte *m.*
talk causer
talk (what are you talking about?) de quoi parlez-vous?
tall grand
tart: cream — gâteau à la crème *m.*
taste goût *m.;* **everyone to his —** chacun son goût
taxi taxi *m.*
tea thé *m.*
teach enseigner; (*— a person*) apprendre (à)
tear déchirer
telegram télégramme *m.*, dépêche *f.*
telephone téléphone *m.*
telephone téléphoner
tell dire, raconter; **tell me** dites-moi; **somebody told me, I have been told** on m'a dit
ten dix
tense temps *m.* (*of a verb*)
term terme *m.*
than que; (*before numerals*) de; **less —** moins de, moins que
thank (for) remercier (de)
thanks, thank you merci; **— very much,** merci bien; **a million thanks** merci infiniment
that (*rel. pro., obj. of verb*) que; (*conjunction*) que; (*dem. pro.*) cela, ça; (*dem. adj.*) ce, cet, cette; **—'s all** voilà tout; **— way** ainsi
that (*conj.*) que; **so —** pour que, afin que
that one celui-là, celle-là
theatre théâtre *m.*
their leur (*pl.* leurs)
theirs le leur, la leur, les leurs
them eux, elles, les, leur
theme thème *m.*
themselves eux-mêmes, elles-mêmes
then donc, puis, alors
there (*pointing out*) là; **y**; **over —** là-bas
there is, there are il y a; (*pointing out*) voilà; **there they are** les voilà
there was, there were, there has been, there have been il y a eu, il y eut
there was, there were il y avait
therefore par conséquent, donc, aussi
Theresa Thérèse
thermometer thermomètre *m.*
these (*adj.*) ces; (*pro.*) celles-ci, ceux-ci
they ils, elles, eux, elles-mêmes, eux-mêmes
thick épais (*f.* épaisse); (*of a voice*) gras (*f.* grasse)
thief voleur *m.*

thin mince
thing chose *f.*
think penser, croire
think of penser à, songer à (nous songeons)
third troisième
thirst soif *f.*
thirteen treize
thirty trente
this (*adj.*) ce, cet, cette; (*pro.*) ceci; **— one** celui-ci, celle-ci
those (*adj.*) ces; (*pro.*) celles-là, ceux-là
thousand mille (*spelled* mil *in dates*)
thread fil *m.*
three trois
throat gorge *f.*
through à travers
throw lancer (nous lançons), jeter (il jette)
Thursday jeudi *m.*
thus ainsi
ticket billet *m.*
tie cravate *f.*
tight étroit
time temps *m.*, fois *f.*, heure *f.*; **a long —** longtemps; **at the same —** à la fois; **at what — ?** à quelle heure?; **each —** chaque fois; **from — to —** de temps en temps; **have a good —** s'amuser; **on —** à l'heure; **take some — to** mettre quelque temps à + *infinitive;* **the first —** la première fois; **the next —** la prochaine fois
time-table affiche *f.*, horaire (des trains) *m.*
timid peureux (*f.* peureuse)
tin fer-blanc *m.*
tip pourboire *m.*
tired fatigué
tireless infatigable
to à, pour (*before inf. to express purpose*); chez; **— it, — them** y
tobacco tabac *m.*
today aujourd'hui
toe doigt de pied *m.*
together ensemble
toilet (le) W. C. (*pronounced* le double vé sé)
told dit (*p. p. of* dire)
tomato tomate *f.*
tomorrow demain; **day after —** après-demain; **I'll see you —** à demain
tongue langue *f.*
tonic: quinine hair — eau de quinine *f.*
tonight ce soir; **I'll see you —** à ce soir
too aussi, trop; **— many, — much** trop (de)
tooth dent *f.*
toothbrush brosse à dents *f.*
toothpaste pâte dentifrice *f.*
tour tournée *f.* (*road tour*)
toward vers
towel serviette (de toilette) *f.*
town ville *f.*; **down —, in —** en ville
train train *m.*
tranquil tranquille
translate traduire
translation traduction *f.*
trap piège *m.*
travel voyager (nous voyageons)
"treat" offrir (*p. p.* offert)
tree arbre *m.*
trip voyage *m.*; **have a good — !** bon voyage!
triumph triompher
trooper gendarme *m.*
trouble peine *f.*
trouble déranger (nous dérangeons)
troublesome pénible
trousers pantalon *m.*
true vrai
truly vraiment
trunk malle *f.*
try on essayer
try to tâcher de, essayer (de)
Tuesday mardi *m.*
Turkey Turquie *f.*
turn tour *m.*; **half- —** demi-tour *m.*
turn tourner
turn around se retourner, faire demi-tour
twelve douze; **(twelve o'clock noon)** midi; **(twelve o'clock midnight)** minuit
twenty vingt

twice (a week) deux fois (par semaine)
two deux; **— days out of three** deux jours sur trois
two hundred deux cents
type taper à la machine
typewriter machine à écrire *f.*

U

umbrella parapluie *m.*
unceasingly sans cesse
uncle oncle *m.*
under sous
undergarment combinaison *f.*
understand comprendre; **— each other** se comprendre
understanding: come to an — se mettre d'accord
understood compris (*p. p.* of comprendre); **make oneself —** se faire comprendre
underwear vêtements de dessous *m. pl.; suit of —* combinaison *f.*
undoubtedly sans aucun doute
unexpected inattendu
unfortunate malheureux (*f.* malheureuse)
unfortunately malheureusement
unhoped for inespéré
unite joindre
United States États-Unis *m. pl.;* **to, in the —** aux États-Unis
university université *f.*
unless à moins que
unpleasant désagréable
until jusqu'à, jusqu'à ce que
up: cut — découper; **give —** renoncer (à); **go —** monter (*with* être); **put — at** (*a hotel*) descendre à
upon sur
upset agité, ému, bouleversé
upset bouleverser
upstairs en haut
up to jusqu'à
us nous; **to —** nous
use emploi *m.;* **make — of** se servir de
use se servir de
usually d'ordinaire

V

vain: in — en vain
veal veau *m.*
vegetable légume *m.*
verb verbe *m.*
veritable véritable
very très, bien, fort, tout; **the — idea!** par exemple!; **this — day** aujourd'hui même; **— close to** tout près de
vest gilet *m.*
victory victoire *f.*
view vue *f.;* **from the point of view** au point de vue
village village *m.*
violet violet (*f.* -te)
visit visite *f.;* **pay a — to** faire une visite à
vocabulary vocabulaire *m.*
voice voix *f.* (*pl.* voix); **in a loud —** à haute voix; **in a low —** à voix basse
voyage voyage *m.*

W

wagon charrette *f.*
wait, wait for attendre; **wait!** attendez!
waiter garçon *m.*
waitress serveuse *f.*
wake up se réveiller
walk promenade *f.;* **go for, take a —** faire une promenade, se promener
walk marcher
walk about se promener (je me promène)
walking marche *f.*
wall mur *m.*
walnut noyer *m.*
want vouloir
wanted voulu (*p. p. of* vouloir)
war guerre *f.*
warm chaud; **be —** avoir chaud (*person*); faire chaud (*weather*)
warmth chaleur *f.*
wash laver; **—** (*oneself*) se laver
watch montre *f.*
watch out! prenez garde!

water eau *f.*
water color aquarelle *f.*
waterproof imperméable
wax cire *f.*, cirage *m.*
wax cirer
way chemin *m.*, route *f.*, façon *f.*, moyen *m.*; **that —** par là; **this —** par ici, de ce côté, de cette façon; **by the —** à propos; **which —?** par où?, de quel côté?
we nous; **— (ourselves)** nous-mêmes; (*emphatic*) nous autres
weak faible
weapon arme *f.*
wear porter
wear out user
weary fatigué
weather temps *m.*; **the — is bad** il fait mauvais (temps); **the — is fine** il fait beau (temps); **in all sorts of —** par tous les temps; **what kind of — is it?, how is the —?** quel temps fait-il?; **it is bad —** il fait mauvais temps; **it is fine —** il fait beau (temps)
Wednesday mercredi *m.*
week semaine *f.*; **last —** la semaine dernière; **next —** la semaine prochaine; **two —s** quinze jours; **a — from (Thursday),** (jeudi) en huit
week-end fin de semaine *f.*
well bien; **well!** eh bien!; **— enough, quite —** assez bien; **as — as** ainsi que
west ouest *m.*, occident *m.*
western occidental (*pl.* occidentaux)
wet mouillé
wharf quai *m.*
what (*adj.*) quel, quelle, quels, quelles; (*pro. subj.*) ce qui, qu'est-ce qui; (*pro. obj.*) que, ce que, qu'est-ce que; (*pro. obj. of prep.*) quoi; **— a pity!** quel dommage!; **— is?** qu'est-ce que c'est que?; **— is that?** qu'est-ce que c'est que cela?
whatsoever: any . . . — n'importe quel . . .
wheel: steering — volant *m.*
when quand, lorsque
where où; **— have I got with** où en suis-je de?
whether si
which (*adj.*) quel, quelle, quels, quelles; (*rel. pro.*) qui, que; **— one, ones** lequel, laquelle, lesquels, lesquelles; **of —** dont
while: (a) — (un) peu *m.*; **be worth —** valoir la peine
while pendant que
whisper souffler
white blanc (*f.* blanche)
who (*rel. pro.*) qui; (*interr. pro.*) qui, qui est-ce qui?
whole entier (*f.* entière), tout; **the — afternoon** toute l'après-midi; **the — day** toute la journée; **the — evening** toute la soirée; **the — morning** toute la matinée
whom (*rel. pro.*) que; (*interr. pro.*) qui, qui est-ce que; **of —** dont
whose dont, duquel, *etc.*; à qui
why pourquoi; **—!** mais!
wide large; **— in the shoulders** large des épaules
widow veuve *f.*
widower veuf *m.*
wife femme *f.*
will volonté *f.*
William Guillaume
will you?, will you have? voulez-vous?; **will you show me?** voulez-vous m'indiquer?
willing: be — vouloir bien
willingly volontiers
win gagner, remporter, vaincre
wind vent *m.*
window fenêtre *f.*; **ticket —** guichet *m.*
window shade store *m.*
windy: it is — il fait du vent
wine vin *m.*
winter hiver *m.*
wire dépêche *f.*
wish désir *m.*; (*to a person*) souhait *m.*
wish désirer; **—** (*somebody something*) souhaiter; **— a happy birthday** souhaiter un heureux anniversaire

with avec; sur (*have money with one*); **come —, go —** accompagner
within dans
without sans; **— the knowledge of** à l'insu de
woman femme *f.*
wonder se demander
wonderful épatant
wonderfully merveilleusement, à merveille
wood forêt *f.*, bois *m.*
wool laine *f.*
word mot *m.*
word: my —! ma foi!
work travail *m.* (*pl.* travaux)
work travailler
world monde *m.*
worn out épuisé
worry se préoccuper, s'inquiéter
worse pire (*adj.*); pis (*adv.*); **so much the —** tant pis
worth: be — valoir; **it's — while** cela vaut la peine; **it's not — while** ça n'en vaut pas la peine
wound blesser
wrist poignet *m.*
write écrire (*p. p.* écrit)
writing-paper papier à lettres *m.*
wrong: be — avoir tort

Y

yard (courtyard) cour *f.*
yawn bâiller
year an *m.*, année *f.*; **every —** tous les ans, chaque année; **last —** l'année dernière
yellow jaune
yes oui; si (*in reply to a negative statement or question*)
yesterday hier; **day before —** avant hier; **— morning** hier matin
yet encore; **not —** pas encore
yield céder (je cède)
you tu (*fam.*); vous (*polite sing. and pl.*); toi, te
young jeune; **— people** jeunes gens *m. pl.*
your ton, ta, tes (*fam.*); votre, vos (*polite sing. and pl.*)
yours le tien, le vôtre, *etc.*; **cordially —** bien à vous, bien amicalement, votre bien cordialement dévoué
yourself toi-même (*fam.*); vous-même (*polite*); vous-mêmes (*pl.*)
Yugoslavia Yougoslavie *f.*
Yvonne Yvonne

INDEX